MW01252301

1001
WINDOWS®98
Tips

Kris Jamsa, Ph.D., MBA

JAMSA
P · R · E · S · S
...a computer user's best friend®

Jamsa Press
A division of Gulf Publishing Company
3301 Allen Parkway
Houston, TX 77019
U.S.A.

http://www.jamsa.com

For information about the translation or distribution of any Jamsa Press book, please write to Jamsa Press at the address listed above.

1001 Windows 98 Tips

Printed in the United States of America.
98765432

ISBN 1-884133-61-4

Performance Manager	*Technical Advisor*	*Proofer*
Kong Cheung	Phil Schmauder	Jeanne K. Smith
Copy Editor	*Cover Photograph*	*Technical Editor*
Rosemary Pasco	O'Gara/Bissell	Phil Schmauder
Composition	*Illustrators*	*Cover Design*
New Vision Media	James Rehrauer	James Rehrauer
James Rehrauer	Phil Schmauder	Debbie Jamsa
Indexer		
Kong Cheung		

Gulf Publishing Company
Book Division
P.O. Box 2608
Houston, TX 77252-2608
U.S.A.

http://www.gulfpub.com

Dedication

To Debbie,

For a lifetime of new beginnings . . .

1 | WHAT'S NEW IN WINDOWS *98*

If you are considering upgrading your Windows 95 system to Windows 98, you will hear considerable debate within the user community as to whether or not you should invest in the upgrade. If you have been using Windows 95 and you have just purchased a system that is running Windows 98, or someone at your office upgraded your system for you, you may be wondering what's new within Windows 98. To start, Windows 98 contains three years of bug fixes and enhancements that alone make it well worth your upgrade investment—in other words, Windows 98 is more stable (will experience fewer errors) than Windows 95. And, in most cases, users should find Windows 98 faster.

If you spend time on the Internet, you will find that Windows 98 provides a variety of powerful Net-based programs—starting with Internet Explorer—that you will use to surf the Web, and Outlook Express, that you will use to send and receive electronic mail. In addition, Windows 98 provides a new chat program, software that you can use to create and then host your own Web site, and the NetMeeting software that you can use to hold virtual-office meetings or to talk with other users (around the globe) across the Internet for free. In short, Windows 98 provides an outstanding collection of Web tools.

Windows 98 also provides a new set of Wizards, software that will walk you through various tasks, that will help you fine-tune your system performance, cleanup your disk space, and even troubleshoot common problems. Using the Windows 98 Wizards, you can direct your system to "wake up" in the middle of the night and to then perform system "clean up" operations.

The biggest visual change you will find within Windows 98 relates to its Active Desktop (which you can turn on and off as your needs require) that you can use to display and update specific Web sites on your Desktop, as you work. In short, there's a lot to Windows 98 and it will take the next 1000 Tips to see it all.

2 | STARTING WINDOWS *98* FOR THE FIRST TIME

Each time your turn on your PC's power, Windows 98 is the first program that your computer runs. Starting Windows 98, therefore, is usually as easy as turning on your PC. If you recently purchased a PC that has Windows 98 installed on its hard drive, simply turn on your PC's power and Windows 98 will start. You can then use your PC to run other programs, such as a word processor or a Web browser.

As Windows 98 starts, it may display a few text messages on your screen, which you can usually ignore (if Windows 98 fails to start, the messages may describe the error that your PC or Windows 98 encountered, and the messages may help you troubleshoot and correct the problem). After a few moments, Windows 98 will start and should display your Desktop, which will appear similar to that shown in Figure 2.1. Depending on the software programs you have installed on your system, your Desktop may contain icons other than those shown in Figure 2.1.

If Windows 98 is not currently on your system, you will have to purchase the Windows 98 Upgrade and then run its installation program (which users refer to as the *Setup program*). If you are currently using Windows 95, simply insert the Windows 98 Upgrade CD-ROM into your CD-ROM drive. On most systems, the Windows 98 *Setup* program will start automatically, displaying a window from within which you can start the Windows 98 upgrade.

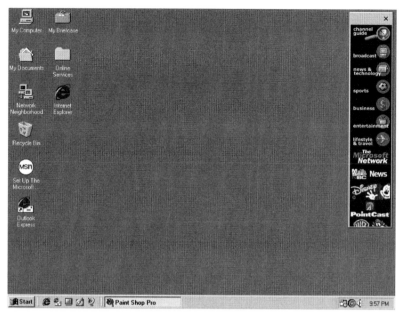

Figure 2.1 *The Windows 98 Desktop.*

In general, installing Windows 98 on your system is straightforward. The *Setup* program will display a series of dialog boxes that contain instructions which will walk you through the upgrade process. If, after you insert the Windows 98 Upgrade CD-ROM into your CD-ROM drive, the Windows 98 *Setup* program does not automatically start, you can start the it yourself by performing these steps:

1. Insert the Windows 98 CD into your CD-ROM drive.
2. If you are currently running Windows 95, click your mouse on the *Start* menu and then select the Run option. If you are running Windows 3.1, select the Program Manager File menu Run option. Windows, in turn, will display the Run dialog box.
3. Within the Run dialog box, type **SETUP** preceded by the drive letter, a colon, and a backslash (such as E:\) that corresponds to your CD-ROM drive. For example, if you are installing Windows 98 from a CD in drive E, you would type **E:\SETUP**.
4. Within the Run dialog box, click your mouse on the OK button, or press ENTER. Windows, in turn, will start the Windows 98 installation.

3   *GETTING FAMILIAR WITH THE WINDOWS 98 DESKTOP*

As you learned in Tip 2, each time you start your system, Windows 98 will display its Desktop which, put simply, is your working area. Just as your regular desk holds a phone, folders, a notepad, incoming and outgoing mail, and even a clock, the Windows 98 Desktop is similar. Within the Desktop (or "on" the Desktop, as some users prefer,) you will find icons upon which you can click your mouse to access your word processor, e-mail software, documents you store within files on your disk, and even sites on the World Wide Web. Figure 3, for example, illustrates several programs running on top of the Windows 98 Desktop. Several of the Tips this book presents will examine ways you can customize your Desktop settings.

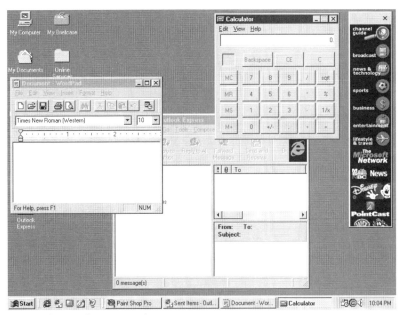

Figure 3 *Program windows sitting on the Windows 98 Desktop.*

| **4** | ***WINDOWS 98 OFFERS TWO USER INTERFACES*** |

As you learned in Tip 2, each time Windows 98 starts, it will display your Desktop. As it turns out, Windows 98 supports two types of Desktop interfaces: the Standard Desktop which resembles the Windows 95 Desktop, and the Active Desktop which lets you display Web-based content, such as a Web page, as well as information from Internet-based sources called *channels*. Within the Active Desktop, for example, you might display real-time information about stock prices or the weather. Figure 4.1 shows the Windows 98 Standard Desktop and the Active Desktop.

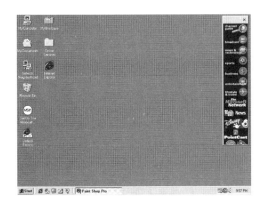

Figure 4.1 *The Windows 98 Standard Desktop and Active Desktop.*

To switch between the Windows 98 Active Desktop and Standard Desktop, perform these steps:

1. Right-click your mouse on an unused area on the Desktop. Windows 98, in turn, will display a small pop-up menu.

2. Within the pop-up menu, select the Active Desktop option and then choose the View as Web

Page option. Windows 98 will treat the menu option as a toggle. If you click your mouse on the option to display a check mark, Windows 98 will turn on the Active Desktop. If you, instead, click your mouse on the option to remove the check mark, Windows 98 will turn off the Active Desktop (which will turn on the Standard Desktop).

5   ***GETTING TO KNOW THE COMMON DESKTOP ICONS***

As you have learned, each time Windows 98 starts, it will display your Desktop. If you examine the Desktop, you will find icons (small pictures) that correspond to various programs you can run, or to folders that contain the documents that you store on your disk. Depending on the programs you have installed on your system, the icons that appear on your Desktop may differ from those you will see on a different system. However, each Desktop will share a set of common icons that this Tip will present. In addition, at the bottom of the Desktop, you will usually find the Windows 98 Taskbar, as shown in Figure 5. Each time you run a program, Windows 98 will display the program's icon within the Taskbar. If you have two or more programs running on your system, you can select the current program by clicking your mouse on the program's icon within the Taskbar.

Figure 5 *Using the Desktop's Taskbar, you can select your current program.*

Table 5 briefly describes several of the common icons that you will encounter on the Windows 98 Desktop. Later, this book will present Tips that describe each icon in detail.

Icon	Element	Description
Internet Explorer	Internet Explorer	Runs the Microsoft Internet Explorer that you can use to surf the World Wide Web.
My Computer	My Computer	Opens a window that contains icons for your PC's disk drives, printers, and other key folders.
Network Neighborhood	Network Neighborhood	Opens a window that contains links to all the omputers within your network.
Recycle Bin	Recycle Bin	Opens a window from within which lets you "undelete" one or more files.
Start	Start button	Displays the Windows 98 Start menu which you will use to run (start) programs.

Table 5 *Descriptions of the Windows 98 screen elements.*

6 — USING THE WELCOME WINDOW TO LEARN ABOUT WINDOWS 98

Depending on your system configuration, each time you start your PC, Windows 98 may display a Welcome to Windows 98 window, as shown in Figure 6, that displays options to help you get started with Windows 98 and to connect to the Internet.

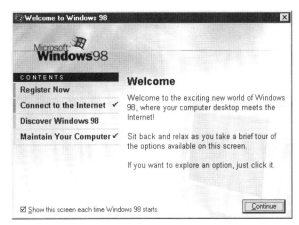

Figure 6 *The Welcome to Windows 98 window.*

Within the Welcome to Windows 98 window, you can use your modem to register with Microsoft as a Windows 98 user, you can start the Internet Connection Wizard to help you connect your system to the Internet, perform the Discover Windows 98 training course that introduces you to various Windows 98 features as well as features within your PC, or you can start the Maintenance Wizard that deletes unnecessary files from your disk, checks your disk for errors, and then defragments your disk to improve your system performance.

If you are new to Windows 98 or to PCs, click your mouse on the Discover Windows 98 option. Windows 98 will then start a tutorial that will introduce you to many of its key features. Next, you can use your modem to register your copy of Windows 98 with Microsoft. By registering Windows 98, you can request that Microsoft keep you abreast of future changes or updates. In Tip 796, you will learn how to connect your PC to the Internet, so you don't need to that now. Likewise, in Tip 636, you will learn how to use the Windows 98 Maintenance Wizard. To close the window, click your mouse on the Close button (the big X that appears within the window's upper-right corner).

7 — DISPLAYING TIPS ON WINDOWS 98 EACH TIME YOUR SYSTEM STARTS

In Tip 6, you learned that when your system starts, Windows 98 may display the Welcome to Windows 98 window. After you traverse the Welcome to Windows 98 window's options the first time, you may not want Windows 98 to display the window in the future.

Before you close the window, click your mouse on the Show this screen each time Windows 98 starts checkbox to remove the check mark. Otherwise, if you leave the check mark, each time your system starts, Windows 98 will display the Welcome to Windows 98 window. Next, to close the window, click your mouse on the window's Close button (the X in the upper-right hand corner).

If your system does not display the Welcome to Windows 98 window when it starts, you can display the window by clicking your mouse on the Start button, choosing the Programs menu Accessories option, and then clicking your mouse on the System Tools submenu Welcome to Windows option, shown in Figure 7. You might, for example, want to use the window to register your use of Windows 98 with Microsoft.

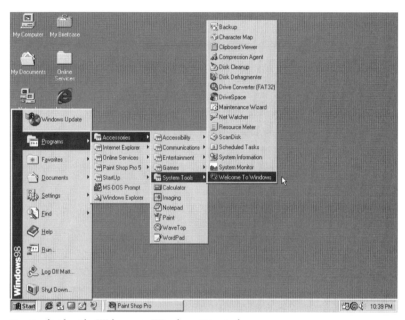

Figure 7 *Using a menu option to display the Welcome to Windows 98 window.*

8 WINDOWS 98 ENHANCES WINDOWS 95 PROGRAMS AND OBJECTS

If you have been using Windows 95 in the past, you will find your transition to Windows 98 easy and fast. Windows 98 supports Windows 95 features such as the Start menu, Taskbar, and software Wizards (which help you accomplish specific tasks, such as installing new hardware or software). As discussed in Tip 1, Windows 98 also provides many new features and programs that will improve your system performance and your productivity.

As Tip 4 briefly discusses, Windows 98 provides an Active Desktop which integrates features of the Internet and the World Wide Web into your Windows environment. If you ignore, just for the moment, the Windows 98 Active Desktop, you will recognize many of the Windows 98 programs and objects from Windows 95. If you have not used Windows 95 in the past, don't worry. The Tips this book presents will cover every aspect of Windows 98 in detail. To help you get started, Table 8 briefly describes several key Windows 98 objects which you will use on a regular basis.

Windows 98 Object	Description
Active Desktop	Lets you integrate parts of the Internet and Web onto your Windows Desktop. Using the Active Desktop, you can display a specific Web site's contents for your screen background or as a screen saver, and you can display "live" Web data, such as stock prices, which Windows 98 constantly updates on your screen as you work.
Explorer	A software program that lets you manage (copy, rename, move, delete, and more) your files and folders.
Internet Explorer	A software program with which you can surf the Web. It includes Outlook Express, a program you can use to send and receive e-mail and view information at on-line newsgroups.
Microsoft Network	Microsoft's online service, which users also refer to as MSN, that provides you with access to the Internet, Web, and even MSN's own services.
My Computer	A special folder within which Windows 98 places icons that correspond to your PC's disk drives. If you double-click your mouse on an icon within the My Computer folder, Windows 98 will display a window within which it will display the drive's files and folders.
Network Neighborhood	A special folder within which Windows 98 places icons that correspond to the PCs, printers, and other shared resources within your local-area network. If you double-click your mouse on an icon within the Network Neighborhood folder, Windows 98 will display a window within which it will display shared resources, such as a shared file folder or printer.
Recycle Bin	A special folder within which Windows 98 places the files you delete. Should you inadvertently delete the wrong file, you may be able to "undelete" the file by removing it from the Recycle Bin.
Right-mouse clicking	Directs Windows 98 to display a context-sensitive, pop-up menu specific to the object on which you click your right-mouse button.
Taskbar	A small bar that Windows 98 displays on your screen which you will use to switch from one program you are running to another. The Taskbar is the Windows 98 "control center."

Table 8 *Common Windows 98 objects.*

9 REMEMBERING WHY MICROSOFT CALLS IT WINDOWS

Over the past few years, Microsoft Windows has become a household word around the world. Microsoft originally named its operating system Windows because it let users view a program's output in a framed screen region called, you guessed it, a *window*.

Windows 98 uses such screen regions, windows, to display a program's output, such as an e-mail message or word-processing document, and program information, such as dialog and message boxes. Although you may use a wide variety of programs, each Windows-based program will display its output within a window. Windows 98 windows contain title bars, sizing buttons, and borders, as they did in Windows 3.1 and Windows 95. Figure 9 illustrates the common parts of a Windows 98 window.

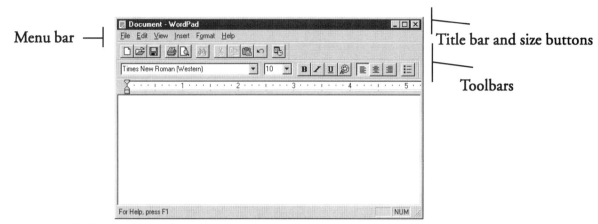

Figure 9 *The common parts of a Windows 98 window.*

10 STARTING PROGRAMS WITHIN WINDOWS 98

Each time you turn on your PC's power, Windows 98 is the first program your PC runs. Using Windows 98, you can then run other programs, such as your word processor, an e-mail program, or even your Web browser. In short, Windows 98 exists to provide you with an environment within which you can run programs. It makes sense, then, that Windows 98 makes it easy for you to start your programs.

If you examine the Taskbar that appears on your Windows 98 Desktop, you will see a Start button. By clicking your mouse on the Start button, you can display a series of menus which will give you access to programs on your computer. Figure 10.1 shows the Taskbar Start button.

Figure 10.1 *The Windows 98 Taskbar Start button.*

When you click your mouse on the Start button, Windows 98 will display the Start menu, as shown in Figure 10.2.

Figure 10.2 *Using the Windows 98 Start menu, you can run the programs that reside on your PC.*

To get you started with the Windows 98 Start button, perform the following steps to run the Calculator, an accessory program that Microsoft ships with Windows 98:

1. Click your mouse on the Start button. Windows 98, in turn, will display the Start menu.
2. Aim your mouse pointer at the Start menu Programs option. Windows 98 will display the Programs submenu as shown in Figure 10.3. (Within the Start menu, you do not have to click your mouse on a menu option to cascade the next menu, you simply must aim your mouse pointer at the menu option.)

Figure 10.3 *Cascading the Start menu Programs submenu.*

3. Within the Programs menu, aim your mouse pointer at the Accessories option. Windows 98, in turn, will display the Accessories menu.
4. Within the Accessories menu, click your mouse on the Calculator option. Windows 98, in turn, will start the Calculator program, as shown in Figure 10.4.

Figure 10.4 *Running the Calculator accessory program within a window.*

Using the Start menu in this way, you can run each program that resides on your PC. Take time now to view a list of your PC's programs by performing these steps:

1. Click your mouse on the Start button. Windows 98 will display the Start menu.
2. Aim your mouse pointer at the Start menu Programs option. Windows 98, in turn, will display the Programs menu, which lists the programs your PC contains.
3. To cancel the Program menu display, click your mouse on an unused location on the Windows 98 Desktop.

11 USING CTRL-ESC TO ACCESS THE WINDOWS 98 START MENU

As you learned in Tip 10, to run programs within Windows 98, you will make extensive use of the Start menu shown in Figure 11.

Figure 11 *Running programs from the Windows 98 Start menu.*

To access the Start menu using your mouse, click your mouse on the Taskbar's Start button. If you are a fast typist and you do not like to take your hands off the keyboard (which you must do to click your mouse), you can press the CTRL-ESC keyboard combination to display the Start menu. After Windows 98 displays the Start menu, you can use your keyboard arrow keys to move through the Start menu options. Also, if you are using a Microsoft keyboard or compatible keyboard that contains a key with the Windows logo, you can press that key to display the Start menu.

12 ENDING A PROGRAM WITHIN WINDOWS 98

In Tip 11, you learned how to use the Windows 98 Start menu to run programs. After you are done using a program, you will want to end the program and close its corresponding window. Just as Windows 98 opens a window for each program you run, Windows 98 closes the window for each program you end. Within Windows 98, there are several ways you can end a program.

First, most Windows-based programs provide a File menu Exit option similar to that shown in Figure 12.1, upon which you can click your mouse to end the program.

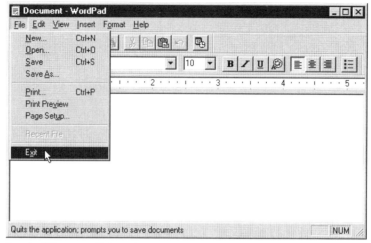

Figure 12.1 *To end a program, select the File menu Exit option.*

Second, most Windows-based programs provide a Control menu that you can access by clicking your mouse on the small icon that appears to the left of the window's title bar.

As shown in Figure 12.2, the Control menu contains a Close option that you can select to end the program.

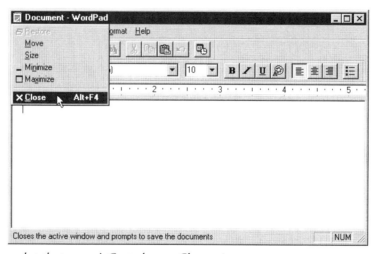

Figure 12.2 *To end a program, select the program's Control menu Close option.*

Third, as a shortcut to selecting the Control menu Close option to end a program, Windows 98 will end a program if you double-click your mouse on the Control menu icon.

Fourth, most Windows-based programs provide a Close button that appears as an X to the right of the window's title bar, as shown in Figure 12.3. To end a program, simply click your mouse on the Close button.

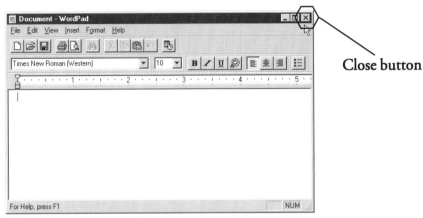

Figure 12.3 To end a program, click your mouse on the program's Close button.

Finally, each time you run a program, Windows 98 will display a button that corresponds to the program on the Windows 98 Taskbar. If you right-click your mouse on a program's Taskbar button, Windows 98 will display the program's control menu, as shown in Figure 12.4, which you can use to close the program.

Figure 12.4 To end a program, right-click your mouse on the program's Taskbar button and then choose the Control menu Close option.

If you started the Calculator program discussed in Tip 10, end the program now using one of the methods this Tip presents.

---

13 | **WINDOWS LETS YOU RUN TWO OR MORE PROGRAMS AT THE SAME TIME**

Windows 98, like most operating systems, exists primarily to help you run programs. Within Windows 98, you can run two or more programs at the same time. For example, assume that while you type an office memo with Microsoft Word, you decide you need more information about your memo's topic. Within Windows 98, with Microsoft Word still running, you can start your Web browser to surf the Web and start your e-mail program to send messages to other users asking for help. Figure 13 shows Windows 98 running Word, Internet Explorer, and the Microsoft Outlook Express e-mail program.

Users refer to Windows 98 running multiple programs simultaneously as *multitasking*. Because your PC probably only has one processing unit (CPU), Windows 98 can only run one program at any given time. By switching between the programs very quickly, however, Windows 98 makes you think the programs are running at the same time. To implement multitasking, Windows 98 assigns each application a small piece of CPU's processing time, called a *time slice*, within which the program can use the CPU to perform its processing. By dividing the CPU's processing time into time slices, Windows 98 can share the CPU among each of your programs. Because the time slices are so small and Windows 98 switches between programs so fast, each program appears to be running at the same time. In actuality, however one program runs for a brief period of time, and then a second program runs, and then a third, and so on. The more programs you run simultaneously, the slower each program becomes, because more programs now have to share the slices of the CPU's time.

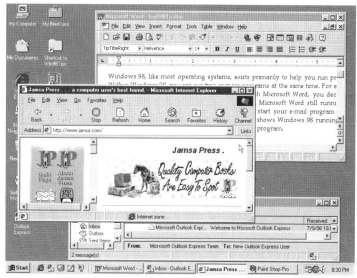

Figure 13 *Windows 98 lets you run two or more programs at the same time.*

14 WITHIN A PROGRAM WINDOW, A PROGRAM MAY DISPLAY ONE OR MORE DOCUMENT WINDOWS

As you have learned, each time you run a program, Windows 98 will display the program's output within a window on your screen. If you run multiple programs at the same time, Windows 98 will display each program's output within a separate window. Because these windows display a program's output, users refer to these windows as *program windows*. Figure 14.1 shows several programs running within their own program windows.

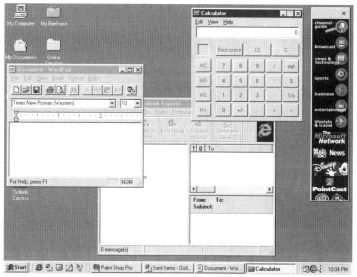

Figure 14.1 *Windows 98 runs each program within a program window.*

Just as Windows 98 lets you run two or more programs at the same time, many programs will let you open two or more documents. For example, if you use the Microsoft Word word-processing software, you might have two documents open within Word, one that contains your company budget and one that contains a memo you will send to your company employees regarding the document. By having both documents open at the same time, you can view information within each document as your needs require. When a program lets you open two or more documents at one time, the program will display each document within a separate document window. Figure 14.2, for example, shows three documents open within Microsoft Word. In this case, your system has one program window (the one running Word) and then, within that window, Word has three open document windows.

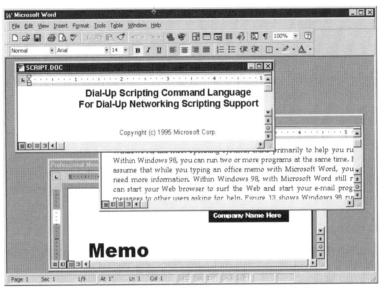

Figure 14.2 Three document windows within the Word program window.

As you work within Windows 98, you must distinguish between program and document windows. If, for example, you maximize a program window, Windows 98 will expand the window to fill your entire screen. If instead, you maximize a document window, Windows 98 will only expand the document window to the size of its surrounding program window. Also, when you close a program window, Windows 98 will end the program. When you close a document window, on the other hand, the program continues to run. Several of the Tips that follow examine operations you can perform with a window, such as sizing or moving the window. In most cases, you can perform the operations on either a program or document window.

15 SWITCHING BETWEEN WINDOWS WITHIN WINDOWS 98

As you learned in Tip 13, within Windows 98 you can run two or more programs at the same time. When you run multiple programs, Windows 98 will display each program's output within its own window on the screen. At any given time, only one of the windows, the *active window*, will respond to your mouse and keyboard operations.

Windows 98 will display the active window in front of other open windows on your screen. If you examine each window's title bar, you will find that Windows 98 highlights the active window's title bar while dimming the title bar of the inactive windows.

It is important that you understand that just because a window is not the active window, its program is still running and the program may continue to display new output within the window.

The active window differs from other open windows in that it is the window that receives and responds to your keyboard and mouse operations.

Windows 98 makes it easy for you to switch between programs that you are running at the same time. When you switch between programs, the new program becomes the active window. The easiest way to select a window as the active window is to click your mouse on any portion of the window, as shown in Figure 15.1.

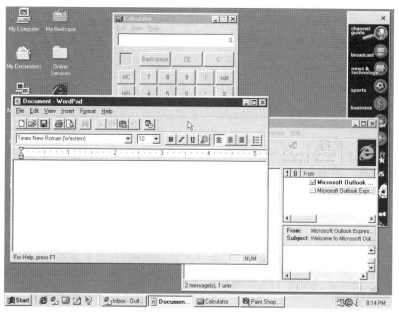

Figure 15.1 *To select a window as the active window, click your mouse on any location within the window frame.*

Second, each time you run a program, Windows 98 will display a button for the program on the Taskbar. To select a program as the active window, click your mouse on the program's Taskbar button, as shown in Figure 15.2.

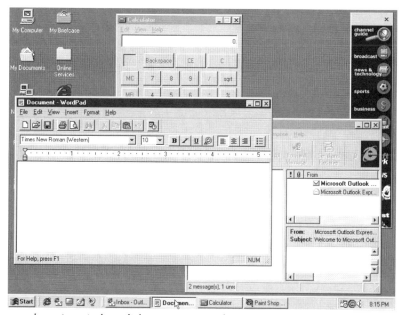

Figure 15.2 *To select a program as the active window, click your mouse on the program's Taskbar button.*

Third, if you do not like to take your fingers off the keyboard, Windows 98 will let you switch between programs by pressing the ALT-TAB keyboard combination. When you hold down the ALT key and then press the TAB key, Windows 98 will display icons within a small box for each of the programs you are running, similar to that shown in Figure 15.3. To highlight the program you desire, continue holding down the ALT key and repeatedly press the TAB key until Windows 98 rests the highlight box on the icon of the program you desire. When you release the keys, Windows 98 will make the program you chose the active window.

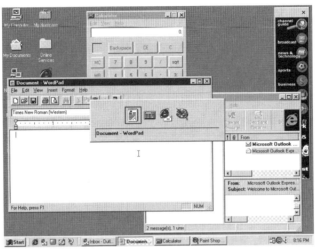

Figure 15.3 *To switch between programs from the keyboard, press the ALT-TAB keyboard combination.*

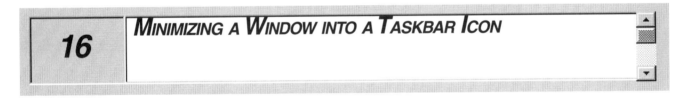

16 MINIMIZING A WINDOW INTO A TASKBAR ICON

When you run two or more programs at the same time, there may be times when the windows you are not currently using simply get in your way. In such cases, Windows 98 will let you shrink (users call it *minimize*) the window so that it appears as a Taskbar button. When you minimize a window, you do not close the window, which means the program continues to run. If the program that you minimize has files open, the files remain open. Also, before you turn off your system, you must end the programs that correspond to each window you have minimized. When you are later ready to use a program whose window you have minimized, click your mouse on the window's Taskbar button and Windows 98 will restore the window to the screen at its previous size. Figure 16.1 shows a crowded Desktop with several open program windows. Figure 16.2 shows the same Desktop after the user minimizes several programs into Taskbar icons.

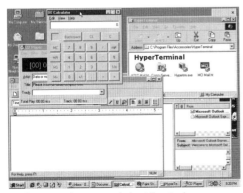

Figure 16.1 *A Desktop crowded with windows.*

Figure 16.2 *Cleaning up the Desktop by minimizing windows.*

Most Windows-based programs provide a Minimize button, which appears as an underscore to the right of the window's title bar, as shown in Figure 16.3. To minimize a window, click your mouse on the Minimize button.

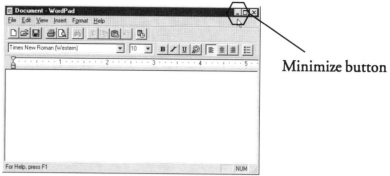

Minimize button

Figure 16.3 *To minimize a window into a Taskbar icon, click your mouse on the window's Minimize button.*

Second, to minimize a window, you can right-click your mouse on the program's Taskbar button. Windows 98, in turn, will display the window's Control menu which may contain a Minimize option similar to that shown in Figure 16.4.

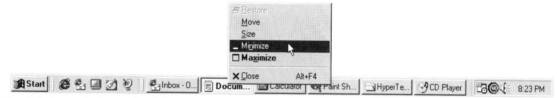

Figure 16.4 *To minimize a window, right-click your mouse on the window's Taskbar button and then choose Minimize.*

Third, most Windows-based programs will provide a Control menu, which appears to the left of the window's title bar. To minimize a window, click your mouse on the Control menu icon. Windows 98, in turn, will display the program's Control menu, as shown in Figure 16.5, from which you can select the Minimize option.

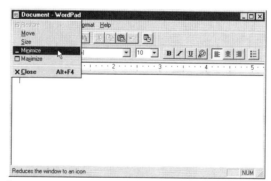

Figure 16.5 *To minimize a window, select the program's Control menu Minimize option.*

17 **MINIMIZING ALL OPEN WINDOWS IN ONE STEP**

In Tip 16, you learned that to improve your screen's appearance (organize your Desktop), Windows 98 will let you minimize an open window into a Taskbar icon. Depending on the number of windows you have open on your Desktop, there may be times when you will find it convenient to minimize all of the windows in one step. Then, you can click your mouse on Taskbar buttons to open the specific windows you require. To minimize all your open windows at the same time, perform these steps:

1. Right-click your mouse on a blank location on the Windows 98 Taskbar. Windows 98, in turn, will display a small pop-up menu, as shown in Figure 17.

Figure 17 *The Taskbar pop-up menu.*

2. Within the Taskbar pop-up menu, select the Minimize All Windows option.

18 **MAXIMIZING A WINDOW TO FILL THE ENTIRE SCREEN**

As you have learned, Windows 98 will let you run two or more programs at the same time. When you run multiple programs at the same time, Windows 98 will display each program's output within its own window. In Tip 16, you learned that by minimizing windows to Taskbar icons, you can control your screen's appearance.

At times, however, you will to want to focus your attention on a specific program. In such cases, Windows 98 will let you maximize the program's window to fill up the entire screen region. For example, Figure 18.1 illustrates two programs, a word processor and a spreadsheet, running on the Desktop. If you maximize the word-processing program's window, Windows 98 will fill the screen with the program's output, as shown in Figure 18.2.

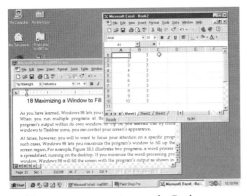

Figure 18.1 *Two programs running on the Desktop.*

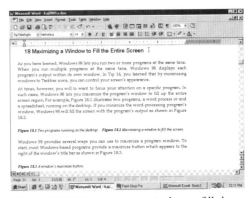

Figure 18.2 *Maximizing a window to fill the screen.*

Windows 98 provides several ways you can maximize a program window. To start, most Windows-based programs provide a Maximize button which appears to the right of the window's title bar, as shown in Figure 18.3.

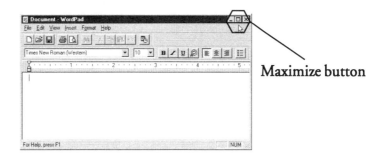

Maximize button

Figure 18.3 *A window's Maximize button.*

Second, most Windows-based programs will provide a Control menu, which appears to the left of the window's title bar. To maximize a window, click your mouse on the Control menu icon. Windows 98, in turn, will display the program's Control menu, as shown in Figure 18.4, from which you can select the Maximize option.

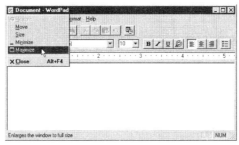

Figure 18.4 *To maximize a window, select the program's Control menu Maximize option.*

Third, if you right-click your mouse on the Taskbar button that corresponds to the program, Windows 98 will display the program's Control menu, which should contain a Maximize option, as shown in Figure 18.5.

Figure 18.5 *To maximize a program window, right-click your mouse on the program's Taskbar button and choose the Control menu Maximize option.*

Finally, if you double-click your mouse on the window's title bar, Windows 98 will maximize the window. Likewise, if you double-click your mouse on the title bar of a maximized window, Windows 98 will restore the window to its previous size. Depending on the information a program displays within a window, you may encounter windows that you cannot maximize.

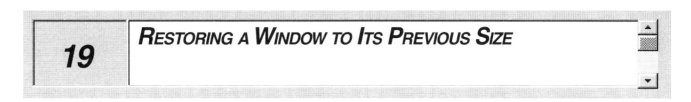

19 RESTORING A WINDOW TO ITS PREVIOUS SIZE

In Tip 18, you learned how to maximize a window to fill your entire screen. Likewise, in Tip 16, you learned how to minimize a window into a Taskbar icon. After you maximize or minimize a window, there may be times when you must restore the window to its previous size. For example, Figure 19.1 displays a maximized window. Figure 19.2 shows the window restored to its previous size.

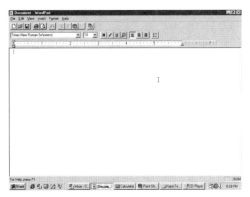

Figure 19.1 *A maximized window.*

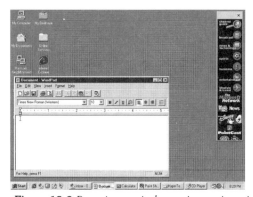

Figure 19.2 *Restoring a window to its previous size.*

Windows 98 provides several ways for you to restore a maximized or minimized window. To restore a maximized window, you can select the window's Restore button, which appears to the right of the window's title bar, as shown in Figure 19.3.

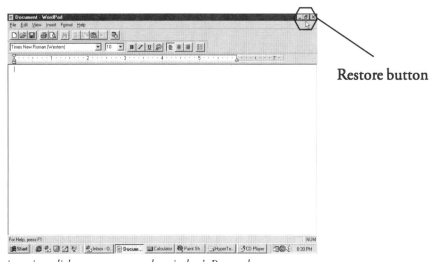

Restore button

Figure 19.3 *To restore a window's previous size, click your mouse on the window's Restore button.*

Second, most Windows-based program will provide a Control menu, which appears to the left of the window's title bar. To restore a maximized window to its previous size, click your mouse on the Control menu icon. Windows, in turn, will display the program's Control menu, as shown in Figure 19.4, from which you can select the Restore option.

Figure 19.4 *To restore a window, select the program's Control menu Restore option.*

Third, if you right-click your mouse on the Taskbar button that corresponds to the program, Windows 98 will display the program's Control menu, which should contain a Restore button, as shown in Figure 19.5.

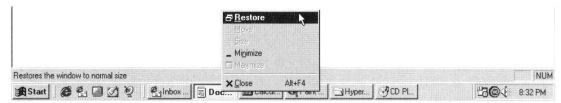

Figure 19.5 *To restore a program window, right-click your mouse on the program's Taskbar button and choose the Control menu Restore option.*

Finally, if your double-click your mouse on the title bar of a maximized window, Windows 98 will restore the window to its previous size.

20 — THINK OF THE WINDOWS 98 TASKBAR AS YOUR CONTROL CENTER

As you have learned, the Windows 98 Taskbar lets you switch between programs, size a program's window, and even close a window. In general, the Windows 98 Taskbar provides you with a "control center" you can use to manage your programs. In addition to letting you manage your programs, you can use the Taskbar to change the way icons appear on your Desktop, to control the volume that Windows 98 uses to play audio CDs and various sounds, to control SCSI devices on a notebook computer, and to display the current date and time. Figure 20.1 illustrates the Windows 98 Taskbar.

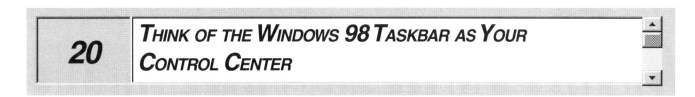

Figure 20.1 *The Windows 98 Taskbar.*

Within the Taskbar, Windows 98 will display the current system time. If you aim your mouse pointer at the Taskbar clock for a few seconds, Windows 98 will display the current system date, as shown in Figure 20.2.

Figure 20.2 *To display the current system date, aim your mouse pointer at the Taskbar clock for a few seconds.*

21 — TILING OR CASCADING WINDOWS USING THE WINDOWS 98 TASKBAR

As you work within Windows 98, there may be times when you have many programs running and many open windows on your Desktop. As you learned in Tip 16, Windows 98 lets you minimize an open window to a Taskbar button. However, depending on your task at hand, there may be times when you need each window visible while you work. In such cases, you can tile or cascade the windows on your Desktop. Figure 21.1 shows a Desktop cluttered with windows.

Figure 21.2 shows the same Desktop with the windows tiled. Likewise, Figure 21.3 shows the same Desktop with the windows cascaded.

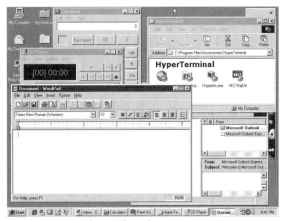

Figure 21.1 *A cluttered Desktop.*

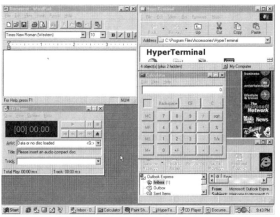

Figure 21.2 *Tiling windows on the Desktop.*

Figure 21.3 *Cascading windows on the Desktop.*

When you tile windows on the Desktop, Windows 98 will place the windows side by side (for vertical tiling) or one on top of each other (horizontal tiling), so a portion of each window is in view. When you cascade windows on the Desktop, Windows 98 stacks the windows at an angle so you can view each window's title bar. To tile or cascade windows on your Desktop, perform these steps:

1. Right-click your mouse on to a blank location on the Taskbar. Windows 98, in turn, will display a small pop-up Taskbar menu, as shown in Figure 21.4.

Figure 21.4 *Tiling and cascading windows using a Taskbar pop-up menu.*

2. Within the Taskbar pop-up menu, select the menu option that will tile or cascade the Desktop windows as you desire.

22 | **SIZING YOUR TASKBAR TO DISPLAY A NUMBER OF PROGRAM BUTTONS**

As you have learned, Windows 98 will let you run several programs at the same time. Usually, the Taskbar makes it easy for you to locate and switch between running programs. You simply scan its buttons and select the one that activates the program window you want to use. (Each button contains an icon and label that tells you the program it represents.)

However, if you run too many programs at the same time, your Taskbar may fill up with so many buttons that you cannot quickly distinguish between them. If you find your Taskbar is getting crowded, like the one shown in Figure 22.1, reevaluate your need for running so many programs at the same time.

Figure 22.1 A crowded Taskbar.

If you are running several programs and your Taskbar is becoming cluttered and the icons are difficult to read, you can increase the Taskbar's width (which will give Windows 98 more room within the Taskbar to display each button's icon and label), as shown in Figure 22.2.

Figure 22.2 Increasing the Taskbar's width to improve its icon display.

To increase the Taskbar's width, perform these steps:

1. Move your mouse pointer to the Taskbar's top edge. (If your Taskbar is on your screen's left, top, or right side, move your mouse pointer to the edge closest to your screen's center.) Windows 98 will change your mouse pointer into a double-pointing arrow.

2. Click your mouse-select button and drag your mouse pointer toward your screen's center. As you drag the mouse, the Taskbar will increase in size.

3. Release your mouse-select button when the Taskbar is the size you want.

Note: *Should you later decide to decrease the Taskbar's width, use your mouse to drag the Taskbar to the smaller width that you desire.*

23 | **USING THE WINDOWS 98 TASKBAR TO ARRANGE ICONS ON YOUR DESKTOP**

Just as you can move and reorder the items on your desk, Windows 98 also lets you arrange the items it displays on your Desktop. For example, Figure 23.1 illustrates icons dispersed about a cluttered Desktop. Figure 23.2 shows the same Desktop with the icons arranged into rows and columns.

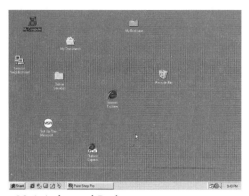

Figure 23.1 *A cluttered Desktop.*

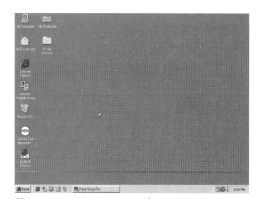

Figure 23.2 *Arranging Desktop icons into rows and columns.*

To arrange your Desktop's icons, perform any of these tasks:

- Using your mouse, drag an icon to a new location.

- To display icons on the Desktop in alphabetical order, right-click your mouse on the Desktop. Within the pop-up menu, click your mouse on the Arrange Icons submenu's By Name option. (You can also use the Arrange Icons submenu to arrange icons by type, size, and date.)

- To arrange the Desktop icons within rows and columns, right-click your mouse on the Desktop. Within the pop-up menu, click your mouse on the Arrange Icons submenu's Auto Arrange option.

- To arrange the Desktop icons in rows, right-click your mouse on the Desktop. Within the pop-up menu, click your mouse on the Line up Icons option.

---

24   USING THE WINDOWS 98 TASKBAR TO LINE UP YOUR DESKTOP ICONS

In Tip 72, you will learn how to create Desktop shortcuts, which are icons Windows 98 associates with specific programs or documents. When you double-click your mouse on a program shortcut, for example, Windows 98 will immediately run the corresponding program. Likewise, if you double-click your mouse on a document shortcut, Windows 98 will run the document's corresponding program (such as Microsoft Word) and will then automatically load the document into the program for editing. As the number of program and document icons you place on your Desktop increases, your Desktop may eventually become quite cluttered with icons, as shown in Figure 24.1.

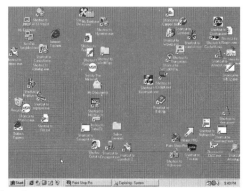

Figure 24.1 *A Windows 98 Desktop cluttered with icons.*

To help you manage your Desktop's appearance, Windows 98 will let you quickly align your icons. To align your Desktop icons, perform these steps:

1. Right-click your mouse on an unused area on the Desktop. Windows 98, in turn, will display the pop-up menu shown in Figure 24.2.

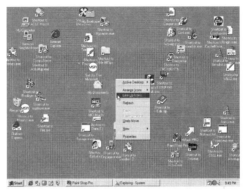

Figure 24.2 *The Windows 98 Desktop's pop-up menu.*

2. Within the pop-up menu, select the Line up Icons option. Windows 98 will align your icons in neat rows and columns, as shown in Figure 24.3.

Figure 24.3 *Lining up icons on the Windows 98 Desktop.*

25   MAKING SURE THAT WINDOWS 98 ALWAYS DISPLAYS THE TASKBAR

As you work within Windows 98, you will use the Taskbar to switch from one program to another. Depending on the programs you run, there may be times when a program window overlaps (covers) the Taskbar. If you find that you have difficulty accessing the Taskbar, you can direct Windows 98 to always keep the Taskbar in view. To direct Windows 98 to keep the Taskbar visible and accessible at all times, perform these steps:

1. Click your mouse on the Start button. Windows 98, in turn, will display the Start menu.
2. Within the Start menu, select the Settings option. Windows 98, in turn, will display the Settings submenu.
3. Within the Settings submenu, select the Taskbar & Start Menu option. Windows 98, in turn, will display the Taskbar Properties dialog box, as shown in Figure 25.

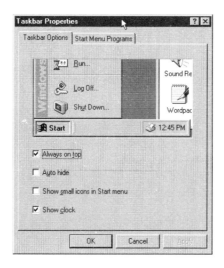

Figure 25 *The Taskbar Properties dialog box.*

4. Within the Taskbar Properties dialog box, make sure the Always on top checkbox contains a check mark. If not, click your mouse on the checkbox.

5. Within the Taskbar Properties dialog box, click your mouse on the OK button.

---

26 DIRECTING WINDOWS 98 TO HIDE THE TASKBAR WHEN IT IS NOT IN USE

Although most users keep the Taskbar in view as they work, if you find that you don't change from one program to another very often, the Taskbar may take up space on your screen. In such cases, you can direct Windows 98 to hide the Taskbar whenever you are are not using it. When you must later use the Taskbar, you simply aim your mouse pointer to the screen location where you keep the Taskbar (which is usually the bottom of your screen), and Windows 98 will bring the Taskbar into view, as shown in Figure 26.1. If you move your mouse pointer off the Taskbar, Windows 98 will again hide the Taskbar.

Figure 26.1 *To bring a hidden Taskbar into view, aim your mouse pointer at the Taskbar location.*

To direct Windows 98 to hide the Taskbar when you are not using it, perform these steps:

1. Click your mouse on the Start button. Windows 98, in turn, will display the Start menu.

2. Within the Start menu, select the Settings option. Windows 98 will display the Settings submenu.

3. Within the Settings submenu, select the Taskbar & Start Menu option. Windows 98, in turn, will display the Taskbar Properties dialog box, as shown in Figure 26.2.

4. Within the Taskbar Properties dialog box, place a check mark in the Auto hide checkbox. If you later decide that you want the Taskbar visible at all times, click your mouse on the checkbox to remove the check mark.

5. Within the Taskbar Properties dialog box, click your mouse on the OK button.

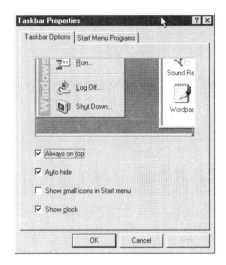

Figure 26.2 *The Taskbar Properties dialog box.*

27 USING THE WINDOWS 98 TASKBAR TO DISPLAY THE CURRENT DATE

As you have learned, within Windows 98 you will use the Taskbar to switch between programs. In addition, you can use the Taskbar to display the current date, as shown in Figure 27.

Figure 27 *Using the Windows 98 Taskbar to display the current date.*

To display the current date using your Taskbar, aim your mouse pointer at the Taskbar clock. After a few seconds, Windows 98 will pop up the small date field, as previously shown in Figure 27. To change the format within which Windows 98 displays the date, select the Control Panel's Regional Settings option.

28 CHANGING YOUR SYSTEM'S DATE OR TIME

In Tip 27, you learned how to display the current date using the Taskbar clock icon. If either your system date or time is wrong, you can update them by performing these steps:

1. Within your Desktop, double-click your mouse on the Taskbar's clock icon. Windows 98, in turn, will display the Date/Time Properties dialog box Date & Time sheet, as shown in Figure 28.

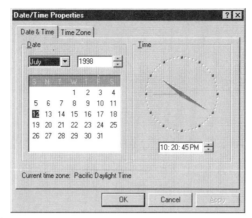

Figure 28 *The Date/Time Properties dialog box.*

2. To change the current month, click your mouse on the Month pull-down list and, within the list, click your mouse on the month you desire.

3. To change the current year, either type in a value within the Year field or use the Year spin buttons to increase or decrease the current year value, one year at a time.

4. To change the current day, click your mouse on the correct number in the monthly calendar.

5. To change the time, click your mouse on the hour, minute, second, and AM/PM fields and either type the value you desire or click your mouse on the spin buttons to change the current value.

6. Within the Date/Time Properties dialog box, click your mouse on the OK button to put your changes into effect.

29 **USING THE DATE/TIME PROPERTIES DIALOG BOX TO CHANGE THE CURRENT TIME ZONE**

In Tip 28, you learned how to change your current system date and time. Within Windows 98, many of your programs will use the current system date and time. For example, each time you create or modify a document, Windows 98 will assign the current date and time to the file's date-and-time stamp. Therefore, you should keep your system date and time correct.

In addition to using your system date and time, some programs will also use your system's time-zone setting. Within Windows 98, you can update your time zone by performing these steps:

1. Within your Desktop, double-click your mouse the Taskbar's clock. Windows 98, in turn, will display the Date/Time Properties dialog box.

2. Within the Date/Time Properties dialog box, click your mouse on the Time Zone tab. Windows 98 will display the Time Zone sheet, as shown in Figure 29.

3. Within the Time Zone sheet, click your mouse on the pull-down list and then click your mouse on the time zone that corresponds to your current region.

4. Within the Time Zone sheet, click your mouse on OK to put your changes into effect.

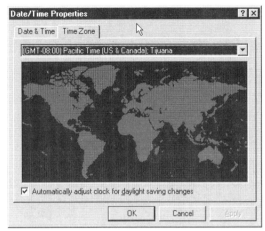

Figure 29 *The Date/Time dialog box TimeZone sheet.*

Note: *Using the Date/Time Properties dialog box Time Zone sheet, you can use the Automatically adjust clock for daylight savings changes checkbox to direct Windows 98 to automatically update your system clock each time daylight savings time changes.*

30	**DIRECTING THE WINDOWS 98 TO DISPLAY OR HIDE THE TASKBAR CLOCK**

As you learned in Tip 27, the Windows 98 Taskbar usually contains a small clock that displays the current system time, as shown in Figure 30.

Figure 30 *The Windows 98 Taskbar displays the current system time.*

Depending on the number of programs you run, you may find that you would prefer that Windows 98 not display the system clock and, instead, use the Taskbar space for program icons. To turn the Taskbar's display of the system clock on or off, perform these steps:

1. Click your mouse on the Start button. Windows 98, in turn, will display the Start menu.

2. Within the Start menu, select the Settings option. Windows 98, in turn, will display the Settings submenu.

3. Within the Settings submenu, select the Taskbar & Start Menu option. Windows 98, in turn, will display the Taskbar Properties dialog box.

4. Within the Taskbar Properties dialog box, place a check mark within the Show Clock checkbox to display the clock, or remove the check mark if you want to cancel the clock's display.

5. Within the Taskbar Properties dialog box, click your mouse on the OK button.

31 | **CONTROLLING YOUR SPEAKER VOLUME FROM THE TASKBAR**

As you have learned, the Windows 98 Taskbar lets you quickly switch between applications. In addition, if you are using your PC's multimedia capabilities to play music or other sounds, you can use the Taskbar speaker icon, shown in Figure 31.1, to adjust your speaker volume.

Figure 31.1 *The Windows 98 Taskbar speaker icon.*

To adjust your PC's volume, click your mouse one time on the Taskbar's speaker icon. Windows 98, in turn, will display a volume control as shown in Figure 31.2.

Figure 31.2 *The Windows 98 volume control.*

To increase the PC's volume, use your mouse to drag the volume control's slider up. To decrease your PC's volume, use your mouse to drag the volume control's slider down. To close the volume control, click your mouse on a screen location outside of the volume control.

32 | **MOVING THE TASKBAR TO A DIFFERENT EDGE OF THE SCREEN**

As you have learned, the Windows 98 Taskbar lets you quickly switch between programs. By default, Windows 98 displays the Taskbar at the bottom of your Desktop. However, depending on your preference, Windows 98 will let you move the Taskbar to the top, bottom, left, or right edge of your Desktop. For example, Figures 32.1 and 32.2 show the Taskbar at the right-hand side of the Desktop and at the top of the Desktop.

Figure 32.1 *Placing the Taskbar at the right of the Desktop.*   ***Figure 32.2*** *Placing the Taskbar at the top of the Desktop.*

To move the Taskbar to an edge of the Desktop, aim your mouse pointer to an empty spot on the Taskbar. Next, hold down your mouse-select button and move your mouse to drag the Taskbar to the edge of the Desktop that you desire.

33 UNDERSTANDING AND USING THE TASKBAR TOOLBARS

Within Windows 98, the Taskbar is your command center. By clicking your mouse on Taskbar icons, you can quickly switch from one program to another. In addition to letting you switch between active programs, you can use Taskbar toolbars to launch specific programs. For example, if you have a set of programs that you run a regular basis, such as Microsoft Word and Excel, you might want to create a toolbar on the Taskbar from which you can start the programs, as shown in Figure 33.1. Tip 38 discusses the steps you must perform to add a toolbar to the Taskbar.

Figure 33.1 *A Taskbar toolbar for Microsoft Word and Excel.*

In addition to letting you create your own Taskbar toolbars, Windows 98 also provides the Address toolbar which you can use to specify a Web address, the Links toolbar within which you can place links to Web sites you visit on a regular basis, the Desktop toolbar which provides you with access to items that appear on your Desktop, and the Quick Launch toolbar that lets you access Internet Explorer and Microsoft Outlook Express, as well as view Internet-based channels and your Desktop.

Within a Taskbar toolbar, you can use toolbar tips, as discussed in Tip 73, to determine the purpose of each toolbar icon. Depending on the toolbar size, there may be times when Windows 98 displays a toolbar with left and right facing scroll arrows on either end of the toolbar. By clicking your mouse on the right or left facing arrows, you can scroll through the list of icons the toolbar contains. Figure 33.2 displays the Windows 98 Taskbar with the Address, Links, Desktop, and Quick Launch toolbars. Several of the Tips that follow discuss each of these toolbars in detail.

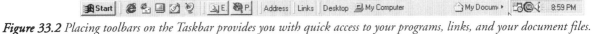

Figure 33.2 *Placing toolbars on the Taskbar provides you with quick access to your programs, links, and your document files.*

To enable or disable a toolbar's display, perform these steps:

1. Right-click your mouse on a blank location within the Taskbar. Windows 98, in turn, will display a pop-up menu.

2. Within the pop-up menu, click your mouse on the Toolbars option. Windows 98, in turn, will display the Toolbars submenu, as shown in Figure 33.3.

Figure 33.3 *The Taskbar's pop-up menu Toolbars submenu.*

3. Within the Toolbars submenu, click your mouse on the option that corresponds to the Toolbar you want to turn on or off.

If you examine the Taskbar closely, you will find that it displays small bars between each of the toolbars. Using your mouse, you can drag these small bars to increase or decrease a toolbar's size.

34 **USING THE TASKBAR'S ADDRESS TOOLBAR TO SPECIFY A WEB ADDRESS**

In Tip 33, you learned that to provide you with easy access to key programs, documents, and sites on the Web, Windows 98 lets you place toolbars on the Taskbar. As you work, there may be times when you want to display a Web site's contents. Rather than starting the Windows Explorer, you can simply type in the Web address you desire within the Taskbar's Address toolbar, as shown in Figure 34. Windows 98, in turn, will launch the Explorer program to display the Web site.

Figure 34 Using the Taskbar's Address toolbar to specify a Web site's address.

To enable the Taskbar's Address toolbar, perform these steps:

1. Right-click your mouse on an unused area within the Taskbar. Windows 98, in turn, will display a pop-up menu.
2. Within the pop-up menu, select the Toolbars option and then click your mouse on the Address option, placing a check mark next to the option.

35 **USING THE TASKBAR'S LINKS TOOLBAR TO BRANCH TO A SPECIFIC WEB SITE**

If you are like most users, you may have a list of Web sites that you visit on a regular basis. To help you access these sites quickly, Windows 98 will let you place the Links toolbar on the your Taskbar, as shown in Figure 35.

Figure 35 Using the Taskbar's Links toolbar to access the Webs you frequently visit.

To enable the Taskbar's Links toolbar, perform these steps:

1. Right-click your mouse on an unused area within the Taskbar. Windows 98, in turn, will display a pop-up menu.
2. Within the pop-up menu, select the Toolbars option and then click your mouse on the Links option, placing a check mark next to the option.

To add a link to the Links toolbar, create a shortcut for the link within the *Windows\Favorites\Links* folder. Tip 141 discusses the steps you must perform to create a shortcut. In addition to removing a link, use the Explorer to delete the link's shortcuts from the *Links* folder.

---

36 USING THE TASKBAR'S DESKTOP TOOLBAR TO OPEN A DESKTOP OBJECT

As you have learned, each time Windows 98 starts, it displays your Desktop, which may contain icons that correspond to the programs you run on a regular basis. Depending on the of number programs you are running, there may be times when your screen fills with windows and locating an icon on the Desktop becomes difficult. To simplify access to your Desktop icons, Windows 98 lets you place the Desktop toolbar on the Taskbar. Within the Desktop toolbar, you will find buttons that correspond to each of your Desktop icons, as shown in Figure 36.

Figure 36 *The Taskbar's Desktop toolbar provides you with quick access to your Desktop icons.*

To enable the Taskbar's Desktop toolbar, perform these steps:

1. Right-click your mouse on an unused area within the Taskbar. Windows 98, in turn, will display a pop-up menu.
2. Within the pop-up menu, select the Toolbars option and then click your mouse on the Desktop option, placing a check mark next to the option.

---

37 USING THE TASKBAR'S QUICK LAUNCH TOOLBAR TO ACCESS THE WINDOWS 98 INTERNET UTILITIES

To help you maximize your use of the Internet and World Wide Web, Windows 98 provides the Internet Explorer (software you can use to browse the Web) and Microsoft Outlook Express (software you can use to send and receive electronic mail). Tip 799 introduces the Internet Explorer and Tip 858 introduces Microsoft Outlook Express. To provide you with quick access to these key Internet-based software programs, Windows 98 lets you display the Quick Launch toolbar on the Taskbar, as shown in Figure 37.

Figure 37 *The Taskbar's Quick Launch toolbar provides you with quick access to key Internet programs.*

To enable the Taskbar's Quick Launch toolbar, perform these steps:

1. Right-click your mouse on an unused area within the Taskbar. Windows 98, in turn, will display a pop-up menu.
2. Within the pop-up menu, select the Toolbars option and then click your mouse on the Quick Launch option, placing a check mark next to the option.

38   CREATING A TASKBAR'S TOOLBAR FOR YOUR OWN FOLDER
OR INTERNET ADDRESS

Over the past several tips, you learned how to use the Address, Links, Desktop, and Quick Launch Taskbar toolbars that Windows 98 predefines for your use. In addition to these four toolbars, Windows 98 will let you use a folder or Web address to create your own toolbar. For example, assume that you have three programs that you run on a regular basis. Using the Windows 98 Explorer, you can create a folder to which you copy the programs or program shortcuts. Then, by assigning the folder to a Taskbar toolbar, you will gain quick access to the programs. To create you own Taskbar toolbar, perform these steps:

1. Right-click your mouse on an unused area within the Taskbar. Windows 98, in turn, will display a pop-up menu.
2. Within the pop-up menu, select the Toolbars option and then click your mouse on the New Toolbar option. Windows 98, in turn, will display the New Toolbar dialog box, as shown in Figure 38.

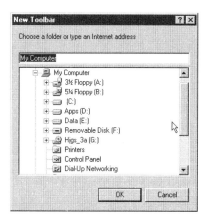

Figure 38 *The New Toolbar dialog box.*

3. Within the New Toolbar dialog box, select the folder for which you want to create the toolbar or type in the Web address of the site for which you want to use a toolbar.
4. Within the New Toolbar dialog box, click your mouse on the OK button. Windows 98, in turn, will place the new toolbar onto your Taskbar.

39   USING THE START MENU RUN OPTION TO RUN
A PROGRAM

Usually, you will run programs by selecting the program from a menu option within the Windows 98 Start menu's Programs submenu or by clicking your mouse on a Desktop icon that corresponds to your program. Using the Start menu is the easiest way to access the programs your PC contains.

However, when you purchase a new program that you want to install onto your system, you need a different way to run the program (because the Start menu only lists the programs that currently reside on your system).

Most of the programs you purchase will come with a special installation program named *Setup*. To run the Setup program, you can use the Start menu Run option. Windows 98, in turn, will display the Run dialog box, as shown in Figure 39.1.

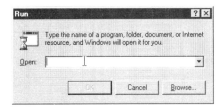

Figure 39.1 *The Run dialog box.*

Within the Run dialog box, you must type the name of the program you want to run, such as Setup, preceded by the drive letter of the disk drive on which the program resides (as well as a colon and a backslash, such D:\). For example, assume that you purchase a program that comes on a CD-ROM. To run the program's installation program, you would type the program name preceded by your CD-ROM drive letter (and a colon and a backslash). For example, if your CD-ROM drive is drive D, you type D:\SETUP as shown in Figure 39.2.

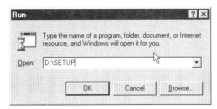

Figure 39.2 *Specifying a program name and disk drive within the Run dialog box.*

---

40 ## USING THE RUN DIALOG BOX PULL-DOWN LIST TO RUN RECENTLY USED COMMANDS

In Tip 39, you learned how to run programs using the Start menu Run option. As you learned, when you select the Run option, Windows 98 will display the Run dialog box. Within the Run dialog box, you can type in the name of the program that you want to run or you can use the Browse button to select the program file that you desire. To help you run programs that you have recently run using the Run dialog box, Windows 98 adds each program you run using the dialog box to a pull-down list that you can access from within the dialog box, as shown in Figure 40. Within the pull-down list, click your mouse on the program you want to run and then click your mouse on the OK button.

Figure 40 *Using the Run dialog box's pull-down list of recently used commands.*

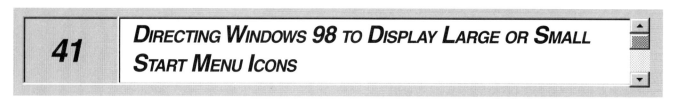

41 DIRECTING WINDOWS 98 TO DISPLAY LARGE OR SMALL START MENU ICONS

Depending on your screen resolution, and possibly on your eyesight or the number of hours you spend at your computer screen, there may be times when your screen's text or icons become a blur. To make it easier for you to view your Start menu icons, Windows 98 lets you display large or small icons on the Start menu, as shown in Figure 41.1.

Figure 41.1 *Windows 98 lets you display large or small Start menu icons.*

If you have difficulty seeing your Start menu icons, you can use the large icons. In contrast, if your Start menu contains many options, you may want to use the small icons simply to improve the menu's appearance. To select the size of the Start menu icons, perform these steps:

1. Click your mouse on the Start button. Windows 98, in turn, will display the Start menu.
2. Within the Start menu, select the Settings option. Windows 98 will display the Settings submenu.
3. Within the Settings submenu, select the Taskbar & Start Menu option. Windows 98, in turn, will display the Taskbar Properties dialog box, shown in Figure 41.2.

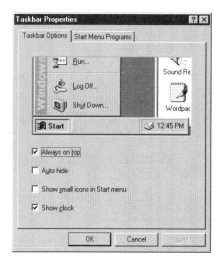

Figure 41.2 *The Taskbar Properties dialog box.*

4. To select the small Start menu icons, place a check mark within the Show small icons in Start menu checkbox. To display the large icons, remove the check mark.

5. Within the Taskbar Properties dialog box, click your mouse on the OK button.

42 **MOVING A WINDOW FROM ONE SCREEN LOCATION TO ANOTHER**

As you have learned, Windows 98 lets you run two or more programs at the same time. Depending on each window's size and position, there may be times when Windows 98 does not display a program's window where you want it. For example, Figure 42.1 shows three programs running within the Windows 98 Desktop. Assume, for example, that you want to move the windows to locations shown in Figure 42.2 so you can better view each window's contents.

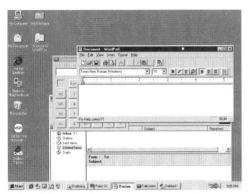

Figure 42.1 Three overlapping program windows.   *Figure 42.2* Moving program windows on the Desktop.

To move a program window, aim your mouse pointer at the window's title bar. Next, with your mouse pointer still aiming at the title bar, hold down your mouse-select button (Usually your left-mouse button) and move your mouse to drag the window to the screen location you desire.

In addition to moving a window using your mouse, Windows 98 lets you move a window using your keyboard arrow keys. To move a window using your keyboard, press the ALT-SPACEBAR keyboard combination to display the window's Control menu. Within the Control menu, select the Move option. Windows 98, in turn, will let you then move the window by pressing your arrow keys. After you move the window to the location you desire, press the ENTER key to end the move operation.

43 **DRAGGING A WINDOW'S FRAME TO SIZE THE WINDOW**

In Tip 42, you learned how to move a window on your Desktop by using your mouse to drag the window's title bar. Likewise, in Tips 16 and 18 you learned how to minimize and maximize a window. Depending on a window's contents, there may be times when you want to increase or decrease a window's size incrementally. For example, Figure 43.1 shows two windows on the Windows 98 Desktop. By sizing each window, you can increase one window's size, while decreasing the second window's size, as shown in Figure 43.2.

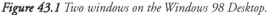

Figure 43.1 *Two windows on the Windows 98 Desktop.*

Figure 43.2 *Sizing windows on the Desktop.*

With the exception of windows that contain dialog or message boxes, Windows 98 lets you size most program windows. To size a window using your mouse, aim your mouse pointer at one of the window's four frames. Windows 98, in turn, will change your mouse pointer into double-ended arrows. Next, hold down your mouse-select button and move your mouse to drag the frame in or out to change the window's size. When the window is the size you desire, release your mouse-select button.

By dragging a window's right or left frames, Windows 98 lets you change a window's width. Likewise, by dragging the window's top or bottom frames, you can change the window's height. To change the window's width and height at the same time, drag one of the window's corner frames.

44 **USING THE CONTROL MENU TO CONTROL A PROGRAM'S WINDOW SETTINGS**

In several of the preceding Tips, you have learned how to move, size, minimize, maximize, and close a program's window. If you examine the upper-left corner of a program window, you will find a small button (the Control menu icon) that corresponds to a special Control menu. If you click your mouse on the Control menu icon, Windows 98 will display the program's Control menu. For example, Figure 44 shows the Control menu for the WordPad accessory which, as you will find, looks almost identical to every program's Control menu.

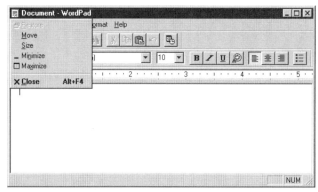

Figure 44 *The Control menu for the WordPad accessory program.*

Within the Control menu, you can select options that will let you move, size, and even close the current window. In general, the Control menu provides you with yet another way to perform common window operations. In addition to accessing the Control menu by clicking your mouse on the Control menu icon, you can usually activate the Control menu by pressing the ALT-SPACEBAR keyboard combination. Finally, in addition to closing a window by clicking your mouse on the window's Close button (the big X that appears in the upper-right side of the window), you can also close a window by double-clicking your mouse on the Control menu icon. As Table 44 explains, the Control menu lets you control the size and placement of windows.

Option	Description
Restore	Restores the window to its former size.
Move	Lets you move the window with the ARROW keys.
Size	Lets you change the size of the window using the ARROW keys.
Minimize	Shrinks the window to a Taskbar icon or, if the window is a document window (a window within a parent window), shrinks the window to an icon within the parent program.
Maximize	Expands the window to consume the entire screen, or to fill the window's parent window if the window is a document window (a window within a window).
Close	Closes the window. If the window is a program, Windows 98 will end the program.

Table 44 *The Control menu lets you control the size and placement of windows.*

45 ***SHUTTING DOWN WINDOWS 98 BEFORE YOU TURN OFF YOUR COMPUTER***

As a rule, never turn off your PC's power before you shut down Windows 98. If you don't shut down Windows 98 before you turn off your PC, you may lose your recent work and, worse yet, the information you have previously stored on your disk. To shut down Windows 98, perform these steps:

1. Using one of the techniques discussed in Tip 12, close all your open programs.

2. Click your mouse on the Start button. Windows 98, In turn, will display the Start menu.

3. Within the Start menu, select the Shut Down option. Windows 98, in turn, will display the Shut Down Windows dialog box, as shown in Figure 45.

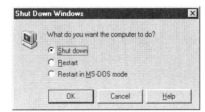

Figure 45 *The Shut Down Windows dialog box.*

4. Within the Shut Down Windows dialog box, click your mouse on the OK button. Windows 98, in turn, will safely record your current data on your disk and will eventually display a message that tells you that you can safely turn off your computer's power.

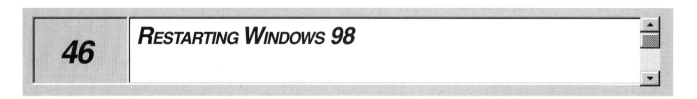

46   *RESTARTING WINDOWS 98*

When you install new software or if your system hangs, you may need to shutdown and restart Windows 98. In Tip 45, you learned how to shut down Windows 98 before you power off your computer. By shutting down your system, turning off your PC's power, and then turning your PC's power back on, you essentially shut down and restart Windows 98. However, Windows 98 lets you restart it without making you turn your PC's power off and on. To restart Windows 98 without toggling your PC's power, perform these steps:

1. Click your mouse on the Start button. Windows 98 will display the Start menu.
2. Within the Start menu, select the Shut Down option. Windows 98, in turn, will display the Shut Down Windows dialog box.
3. Within the Shutdown dialog box, select the Restart the computer option.

Depending on the number of programs you run throughout your day, you may find that you can improve your system performance by restarting your computer once a day—such as every morning before you start your work.

47   *A FASTER WAY TO RESTART WINDOWS 98*

In Tip 46, you learned how to shut down Windows 98 by selecting the Start menu Shut Down option. As you learned, when you select the Shut Down option, Windows 98 will display the Shut Down Windows dialog box, as shown in Figure 47, that you can use to shut down or restart your system.

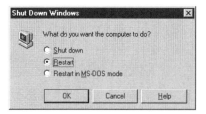

Figure 47 The Shut Down Windows dialog box.

Usually, when you select the Shut Down menu Restart option, Windows 98 will first reboot your computer and will then restart Windows 98. If, for example, you are restarting your system because you have installed new software, you can speed up the restart process by directing Windows 98 to restart itself without rebooting your PC. To restart only Windows 98 (without rebooting the PC), select the Start menu Shut Down option. Windows 98, in turn, will display its Shut Down Windows dialog box. Within the Shut Down Windows dialog box, click your mouse on the Restart option. Next, hold down the SHIFT key as you click your mouse on the OK button.

48 ENDING AN APPLICATION USING A LOCAL REBOOT OPERATION

As you run programs within Windows 98, there will be times when a program simply will not run or when the program stops working (users describe this situation as "the program hangs" or the "program is hung"). If you think that a program is no longer working, try to end the program using any of the steps Tip 12 presents.

If you cannot end the program using normal steps, Windows 98 may be able to shut down by performing a "local reboot" of a specific program window. When you direct Windows 98 to perform a local reboot, Windows 98 will shut down only the program you select, and not the entire computer. To perform a local reboot within Windows 98, perform these steps:

1. Press the CTRL-ALT-DEL keyboard combination by first holding down the CTRL key, and then pressing down the ALT key, followed by the DEL (or DELETE) key. Windows 98, in turn, will display the Close Program dialog box, as shown in Figure 48. Usually, the name of the program you want Windows 98 to end will appear at the top of the list of program names within the Close Program dialog box.

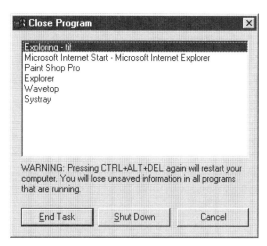

Figure 48 *The Close Program dialog box.*

2. Within the Close Program dialog box, click your mouse on the name of the program you want to end. Windows 98, in turn, will highlight the program name.

3. Within the Close Program dialog box, click your mouse on the End Task button to close the program.

Note: *In some cases, Windows 98 may have trouble ending the program on its first try, and you may need to repeat these steps several times to end the program. Use a local reboot as a "last resort" to end a program. In most cases, after you end a program using a local reboot, you will lose any work you had performed within the program, but not yet saved.*

As you work with large documents, such as a report or spreadsheet, your program windows will not always be large enough to display a document's entire contents. In some cases, you may be able to display the document within the window by maximizing the window. If, however, you still cannot see your entire document, you can use window's *scroll bars* (which you will find at the right and, sometimes, at the bottom of the window) to move (scroll) through the window's contents. Figure 49 displays vertical scroll bar within a window. If your current window does not contain a scroll bar, the window is currently displaying your entire document and there is nothing for you to scroll through.

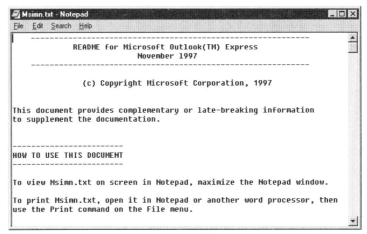

Figure 49 *To move through a large document, you can use the window's scroll bars.*

As you move through your document, Windows 98 will move a small *scroll box* within the scroll bar that you can use as a guide to your relative position within the document. For example, if a scroll box appears near the top of the vertical scroll bar, you are viewing information that appears near the start of your document. Likewise, if the scroll box appears at the bottom of the scroll bar, the program window is displaying content at the document's end.

To scroll through a document using a scrollbar, use your mouse to drag the scroll box within the scroll bar in the direction you want to move through the document. In addition, if you examine each end of a scroll bar, you will find up and down or right and left facing arrows. If you click your mouse on one of the arrow buttons, Windows 98 will move the scroll box in the corresponding direction. Finally, if you click your mouse on the scroll bar itself, Windows 98 will advance through your document using large steps, about the size of the window's current display size.

Within Windows 98 and the programs you run, you will make extensive use of pull-down menus to perform a variety of operations. For example, the WordPad word-processing accessory that Tip 565 introduces. Beneath the window's title bar, you will find a menu bar within which WordPad displays the names of each of its menus, as shown in Figure 50.1.

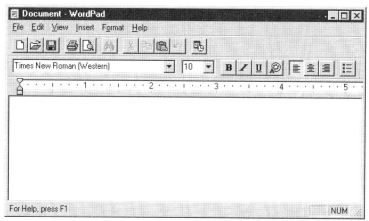

Figure 50.1 *Within WordPad, as is the case with most programs, the menu bar appears beneath the window's title bar.*

Within a menu bar, you will usually access a pull-down menu by clicking your mouse on the menu name of the menu you want to view. In addition, you can use your keyboard to access a pull-down menu by holding down the ALT key as you type the letter that the program underlines within the menu's name. Within WordPad, for example, you can access the File menu by pressing the ALT-F keyboard combination. Likewise, to access the Edit menu, you would press ALT-E.

Figure 50.2 shows the WordPad File menu. To select an option from within a pull-down menu, click your mouse on the option you desire, or, using your keyboard, press the ARROW keys to highlight the correct option and then press ENTER.

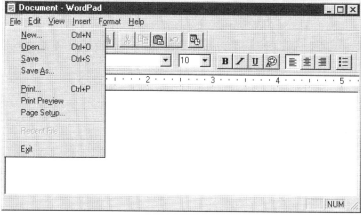

Figure 50.2 *The WordPad File menu.*

Within a pull-down menu, you will often encounter options that include ellipses (the dots, …). After you select a menu option that contains ellipses, the program will display a dialog box that asks you for more information. For example, if you select the WordPad File menu Save As option (an option that includes ellipses), WordPad will display the Save As dialog box.

As you examine options within a menu, you will find that the menu usually underlines a specific letter within each option. For example, within the File menu New option, the menu underlines the letter N. Within a menu, you can select an option by typing the corresponding underlined character.

If you examine the Start menu, you will find several menu options that include a right-facing arrow (such as the Settings option or the Programs option). When you move your mouse pointer over such an option, Windows 98 will cascade the option to display a submenu. For example, Figure 50.3 shows Windows 98 *cascading* the Start menu Programs option to display the Programs submenu.

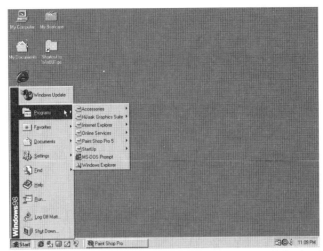

Figure 50.3 *When you click your mouse on a menu with a right-facing arrow, the program will display (cascade) a submenu.*

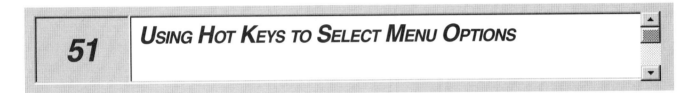

51 | **USING HOT KEYS TO SELECT MENU OPTIONS**

As you have learned, Windows 98 (as well as most Windows-based programs) makes extensive use of menus to help you simplify specific tasks. Within a menu, you can select an option by clicking your mouse on the option or by using your keyboard arrow keys to highlight the option, then pressing ENTER. In addition, many menus define one or more hot-key combinations you can press to perform an operation without having to open the menu and select the corresponding option. For example, Figure 51 shows the WordPad File menu. To the right of several options within the WordPad File menu, you will see the option's corresponding hot-key combination.

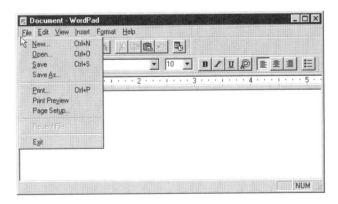

Figure 51 *The WordPad File menu.*

Within the WordPad File menu, for example, you can press the CTRL+N hot-key combination to create a new document, CTRL+O to open an existing document, CTRL+S to save the current document, and CTRL+P to print the current document. By using the hot-hey combinations, you can perform operations without having to select the options from the File menu.

52 MOVING THROUGHOUT DIALOG BOX SHEETS, PAGES, AND TABS

As you work with Windows 98 and Windows-based programs, you will make extensive use of dialog boxes, which your programs will display when they need you to enter more information. For example, when you save a document to a file on disk, your program will display the Save As dialog box, within which you can specify the file's name. Likewise, when you print a document, your program may display the Print dialog box, within which you can select the printer you desire or specify the number of copies you want the program to print.

Within a dialog box, you will usually find text fields, checkboxes, radio buttons, and a pull-down list. Depending on the dialog box's purpose, the fields for which you must provide values will differ. Figure 52.1, for example, illustrates the WordPad Print dialog box. which contains a pull-down list which you can use to select a printer, radio buttons which you can use to specify the print range, text fields which you can use to specify the starting and ending pages, and checkboxes which you can use to direct WordPad to print to a file or to collate your output.

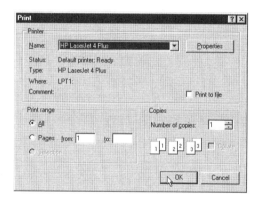

Figure 52.1 The WordPad Print dialog box.

Depending on the amount of information the dialog box requires, there may be times when the dialog box cannot place all its fields on a page. In such cases, the dialog box will have two or more tabs upon which you can click your mouse to display a specific sheet. For example, Figure 52.2 displays the Taskbar Properties dialog box, which contains two tabs.

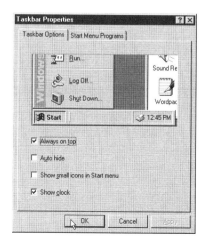

Figure 52.2 The Taskbar Properties dialog box.

Within the Taskbar Properties dialog box, if you click your mouse on the Start Menu Programs tab, Windows 98 will display the Start Menu Programs sheet, as shown in Figure 52.3.

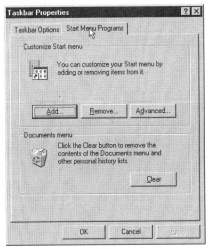

Figure 52.3 *The Taskbar Properties dialog box Start Menu Programs sheet.*

53 TO CANCEL A DIALOG BOX, PRESS THE ESC KEY

As you have learned, Windows 98, as well as most Windows-based programs, make extensive use of dialog boxes to prompt you for more information. As you work, there may be times when you decide you do not want to perform the dialog box operation. To cancel the current dialog box, you can click your mouse on the dialog box's Cancel button. Likewise, you can also press your keyboard's ESC button to cancel the dialog box.

54 USING YOUR MOUSE OR KEYBOARD TO SELECT DIALOG BOX OPTIONS

Most dialog boxes contain several different fields for which you may have to assign values. Within a dialog box, you can select a field by simply clicking your mouse on the field. If you feel more comfortable using your keyboard than your mouse, you can move from one field to another within a dialog box by pressing your keyboard's Tab key. Each time you press Tab, Windows 98 will advance to the next field within the dialog box. To move back to the previous field, you can press the Shift-Tab keyboard combination. Finally, if you examine a dialog box's fields closely, you will find that the dialog box underlines one character within each field name. To select a field, you can hold down your keyboard's Alt key and then type the field's underlined character.

Note: *Within a dialog box, press the TAB key to move from one field to the next, not the ENTER key. Often, after a user types an entry for a text field, they will press the ENTER key, which usually corresponds to the OK button. As a result, the user does not specify all the information the dialog box requires.*

---

55 | **USING CHECKBOXES WITHIN A DIALOG BOX TO CHOOSE MULTIPLE OPTIONS**

As you have learned, Windows-based programs display dialog boxes when they require you to provide more information. Within a dialog box, programs often use checkboxes to let you specify which options you desire. For example, Figure 55 shows the Taskbar Properties dialog box. Within the dialog box, Windows 98 uses checkboxes to let you select various Taskbar settings.

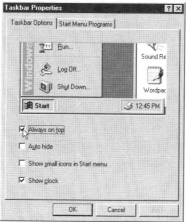

Figure 55 *Checkboxes within the Taskbar Properties dialog box.*

Windows 98 treats checkboxes as toggle controls meaning, if a checkbox currently contains a check mark, clicking your mouse on the checkbox will remove the mark. Likewise, if the checkbox does not contain a check mark, clicking your mouse on the checkbox will add one. To select and deselect checkboxes within a dialog box, perform any of these steps:

- Click your mouse-select button on the checkbox.

- Hold down your keyboard's ALT key and type the letter that appears underlined within the checkbox caption.

- Press your keyboard's TAB key to highlight the checkbox field and then press the SPACEBAR.

---

56 | **USING RADIO BUTTONS WITHIN A DIALOG BOX TO SELECT A SPECIFIC OPTION**

As you learned in Tip 55, Windows-based programs often display checkboxes within a dialog box to let you choose a specific option. Often, a program will require that you choose one of a specific number of options. In such cases, the program will use two or more radio buttons—so named because they operate much like a car radio that only lets you push one station button at a time. For example, Figure 56 displays the WordPad Print dialog box which uses radio buttons to let you specify the range of the document that you want to print. Within the dialog box, you can print the entire document, a specific number of pages, or the text you have currently selected. You cannot, however, select all three options for printing at one time—you must pick one.

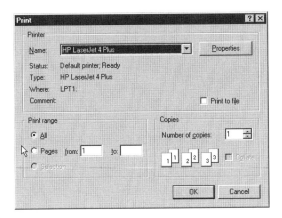

Figure 56 *The WordPad Print dialog box.*

To select a radio button within a dialog box, perform any of these steps:.

- Click your mouse-select button on the radio button.

- Hold down your keyboard's ALT key and type the letter that appears underlined within the checkbox caption.

- Press your keyboard's TAB key to highlight the first radio button within the field and then press your keyboard's ARROW keys to highlight the button you desire.

57   USING A PULL-DOWN LIST WITHIN A DIALOG BOX TO SELECT AN OPTION

Windows-based programs display dialog boxes to prompt you for specific information. Depending on the dialog box's purpose, the fields within dialog boxes will vary. Often, a dialog box will want you to select an item from a list of available options. In such cases, the dialog box will use a pull-down list. For example, Figure 57.1 displays the WordPad Print dialog box, which uses a pull-down list to let you select the printer to which you want WordPad to print your output.

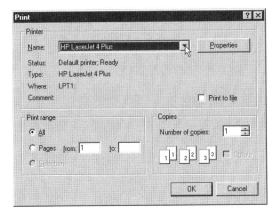

Figure 57.1 *The WordPad Print dialog box.*

When you open a pull-down list, the dialog box will display the list's entries (possibly with a scroll bar you can use to move through a long list). For example, Figure 57.2 shows the Print dialog box with the Printer pull-down list open. To select an item within the pull-down list, click your mouse on the option you desire or use your keyboard arrow keys to move through the list of options to highlight the option you desire and then press E*NTER*.

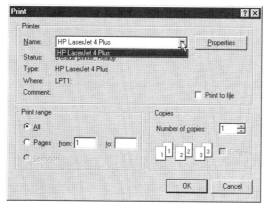

Figure 57.2 *Pulling down the Printer pull-down list to reveal a list of available printers.*

To open a pull-down list within a dialog box, you can perform any of these steps:

- Click your mouse on the arrow that appears to the right of the pull-down list.

- Press your keyboard's T*AB* key to highlight the list and then press the S*HIFT*-D*OWN* A*RROW* keyboard combination to open the list.

- Hold down your keyboard's **A**LT key and type the letter that appears underlined within the list caption. Next, press the S*HIFT*-D*OWN* A*RROW* keyboard combination to open the list.

---

58 USING A TEXTBOX WITHIN A DIALOG BOX TO TYPE INFORMATION

As you have learned, dialog boxes exist within Windows 98 and Windows-based programs to help you provide a program with additional information. Depending on the dialog box's purpose, there may be times when you must type in text, such as your name, a filename, or a Web-site address. In such cases, the dialog box will display a text field. For example, Figure 58 illustrates the Run dialog box that uses the Open text field to prompt you for the name of the program you want to run.

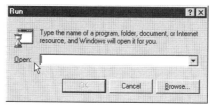

Figure 58 *The Open text field within the Run dialog box.*

Within a text field, you simply type the text that you desire. After you type your text, however, you should not press ENTER unless you are done using the dialog box. Usually, the ENTER key corresponds to the OK button. If you type your text and then press ENTER, Windows 98 will assume you are done with the dialog box. If you have other fields within the dialog box to which you must assign values, press the TAB key to select the fields or click your mouse on the next field. After you are done entering information into the dialog box, you can then click your mouse on the OK button or press the ENTER key.

If a textbox contains text, you can select the box (by clicking your mouse on the box, by pressing the TAB key to cycle through the other fields to the textbox, or by holding down the ALT key as you type the letter that appears underlined within the field name) and then, using your keyboard arrow keys, as well as the DEL and BACKSPACE keys, edit the existing text.

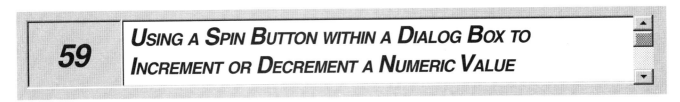

59 **USING A SPIN BUTTON WITHIN A DIALOG BOX TO INCREMENT OR DECREMENT A NUMERIC VALUE**

Depending on a dialog box's purpose, there may be times when you must enter or change a numeric value. In such cases, the dialog box will often use spin buttons upon which you can click your mouse to increment or decrement the value by one. For example, Figure 59 displays the Date/Time Properties dialog box that uses spin buttons to let you increment the current year as well as the current hours, minutes, and seconds.

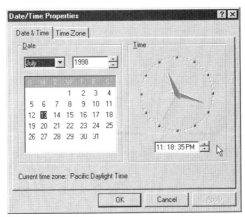

Figure 59 *Spin buttons within the Date/Time Properties dialog box.*

To increment or decrement a numeric value using a spin button, you can perform any of these steps:

- To increment the current value, click your mouse on the up-arrow that appears to the right of the spin button. To decrement the current value, click your mouse on the down-arrow.

- Press your keyboard's TAB key to highlight the spin-button field. To increment the current value, press the CTRL-UP ARROW keyboard combination. To decrement the current value, press CTRL-DOWN ARROW.

- Hold down your keyboard's ALT key and type the letter that appears underlined within the spin-button caption. To increment the current value, press the CTRL-UP ARROW keyboard combination. To decrement the current value, press CTRL-DOWN ARROW.

60 UNDERSTANDING AND USING THE OK, CANCEL, AND APPLY BUTTONS WITHIN A DIALOG BOX

After you provide values for the fields within a dialog box, you must tell your program that you have completed your input. Most dialog boxes will display OK and Cancel buttons. In some cases, the dialog box will include an Apply button as well. For example, Figure 60 displays the Date/Time Properties dialog box that includes the OK, Cancel, and Apply buttons.

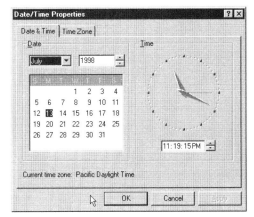

Figure 60 *The Date/Time Properties dialog box.*

When you are done with the dialog box and you want your program to use your input values, click your mouse on the OK button. The program, in turn, will close the dialog box and process your entries. If, however, you don't want the program to use your input or you simply want the program to cancel the current operation, click your mouse on the Cancel button. The program will close the dialog box and will ignore any inputs you made. Finally, there may be times when you want the program to put your values to immediate use while leaving the dialog box open. In such cases, you should click your mouse on the dialog box Apply option. The program, in turn, will immediately use (apply) your inputs but will leave the dialog box open for additional processing. To select the OK, Cancel, or Apply buttons, you can perform any of these steps:

- Click your mouse on the button you desire.

- Press your keyboard's TAB key to highlight the button you desire and then press ENTER.

- Hold down your keyboard's ALT key and type the letter that appears underlined within the button name (often, only the Apply button will have an underlined character).

61 WINDOWS 98 ONLINE HELP PROVIDES A WIDE RANGE OF SOLUTIONS

As you will learn throughout this book's Tips, Windows 98, and the programs it includes, provides you with a wide range of capabilities. If, as you work with Windows 98, you encounter a problem and you do not have this book close at hand, you can quite likely find an answer to situation within Windows 98 on-line help. Several of the tips that follow examine the Windows 98 Help system in detail. You should take time now to learn how to use Windows 98 Help. As you will learn, most Windows-based programs provide an on-line help facility which is identical to the one you will learn how to use now. By learning how to use Windows 98 on-line Help, you are actually learning how to use the help facility for most programs you will run. To start the Windows 98 on-line Help, perform these steps:

1. Click your mouse on the Start button. Windows 98, in turn, will display the Start menu.
2. Within the Start menu, select the Help option. Windows 98, in turn, will display the Windows Help window, as shown in Figure 61.1.

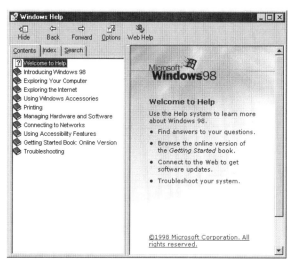

Figure 61.1 *The Windows Help window.*

Windows 98 organizes the Windows Help window by displaying three sheets. Within the Contents sheet shown in Figure 61.1, you will encounter a table of contents that presents the Help topics much like the table of contents you would find at the front of a book. To start, the Contents sheet displays a book icon next to key topics. If you click your mouse on the book icon, Windows 98 will further expand the topic, showing additional levels of detail, as shown in Figure 61.2.

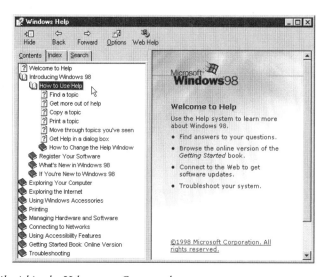

Figure 61.2 *Displaying levels of detail within the Help system Contents sheet.*

When you encounter a question mark icon in front of a topic, you have located a topic for which Help will display textual instructions. For example, if you click your mouse on the Find a Topic entry, shown in Figure 61.2, Help will display the corresponding instructional text within its right-hand window frame, as shown in Figure 61.3.

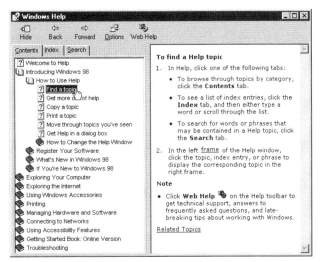

Figure 61.3 *Displaying Help text on a specific topic from within the Contents sheet.*

If you click your mouse on the Help window Index tab, Help will display an index (a list) that contains an entry for each topic it discusses, as shown in Figure 61.4. Using your mouse or keyboard arrow keys, you can scroll through the list of topics.

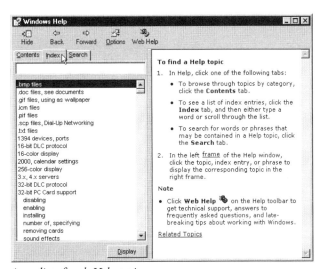

Figure 61.4 *The Help Index sheet contains a list of each Help topic.*

Within the Index sheet's text field, you can type the topic you desire. With each letter that you type, Help will display the corresponding matching terms. For example, assume that you want information on Printers. As you type the letter **P**, Help will display its topics that start with the letter P.

After you type the letter **r**, Help will display the topics that start with **Pr**. By the time you type the letters **Prin**, Help will display the Printer topics shown in Figure 61.5. After you locate the entry you desire, click your mouse on the Display button. Help, in turn, will display its instructional text within its right-hand window frame.

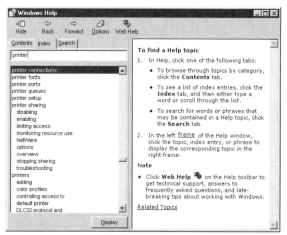

Figure 61.5 *Using the Help Index sheet to locate a topic.*

Depending on the entry you choose from Help's index list, there may be times when Help provides multiple topics that discuss your entry. In such cases, Help will display a pop-up Topics Found window within which it lists the available topics, as shown in Figure 61.6. Within the Topics Found window, click your mouse on the Topic you desire and then click your mouse on the Display button.

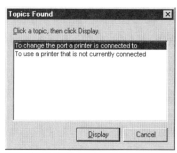

Figure 61.6 *Selecting a topic from within the Topics Found pop-up window.*

If you click your mouse on the Help window Search button, Help will display the Search sheet, as shown in Figure 61.7. Within the Search sheet's textbox, you can type in your topic of interest, such as Printers, and then click your mouse on the List Topics button. Help, in turn, will search all its topics for a match and will display the matching topics within a topic list. If you find the topic you desire, click your mouse on the topic and then click your mouse on the Display button. Help, in turn, will display its instructional text within its right-hand window frame.

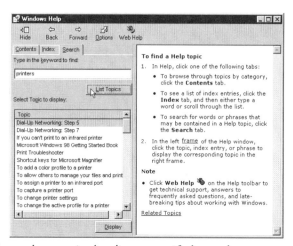

Figure 61.7 *Using the Help Search sheet to locate topics that discuss a specific keyword.*

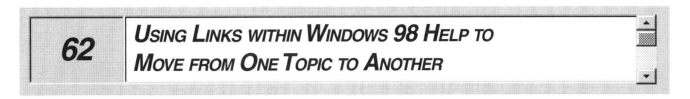

62 USING LINKS WITHIN WINDOWS *98* HELP TO MOVE FROM ONE TOPIC TO ANOTHER

In Tip 61, you learned how to start the Windows 98 Help system and how to look up a topic within Help. As you also learned, when you direct Help to display its instructional text, Help will show the text within its right-hand window frame. As you examine Help's instructional text, you will often encounter one or more words that Help underlines. Such underlined text is a *Help link*. If you click your mouse on the link, Help will immediately display the corresponding text within the right-hand window frame. By clicking your mouse on links as you read Help's instructional text, you can quickly move from one related topic to another. To better understand how Help links work, perform these steps:

1. Within the Help Search sheet, type in the text **Internet** and then click your mouse on the List Topics button. Help, in turn, will display a list of topics that use the term Internet.

2. Within Help's topic list, click your mouse on the Active Desktop topic and then click your mouse on the Display button. Help, in turn, will display the instructions shown in Figure 62.1.

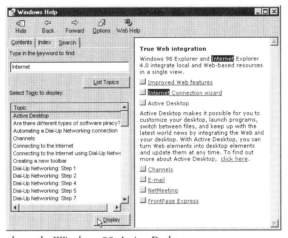

Figure 62.1 *Displaying instructional text about the Windows 98 Active Desktop.*

3. Within Help's instructional text, each topic that appears underlined is a Help link. In this case, click your mouse on the Improved Web features link. Help will display text that corresponds to the new features built into the Windows 98 Explorer, as shown in Figure 62.2.

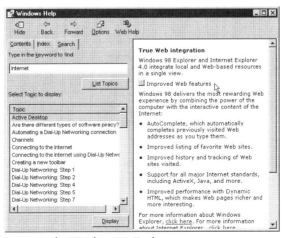

Figure 62.2 *Using a Help link to branch to text on the Windows 98 Explorer.*

4. If you scroll through Help's text on the Windows 98 Explorer, you will encounter other links. If you click your mouse on a link, Help, will again, display the related text.

63   **RETURNING TO A HELP TOPIC YOU PREVIOUSLY VIEWED**

In Tip 62, you learned how to use Help links to move from one topic within Help's instructional text to another. When you use links to move from topic to topic in this way, there may be times when you want to return to a previous topic. In such cases, click your mouse on the Back button that appears within Help's toolbar, as shown in Figure 63.

In a similar way, as you move back several topics using the Back button, there may be times when you will then want to move in the opposite direction. For example, assume that you use Help to view a topic that, for the sake of this example, is Topic 1. Then, you view Topic 2, followed by Topic 3. If you click your mouse on the Back button, Help will display Topic 2. At that point, you can click your mouse on the Back button a second time to display Topic 1 or you can click your mouse on the Previous button to display Topic 3. By using the Back and Previous buttons, you can move back and forth throughout your recent Help topics.

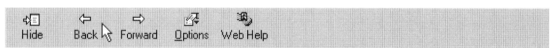

Figure 63 *To return to a topic, click your mouse on the Help toolbar Back button.*

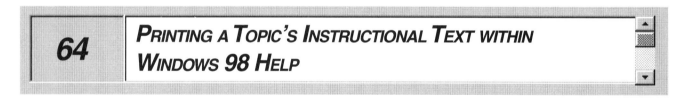

64   **PRINTING A TOPIC'S INSTRUCTIONAL TEXT WITHIN WINDOWS 98 HELP**

After you find the Help topic you desire, you may find it convenient to print a hard copy of Help's instructional text. In that way, you do not have to continually switch between your program and Help. To print the current instructional text within Help, perform these steps:

1. After you display the Help text that you want to print, right-click your mouse within Help's right-hand frame. Windows 98, in turn, will display a pop-up menu.
2. Within the pop-up menu, click your mouse on the Print option. Help will print the corresponding instructional text.

65   **WINDOWS 98 LETS YOU COPY AND PASTE A HELP TOPIC'S TEXT TO THE CLIPBOARD**

If you work in an office with other users, you may have to assist them with problems or questions regarding Windows 98. In such cases, by using Windows 98 Help, you can look up an answer to the user's problem and then print Help's instructional text, as discussed in Tip 64. In addition, if your office uses electronic mail, you can copy Help's instructional text to the Clipboard and then paste the text into an e-mail message that you send to the user. To copy Help text to the Clipboard, perform these steps:

1. Within Help's instructional text, drag your mouse over the text you desire. As you drag your mouse, Help will highlight your selected text.

2. Right-click your mouse within your selected text. Windows 98, in turn, will display a small pop-up menu.

3. Within the pop-up menu, click your mouse on the Copy option. Help, in turn, will copy your selected text to the Clipboard.

Note: *If you want to select all the text regarding the current topic, right-click your mouse within the instructional text and then choose the Select All option from within the pop-up menu.*

66 **HIDING AND LATER REDISPLAYING HELP'S CONTENT, INDEX, AND SEARCH TABS**

As you have learned, the Windows on-line Help window displays two window frames, as shown in Figure 66.1. Within the Help window's left-hand frame, Help displays the Contents, Index, and Search tabs. Within the right-hand frame, Help displays its instructional text.

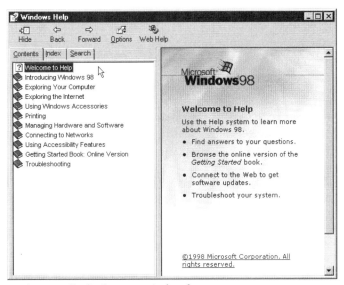

Figure 66.1 *The Windows 98 Help window usually displays two window frames.*

Depending on the number of items Windows 98 displays on your screen, there may be times when you want to reduce your screen clutter by only displaying Help's instructional text (but not the Contents, Index, and Search tabs). To turn off the Help window's left-hand frame display, click your mouse on the Help toolbar Hide button. Help, in turn, will only display its instructional text, as shown in Figure 66.2. If you later want to display the left-hand frame, click your mouse on the toolbar Show button.

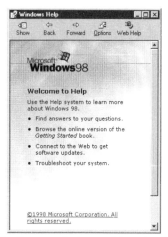

Figure 66.2 Suppressing the Help window display of the Contents, Index, and Search tabs.

67 **USING HELP TO SEARCH FOR TOPICS ON THE WEB**

Although the Windows 98 on-line Help is very complete, there may still be times when you cannot find the information that you need within Help. In such cases, you can try finding information on your topic at the Microsoft site on the World Wide Web. To look for Help on a specific subject on the Web, perform these steps:

1. Within the Help window, click your mouse on the Help toolbar Web button and then click your mouse on the Support Online link. If you are not currently connected to the Internet, Windows 98 will connect you. (You will have to specify the username and password that you use to connect to your Internet Service Provider.) Next, Windows 98 will start the Internet Explorer which, in turn, will connect you to the Microsoft Web site.

2. Within the Microsoft Web site, you must first register to use the on-line Help facility by providing Microsoft with your name, e-mail address, and other information. After you register, the Explorer will display a Web page, similar to that shown in Figure 67.1, within which you can search for your topic of interest.

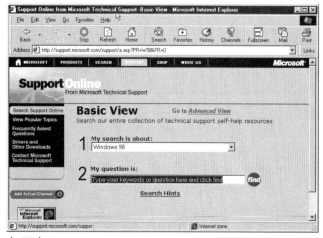

Figure 67.1 Searching for Help using the Web.

3. Type in a subject, such as Web TV, and the Microsoft Web site will display a Web page that contains Help text, troubleshooting techniques, and possibly software updates.

68   TROUBLESHOOTING PROBLEMS WITHIN HELP

In later Tips, you will learn how to use the Windows 98 Control Panel to configure your hardware and software settings. As you add hardware or change system settings, there will be times your change simply will not work. Fortunately, Help provides several step-by-step troubleshooting guides that will walk you through some common fixes. If you experience a problem within Windows 98 that you must fix, select the Help window Search tab and direct Help to search for the term Troubleshooting. Help, in turn, will display the topic list shown in Figure 68.

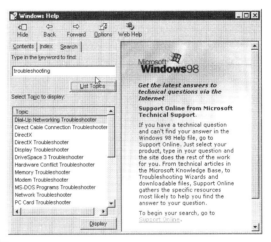

Figure 68 *Help's list of troubleshooting topics.*

Within Help's list of troubleshooting topics, click your mouse on the topic you desire and then click your mouse on the Display button. Help, in turn, will display a page within which you start one of Help's troubleshooters, which will ask you a series of questions about the problem you are experiencing and will offer step-by-step instructions to help you resolve the problem.

69   UNDERSTANDING AND USING WINDOWS 98 CONTEXT-SENSITIVE HELP

In addition to using the Windows 98 on-line Help facility to find information on specific topics, Windows 98 also lets you perform context-sensitive Help operations for which Windows 98 displays help text based upon your current operation. Depending on the operation you are performing, Windows 98 may or may not provide context-sensitive help. For those times that Windows 98 supports context-sensitive help, you will usually see a button that contains a question mark (?) icon. For example, Figure 69.1 shows the WordPad Print dialog box. At the right end of the Print dialog box title bar, you will find a button that contains a question mark.

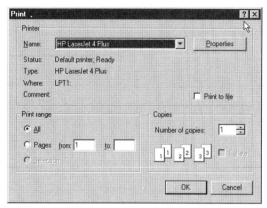

Figure 69.1 *The WordPad Print dialog box supports context-sensitive help.*

To use the context-sensitive Help, click your mouse on the question-mark button. Windows 98, in turn, will change your mouse pointer into an arrow with a question mark. Next, click your mouse on the object for which you want help. In the case of the Print dialog box, you might click your mouse on the Copies field. Windows 98, in turn, will display a context-sensitive pop-up window that contains help text, as shown in Figure 69.2. To close the pop-up window, click your mouse.

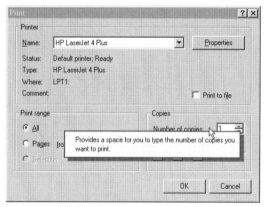

Figure 69.2 *Displaying context-sensitive help within a pop-up window.*

---

70 WINDOWS 98 LETS YOU START MANY OPERATIONS FROM WITHIN HELP

In Tip 68, you learned that within Windows 98 Help, you can start a variety of troubleshooters that will help you resolve common system problems. In addition, as you read through Help's instructional text, there may be times when you can initiate an operation from within Help. For example, another user tells you that you can improve your system performance if you defragment your hard disk. Within the Help Search sheet, you type in the term Defragment and click your mouse on the List Topics button. Help, in turn, will display its topic list. Within the Topic list, click your mouse on the To make files open quickly option and then click your mouse on the Display button. Help will display instructional text about steps you must perform to defragment your disk, as shown in Figure 70.

If you examine Help's instructional text, you will find that the help link within Step 1 of the text's discussion lets you start the Windows 98 Disk Defragmenter. If you click your mouse on the link, Help will start the Disk Defragmenter program. Then, you can read and perform Help's remaining text with the Disk Defragmenter program running. In this way, the Help text essentially takes you step by step through the process of defragmenting your disk. As you examine various topics within Help, you will encounter numerous links that will let you start a specific program from within Help.

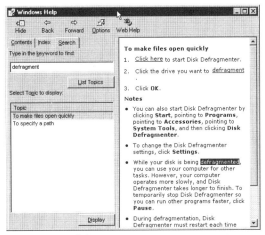

Figure 70 *Help's instructional text on defragmenting your disk.*

71	**ADDING THE CURRENT HELP TOPIC TO YOUR FAVORITES FOLDER**

In Tip 176, you will learn that to help you access key documents, programs, or Web sites quickly, Windows 98 lets you place such objects within a folder on your disk that Windows 98 names Favorites. If you browse the Yahoo Web site, for example, on a regular basis, you might add that Web site to the Favorites folder (which you will learn how to do in Tip 832). Later, when you want to visit the site, you can access the site from the Start menu Favorites submenu, shown in Figure 71.1.

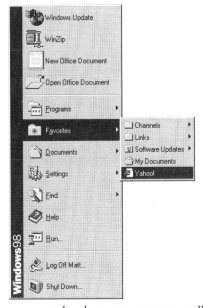

Figure 71.1 *The Start menu Favorites submenu lets you access key documents, programs, or Web sites quickly.*

If, as you use Windows 98 Help, you find a topic whose contents you may need in the future, you can direct Help to place the topic's text within your Favorites folder. Later, to view the text, you can select the corresponding entry from the Favorites submenu. Windows 98, in turn, will open an Internet Explorer window, within which it will display the Help text. To add the current Help topic to the Favorites submenu, perform these steps:

1. Right-click your mouse on the Help topic text. Windows 98will display a pop-up menu.
2. Within the pop-up menu, click your mouse on the Add to Favorites option. Help will display the Add Favorite dialog box, as shown in Figure 71.2.

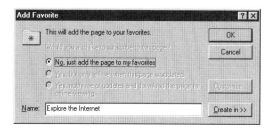

Figure 71.2 *The Add Favorite dialog box.*

3. Within the Add Favorite dialog box Name field, type the name you want Windows 98 to display for this topic within the Favorites submenu and then click your mouse on OK.

72 ADDING THE CURRENT HELP TOPIC TO A SHORTCUT ON YOUR DESKTOP

In Tip 71, you learned how to add a Help topic to the Windows 98 Favorites submenu, which lets you display the Help topic's text without having to search for the topic within Help. In a similar way, after you find the text you desire within Help, there may be times when you will want to store a link (a shortcut) to the text on your Desktop. To create a Desktop shortcut for the current topic within Help, perform these steps:

1. Right-click your mouse on the Help topic text. Windows 98 will display a pop-up menu.
2. Within the pop-up menu, click your mouse on the Create Shortcut option. Help will display a message box telling you it will create the shortcut on your Desktop. Click your mouse on OK.

When you later click your mouse on the Desktop shortcut, Windows 98 will open an Internet Explorer window, within which it will display the Help topic's text. When you no longer need to reference the Help topic, you can use your mouse to drag the shortcut onto the Recycle Bin icon to delete the shortcut from your Desktop.

73 USING TOOLBAR TIPS TO IDENTIFY TOOLBAR BUTTONS

To simplify common operations, many programs provide a toolbar (which often resides beneath the program's menu bar) that contains icons upon which you can click your mouse to perform specific operations. For example, Figure 73.1

illustrates the WordPad accessory program's toolbar that you can use to create a new document, open an existing document, save or print the current document, and so on.

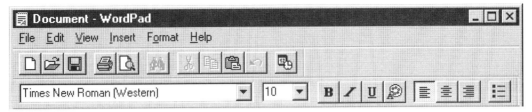

Figure 73.1 *The WordPad toolbar icons.*

Throughout this book, you will examine the toolbars for each of the Windows 98 programs. If, however, you are running a program and you do not have this book close at hand, you can take advantage of Windows 98 toolbar tips to help remind you what operation a toolbar button performs. Within most programs, you can aim your mouse pointer at an icon within the toolbar. After a short delay, the program will display a small tip pop-up that identifies the button. For example, Figure 73.2 shows the toolbar tip pop-up for WordPad's toolbar Print button.

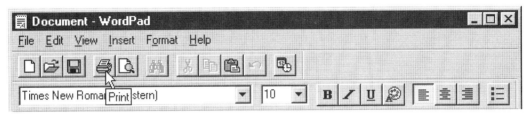

Figure 73.2 *Using toolbar tips to determine a button's purpose.*

74 USING FILES TO STORE INFORMATION AND FOLDERS TO ORGANIZE YOUR FILES

Windows 98, like all operating systems, exists to perform three key operations: to let you run programs, to let your programs interact with your hardware devices, and to let you store information on your disk. Each time you store information on your disk, you must place the information within a file. When you create a word processing document, for example, you will later store that document within a file. Likewise, if you use a spreadsheet program to create a budget, you will store your budget within a file on your disk. In addition, each of the programs that you run resides in a file on your disk. Each time you create a file, you must specify the name you want Windows 98 to assign to your file. Later, when you are ready to use the file, you simply tell Windows 98 (or your application program, such as your word processor) the file's name.

As you might guess, over time, your disk may contain hundreds, if not thousands, of files. To help you organize your files, Windows 98 lets you group related files within file folders on your disk, much as you would place paper files in folders within a filing cabinet. Like the files you store on disk, each folder you create must have a unique name. Using file folders, you might group your word processing documents into one folder, your spreadsheet documents into a second folder, and so on. If you create a variety of word processing documents, for example, Windows 98 lets you create subfolders. Within your Word Processing folder, you might create a subfolder for your home documents, a different subfolder for your work documents, and a third subfolder for your school documents. Several of the Tips that follow examine documents and folders in detail. Then, the Tips will examine the Windows 98 Explorer, a powerful program you can use to create, copy, rename, and delete files and folders on your disk.

75 | **WINDOWS 98 LETS YOU USE UP TO 255 CHARACTERS WITHIN FILENAMES**

As you learned in Tip 74, each file you store on your disk must have a unique name. As you assign names to your files, you should choose names that meaningfully describe your file's contents. For example, if you use a word-processing program to create a memo, you may be tempted to simply name your document's file *Memo*. However, a more meaningful name might be *Memo Regarding Office Equipment*. Within Windows 98, you can use up to 255 characters, including spaces, to name your files. As you name your files, ask yourself if another user reads the file's name, would the user have a good idea of the contents the file contains? To help organize your files, include the current date at the start of the filename, as shown in these examples:

98-01-04 Memo Regarding Office Move

98-02-13 Memo Regarding Valentine's Day Holiday

98-12-24 Note to Staff Regarding End of Year Review

As you can see, each document name starts with the current year, followed by the month, and then the day. By naming files in this fashion, many Windows-based programs will automatically sort your files by the date, which may make it easier for you to locate a specific file. For example, Figure 75 illustrates several files within the Windows 98 Explorer. As you can see, the Explorer is sorting the files by date.

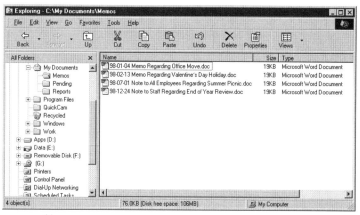

Figure 75 *Assigning meaningful names to files.*

76 | **USING THE DOCUMENTS MENU TO ACCESS YOUR RECENTLY USED DOCUMENTS QUICKLY**

As you learned in Tip 74, each time you store information on your disk, you must place the information within a file. Everything on your disk resides within a file. Your word processing documents will each reside within a file, your spreadsheets will reside within a file, your electronic mail messages will reside within a file, and every program on your system will reside within a file. As you work within Windows 98 and other Windows-based programs, you often encounter the term *document*. In general, a document is simply a file whose contents you can view, print, and even edit.

Examples of documents include word-processing memos, reports, spreadsheets, and even illustrations you create using a drawing program, such as Paint accessory that Windows 98 provides. A program, which also resides within a file on your disk, is not a document because you will not view, edit, or print the program's contents.

Usually, to open a document, such as a word-processing memo, you will start the application program that you used to create the document (such as Microsoft Word), and then you will open the document (which directs the program to load the document's contents from your disk into your PC's random-access memory (RAM). To simplify the steps you must perform to open your recently used documents, Windows 98 provides the Documents menu, shown in Figure 76.

Figure 76 *The Windows 98 Documents menu.*

Within the Documents menu, Windows 98 lists the documents you have most recently used. For example, assume that you use Microsoft Word to create a report, which you store within a file on your disk. Later, to open the report, you have two choices. First, you can start Microsoft Word and then use Word's File menu Open option to open the document. Or, second, you can click your mouse on the document's name from within the Windows 98 Documents menu. To access the Documents menu, simply click your mouse on the Start menu Documents option.

77 CLEARING THE DOCUMENTS MENU LIST OF YOUR RE-CENTLY-USED DOCUMENTS

In Tip 76, you learned that the Windows 98 Start menu provides the Documents submenu which you can use to quickly open the documents you have recently used. Although the Documents submenu is very convenient, there may be times when you will want Windows 98 to erase the menu's contents. For example, within an office, another user who gains access to your computer can determine which documents you have been working with lately simply by viewing your Documents menu. For example, Figure 77.1 shows a list of documents within the Documents menu. By studying the menu's contents, you can determine the files with which the user has been recently working.

Figure 77.1 *Documents within the Start menu Documents submenu.*

To clear the Documents menu list, perform these steps:

1. Click your mouse on the Start button. Windows 98, in turn, will display the Start menu.
2. Within the Start menu, select the Settings option. Windows 98, in turn, will display the Settings submenu.
3. Within the Settings submenu, click your mouse on the Taskbar option. Windows 98, in turn, will display the Taskbar Properties dialog box shown, in Figure 77.2.

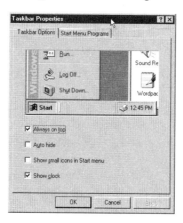

Figure 77.2 *The Taskbar Properties dialog box.*

4. Within the Taskbar Properties dialog box, select the Start Menu Programs tab. Windows 98, in turn, will display the Start Menu Programs sheet shown in Figure 77.3.

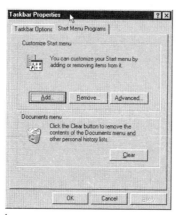

Figure 77.3 *The Windows 98 Start Menu Programs sheet.*

5. Within the Start Menu Programs sheet, click your mouse on the Clear button to clear the Documents menu.

78   *OPENING THE WINDOWS 98 MY COMPUTER FOLDER*

If you examine your Windows 98 Desktop, you will find the My Computer icon. As it turns out, My Computer is a special folder within which Windows 98 groups each of your PC's disk drives, printers, as well as other device folders. Depending on your PC's configuration, the contents of the My Computer folder on your system may differ slightly from that of another user. However, as shown in Figure 78, the My Computer folder will provide you with access to your system's disk drives. To open the My Computer folder on your system, double-click your mouse on the Desktop's My Computer icon.

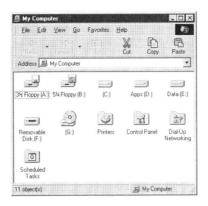

Figure 78 A typical My Computer folder.

As you can see, the My Computer folder contains icons for each of your disk drives as well as folders for other objects. Also, because Windows 98 displays the My Computer folder within a window, you can move, size, or close the My Computer folder just as you would any window. Several of the Tips that follow discuss how you can use the My Computer folder to view the files and folders that reside on your disk.

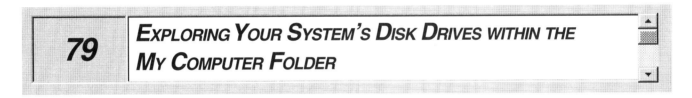

79 **EXPLORING *YOUR* SYSTEM'S DISK DRIVES WITHIN THE MY COMPUTER FOLDER**

In Tip 78, you learned that Windows 98 provides a special folder, named My Computer, within which Windows 98 places icons that correspond to your system's disk drives and other devices. From within the My Computer folder, you can view a disk drive's contents by double-clicking your mouse on the corresponding disk-drive icon. Windows 98, in turn, will open a second window that lists the drive's top-level folders, as shown in Figure 79. For example, within the My Computer folder on your PC, you can display a list of the top-level folders on your hard disk by double-clicking your mouse on the drive C: icon.

Figure 79 *Viewing a disk drive's top-level folders within a My Computer window.*

The best way to understand disk drives, folders, subfolders, and files is to compare your disk drive to a filing cabinet. Within a filing cabinet, you have multiple drawers. Think of each drawer as one of your disk's top-level folders. Unlike a filing cabinet that has a fixed number of drawers, you can generally create as many top-level folders on your disk as you will require.

Within each drawer of a filing cabinet, you may place one or more file folders. Depending on how you organize your paper documents, you may have one large paper folder within which you insert several smaller subfolders. Eventually, within your folders, you may place one or more files. The same is true for how you store information on your disk. You will begin with several top-level folders within which you create additional subfolders. Within each subfolder, you may store files, or to further organize your files, you may create additional subfolders. Within Windows 98, you can create many levels of subfolders.

80 EXPLORING A DISK DRIVE'S FOLDERS WITHIN THE MY COMPUTER FOLDER

In Tip 79, you learned how to view a disk drive's top-level folders within a My Computer folder. When you view a disk drive's contents, you will usually encounter more file folders. As discussed, Windows 98 provides file folders to help you group related files (documents) on your disk. You might, for example, keep all your work documents within a folder named *Work* and your school documents within a folder named *School*. Depending on the number of documents you create, you might create a subfolder within your *Work* folder named *Memos* and a second subfolder named *Reports*. Likewise, within your *School* folder, you might create a subfolder for each of your classes. In later Tips, you will learn how to create your own folders.

For now, however, to view the contents of a folder on your disk, double-click your mouse on the folder's icon. For example, if you double-click your mouse on the Windows folder that you will find within the drive C: folder (you may have to use the scroll bar to locate the folder), Windows 98 will open another window, as shown in Figure 80.1, within which it will display the folder's contents.

Figure 80.1 *Viewing the Windows folder's contents.*

If you scroll through the Windows folder, you will see icons for additional subfolders and icons for files that reside within the Windows folder. To close the Windows folder, click your mouse on the window's Close button, as shown in Figure 80.2.

Figure 80.2 *To close a folder's window, click your mouse on the Close button.*

81 CLOSING A MY COMPUTER SUBFOLDER WINDOW AND THAT OF ITS PARENT IN ONE STEP

In Tip 80, you learned that by using the My Computer window, you can quickly search your PC's disks, folders, and files. As you traverse your system within the My Computer window, there may be times when you end up with several windows open at the same time, as shown in Figure 81.

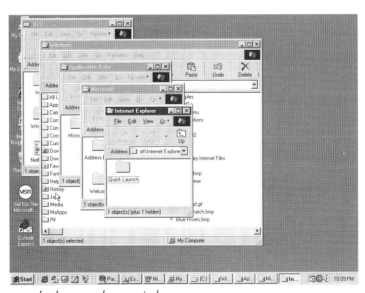

Figure 81 *Traversing My Computer can lead to several open windows.*

To close the Explorer windows, you have two choices. First, you can close the windows one at a time by selecting each window's File menu Close option or by clicking your mouse on the window's Close button. Second, the Explorer lets you close a subfolder window and that of its parents in one step by holding down they SHIFT key and then clicking your mouse on the subfolder window's Close button. If you do not hold down the SHIFT key, Windows 98 will close only the current subfolder window.

82   TO OPEN A FILE FOLDER USING THE SAME MY COMPUTER WINDOW, USE THE CTRL KEY

In several of the previous Tips, you learned how to use the My Computer folder to view the disks, files, and folders that reside on your system. As you found each time you double-clicked your mouse on a disk or folder icon, Windows 98 opened a new window within which it displayed the disk's or folder's contents. Depending on the number of folders you must traverse to locate a file, you might quickly open a large number of windows.

Rather than having Windows 98 open a new window each time you double-click your mouse on a disk or folder within a My Computer window, you can instead hold down your keyboard's CTRL key and then double-click your mouse on the disk or folder. Windows 98, in turn, will display the disk's or folder's contents within the current window.

Note: When you hold down the CTRL key and double-click your mouse on a disk or folder icon, the Explorer will actually perform the opposite action that you have currently selected within the Custom Settings dialog box, meaning, that if you have instructed the Explorer to normally display a new folder's contents within the existing window, holding down the CTRL key directs the Explorer to open a new window. Likewise, if the Explorer would normally open a new window, holding down the CTRL key directs the Explorer to use the existing window.

83   WINDOWS 98 PROVIDES THE EXPLORER PROGRAM TO HELP YOU MANAGE YOUR FOLDERS AND FILES

As you have learned, everything you store on your disk must reside within a file. To help you organize the files on your disk, you can create folders within which you group related files. As you create and store documents, you will want to create your own folders and subfolders, and you will have to copy, move, rename, and delete files. To help you manage your files and folders, Windows 98 provides the Explorer program, shown in Figure 83.

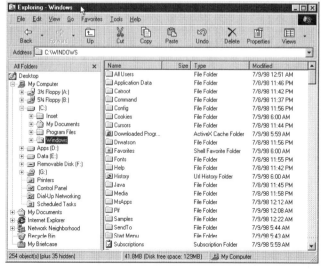

Figure 83 *The Windows 98 Explorer program.*

The Windows 98 Explorer may look quite similar to the My Computer folder you used in Tip 79 to display your disk's files and folders. That is because the My Computer folder uses a slight variation of the Explorer to display your system's disks, folders, and files. Several of the Tips that follow discuss the Explorer in detail. To start the Explorer, perform these steps:

1. Click your mouse on the Start button. Windows 98, in turn, will display the Start menu.
2. Within the Start menu, click your mouse on the Programs option. Windows 98, in turn, will display the Programs submenu.
3. Within the Programs submenu, click your mouse on the Windows Explorer option. Windows 98, in turn, will open the Explorer window, previously shown in Figure 83.

Note: *To start the Explorer, you can also right-click your mouse on the Start menu button and then choose Explore from within pop-up menu.*

84 **THE EXPLORER WINDOW CONSISTS OF TWO PARTS: A FOLDER LIST AND THE CURRENT FOLDER'S CONTENTS**

In Tip 83, you learned that Windows 98 provides the Explorer to help you manage files and folders on your disk. If you examine the Explorer program window, you will find that the window consists of two parts. As shown in Figure 84.1, the left side of the Explorer lists your computer's disks and the folders each contains. Likewise, the Explorer's right side displays the folders that reside within a specific folder.

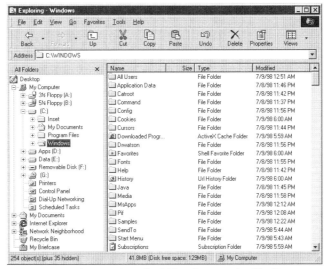

Figure 84.1 *The Windows 98 Explorer program window consists of a folders frame and a files frame.*

Several of the Tips that follow discuss Explorer operations in detail. Like most program windows, Windows 98 lets you size the Explorer window. You can, for example, use the Maximize button to expand the Explorer window to fill the entire screen. Likewise, you can use your mouse to drag one of the window frames to increase or decrease the window size. In addition, if you drag the bar that separates the folders and files window frames, you can increase the size of either frame, as shown in Figure 84.2.

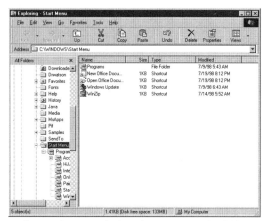 

Figure 84.2 *By dragging the bar that separates the folders and files frames, you can change either frame's size.*

85	EXPANDING THE DISPLAY OF A FOLDER'S SUBFOLDERS WITHIN THE EXPLORER

In Tip 74, you learned that you should use folders to organize the documents (files) that you store on your disk. As you work within Windows 98, you will eventually need to create, copy, move, or delete file folders, all of which you can do from within the Explorer. In Tip 84, you learned that the Explorer divides its program window into two frames, a folders frame and a files frame.

Within the Explorer, you can use your mouse to scroll through a list of the folders a disk contains. If you examine the Explorer's folders frame, you may see disk drive icons or folder icons beside which the Explorer displays a plus sign (+), as shown in Figure 85.1.

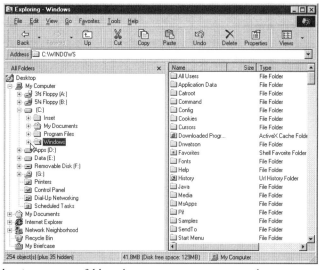

Figure 85.1 *The Explorer displays a plus sign next to a folder whose contents you can expand.*

If you click your mouse on the plus sign, the Explorer will expand the folder's display to list the subfolders the folder contains, as shown in Figure 85.2.

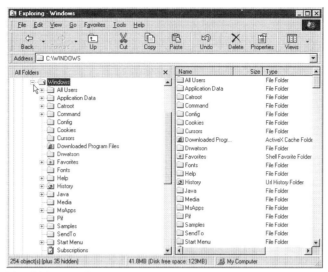

Figure 85.2 *By clicking on an expandable folder, you direct the Explorer to display a list of the subfolders the folder contains.*

When the Explorer expands a folder, it changes the plus sign that appears beneath the folder's icon to a minus sign. If you click your mouse on the minus sign, Windows 98 will compress the display of the folder's subfolders.

86 DISPLAYING THE FILES A FOLDER CONTAINS

As you have learned, file folders help you organize the files you store on your disk. Using the Windows 98 Explorer, you can view a list of the files a folder contains. To view a folder's contents, click your mouse on the folder's icon within the Explorer's folders frame. The Explorer, in turn, will display a list of the files the folder contains, as shown in Figure 86.

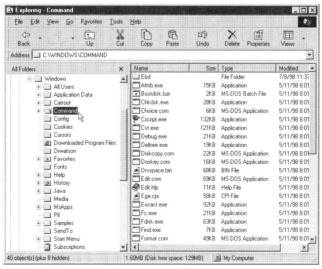

Figure 86 *To display a list of the files a folder contains, click your mouse on the folder's icon within the Explorer's folders frame.*

87	**USING FILE ICONS TO IDENTIFY FILES WITHIN THE WINDOWS 98 EXPLORER**

In Tip 86, you learned that if you click your mouse on a folder's icon within the Explorer's folders frame, the Explorer, in turn, will display a list of the files a folder contains, as shown in Figure 87.

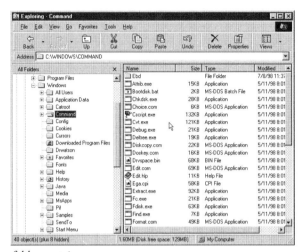

Figure 87 *The Explorer's list of the files a folder contains.*

As you examine the list of files that a folder contains, you can often determine the file's type by examining the icon that the Explorer displays to the left (or possibly above, depending on how the Explorer is displaying your file list) of the file's name. To help you identify file types, Table 87 defines common file icons that you will encounter within the Explorer.

Icon	File Contents
	A folder that contains files
	A Windows 98 operating system file
	A Microsoft Word or WordPad word-processing document
	A Microsoft Excel spreadsheet document
	A text file whose contents you can view with an editor or the WordPad accessory program
	An audio file whose contents you can play using the Sound Recorder or Media Player

Table 87 *Using file icons to determine a file's contents. (continued on the following page)*

Icon	File Contents
	A video file whose contents you can play using the Media Player
	A graphics file stored in a bitmap format you can view or edit within the Paint program
	An HTML document you can view using the Explorer or Internet Explorer
	A generic file type that Windows 98 does not recognize
	An MS-DOS system program
	An MS-DOS application program
	A TrueType font file description

Table 87 Using file icons to determine a file's contents. (continued from previous page)

88 USING THE EXPLORER TO DISPLAY A PAGE ON THE WORLD WIDE WEB

As briefly discussed in Tip 83, using the Windows 98 Explorer, you can manage the files and folders that reside on your disk. If your PC is connected to the Internet, you can also use the Explorer to "surf" the Web. To use the Explorer to view a Web page, make sure the Explorer is displaying its Address bar, as discussed in Tip 34. Next, within the Address bar, type in the Web site you desire, such as *www.microsoft.com* or *www.jamsa.com*. The Explorer, in turn, will display the Web site, as shown in Figure 88.1.

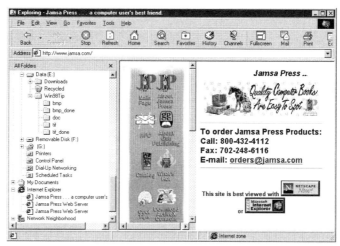

Figure 88.1 Using the Explorer to surf the World Wide Web.

After you use the Explorer to visit sites on the Web, you can quickly return to a site you previously visited by selecting the site from the Address bar's pull-down list, as shown in Figure 88.2.

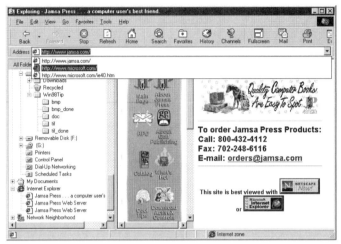

Figure 88.2 Using the Address bar's pull-down list to select a previous Web site.

Note: *Tip 796 discusses ways you can connect to the Internet and the World Wide Web.*

89 USING THE EXPLORER'S LINKS BAR TO ACCESS SPECIFIC SITES ON THE WORLD WIDE WEB

In Tip 88, you learned that if your PC is connected to the Internet, you can use the Explorer to surf sites on the World Wide Web. To help you get started on your Web travels, Windows 98 predefines several links that will take you to such sites as Microsoft, the Windows 98 Update, Microsoft Product News, and more. To access these sites within the Explorer, turn on the Explorer's Links toolbar, as discussed in Tip 35 and as shown in Figure 89.1.

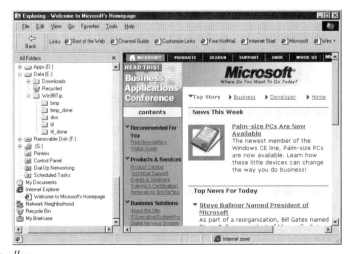

Figure 89.1 The Explorer's Links toolbar.

To visit a site whose button appears on the Links toolbar, simply click your mouse on the corresponding button. The Explorer, in turn, will display the site's Web page. If you examine the right and left ends of the Links toolbar, you might find a small arrow, upon which you can click your mouse to bring more site buttons into view. As it turns out, the Explorer stores each link as a shortcut within the Links folder, which itself resides within the *Windows\Favorites* folder, whose contents you can view within the Explorer simply by clicking on the folder within the Explorer folder list. Within the Links folder, you can double-click your mouse on a shortcut icon to direct the Explorer to display the corresponding Web site. In addition, you can also select a Link from the Explorer Favorites menu Links submenu shown in Figure 89.2.

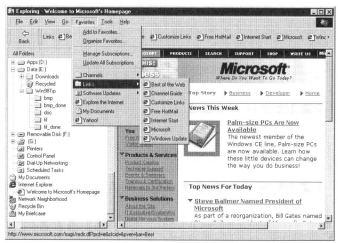

Figure 89.2 *Selecting a Web site from the Links submenu.*

90 | TAKING ADVANTAGE OF THE EXPLORER'S TOOLBAR BUTTONS

Like most Windows-based programs, the Explorer provides several toolbars you can use to simplify common operations. To turn a toolbar's display on or off, click your mouse on the Explorer's View menu Toolbars option. The Explorer, in turn, will display its Toolbars submenu, as shown in Figure 90.1. To turn on a toolbar's display, click your mouse on the corresponding menu option, placing a check mark next to the option. To turn off a toolbar's display, click your mouse on the option, removing the check mark. Several of this book's Tips examine the Explorer toolbars in detail.

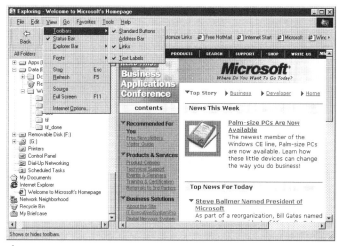

Figure 90.1 *The Explorer Toolbars submenu.*

Figure 90.2 briefly describes each of the Standard toolbar buttons.

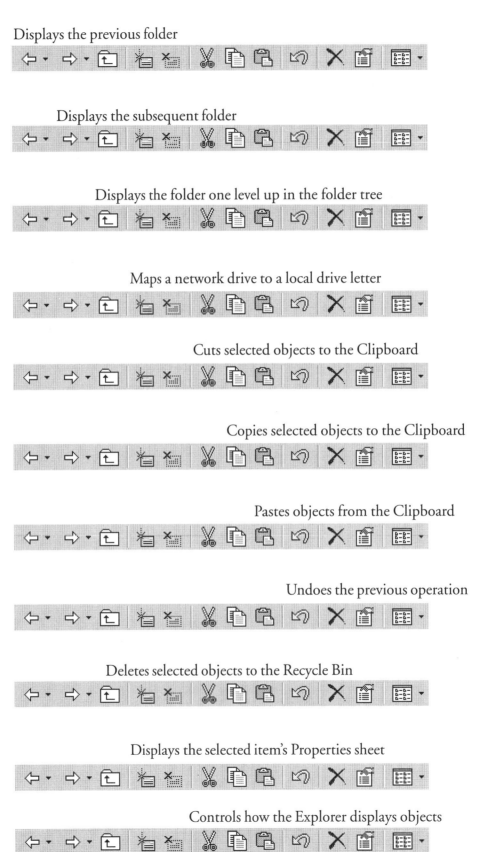

Figure 90.2 The Explorer's Standard toolbar buttons.

The Explorer Address bar, shown in Figure 90.3, lets you access a file, folder, or a Web site by typing in the corresponding path or Internet address.

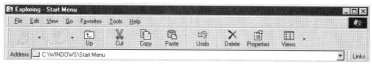

Figure 90.3 *The Explorer's Address toolbar.*

Finally, the Explorer's Links toolbar, shown in Figure 90.4, lets you connect quickly to specific sites across the World Wide Web.

Figure 90.4 *The Explorer's Links toolbar.*

91 CREATING YOUR OWN FILE FOLDERS TO BETTER ORGANIZE YOUR DOCUMENTS

As you have learned, Windows 98 provides folders to help you organize the files that you store on your disk. Using the Windows 98 Explorer, you can manage your folders by viewing their contents, or by moving, copying, and deleting files as your needs require. As the number of documents you store on your disk increases, you will eventually want to create your own folders. In this Tip, you will learn how to create your own folders using the Explorer. In Tip 181, you will learn how to create a folder from within an application program, such as Microsoft Word, by using the Save As dialog box. To create a folder within the Explorer, perform these steps:

1. Within the Explorer folder list, click your mouse on the disk drive icon or on the folder icon within which you will create your new folder. The Explorer, in turn, will display the disk's or folder's contents within its file list.

2. Within the Explorer, click your mouse on the File menu New option. Windows 98 will cascade the New submenu as shown in Figure 91.

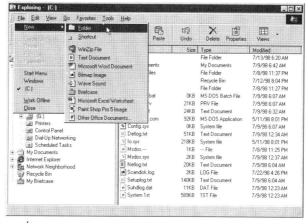

Figure 91 *The Explorer's File menu New submenu.*

3. Within the New submenu, click your mouse on the Folder option. The Explorer, in turn, will place a folder icon in the current file list window and will name the folder "New Folder."

4. Within the folder's name field, type in the folder name that you desire and press ENTER.

92 USING SUBFOLDERS (A FOLDER WITHIN A FOLDER) TO BETTER ORGANIZE YOUR DOCUMENTS

In Tip 91, you learned how to use the Windows 98 Explorer to create a folder on your disk. Over time, as the number of documents that you create increases, you will eventually create subfolders within your folders to better organize your files. For example, assume that you store your documents for work in a folder named *Work*.

To better organize your documents, you might create subfolders named *Memos*, *Reports*, *Drafts*, and *Pending*. Then, using file-move operations, as discussed in Tip 100, you can move your documents into the correct folders. Figure 92.1 illustrates how such a folder and subfolder would appear within the Explorer.

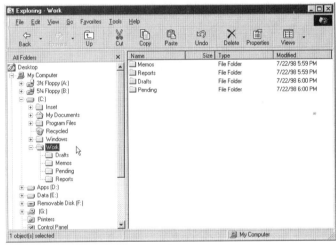

Figure 92.1 *Viewing the Work folder and its subfolders within the Explorer.*

In general, your Windows 98 folders can hold as many subfolders as your needs require. Likewise, you can usually create as many levels of subfolders as you require to organize your files.

1. Within the Explorer folder list, click your mouse on the folder icon within which you create your new subfolder. The Explorer, in turn, will display the disk's or folder's contents within its file list.

2. Within the Explorer, click your mouse on the File menu New option. Windows 98 will cascade the New submenu as shown in Figure 92.2.

3. Within the New submenu, click your mouse on the Folder option. The Explorer, in turn, will place a folder icon in the current file list window and will name the folder "New Folder."

4. Within the folder's name field, type in the folder name that you desire and press ENTER.

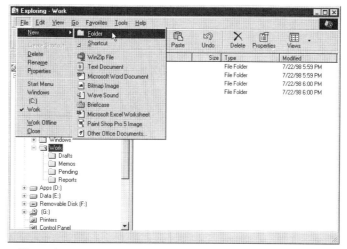

Figure 92.2 *The Explorer's File menu New submenu.*

---

93 | MOVING UP ONE LEVEL WITHIN AN EXPLORER FOLDER LIST

In Tip 92, you learned how to traverse folders within the Explorer. As you also learned, by clicking your mouse on the folders that the Explorer displays within its folder list, you can quickly display a specific folder's contents. As discussed, within a folder you have several other subfolders, each of which may contain their own subfolders. By clicking your mouse on subfolders within the Explorer, you can quickly find yourself several folders deep within the Explorer's folder list. To better understand the process of moving between folders, start the Explorer as discussed in Tip 83 and then double-click your mouse on the *Windows* folder. Within the *Windows* folder, double-click your mouse on the *Favorites* folder. Then, within the *Favorites* folder, double-click your mouse on the *Channels* folder. If you examine the Explorer Address bar, you will find that you are now several folder levels deep within the folder tree. To move up one level, in this case from the *Channels* folder to the *Favorites* folder, click your mouse on the Explorer's toolbar Up button, as shown in Figure 93.

Figure 93 The Explorer's toolbar Up button displays the current folder's parent folder.

If you click your mouse on the Up button a second time, the Explorer will move you from the *Favorites* folder back into the *Windows* folder. Finally, if you click on the Up button one last time, the Explorer will move you back to the drive C: icon. As you store and open files that reside within folders, you will use the Explorer's toolbar Up button on a regular basis. Likewise, in Tip 173, you will learn how to use the Up button within the Save As and Open dialog boxes to move up one level within the folder tree.

Note: In addition to clicking your mouse on the Explorer's toolbar Up arrow button to move up one level from the current subfolder, you can also press your keyboard's BACKSPACE key.

94   CUSTOMIZING THE EXPLORER'S FILE LIST DISPLAY

As you have learned, the Explorer exists to help you manage your files and folders. After you click your mouse on a folder within the Explorer's folder list, the Explorer will display the folder's contents within its file list. Depending on your preferences, the Explorer lets you view the file list using a variety of formats (the Explorer refers to the display formats as *views*). For example, Figure 94.1 shows the Explorer's large icon view and small icon view. Likewise, Figure 94.2 shows the Explorer's list display and details display. The Explorer view that you select is simply your preference.

Figure 94.1 The Explorer large and small icon views.

Figure 94.2 The Explorer list and details views.

To change the Explorer's current view, click your mouse on the Explorer View menu and choose the option that you desire. In addition, you can click your mouse on the downward arrow that appears next to the Explorer toolbar Views button and then select the view you desire from the pull-down list.

95 | **DISPLAYING THE EXPLORER WINDOW AS A WEB PAGE**

As you will learn in Tip 34, by typing a Web address, such as *www.jamsa.com*, within the Explorer's address bar, you can use the Explorer to surf sites on the World Wide Web. In addition to letting you view Web sites, the Explorer also lets you display the current folder's contents as a Web document. For example, Figure 95.1 shows the Program Files folder as a Web document within the Explorer.

Figure 95.1 *Viewing a folder's contents as a Web document within the Explorer.*

As you can see, within its Web-format display, the Explorer displays information about the current folder to the left of the folder's file list. If you select a file within the folder, the Explorer will display specifics about the file, as shown in Figure 95.2.

Figure 95.2 *Displaying specifics about a selected file within the Explorer's Web-format display.*

In Tip 119, you will learn how to create an HTML page for a folder with which you can customize how the Explorer displays the folder's contents. To turn the Explorer's Web-format display on or off, select the Explorer View menu and choose the menu's as Web Page option.

96 DISPLAYING TEXT LABELS WITHIN THE EXPLORER'S TOOLBAR ICONS

As you have learned, the Windows 98 Explorer provides a toolbar whose icons correspond to common file or folder manipulation tasks. If you are new to the Explorer, you may find it convenient for the Explorer to label its toolbar icons, as shown in Figure 96.1.

Figure 96.1 *Displaying text labels within the Explorer's toolbar icons.*

However, as you become more proficient with the Explorer, you may find that removing the text labels reduces each icon's size, which lets you display more files or folders within the Explorer window. Figure 96.2 shows the Explorer toolbar without text labels.

Figure 96.2 *Displaying the Explorer's toolbar icons without text labels.*

To turn the Explorer's display of text labels within its toolbar icons on or off, perform these steps:

1. Select the Explorer View menu and choose the Toolbars option. The Explorer, in turn, will display the Toolbars submenu.
2. Within the Toolbars submenu, click your mouse on the Text Labels option. If you remove the check mark that appears to the left of the menu option, the Explorer will remove the text labels from the toolbar icons. If you instead add a check mark, the Explorer will display the text labels.

97 TAKING ADVANTAGE OF THE EXPLORER'S STATUS BAR

As you have learned, you can direct the Explorer to display up to three different toolbars near the top of the Explorer window upon whose buttons you can click your mouse to perform various operations. As the Explorer performs its operations, the Explorer will often display status information within its Status bar, which you can display near the bottom of the Explorer window, as shown in Figure 97.1.

If the Explorer is not currently displaying its Status bar, select the Explorer View menu and choose the Status bar option, placing a check mark next to the option. Depending on the operation you are performing, the information the Explorer displays within its Status bar will differ.

Figure 97.1 *The Explorer provides status information about the current operation within its Status bar.*

For example, if you click your mouse on a folder within the Explorer's folders frame, the Explorer will display a count of the number of objects the folder contains as well as the amount of disk space available on your disk, as shown in Figure 97.2.

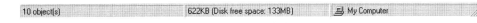

Figure 97.2 *Using the Explorer's Status bar to display information about a folder.*

Likewise, if you click your mouse on a file, the Explorer will display the file's size within the Status bar, as shown in Figure 97.3.

Figure 97.3 *Using the Explorer's Status bar to display a file's size.*

If you click your mouse within on a disk drive icon within the Explorer's folders frame, the Explorer will display the disk's storage capacity and available disk space within the Status bar, as shown in Figure 97.4.

Figure 97.4 *Using the Explorer's Status bar to display a disk's size.*

In Tip 100, you will learn how to copy one or more files using the Explorer. By examining the Explorer's Status bar, you can determine the size of the file or files you are going to copy and then determine if the files will fit on the target drive.

98 USING THE EXPLORER TO DELETE A FILE OR FOLDER

As you learned in Tip 83, the Windows 98 Explorer helps you manage your disk's files and folders. As you have learned, everything that you store on your disk must reside within a file. To organize your disk, you can group related files within folders. Eventually, you will have files or folders of files on your disk that you no longer need. To delete a file within the Explorer, perform these steps:

1. Within the Explorer window's folder list, click your mouse on the folder that contains the file you want to delete. The Explorer, in turn, will display the folder's files within its right-hand frame.

2. Within the Explorer's right-hand frame, click your mouse on the file you want to delete and then press the DEL key or click your mouse on the Explorer's toolbar Delete button. The Explorer will remove the file from the folder.

To delete a folder (and all the files the folder contains) using the Explorer, perform these steps:

1. Within the Explorer window's folder list, click your mouse on the folder that contains the file you want to delete. The Explorer, in turn, will display the folder's files within its right-hand frame.

2. Press the DEL key or click your mouse on the Explorer's toolbar Delete button. The Explorer, in turn, will display a dialog box asking you to confirm that you want to delete the folder and its contents. Click your mouse on the Yes button.

When you delete a folder or file using the Explorer, Windows 98 removes the file or folder from its current location on your disk. However, Windows 98 does not immediately erase the information from your disk. Instead, Windows 98 moves the file or folder into a special folder, called the Recycle Bin. Should you later decide you wish that you had not deleted the file or folder, you may be able to "undelete" the object from within the Recycle Bin. Tip 150 introduces the Windows 98 Recycle Bin.

99 USING THE EXPLORER TO RENAME A FILE OR FOLDER

As you learned in Tip 75, when you create a file or folder, you should assign a meaningful name to the object that describes its contents. After you create a file or folder, should you decide that you want to change the object's name, you can rename the object using the Explorer. To rename a file using the Explorer, perform these steps:

1. Within the Explorer window's folder list, click your mouse on the folder that contains the file you want to rename. The Explorer, in turn, will display the folder's files within its right-hand frame.

2. Within the Explorer's right-hand frame, right-click your mouse on the file you want to rename. The Explorer, in turn, will display a pop-up menu.

3. Within the pop-up menu, select the Rename option. The Explorer will highlight the file's current name using reverse video. Within the highlighted filename box, type in the filename you desire and press ENTER.

Note: *Within the highlighted filename box, you can type in a new name, or you can use your keyboard's **ARROW**, **INS**, and **DEL** keys to edit characters in the existing name as your needs require.*

To rename a folder within the Explorer, perform these steps:

1. Within the Explorer window's folder list, right-click your mouse on the folder that you want to rename. The Explorer, in turn, will display a pop-up menu.

2. Within the pop-up menu, select the Rename option. The Explorer will highlight the folder's current name using reverse video. Within the highlighted folder-name box, type in the folder name you desire and press ENTER.

Note: *As a rule, you should only rename files or folders you created yourself. Should you rename a file or folder that you did not create, you may keep a program from running successfully later.*

Note: *To rename a file or folder within the Explorer, you can also double-click your mouse on the file's name. The Explorer, in turn, will display the folder-name box, within which you can type the new name.*

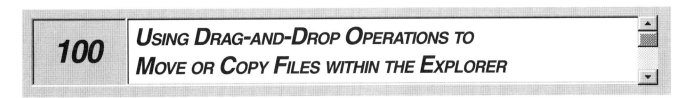

100   USING DRAG-AND-DROP OPERATIONS TO MOVE OR COPY FILES WITHIN THE EXPLORER

As you have learned, the Explorer exists to help you manage your files. Over time, you may eventually copy one or more files to another folder or disk. Within the Explorer, you can use your mouse to drag-and-drop the file into the folder or onto the disk that you desire. To copy a file using a drag-and-drop operation, perform these steps:

1. Within the Explorer's folder list, click your mouse on the icon that corresponds to the folder that contains the file (or files) that you want to copy. The Explorer, in turn, will display the folder's file list.

2. Next, within the Explorer's folder list, use your mouse to scroll through the list until you see the drive and folder to which you want to copy the file (do not click your mouse on the drive or folder). To locate the folder that you desire, you may have to expand one or more folder's within the list (by clicking your mouse on the plus sign (+) that precedes the folder name).

3. Next, hold down your keyboard's CTRL key and use your mouse to drag the file from the Explorer's file list onto the target folder or drive folder that appears within the Explorer's folder list. As you drag the file over the folder or disk drive that you desire, the Explorer will highlight the icon.

4. Release your mouse-select button. The Explorer, in turn, will display the Copying dialog box, telling you that it is performing the file copy operation, as shown in Figure 100.

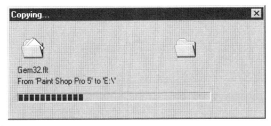

Figure 100 *The Explorer's Copying dialog box.*

Note: *To move a file, as opposed to copying a file, perform Steps 1 through 4 without holding down your keyboard's Ctrl key as you drag the file to its target destination. When you hold the mouse pointer over the target location, the Explorer will display a small plus sign within the mouse pointer if you are performing a copy operation. If you are performing a move operation, the Explorer will not display the plus sign. In Tip 113, you will learn how to select multiple files for use in a file copy or move operation.*

Note: *If your source and file destinations reside on different drives, the Explorer will perform a file-copy operation by default. To perform a file-move operation across two drives, you must hold down your keyboard SHIFT key as you drag-and-drop the object.*

---

101 USING DRAG-AND-DROP OPERATIONS TO PRINT A FILE WITHIN THE EXPLORER

In Tip 100, you learned how to move or copy files by performing a drag-and-drop operation within the Explorer. In addition to letting you drag a file onto a folder or disk to move or copy the file, the Explorer also lets you perform a drag-and-drop operation to print a file's contents. To print a file using a drop-and-drag operation, perform these steps:

1. Within your Desktop, double-click your mouse on the My Computer option. Windows 98 will open the My Computer window.

2. Within the My Computer window, double-click your mouse on the Printers icon. Windows 98 will display the Printers folder.

3. Within the Explorer's folder list, click your mouse on the folder that contains the file you want to print. The Explorer, in turn, will display the folder's contents within its file list.

4. Within the Explorer's file list, use your mouse to drag the file that you want to print onto your printer icon that appears within the Printers folder. When you release your mouse-select button, Windows 98 will start the program that created the document file and direct the program to print the document's contents. After the program ends its printing, Windows 98 will end the program, closing the program's window.

Note: *If you find that you perform drag-and-drop print operations on a regular basis, follow the steps Tip 369 presents to place a shortcut to your printer on your Desktop. Later, to print a file using a drag-and-drop operation, you can simply drag the file from the Explorer file list onto the Desktop printer icon.*

---

102 USING DRAG-AND-DROP OPERATIONS TO ADD A PROGRAM TO THE START MENU

In several of the previous Tips, you have learned how to use mouse drag-and-drop operations to move, copy, print, and delete files. In addition, using drag-and-drop operations, Windows 98 lets your add a program to the Start menu. Assume, that you have a program that you use on a regular basis. Rather than forcing you to traverse several menus to run the program, you can place the program on the Start menu itself. For example, Figure 102 shows a Start menu with a menu option that runs Microsoft Word.

To drag and drop a program onto the Start menu, perform these steps:

1. Within the Explorer's folder list, click your mouse on the folder that contains the file you want to add. The Explorer, in turn, will display the folder's contents within its file list.

2. Within the Explorer's file list, use your mouse to drag the file that you want to add to the Start menu onto the Start button.

3. Within the Explorer window, click your mouse on the Close button to close the window.

Figure 102 By placing programs onto the Start menu, you can run the program in fewer steps.

103 USING DRAG-AND-DROP OPERATIONS TO DELETE A FILE OR FOLDER

As you have learned in previous Tips, using drag-and-drop operations, you can move and copy files and folders from one location to another. In addition, by dragging a file or folder onto the Desktop Recycle Bin icon, you can quickly delete the item.

To delete a file or folder using a drag-and-drop operation, perform these steps:

1. Within the Explorer's folder list, click your mouse on the folder that contains the file you want to delete. The Explorer, in turn, will display the folder's contents within its file list.

2. Within the Explorer's file list, use your mouse to drag the file or folder that you want to delete onto your Desktop's Recycle Bin. Windows 98, in turn, will display a dialog box asking you to confirm the deletion.

3. Within the dialog box, click your mouse on the Yes button.

---

104 | **USING THE ESC KEY TO CANCEL A DRAG-AND-DROP OPERATION WITHIN THE EXPLORER**

Several of the previous Tips have presented steps you can perform to copy, move, print, and delete files and folders using mouse drag-and-drop operations. Should you begin a drag-and-drop operation within the Explorer that you decide you do not want to complete, simply press your keyboard's ESC key before you release the mouse-select button. The Explorer, in turn, will cancel the operation.

---

105 | **STARTING THE EXPLORER FROM THE MS-DOS PROMPT**

If you periodically work from within an MS-DOS window, there may be times you will want to perform a file operation from within the Windows Explorer. In such cases, you can launch the Windows Explorer by typing the Explorer command at the MS-DOS prompt, as shown here:

```
C:\> Explorer   <ENTER>
```

To start the Explorer within a specific folder, simply include the folder name within the Explorer command line. For example, the following command launches the Explorer, directing it to display the Windows folder:

```
C:\> Explorer  \Windows  <ENTER>
```

---

106 | **USING CUT-AND-PASTE OPERATIONS TO MOVE OR COPY FILES WITHIN THE EXPLORER**

In Tip 100, you learned how to copy and move files within the Explorer using drag-and-drop operations. As you have learned, Windows 98 supports cut-and-paste operations that let you move or copy an object from one location to another. Usually, users perform cut-and-paste operations within a word-processing document to move or copy text.

As it turns out, however, the Explorer lets you use such operations to move or copy files. To copy a file using a copy-and-paste operation within the Explorer, perform these steps:

1. Within the Explorer's folder list, click your mouse on the icon that corresponds to the folder that contains the file (or files) that you want to copy. The Explorer, in turn, will display the folder's file list.

2. Within the folder's file list, click your mouse on the file you want to copy. The Explorer will select (and highlight) the file.

3. Select the Explorer Edit menu Copy option. The Explorer, in turn, will copy the file to the Clipboard.

4. Within the Explorer's folder list, use your mouse to scroll through the list until you see the drive and folder to which you want to copy the file and click your mouse on the folder's icon. The Explorer, in turn, will display the folder's contents. To locate the folder that you desire, you may have to expand one or more folder's within the list (by clicking your mouse on the plus sign (+) that precedes the folder name).

5. Select the Explorer Edit menu Paste option. The Explorer will copy the file from the Clipboard into the current folder.

Note: *To move a file, as opposed to copying a file, perform Steps 1 through 5; however, in Step 3, rather than selecting the Explorer Edit menu Copy option, choose the Edit menu Cut option. In Tip 113, you will learn how to select multiple files for use in a file copy or move operation.*

107	**MOVING OR COPYING A FOLDER USING THE EXPLORER FOLDER LIST**	

In Tip 100, you learned how to copy a file or folder by using your mouse to drag and drop the file or folder from the Explorer file list onto the destination drive or folder within the Explorer folder list. Then, in Tip 106, you learned how to copy or move a file or folder using cut-and-paste operations.

If you are moving or copying a folder within the Explorer, you can perform a drag-and-drop operation using the Explorer folder list. To copy a folder using the Explorer folder list, for example, perform these steps:

1. Within the Explorer folder list, locate the disk drive or folder to which you want to copy the folder. To locate a folder, you may have to expand one or more folder trees by clicking your mouse on the plus sign (+) that precedes the folder name.

2. Within the Explorer folder list, hold down your keyboard's CTRL key and click your mouse on the folder that you want to copy. While holding down the CTRL key, drag the folder onto its target folder. As you position the mouse pointer over the target folder, the Explorer will high-light the folder using reverse video. If you cannot see the target location in the Explorer's folder list, simply hold the mouse pointer (while you are dragging the folder) over the top or bottom folder in the list. The Explorer, in turn, will scroll the list up or down to bring other folders into view.

Note: *To move a folder, as opposed to copying the folder, perform Steps 1 and 2 without holding down your keyboard's CTRL key as you drag the folder to the target location. When you hold the mouse pointer over the target location, the Explorer will display a small plus sign within the mouse pointer if you are performing a copy operation. If you are performing a move operation, the Explorer will not display the plus sign.*

108 UNDOING AN OPERATION WITHIN THE EXPLORER

In Tip 98, you learned how to delete a file or folder within the Explorer. Likewise, in Tip 99, you learned how to rename objects. If, after you perform an operation within the Explorer you wish you had not done the operation, you can use the Explorer's "undo" facility to cancel the operation, restoring your file or folder to its previous state. To undo the previous operation within the Explorer, click your mouse on the Explorer's toolbar Undo button, or click your mouse on the Explorer Edit menu Undo option.

In the Tips that follow, you will learn how to copy and move files and folders using the Explorer. Should you later decide that you wished you had not performed the operation, use the Explorer's undo feature to restore your system's previous settings.

109 SELECTING TWO OR MORE SUCCESSIVE FILES FOR AN EXPLORER FILE OPERATION

In several of the previous Tips, you have learned how to copy, move, and delete files. Often, within the Explorer, you will want to perform your file operations on two or more files. In such cases, you must simply select the files with which you want the Explorer to work. If you are fortunate enough that the files you want appear in successive order within the Explorer's file list, you can select the files you desire by performing these steps:

1. Within the Explorer's file list, click your mouse on the first file within the group of files that you desire. The Explorer, in turn, will highlight the file as a selected file.

2. Also within the Explorer's file list, hold down your keyboard's SHIFT key and then click your mouse on the last file within the group of files that you desire. The Explorer will select (and highlight) each file that appears between the first and last files, as shown in Figure 109. You can now perform your file operation on your selected files.

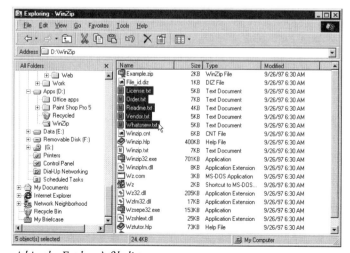

Figure 109 Selecting successive files within the Explorer's file list.

110 SELECTING TWO OR MORE FILES DISPERSED THROUGH-OUT THE EXPLORER'S FILE LIST FOR A FILE OPERATION

In Tip 109, you learned how to use the SHIFT key to select a group of successive files within the Explorer's file list. Often, however, the files on which you want to perform an operation may reside at locations dispersed throughout the Explorer's file list, as shown in Figure 110.

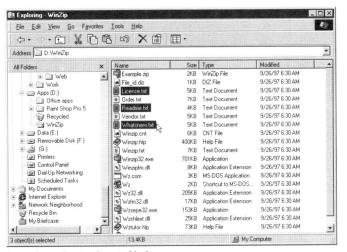

Figure 110 *Selecting files dispersed throughout the Explorer's file list.*

To select a group of dispersed files within the Explorer, hold down your keyboard's CTRL key as you click your mouse on each file. After you select the files that you desire, you can perform your file operation.

111 SELECTING ALL THE FILES IN A FOLDER FOR AN EXPLORER FILE OPERATION

As you have learned, the Explorer exists to help you manage your files and folders. In previous Tips, you have learned how to copy, move, rename, and delete files. Often, you will want to perform your files operation on all the files within a folder. You might, for example, want to copy all the files in a folder to a floppy disk. To perform a file operation using all the files in a folder, you must first select all the files.

Within the Explorer, you can select the current folder's files by selecting the Edit menu Select All option. The Explorer, in turn, will select (and highlight) all the folder's files, as shown in Figure 111.

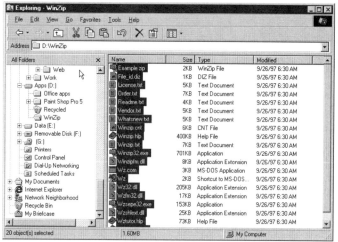

Figure 111 Selecting all the files within a folder for a file operation.

112 INVERTING YOUR FILE SELECTION WITHIN THE EXPLORER

In Tip 111, you learned how to select all the files within a folder for an Explorer file operation. Depending on the files with which you want to work, there may be times when you want to perform a file operation with all but a few select files, as shown in Figure 112.

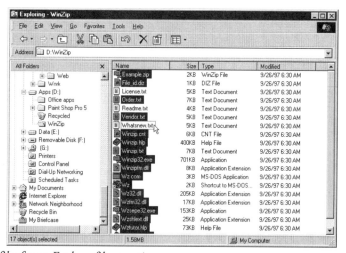

Figure 112 Selecting all but a few files for an Explorer file operation.

In Tip 107, you learned how to select specific files within the Explorer's file list by holding down the CTRL key as you clicked your mouse on each file. To select all but a few files within an Explorer file list, you will use a similar technique:

1. Within the Explorer window, select the Edit menu Select All option. The Explorer, in turn, will highlight each file within the file list.

2. Within the Explorer's file list, hold down the CTRL key and click your mouse on the files you want to "deselect." As you click your mouse on a file, Explorer will remove the file's highlight.

DRAGGING YOUR MOUSE TO SELECT MULTIPLE FILES AND FOLDERS WITHIN THE EXPLORER

Several of the previous Tips have discussed ways you can select one or more files and folders within the Explorer's file list. In addition to the methods discussed, the Explorer also lets you drag your mouse in a rectangular pattern around the file list to select files, as shown in Figure 113.

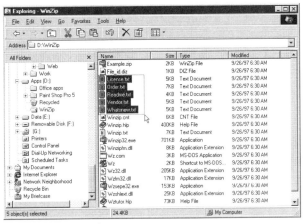

Figure 113 Selecting files within the Explorer by dragging the mouse.

To select files by dragging your mouse, first click your mouse in an unused location within the file list and hold down your mouse-select button. Then, as you drag your mouse around the list, the Explorer will select the files you surround.

PREVIEWING A FILE'S CONTENTS WITHIN THE EXPLORER USING QUICK VIEW

When you double-click your mouse on a file within the Explorer's file list, Explorer will launch the program that created the file and will load the file into the program. Before you open a file, you can first preview the file's contents by using the Quick View utility. As shown in Figure 114, you can use Quick View to preview a variety of file formats.

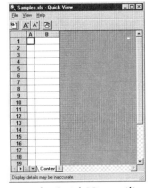 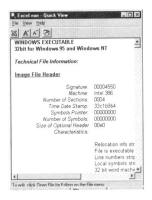

Figure 114 Previewing files using the Quick View utility program.

To use the Quick View program to preview a file's contents, perform these steps:

1. Within the Explorer folder list, click your mouse on the folder that contains the file you want to preview. The Explorer will display the folder's contents within its file list.
2. Within the Explorer's file list, right-click your mouse on the file. Windows 98 will display a pop-up menu. Within the pop-up menu, click your mouse on the Quick View option. The Explorer, in turn, will open a Quick View window within which it previews the file's contents. To close the Quick View window, click your mouse on the Close button.

---

115   SORTING THE ORDER OF FILES WITHIN AN EXPLORER FILE LIST

After you click your mouse on a folder within the Explorer's folder list, the Explorer will display a list of the files and subfolders the folder contains. Depending on the number of files and folders in the file list, you may have trouble finding a specific object. In such cases, you may want the Explorer to sort its file list, displaying the files sorted by name, size, or based on the file's date-and-time stamp. To sort the files within an Explorer file list, click your mouse on the View menu Arrange Icons option. The Explorer will display the Arrange Icons submenu, as shown in Figure 115. Within the Arrange Icons submenu, click your mouse on the option that corresponds to the sort order that you desire.

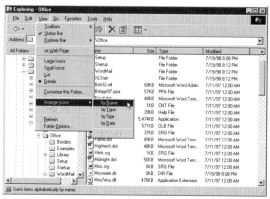

Figure 115 *The View menu Arrange Icons submenu.*

---

116   REFRESHING THE EXPLORER WINDOWS

As you have learned, Windows 98 lets you run multiple programs at the same time. If you open an Explorer window while other programs are running, there may be times when one of the programs changes the current folder's contents in some way, possibly by creating, renaming, or deleting a file or folder. Usually, the Explorer will detect the change and update its folder or file list, as appropriate. To ensure that the Explorer window's contents are current, however, you can direct the Explorer to "refresh" the folder and file list contents. In other words, you can tell the Explorer to check to see if anything has changed and, if so, to update its list. To direct the Explorer to refresh the current folder and file list, click your mouse on the Explorer view menu and choose Refresh.

> ## 117 | CUSTOMIZING THE CURRENT FOLDER'S DISPLAY WITHIN THE EXPLORER

As you have learned, using the Explorer, you can display and manage a folder's list of the files and subfolders. Within Windows 98, users make extensive use of the Explorer to copy, move, rename, and delete files and folders. In addition, using the Explorer you can specify an address on the World Wide Web and if your PC is currently connected to the Net, the Explorer will display the Web site's contents. Because it includes such capabilities, the Explorer also lets you customize the current folder's display by creating an HTML document for the folder (Tip 119 discusses HTML in detail) or by adding a background graphic to the folder. For example, Figure 117.1 shows two Explorer windows. The first window includes a background image. The second window displays the folder's contents using an HTML document within which a user who knows HTML can customize the folder's display format.

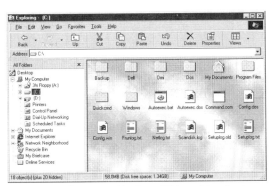 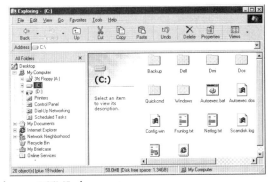

Figure 117.1 *Displaying an Explorer folder with a background image and as an HTML document.*

To customize the current folder's display, perform these steps:

1. Within the Explorer's folder list, click your mouse on the folder whose appearance you want to change. The Explorer will display the folder's current contents within its file list.
2. Click your mouse on the Explorer View menu and choose Customize this Folder. The Explorer, in turn, will start the Customize this Folder Wizard, as shown in Figure 117.2, that will walk you through the steps you must perform to add a background graphic to the current folder's display or to create an HTML document for the current folder.

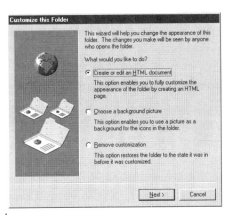

Figure 117.2 *The Customize this Folder Wizard.*

3. Within the Customize this Folder Wizard, select the option you desire and then click your mouse on the Next button. To help you perform each operation, Later Tips discusses how you can add a background image to the current folder how you create an HTML document that controls the folder's display.

Note: *Within the Customize this Folder dialog box, you can select the Remove customization option to turn off the current folder's custom display.*

118 DISPLAYING A BACKGROUND IMAGE BEHIND THE CURRENT FOLDER'S FILE LIST

In Tip 117, you learned that the Windows 98 Explorer lets you display a graphic image behind the current folder's file list. To add or remove a background image to the Explorer file list, you will use the Customize this Folder option. Specifically, to add a background image to the current folder, perform these steps:

1. Within the Explorer's folder list, click your mouse on the folder whose appearance you want to change. The Explorer will display the folder's current contents within its file list.

2. Click your mouse on the Explorer View menu and choose Customize this Folder. The Explorer, in turn, will start the Customize this Folder Wizard that will walk you through the steps you must perform to add a background graphic to the current folder's display or to create an HTML document for the current folder.

3. Within the Customize this Folder Wizard, click your mouse on the Choose a background picture option and then click your mouse on the Next button. The Wizard, in turn, will display a dialog box, as shown in Figure 118, within which you can select the background image you desire.

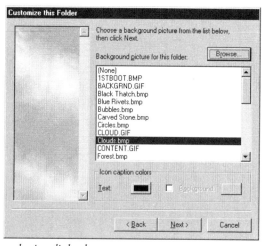

Figure 118 *The Customize this Folder image-selection dialog box.*

4. Within the image-selection dialog box, select an image from the list of image files that reside in the Windows folder, or click your mouse on the Browse button to locate a specific image file on your disk. The Wizard, in turn, will preview your image selection with the rectangle that ap-

pears at the left-hand side of the dialog box.

5. Within the image-selection dialog box, use the Icon caption colors field to select the color you want the Explorer to use to display icon captions within the folder list. If your background is dark, for example, you will want to choose a light color for the icon captions.

6. Within the image-selection dialog box, click your mouse on the Next button. The Wizard will display a dialog box that congratulates you for successfully assigning a background image. Within the dialog box, click your mouse on the Finish button.

119 Using an HTML Document to Customize the Current Folder's Display

As you have learned, using the Explorer, you can view sites on the World Wide Web. To display a Web site, the Explorer must interpret HTML documents which contain special codes that Web-page designers use to build Web sites. Within an HTML document, for example, you might encounter the symbol <B> which directs the browser to display bold text, or the symbol </B> which directs the browser to turn off its bold text display. Because the Explorer understands HTML codes, the Explorer lets you design an HTML document to customize a folder's display. Figure 119.1, for example, illustrates a folder that uses HTML to format the Explorer's display.

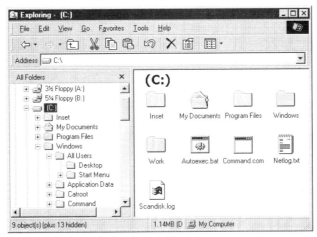

Figure 119.1 *Using HTML codes to format a folder's display within the Explorer.*

If you understand HTML, you can direct the Explorer to customize the current folder's display using HTML by performing these steps:

1. Within the Explorer's folder list, click your mouse on the folder whose appearance you want to change. The Explorer will display the folder's current contents within its file list.

2. Click your mouse on the Explorer View menu and choose Customize this Folder. The Explorer, in turn, will start the Customize this Folder Wizard that will walk you through the steps you must perform to add a background graphic to the current folder's display or to create an HTML document for the current folder.

3. Within the Customize this Folder Wizard, click your mouse on the Create or edit an HTML

document option and then click your mouse on the Next button. The Wizard, in turn, will display a dialog box that tells you it will start an HTML editor within which you can edit and save the document's HTML codes. Within the dialog box, click your mouse on the Next button. Windows 98 will open a text editor (such as the Notepad accessory program), as shown in Figure 119.2.

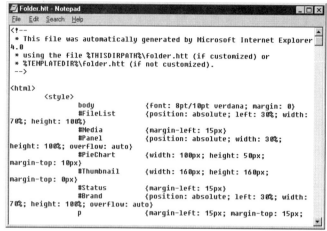

Figure 119.2 *Editing the folder's HTML codes within a text editor.*

4. Within the text editor, edit the folder's HTML codes as your needs require and then use the editor's file menu Save option to save the file's contents. (The Explorer will provide the filename *Folder.HTT*, which it will store in the current folder.) Then, close the text editor window.

5. Within the Wizard, click your mouse on the Finish button. The Explorer, in turn, will display your folder using your HTML entries.

Later, if you want to make changes to the folder's HTML codes, simply open the file *Folder.HTT* (which you will find within the folder) and change the HTML entries to meet your needs.

120 DISPLAYING A FILE OR FOLDER'S PROPERTIES WITHIN THE EXPLORER

As you will learn in Tips this book presents, Windows 98 tracks a variety of properties (characteristics) about your files, folders, and even your hardware devices. With respect to your files, for example, Windows 98 tracks such items as the file's name, size, and even the date and time you created or last changed the file's contents. To display a file's properties within the Explorer, perform these steps:

1. Within the Explorer's folder list, click your mouse on the folder that contains your file of interest. The Explorer, in turn, will display the folder's file list.

2. Within the Explorer's file list, right-click your mouse on the file you desire. The Explorer will display a small pop-up menu. Within the pop-up menu, click your mouse on the Properties option. The Explorer will display the Properties dialog box, as shown in Figure 120.

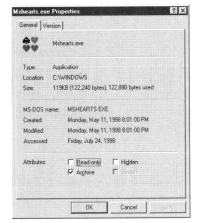

Figure 120 *Displaying a file's Properties dialog box.*

Depending on the file's type, the Properties dialog box contents may differ, possibly containing additional tabs. Within the General sheet, however, the dialog box will display the file's name, folder location, size, date-and-time fields, as well as the file's attributes. To display a folder's properties within the Explorer, perform these steps:

1. Within the Explorer's folder list, right-click your mouse on the folder of interest. The Explorer will display a small pop-up menu.

2. Within the pop-up menu, click your mouse on the Properties option. The Explorer will display the folder's Properties dialog box.

121 DISPLAYING THE NUMBER OF FILES OR SUBFOLDERS A FOLDER CONTAINS

As you have learned, folders exist within Windows 98 to help you organize your files. As you work, there may be times when you need to know the number of files or subfolders a folder contains. Depending on the folder's contents, counting the files and folders can become quite time consuming and is a process prone to errors. Fortunately, by displaying the folder's Properties dialog box, you can quickly determine the number of files and subfolders a folder contains, as shown in Figure 121.

Figure 121 *Using a folder's Properties dialog box to determine the number of files and subfolders the folder contains.*

To display a count of the number of files or subfolders a folder contains, perform these steps:

1. Within the Explorer, right-click your mouse on the folder you desire. Windows 98, in turn, will display a pop-up menu.

2. Within the pop-up menu, click your mouse on the Properties option. Windows 98 will display the folder's Properties dialog box, within which you can find a count of the number of files and subfolders the folder contains.

122 *UNDERSTANDING AND USING FILE ATTRIBUTES*

In Tip 120, you learned how to display a file's properties within the Explorer, using a file's Properties dialog box. Near the bottom of a file's Properties dialog box, you will find an Attributes field that contains several checkboxes that correspond to the file's attributes, as shown in Figure 122.

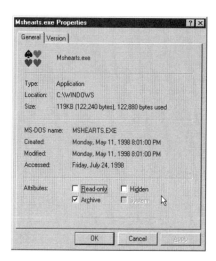

Figure 122 A file's Properties dialog box.

The term *file attributes* is a holdover from the MS-DOS operating system which lets users change four specific file properties. By selecting or clearing an attribute checkbox within the Properties dialog box, you can set a file's attributes. As you will learn, each of the four file attributes controls how Windows 98 can use the file. For example, if you have a file whose contents you do not want to change or delete (and whose contents you do not want others to change or delete), you can protect the file by selecting the file's read-only attribute. By setting the read-only attribute, you prevent another program from changing the file.

A file's hidden attribute controls whether not the file will appear within an MS-DOS directory listing (and possibly whether the file will appear within an Explorer file list). By selecting a file's hidden attribute, you hide the file, preventing it from appearing within the directory list. Users hide files in this way to prevent other users from knowing that the file exists. In general, however, only the Windows 98 operating system (which hides key files so you do not accidentally delete them) should use a file's hidden attribute. A file's system attribute combines the hidden and read-only attributes, meaning that Windows 98 will not let a program change the file and the file will not appear within an MS-DOS directory listing. Users should not set or remove a file's system attribute. Instead, only Windows 98 should use the system attribute.

In later Tips, you will learn how to use the Windows 98 Backup utility to make backup copies of the files that reside on your disk. When you perform a backup operation, you can direct the Backup program to only backup those files whose contents have changed since your last backup (so you don't have to repeatedly backup all the files on your disk). To keep track of which files have changed and which have not, Windows 98 uses the archive attribute. As it turns out, each time you backup a file, Windows 98 clears the file's archive attribute. Should you later change the file's contents, Windows 98 will set the archive attribute which tells the Backup utility that it should backup the file's new contents.

Within a file's Properties dialog box, you can click your mouse on an attribute checkbox to set or clear the check mark. Then, click your mouse on the OK button to put your changes into effect.

123 CONTROLLING THE DISPLAY OF HIDDEN FILES WITHIN THE EXPLORER

In Tip 122, you learned that the hidden file attribute lets you control whether or not Windows 98 will display a file's listing within an MS-DOS directory listing and sometimes, within an Explorer window's file list. Usually, the Explorer will not display hidden files within a file list. In addition, the Explorer usually does not list the following file types:

- Dynamic link library files that use the DLL extension

- System files that use the SYS extension

- Virtual-device drivers that use the VXD, 386, or DRV extensions

To direct the Explorer to display these file types and files whose hidden attributes are set, perform these steps:

1. Within the Explorer window, click your mouse on the View menu and choose Folder Options. Windows 98 will display the Folder Options dialog box, as shown in Figure 123.1.

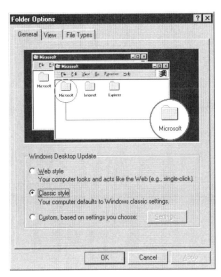

Figure 123.1 *The Folder Options dialog box.*

2. Within the Folder Options dialog box, click your mouse on the View tab. Windows 98 will display the View sheet, as shown in Figure 123.2.

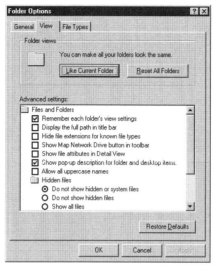

Figure 123.2 *The Folder Options dialog box View sheet.*

3. Within the View sheet Advanced Settings field, use your mouse to scroll through the settings list and locate the Hidden file section. Then, click your mouse on the Show all files radio button.

4. Within the View sheet, click your mouse on the OK button to put your changes into effect.

124 FINE TUNING THE EXPLORER WINDOW'S DISPLAY

In several of the preceding Tips, you have learned ways you can customize how the Explorer displays a folder's contents. In addition to controlling how the Explorer displays a specific folder's contents, you can also customize the Explorer's general settings using the Folder Options dialog box shown in Figure 124.1.

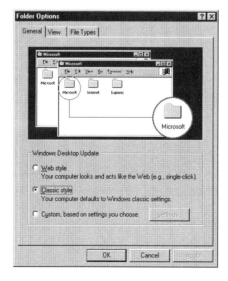

Figure 124.1 *The Folder Options dialog box.*

Within the Folder Options dialog box, you can enable the Explorer's Web style display, its classic display, or you can click your mouse on the Settings button to display the Explorer's Custom Settings dialog box, as shown in Figure 124.2.

Figure 124.2 *The Custom Settings dialog box.*

Within the Custom Settings dialog box, you can control how the Explorer displays Active (Web-based content), whether not the Explorer opens a new window for each folder you view, whether or not the Explorer displays Web content for all folders or just special folders, and whether or not the Explorer responds to single-click or double-click mouse operations.

Also, if you click your mouse on the Folder Options dialog box View tab, Windows 98 will display the View sheet, as shown in Figure 124.3. Within the View sheet, you can select specific settings by checking or unchecking the various checkboxes. After you make the selections you desire, click your mouse on the OK button to put your changes into effect.

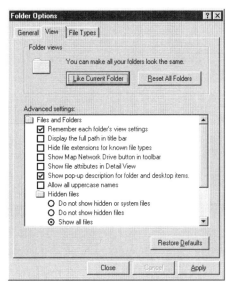

Figure 124.3 *The Folder Options dialog box View sheet.*

125	REGISTERING A NEW FILE TYPE

As you have learned, if, within the Explorer, you double-click your mouse on a document file, Windows 98 will run the program that corresponds to the document and will load it for use within the program. If Windows 98 does not recognize the document's type, Windows 98 will display the Open With dialog box that asks you to specify the corresponding program. In addition to using the Open With dialog box to associate a program with a specific document type, you can use the Folder Options dialog box File Types sheet, shown in Figure 125.1.

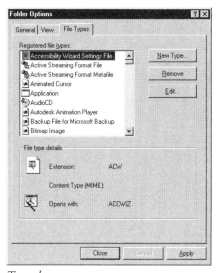

Figure 125.1 *The Folder Options dialog box File Types sheet.*

To register a file type using the Explorer, perform these steps:

1. Within the Explorer, click your mouse on the View menu Folder Options option. Windows 98, in turn, will display the Folder Options dialog box.

2. Within the Folder Options dialog box, click your mouse on the File Types tab. Windows 98 will display the File Types sheet, previously shown in Figure 125.1.

3. Within the File Types sheet, click your mouse on the New Type button. Windows 98, in turn, will display the Add New File Type dialog box shown in Figure 125.2.

4. To select a new icon for the file type, click your mouse on the Change Icon button. Windows 98 will display the Change Icon dialog box, within which you can select the icon you desire.

5. Within the Add New File Type dialog box, click your mouse on the Description of type field and type in a brief description of the type's typical contents. The Explorer will display this information within its Type column when you enable the Explorer's Detail view.

6. Within the Add New File Type dialog box, click your mouse on the Associated extension field and type in the new type's file extension.

7. Within the Add New File Type dialog box, click your mouse on the Content_Type (MIME) field and type in (if you know it) a MIME (Multimedia Internet Mail Extension) content label that corresponds to your new type.

8. Within the Add New File Type dialog box, click your mouse on the Actions field and type in the commands you want the Explorer to display on type's pop-up menu. For example, you might add a command such as Open with WordPad or Print with WordPad. To add a new command, click your mouse on the New button.

9. At the bottom of the Add New File Type dialog box, use the checkboxes to select the settings you desire and then click your mouse on the OK button to put your changes into effect.

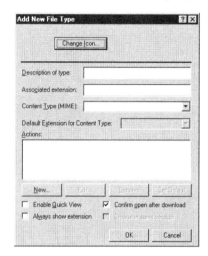

Figure 125.2 The Add New File Type dialog box.

126 REMOVING A REGISTERED FILE TYPE

In Tip 125, you learned how to register a new file type within the Windows 98 Explorer. Each time you double-click your mouse on a file of that type, Windows 98 will run the corresponding program. Should you remove the program from your system, you may want to remove the type registration. To unregister a file type within the Explorer, perform these steps:

1. Within the Explorer, click your mouse on the View menu Folder Options option. Windows 98 will display the Folder Options dialog box.

2. Within the Folder Options dialog box, click your mouse on the File Types tab. Windows 98, in turn, will display the File Types sheet.

3. Within the File Types sheet, use your mouse to scroll through the list of Registered file types and then click your mouse on the file type you want to remove. Windows 98 will highlight the file type.

4. Within the File Types sheet, click your mouse on the Remove button. Windows 98, in turn, will display the File Types dialog box asking you to confirm the file deletion. Click your mouse on the Yes option.

5. Within the File Types sheet, click your mouse on the OK button.

---

127 | ***USING THE EXPLORER TO LAUNCH (RUN) A PROGRAM***

In Tip 39, you learned how to run your programs using the Start menu. Usually, within Windows 98, you will run your programs using the Start menu. However, as you have learned, each of your programs reside in a file on your disk. As you view your disk's contents within the Explorer, you will encounter program icons. For example, if you use the Explorer to examine the Windows folder, you will find several different program files, as shown in Figure 127.

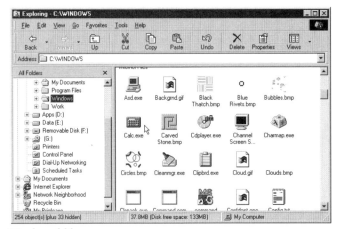

Figure 127 *Program files within the Windows folder.*

To run a program from within the Explorer, simply double-click your mouse on the program's icon. Windows 98, in turn, will launch the program, displaying the program window. Within the Windows folder, for example, you can double-click your mouse on the *Calc.EXE* file to launch the Calculator accessory or the *MSHearts.EXE* file to launch the Hearts card game. To end the programs, simply click your mouse on the program window's Close button.

---

128 | ***LAUNCHING A PROGRAM AND PRELOADING A DOCUMENT WITHIN THE EXPLORER***

In Tip 127, you learned how to run a program within the Explorer by double-clicking your mouse on the program icon that appears within an Explorer file list. The Explorer also lets you run a program by double-clicking your mouse on a program document within the Explorer file list. For example, if you double-click your mouse on a document that you created using Microsoft Word, the Explorer will start Word and load the document for editing. Likewise, if you double-click your mouse on a spreadsheet document that you created using Microsoft Excel, the Explorer will start Excel and load your spreadsheet.

In Tip 143, you learned that a filename extension tells other users (and the Explorer) about the file's contents as well as the program that created the document. When you double-click your mouse on a document file within the file list, the Explorer will examine the file's extension to determine which program it should start. The Explorer will then launch that program and direct it to load your document file.

---

129 | **USING A FILE ASSOCIATION TO START THE PROGRAM THAT CORRESPONDS TO A SPECIFIC DOCUMENT TYPE**

In Tip 127, you learned how to preload a document within a program by double-clicking your mouse on the document file within the Explorer file list. As discussed, when you double-click your mouse on a document, the Explorer examines the document's file extension to determine which program to run. In other words, the Explorer associates specific programs with specific file extensions. For example, the Explorer might associate Microsoft Word with documents that use the DOC extension. Likewise, the Explorer will associate documents with the XLS extension to Microsoft Excel. If you double-click your mouse on a document for which the Explorer does not have an association, Windows 98 will display the Open With dialog box, as shown in Figure 129, within which you can select the program you want Windows 98 to use to open the file.

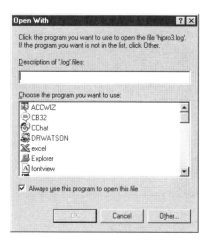

Figure 129 *The Open With dialog box.*

Within the Open With dialog box, use your mouse to scroll through the list of programs installed on your system. Click your mouse on the program that you want Windows 98 to associate with the document type and then click your mouse on the OK button. Windows 98, in turn, will open the document using your selected program and will record your newly created association for future use.

---

130 | **RUNNING THE EXPLORER FROM WITHIN THE RUN DIALOG BOX**

As you learned in Tip 83, you will use the Windows 98 Explorer on a regular basis to copy, move, rename, and delete your files and folders. Depending on the number of entries in your Start menu's Programs submenu, it may take you a little time to find the Explorer option. To save time, consider starting the Explorer one time using the Start menu Run option. Then, you can later use the Run option to quickly start the Explorer. As Tip 40 discussed, within the Windows 98 Run dialog box, Windows 98 also displays your most recently used command and keeps track of your recent commands within its pull-down command list. By starting the Explorer using the Run option, you place the Explorer command within this list. To run the Explorer using the Start menu Run option, perform these steps:

1. Click your mouse on the Start menu Run option. Windows 98, in turn, will display the Run dialog box.

2. Within the Run dialog box, type EXPLORER and press ENTER. Windows 98, in turn, will open the Explorer window. (If you want the Explorer to display a specific folder when it starts, simply include the folder's path within the command line, such as EXPLORER C:\MyStuff.)

131 DISPLAYING SPECIFICS ABOUT A DISK DRIVE WITHIN THE EXPLORER

As you have learned, using the Windows 98 Explorer, you can manage your folders and the files they contain. In addition, using the Explorer, you can display specifics about a disk drive, as shown in Figure 131.

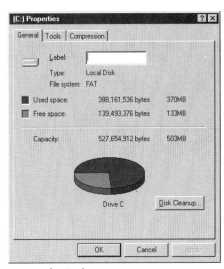

Figure 131 Displaying specifics about a disk drive using the Explorer.

Within the disk's Properties dialog box, you can display the disk's current storage capacity as well as the amount of space available for use. Several of the Tips that follow will examine ways you can use a disk's Properties dialog box to display information about the disk or to customize various disk-drive settings.

To display a disk's Properties dialog box, perform these steps:

1. Within the Explorer's folder list, click your mouse on the icon that corresponds to the disk you desire. The Explorer, in turn, will display the disk's upper-level folders and files within its file list.

2. Select the Explorer File menu Properties option. The Explorer, in turn, will display the disk's Properties dialog box, as previously shown in Figure 131.

Note: *You can also display a disk's Properties dialog box by right-clicking your mouse on the disk within the Explorer folder list or within the My Computer window and then selecting the Properties option from the pop-up menu that Windows 98 displays.*

132 ASSIGNING A NAME (A LABEL) TO A DISK DRIVE

Depending on the number of disk drives attached to your PC, you might have disks named C:, D:, E:, F:, and so on. As you work, you must remember which disk drive contains specific files. To help you track your drives and files, Windows 98 lets you assign a name (users refer to disk names as *labels*) to a disk drive. After you assign a name to a disk drive, the Explorer will precede the drive letter with its disk name, as shown in Figure 132.1.

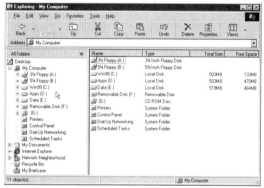

Figure 132.1 *The Windows Explorer displays a disk drive's label within its folder window.*

Using disk labels, you might name your disks Reports, Budgets, Sales, and so on. Later, if you can store your related files on the corresponding disk drive, you can use the disk label to quickly locate the disk that contains the files you desire. To assign a disk label to a disk drive, perform these steps:

1. Click your mouse on the Start menu Programs option and then select Windows Explorer. Windows 98, in turn, will start the Explorer.

2. Within the Explorer window, right-click your mouse on the disk drive to which you want to assign a disk label. Windows 98, in turn, will display a pop-up menu.

3. Within the pop-up menu, click your mouse on the Properties option. The Explorer, in turn, will display the disk's Properties dialog box, as shown in Figure 132.2.

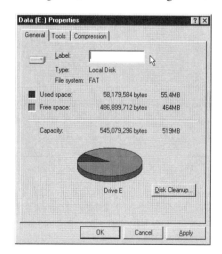

Figure 132.2 *A disk's Properties dialog box.*

4. Within the Properties dialog box, click your mouse within the Label field and type in the disk name that you desire. The label can contain up to 11 characters.

5. Within the Properties dialog box, click your mouse on the OK button. The Explorer, in turn, will display your disk label within its folders window.

---

133 FREEING UP SPACE ON A DISK USING THE WINDOWS 98 DISK CLEANUP WIZARD

Regardless of the amount of space their disk drives contain, users usually have no problem filling up their available space. After your disk fills, you will have to delete files that you no longer use to make room for new files.

To help you remove unnecessary files from your disk, Windows 98 provides the Disk Cleanup Wizard, which will help you delete unnecessary files from your disk. To start the Disk Cleanup Wizard from within the Explorer, perform these steps:

1. Click your mouse on the Start menu Programs option and then select Windows Explorer. Windows 98, in turn, will start the Explorer.

2. Within the Explorer window, right-click your mouse on the disk drive from which you want the Disk Cleanup Wizard to remove unnecessary files. Windows 98 will display a pop-up menu.

3. Within the pop-up menu, click your mouse on the Properties option. The Explorer, in turn, will display the disk's Properties dialog box, as shown in Figure 133.1.

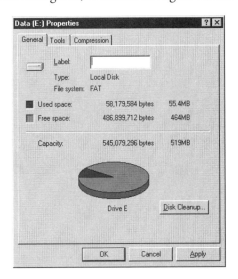

Figure 133.1 A disk's Properties dialog box.

4. Within the Properties dialog box, click your mouse on the Disk Cleanup button. Windows 98, in turn, will start the Disk Cleanup Wizard, as shown in Figure 133.2.

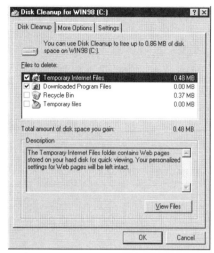

Figure 133.2 *The Windows 98 Disk Cleanup Wizard.*

5. Within the Disk Cleanup Wizard, click your mouse on the checkboxes that correspond to the files you want the Wizard to delete, placing a check mark within the box. As you select the files you want to remove, the Wizard will display the amount of disk space you will recover.

6. Within the Disk Cleanup Wizard, click your mouse on the OK button. The Wizard, in turn, will display a dialog box asking you to confirm the file deletion. Click your mouse on the Yes button.

134 **DETERMINING A DISK'S ERROR-CHECKING STATUS**

In Tip 643, you will learn how to use the ScanDisk utility to check your disk for errors. As you troubleshoot system errors, there may be times you will want to know the last time someone ran the ScanDisk utility program on your disk. In such cases, you can use the disk's Properties dialog box Tools sheet, as shown in Figure 134.

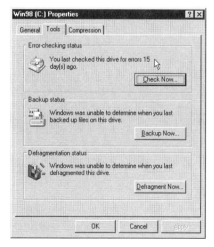

Figure 134 *The Properties dialog box Tools sheet.*

If you examine the Error-checking status field within the Tools sheet, you will find that Windows 98 will display the number of days since the last time you (or someone) checked your disk drive for errors. Depending on the number of days that have passed since the last ScanDisk operation, you may want to run the ScanDisk utility now. To run the ScanDisk utility from within the Tools sheet, click your mouse on the Check Now button. Windows 98, in turn, will start the ScanDisk utility, as discussed in Tip 643.

To display the Properties dialog box Tools sheet, perform these steps:

1. Click your mouse on the Start menu Programs option and then select Windows Explorer. Windows 98, in turn, will start the Explorer.
2. Within the Explorer window, right-click your mouse on the disk drive whose error status you want to check. Windows 98 will display a pop-up menu.
3. Within the pop-up menu, click your mouse on the Properties option. The Explorer, in turn, will display the disk's Properties dialog box.
4. Within the Properties dialog box, click your mouse on the Tools tab. Windows 98 will display the Tools sheet.
5. Within the Tools sheet, click your mouse on the Check Now button.

135   DETERMINING A DISK'S BACKUP STATUS

In later tips, you will learn how to use the Windows 98 Backup utility to backup the files on your disk. As you work, there may be times when you must know the last time you (or someone else) backed up the files on your disk. In such cases, you can use the disk's Properties dialog box Tools sheet, as shown in Figure 135.

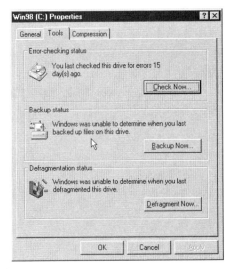

Figure 135 *The Properties dialog box Tools sheet.*

If you examine the Backup status field within the Tools sheet, you will find that Windows 98 displays the number of days since your disk was last backed up. Depending on the number of days that have passed since the last backup operation, you may want to run the Backup utility now. To run the Backup utility from within the Tools sheet, click your mouse on the Backup Now button. Windows 98, in turn, will start the Backup utility. To display the Properties dialog box Tools sheet, perform these steps:

1. Click your mouse on the Start menu Programs option and then select Windows Explorer. Windows 98, in turn, will start the Explorer.

2. Within the Explorer window, right-click your mouse on the disk drive whose backup status you want to check. Windows 98 will display a pop-up menu.

3. Within the pop-up menu, click your mouse on the Properties option. The Explorer, in turn, will display the disk's Properties dialog box.

4. Within the Properties dialog box, click your mouse on the Tools tab. Windows 98 will display the Tools sheet.

5. Within the Tools sheet, click your mouse on the Backup Now button.

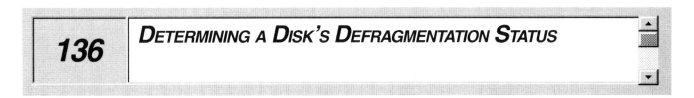

136   *DETERMINING A DISK'S DEFRAGMENTATION STATUS*

In Tip 615, you will learn how to use the Windows 98 Disk Defragmenter to defragment the files on your disk. In general, by defragmenting the files on your disk, you improve your system performance by reducing the amount of time Windows 98 must spend to locate and read your files from disk. If your system performance seems slow, you may want to know the last time you (or someone else) defragmented your disk. In such cases, you can use the disk's Properties dialog box Tools sheet, as shown in Figure 136.

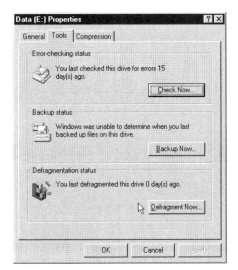

Figure 136 *The Properties dialog box Tools sheet.*

If you examine the Defragmentation status field within the Tools sheet, you will find that Windows 98 displays the number of days since your disk was defragmented. Depending on the number of days that have passed since the last defragmentation operation, you may want to run the Disk Defragmenter utility now. To run the Disk Defragmenter utility from within the Tools sheet, click your mouse on the Defragment Now button. Windows 98, in turn, will start the Disk Defragmenter utility.

To display the Properties dialog box Tools sheet, perform these steps:

1. Click your mouse on the Start menu Programs option and then select Windows Explorer. Windows 98, in turn, will start the Explorer.

2. Within the Explorer window, right-click your mouse on the disk drive whose fragmentation status you want to check. Windows 98 will display a pop-up menu.

3. Within the pop-up menu, click your mouse on the Properties option. The Explorer, in turn, will display the disk's Properties dialog box.

4. Within the Properties dialog box, click your mouse on the Tools tab. Windows 98 will display the Tools sheet.

137 DETERMINING A DISK'S COMPRESSION OPTIONS

In Tip 626, you will learn how to use the Windows 98 DriveSpace utility program to compress the files on your disk which, in turn, increases your disk's storage capacity. By compressing the files on a disk using DriveSpace, you may double the disk's storage capacity. Within a disk's Properties dialog box Compression sheet, you can display the disk's current storage use and learn how much space you will gain by compressing the disk's files, as shown in Figure 137.

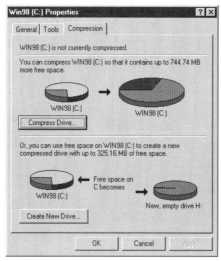

Figure 137 *The Properties dialog box Compression sheet.*

Within the Compression sheet, you can view how much space you will gain by compressing your entire disk as well as the amount of space you can gain by compressing only the free space. Tip 621 discusses the DriveSpace utility and disk compression in detail. Do not compress your disk until you have read Tip 621's discussion. If, however, you understand how Windows 98 file compression works (and how it may decrease your system performance), you can use the Compress Drive button to compress your entire drive or the Create New Drive button to compress the disk's available space.

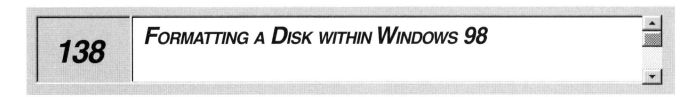

138 *FORMATTING A DISK WITHIN WINDOWS 98*

Before you can store information on a disk, you must first format the disk for use by Windows 98. Within Windows 98, you can format a disk using the Explorer. To format a disk within the Explorer, perform these steps:

1. Click your mouse on the Start menu Programs option and then select Windows Explorer. Windows 98, in turn, will start the Explorer.

2. Within the Explorer window, right-click your mouse on the disk drive you want to format. Windows 98 will display a pop-up menu.

3. Within the pop-up menu, click your mouse on the Format option. The Explorer, in turn, will display the disk's Format dialog box.

4. Within the Format dialog box, select the options you desire and then click your mouse on the Start button.

Note: *Windows 98 will not let you format a disk that has open files.*

139 *OPENING A SECOND EXPLORER WINDOW TO DISPLAY A FOLDER'S FILE LIST*

As you learned in Tip 86, each time you click your mouse on a folder within the Explorer's folders list, the Explorer will display the folder's list of files and subfolders within its file list. As you perform file copy and move operations, there may be times when you will want to view the contents of your source and destination folders at the same time. In such cases, you can direct Explorer to open a new window, within which it will display a folder's contents, as shown in Figure 139.

Figure 139 *Displaying multiple folders' contents within multiple Explorer windows.*

To direct the Explorer to open a new window for a folder, perform these steps:

1. Within the Explorer's folder list, right click your mouse on the folder for which you want the Explorer to open a new window. Windows 98, in turn, will display a pop-up menu.

2. Within the pop-up menu, click your mouse on the Open option. The Explorer, in turn, will open a new window within which it will display the folder's file list.

140 USING EXPLORER'S SEND TO OPTION TO FAX OR E-MAIL A DOCUMENT

As you have learned, the Windows 98 Explorer makes it easy for you to copy, move, rename, and delete files. In addition, within the Explorer, you can quickly send a document to another user via e-mail or by fax. Also, if your PC has infrared devices, you can use the Explorer to send a document to an infrared device, such as an infrared printer. To use the Explorer to send a document to another user, a device, or even to a floppy disk, perform these steps:

1. Within the Explorer file list, right-click your mouse on the document you desire. Windows 98, in turn, will display a pop-up menu.

2. Within the pop-up menu, click your mouse on the Send To option. Windows 98, in turn, will display the Send To submenu, as shown in Figure 140.

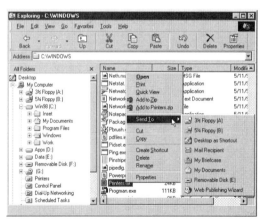

Figure 140 *The Windows 98 Send To submenu.*

3. Within the Send To submenu, select the menu option that corresponds to the operation you want to perform. Depending on the option you select, Windows 98 will start software, such as your fax or e-mail program, to perform the operation.

141 CREATING A SHORTCUT FOR A FILE, FOLDER, OR EVEN AN WEB LINK

Within your Desktop, Windows 98 will display program icons and shortcuts. Usually, you can distinguish between a program and shortcut icon by the presence of an arrow within the shortcut icon, as shown in Figure 141.1.

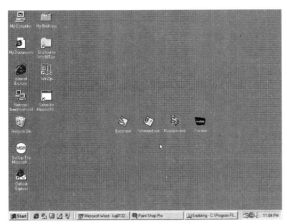 

Figure 141.1 *Windows 98 distinguishes a shortcut icon from a program icon by including an arrow within the shortcut item.*

A shortcut is simply a link to an object that exists on your disk. For example, assume that you have a program named *Budget.Exe* within a folder named *Programs*. Using the Explorer, you can copy the program file from the *Programs* folder into a different folder. Likewise, using the Explorer, you can place a shortcut to the program within a second folder as well. The difference between copying the file into a folder and placing a shortcut to the object within the folder is that, with the shortcut, you only have one copy of the program file on your disk. The shortcut is not the object—it simply points to the object. Within Windows 98, you can create a shortcut to a file, a folder, a program, and even to a Web site. To create a shortcut within the Explorer, perform these steps:

1. Right-click your mouse on your Desktop (to create a Desktop shortcut) or within the folder within which you want to place the shortcut. Windows 98 will display a pop-up menu.

2. Within the pop-up menu, click your mouse on the File menu New option and then choose Shortcut. Windows 98 will display the Create Shortcut dialog box, as shown in Figure 141.2.

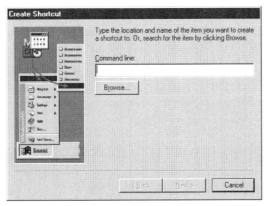

Figure 141.2 *The Create Shortcut dialog box.*

3. Within the Create Shortcut dialog box, type in the name and location of the file or folder for which you want to create a shortcut or click your mouse on the Browse button to locate the file or folder. If you are creating a shortcut for a Web address (such as *www.jamsa.com*), simply type in the address. Click your mouse on the Next button. Windows 98, in turn, will display the Select a Title for the Program dialog box asking you to type in the shortcut name.

4. Within the Select a Title for the Program dialog box, type in the shortcut name you desire and then click your mouse on the Finish button. Windows 98 will create the shortcut.

Note: *If you inadvertently delete a shortcut, the original file remains intact.*

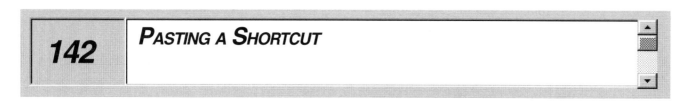

142 | PASTING A SHORTCUT

In Tip 106 you learned how to copy a file or document using cut-and-paste operations. When you perform such cut-and-paste operations, you can make an actual copy of an object, or you can paste a shortcut to the object. By creating a shortcut, you provide a quick way to access the object, but you do not actually create a duplicate of the object. To create a shortcut using cut-and-paste operations, perform these steps:

1. Start the Windows Explorer and locate the file for which you want to create a shortcut.
2. Within the Explorer, right-click your mouse on the file. Windows will display a pop-up menu.
3. Within the pop-up menu, select the Copy option.
4. Within the Explorer, click your mouse on the folder into which you want to place the shortcut.
5. Right-click your mouse in the Explorer's right frame. Windows will display a pop-up menu.
6. Within the pop-up menu, select the pop-up menu's Paste Shortcut option.

143 | UNDERSTANDING FILE TYPES AND EXTENSIONS

When you store a document on your disk, you should use a name that describes the file's contents. Document names consist of two parts: a filename and an extension. Within a document's name, you separate the filename from its extension using a period. For example, users usually use the *DOC* extension for documents they create using Microsoft Word, such as *SalaryReport.DOC* or *TravelBudget.DOC*. Usually, when you save a document to a file, your programs will assign an extension for you. Microsoft Excel, for example, will assign the *XLS* extension (for Excel spreadsheet) to your spreadsheet documents. The Windows 98 Paint utility discussed in Tip 500 will assign the *BMP* extension (for bitmap graphic).

In Tip 127, you learned that when you double-click your mouse on a document file within the Explorer, Windows 98 will run the corresponding program and will load the document within the program for use. To determine which program to run, the Explorer examines your document's file extension. If, for example, you double-click your mouse on a file with the *DOC* extension, Windows 98 will start Word. Likewise, if you double-click your mouse on a file with the *XLS* extension, Windows 98 will start Excel, loading your spreadsheet for editing. As you name your documents, make sure you assign extensions that are consistent with your application's use.

144 | DISPLAYING FILE TYPES (EXTENSIONS) WITHIN THE EXPLORER

In Tip 143, you learned that the Explorer uses a file's extension to determine which program it should run when you double-click your mouse on a document file. As you work with files within the Explorer, there may be times when you will want the Explorer to display file extensions, as shown in Figure 144.1.

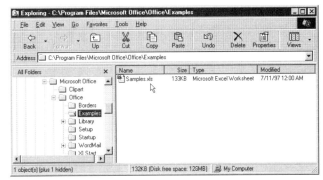

Figure 144.1 *Displaying file extensions within the Explorer.*

To direct the Explorer to display file extensions, perform these steps:

1. Within the Explorer, click your mouse on the View menu Folder Options option. Windows 98 will display the Folder Options dialog box.

2. Within the Folder Options dialog box, click your mouse on the View tab. Windows 98, in turn, will display the View sheet, as shown in Figure 144.2.

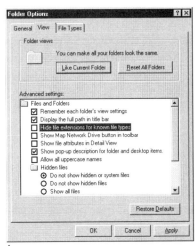

Figure 144.2 *The Folder Options dialog box View sheet.*

3. Within the View sheet, click your mouse on the Hide file extensions for known file types checkbox, removing the check mark from the box.

4. Within the View sheet, click your mouse on the OK button to put your changes into effect.

145 USING THE EXPLORER'S GO MENU TO BRANCH TO A SPECIFIC LOCATION

Several of the previous Tips discussed ways you can use the Explorer's toolbar Back, Forward, and Up buttons to move from one folder to another, the Address toolbar to specify a Web site's address, or the Links toolbar to select a specific Web site. In addition to these techniques, you can use the Explorer's Go menu, shown in Figure 145, to branch to a specific location. Using Go menu options, you can select a specific folder, channel, or even a specific program, such as your e-mail software.

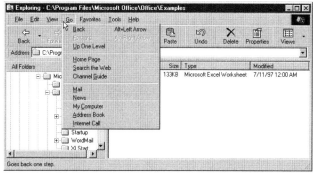

Figure 145 *Using the Explorer's Go menu to branch to a specific location.*

146 CREATING DESKTOP SHORTCUTS TO LAUNCH THE EXPLORER

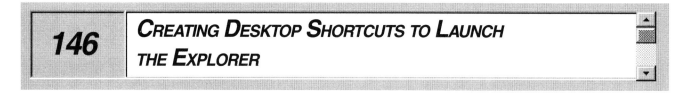

If you are like many users, you probably have a few key folders with which you often use the Explorer to copy, rename, or delete files. Rather than forcing you to start the Explorer and then select your folder, Windows 98 lets you create a Desktop shortcut that launches the Explorer with the folder you desire. For example, assume that you store your key documents within a folder on drive C named *MyWork*. By creating a shortcut to the command line, *Explorer C:\MyWork*, you can quickly start the Explorer and display your folder's contents. To create a Desktop shortcut for a specific folder, perform these steps:

1. Right-click your mouse on your Desktop. Windows 98, in turn, will display a pop-up menu.

2. Within the pop-up menu, click your mouse on the File menu New option and then choose Shortcut. Windows 98 will display the Create Shortcut dialog box, as shown in Figure 146.

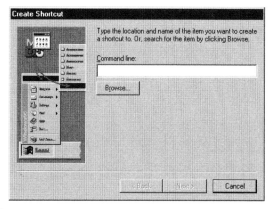

Figure 146 *The Create Shortcut dialog box.*

3. Within the Create Shortcut dialog box, type in the command **Explorer C:\MyWork** and click your mouse on the Next button. Windows 98, in turn, will display the Select a Title for Program dialog box.

4. Within the Select a Title for the Program dialog box, type in the shortcut name that corresponds to your folder, such as MyWork, and then click your mouse on the Finish button. Windows 98 will create the shortcut.

147 USING THE EXPLORER TO TRAVERSE MY COMPUTER

As you learned in Tip 78, when you double-click your mouse on the My Computer icon, Windows 98 will open the My Computer window, within which it displays icons for your system's disks and folders, as shown in Figure 147.1.

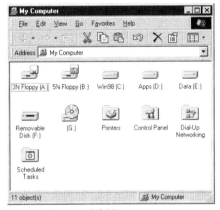

Figure 147.1 The My Computer window represents disks, files, and folders using icons.

If you use the Explorer on a regular basis, you will likely find that the Explorer's directory tree structure makes it easier for you to quickly traverse a disk than using the My Computer window. Fortunately, you can have the best of the Explorer and the My Computer window. To view the My Computer window using the Explorer format, hold down the **SHIFT** key when you double-click your mouse on the My Computer icon. Windows 98, in turn, will start the Explorer, displaying the contents of the My Computer window, as shown in Figure 147.2.

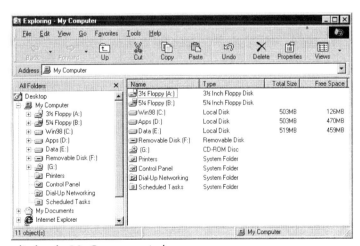

Figure 147.2 Using the Explorer to display the My Computer window.

148   VIEWING A LIST OF YOUR RECENTLY USED DOCUMENTS WITHIN THE EXPLORER

In Tip 76, you learned that to help you quickly access your recently used documents, Windows 98 provides the Start menu Documents submenu, as shown in Figure 148.1. Using the Documents submenu, you can select and open a document. Windows 98, in turn, will launch the program that you used to create the document and will then load the document within the program.

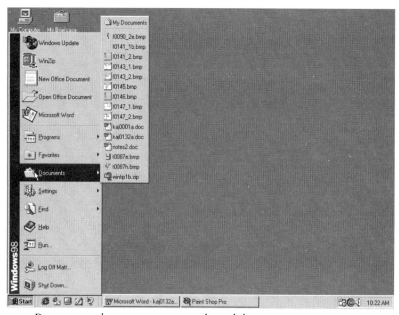

Figure 148.1 *Using the Start menu Documents submenu to access recently used documents.*

As it turns out, Windows 98 stores shortcuts (links) to your recently used documents that it displays on the Documents submenu within a folder named *Recent* (a hidden folder) that resides within the *Windows* folder. Using the Explorer, you can open the *Recent*, folder as shown in Figure 148.2.

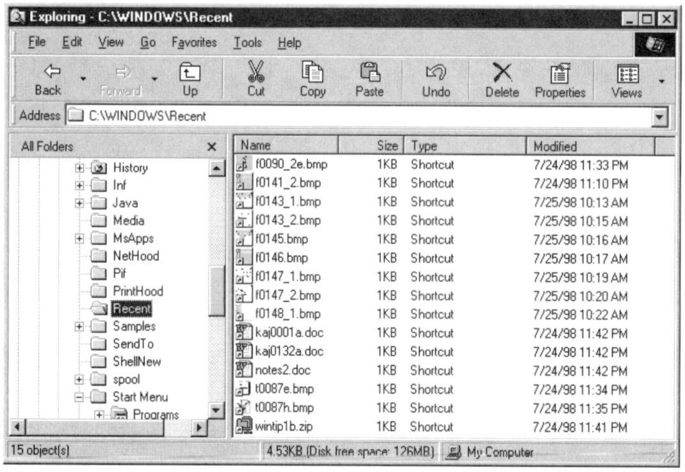

Figure 148.2 *Displaying your recently used documents within the **Windows** folder **Recent** subfolder.*

Within the *Recent* folder, you can open a document by double-clicking your mouse on the document's icon. Likewise, you can move or delete the document's shortcut by using your mouse to drag the shortcut to another folder or to the Recycle Bin. When you delete a document's icon from within the *Recent* folder, Windows 98 will remove the document from its Start menu Documents submenu.

149 USING THE EXPLORER'S SHORTCUT KEYS

As you have learned, using the Windows 98 Explorer, you can quickly traverse a disk and the files and folders it contains. If you prefer to keep your hands on your keyboard (rather than using your mouse), you may want to take advantage of the Explorer's keyboard shortcut keys Table 149 describes.

Shortcut Key	Action
F6 function key	Toggles between the folder list and file list.
Left arrow	If the current selection is expanded, collapses the selection.
	If the current section is not expanded, selects its parent folder.
Right arrow	If the current selection is collapsed, expands the selection.
	If the current select is not collapsed, selects the first subfolder.
NumLock+Minus key	Collapses the current folder.
NumLock+Plus key	Expands the current folder.
NumLock+Asterisk	Expands all folders beneath the current folder.

Table 149 *The Explorer's shortcut key combinations.*

150 RETRIEVING DELETED FILES FROM THE WINDOWS 98 RECYCLE BIN

In Tip 98, you learned how to delete files and folders from your system using the Windows 98 Explorer. As it turns out, within Windows 98, when you delete a file, Windows 98 does not actually remove the file from your disk. Instead, Windows 98 moves the file into a special folder named the Recycle Bin. Should, after you delete a file, you find that you want the file back, you may be able to use the Recycle Bin to "undelete" your file.

Windows 98 will keep each of the files you delete in the Recycle Bin until you either empty the bin's contents, as discussed in Tip 152, or the bin becomes full and Windows 98 must start to discard the bin's oldest contents. To view the contents of your system's Recycle Bin, double-click your mouse on the Recycle Bin icon that appears on your Desktop. Windows 98, in turn, will open the Recycle Bin folder, as shown in Figure 150.

Figure 150 *Windows 98 moves the files you delete into the Recycle Bin folder.*

To retrieve a file or folder from within the Recycle Bin, perform these steps:

1. Within the Recycle Bin window, right-click your mouse on the file or folder that you want to "undelete." Windows 98, in turn, will display a small pop-up menu.

2. Within the pop-up menu, click your mouse on the Restore option. Windows 98, in turn, will place the file or folder back at its original location.

3. To close the Recycle Bin window, click your mouse on the Close button.

Note: *If you want to undelete two or more files or folders in one step, simply hold down your keyboard's CTRL key and click your mouse on each file or folder that you desire. Then, right-click your mouse on an object and select the pop-up menu Restore option.*

151 **USING A DRAG-AND-DROP OPERATION TO RESTORE A DELETED FILE OR FOLDER**

In Tip 100, you learned how to use a drag-and-drop operation to move a file or folder from one location to another. In general, the Recycle Bin is simply a Windows 98 folder. As such, when you open the Recycle Bin, you can drag-and-drop (or cut-and-paste) a file or folder to a different location.

Usually, when you use the Recycle Bin to "undelete" a file or folder, the Recycle Bin places the object back to its original location. There may be times, however, when you want to place the file or folder somewhere else. In those cases, you should use a drag-and-drop operation to move the file or folder from the Recycle Bin into the folder you desire. To "undelete" a file or folder using a drag-and-drop operation, perform these steps:

1. Click your mouse on the Start menu Programs option and choose Explorer to start the Windows 98 Explorer.

2. Within the Explorer's folder list, click your mouse on the folder into which you want to place the files from the Recycle Bin.

3. If the Recycle Bin is not currently open, double-click your mouse on the Recycle Bin icon that appears on your Desktop.

4. Within the Recycle Bin window, click your mouse on the file or folder you want to "undelete" and then use your mouse to drag the item into the Explorer folder. After you release your mouse-select button, Windows 98, in turn, will move the file or folder from the Recycle Bin into its new location.

5. To close the Recycle Bin window, click your mouse on the Close button. Then, close the Explorer window.

Note: *If you want to undelete two or more files or folders in one step, simply hold down your keyboard's CTRL key and click your mouse on each file or folder that you desire. Then, use your mouse to drag all the files to the new location.*

152   EMPTYING THE WINDOWS 98 RECYCLE BIN

As you have learned, when you delete a file within Windows 98, you do not really remove the file from your system but, rather, into the Recycle Bin. Because Windows 98 places the file into the Recycle Bin, which is a folder that stores information on your disk, files within the Recycle Bin continue to consume disk space on your PC. When you delete many files or a very large file, you may want to open and empty the Recycle Bin, telling Windows 98 to remove the files from your system once and for all. After you empty the Recycle Bin, the files you have previously deleted no longer consume space on your disk. To empty the Recycle Bin, perform these steps:

1. Within the Windows 98 Desktop, right-click your mouse on the Recycle Bin icon. Windows 98, in turn, will display a pop-up menu, as shown in Figure 152.1.

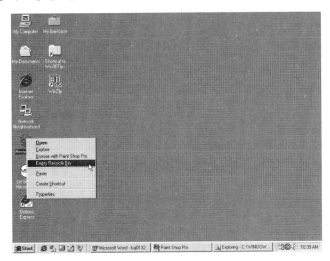

Figure 152.1 The Recycle Bin pop-up menu.

2. Within the pop-up menu, select the Empty Recycle Bin option. Windows 98, in turn, will display a dialog box asking you to confirm the deletion.

3. Within the dialog box, click your mouse on the Yes button. Windows 98, in turn, will empty the Recycle Bin.

As shown in Figure 152.2, Windows 98 displays one icon when the Recycle Bin contains files and a second icon when the Recycle Bin is empty.

Recycle Bin   Recycle Bin

Figure 152.2 *The Recycle Bin displays one icon when the Recycle Bin contains files and a second icon when the Recycle Bin is empty.*

153 **DIRECTING THE RECYCLE BIN TO DISCARD SPECIFIC FILES**

In Tip 152, you learned how to empty (flush) the Recycle Bin's contents to free up space on your disk. Before you flush the Recycle Bin's contents in this way, it is a good idea to take one last look at the list of files the Recycle Bin contains. As you examine the file list, you may find one or more files that you are not quite sure that you want to throw out. Rather than discarding all the files in the Recycle Bin at one time, you may instead want to select specific files for the Recycle Bin to discard—leaving other files in the Bin. To direct the Recycle Bin to discard specific files, perform these steps:

1. Within your Desktop, double-click your mouse on the Desktop's Recycle Bin icon. Windows 98, in turn, will open the Recycle Bin window.

2. Within the Recycle Bin, hold down your keyboard CTRL and click your mouse on each file you want the Recycle Bin to discard.

3. Within the Recycle Bin toolbar, click your mouse on the Delete button or simply press your keyboard's DEL key. Windows 98 will display a dialog box asking you to confirm your file deletion. Within the dialog box, click your mouse on the Yes button.

4. To close the Recycle Bin window, click your mouse on the window's Close button.

154 **CONTROLLING THE RECYCLE BIN'S CAPACITY**

As you have learned, when the Recycle Bin becomes full, Windows 98 discards the files that have been in the Recycle Bin for the longest period of time. Depending on your disk size and the frequency with which you must use the Recycle Bin, you may want to increase or decrease your Recycle Bin's size. Windows 98 bases the Recycle Bin's size as a percentage of your disk space. To change the Recycle Bin's capacity, perform these steps:

1. Within your Windows 98 Desktop, right-click your mouse on the Recycle Bin icon. Windows 98, in turn, will display a pop-up menu.

2. Within the pop-up menu, click your mouse on the Properties option. Windows 98 will display the Recycle Bin Properties dialog box, as shown in Figure 154.

3. Within the Recycle Bin Properties dialog box, use your mouse to drag the percentage slider to the right or to the left to increase or decrease the Recycle Bin's storage capacity.

4. Within the Recycle Bin Properties dialog box, click your mouse on the OK button to put your changes into effect.

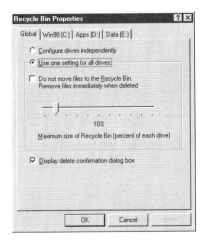

Figure 154 *The Recycle Bin Properties dialog box.*

155	*TURNING OFF WINDOWS 98 RECYCLE BIN USE*

In Tip 150, you learned that using the Recycle Bin folder, you can often "undelete" one or more files. If you find that you never use the Recycle Bin to recover your deleted files and you perform backup operations on a regular basis, you can direct Windows 98 not to use the Recycle Bin. By turning off Windows 98 use of the Recycle Bin, Windows 98 will delete files faster (because it no longer has to move the files into the Recycle Bin) and the Recycle Bin will not consume disk space. To turn Windows 98 use of the Recycle Bin off or on, perform these steps:

1. Within your Windows 98 Desktop, right-click your mouse on the Recycle Bin icon. Windows 98, in turn, will display a pop-up menu.

2. Within the pop-up menu, click your mouse on the Properties option. Windows 98 will display the Recycle Bin Properties dialog box, as shown in Figure 155.

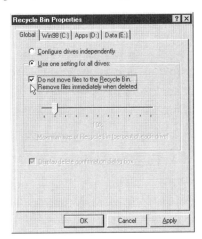

Figure 155 *The Recycle Bin Properties dialog box.*

3. Within the Recycle Bin Properties dialog box, click your mouse on the Do not move files to the Recycle Bin checkbox to place a check mark in the box, if you want to turn off the Recycle Bin, or to remove the check mark if you want Windows 98 to use the Recycle Bin.

4. Within the Recycle Bin Properties dialog box, click your mouse on the OK button to put your changes into effect.

156 ASSIGNING DIFFERENT RECYCLE BIN SETTINGS TO EACH OF YOUR DRIVES

As you have learned, within Windows 98, each time you delete a file, Windows 98 moves the file into the Recycle Bin, which gives you a chance to "undelete" the file should you decide you still need the file's contents. If your PC has multiple hard disks, you can direct the Recycle Bin to perform different operations for each drive. For example, you might want to turn off the Recycle Bin for drive C, and you might want to increase the size of the Recycle Bin on drive D. To direct the Recycle Bin to use different settings for each of your disk drives, perform these steps:

1. Within your Windows 98 Desktop, right-click your mouse on the Recycle Bin icon. Windows 98, in turn, will display a pop-up menu.

2. Within the pop-up menu, click your mouse on the Properties option. Windows 98 will display the Recycle Bin Properties dialog box.

3. Within the Recycle Bin Properties dialog box, click your mouse on the Configure drives independently radio button. Then, click your mouse on the dialog box tab that corresponds to each drive and assign the settings you desire. Within the Recycle Bin Properties dialog box, click your mouse on the OK button to put your changes into effect.

157 USING SHIFT-DEL TO DELETE A FILE AND BYPASS THE RECYCLE BIN

When you delete a file within Windows 98 (unless you delete the file from within an MS-DOS window), Windows 98 moves the file into the Recycle Bin, which provides you with the ability to later undelete the file. As you delete files, there will be times when you are sure you will never need a particular file's contents again, so there is no reason for Windows 98 to move the file to the Recycle Bin. In such cases, you can direct Windows 98 to delete the file from your system (and not use the Recycle Bin) by holding down your keyboard SHIFT key when you delete the file (which you can do either by pressing the DEL key or by clicking your mouse on the Explorer Delete button).

158 "UNDOING" A DELETE OPERATION WITH THE PROPERTIES MENU UNDO OPTION

In Tip 150, you learned that when you delete a file, Windows 98 moves the file into the Recycle Bin, which gives you a chance to later "undelete" the file. When you delete a file within the Windows 98 Explorer, you may be able to recover the file without having to open the Recycle Bin by performing an "Undo" operation. To undelete your recently deleted files using an Undo operation, perform these steps:

1. Within the Explorer, right-click your mouse pointer at the file's previous location. Windows 98, in turn, will display a pop-up menu similar to that shown in Figure 158.

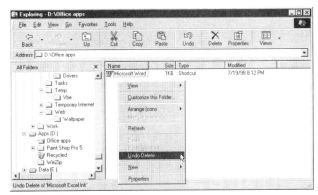

Figure 158 *A pop-up menu within the Windows 98 Explorer.*

2. Within the pop-up menu, click your mouse on the Undo Delete option. Windows 98, in turn, will place the file back into the folder.

If you have deleted multiple files, you can repeat Steps 1 and 2 to undelete each file.

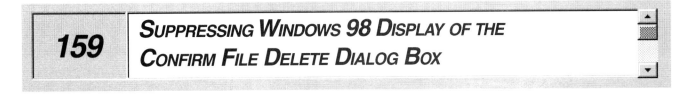

159 SUPPRESSING WINDOWS 98 DISPLAY OF THE CONFIRM FILE DELETE DIALOG BOX

In previous Tips, you learned to delete files and folders from your disk drive using the Windows 98 Explorer. As you learned, each time you delete a file, Windows 98 displays the Confirm File Delete dialog box, as shown in Figure 159, asking you to confirm that you really want to delete the file.

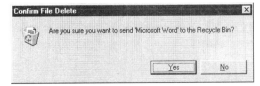

Figure 159 *The Confirm File Delete dialog box.*

Although the Confirm File Delete dialog box may prevent you from accidentally deleting the wrong files, most users will find confirming file-delete operations an unnecessary step. After all, should you accidentally delete a file, you can recover the file using the Recycle Bin. To direct Windows 98 not to display the Confirm File Delete dialog box, perform these steps:

1. Within your Windows 98 Desktop, right-click your mouse on the Recycle Bin icon. Windows 98, in turn, will display a pop-up menu.

2. Within the pop-up menu, click your mouse on the Properties option. Windows 98 will display the Recycle Bin Properties dialog box.

3. Within the Properties dialog box, click your mouse on the Display delete confirmation dialog box checkbox, removing the check mark in the box if you want to turn off the dialog box display, or to display the check mark if you want Windows to display the dialog box.

4. Within the Recycle Bin Properties dialog box, click your mouse on the OK button to put your changes into effect.

160 EXPLORING YOUR COMPUTER'S NETWORK NEIGHBORHOOD

If you use your PC within an office, it is more likely than not that your PC is connected to a local-area network (LAN). Several Tips within this book will examine Windows 98 networking in detail. For now, you need only to know that networks let you and other users share resources such as files, folders, and printers. In addition, using a network, you send can send and receive electronic mail (e-mail). If you are connected to a network, you can double-click your mouse on your Desktop's Network Neighborhood icon, shown in Figure 160.1, to view your network's PCs and printers.

Figure 160.1 To view PCs and printers within your network, double-click your mouse on the Desktop's Network Neighborhood icon.

In later Tips, you will use the Desktop's My Computer icon to display your PC's disks and folders. In a similar way, you use the Network Neighborhood icon to traverse your network resources. When you double-click your mouse on the Network Neighborhood icon, Windows 98 will display a listing of the PCs and printers connected to your network, as shown in Figure 160.2.

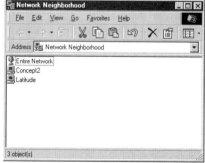

Figure 160.2 The Network Neighborhood window lists PCs and printers connected to your network.

If you double-click your mouse on a specific PC, the Network Neighborhood will display the files, folders, and printers that PC will share with you, as shown in Figure 160.3.

Figure 160.3 *Displaying a PC's shared resources.*

161 **MAPPING TO A NETWORK DRIVE**

In Tip 340, you will learn how to share disks and folders with other users across a network. Assume, for example, that you are working a project with several users and that you all store your files within a shared folder named *KeyProject*. Rather than forcing you to traverse the network each time you want to use the folder, Windows 98 lets you map a disk drive letter to the folder. In this way, to access the folder, you would use a drive letter, such as F: drive. Depending on the disk drives you are currently using, the drive letter you will use to access the network folder may vary. Likewise, another user in your group may use a different drive letter on his or her PC to map to the network folder. To map a shared network folder to a local drive name, perform these steps:

1. Click your mouse on the Start menu Programs option and choose Windows Explorer.

2. Within the Explorer window, click your mouse on the Tools menu Map Network Drive option. Windows 98, in turn, will display the Map Network Drive dialog box, as shown in Figure 161.

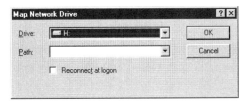

Figure 161 *The Map Network Drive dialog box.*

3. Within the Map Network Drive dialog box, click your mouse on the Drive pull-down list and click your mouse on the drive letter you want to map to the network folder.

4. Within the Map Network Drive dialog box Path field, type in the shared folder's complete network path. For example, if you want to map a folder named "BusinessPlan" on a networked computer named "Office Server", you would type **\\Office Server\BusinessPlan**. If you do not know the folder's exact name, click your mouse on the Path pull-down list and select from the computer and paths displayed. The Path pull-down list will contain a list of the network locations to which you have recently mapped a drive letter.

5. Within the Map Network Drive dialog box, click your mouse on the OK button to put your changes into effect.

162

MAPPING TO A NETWORK DRIVE EACH TIME WINDOWS 98 STARTS

In Tip 161, you learned how to map a drive to a shared network folder to simplify the steps you must perform to access the folder's files. If you use the same network drives on a regular basis, you can eliminate the time you spend creating the network connection each time you start your system by telling Windows to connect to the disk automatically, each time you start Windows 98. To create a *persistent connection* (a mapped-drive connection that Windows 98 re-establishes each time your system starts), perform these steps:

1. Click your mouse on the Start menu Programs option and choose Windows Explorer.
2. Within the Explorer window, click your mouse on the Tools menu Map Network Drive option. Windows 98, in turn, will display the Map Network Drive dialog box.
3. Within the Map Network Drive dialog box, click your mouse on the Drive pull-down list and click your mouse on the drive letter you want to map to the network folder.
4. Within the Map Network Drive dialog box Path field, type in the shared folder's complete network path. For example, if you want to map a folder named "BusinessPlan" on a networked computer named "Office Server", you would type **\\Office Server\BusinessPlan**. If you do not know the folder's exact name, click your mouse on the Path pull-down list and select from the computer and paths displayed.
5. Within the Map Network Drive dialog box, click your mouse on the Reconnect at logon checkbox, placing a check mark within the box. Then, click your mouse on the OK button to put your changes into effect.

163

DISCONNECTING FROM A NETWORK DRIVE

In Tip 161, you learned how to map a shared network folder to a local disk drive. Using the drive letter, you can then access the folder within the Explorer and your application programs. When you will no longer use the folder, you can direct Windows 98 to disconnect the mapped drive by performing these steps:

1. Click your mouse on the Start menu Programs option and choose Windows Explorer. Windows 98, in turn, will open the Explorer window.
2. Within the Explorer window, click your mouse on the Tools menu Disconnect Network Drive option. The Explorer, in turn, will display the Disconnect Network Drive dialog box, as shown in Figure 163, that shows your mapped drives.
3. Within the Disconnect Network Drive dialog box, select the mapped drive that you want to remove and then click your mouse on the OK button.

Figure 163 *The Disconnect Network Drive dialog box.*

164	**CREATING DESKTOP SHORTCUTS FOR THE DOCUMENTS OR PROGRAMS YOU COMMONLY USE**

As you have learned, using the Windows 98 Start menu, you can run most programs quickly. As you work, you may find that there are several key programs that you run on a regular basis. Rather than forcing you to continually traverse the Start menu to run these programs, Windows 98 lets you create shortcuts, which you place on your Desktop to run the programs with one double-click mouse operation.

In addition to letting you create shortcuts for programs, Windows 98 also lets you create shortcuts for your commonly used documents. For example, assume that you work with a database file on a daily basis. If you create a shortcut to the database file (the database document), you can later double-click your mouse on the document shortcut. Windows 98, in turn, will run the database program and automatically load the document. To create a shortcut to a program or document file, perform these steps:

1. Within the Windows Explorer, locate the file for which you want to create a shortcut.

2. Right-click your mouse on the file icon. Windows 98, in turn, will display the pop-up menu, as shown in Figure 164.1.

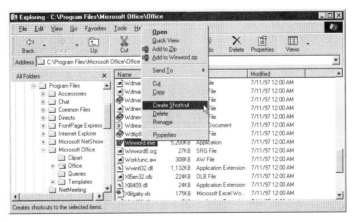

Figure 164.1 *The Explorer pop-up menu.*

3. Within the pop-up menu, select the Create Shortcut option. Windows 98, in turn, will create a shortcut icon for the file.

4. Within the Explorer, drag the shortcut icon onto the Desktop, as shown in Figure 164.2.

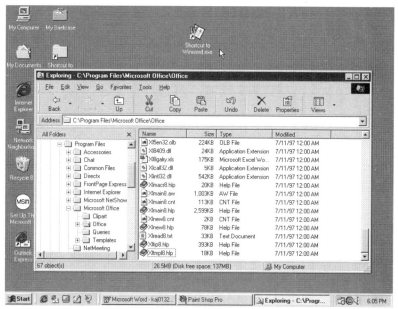

Figure 164.2 *Windows 98 represents shortcuts as an icon with a small arrow.*

In addition to creating a Desktop shortcut using the Steps 1-4 just discussed, you can also create a Desktop shortcut by performing these steps:

1. Within the Windows Explorer, locate the file for which you want to create a shortcut.

2. Click your mouse on the file icon. Windows 98 will highlight the file.

3. Hold down the **CTRL-SHIFT** keyboard combination and drag the file icon onto your Desktop. Windows 98, in turn, will display a small pop-up menu. Within the menu, click your mouse on the Create Shortcut option.

Note: *When you delete a shortcut to a file, Windows 98 will delete only the shortcut and not the file itself. A shortcut is simply a link to the file, not the actual file itself.*

165

USING COPY-AND-PASTE OPERATIONS WITHIN WINDOWS 98 TO COPY OBJECTS

If you use a word processor, you may have used cut-and-paste operations to move text from one location in a document to another. To perform the cut-and-paste operation, you first chose the text you wanted to move. Then, you selected an Edit menu Cut option which removed the text from its current location. Using your mouse or the keyboard arrow keys, you then positioned the cursor at the location within the document at which you wanted to place the text. Using an Edit menu Paste option, you placed the text at the current location.

When you move or copy items using cut-and-paste operations, Windows 98 (and your programs) use a special memory location called the Clipboard to hold the information you are moving or copying. When you copy an item to the Clipboard, the item remains in the Clipboard until you copy a different item to the Clipboard.

In addition to letting you move or copy text using the Clipboard, Windows 98 lets you move or copy files, folders, and other Desktop items using cut-and-paste or copy-and-paste operations. A copy-and-paste operation differs from a cut-and-paste operations in that you use a Copy option to place a copy of the item within the Desktop, instead of the item itself. To use copy-and-paste operations to copy a file or folder from one location to another, perform these steps:

1. Within the Explorer, click your mouse on the file or folder you want to copy. Windows 98, in turn, will highlight the item.

2. Within the Explorer, select the Edit menu Copy option. (Likewise, you can right-click your mouse on the file or folder and then select the pop-up menu's Copy option.) Windows 98, in turn, will place a copy of the item into the Clipboard.

3. Within the Explorer, locate the folder into which you want to paste the object.

4. Within the Explorer, select the Edit menu Paste option. Windows 98, in turn, will place a copy of the item into the current folder.

166   *PASTING ITEMS ONTO THE WINDOWS 98 DESKTOP*

In Tip 165, you learned that Windows 98 lets you copy or move items using copy-and-paste or cut-and-paste operations. In addition to letting you move items from one folder to another, Windows 98 also lets you place items onto the Desktop. When you paste an item onto the Windows 98 Desktop, you can place an actual copy of the item itself on the Desktop, or you can place a shortcut (a link) to the item. To copy or move an item to the Desktop, perform these steps:

1. Within the Explorer, click your mouse on the file or folder you want to copy. Windows 98, in turn, will highlight the item.

2. Within the Explorer, select the Edit menu Copy option to copy the item or the Edit menu Cut option to move the item.

3. Right-click your mouse on the Desktop. Windows 98, in turn, will display a pop-up menu similar to that shown in Figure 166.1.

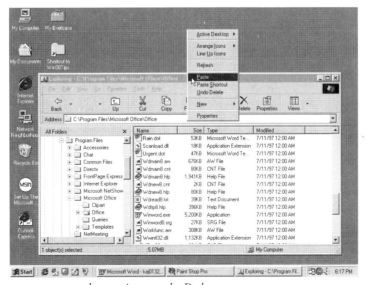

Figure 166.1 Using the Desktop pop-up menu to place an item on the Desktop.

4. To place the item on the Desktop, select the pop-up menu Paste option. To place a shortcut to the item on the Desktop, select the pop-up menu Paste Shortcut option.

In addition to letting you move files and folders onto the Desktop using cut-and-paste operations, Windows 98 lets you copy a text (which Windows 98 users refer to as a *scrap*) from a document to the Desktop. When you place a scrap on the Desktop, Windows 98 will include the word "scrap" in the icon's caption, as shown in Figure 166.2.

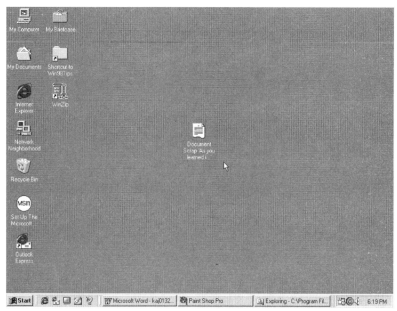

Figure 166.2 Windows 98 lets you place document text onto the Desktop as a scrap.

167	UNDERSTANDING AND WORKING WITH DOCUMENT SHORTCUTS (SCRAPS)

As you learned in Tip 166, if you use your mouse to drag and drop a folder or file onto your Desktop, Windows 98 will place a shortcut icon on the Desktop upon which you can click your mouse to open the file or folder. In a similar way, Windows 98 lets you place the current Clipboard contents onto the Desktop as well. For example, assume that you have cut or copied text from a document into the Clipboard using the WordPad word processor. By creating a scrap on the Desktop, you create a shortcut icon that corresponds to the scrap's contents. Later, you can drag and drop the scrap icon into your program's window to edit the scrap's contents.

When you create a scrap, Windows 98 will place the scrap's icon on the Desktop using the name *Document Shortcut* followed by the first few words of the scrap's text. To rename the scrap, right-click your mouse on the icon and then select the pop-up menu Rename option. Using a scrap is one of the quickest ways to select text from a document and then to save the text to its own separate file. If you drag a scrap onto the Start button, Windows 98 will create an option for the scrap to your Start menu. When you subsequently click your mouse over the Start menu scrap, Windows 98 starts the associated program with which you can edit, copy, and print that scrap. To create a scrap on your Desktop, perform these steps:

1. Within your application program, cut or copy the information you want to save within the scrap to the Clipboard.

2. Within your Desktop, right-click your mouse on an unused location. Windows 98, in turn, will display a pop-up menu.

3. Within the pop-up menu, click your mouse on the Paste Shortcut option.

168 **PASTING A SCRAP INTO A DOCUMENT BY DRAGGING THE SCRAP OVER THE TASKBAR'S PROGRAM ICON**

In Tip 167, you learned how to create a scrap for a document that you store as an icon on your Desktop. As you learned, if you double-click your mouse on the scrap, Windows 98 will start the corresponding program, loading the scrap's contents for editing. Likewise, if the program is running, you can use your mouse to drag and drop the scrap into the program's window. If the program is currently minimized (to a Taskbar icon), simply use your mouse to drag the scrap's icon over the Taskbar's program icon. Windows 98, in turn, will restore the program window and will load the scrap for editing.

169 **TUNE YOUR START MENU**

Within Windows 98, you make extensive use of the Start menu to run your programs. As you have learned, the Start menu contains cascading submenus that you can use to access your programs—with the Programs submenu being the one you will use most often. As you add more programs to your system, your Start menu and its submenus may eventually become cluttered, as shown in Figure 169.1.

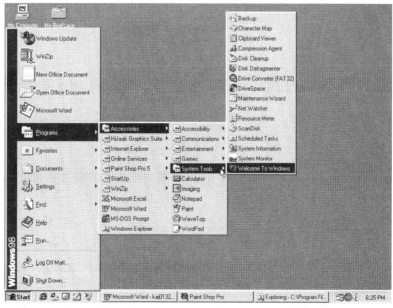

Figure 169.1 *As your Start menu becomes cluttered, finding your programs becomes more difficult.*

When Windows 98 can no longer display each menu's program options, Windows 98 may display a small arrow at the top or bottom of the menu. To scroll up or down through the menu options, simply click your mouse on the corresponding arrow. If your Start menu (or its submenus) are becoming cluttered, you may want to create additional submenus, within which you can group related programs, much like you might use folders and subfolders to organize your files on disk. To manage (move, delete, rename, and so on) the Start menu options, perform these steps:

1. Click your mouse on the Start menu Settings option and choose the Taskbar & Start menu option. Windows 98, in turn, will display the Taskbar Properties dialog box.

2. Within the Taskbar Properties dialog box, click your mouse on the Start Menu Programs tab. Windows 98 will display the Start Menu Programs sheet, as shown in Figure 169.2.

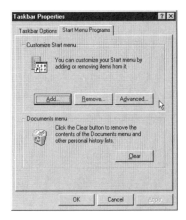

Figure 169.2 *The Start Menu Programs sheet.*

3. Within the Start menu Programs sheet, click your mouse on the Advanced button. Windows 98 will start the Explorer, displaying the Start Menu folder, as shown in Figure 169.3.

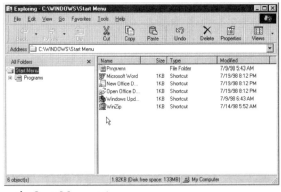

Figure 169.3 *Using the Explorer to manage the Start Menu options.*

4. Within Explorer, you can move, rename, and create folders to organize your Start menu.

170   *ADDING OPTIONS TO THE WINDOWS 98 START MENU*

As you have learned, the Windows 98 Start menu makes it easy for you to run your programs by letting you select your programs from a menu option. Depending on the program you must run, however, there may be times when you need to traverse a series of menus to access the program's menu option. For example, assume that you want to run the Windows 98 CD Player accessory program. To locate the CD Player program, you must traverse a series of menus, as shown in Figure 170.1.

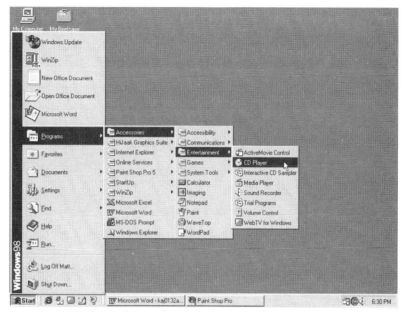

Figure 170.1 *Traversing Start menu options to locate the Windows 98 CD Player accessory program.*

To make it easier for you run the programs you use on a regular basis, Windows 98 lets you add the programs to the first level of the Start menu itself. For example, Figure 170.2 shows the Start menu after a user has added the CD Player accessory program as a menu option.

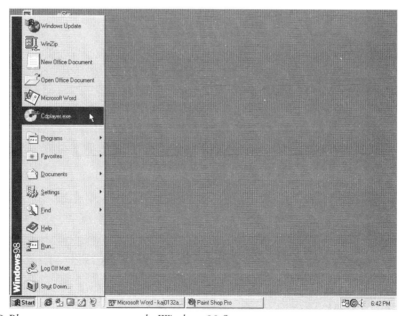

Figure 170.2 *Adding the CD Player accessory program to the Windows 98 Start menu.*

To add a program to the Windows 98 Start menu, perform these steps:

1. Select the Start menu Settings option and choose Taskbar. Windows 98, in turn, will display the Taskbar Properties dialog box.

2. Within the Taskbar Properties dialog box, select the Start Menu Programs tab. Windows 98 will display the Start Menu Programs sheet.

3. Within the Start Menu Programs sheet, click your mouse on the Add button. Windows 98, in turn, will display the Create Shortcut dialog box shown in Figure 170.3.

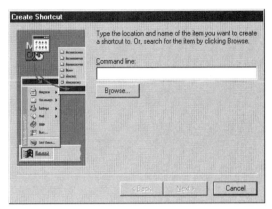

Figure 170.3 *The Create Shortcut dialog box.*

4. Within the Create Shortcut dialog box Command line field, type in the command that corresponds to the program you want to run, including the disk drive letter and directory path that identifies the program file's location on your disk. If you are not sure of the program's command line, click your mouse on the Browse button to locate the program file.

5. Within the Create Shortcut dialog box, click your mouse on the Next button. Windows 98 will display the Select Program Folder dialog box, as shown in Figure 170.4.

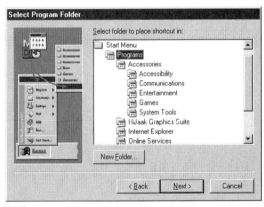

Figure 170.4 *The Select Program Folder dialog box.*

6. Within the Select Program Folder dialog box, click your mouse on the Start Menu folder and then click your mouse on the Next button. Windows 98 will display the Select a Title for the Program dialog box.

7. Within the Select a Title for the Program dialog box, type in the title that you want Windows 98 to display as a Start menu option. Then, click your mouse on the Finish button. Windows 98 will return you to the Taskbar Properties dialog box.

8. Within the Taskbar Properties dialog box, click your mouse on the OK button.

171	USING THE OPEN DIALOG BOX TO OPEN A DOCUMENT (A FILE)

In several of the preceding Windows 98 Explorer Tips, you learned how to open a document by double-clicking your mouse on the document's file within the Explorer's file list. Likewise, in Tip 76, you learned how to open a document you have recently used from within the Start menu Documents submenu. Usually, you will open your documents from within the program you used to create the document. For example, you will open your word-processing documents within a program such as Microsoft Word and you would open your spreadsheet documents within Microsoft Excel. To help you open documents, virtually every Windows-based program that you will run will provide a File menu Open option. When you select the Open option, the program will display an Open dialog box, similar to that shown in Figure 171.

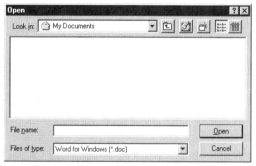

Figure 171 An application's Open dialog box.

Within the Open dialog box, the application will display your document files that reside within the current folder. To open a document, simply click your mouse on the document and then click your mouse on the OK button. (Also, you can usually open a document within an Open dialog box by simply double-clicking your mouse on the document.)

Note: *Depending on the folder within which you stored your document, you may need to change folders within the Open dialog box to locate your document file.*

172	USING THE OPEN DIALOG BOX LOOK IN FIELD TO LOCATE A DOCUMENT'S FOLDER

As you learned in Tip 171, most Windows-based programs provide an Open dialog box within which you can open a document for use. Within the Open dialog box, your application will display a list of the documents and subfolders that reside within the current folder. If your document does not reside within the current folder, you must use the Open dialog box to change folders.

In general, you locate files within the Open dialog box much like you do within the Windows 98 Explorer—meaning, you click your mouse on a folder's icon to open the folder. In addition, most Open dialog boxes will provide a Look in pull-down list, as shown in Figure 172, within which you can start searching for your folder.

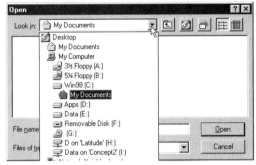

Figure 172 *The Open dialog box Look in pull-down list.*

To use the Look in pull-down list, simply click your mouse on the list to open it. Then, click your mouse on the disk drive or folder icon you desire, just as you would within the Windows 98 Explorer.

173	USING THE MOVE-UP-ONE-FOLDER BUTTON WITHIN WINDOWS 98 DIALOG BOXES

As you learned in Tip 172, depending on the folder you use to store your documents, there may be times when you must change the current folder within an Open dialog box. For example, assume that you organize the documents you create for work within a folder you name *Work*. Within the Work folder, you further organize your folders using the *Memos*, *Reports*, and *Pending* subfolders. Assume that your current folder is the *Memos* folder and that you want to open a file that resides in the *Pending* folder.

To open the file that resides in the *Pending* folder, you must move up one level in your folder tree (to the *Work* folder), and then open the *Pending* folder. Within an Open dialog box, you can move up one folder level by clicking your mouse on the Move-Up-One-Level button, as shown in Figure 173.

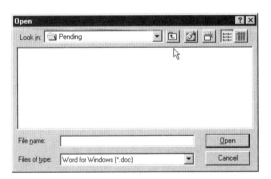

Figure 173 *The Open dialog box Move-Up-One-Level button.*

Each time you click your mouse on the Move-Up-One-Level button, Windows 98 will display your current folder's parent folder (or disk).

Note: *In addition to using the Move-Up-One-Level button within an Open dialog box to move to the current folder's parent folder, you can also press the BACKSPACE key.*

174 | **USING THE FILE MENU RECENTLY USED DOCUMENTS LIST**

In Tip 76, you learned that Windows 98 provides the Start menu Documents submenu that you can use to open your recently used documents. In a similar way, most Windows-based programs also let you open your most recently used documents from the File menu. For example, if you examine the Microsoft Word File menu shown in Figure 174, you will find that the menu's bottom entries correspond to files you have recently used. To open one of these files, simply click on the corresponding File menu option.

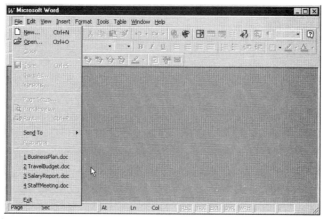

Figure 174 Opening a recently used document from within an application's File menu.

175 | **UNDERSTANDING AND USING THE WINDOWS 98 MY DOCUMENTS FOLDER**

As you have learned, folders exist within Windows 98 to help you organize your document files by grouping related documents within specific locations on your disk. To help you get started with your file management, Windows 98 provides the My Documents folder, within which you can create your own subfolders to further organize you files. Often, when you select the File menu Open option or the Save As option, your application program will display the My Documents folder's contents within the corresponding dialog box. You may find the My Documents folder a convenient place to store your document files. However, within the My Documents folder, you should further group related files within their own subfolders. Figure 175 shows the My Documents folder's contents within an Open dialog box.

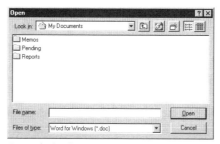

Figure 175 The My Documents folder within an Open dialog box.

176 | **KEEPING THE PROGRAMS, DOCUMENTS, AND LINKS YOU USE MOST OFTEN WITHIN THE FAVORITES FOLDER**

As you have learned, to make it easier for you to open your recently used documents, Windows 98 tracks your most recently used documents within the Documents folder. In a similar way, as you work, you may have one or more folders or Web sites that you use on a regular basis. To help you quickly access such objects, Windows 98 provides the Start menu Favorites submenu, as shown in Figure 176.1.

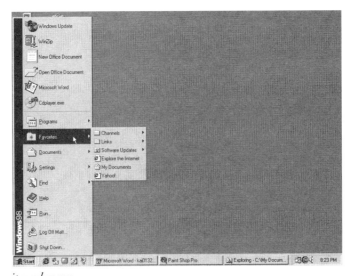

Figure 176.1 The Start menu Favorites submenu.

Within the Favorites submenu, you can click on a file, folder, or Web site menu option to access the object. As you work, you can add an object to the Favorites folder from within the Explorer, using the Explorer's Favorites menu, shown in Figure 176.2.

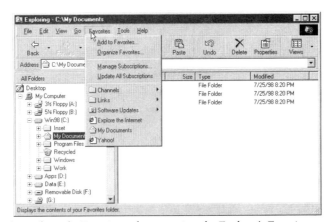

Figure 176.2 Adding and removing objects from the Favorites submenu using the Explorer's Favorites menu.

To add an object to the Favorites submenu, select the Explorer's Favorites menu Add to Favorites option. To remove an item, select the Organize Favorites option. The Explorer, in turn, will display the Organize Favorites dialog box, as shown in Figure 176.3. Within the Organize Favorites dialog box, click your mouse on the item you want to remove and then press the DEL key.

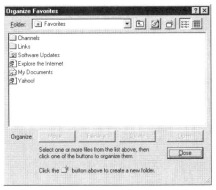

Figure 176.3 *The Organize Favorites dialog box.*

177	**LISTING ONLY THE FILENAMES FOR A SPECIFIC TYPE WITHIN THE OPEN DIALOG BOX**

In Tip 143, you learned when you name a document's file, you should assign a file extension that corresponds to the file's contents. For example, you would use the *DOC* extension for a word-processing document, the *XLS* extension for a spreadsheet, and the *BMP* extension for a bitmap file. By assigning the correct extension to a document's filename, you make it easier for another user to determine the file's contents. Likewise, as you learned in Tip 143, many Windows-based programs (such as the Explorer) use the document's file extension to determine which program it should run to open the file. Within the Open dialog box, an application program will usually only display files whose extensions correspond to its standard file type. For example, within the Microsoft Word Open dialog box, Word will usually only display files that use the *DOC* extension.

If you have trouble locating a file within an Open dialog box, your problem may not be that you canot find the document's folder but, rather, that the program is not listing your file within the Open dialog box file list. If you examine the Open dialog box shown in Figure 177, you will find the Files of Type pull-down list. Using the pull-down list, you can specify the type of files (based on the file's extension) the program displays within the Open dialog box. If you cannot find a file that you know exists on your disk, try setting the Files of type option to All files. Also, if you find that the Open dialog box displays a variety of files, you can use the pull-down list to restrict the type of files the program includes within the dialog box file list.

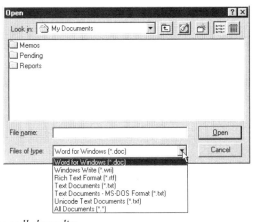

Figure 177 *The Open dialog box Files of Type pull-down list.*

178	**LISTING FILE ICONS OR FILE DETAILS WITHIN A WINDOWS 98 DIALOG BOX**

As you have seen in previous tips, within an Open dialog box, Windows 98 usually displays an icon for each document file, as shown in Figure 178.1.

Figure 178.1 *Displaying file icons within an Open dialog box.*

If you are having trouble locating a specific file on your disk, you may want Windows 98 to display more information about your files within an Open dialog box, as shown in Figure 178.2.

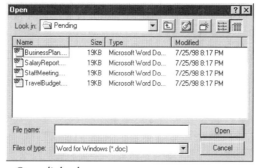

Figure 178.2 *Displaying file details within an Open dialog box.*

To switch between the Windows 98 display of icons or file details within an Open dialog box, click your mouse on either the List or Details button, as shown in Figure 178.3.

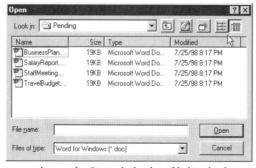

Figure 178.3 *Using the List and Details buttons to change the Open dialog box file list display.*

179 USING THE SAVE AND SAVE AS OPTIONS WITHIN WINDOWS 98 PROGRAMS

As you have learned, when you select the File menu Open option, most applications will display the Open dialog box, within which you can open a specific document file. After you make changes to a file, you must direct your application to save your changes back to a file on disk. If you are editing a named document, you can save your changes back to the document's current file on disk by selecting the File menu Save option.

If you have not yet named your document (or if you want to save your changes to a different document on your disk), you should select the File menu Save As option. When you select the Save As option, your program will display the Save As dialog box, as shown in Figure 179.

Figure 179 *The Save As dialog box.*

Within the Save As dialog box, use the Save In pull-down list to select the folder within which you want to save your document. Next, within the File name field, type in the filename that you desire and press ENTER. Remember, your filename should accurately reflect your document's contents.

After you use the Save As option to name your document's file, you can later save changes to your document by simply clicking your mouse on the File menu Save option. When you select the Save option, your application knows that you want to save your changes to the current document file on disk. When you select the Save As option, the application lets you save your current document to the file on disk whose name you specify within the Save As dialog box.

Note: *If, within the Save As dialog box, you specify the name of a file that already exists on your disk, most applications will display a dialog box telling that a file with the name you are wanting to use already exists on your disk. The dialog box will ask you if you want to overwrite the file with your current document. To overwrite the existing file on disk, click your mouse on the Yes button. If you do not want to overwrite the existing file, click your mouse on the No button and then specify a different filename.*

Note: *If you try to end a program before you save your document's changes to a file on disk, most application programs will display a dialog box asking you if you want to save your changes. If you click your mouse on the Yes button, the application will display the Save As dialog box if you have not already named your document, or the application will simply save your changes to the document's current contents on disk. If you click your mouse on the No button, the application will discard your current changes.*

180 SAVING A FILE IN A SPECIFIC FOLDER USING THE
SAVE IN FIELD

In Tip 179, you learned how to use the Save As dialog box to save your current document to a file on your disk. As you save your documents, you should store them within a folder that corresponds to the document's contents. For example, you might store a memo within a folder named *Memos* and a report within a folder named *Reports*.

Within the Save As dialog box, shown in Figure 180, you will find a Save in pull-down list. Using the pull-down list, you can select the folder within which you want to store your document. As was the case with the Open dialog box's Look in field that Tip 172 presents, within the Save As dialog box Save in field, you can select a folder by double-clicking your mouse on the folder's icon. Should you decide that you do not have an appropriate folder within which you can store your document, perform the steps Tip 181 presents to create a new folder on your disk.

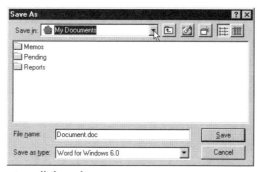

Figure 180 *Using the Save As dialog box Save in pull-down list.*

181 CREATING A FOLDER WITHIN THE SAVE AS
DIALOG BOX

As you have learned, folders exist within Widows 98 to help you organize your files. When you save a document using the Save As dialog box, you should always store the document within a meaningful folder, rather than storing all your documents within the My Documents folder. Often, as you prepare to save a document, you will realize that you do not have the correct folder for your current document on your disk. Fortunately, within the Save As dialog box, you can first create the folder you desire, and then store your document within the folder. To create a folder within the Save As dialog box, perform these steps:

1. Within the Save As dialog box, use the Save In field to select the folder within which you want to create your new subfolder.

2. Within the Save As dialog box, click your mouse on the Create New Folder button, shown in Figure 181. Windows 98, in turn, will place a new folder icon within the dialog box file list, naming the icon New folder.

3. Within the New folder textbox, type in the folder name that you desire and press ENTER.

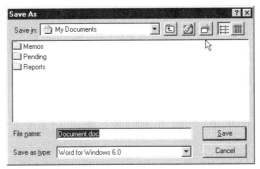

Figure 181 *The Save As dialog box Create New Folder button.*

182	SAVING A FILE IN A SPECIFIC FORMAT USING THE SAVE AS DIALOG BOX

As you learned in Tip 179, to save your current document to a file on your disk, you will use the Save As dialog box. Within the Save As dialog box, you can specify the filename that you desire and the folder within which you want to place the file. In addition, many application programs let you specify the file format you want the program to use to save the file. For example, assume that you have created a report using Microsoft Word on your home PC and the PC's at your office use WordPerfect. Within Word's Save As dialog box, you can use the Save as type pull-down list, shown in Figure 182, to direct Word to store your document using WordPerfect format.

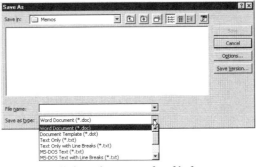

Figure 182 *Using the Save As dialog box Save as type pull-down list to specify a file format.*

Depending on the program you are using, the formats the program may offer within the Save as type pull-down list will vary. To better understand your program's capabilities, take time to examine the pull-down list entries the next time you use the Save As dialog box to save a document to a file on your disk.

183	CREATING A NEW DOCUMENT WITHIN AN APPLICATION

Within your Windows-based programs, you will make extensive use of the File menu Open option to open an existing document. In a similar way, there will be many times when you will want to create a new document within your programs. In such cases, you will simply select the File menu New option.

Most Windows-based programs let you open two or more documents at the same time, displaying each document's contents within its own *document window*. When you use the File menu New option to create a new document within an application, your program will simply open a new document window, which it will probably display over any other document windows you have open. To switch between document windows within a program, you will select the window you desire using the program's Window menu, within which the program will display a menu option that corresponds to each window. Some programs, such as the Paint accessory, only let you open one document at a time. Within such a program, you must close your open document (saving or discarding any changes as you desire) before the program can create your new document.

184 USING THE BROWSE BUTTON WITHIN A DIALOG BOX TO LOCATE FILES OR FOLDERS

As you perform different operations within Windows 98, there will be times when you must specify a document or program file that Windows 98 will use to perform a specific task. Usually, when Windows 98 requires a specific file, Windows 98 will display a Browse button, similar to the one shown in Figure 184.1.

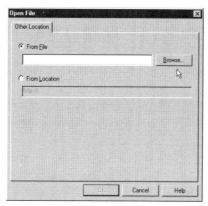

Figure 184.1 *A Browse button within a Windows 98 dialog box.*

After you click your mouse on a Browse button, Windows will display the Browse dialog box, shown in Figure 184.2.

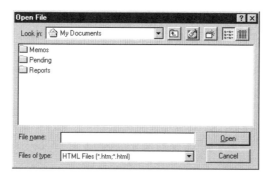

Figure 184.2 *The Browse dialog box.*

Using the Browse dialog box, you can search the folders on your disk until you locate the file that you desire. If you examine the Browse dialog box, you will find the Look in pull-down list which you can use to locate a specific folder on your disk. As you click your mouse on folders within the Look in pull-down list, Windows 98 will display the folder's contents within the Browse dialog box file list. To select the file you want Windows 98 to use to perform the current operation, click your mouse on the file within the file list and then click your mouse on the OK button.

185 **USING COMMON APPLICATION ICONS TO CREATE, OPEN, SAVE, OR PRINT A DOCUMENT**

In several of the previous tips, you have learned how to use the File menu New, Open, Save, and Print options within an application. To simplify these common operations, most Windows-based programs provide a toolbar that contains a button for each operation. For example, Figure 185 shows the WordPad toolbar which contains a button for each operation. As you run various programs within Windows 98, you will usually find each of the icons shown in Figure 185 within your program's toolbar.

Figure 185 *Toolbar buttons for common operations.*

186 **RENAMING FOLDERS AND FILES WITHIN AN APPLICATION'S DIALOG BOXES**

In a previous Tip, you learned how to rename a file using the Windows 98 Explorer. In addition to renaming files using the Explorer, you can often rename a file from within an application's Open or Save As dialog box. To rename a file within an application's dialog box, perform these steps:

1. Within the dialog box, right-click your mouse on the file that you want to rename. Windows 98, in turn, will display a pop-up menu.

2. Within the pop-up menu, click your mouse on the Rename option. Windows 98, in turn, will highlight the file's current name using reverse video and will display a textbox around name.

3. Within the textbox, type in the name that you desire and press ENTER. (If you want to use part of the file's existing name, use your keyboard arrow, DEL, and INS keys to edit the filename characters as you desire.)

Note: *In addition to renaming a file by clicking your right-mouse button on the file, you can also click your left-mouse button on the file and then press the F2 function key. Windows 98 will then highlight the filename using reverse video. Within the textbox, type in the filename you desire.*

187 **USING THE EXPLORER TO FIND A FILE, FOLDER, PC IN YOUR NETWORK, OR EVEN PEOPLE ON THE NET**

As the number of files and folders on your disk increases, there may be times when you will have trouble locating a specific file or folder. If your PC is connected to a local-area network, there may be times when you cannot find a specific PC. Likewise, if you connect your PC to the Internet, there may be times when you must find a specific user's e-mail address. In such cases, you can use the Start menu Find submenu as shown in Figure 187.1.

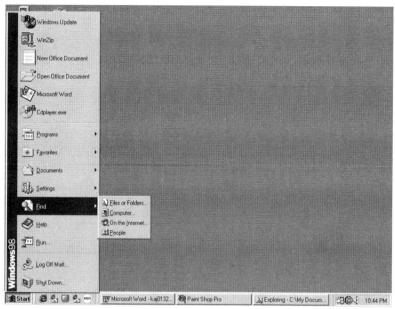

Figure 187.1 *Using the Start menu Find submenu.*

Several of the Tips that follow examine the Find submenu in detail. In addition to performing the find operations from the Start menu, you can also perform them using the Explorer Tools menu Find submenu shown in Figure 187.2.

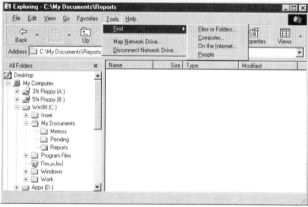

Figure 187.2 *Using the Explorer Tools menu Find submenu.*

188 FINDING A FOLDER THAT CONTAINS A FILE

Although file folders exist to help you organize your files, you may still have times when you cannot locate a file on your system. If you have recently used the file, start your search in the Start menu Documents submenu. As you learned in Tip 174, Windows 98 lists your most recently used files within the Documents submenu. Next, if you still cannot find the file, select the Start menu Find option and choose the Files or Folders option. Windows 98, in turn, will display the Find: All Files dialog box, as shown in Figure 188.1.

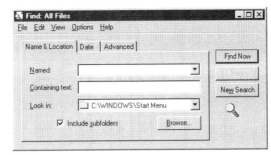

Figure 188.1 *The Find: All Files dialog box.*

To use the Find: All Files dialog box to locate a file on your disk, perform these steps:

1. Within the Find: All Files dialog box Name field, type in name of the file you are trying find.

2. Within the Look in field, use the pull-down list to select the folder within which you want Windows 98 to start its search. To search your entire drive, select your disk's icons as the starting location. Then, if the Include subfolders checkbox does not contain a check mark, click your mouse on the checkbox to display the check mark, which directs Windows 98 to search all the subfolders that reside beneath your starting location.

3. Click your mouse on the Find Now button. Windows 98, in turn, will start searching your disk. If Windows 98 locates a matching file, Windows 98 will display each matching file within a list box that it displays near the bottom of the Find dialog box, as shown in Figure 188.2. If Windows 98 does not find a matching file, it will display a message so stating within the Find dialog box's list box.

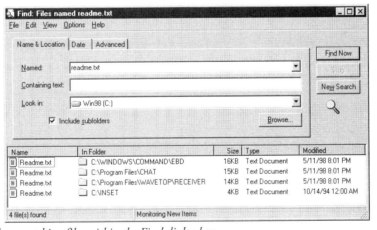

Figure 188.2 *Windows 98 displays matching files within the Find dialog box.*

4. To direct Windows 98 to open one of the matching files, double-click your mouse on the file's name within the Find dialog box list.

5. To close the Find dialog box, click your mouse on the dialog box's Close button.

Depending on the number of files your disk contains, you may find that your file-find operation consumes a considerable amount of time. Should Windows 98 display the file that you desire, you can click your mouse on the Stop button to end the search operation.

189	**USING WILDCARD CHARACTERS WITHIN THE FIND: ALL FILES DIALOG BOX**	

In Tip 188, you learned how to use the Start menu Find option to locate a file on your disk using the file's name. When you use the Find: All Files dialog box to locate a file, you can use the asterisk (*) and question mark (?) wildcard characters within your search. Using such wildcards within a search, you can locate one or more files whose names start with the pattern you specify.

The asterisk wildcard, for example, directs Windows 98 to match zero or more characters that follow. For example, if you tell Windows 98 to find the file A*, Windows 98 would match the following filenames:

> A   AB   ABC   ABCD ABCDE
>
> AZZ   Apple   Alaska   A1234   AAAAA

The question mark wildcard directs Windows 98 to match a single character. For example, if you use the filename AB?DE, Windows 98 will match the following filenames:

> AB1DE   ABKDE   AB_DE   AB5DE

If you cannot remember what you named a file, you can use the wildcard characters to help you match files whose names start with a specific pattern.

190	**DIRECTING WINDOWS 98 TO SEARCH YOUR DISK FOR A FILE THAT CONTAINS SPECIFIC TEXT**	

In Tip 187, you learned how to use the Start menu Find option to locate a file on your disk by name. If you misplace a file whose name you can no longer remember, you can use the Start menu Find option to locate a file or files on your disk that contain specific text. For example, if you recently created a letter whose filename you cannot remember, you might search your disk for a file that contains the text, Dear Mr. Johnson. To search your disk for a file that contains specific text, perform these steps:

1. Click your mouse on the Start menu Find option and choose the Files or Folders option. Windows 98, in turn, will display the Find: All Files dialog box.

2. Within the Find: All Files dialog box Containing text field, type in the text for which you want Windows 98 to search.

3. Within the Look in field, use the pull-down list to select the folder within which you want Windows 98 to start its search. To search your entire drive, select your disk's icons as the starting location. Then, if the Include subfolders checkbox does not contain a check mark, click your mouse on the checkbox to display the check mark, which directs Windows 98 to search all the subfolders that reside beneath your starting location.

4. Click your mouse on the Find Now button. Windows 98 will start searching your disk. If Windows 98 locates a matching file, Windows 98 will display each matching file within a list

box that it displays near the bottom of the dialog box. If Windows 98 does not find a matching file, it will display a message so stating within the Find dialog box's list box.

5. To direct Windows 98 to open one of the matching files, double-click your mouse on the file's name within the Find dialog box list.

6. To close the Find dialog box, click your mouse on the dialog box's Close button.

---

191 DIRECTING WINDOWS 98 TO PERFORM CASE-SENSITIVE SEARCH OPERATIONS

In Tip 190, you learned how to search your disks for files that contain specific text. When you direct Windows 98 to search the files on your disk for specific text, Windows 98, unless you tell it to do otherwise, will not perform a *case-sensitive search*. In other words, as Windows 98 searches your files for the text, Windows 98 does not care whether the characters appear in upper- or lowercase letters. As a result, if you search your files for the word Happy, Windows 98 would match the words Happy, happy, and even HAPPY.

If, however, you want Windows 98 to perform a case-sensitive search, click your mouse on the Find: All Files dialog box Options menu shown in Figure 191 and select the Case Sensitive option, placing a check mark next to the option.

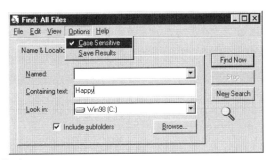

Figure 191 *The Find: All Files dialog box Options menu.*

---

192 DIRECTING WINDOWS 98 TO SEARCH YOUR DISK FOR A FILE OR FOLDER BASED ON THE DATE-AND-TIME STAMP

As the number of files you create increases, you may have times you cannot remember the name you assigned to a document and Windows 98 did not find the file when you searched your disk for a file that contained specific text. In such cases, you can direct Windows 98 to list the files that you have created within the last day, week, month, or even several months. For example, if you misplace the file that contains your company budget, you can direct Windows 98 to search for documents you created between January 1 and January 31 (the month you created the budget).

Each time you create or change a file's contents, Windows 98 updates the file's date-and-time stamp. By using the file's date-and-time stamp, Windows 98 can determine when you created or last changed a file. To direct Windows 98 to search your disk for a file based on the file's date-and-time stamp, perform these steps:

1. Click your mouse on the Start menu Find option and choose the Files or Folders option. Windows 98 will display the Find: All Files dialog box.

2. Within the Look in field, use the pull-down list to select the folder within which you want Windows 98 to start its search. To search your entire drive, select your disk's icons as the starting location. Then, if the Include subfolders checkbox does not contain a check mark, click your mouse on the checkbox to display the check mark, which directs Windows 98 to search all the subfolders that reside beneath your starting location.

3. Within the Find: All Files dialog box, click your mouse on the Date tab. Windows 98, in turn, will display the Date sheet, as shown in Figure 192.

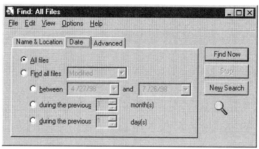

Figure 192 *The Find: All Files dialog box Date sheet.*

4. Within the Date sheet, you can direct Windows 98 to find a file that you created between two dates, during the previous month (or months), or during the previous day (or days). After you specify your date interval, click your mouse on the Find Now button. Windows 98, in turn, will start searching your disk. If Windows 98 locates a matching file, Windows 98 will display each matching file within a list box that it displays near the bottom of the dialog box. If Windows 98 does not find a matching file, it will display a message so stating within the Find dialog box's list box.

5. To direct Windows 98 to open one of the matching files, double-click your mouse on the file's name within the Find dialog box list.

6. To close the Find dialog box, click your mouse on the dialog box's Close button.

---

193   DIRECTING WINDOWS 98 TO SEARCH YOUR DISK FOR A FILE OR FOLDER BASED ON THE FILE'S SIZE

As you use Windows 98, there may be times when you want Windows 98 to locate files based on the file's size. For example, assume that your disk is running out of available space and you want to delete some unused files to free up space. By directing Windows 98 to search your disk for files that exceed 1Mb, you can quickly identify the files that are consuming the most disk space. To direct Windows 98 to search your disk for files based on the file's size, perform these steps:

1. Click your mouse on the Start menu Find option and choose the Files or Folders option. Windows 98, in turn, will display the Find: All Files dialog box.

2. Within the Look in field, use the pull-down list to select the folder within which you want Windows 98 to start its search. To search your entire drive, select your disk's icons as the starting location. Then, if the Include subfolders checkbox does not contain a check mark, click your mouse on the checkbox to display the check mark, which directs Windows 98 to search all

the subfolders that reside beneath your starting location.

3. Within the Find: All Files dialog box, click your mouse on the Advanced tab. Windows 98, in turn, will display the Advanced sheet, as shown in Figure 193.

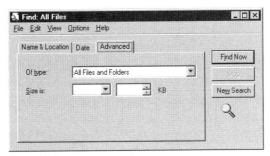

Figure 193 *The Find: All Files dialog box Advanced sheet.*

4. Within the Advanced sheet Size is field, use the pull-down list to select the "At least" or "At most" search criteria and then type in the file size you desire. Then, click your mouse on the Find Now button. Windows 98 will start searching your disk. If Windows 98 locates a matching file, Windows 98 will display each matching file within a list box that it displays near the bottom of the dialog box. If Windows 98 does not find a matching file, it will display a message so stating within the Find dialog box's list box.

5. To direct Windows 98 to open one of the matching files, double-click your mouse on the file's name within the Find dialog box list.

6. To close the Find dialog box, click your mouse on the dialog box's Close button.

194 USING WINDOWS 98 TO FIND A PC WITHIN YOUR NETWORK

If your PC is connected to a local-area network, you may have times when you must locate a specific computer within the network. In such cases, you can use the Start menu Find option. To locate a computer within your network, perform these steps:

1. Click your mouse on the Start menu Find option and choose the Computer option. Windows 98 will display the Find: Computer dialog box.

2. Within the Find: Computer dialog box Named field, type in the name of the computer for which you want Windows 98 to search. (You can use wildcards within your search text.)

3. Click your mouse on the Find Now button. Windows 98 will start searching your disk. If Windows 98 locates a matching computer, Windows 98 will display each matching computer name within a list box that it displays near the bottom of the dialog box. If Windows 98 does not find a matching computer, it will display a message so stating within the Find dialog box's list box.

4. To direct Windows 98 to show the shared objects on one of the matching computers, double-click your mouse on the computer's name within the Find dialog box list.

5. To close the Find dialog box, click your mouse on the dialog box's Close button.

195   USING WINDOWS *98* TO FIND A USER'S E-MAIL ADDRESS

In later tips, you will learn how to use Microsoft Outlook to send and receive electronic mail across a local-area network or across the Internet. If you misplace a user's e-mail address, you may be able to find the address using the Find submenu's People option. To search for a user's e-mail address, perform these steps:

1. Click your mouse on the Start menu Find option and choose People. Windows 98, in turn, will display the Find People dialog box, as shown in Figure 195.

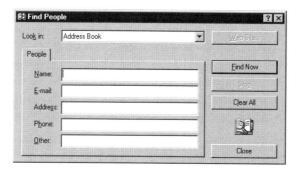

Figure 195 *The Find People dialog box.*

2. Within the Find People dialog box, use the Look in pull-down list to select the location (the directory, so to speak) within which you want Windows 98 to look for the individual's e-mail address. (If you have sent or received e-mail to or from the individual in the past, you should first try searching your Address Book. After that, you can try some of the Web-based e-mail directories to see if they can provide information about the user.)

3. Within the Find People dialog box Name field, type in the individual's name and then click your mouse on the Find Now button. If you are searching one of the Web-based directories and you are not connected to the Web, Windows 98 will connect you.

4. If Windows 98 finds a matching entry, Windows 98 will display the user's e-mail address within the dialog box.

196   USING WINDOWS UPDATE TO RETRIEVE CURRENT
SOFTWARE AND DEVICE DRIVERS FROM MICROSOFT

In addition to providing several new programs that were not present in Windows 95, the Windows 98 operating system updates several device drivers (the software that Windows 98 uses to interact with hardware devices, such as your screen, keyboard, and disk drives). In the past, experienced users would visit sites on the Web, such as Microsoft, in search of new or updated device drivers which they would then install on their system. Most users, however, were unaware of the fact that the new device drivers existed, let alone how to download and install the new software.

Fortunately, Windows 98 now makes such on-line software updates easy for all users. If your PC has a modem, you can use the Start menu Windows Update option to direct Windows 98 to connect to the Microsoft Web site and search for device-driver updates for your system. If the Windows Update software locates a new device driver, the software will install the update onto your system. As a rule, you should run the Windows Update about once a month. To start the Windows Update, simply click your mouse on the Start menu Windows Update option. Windows 98, in turn, will start the Internet Explorer and connect you to the update site, as shown in Figure 196. Within the site, you can follow links to update your software as you require.

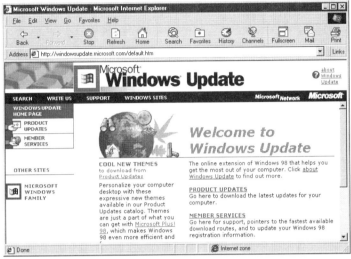

Figure 196 *Using the Windows Update site to update your system software.*

---

197 | USING THE WINDOWS 98 CONTROL PANEL TO CUSTOMIZE YOUR SYSTEM SETTINGS

Although Windows 98 supports plug-in-play hardware, as discussed in Tip 214, there may still be times when you install new hardware into your system when you must tell Windows 98 about your new device. In such cases, you will use one of the programs you will find within the Windows 98 Control Panel, shown in Figure 197.1.

Figure 197.1 *The Windows 98 Control Panel.*

The Windows 98 Control Panel is simply a folder that contains programs and Wizards that you use to customize your system settings—in other words, programs you use to "control" key hardware and software settings. Several of the Tips this book presents examine the Control Panel programs and Wizards in detail. To open the Windows 98 Control Panel, perform these steps:

1. Click your mouse on the Start button. Windows 98, in turn, will display the Start menu.
2. Within the Start menu, select the Settings option. Windows 98, in turn, will cascade the Settings menu, displaying the menu options shown in Figure 197.2.

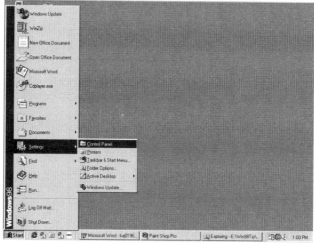

Figure 197.2 *The Windows 98 Settings menu.*

3. Within the Settings menu, select the Control Panel option. Windows 98 will open the Control Panel window.

198   WINDOWS 98 WIZARDS HELP YOU ACCOMPLISH SPECIFIC TASKS

Throughout this book, you have made extensive use of the dialog boxes to interact with Windows 98 and Windows-based programs. To help you perform key tasks, Windows 98 provides a series of Wizards, which are programs that walk you, step-by-step, through the operations you must perform to complete a task by displaying a series of dialog boxes. For example, when you install new hardware, you must install the software that lets Windows 98 interact with the device. To install software for a new device, you can use the Windows 98 Add Hardware Wizard. Likewise, if you need to configure a new printer, you can use the Add Printer Wizard that will display a series of dialog boxes that let you identify your printer type, the port you use to attach the printer to your PC, and so on.

In general, a Wizard will simply display a series of dialog boxes, each of which corresponds to a specific step in your operation. For example, Figure 198 shows a step within the Windows Add Hardware Wizard. After you perform the step's instructions, you simply click your mouse on the Wizard's Next button to continue.

In addition to using Wizards to help you configure new hardware and software, Windows 98 also provides Wizards that you can use to troubleshoot your printers, networks, modem connections, and much more.

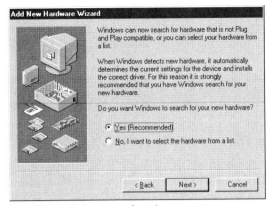

Figure 198 *Windows 98 Wizards display dialog boxes to help you perform key operations.*

199   WHY YOU MUST CUSTOMIZE WINDOWS 98

Today, Microsoft Windows is the most widely used operating system in the world. Although the way users interact with Windows is quite similar (users run the same programs, respond to similar dialog boxes and menus), each user's PC may have slightly different hardware. As a result, it is not uncommon for users to have to configure specific parts of Windows 98. For example, if you install a new modem, you must configure Windows 98 to use your new hardware. Within Windows 98, users customize their hardware and software settings from within a special folder called the Control Panel. As shown in Figure 199.1, the Control Panel folder holds a series of icons that correspond to different system objects (such as your printer, modem, keyboard, and mouse) that you can customize. The Control Panel is so named because you use its icons to control (configure) your hardware and software settings.

Figure 199.1 *Users configure specific Windows 98 settings from within the Control Panel.*

To display the Windows 98 Control Panel, perform these steps:

1. Click your mouse the Start menu Settings Options. Windows 98, in turn, will display the Settings submenu, as shown in Figure 199.2.

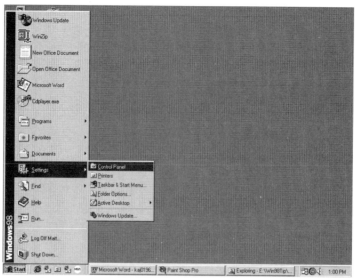

Figure 199.2 The Windows 98 Settings submenu.

2. Within the Settings submenu, click your mouse on the Control Panel option. Windows 98, in turn, will open the Control Panel folder.

The Tips that follow examine the Control Panel icons in detail.

200 ADDING A CONTROL PANEL OPTION TO THE START MENU ITSELF

In Tip 382, you will learn that you can save mouse clicks by placing a Printers option on the Start menu itself (rather than having the user select the Start menu and then Settings submenu). In a similar way, Windows 98 lets you place a Control Panel option on the Start menu, as shown in Figure 200.

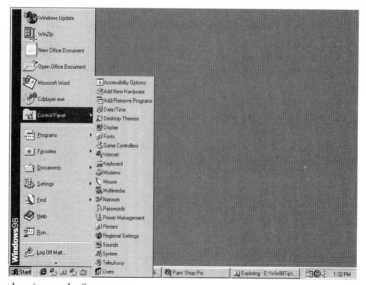

Figure 200 Adding a Control Panel option to the Start menu.

By placing the Control Panel onto the Start menu in this way, you no longer have to open the Control Panel window to access a specific program. Instead, you can quickly access the program from the Control Panel submenu. To add a Control Panel submenu to the Start menu, perform these steps:

1. Right-click your mouse on the Start button. Windows 98, in turn, will display a pop-up menu.

2. Within the pop-up menu, select the Explore option. Windows 98 will open an Explorer window, displaying within the window the Start menu tree.

3. Within the Explorer window, click your mouse on the File menu New Folder option. Windows 98, in turn, will display a new folder within the Start menu tree.

4. Within the folder's name field, type the following folder name, including the period and two curly braces:

   Control Panel.{21EC2020-3AEA-1069-A2DD-08002B30309D}

5. After you verify your typing, press ENTER.

6. Close the Explorer window.

7. Click your mouse on the Start button to display the Start menu. If you typed the folder name correctly, your Start menu will contain a Control Panel option, as shown in Figure 200.

Should you later decide that you want to remove the Control Panel option from the Startup menu, use Explorer to open the Startup Menu folder and then use your mouse to highlight the folder. Press the DEL key. Windows 98, in turn, will delete the folder, restoring your Start menu to its previous state.

201   UNDERSTANDING THE ACCESSIBILITY OPTIONS

To meet the goal of having Windows running on every PC, everywhere, Microsoft must make Windows 98 easy for everyone to use. With user ease in mind, Microsoft built several features into Windows 98 to support users with special vision, hearing, or mobility needs. In Tip 202, you will learn how you can use the Windows 98 Accessibility Wizard to customize the Windows 98 Accessibility options. In addition, several of the Tips that follow will discuss ways you can use the Control Panel Accessibility Options entry to customize various settings. When you double-click your mouse on the Accessibility Options icon, Windows 98 will open the Accessibility Properties dialog box, as shown in Figure 201.

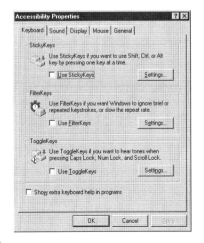

Figure 201 *The Accessibility Properties dialog box.*

Within the Accessibility Properties dialog box, you can configure your keyboard, mouse, sound, and display settings.

Note: If you will not use the Accessibility Options, you can remove them from your system to free up disk space.

---

202 USING THE ACCESSIBILITY WIZARD TO CUSTOMIZE YOUR SYSTEM SETTINGS

In Tip 201, you learned that Windows 98 provides a variety of tools to assist users who may have specific vision, hearing, or mobility needs. To help such users configure their system quickly, Windows 98 provides an Accessibility Wizard. To start the Accessibility Wizard, perform these steps:

1. Click your mouse on the Start menu Programs option and choose Accessories. Windows 98, in turn, will display the Accessories submenu.

2. Within the Accessories submenu, click your mouse on the Accessibility option and choose Accessibility Wizard. Windows 98, in turn, will start the Accessibility Wizard, as shown in Figure 202.

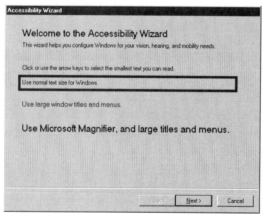

Figure 202 The Windows 98 Accessibility Wizard.

3. The Accessibility Wizard will present a series of dialog boxes that will help the Wizard configure your system to best suit your needs. Within each dialog box, click your mouse on the option you desire and then select the Next button.

---

203 USING THE MAGNIFIER ACCESSORY TO ENHANCE YOUR SCREEN DISPLAY

If you have difficulty viewing the items that appear on your screen, you can take advantage of the Windows 98 Magnifier accessory program. When you run the Magnifier program, Windows 98 allocates a small portion of your screen as a magnified window. As you move your mouse pointer about your screen, Windows 98 will display the area that surrounds the mouse pointer in the magnified window, as shown in Figure 203.1.

Figure 203.1 *Using the Magnifier accessory program to magnify the screen's contents.*

To run the Magnifier accessory program, perform these steps:

1. Click your mouse on the Start menu Programs option and choose Accessories. Windows 98, in turn, will display the Accessories submenu.

2. Within the Accessories submenu, click your mouse on the Accessibility option and choose Magnifier. Windows 98, in turn, will start the Magnifier program, displaying the window magnification window on your screen.

3. In addition to showing the Magnifer window, Windows 98 will display the Magnifer dialog box, within which you can customize the Magnifier's properties, such as its zoom percentage, as shown in Figure 203.2.

Figure 203.2 *The Magnifier dialog box.*

4. Within the Magnifier dialog box, select the options you desire and then click your mouse on the OK button. Windows 98, in turn, will minimize the dialog box to a Taskbar button.

5. To later end the Magnifier program, click your mouse on the Magnifier's Taskbar button. Windows 98 will display the Magnifier dialog box, within which you can click your mouse on the Exit button to end the program.

Note: *If you want Windows 98 to automatically run the Magnifier program each time your system starts, perform the steps Tip 102 presents to add the Magnifier program file, Magnify.EXE, to the Start menu.*

204 MOVING THE MAGNIFIER WINDOW ABOUT YOUR SCREEN DISPLAY

In Tip 203, you learned how to run the Magnifier accessory program, which lets you magnify the portion of your screen display that surrounds your mouse pointer, to make your screen contents easier to view. By default, when you start the Magnifier program, Windows 98 displays the Magnify window at the top of your screen. Depending on your needs or preferences, you may want to move the Magnify window, as shown in Figure 204.

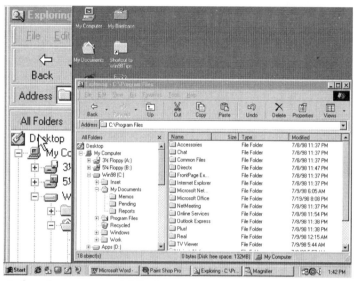

Figure 204 Docking the Magnify window along your screen's left edge.

To move the Magnify window from one location on your screen to another, aim your mouse pointer to the top edge of the window until the Magnifier displays a thick window frame. Then, use your mouse to drag the frame to the screen location that you desire.

205 TAKING ADVANTAGE OF STICKYKEYS TO SIMPLIFY KEYBOARD COMBINATIONS

As you have learned, Windows 98 programs often define shortcut key combinations that you can press to perform an operation. Usually, the shortcut key combinations use one or more of the ALT, CTRL, and SHIFT keys. If you are unable to hold down any of these keys while you press with another key, such as the CTRL-V keyboard combination, which many programs use to paste the current contents of the Clipboard, you should activate Windows 98 support for StickyKeys. After you enable Windows 98 StickyKeys support, you can press one of these three keys, such as the CTRL key, release the key, and then press another key, such as V. To Windows 98, the CTRL key appears to stick (stay down) until you press a second key. To activate Windows 98 StickyKeys support, perform these steps:

1. Click your mouse on the Start menu Settings option and choose Control Panel. Windows 98, in turn, will open the Control Panel window.

2. Within the Control Panel window, double-click your mouse on the Accessibility Options icon. Windows 98, in turn, will display the Accessibility Properties dialog box Keyboard sheet.

3. Within the Keyboard sheet, click your mouse on the Use StickyKeys checkbox, placing a check mark within the box.

4. Within the Keyboard sheet, click your mouse on the StickyKeys Settings button. Windows 98 will display the Settings for StickyKeys dialog box, as shown in Figure 205.

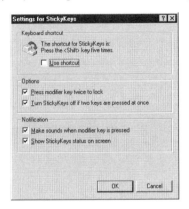

Figure 205 *The Settings for StickyKeys dialog box.*

5. Within the Settings for StickyKeys dialog box, select the options you desire and click your mouse on the OK button. Table 205 briefly describes the StickyKey settings.

6. Within the Accessibility Properties dialog box, click your mouse on the OK button to put your settings into effect.

Setting Option	Description
Use shortcut	Turns StickyKeys support on and off if you press the SHIFT five times.
Press modifier key twice to lock	Requires you to press a sticky key two times before the key sticks.
Turn StickyKeys off if two keys are pressed at once	Turns off StickyKey support if you press two keys at the same time.
Make sounds when modifier key is pressed	Directs Windows 98 to generate a sound each time you press a the StickyKey modifier.
Show StickyKeys status on screen	Directs Windows 98 to display a visual indication of the current StickyKeys operation.

Table 205 *The StickyKey Settings.*

---

206 TAKING ADVANTAGE OF FILTERKEYS TO REDUCE ERRANT KEYSTROKES

Depending on a user's mobility, the user may periodically strike errant keyboard keys or hold down a key too long (which causes the PC to repeat the keystroke). To assist the user with keyboard operations, Windows 98 supports FilterKeys which directs Windows 98 to ignore keystrokes that occur rapidly, such as when a user inadvertently presses two keys or when the user holds down a key for too long. After you enable Windows 98 FilterKeys support, Windows 98 will only repeat a keystroke when the user presses the key twice (holding the key down on the second keystroke) or when the user holds the key down for an extended period of time. To activate FilterKeys support, perform these steps:

1. Click your mouse on the Start menu Settings option and choose Control Panel. Windows 98, in turn, will open the Control Panel window.

2. Within the Control Panel window, double-click your mouse on the Accessibility Options icon. Windows 98, in turn, will display the Accessibility Properties dialog box Keyboard sheet.

3. Within the Keyboard sheet, click your mouse on the Use FilterKeys checkbox, placing a check mark within the box.

4. Within the Keyboard sheet, click your mouse on the FilterKeys Settings button. Windows 98, in turn, will display the Settings for FilterKeys dialog box as shown in Figure 206.

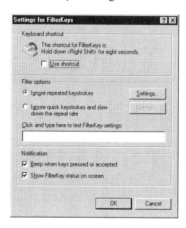

Figure 206 *The Settings for FilterKeys dialog box.*

5. Within the Settings for FilterKeys dialog box, select the options you desire and click your mouse on the OK button. Table 206 briefly describes the FilterKey settings.

6. Within the Accessibility Properties dialog box, click your mouse on the OK button to put your settings into effect.

Setting Option	Description
Use shortcut	Turns FilterKeys support on and off if you hold down the keyboard's RIGHT SHIFT key for eight seconds.
Ignore repeated keystrokes	Directs Windows 98 to ignore keystrokes that occur in quick succession.
Ignore quick keystrokes	Directs Windows 98 to ignore keys that are only pressed quickly (such as an errant brush of a key).
Click and type here to test FilterKey settings	Provides a text field within which you test your current key settings by holding down a specific key and waiting for the keystroke to repeat.
Beep when keys pressed or accepted	Directs Windows 98 to sound a beep each time a key is pressed or accepted.
Show FilterKeys status on screen	Directs Windows 98 to display a visual indication of the current FilterKey operation.

Table 206 *The FilterKey Settings.*

207 TAKING ADVANTAGE OF TOGGLEKEYS TO SIGNAL KEY LOCK OPERATIONS

As you know, you keyboard contains the CAPS LOCK, NUM LOCK, or SCROLL LOCK keys which you can turn on or off to change your keyboard's behavior. To help users who have visual impairments recognize when to press one of these special keys, Windows 98 provides ToggleKey support. After you enable Windows 98 ToggleKey support, Windows 98 will beep each time you press one of these keys. To enable Windows 98 ToggleKey support, perform these steps:

1. Click your mouse on the Start menu Settings option and choose Control Panel. Windows 98, in turn, will open the Control Panel window.

2. Within the Control Panel window, double-click your mouse on the Accessibility Options icon. Windows 98, in turn, will display the Accessibility Properties dialog box Keyboard sheet.

3. Within the Keyboard sheet, click your mouse on the Use ToggleKeys checkbox, placing a check mark within the box.

4. Within the Keyboard sheet, click your mouse on the ToggleKeys Settings button. Windows 98 will display the Settings for ToggleKeys dialog box, as shown in Figure 207.

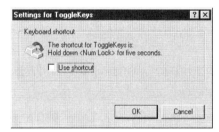

Figure 207 *The Settings for ToggleKeys dialog box.*

5. Within the Settings for ToggleKeys dialog box, click your mouse on the checkbox, placing a check mark within the box to enable the shortcut and then click your mouse on the OK button.

6. Within the Accessibility Properties dialog box, click your mouse on the OK button to put your settings into effect.

208 TAKING ADVANTAGE OF SOUNDSENTRY TO DISPLAY VISUAL WARNING EACH TIME YOUR SYSTEM GENERATES A SOUND

When specific events occur, Windows 98 often generates a sound to notify the user of the event. To help notify users who may have special hearing needs, Windows 98 provides SoundSentry support. After you enable SoundSentry support, Windows 98 will display a visual warning each time your system generates sounds. To enable Windows 98 SoundSentry support, perform these steps:

1. Click your mouse on the Start menu Settings option and choose Control Panel. Windows 98, in turn, will open the Control Panel window.

2. Within the Control Panel window, double-click your mouse on the Accessibility Options icon. Windows 98 will display the Accessibility Properties dialog box.

3. Within the Accessibility Properties dialog box, click your mouse on the Sounds tab. Windows 98, in turn, will display the Sounds sheet, as shown in Figure 208.1.

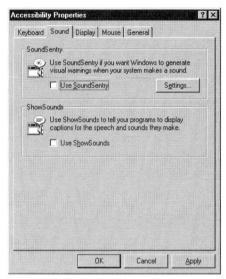

Figure 208.1 *The Accessibility Properties dialog box Sounds sheet.*

4. Within the Sounds sheet, click your mouse on the Use SoundSentry checkbox, placing a check mark within the box.

5. Within the Keyboard sheet, click your mouse on the SoundSentry Settings button. Windows 98, in turn, will display the Settings for SoundSentry dialog box, as shown in Figure 208.2.

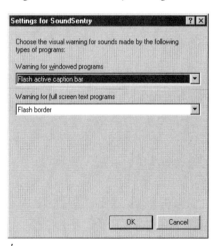

Figure 208.2 *The Settings for SoundSentry dialog box.*

6. Within the Settings for SoundSentry dialog box, use the pull-down list to select the method you want Windows 98 to use to warn you of a sound. Next, click your mouse on the OK button.

7. Within the Accessibility Properties dialog box, click your mouse on the OK button to put your settings into effect.

209   TAKING ADVANTAGE OF SHOWSOUNDS TO DISPLAY A VISUAL CAPTION FOR PROGRAM SOUNDS AND SPEECH

In Tip 208, you learned how to use Windows 98 SoundSentry support to direct Windows 98 to display a visual warning each time your system makes a sound. In a similar way, using Windows ShowSounds support, you can direct Windows 98 and programs that support ShowSounds features to display a visual caption for each sound or speech they play. To enable Windows 98 ShowSounds support, perform these steps:

1. Click your mouse on the Start menu Settings option and choose Control Panel. Windows 98, in turn, will open the Control Panel window.
2. Within the Control Panel window, double-click your mouse on the Accessibility Options icon. Windows 98, in turn, will display the Accessibility Properties dialog box.
3. Within the Accessibility Properties dialog box, click your mouse on the Sounds tab. Windows 98, in turn, will display the Sounds sheet, as shown in Figure 209.

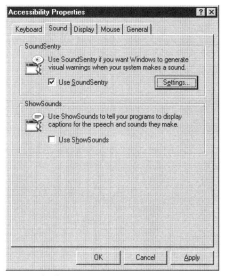

Figure 209 *The Accessibility Properties dialog box Sounds sheet.*

4. Within the Sounds sheet, click your mouse on the Use ShowSounds checkbox, placing a check mark within the box. Then, click your mouse on the OK button to put your settings into effect.

210   USING A HIGH-CONTRAST SCREEN TO IMPROVE THE SCREEN'S VISIBILITY

In Tip 203, you learned how to use the Windows 98 Magnifier accessory to help users view the information on their screen. Depending on a user's visual needs, there may be times when the user will find that high-contrast (almost bright white text on a dark screen) will improve the user's ability to view the screen's contents. To direct Windows 98 to use its high-contrast display, perform these steps:

1. Click your mouse on the Start menu Settings option and choose Control Panel. Windows 98, in turn, will open the Control Panel window.

2. Within the Control Panel window, double-click your mouse on the Accessibility Options icon. Windows 98, in turn, will display the Accessibility Properties dialog box.

3. Within the Accessibility Properties dialog box, click your mouse on the Display tab. Windows 98, in turn, will display the Display sheet, as shown in Figure 210.1.

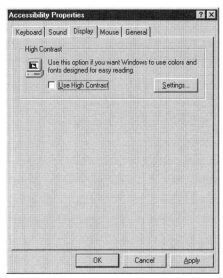

Figure 210.1 *The Accessibility Properties dialog box Display sheet.*

4. Within the Display sheet, click your mouse on the Use High Contrast checkbox, placing a check mark within the box.

5. Within the Keyboard sheet, click your mouse on the High Contrast Settings button. Windows 98, in turn, will display the Settings for High Contrast dialog box as shown in Figure 210.2.

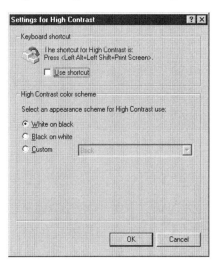

Figure 210.2 *The Settings for High Contrast dialog box.*

6. Within the Settings for High Contrast dialog box, select the color scheme you desire. Next, click your mouse on the OK button.

7. Within the Accessibility Properties dialog box, click your mouse on the OK button to put your settings into effect.

211 USING MOUSEKEYS TO SIMULATE MOUSE OPERATIONS WITH THE KEYBOARD

Depending on a user's mobility needs, some users may prefer using a keyboard over the mouse. To help such users control the mouse cursor using their keyboard, Windows 98 provides MouseKeys support. After you enable MouseKeys support, Windows 98 will let you move the mouse pointer by pressing keys on the numeric keypad. To perform a double-click operation, the user presses the number **5**.

Likewise, to hold down the mouse-select button for a mouse-drag operation, the user presses the **0** key. To release the mouse-select button, the user presses the decimal point (.). To perform a left-click operation, the user presses the slash (/) and to perform a right-click operation, the user presses the minus sign (-). To enable Windows 98 MouseKey support, perform these steps:

1. Click your mouse on the Start menu Settings option and choose Control Panel. Windows 98, in turn, will open the Control Panel window.

2. Within the Control Panel window, double-click your mouse on the Accessibility Options icon. Windows 98, in turn, will display the Accessibility Properties dialog box.

3. Within the Accessibility Properties dialog box, click your mouse on the Mouse tab. Windows 98, in turn, will display the Mouse sheet.

4. Click your mouse on the Use MouseKeys checkbox, placing a check mark within the box. Within the Mouse sheet, click your mouse on the MouseKeys Settings button. Windows 98 will display the Settings for MouseKeys dialog box.

6. Within the Settings for MouseKeys dialog box, select the settings you desire and then click your mouse on the OK button. Table 211 briefly describes each of the MouseKey settings.

7. Within the Accessibility Properties dialog box, click your mouse on the OK button to put your settings into effect.

Setting Option	Description
Keyboard shortcut	Turns MouseKeys on or off if you press the LEFT ALT-LEFT SHIFT-NUM LOCK keyboard combination.
Top speed	Sets how fast Windows 98 will move the mouse pointer.
Acceleration	Sets how fast Windows 98 will accelerate the mouse pointer moves from a stopped position to its top speed.
Hold down Ctrl to speed up and Shift to slow down	Lets you speed up or slow down the MouseKeys operation by holding down the CTRL or SHIFT keys.
Use MouseKeys	Directs Windows 98 to use MouseKeys when the NumLock is on or when it is off
Show MouseKeys status on screen	Directs Windows 98 to display the status of MouseKey operations.

Table 211 The MouseKeys Settings.

212   *TAKING ADVANTAGE OF SERIALKEY DEVICES*

Depending on a user's mobility needs, the user may or may not be able to use a mouse or a keyboard. Fortunately, hardware manufacturers have created a wide range of devices that users can attach to their PC's serial port and then use instead of a keyboard. To enable Windows 98 support for such SerialKey devices, perform these steps:

1. Click your mouse on the Start menu Settings option and choose Control Panel. Windows 98, in turn, will open the Control Panel window.

2. Within the Control Panel window, double-click your mouse on the Accessibility Options icon. Windows 98, in turn, will display the Accessibility Properties dialog box.

3. Within the Accessibility Properties dialog box, click your mouse on the General tab. Windows 98, in turn, will display the General sheet, as shown in Figure 212.1.

Figure 212.1 The Accessibility Properties dialog box General sheet.

4. Within the General sheet, click your mouse on the Support SerialKey Devices checkbox, placing a check mark within the box.

5. Within the General sheet, click your mouse on the Support SerialKey Devices Settings button. Windows 98 will display the Settings for SerialKeys dialog box, as shown in Figure 212.2.

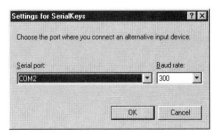

Figure 212.2 The Settings for SerialKeys dialog box.

6. Within the Settings for SerialKeys dialog box, specify the serial port to which you have attached the SerialKey device and then specify the device's baud rate. Next, click your mouse on the OK button.

7. Within the Accessibility Properties dialog box, click your mouse on the OK button to put your settings into effect.

213 CUSTOMIZING SETTINGS FOR WINDOWS 98 ACCESSIBILITY OPTIONS

As you have learned, using the Accessibility Properties dialog box, Windows 98 provides you with a wide range of features to make Windows 98 easier to use. If the PC you are configuring is used by a wide range of users, you may want Windows 98 to disable its support for various accessibility options after the PC is idle for a specific period of time. That way, should another user sit down at the system, the accessibility options will be off and will therefore not confuse the user. To further customize the Windows 98 Accessibility Options, perform these steps:

1. Click your mouse on the Start menu Settings option and choose Control Panel. Windows 98, in turn, will open the Control Panel window.

2. Within the Control Panel window, double-click your mouse on the Accessibility Options icon. Windows 98, in turn, will display the Accessibility Properties dialog box.

3. Within the Accessibility Properties dialog box, click your mouse on the General tab. Windows 98, in turn, will display the General sheet, as shown in Figure 213.

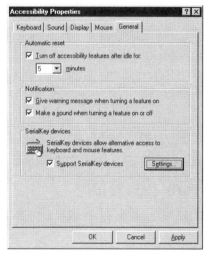

Figure 213 *The Accessibility Properties dialog box General sheet.*

4. Within the General sheet, customize the settings you desire and then click your mouse on the OK button to put your settings into effect.

3. Within the Keyboard Properties dialog box, click your mouse on the Language tab. Windows 98 will display the Language sheet.

4. Within the Language sheet, click your mouse on the keyboard language that you want to remove and then click your mouse on the Remove button. Then, click your mouse on the OK button to close the dialog box.

214 WINDOWS 98 FULLY SUPPORTS PLUG-AND-PLAY DEVICES

As you will learn, Windows 98 makes its easy for you to get new hardware up and running. To start, Windows 98 fully supports plug-and-play hardware. In general, "plug and play" is a hardware technology which lets the hardware cards that you install in your system communicate with one another to determine which resources they can use without conflicting with another device. In the past, users first had to determine which resources (such as wires to the CPU, called IRQ, or interrupt request lines) each device was using. Next, the users had to set jumpers and switches on their new hardware cards to select resources that were not in use. When the users made a mistake, and assigned resources to a new device that another card was already using, either the user's system did not start, or one of their hardware devices did not work.

Plug-and-play hardware, on the other hand, communicates with the other devices in your system to determine which settings are in use. By managing their own settings, plug-and-play devices make hardware installations very easy. Usually, you can install a plug-and-play hardware card, such as a new modem, in your system by performing these steps:

1. Shut down Windows 98 and turn off your computer.
2. Unplug and then open your PC, installing the new device.
3. Close your PC and then plug in your PC's power.
4. Turn on your computer. After Windows 98 starts, it will usually recognize the new hardware device and start the steps it must perform to install the device's software.

If, for some reason, Windows 98 does not recognize your new plug-and-play device, you can use the Windows 98 Add Hardware Wizard Tip 216 discusses to install the software Windows 98 needs to interact with the device.

215 CONTRASTING LEGACY HARDWARE WITH PLUG-AND-PLAY DEVICES

As you learned in Tip 214, when you install a plug-and-play device within your PC, the device communicates with your system's other plug-and-play devices to determine its proper settings. By communicating in this way, plug-and-play devices eliminate your need to change jumpers or switches on the devices that specify the device settings. Unfortunately, not all hardware devices are plug-and-play. Most articles and books refer to non-plug-and-play devices as legacy devices (they are left over from an older hardware technology).

When you install a legacy within your PC, Windows 98 may perform a series of different tests on the device trying to determine the device type and its manufacturer. By testing legacy hardware in this way, Windows 98 can often determine, on its own, which device drivers it must install. Unfortunately, for legacy devices that require you to assign their memory and interrupt settings (using jumpers and switches), Windows 98 has no way to help you. Instead, you must examine the settings for each card in your PC and then determine and assign the correct settings to your new card. If the settings you assign conflict with another device, your system may fail or one or both of the devices will not work. When such conflicts occur, you must again try to determine settings that do not conflict with other devices.

216	USING THE ADD NEW HARDWARE WIZARD TO INSTALL SOFTWARE WINDOWS 98 REQUIRES FOR NEW HARDWARE	

In Tip 214, you learned that usually, when you install a new hardware device, such as a modem, Windows 98 will recognize the device the next time your system starts and will perform steps to install software for the device. If, however, Windows 98 does not recognize your new hardware, you can use the Windows 98 Add New Hardware Wizard to install the software Windows 98 will use to interact with the device.

To use the Windows 98 Add New Hardware Wizard, perform these steps:

1. Click your mouse on the Start menu Settings option and choose Control Panel. Windows 98, in turn, will open the Control Panel folder.

2. Within the Control Panel, double-click your mouse on the Add New Hardware icon. Windows 98 will start the Add New Hardware Wizard, as shown in Figure 216.1.

Figure 216.1 *The Add New Hardware Wizard.*

3. Within the Add New Hardware Wizard, click your mouse on the Next button. The Wizard, in turn, will display a dialog box telling you that it will search your system for new plug-and-play devices. Click your mouse on the Next button. The Wizard will begin its search. After the Wizard performs its search for new plug-and-play devices, the Wizard will display a dialog box telling you that it will now search for other hardware, as shown in Figure 216.2.

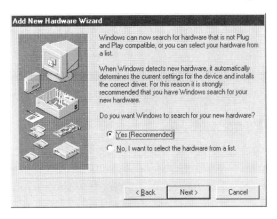

Figure 216.2 *The Add New Hardware Wizards will search your PC for new hardware devices.*

4. Within the Wizard's dialog box, click your mouse on the Next button to direct the Wizard to perform its search. Depending on your system configuration, the Wizard's hardware search may take several minutes. After the Wizard completes its search, it will display a list of devices it found. To continue the installation, click your mouse on the Next button. Depending on the hardware you have installed, the Wizard may prompt you to insert your Windows 98 CD-ROM or the software that accompanied your device. Perform the steps the Wizard specifies and continue to click your mouse on the Next button after you complete each step.

217 USING THE *DETLOG.TXT* FILE TO DETERMINE WHICH HARDWARE WINDOWS 98 DETECTED

In Tip 216, you learned how to use the Control Panel Add New Hardware Wizard to direct Windows 98 to search your system for a new hardware device and then to install the software it requires to use the device. Each time you use the Add New Hardware Wizard, Windows 98 creates a log file within your root directory named *DETLOG.TXT* within which it records information about each hardware device it detected. (The Windows 98 installation program also creates the log file when you first install Windows 98 on your system.)

If you have problems getting Windows 98 to recognize a new hardware device, the technical support staff who will help you troubleshoot your installation may ask you to print a copy of the *DETLOG.TXT* file. To view and to print the *DETLOG.TXT* file's contents, you can use the WordPad accessory program, as shown in Figure 217.

Figure 217 *Using the **DETLOG.TXT** file to view the hardware Windows 98 detected.*

218 GENERAL RULES FOR INSTALLING SOFTWARE WITHIN WINDOWS 98

The Tips in this book present each of the software programs Microsoft includes within Windows 98. Depending on your Windows 98 installation, there may be times when a Tip presents a software program that is not currently installed on your system. To install the software, you will need your Windows 98 CD-ROM and you will use the Control Panel's Add/Remove Programs icon. Tip 220 discusses the steps you must perform to install a Windows 98 component (one of the groups of Windows 98 programs, such as the Accessories component). In addition, Tip 219 discusses how you can use the Windows 98 Install Program Wizard to simplify your software installations. In addition to installing Windows 98 software, you may eventually have to install software for other programs, such as a word processor or spreadsheet. Depending on the program you are installing, the exact steps you must perform may differ. However, in general, to install a software program on your PC, perform these steps:

1. Insert the software's CD-ROM or floppy disk into your disk drive. If you are inserting a CD-ROM, Windows 98 may automatically start the installation program for you.

2. If Windows 98 did not automatically start the installation, click your mouse on the Start menu Run option. Windows 98, in turn, will display the Run dialog box.

3. Within the Run dialog box, click your mouse on the Browse button. Windows 98 will display the Browse dialog box, as shown in Figure 218.

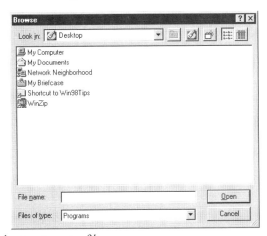

Figure 218 Using the Browse dialog box to locate a program file.

4. Within the Browse dialog box, locate the disk that contains the program you want to install. Within the disk's folder, you will usually find a program named *Setup*. Double-click your mouse on the *Setup* program to start the installation. The *Setup* program will usually display a set of dialog boxes that will walk you through the installation. After the installation completes, you can run your program from the Start menu Programs submenu.

219   USING THE WINDOWS 98 INSTALL PROGRAM WIZARD TO INSTALL SOFTWARE ON YOUR SYSTEM

In Tip 218, you learned the general steps you can perform to install a software program on your system. To make it even easier for you to install software, Windows 98 provides the Install Program Wizard. As you have learned, a Wizard is a program that displays a series of dialog boxes that walk you through a specific task. In this case, the Install Program Wizard walks you through the steps you must perform to install a new software program on your PC. To use the Windows 98 Install Program Wizard, perform these steps:

1. Click your mouse on the Start menu Settings button and choose Control Panel. Windows 98, in turn, will open the Control Panel window.

2. Within the Control Panel window, double-click your mouse on the Add/Remove Programs icon. Windows 98 will display the Add/Remove Programs Properties dialog box.

3. Within the Add/Remove Programs Properties dialog box Install/Uninstall sheet, click your mouse on the Install button. Windows 98, in turn, will start the Install Program Wizard, as shown in Figure 219.

Figure 219 *The Windows 98 Add/Remove Program Wizard.*

4. Within the Add/Remove Program Wizard, perform each operation a dialog box presents and then click your mouse on Next. The Wizard will walk you though your software installation.

220   ADDING WINDOWS 98 COMPONENTS

As you have learned, depending on your Windows 98 installation, there may be times when you do not have one or more of the programs that this book presents installed on your system. In such cases, you will need your Windows 98 CD-ROM. To install a Windows 98 component (one of the groups of programs Microsoft includes within Windows 98), perform these steps:

1. Click your mouse on the Start menu Settings button and choose Control Panel. Windows 98, in turn, will open the Control Panel window.

2. Within the Control Panel window, double-click your mouse on the Add/Remove Programs icon. Windows 98 will display the Add/Remove Programs Properties dialog box.

3. Within the Add/Remove Programs Properties dialog box, click your mouse on the Windows Setup tab. Windows 98 will display the Windows Setup sheet, as shown in Figure 220.

Figure 220 *The Add/Remove Programs Properties dialog box Windows Setup sheet.*

4. Within the Windows Setup sheet, click your mouse on the checkbox that corresponds to the component that you want to install. Depending on the component that you select, Windows 98 may install several related programs. Within the dialog box Description field, Windows 98 will display the number of programs it will install. If Windows 98 is not installing all the component's programs (the field will says something like 5 of 11 components selected), you can use the Details button, as discussed in Tip 221, to then select or not select specific programs within the component group.

5. After you select the component programs you desire, click your mouse on the OK button. Windows 98, in turn, will prompt you to insert your Windows 98 CD-ROM. Insert the CD-ROM and then click your mouse on the OK button. Windows 98, in turn, will install your selected programs.

221 VIEWING DETAILS ABOUT A WINDOWS 98 SOFTWARE COMPONENT

In Tip 220, you learned that using the Control Panel Add/Remove Programs icon, you can add or remove specific Windows 98 programs. In some cases, you may remove a program that you are not using to free up space on your disk. In other cases, you may learn about a Windows 98 program from a Tip in this book and then realize that the program is not installed on your system. Figure 221.1 shows the Windows Setup sheet within the Add/Remove Program Properties dialog box.

Figure 221.1 The Add/Remove Programs Properties dialog box Windows Setup sheet.

As you examine the Windows Components list, you will find that the dialog box displays the amount of disk space each component will require. Depending on your needs, however, there may be times when you do not need all the programs that Windows 98 provides for a specific component. You might, for example, only want to install the Paint and WordPad accessories (2 out of 11 accessory programs).

To view the programs that make up a specific component, click your mouse on the component you desire and then click your mouse on the Details button. In the case of the Windows 98 Accessories component, for example, Windows 98 will display a dialog box that lists program and its disk requirements, as shown in Figure 221.2. Within the dialog box, you can use the checkbox to add or remove the component. If you select the checkbox, Windows 98 will install the component. If you remove the check mark, Windows 98 will remove the component from your system.

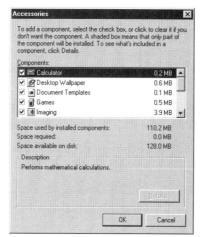

Figure 221.2 Viewing details about a Windows 98 component.

222 REMOVING A WINDOWS 98 COMPONENT FROM YOUR SYSTEM

In Tip 221, you learned how to use the Control Panel's Add/Remove Programs icon to install a Windows 98 component, such as the Windows 98 Accessories, or a specific component program, such as the WordPad accessory. If you later find, however, that you are not using the program or component, you may want to remove the component from your disk to free up space for other purposes. As you will learn, removing a Windows 98 component is much like adding one—with one exception. Rather than selecting a checkbox within the Windows Setup sheet, you will remove the check mark. Specifically, to remove a Windows 98 component from your system, perform these steps:

1. Click your mouse on the Start menu Settings button and choose Control Panel. Windows 98, in turn, will open the Control Panel window.

2. Within the Control Panel window, double-click your mouse on the Add/Remove Programs icon. Windows 98 will display the Add/Remove Programs Properties dialog box.

3. Within the Add/Remove Programs Properties dialog box, click your mouse on the Windows Setup tab. Windows 98, in turn, will display the Windows Setup sheet.

4. Within the Windows Setup sheet, highlight the component that you want to remove. In many cases, you may not want to remove the entire component but, rather, a specific program within component. To select the program you want to remove, click your mouse on the Details button. Windows 98 will display a list of the component's programs. Within the list, click your mouse on the program's checkbox, removing the check mark from the box. After you remove the check mark from each program you want to remove, click your mouse on the OK button.

5. After you select the component programs you desire, click your mouse on the OK button. Windows 98, in turn, may prompt you to insert your Windows 98 CD-ROM. Insert the CD-ROM and then click your mouse on the OK button. Windows 98, in turn, will then remove your selected programs from your disk. Windows 98 will also remove the component's Start menu options.

223 REMOVING OTHER SOFTWARE FROM YOUR SYSTEM

In Tip 222, you learned how to remove a Windows 98 component from your system. Just as you may find that you no longer use a specific Windows 98 component program, there may also be times when you find that you no longer use one of your application programs. By removing the program from your system, you can free up space on your disk.

Depending on when and how you installed the program, you may be able to remove the program from your system using the Control Panel's Add/Remove Programs option. Specifically, if you installed the program after you installed Windows 98, it is likely that Windows 98 knows the program's specifics, such as where the program files reside on your disk as well as the program's Start menu options. If Windows 98 knows this information, it can help you remove the program. To remove a software program from your disk, perform these steps:

1. Click your mouse on the Start menu Settings button and choose Control Panel. Windows 98, in turn, will open the Control Panel window.

2. Within the Control Panel window, double-click your mouse on the Add/Remove Programs icon. Windows 98 will display the Add/Remove Programs Properties dialog box.

3. Within the Add/Remove Programs Properties dialog box Install/Uninstall sheet, use your mouse to scroll through the list of programs Windows 98 displays within the Add/Remove field to locate the program you want to remove from your system. Next, click your mouse on the Add/Remove button. Windows 98, in turn, will start a program that will walk you through the steps you must perform to remove the software from your disk.

If you cannot find the program you want to remove within the Add/Remove program list, Windows 98 does not have enough information about the program to help you remove it. In such cases, you can use the Windows 98 Explorer to remove the program's folder (which you will likely find within the Program Files folder on your hard disk). Next, you can update the Start menu to remove the program's menu options. Finally, you can drag any shortcuts you have created for the program to the Recycle Bin.

224 CREATING A STARTUP FLOPPY DISKETTE

If you travel with a notebook PC, you should always keep a Windows 98 Startup Disk within your computer bag. Should your notebook ever fail to start Windows 98 in the future (for example, you accidentally drop your PC in the airport and now it won't start Windows 98 from your hard disk), you may be able to start your PC from its floppy drive using your Startup Disk. Then, after your system is running, you can copy key files from your hard drive to the floppy. Likewise, for the same reason, you should keep a Startup Disk close to your Desktop PC. A Startup Disk is simply a disk that contains the software Windows 98 needs to start and display a system prompt. To create a Startup Disk, perform these steps:

1. Click your mouse on the Start menu Settings button and choose Control Panel. Windows 98, in turn, will open the Control Panel window.

2. Within the Control Panel window, double-click your mouse on the Add/Remove Programs icon. Windows 98 will display the Add/Remove Programs Properties dialog box.

3. Within the Add/Remove Programs Properties dialog box, click your mouse on the Startup Disk tab. Windows 98, in turn, will display the Startup Disk sheet, as shown in Figure 224.

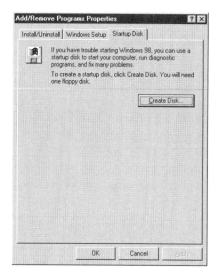

Figure 224 *The Windows 98 Startup Disk sheet.*

4. Within the Startup Disk sheet, click your mouse on the Create Disk button. Windows 98 will prompt you to insert your Windows 98 CD-ROM. Insert the CD and then click your mouse on the OK button. Windows 98, in turn, will then display a series of dialog boxes that will walk you through the steps you must perform.

5. After you create your Startup Disk, label the disk as Windows 98 Startup Disk and then place the disk in a safe location.

225 USING THE CONTROL PANEL TO SET THE DATE AND TIME

In Tip 30, you learned how to use the Taskbar clock to set your system's current date and time. As you have learned, because Windows 98 uses the system date and time to timestamp your files and e-mail messages, you should keep your system clock accurate.

If your Taskbar does not display the clock, you can use the Control Panel's Date/Time entry to set or display the current date and time. To set your system clock using the Date/Time entry, perform these steps:

1. Click your mouse on the Start menu Settings button and choose Control Panel. Windows 98, in turn, will open the Control Panel window.

2. Within the Control Panel window, double-click your mouse on the Date/Time icon. Windows 98 will display the Date/Time Properties dialog box, as shown in Figure 225.

3. Within the Date/Time Properties dialog box, set the date, time, and time zone.

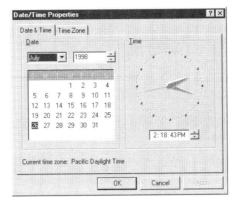

Figure 225 *The Date/Time Properties dialog box.*

226 **USING THE WINDOWS 98 DESKTOP THEMES**

In Tip 229, you learned how to customize your Desktop's look and feel by using the Display Properties dialog box Appearance sheet to assign various colors to define Desktop elements. For example, you might direct Windows 98 to display title bars in yellow, the current menu option in green, and so on. To help you customize your Desktop settings, Windows 98 predefines several Desktop themes, which will assign complimentary colors to your Desktop components, customize your Desktop icons and background, and even provide a multimedia screen saver. In addition to using the Display Properties dialog box Appearance sheet to select or configure Desktop themes, Windows 98 also lets you use the Control Panel Desktop Themes icon. When you double-click your mouse on the Desktop Themes icon within the Control Panel, Windows 98 will open the Desktop Themes dialog box, as shown in Figure 226.1.

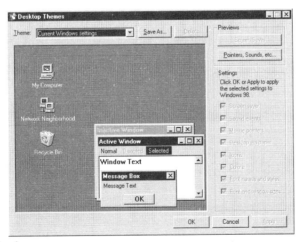

Figure 226.1 *The Desktop Themes dialog box.*

To select an existing theme from within the Desktop Themes dialog box, perform these steps:

1. Within the Desktop Themes dialog box, click your mouse on the Theme pull-down list.

2. Within the Theme pull-down list, click your mouse on the theme you desire. Windows 98, in turn, will preview the theme within the Desktop Themes dialog box. For example, Figure 226.2 shows the Dangerous Creatures Desktop theme.

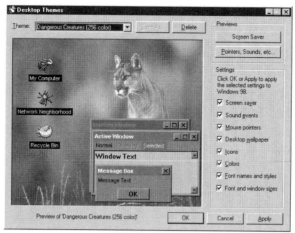

Figure 226.2 *Previewing the Dangerous Creatures Desktop theme.*

3. Within the Desktop Themes dialog box Settings field, use the checkboxes to specify which of the theme's attributes you want Windows 98 to apply.

4. Within the Desktop Themes dialog box, click your mouse on the OK button to put your changes into effect.

227 PREVIEWING A DESKTOP THEME'S SCREEN SAVER

In Tip 226, you learned that Windows 98 provides several built-in Desktop themes that define screen colors, sounds, icons, and much more. Take time now to entertain yourself for a few minutes with the Desktop themes that Windows 98 defines. Several of the themes are quite fun. The Baseball theme, for example, provides a screen saver that generates the sights and sounds of a major-league baseball game. To preview the theme screen savers, perform these steps:

1. Within the Windows 98 Control Panel, double-click your mouse on the Desktop Themes icon. Windows 98, in turn, will open the Desktop Themes dialog box.

2. Within the Desktop Themes dialog box, click your mouse on the Theme pull-down list and select the theme you desire.

3. Within the Desktop Themes dialog box, click your mouse on the Screen Saver button. Windows 98 will preview the screen saver.

228 PREVIEWING A DESKTOP THEME'S MOUSE POINTERS AND EVENT SOUNDS

In Tip 226, you learned that Windows 98 provides several Desktop themes that you can use to customize your Desktop appearance. Before you select a Desktop theme, you may want to first preview the theme's settings. To preview a Desktop theme's pointers, sounds, and icons, perform these steps:

1. Within the Windows 98 Control Panel, double-click your mouse on the Desktop Themes icon. Windows 98, in turn, will open the Desktop Themes dialog box.

2. Within the Desktop Themes dialog box, click your mouse on the Theme pull-down list and select the theme you desire.

3. Within the Desktop Themes dialog box, click your mouse on the Pointers, Sounds, etc. button. Windows 98, in turn, will display a Preview dialog box, similar to that shown within Figure 228.1, that you can use to preview the theme's settings.

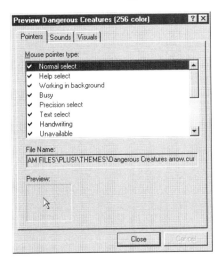

Figure 228.1 *Previewing a Desktop theme.*

4. To preview the theme's mouse pointers, click your mouse on the Pointers tab (if it is not already selected). Windows 98 will display the Pointers sheet. Within the Pointers sheet's list of mouse pointers, click your mouse on the pointer you desire. Windows 98, in turn, will preview the pointer's shape within the Preview dialog box Preview field.

5. To preview the theme's sounds, click your mouse on the Preview dialog box's Sounds tab. Windows 98, in turn, will display the Sounds sheet, as shown in Figure 228.2. Within the Sounds sheet's list of sound events, click your mouse on the event you desire and then click your mouse on the play button. Windows 98, in turn, will preview the sound.

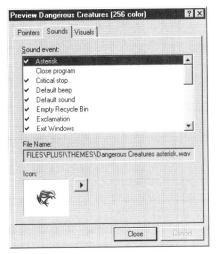

Figure 228.2 *The Preview dialog box Sounds Sheet.*

6. To preview the icons that the theme will use for key Desktop components, click your mouse on the Preview dialog box Visuals tab. Windows 98 will display the Visuals sheet as shown in Figure 228.3. Within the Visuals sheet, click your mouse on the item you desire. Windows 98, in turn, will preview the icon within the Preview dialog box Picture field.

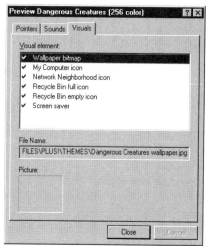

Figure 228.3 *The Preview dialog box Visuals sheet.*

229 USING THE CONTROL PANEL FOR SCREEN DISPLAY SETTINGS

As you have learned, the Windows 98 Control Panel exists to help you customize your system settings. Although you may never have a need to configure your system's low-level hardware settings, many users like to customize the Windows 98 Desktop, either by changing screen colors, the Desktop's background image, or even by directing Windows 98 to display Web-based information, such as a stock ticker-tape or a real-time weather report within a window on their screen. To customize your Desktop settings, you will use the Display Properties dialog box, shown in Figure 229.

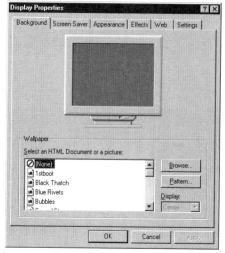

Figure 229 *Using the Display Properties dialog box to customize your screen and Desktop settings.*

Several of the Tips that follow examine the Display Properties dialog box in detail. To display the Display Properties dialog box, perform these steps:

1. Click your mouse on the Start menu Settings options and choose Control Panel. Windows 98, in turn, will open the Control Panel window.
2. Within the Control Panel, double-click your mouse on the Display icon. Windows 98 will display the Display Properties dialog box.

Note: *In addition to using the Control Panel display entry to open the Display Properties dialog box, you can also right-click your mouse on the Windows 98 Desktop and then select the Properties option from within the pop-up menu.*

As you have learned, Windows 98 provides you with several ways to customize your Desktop. In Tip 232, you will learn how to display a graphics file on your Desktop as a background image. In addition, if you are using the Active Desktop, Windows 98 lets you assign a Web page as your system background. At the low end of the Desktop designs, Windows 98 lets you assign a simple pattern to your Desktop. For example, Figure 230.1 shows three Desktops, each using a different background pattern.

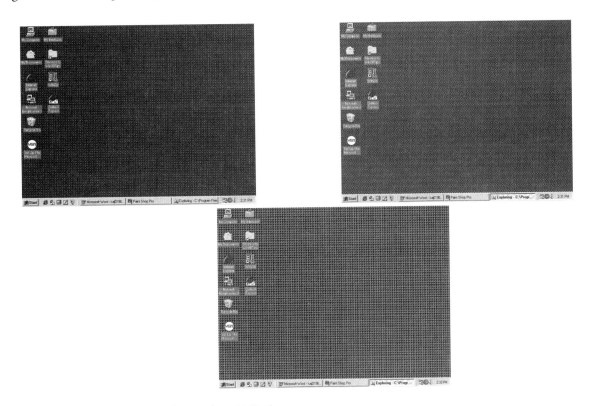

Figure 230.1 *Applying a pattern to the Windows 98 Desktop.*

To assign a pattern to your Desktop, perform these steps:

1. Right-click your mouse on an unused part of the Desktop. Windows 98, in turn, will display a small pop-up menu.

2. Within the pop-up menu, select the Properties option. Windows 98, in turn, will open the Display Properties dialog box.

3. Within the Background sheet, click your mouse on the Wallpaper list and select the None option. Windows 98 will enable the Pattern button.

4. Within the Background sheet, click your mouse on the Pattern button. Windows 98, in turn, will display the Pattern dialog box.

5. Within the Pattern dialog box, click your mouse on the pattern you desire. Windows 98, in turn, will display the pattern within the Preview box.

6. Within the Pattern dialog box, click your mouse on the OK button.

7. Within the Display Properties dialog box, click you mouse on the OK button. Windows 98, in turn, will update your Desktop to show the pattern you have selected.

---

231 ASSIGNING A BACKGROUND WALLPAPER TO YOUR DESKTOP

In Tip 230, you learned how to assign a pattern to your Desktop background. As briefly discussed, a background pattern is a simple design. Rather than using patterns on their Desktop, most Windows 98 users apply a graphics image, which Windows 98 refers to as a wallpaper, to their Desktop, as shown in Figure 231.

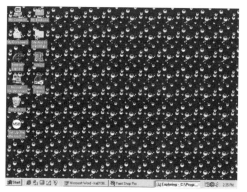
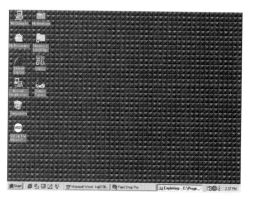

Figure 231 *Assigning a graphics image to the Windows 98 Desktop.*

Just as Windows 98 defines several different background patterns, it also provides several different images you can apply to a Desktop wallpaper. To assign one of the Windows 98 images as a Desktop wallpaper, perform these steps:

1. Right-click your mouse on an unused part of the Desktop. Windows 98, in turn, will display a small pop-up menu.

2. Within the pop-up menu, select the Properties option. Windows 98 will open the Display Properties dialog box.

3. Within the Background sheet, click your mouse on the Wallpaper list and select the wallpaper you desire. Windows 98, in turn, will display the wallpaper within the monitor that appears in the dialog box.

4. If the wallpaper that you select does not fill the dialog box's preview monitor, click your mouse on the Display pull-down list (which appears on the Background sheet) and click your mouse on the Tile option. Windows 98, in turn, will tile the number of image copies it requires to fill the screen. After you select the wallpaper image you desire, click your mouse on OK.

232   *DISPLAYING A SPECIFIC GRAPHICS FILE AS A DESKTOP WALLPAPER*

In Tip 231, you learned how to apply one of Windows 98 predefined wallpapers as a Desktop background image. In addition to letting you display one of its predefined wallpaper images, Windows 98 lets you assign other graphics files to your Desktop. To create a wallpaper using your own bitmap graphic file, perform these steps:

1. Right-click your mouse on an unused part of the Desktop. Windows 98, in turn, will display a small pop-up menu.

2. Within the pop-up menu, select the Properties option. Windows 98, in turn, will open the Display Properties dialog box.

3. Within the Background sheet, click your mouse on the Browse button. Windows 98, in turn, will display the Browse dialog box, within which you can locate the graphics image files you want to assign to the Desktop.

4. If the image you select does not fill the dialog box's preview monitor, click your mouse on the Display pull-down list (which appears on the Background sheet) and click your mouse on the Tile option. Windows 98 will tile the number of image copies it requires to fill the screen.

5. After you select the wallpaper image you desire, click your mouse on the OK button.

233   *DISPLAYING A WEB PAGE AS A DESKTOP WALLPAPER*

In Tip 232, you learned how to assign a graphics file to your Desktop's background. Using the Windows 98 Active Desktop, you can display a Web page as your Desktop background. For example, Figure 233 displays the Microsoft Web page as the Desktop background.

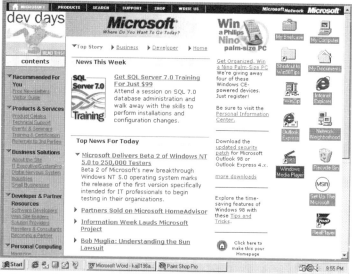

Figure 233 *Windows 98 lets you display a Web page as your Desktop background.*

If you are connected to the Web, you can click your mouse on the Web page's links to move from one site to another. Likewise, if the Web site has active content (which your browser will download automatically), the Internet Explorer will update your Desktop background automatically. To display a Web site as your Desktop background, perform these steps:

1. Right-click your mouse on an unused part of the Desktop. Windows 98, in turn, will display a small pop-up menu.

2. Within the pop-up menu, select the Properties option. Windows 98, in turn, will open the Display Properties dialog box.

3. Within the Display Properties dialog box, click your mouse on the Web tab. Windows 98, in turn, will display the Web sheet.

4. Within the Web sheet, click your mouse on the View my Active Desktop as a Web page checkbox, placing a check mark within the box. Then, click your mouse on the Background button. Windows 98 will display the Background sheet.

5. Within the Background sheet, click your mouse on the Browse button. Windows 98, in turn, will display the Browse dialog box, within which you can locate the HTML file you want to assign to the Desktop. Within the Browse dialog box, locate the HTML document that you want to display as your background and then click your mouse on the OK button.

6. Within the Display Properties dialog box, click your mouse on the OK button to put your changes into effect.

---

234 STRETCHING AN IMAGE TO FILL THE DESKTOP'S BACKGROUND

In Tip 232, you learned how to display a graphics images as your Desktop's background. Depending on your image size, there may be times when the image is not large enough to fill your Desktop. In such cases, you can direct Windows 98 to simply the center the image, to repeat or tile the image, or to stretch the image so that it fits. For example, Figure 234 shows the Clouds background image centered, tiled, and stretched on the Desktop.

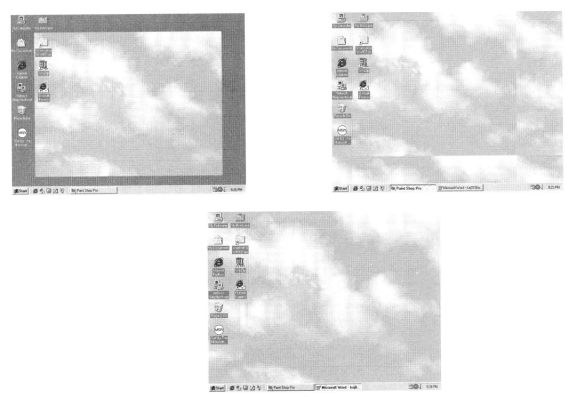

Figure 234 *Centering, tiling, and stretching a Desktop background.*

Depending on your image size, you may find when you stretch a background image, the result becomes distorted or pixelized. You may have to experiment until you find an image that stretches well. To stretch an image on your Desktop, perform these steps:

1. Right-click your mouse on an unused part of the Desktop. Windows 98, in turn, will display a small pop-up menu.

2. Within the pop-up menu, select the Properties option. Windows 98 will open the Display Properties dialog box.

3. Within the Background sheet, click your mouse on the Browse button. Windows 98, in turn, will display the Browse dialog box, within which you can locate the graphics image files you want to assign to the Desktop.

4. If the image you select does not fill the dialog box's preview monitor, click your mouse on the Display pull-down list (which appears on the Background sheet) and click your mouse on the Stretch option. Windows 98, in turn, will stretch your image to fill the Desktop.

5. After you select the wallpaper image you desire, click your mouse on the OK button.

235 SELECTING A SCREEN SAVER WITHIN WINDOWS 98

Computer screens display images by illuminating small red, green, and blue phosphors within the screen display. When the screen applies energy to the phosphors, they essentially burn, producing colored light. Over time, if the image on your screen does not change, the phosphors can actually burn the image into your screen, creating a ghost-like image that you can see even after you turn off your monitor's power.

To prevent such monitor damage from occurring, programmers created screen savers, which are simply programs that display different images on your screen when your screen is not in use. By constantly changing the screen images, the screen savers prevent image "burn in." Windows 98 provides several different screen savers you can use on your system. After you select a screen saver, you can tell Windows 98 how long you want it to wait, after your most recent use, before it starts the screen saver. In other words, you might want Windows 98 to wait for you to not use your system for 10 minutes before its starts the screen saver. Later, when you are ready to resume your work, you simply need to press any key or move your mouse. Windows 98, in turn, will turn off your screen saver and will display your previous screen contents. To select a Windows 98 screen saver, perform these steps:

1. Right-click your mouse on an unused part of the Desktop. Windows 98, in turn, will display a small pop-up menu, as shown in Figure 235.1.

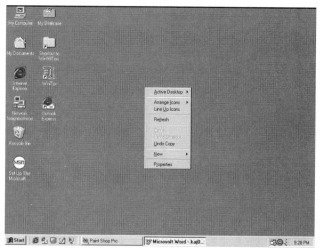

Figure 235.1 *The Windows 98 Desktop pop-up menu.*

2. Within the pop-up menu, select the Properties option. Windows 98 will open the Display Properties dialog box.
3. Within the Display Properties dialog box, click your mouse on the Screen Saver tab. Windows 98, in turn, will display the Screen Saver sheet, as shown in Figure 235.2.

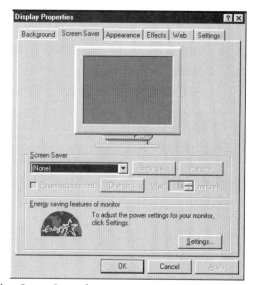

Figure 235.2 *The Display Properties dialog box Screen Saver sheet.*

4. Within the Screen Saver sheet, click your mouse on the Screen Saver pull-down list. Windows 98, in turn, will display a list of screen savers installed on your system.

5. Within the Screen Saver pull-down list, click your mouse on the screen saver you desire. If you are not sure which screen saver you want, simply pick one. You can later follow these steps to select a different screen saver.

6. Within the Screen Saver sheet, click your mouse within the Wait field, and type in the number of minutes you want Windows 98 to wait before its starts the screen saver you selected.

7. Within the Screen Saver sheet, click your mouse on the OK button.

Note: *Tip 236 discusses how you can preview a screen saver within the Screen Saver sheet.*

236 *PREVIEWING A SCREEN SAVER WITHIN WINDOWS 98*

In Tip 235, you learned how to select a screen saver using the Display Properties dialog box. As you found in Tip 235, Windows 98 provides many different screen savers from which you can select. To help you choose a screen saver, Windows 98 lets you preview the screen saver within the Display Properties dialog box. To preview a screen saver, perform these steps:

1. Within the Display Properties dialog box Screen Saver sheet, click your mouse on the Screen Saver pull-down list and then click your mouse on the screen saver that you want to preview.

2. Within the Screen Saver sheet, click your mouse on the Preview button. Windows 98, in turn, will blank your screen and activate the screen saver. To end the preview, simply move your mouse or press a key.

After you select the screen saver that you desire, you may want to use the Screen Saver sheets Settings button to customize the screen saver's processing. After you apply the settings you desire, you can again use the Preview button to view the screen saver.

237 *USING YOUR SCREEN SAVER'S PASSWORD PROTECTION TO INCREASE YOUR SYSTEM SECURITY*

If you work within an office with other employees, you can password protect your screen saver to keep other users from accessing your system when you step away from your office for a few minutes. When you password protect your screen saver, Windows 98 will display the Windows Screen Saver dialog box, similar to that shown in Figure 237.1, when a user moves your mouse or presses a key to end your screen saver.

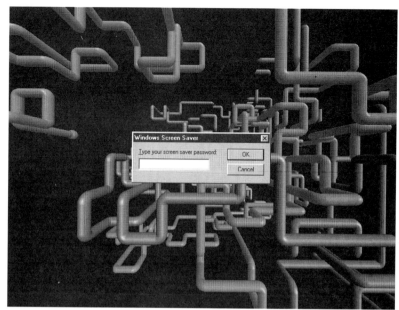

Figure 237.1 *The Windows Screen Saver dialog box prompting the user for a screen saver password.*

If the user does not type in the correct password, the screen saver will remain active and the user cannot access your system. To password protect your system, perform these steps:

1. Right-click your mouse on an unused part of the Desktop. Windows 98, in turn, will display a small pop-up menu.

2. Within the pop-up menu, select the Properties option. Windows 98 will open the Display Properties dialog box.

3. Within the Display Properties dialog box, click your mouse on the Screen Saver tab. Windows 98, in turn, will display the Screen Saver sheet.

4. Within the Screen Saver sheet, click your mouse on the Password protected checkbox, placing a check mark in the box.

5. Within the Screen Saver sheet, click your mouse on the Change button. Windows 98, in turn, will display the Change Password dialog box, as shown in Figure 237.2.

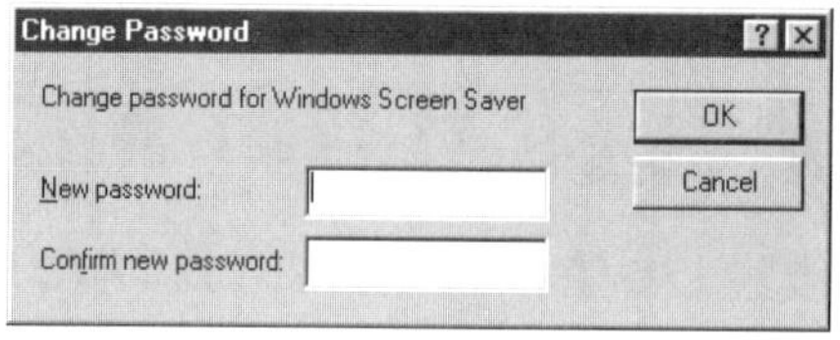

Figure 237.2 *The Change Password dialog box.*

6. Within the Change Password dialog box, type in your password within the two text boxes. As you type, Windows 98 will display the characters in your password as asterisks (*) to prevent another user from seeing your password.

7. Within the Change Password dialog box, click your mouse on the OK button. Windows 98 will display a dialog box telling you the password has been successfully changed. Click your mouse on the OK button.

8. Within the Screen Saver sheet, click your mouse on the OK button to close the dialog box and to put your password into effect.

238 CUSTOMIZING SCREEN SAVER SETTINGS WITHIN WINDOWS 98

With the exception of the Windows 98 Blank Screen screen saver, which simply displays a blank screen when your system is not in use, you can customize the screen savers that Windows 98 provides. For example, within the 3D Text screen saver, you can direct Windows 98 to display a specific message (using a 3D font) across your screen each time the screen saver becomes active. To customize the current screen saver settings, perform these steps:

1. Right-click your mouse on an unused part of the Desktop. Windows 98, in turn, will display a small pop-up menu.

2. Within the pop-up menu, select the Properties option. Windows 98 will open the Display Properties dialog box.

3. Within the Display Properties dialog box, click your mouse on the Screen Saver tab. Windows 98, in turn, will display the Screen Saver sheet.

4. Within the Screen Saver sheet, click your mouse on the Settings button. Windows 98 will display a dialog box, within which you can adjust settings specific to your current screen saver.

5. Within the Settings dialog box, assign the values you desire and click your mouse on the OK button. Windows 98, in turn, will redisplay the Screen Saver sheet.

6. Within the Screen Saver sheet, click your mouse on OK to put your changes into effect.

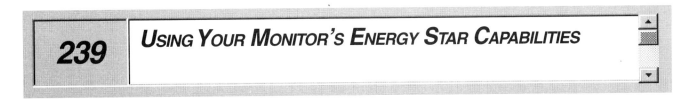

239 USING YOUR MONITOR'S ENERGY STAR CAPABILITIES

Over the past ten years, over 100 million PCs have emerged worldwide. As you might guess, these PC's have had a significant impact on the amount of electricity the world consumes. At the end of the day, for example, most employees leave the office with their PCs still running.

To help reduce the amount of electricity that PC components consume, hardware manufacturers created the Energy Star standards which turn devices, such as monitors, printers, and even some PCs, off (or to a low-power standby mode). Devices that are Energy Compliant work much like a screen saver. If you do not use your PC for a specific time interval, which you specify, Windows 98 can power down the device. Later, when you are ready to resume your work, and you press a key or move your mouse, Windows 98 can power the device back on.

Usually, if your device is Energy Star compliant, your hardware manufacturer will place an Energy Star logo somewhere on the device. To enable Windows 98 support for Energy Star compliant devices, perform these steps:

1. Right-click your mouse on an unused part of the Desktop. Windows 98, in turn, will display a small pop-up menu.

2. Within the pop-up menu, select the Properties option. Windows 98 will open the Display Properties dialog box.

3. Within the Display Properties dialog box, click your mouse on the Screen Saver tab. Windows 98, in turn, will display the Screen Saver sheet.

4. Within the Screen Saver sheet, click your mouse on the Settings button that appears within the Energy Star field within the dialog box. Windows 98, in turn, will display the Power Management Properties dialog box, as shown in Figure 239. If your system does not enable the Settings button, your monitor or PC is not Energy Star compliant.

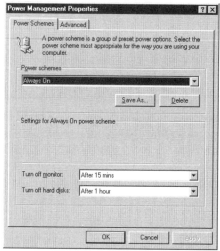

Figure 239 *The Power Management Properties dialog box.*

5. Within the Properties dialog box, click your mouse on the Turn off monitor pull-down list or the Turn off hard disks pull-down list to configure your PC's Energy Star settings.

6. Within the Power Management Properties dialog box, click your mouse on the OK button to put your power-management settings into effect.

7. Within the Display Properties dialog box, click your mouse on the OK button.

240 | **ASSIGNING A COLOR SCHEME TO YOUR DESKTOP**

As you have learned, within Windows 98, the Desktop is your personal workspace. To help you feel "more at home" with your Desktop, Windows 98 lets you customize various settings. As you will learn in Tip 241, for example, Windows 98 lets you assign different colors to various items that appear on the Desktop, such as menu options, window boards, title bars, and so on. In addition to letting you assign colors to items individually, Windows 98 provides you with several color schemes which have selected combinations of matching colors. To change your Desktop's current color scheme, perform these steps:

1. Right-click your mouse on an unused part of the Desktop. Windows 98, in turn, will display a small pop-up menu.

2. Within the pop-up menu, select the Properties option. Windows 98, in turn, will open the Display Properties dialog box.

3. Within the Display Properties dialog box, click your mouse on the Appearance tab. Windows 98, in turn, will display the Appearance sheet, as shown in Figure 240.1.

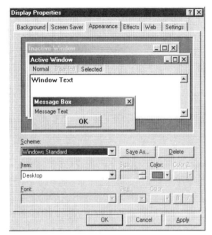

Figure 240.1 *The Display Properties Appearance sheet.*

4. Within the Appearance sheet, click your mouse on the Scheme pull-down list. Windows 98 will open the Scheme pull-down list, as shown in Figure 240.2.

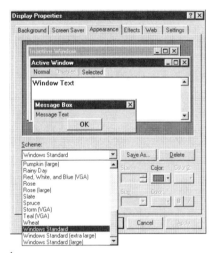

Figure 240.2 *The Display Properties Appearance sheet.*

5. Within the Scheme pull-down list, click your mouse on the color scheme that you want to use. Windows 98, in turn, will display the scheme's colors in the sample area that appears at the top of the dialog box. If you do not like the scheme's colors, simply click your mouse on a different scheme whose name appears within the pull-down list.

6. Click your mouse on the OK button to put your color scheme selection into effect.

241 ASSIGNING COLORS TO SPECIFIC ITEMS ON YOUR DESKTOP

As you learned in Tip 240, Windows 98 lets you customize your work environment by assigning a color scheme to the items that appear on your Desktop. If you cannot find a color scheme that suits your tastes, Windows 98 also lets you assign colors to individual screen elements. To assign a color to a specific Desktop item, perform these steps:

1. Right-click your mouse on an unused part of the Desktop. Windows 98, in turn, will display a small pop-up menu.

2. Within the pop-up menu, select the Properties option. Windows 98 will open the Display Properties dialog box.

3. Within the Display Properties dialog box, click your mouse on the Appearance tab. Windows 98, in turn, will display the Appearance sheet.

4. Within the Appearance sheet, click your mouse on the Item pull-down list. Windows 98 will display a list of Desktop items, as shown Figure 241.1.

Figure 241.1 The Desktop Item pull-down list.

5. Within the Item pull-down list, click your mouse on the item whose color you want to change.

6. Within the Appearance sheet, click your mouse on the Color pull-down list. Windows 98, in turn, will display a Color palette, as shown in Figure 241.2.

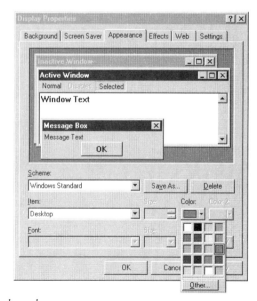

Figure 241.2 Displaying the Desktop item color palette.

7. Within the Color palette, click your mouse on the color you desire.

8. Repeat Steps 4-7 until you have assigned colors to each Desktop item that you desire.

9. Within the Appearance sheet, click your mouse on the OK button.

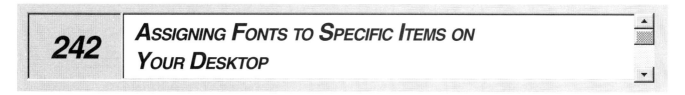

Unless you tell Windows 98 to do otherwise, Windows 98 uses the MS Sans Serif font within Desktop items, such as a title bar, that contain text. Like most of the items that appear on your Desktop, Windows 98 lets you customize different settings to better suit your needs and desires. As such, Windows 98 lets you specify the font you want Windows 98 to display within items that appear on your Desktop. To change the Windows 98 default Desktop font, perform these steps:

1. Right-click your mouse on an unused part of the Desktop. Windows 98, in turn, will display a small pop-up menu.

2. Within the pop-up menu, select the Properties option. Windows 98, in turn, will open the Display Properties dialog box.

3. Within the Display Properties dialog box, click your mouse on the Appearance tab. Windows 98, in turn, will display the Appearance sheet.

4. Within the Appearance sheet, click your mouse on the Item pull-down list. Windows 98, in turn, will display a list of Desktop items.

5. Within the Desktop Item pull-down list, click your mouse on the item to which you want to assign a new font.

6. Within the Appearance sheet, click your mouse on the Font pull-down list. Windows 98 will display a list of available fonts, as shown in Figure 242.

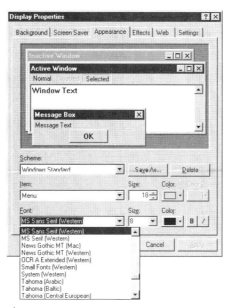

Figure 242 *The list of available fonts for Desktop items.*

7. Within the Font pull-down list, click your mouse on the font you desire. To change the font size, click your mouse on the Size field and type in the size you desire. Likewise, to select a bold or italic font, click your mouse on the **B** or *I* buttons.

8. Repeat Steps 4-7 for each Desktop item for which you want to assign a specific font.

9. Within the Appearance tab, click your mouse on the OK button to put your font selections into effect.

243 — CREATING A CUSTOM COLOR TO ASSIGN TO AN ITEM ON YOUR DESKTOP

In Tip 240, you learned that Windows 98 lets you assign colors to specific Desktop items. If you find that the colors Windows 98 provides in its default palette do not suit your tastes, you can create your own custom color. To create a custom color which you can later assign to Desktop items, perform these steps:

1. Right-click your mouse on an unused part of the Desktop. Windows 98, in turn, will display a small pop-up menu.

2. Within the pop-up menu, select the Properties option. Windows 98 will open the Display Properties dialog box.

3. Within the Display Properties dialog box, click your mouse on the Appearance tab. Windows 98, in turn, will display the Appearance sheet.

4. Within the Appearance sheet, click your mouse on the Item pull-down list. Windows 98 will display a list of Desktop items.

5. Within the Item pull-down list, click your mouse on the item whose color you want to change.

6. Within the Appearance sheet, click your mouse on the Color pull-down list. Windows 98, in turn, will display a Color palette.

7. Within the Color palette, click your mouse on the Other button. Windows 98, in turn, will display the Color dialog box, as shown in Figure 243.

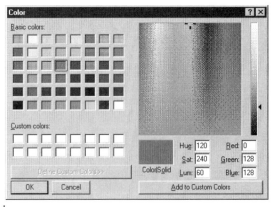

Figure 243 *The Windows 98 Color dialog box.*

8. Within the Color dialog box, experiment by assigning different values to the hue, saturation, luminosity, and RGB fields. As you change each setting, the Color dialog box will display a color that matches your values.

9. To add your new color to the list of available custom colors, click your mouse on the Add to Custom Colors button. The Color dialog box, in turn, will display your new color as one of 16 custom colors.

10. Within the Color dialog box, click your mouse on the OK button. Windows 98, in turn, will make your new color the current color selection and will redisplay the Appearance sheet.

244 CREATING YOUR OWN DESKTOP COLOR SCHEME

In Tip 240, you learned that Windows 98 lets you apply one of several predefined color schemes to the items that appear on your Desktop. Likewise, in Tip 241, you learned that Windows 98 lets you apply a color to a specific Desktop item.

If you use the steps Tip 241 discusses to assign colors to several Desktop items, you can save your current color assignments to a custom color scheme. To save your own color scheme, perform these steps:

1. Perform the steps that Tip 241 discusses to assign colors to various Desktop items.

2. Next, within the Display Properties sheet Appearance sheet, click your mouse on the Save As button. Windows 98, in turn, will open the Save Scheme dialog box, as shown in Figure 244.

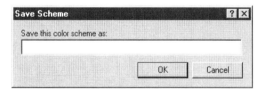

Figure 244 *The Save Scheme dialog box.*

3. Within the Save Scheme dialog box, type in the name you want Windows 98 to use for your color scheme and then click your mouse on the OK button.

4. Within the Appearance sheet, click your mouse on the OK button.

245 CUSTOMIZING THE DESKTOP'S VISUAL EFFECTS

As you have learned, the Control Panel Display entry lets you customize your Desktop appearance. In addition to using the Display Properties dialog box to select screen colors, a screen saver, and even the use of the Active Desktop, you can use the Effects sheet, shown in Figure 245, to control the size of Desktop icons, whether or not Windows 98 displays a window's contents or simply the window's frame when you move a window, and even the Active Desktop's display of icons.

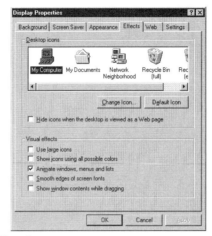

Figure 245 *The Display Properties dialog box Effects sheet.*

To use the Effects sheet to customize your Desktop, perform these steps:

1. Right-click your mouse on an unused part of the Desktop. Windows 98, in turn, will display a small pop-up menu.

2. Within the pop-up menu, select the Properties option. Windows 98 will open the Display Properties dialog box.

3. Within the Display Properties dialog box, click your mouse on the Effects tab. Windows 98, in turn, will display the Effects sheet.

4. Within the Effects sheet, use the checkboxes to select the Desktop visual effects that you desire and then click your mouse on the OK button to put your changes into effect.

---

246   USING THE DISPLAY PROPERTIES DIALOG BOX TO ENABLE AND DISABLE THE ACTIVE DESKTOP

As you have learned, Windows 98 supports an Active Desktop that lets you display Web-based information, such as a stock ticker-tape machine or real-time weather information, on your Desktop. For example, Figure 246.1 shows an Active Desktop.

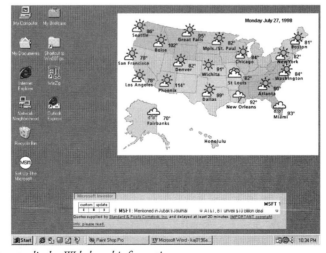

Figure 246.1 *Using the Active Desktop to display Web-based information.*

If you are working off-line (not connected to the Web), you may want to turn off the Active Desktop. To enable or disable Windows 98 use of the Active Desktop, select the Start menu Settings Option and then choose Active Desktop. Windows 98 will cascade the Active Desktop submenu, as shown in Figure 246.2.

Within the Active Desktop submenu, click your mouse on the View as Web page option. If you place a check mark next to the option, Windows 98 will enable the Active Desktop. If, instead, you remove the check mark, Windows 98 will turn off the Active Desktop.

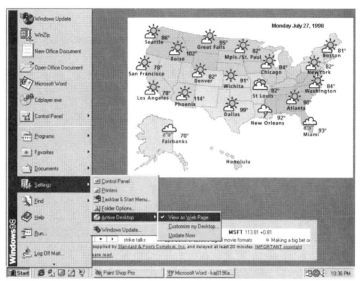

Figure 246.2 *The Windows 98 Active Desktop submenu.*

Note: *You can also enable or disable the Active Desktop using the View my Active Desktop as a Web page checkbox within the Display Properties dialog box Web sheet.*

247 **TELLING WINDOWS 98 THE MAXIMUM NUMBER OF COLORS YOUR MONITOR CAN DISPLAY**

The Display Properties sheet Settings page lets you change the number of colors Windows 98 offers for display. If you change monitors or want to adjust the number of colors Windows 98 displays at any one time for screen captures, perform these steps:

1. Right-click your mouse on an unused part of the Desktop. Windows 98, in turn, will display a small pop-up menu.

2. Within the pop-up menu, select the Properties option. Windows 98 will open the Display Properties dialog box.

3. Within the Display Properties dialog box, click your mouse on the Settings tab. Windows 98, in turn, will display the Settings sheet, as shown in Figure 247.1.

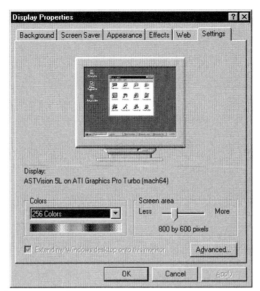

Figure 247.1 *The Display Properties dialog box Settings sheet.*

4. Within the Settings tab, click your mouse on the Colors pull-down list. Windows 98 will display the list of color settings, as shown in Figure 247.2.

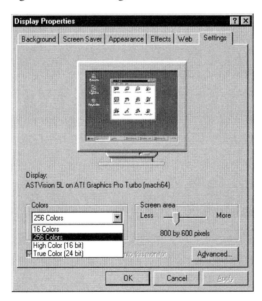

Figure 247.2 *The Colors pull-down list.*

5. Within the Colors pull-down list, click your mouse on the option that corresponds to the number of colors that you desire.

6. Within the Display Properties dialog box, click your mouse on OK. Windows 98 will display a dialog box asking you if you want to Restart your system to put your changes into effect.

7. Select Yes. Windows 98, in turn, will restart your system.

Depending on your monitor and video card type, the number of colors your system supports may differ. If your system does not support a specific number of colors, Windows 98 will dim the corresponding color option within the Colors pull-down list.

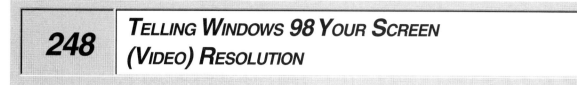

248 | **TELLING WINDOWS 98 YOUR SCREEN (VIDEO) RESOLUTION**

If the images your monitor displays do not seem quite as sharp as you would like, you may be able to change your current video resolution to improve your screen's sharpness. In general, your display's *resolution* defines its display sharpness. The higher the display resolution, the greater the image detail your screen can display. In Tip 247, you learned how to change the number of colors your video card uses to display images. In a similar way, you can also change your video card's current resolution. Depending on your video card type, the number of colors, like the resolutions your card supports, will differ. Resolution refers to the number of *pixels* (*picture elements* or screen dots) your monitor displays. The more pixels on your screen, the higher the resolution. The maximum number of pixels across and down your screen (the number of rows and columns of dots) determine your screen resolution. To change your display resolution, perform these steps:

1. Right-click on a blank spot on the Desktop. Windows 98, in turn, will display a pop-up menu.
2. Within the pop-up menu, click your mouse on the Properties option. Windows 98 will display the Display Properties dialog box.
3. Within the Display Properties dialog box, click your mouse on the Settings tab. Windows 98 will display the Settings sheet, as shown in Figure 248.

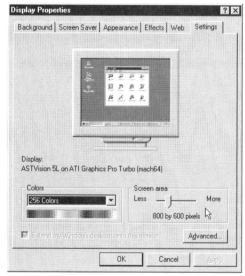

Figure 248 *The Display Properties Settings sheet.*

4. Within the Settings sheet, use your mouse to drag the Desktop area slider to the right or to the left to increase or decrease the current resolution. As you drag the control, Windows 98 will change the control's caption to reflect the new resolution. In addition, Windows 98 will preview the resolution within the dialog box monitor.
5. After you select the resolution you desire, click your mouse on the OK button to save your changes. Windows 98 may display a dialog box telling you that you must restart your system for the changes to take effect. If this dialog box appears, select Yes.

Note: *Depending on your video card type, as you increase the resolution, you may have to decrease the number of colors the card can display.*

249 TELLING WINDOWS 98 YOUR SCREEN'S DEFAULT FONT SIZE

In Tip 248, you learned how to change your screen resolution. Depending on the resolution you select, you may have difficulty reading the characters your screen displays, either because the characters are too large or because the characters are too small. In such cases, you may want to increase the Windows font size. To change the Windows 98 font size, perform these steps:

1. Right-click your mouse on an unused part of the Desktop. Windows 98, in turn, will display a small pop-up menu.

2. Within the pop-up menu, select the Properties option. Windows 98 will open the Display Properties dialog box.

3. Within the Display Properties dialog box, click your mouse on the Settings tab. Windows 98 will display the Settings sheet.

4. Within the Settings sheet, click your mouse on the Advanced button. Windows 98 will display a dialog box whose contents are specific to your monitor and video adapter. Within the dialog box, click your mouse on the General tab. Windows 98 will display the General sheet.

5. Within the General sheet, click your mouse on the Font size pull-down list and select Other. Windows 98 will display the Custom Font Size dialog box, as shown in Figure 249.

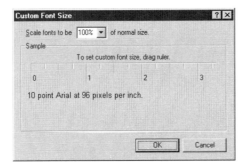

Figure 249 *The Custom Font Size dialog box.*

6. Within the Custom Font Size dialog box, click your mouse on the pull-down Scale list and choose the font size you desire. Then, click your mouse on the OK button to put your changes into effect.

7. Within the Advanced Settings dialog box, click your mouse on the OK button.

8. Within the Display Properties dialog box, click your mouse on the OK button.

250 CUSTOMIZING ADVANCED DISPLAY ADAPTER SETTINGS

In several of the previous Tips, you have learned to change your video resolution, the Windows font size, and even the number of colors your system will display. However, depending on your video adapter type (your video card), you may be able to control advanced settings that let you maximize the card's performance. For example, you may find that by changing your video card's refresh rate, your monitor's appearance becomes clearer and less wavelike. Unfortunately, the settings you can control will vary from one video card to another. However, to display your video card's settings, you can perform these steps:

1. Right-click your mouse on an unused part of the Desktop. Windows 98, in turn, will display a small pop-up menu.

2. Within the pop-up menu, select the Properties option. Windows 98 will open the Display Properties dialog box.

3. Within the Display Properties dialog box, click your mouse on the Settings tab. Windows 98, in turn, will display the Settings sheet.

4. Within the Settings sheet, click your mouse on the Advanced button. Windows 98 will display a dialog box whose contents are specific to your monitor and video adapter. Within the dialog box, you may need to search before you find the low-level settings.

---

251   CONNECTING MULTIPLE MONITORS TO YOUR PC

If you shop in one of the larger TV stores, you may have seen a display that uses three rows of three TVs to create one large screen, within which each TV displays a specific piece of the picture. The upper-left TV, for example, displays the upper-corner of the picture, whereas the lower-right TV displays the lower-right part of the picture. In a similar way, if you install multiple video cards within your PC (either PCI or AGP (Accelerated Graphics Port) cards), Windows 98 will let you display different parts of the Desktop on each PC. To configure Windows 98 to take advantage of multiple monitors, perform these steps:

1. Install and configure each of the PCI or AGP video cards.

2. Right-click your mouse on an unused part of the Desktop. Windows 98, in turn, will display a small pop-up menu.

3. Within the pop-up menu, select the Properties option. Windows 98 will open the Display Properties dialog box.

4. Within the Display Properties dialog box, click your mouse on the Settings tab. Windows 98, in turn, will display the Settings sheet.

5. Within the Settings sheet, use your mouse to drag the monitor icons to their respective positions on the screen display.

6. Click your mouse on the OK button to put your changes into effect.

---

252   CALIBRATING YOUR MONITOR SETTINGS TO ITS ACTUAL DISPLAY DIMENSIONS

If you use your PC for Desktop publishing, there may be times when you want Windows 98 to display fonts in a window at their exact size. In such cases, you can calibrate the Windows 98 font size by performing these steps:

1. Right-click your mouse on an unused part of the Desktop. Windows 98, in turn, will display a small pop-up menu.

2. Within the pop-up menu, select the Properties option. Windows 98 will open the Display Properties dialog box.

3. Within the Display Properties dialog box, click your mouse on the Settings tab. Windows 98, in turn, will display the Settings sheet.

4. Within the Settings sheet, click your mouse on the Advanced button. Windows 98 will display a dialog box whose contents are specific to your monitor and video adapter. Within the dialog box, click your mouse on the General tab. Windows 98 will display the General sheet.

5. Within the General sheet, click your mouse on the Font size pull-down list and select Other. Windows 98, in turn, will display the Custom Font Size dialog box, as shown in Figure 252.

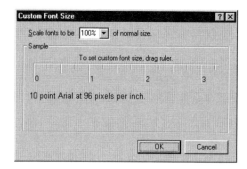

Figure 252 *The Custom Font Size dialog box.*

6. Hold a ruler up to your screen, just below the ruler within the dialog box. Next, using your mouse, drag the dialog box's ruler in or out until it matches your actual ruler. Then, click your mouse on the OK button. Windows 98, in turn, will calibrate its font size to match your display.

7. Within the Advanced Settings dialog box, click your mouse on the OK button.

8. Within the Display Properties dialog box, click your mouse on the OK button.

253 **MANAGING FONTS WITHIN WINDOWS 98**

If you have used a word processor, such as Microsoft Word or even the WordPad accessory Windows 98 provides, you may have assigned different fonts to characters within a document. In the simplest sense, a font is a specification that tells your system how to display letters, numbers, and even special symbols (such as ☺ and ©). In other words, a font determines a character's shape, size, and appearance.

As discussed, a font not only describes a character's typeface, the font also defines the character's size. You specify font sizes in terms of *points*, which are 1/72nd of an inch each. A 12-point font, for example, is 12/72 or 1/6 of an inch. Likewise, a 36-point is 36/72 or1/2 of an inch.

Each time Windows 98 displays a character on your screen, Windows 98 draws that character using the current font's rules. Within your applications, you usually select the current font using the Font menu or even a Font pull-down list that appears within a toolbar, such as that shown in Figure 253.1.

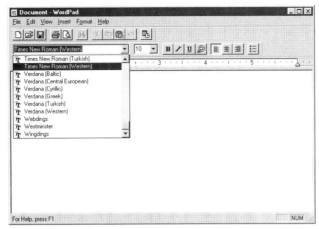

Figure 253.1 *An application toolbar that contains a Font pull-down list.*

Usually, an application's Font dialog box or pull-down list will include all of your system fonts. In addition, you can view the fonts on your system using the Fonts folder, as shown in Figure 253.2.

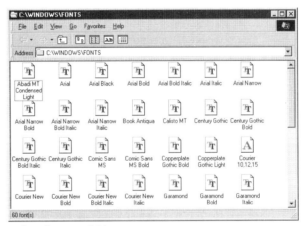

Figure 253.2 *Viewing your system fonts within the Fonts folder.*

To display the Fonts folder, perform these steps:

1. Click your mouse on the Start menu Settings option and choose Control Panel. Windows 98 will display the Control Panel window.

2. Within the Control Panel window, double-click your mouse on the Fonts option. Windows 98, in turn, will display the Fonts folder previously shown in Figure 253.2.

254   *VIEWING AND PRINTING A FONT SAMPLE FROM WITHIN THE FONTS FOLDER*

In Tip 253, you learned how to display your system's fonts within the Fonts folder. Within the Fonts folder, you can display a specific font's character set. For example, Figure 254 shows characters within the Arial font. To display a font's character set, perform these steps:

1. Click your mouse on the Start menu Settings option and choose Control Panel. Windows 98 will display the Control Panel window.

2. Within the Control Panel window, double-click your mouse on the Fonts option. Windows 98, in turn, will display the Fonts folder.

3. Within the Fonts folder, double-click your mouse on the icon that corresponds to the font you desire. Windows 98, in turn, will open a window within which you can scroll through samples of the font's characters. If you want to print the font sample, click your mouse on the Print button that appears near the top of the window.

4. Windows 98, in turn, will display the Print dialog box. Within the Print dialog box, click your mouse on OK to print the sample.

5. To close the font sample window, click your mouse on the Done button which appears near the top of the window.

Figure 254 *Displaying the characters within a font.*

255 **REDUCING CLUTTER WITHIN THE WINDOWS 98 FONTS WINDOW**

In Tip 254, you learned how to display your system fonts within the Fonts folder. Depending on the number of fonts your system contains, the Font folder may become quite cluttered, making it harder for you to locate a specific font. Within the Fonts folder, you can reduce the number of font icons the folder displays by directing Windows 98 not to display an icon for each variation of the font.

Usually, Windows 98 displays an icon for a font, the bold variation, the italic variation, and so on. To reduce the number of font icons in the Fonts folder, click your mouse on the Fonts folder View menu and choose the Hide Variations option. Windows 98, in turn, will reduce the window's icon list, as shown in Figure 255.1.

In addition to reducing the number of icons the Fonts folder displays, you can also reduce the Fonts folder clutter by displaying small icons, as shown in Figure 255.2. To display small icons within the Fonts folder, click your mouse on the Fonts folder View menu List option.

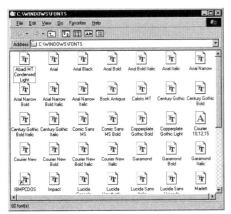 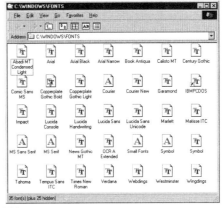

Figure 255.1 *Reducing the number of icons that appear within the Fonts folder.*

Figure 255.2 *Displaying a list of fonts within the Fonts folder.*

256 LISTING FONTS BY SIMILARITY WITHIN THE FONTS FOLDER

As you have learned, using the Fonts folder, you can display specifics about each of your system fonts. As you examine various fonts, you will find that two or more fonts may look quite similar. For example, the bitmap Courier font looks like the TrueType Courier New font, as shown in Figure 256.

Suppose, for example, that you have selected a TrueType font, such as TrueType Courier New, and your application does not support TrueType fonts. You must then find a non-TrueType font as a substitute. To help you identify similar fonts, you can select the Fonts folder View menu and choose the List By Similarity option. The Fonts folder, in turn, will group similar fonts within its fonts list.

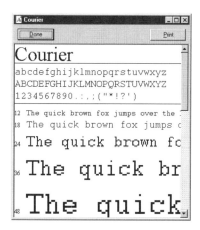 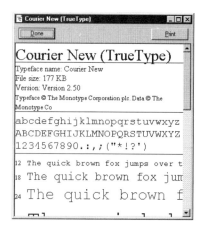

Figure 256 *The Courier font is quite similar to the TrueType Courier New font.*

257 | **INSTALLING A NEW FONT ON YOUR SYSTEM**

Depending on the applications you run, there may be times when you must add a new font. For example, if you use a word processor or page-layout software to create fliers or other graphics arts, you will likely need one or more special fonts. To install a new font on your system, perform these steps:

1. Click your mouse on the Start menu Settings option and choose Control Panel. Windows 98 will display the Control Panel window.

2. Within the Control Panel window, double-click your mouse on the Fonts option. Windows 98, in turn, will display the Fonts folder.

3. Within the Fonts folder, click your mouse on the File menu Install New Font option. Windows 98, in turn, will display the Add Fonts dialog box, as shown in Figure 257.

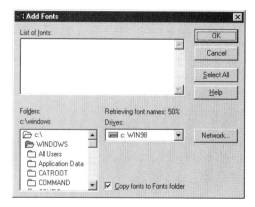

Figure 257 *The Add Fonts dialog box.*

4. Within the Add Fonts dialog box, select the drive and folder that contain the new font that you want to install and then click your mouse on the OK button. Windows 98 will display a list of the fonts the drive and folder contains.

5. Within the list, click your mouse on the font that you want to install. (To select multiple fonts, hold down the CTRL key while you click your mouse on each font you want to install. To install all of the fonts within the list, click your mouse on the Select All button.)

6. To install the fonts, click your mouse on the OK button.

258   REMOVING ONE OR MORE FONTS FROM YOUR SYSTEM

In Tip 254, you learned how to display your system fonts using your system folder. If you have fonts on your system that you do not use (and Windows 98 itself does not use for dialog boxes or other objects), you can free up disk space by removing the font from your system. To remove a font from your system, perform these steps:

1. Click your mouse on the Start menu Settings option and choose Control Panel. Windows 98 will display the Control Panel window.

2. Within the Control Panel window, double-click your mouse on the Fonts option. Windows 98, in turn, will display the Fonts folder.

3. Within the Fonts folder, right-click your mouse on the icon that corresponds to the font that you want to delete. Windows 98, in turn, will display a pop-up menu.

4. Within the pop-up menu, select the Delete option. Windows 98, in turn, will display a dialog box asking you to verify that you want to delete the file. Click your mouse on the Yes button.

259   RESTRICTING THE FONTS FOLDER LIST TO ONLY TRUETYPE FONTS

If you discuss fonts with other users, you may hear the term TrueType font. In general, TrueType is a new font technology that your programs display on your screen just as the font will print. In other words, the font's screen appearance is true to how the printer will print the font.

Within the Fonts folder, fonts whose icons appear with the letters TT are TrueType fonts. As a rule, TrueType fonts will better match the characters on your screen. Within your programs, you can restrict the Font dialog box's or Font list's display to TrueType only fonts by performing these steps:

1. Within the Fonts folder, click your mouse View menu and choose Options. Windows 98, in turn, will display the Options dialog box.

2. Within the Options dialog box, click your mouse on the TrueType tab. Windows 98 will display the TrueType sheet, as shown in Figure 259.

3. Within the TrueType sheet, click your mouse on the Show only TrueType fonts in the programs on my computer checkbox and then click your mouse on the OK button.

4. Click your mouse on the Close button to close the Fonts window.

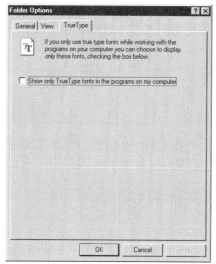

Figure 259 *The Options dialog box TrueType sheet.*

260 **CUSTOMIZING YOUR GAME CONTROLLER SETTINGS**

With the PC's processor speeds ever increasing, Windows 98 is now capable of running very complex high-performance computer games. If you use your PC to play computer games, you will likely have a game controller (a joystick) that you use to interact with the games. Within Windows 98, you can use the Control Panel Game Controllers entry to customize your game controller's settings. When you double-click your mouse on the Game Controllers icon, Windows 98, in turn, will display the Game Controllers dialog box, as shown in Figure 260.1.

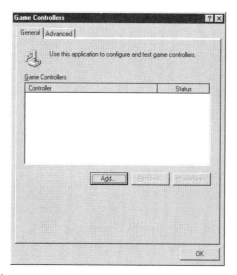

Figure 260.1 *The Game Controllers dialog box.*

Within the Game Controllers dialog box, you can use the Add button to add a new game controller to your system. Windows 98, in turn, will display the Add Game Controller dialog box, as shown in Figure 260.2, from which you can select your game controller and install its software.

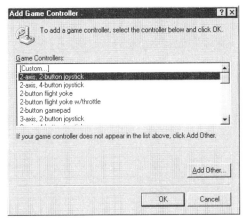

Figure 260.2 *The Add Game Controller dialog box.*

If you must configure your game controller's port driver, or if you must assign a specific controller to a controller ID, click your mouse on the Advanced tab. Windows 98, in turn, will display the Advanced sheet, within which you can configure the port settings.

261 CUSTOMIZING INFRARED HARDWARE DEVICES

To make PCs easier to use, hardware manufacturers are going "wireless." Today, many notebook computers support infrared communications, which use a high-frequency light, much like your TV's remote control. If your notebook PC supports infrared operations, you might use an infrared printer, keyboard, or even transfer files (using the Windows 98 Direct-Connection software discussed in Tip 330). Within the Windows 98 Control Panel, you can monitor and adjust your PC's infrared settings. When you double-click your mouse on the Control Panel's Infrared icon, Windows 98 will display the Infrared Monitor dialog box, as shown in Figure 261.1.

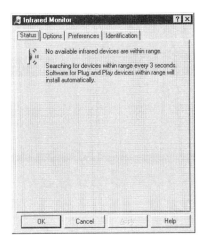

Figure 261.1 *The Infrared Monitor dialog box.*

Within the Infrared Monitor dialog box, you can view the current status of your infrared-device operations. To customize those operations, click your mouse on the Options tab. Windows 98, in turn, will display the Options sheet, as shown in Figure 261.2.

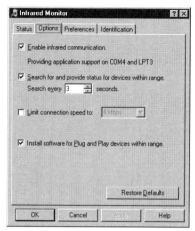

Figure 261.2 *The Infrared Monitor dialog box Options sheet.*

Within the Options sheet, you can enable or disable infrared operations, control how Windows 98 responds to infrared plug-and-play devices, and control how often your PC scans for infrared devices. In addition, the dialog box tells you which ports your programs should use to communicate to your infrared devices. If you click your mouse on the Preferences tab, Windows 98 will display the Preferences sheet, as shown in Figure 261.3.

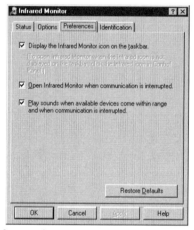

Figure 261.3 *The Infrared Monitor dialog box Preferences sheet.*

Within the Preferences sheet, you can enable or disable the Taskbar's display of the Infrared Monitor icon. You can also control when and how Windows 98 displays the Infrared Monitor dialog box. Finally, if you click your mouse on the Identification tab, Windows 98 will display the Identification sheet, within which you can specify the computer name and description Windows 98 will report to other infrared devices and PCs within a Microsoft network.

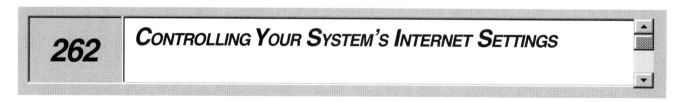

262   CONTROLLING YOUR SYSTEM'S INTERNET SETTINGS

Several of this book's Tips cover the Internet, electronic mail, as well as the World Wide Web in great detail. Within those Tips, you will learn how to configure your system for optimal performance and security. Several of the Tips may require you to use the Internet Properties dialog box, as shown in Figure 262.

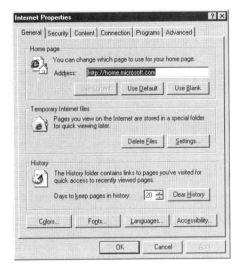

Figure 262 *The Internet Properties dialog box.*

Within the Internet Properties dialog box, you can customize many browser settings, the program Windows 98 uses for your e-mail, your security levels, and much more. To display the Internet Properties dialog box, perform these steps:

1. Click your mouse on the Start menu Settings option and choose Control Panel. Windows 98, in turn, will open the Control Panel window.

2. Within the Control Panel, double-click your mouse on the Internet icon. Windows will open the Internet Properties dialog box. Several Tips will examine the dialog box options in detail.

263 CONTROLLING YOUR KEYBOARD'S RESPONSIVENESS WITHIN WINDOWS 98

Within the Windows 98 Control Panel, you can use the Keyboard entry to customize your keyboard settings, to improve your keyboard's responsiveness, and to control the speed at which Windows 98 blinks the text cursor. When you double-click your mouse on the Control Panel's Keyboard entry, Windows 98 will display the Keyboard Properties dialog box, as shown in Figure 263.

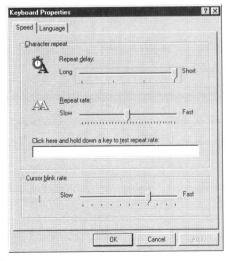

Figure 263 *The Keyboard Properties dialog box.*

Within the Keyboard Properties dialog box, you can control your keyboard's responsiveness (the speed at which the keyboard repeats the characters you type when you hold down a key) by setting two values. To start, the keyboard's *repeat delay* specifies the amount of time Windows 98 waits (delays) before repeating a character when you hold down a key. If your fingers are a little slow and your typing is still a little rusty, you may want your keyboard controller (a chip inside the keyboard) to delay longer before it repeats a character simply to give you time to press and release a key. If, instead, you type fast, you will want to minimize the delay. To decrease the keyboard's delay rate, use your mouse to drag the Repeat delay slider to the right. Likewise, to increase the delay, drag the slider to the left. After your keyboard starts to repeat characters, your keyboard's *repeat rate* specifies how fast it will repeat the character. To increase the rate at which your keyboard repeats the character that corresponds to the key you are holding down, use your mouse to drag the repeat rate slider to the right. Likewise, to decrease the repeat rate, drag the slider to the left. To test your keyboard settings, click your mouse within the dialog box's text field and then hold down a key. As you change the settings, note how long your keyboard waits to start repeating the character and then the speed at which the character repeats.

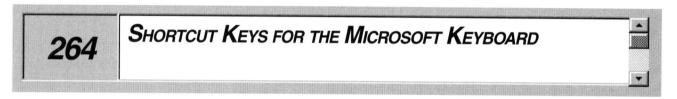

264 SHORTCUT KEYS FOR THE MICROSOFT KEYBOARD

If you are using a Microsoft keyboard or a keyboard that contains a Windows key, you can press that key to activate the Windows 98 Start menu. In addition, you can use the Windows key with the keyboard combinations Table 264 lists to perform other common operations.

Keyboard	Combination Description
WIN+R	Displays the Start menu's Run dialog box
WIN+M	Minimizes all open windows
SHIFT+WIN+M	Reverses a minimize all open windows operation by restoring all minimized windows to their original state
CTRL+WIN+V	Increases the speaker volume
SHIFT+WIN+ V	Decreases the speaker volume
WIN+F1	Starts the Windows 98 online help
WIN+E	Starts Explorer
CTRL+WIN+F	Finds files and folders
WIN+TAB	Cycles through Taskbar buttons
WIN+BREAK	Displays the System Properties dialog box

Table 264 The Microsoft keyboard Windows-key shortcuts.

265 CONTROLLING THE TEXT CURSOR BLINK RATE

When you use an application program, such as the WordPad accessory, to create a document, Windows 98 will display a small text cursor within your document that shows you the location at which it will place the next character you type.

To help you spot the cursor, Windows 98 blinks the cursor. Within the Keyboard Properties dialog box, previously shown in Figure 263, you can control the speed at which Windows 98 blinks the cursor.

To specify your text-cursor blink rate, perform these steps:

1. Click your mouse on the Start menu Settings option and choose Control Panel. Windows 98, in turn, will display the Control Panel window.

2. Within the Control Panel window, double-click your mouse on the Keyboard icon. Windows 98 will display the Keyboard Properties dialog box.

3. Within the Keyboard Properties dialog box, use your mouse to drag the Cursor blink rate slider to the right or left to speed up or to slow down the blink rate. As you change the blink rate, Windows 98 will preview a small cursor that blinks at your current rate.

4. After you select the blink rate that you desire, click your mouse on the OK button to put your changes into effect.

266 UNDERSTANDING AND USING KEYBOARD LANGUAGES

As you know, different countries use different languages which often require different letters of the alphabet. If you must type a letter or memo within such a language, you may want Windows 98 to use the corresponding language's keyboard layout. In such cases, you can use the Keyboard Properties dialog box Language sheet, as shown in Figure 266.1.

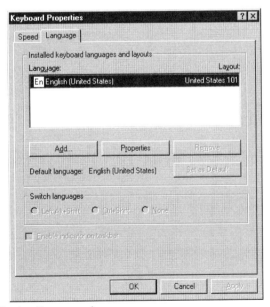

Figure 266.1 *The Keyboard Properties dialog box Language sheet.*

Within the Language sheet, you can click your mouse on the Add button to add Windows 98 support for a different language's keyboard. Windows 98, in turn, will display the Add Language dialog box, as shown in Figure 266.2.

Figure 266.2 *The Add Language dialog box.*

Within the Add Language dialog box, click your mouse on the Language pull-down list and select the language that you desire. Then, click your mouse on the OK button. Within the Languages sheet, you can then click your mouse on the Keyboard language that you desire.

267 SWITCHING BETWEEN KEYBOARD LANGUAGES

In Tip 266, you learned how to use the Keyboard Properties dialog box to add Windows 98 support for a different language's keyboard template. After you add a language to your system, Windows 98 makes it is easy for you to switch between keyboard layouts. To start, you can select the language you desire by clicking on the language from within the Keyboard Properties dialog box Language sheet. Second, within the Languages sheet, you can direct Windows 98 to use either the LEFT ALT-SHIFT keyboard combination or the CTRL-SHIFT keyboard combination to toggle between keyboard layouts. If you select the None option for the keyboard combination, you will only be able to change keyboard settings using the Languages sheet.

Within the Languages sheet, place a check mark within the Enable indicator on Taskbar checkbox. Windows 98, in turn, will display, to the left of the Taskbar clock, the first two letters of the keyboard language you are currently using, as shown in Figure 267.

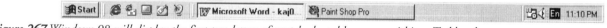

Figure 267 *Windows 98 will display the first two letters of your keyboard language within a Taskbar button.*

268 REMOVING WINDOWS 98 SUPPORT FOR A KEYBOARD LANGUAGE

In Tip 266, you learned how to add Windows 98 support for a specific keyboard language. If you find that you no longer use a keyboard language, you can use the Keyboard Properties dialog box Languages sheet to remove the keyboard language from your system, which will free up some disk space and other resources. To remove Windows 98 support for a keyboard language, perform these steps:

1. Click your mouse on the Start menu Settings option and choose Control Panel. Windows 98, in turn, will open the Control Panel window.

2. Within the Control Panel, double-click your mouse on the Keyboard icon. Windows 98, in turn, will display the Keyboard Properties dialog box.

3. Within the Keyboard Properties dialog box, click your mouse on the Language tab. Windows 98 will display the Language sheet.

4. Within the Language sheet, click your mouse on the keyboard language that you want to remove and then click your mouse on the Remove button. Then, click your mouse on the OK button to close the dialog box.

269 TAKING ADVANTAGE OF KEYBOARD SPECIAL FUNCTION KEYS

If you are using a notebook computer with a compact keyboard, you may find several keys that have multiple purposes. Usually, these keys will indicate their standard characters using black ink and their special-purpose characters in white. Notebook computers often use these special-purpose keys, for example, to provide a numeric keypad, to toggle the display between the notebook's monitor and external monitor, to display the notebook's current battery settings.

To use these special keys, you must locate your keyboard's function key (not the function keys F1 through F12, but a key usually labeled Fn, for function). Next, hold down the function key and then press one of the special-purpose keys. You should take time now to read your notebook's documentation so you can learn each key's purpose. That way, should you inadvertently press one of the keys while you are traveling, you can later "undo" whatever operation the function key caused.

270 CUSTOMIZING MODEM SETTINGS WITHIN WINDOWS 98

Today, users make extensive use of their PC's modem to connect to the Internet so they can surf the World Wide Web or send and receive electronic mail. Several of the Tips that follow examine ways you can configure your modem for ease of use and top performance. To perform the operations the Tips present, you will make extensive use of the Modems Properties dialog box, as shown in Figure 270.

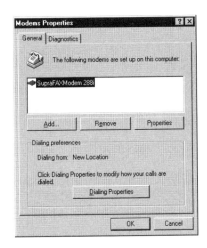

Figure 270 The Modems Properties dialog box.

To display the Modems Properties dialog box, perform these steps:

1. Click your mouse on the Start menu Settings option and choose Control Panel. Windows 98, in turn, will open the Control Panel window.

2. Within the Control Panel, double-click your mouse on the Modems icon. Windows will display the Modems Properties dialog box.

271   INSTALLING SOFTWARE FOR A NEW MODEM UNDER WINDOWS 98

Today, telephone, cable, and modem manufacturers are constantly coming up with faster and more efficient ways for users to connect to the Internet and the World Wide Web. As a result, to save time, you may find that you purchase a new modem every six months, simply to keep up with technology. When you install a new modem, you must tell Windows 98 about your new hardware. Depending on the modem you purchase, you will tell Windows 98 about your modem using one of three techniques:

- Windows 98 will recognize your new modem using its plug-and-play capabilities.

- From within the Window 98 Control Panel, you can start the Install New Modem wizard which will help you install the software you need.

- From within the Windows 98 Control Panel, you can start the Add New Hardware Wizard which, in turn, will recognize that you have installed a new modem and will help you install the software you need.

If you install a plug-and-play modem, Windows 98 will display a dialog box that identifies your modem and tells you that it must now install software to support it, as shown in Figure 271.1.

Figure 271.1 Windows 98 identifying a plug-a-play modem.

In most cases, you can simply follow the dialog boxes Windows 98 displays to install your plug-and-play modem's software. If, for some reason, Windows 98 does not recognize your new modem, the easiest way to install your modem software is to start Install New Modem Wizard from within the Control Panel, by performing these steps:

1. Select the Start menu Settings option. Windows 98, in turn, will display the Settings submenu.

2. Within the Settings submenu, select the Control Panel option. Windows 98 will open the Control Panel window.

3. Within the Control Panel window, click your mouse on the Modems icon. Windows 98, in turn, will display the Modems Properties dialog box, as shown in Figure 271.2.

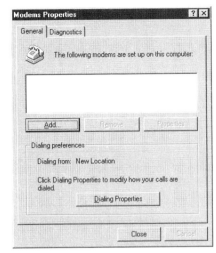

Figure 271.2 *The Modems Properties dialog box.*

4. Within the Modems Properties dialog box, click your mouse on the Add button. Windows 98, in turn, will start the Install New Modem Wizard which will walk you through the modem installation. Follow the instructions the Wizard displays on your screen to install your modem software. At some point during the installation, the Wizard will prompt you to insert the CD-ROM or floppy disk that accompanied your modem.

Note: *If the Install New Modem Wizard fails to identify your modem, you may need to run the SETUP program which resides on the floppy disk that accompanies your modem. For more information on installing new software, refer to Tip 218.*

272 **REMOVING YOUR OLD MODEM FROM THE WINDOWS 98 MODEM LIST**

In Tip 271, you learned how to install software for a new modem using the Control Panel Modems icon. After you install your new modem and have it up and running, you will want to remove your old modem from the Windows 98 modem list. If you do not remove your modem, many modem-based programs will continue to list the modem as available for use. To remove your modem from the list of available modems, perform these steps:

1. Select the Start menu Settings option. Windows 98, in turn, will display the Settings submenu.
2. Within the Settings submenu, select the Control Panel option. Windows 98 will open the Control Panel window.
3. Within the Control Panel window, click your mouse on the Modems icon. Windows 98, in turn, will display the Modems Properties dialog box.
4. Within the Modems Properties dialog box, click your mouse on the Remove button. Windows 98, in turn, will remove the modem from the list of available modems.
5. Within the Modems Properties dialog box, click your mouse on the Close button.

When you remove a modem from the Windows 98 list of available modems, Windows 98 will not remove the modem's device drivers from your system. As a result, should you later place the modem back into your system, the software Windows 98 needs to run the modem already resides on your disk. To add the old modem, you simply must follow the steps Tip 216 describes.

273 DISPLAYING YOUR MODEM PROPERTIES

Using the Windows 98 Control Panel, you can view or change various configuration settings for many of your hardware devices—modems being no exception. Several of the Tips that follow discuss ways you can configure your modem. To change your modem settings, you will use the Modems Properties dialog box, as shown in Figure 273.

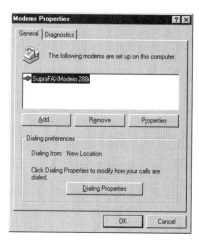

Figure 273 *The Windows 98 Modems Properties dialog box.*

To display the Modems Properties dialog box, perform these steps:

1. Select the Start menu Settings option. Windows 98, in turn, will display the Settings submenu.
2. Within the Settings submenu, select the Control Panel option. Windows 98 will open the Control Panel window.
3. Within the Control Panel window, click your mouse on the Modems icon. Windows 98, in turn, will display the Modems Properties dialog box.

Within the Modems Properties dialog box, you will click your mouse on the Properties button to display and configure information about your modem's hardware settings. Likewise, you will click your mouse on the Dialing Properties button to set your modem's phone characteristics, such as whether or not your modem must dial 9 to access an outside line, or what number your modem must dial to disable call waiting. Several of the Tips that follow discuss your modem's hardware settings and call settings in detail.

274 CONFIGURING YOUR MODEM'S DIALING PROPERTIES

As you know, a modem lets you connect your PC to another computer over standard telephone lines. Using your PC's modem to connect to another computer is very much like making a phone call. You must tell your data-communication software the number you want to call and then your modem will dial the number. If the number corresponds to a long-distance call, you will pay the same long-distance rates for your modem call as you would for your phone call.

Depending from where you place your call, you may also need to tell your modem to dial 9 to access an outside line or that your modem should disable call waiting to prevent an incoming call from disabling your modem connection. To simplify your modem use, Windows 98 lets you define these call settings one time for your modem. Then, each time you make a modem connection, Windows 98 will automatically use the settings. To define your modem's dialing settings, perform these steps:

1. Select the Start menu Settings option. Windows 98, in turn, will display the Settings submenu.

2. Within the Settings submenu, select the Control Panel option. Windows 98 will open the Control Panel window.

3. Within the Control Panel window, click your mouse on the Modems icon. Windows 98, in turn, will display the Modems Properties dialog box.

4. Within the Modems Properties dialog box, click your mouse on the Dialing Properties button. Windows 98, in turn, will display the Dialing Properties dialog box, as shown in Figure 274. Several of the Tips that follow discuss the steps you must perform to configure specific settings within the Dialing Properties dialog box.

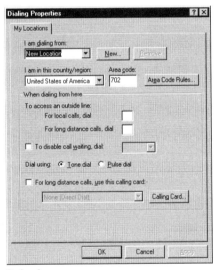

Figure 274 The Windows 98 Dialing Properties dialog box.

275 USING THE DIALING PROPERTIES DIALOG BOX TO TELL WINDOWS 98 YOUR AREA CODE

Placing a long-distance call using your modem is no different than placing a long-distance call with your phone. Your modem software must dial the area code and the phone number. To simplify your modem calls, you should use the Dialing Properties dialog box to tell Windows 98 your current area code. Most data-communication software programs will use the area code value that you specify to determine when they are placing a long-distance call, and can then determine, on their own, what prefixes they must dial, and even if you want the software to charge the call to your phone card. To assign your current area code to your modem settings, perform these steps:

1. Select the Start menu Settings option. Windows 98, in turn, will display the Settings submenu.

2. Within the Settings submenu, select the Control Panel option. Windows 98 will open the Control Panel window.

3. Within the Control Panel window, click your mouse on the Modems icon. Windows 98, in turn, will display the Modems Properties dialog box.

4. Within the Modems Properties dialog box, click your mouse on the Dialing Properties button. Windows 98, in turn, will display the Dialing Properties dialog box.

5. Within the Dialing Properties dialog box, click your mouse on the I am in this country/region pull-down list. Windows 98, in turn, will display a list of countries similar to that shown in Figure 275.

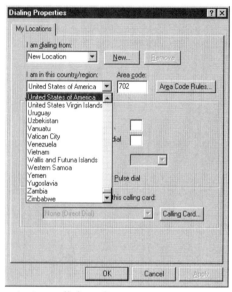

Figure 275 *The Windows 98 I am in this country/region pull-down list.*

6. Within the pull-down list, click your mouse on the country within which you currently reside. Windows 98, in turn, will later use this information when you place calls to other countries.

7. Within the Dialing Properties dialog box, click your mouse within the Area code field and type in your area code.

8. Depending on where you live, you may have local area codes that differ from your area code, but that do not require you to dial a 1 to place the call as a long distance number. To inform Windows 98 about such area-code rules, click your mouse on the Dialing Properties dialog box Area Code Rules button. Windows 98, in turn, will display the Area Code Rules dialog box, within which you can specify how your modem software should treat different local area codes.

276 CONTROLLING PHONE LINE SPECIFIC MODEM SETTINGS

Depending from where you are placing your modem calls, there may be times when you must dial 9 to access an outside line (which is common in hotels, for example), or you must dial a different access number before you can place a long-distance call (which is common in many businesses). In addition, if you are making modem calls over a phone line that supports call waiting, you may want to disable the call waiting feature during your modem calls to prevent an incoming call from disconnecting your modem connection.

To specify settings which are specific to your current phone line, perform these steps:

1. Select the Start menu Settings option. Windows 98, in turn, will display the Settings submenu.
2. Within the Settings submenu, select the Control Panel option. Windows 98 will open the Control Panel window.
3. Within the Control Panel window, click your mouse on the Modems icon. Windows 98, in turn, will display the Modems Properties dialog box.
4. Within the Modems Properties dialog box, click your mouse on the Dialing Properties button. Windows 98, in turn, will display the Dialing Properties dialog box.
5. If you must dial a specific number to access an outside line for local calls, click your mouse in the For local calls, dial text box and type the number you must dial to access the outside line.
6. If you must dial a specific access code before you can place a long distance call, click your mouse in the For long distance calls, dial text box and type your access code.
7. If you want to disable call waiting for the duration of your modem call, click your mouse on the checkbox that appears to the left of the To disable call waiting, dial field, placing a check mark within the box. Then, click your mouse on the To disable call waiting pull-down list. Windows 98, in turn, will display a list of codes that disable call waiting. Within the pull-down list, select the code that disables call waiting for your current phone service.
8. Within the Dialing Properties dialog box, click your mouse on the OK button to put your changes into effect.

277 DIRECTING WINDOWS 98 TO USE YOUR CALLING CARD FOR LONG-DISTANCE MODEM CALLS

As you have learned, placing a long-distance modem call is very similar to placing a long-distance phone call. Your modem software must specify the long-distance area codes and the phone company will charge you the same rate for your modem call as it would for a phone call. To simplify your modem calls, Windows 98 lets you charge your calls to a calling card.

To assign your calling-card number to your modem settings, perform these steps:

1. Select the Start menu Settings option. Windows 98, in turn, will display the Settings submenu.
2. Within the Settings submenu, select the Control Panel option. Windows 98 will open the Control Panel window.
3. Within the Control Panel window, click your mouse on the Modems icon. Windows 98, in turn, will display the Modems Properties dialog box.
4. Within the Modems Properties dialog box, click your mouse on the Dialing Properties button. Windows 98, in turn, will display the Dialing Properties dialog box.
5. Within the Dialing Properties dialog box, click your mouse on the Calling Card button. Windows 98, in turn, will display the Calling Card dialog box, as shown in Figure 277.1.

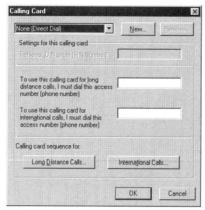

Figure 277.1 *The Windows 98 Calling Card dialog box.*

6. Within the Calling Card dialog box, click your mouse on the pull-down list which appears near the top of the dialog box. Windows 98, in turn, will display a list of the common calling cards, as shown in Figure 277.2.

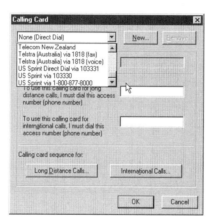

Figure 277.2 *A pull-down list of common calling cards.*

7. Within the pull-down list, click your mouse on your calling card plan. Windows 98, in turn, will display the calling card access numbers within the Calling Card dialog box.

8. Within the Calling Card dialog box, click your mouse on the Settings for this calling card field and type in the Personal ID Number (your PIN number) that your phone company gave you with the card. Within the Calling Card dialog box, click your mouse on the OK button.

Note: *If Windows 98 does not list your calling card within its pull-down list, click your mouse on the Calling Card New button and define a name for your card. Next, within the Calling Card dialog box, you must enter your PIN number and your calling card company's long distance and international dialing codes.*

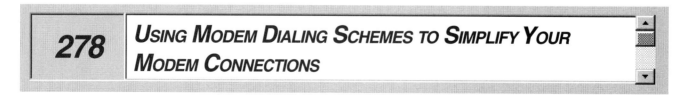

278   USING MODEM DIALING SCHEMES TO SIMPLIFY YOUR MODEM CONNECTIONS

In several of the previous Tips, you have learned ways to define settings for your current phone line. If you are like many users who use a notebook PC at work, at home, and on the road, you can simplify your modem operations by defining a modem dialing scheme, which defines the dialing settings for a specific location. You might, for example, create one dialing scheme that you name *Work Office*, for which you enter the numbers you must dial to access an outside line, and so forth. Then, you might create a scheme that you call *Home Office*. In addition, if you travel on a regular basis and your company provides you with a calling card, you might create a scheme that you call *Business Travel*, within which you direct Windows 98 to use your calling card for all long-distance calls. To create a modem dialing scheme, perform these steps:

1. Select the Start menu Settings option. Windows 98, in turn, will display the Settings submenu.
2. Within the Settings submenu, select the Control Panel option. Windows 98 will open the Control Panel window.
3. Within the Control Panel window, click your mouse on the Modems icon. Windows 98, in turn, will display the Modems Properties dialog box.
4. Within the Modems Properties dialog box, click your mouse on the Dialing Properties button. Windows 98, in turn, will display the Dialing Properties dialog box.
5. Within the Dialing Properties dialog box, click your mouse on the New button. Windows 98, in turn, will create an entry within the I am dialing from pull-down list named New Location.
6. Within the Dialing Properties dialog box, click your mouse within the I am dialing from text field and type in your modem dialing scheme name, such as Work Office, overwriting the name New Location.
7. Within the Dialing Properties dialog box, change the phone settings to match the location for which you are defining your new scheme.
8. Within the Dialing Properties dialog box, click your mouse on the OK button to save your new scheme. Tip 279 will discuss how you select a scheme before you place your modem calls.

279   *USING A MODEM DIALING SCHEME*

In Tip 278, you learned how creating a modem dialing scheme for each location from which you use your modem can simplify your modem operations. After you define a modem dialing scheme, you will want to select the scheme that corresponds to your current location before you try to place a modem call. To select a modem dialing scheme, perform these steps:

1. Select the Start menu Settings option. Windows 98, in turn, will display the Settings submenu.
2. Within the Settings submenu, select the Control Panel option. Windows 98 will open the Control Panel window.
3. Within the Control Panel window, click your mouse on the Modems icon. Windows 98, in turn, will display the Modems Properties dialog box.
4. Within the Modems Properties dialog box, click your mouse on the Dialing Properties button. Windows 98, in turn, will display the Dialing Properties dialog box.
5. Within the Dialing Properties dialog box, click your mouse on the I am dialing from pull-down list. Windows 98 will display a list of your modem dialing schemes, as shown in Figure 279.

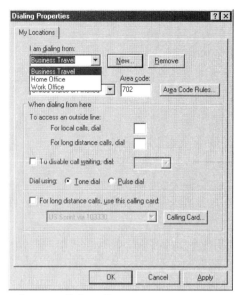

Figure 279 *Selecting your modem dialing scheme from a pull-down list.*

6. Within the pull-down list, click your mouse on the modem dialing scheme that corresponds to your current location.

7. Within the Dialing Properties dialog box, click your mouse on the OK button to put your changes into effect.

8. Within the Modems Properties dialog box, click your mouse on the OK button. You are now ready to place your modem calls.

280 CONTROLLING YOUR MODEM'S HARDWARE SETTINGS

In several of the previous Tips, you learned how to configure the settings your modem uses to place calls. Usually, newer plug-and-play modems work fine from the moment you take them out of the box and install them into your PC. Periodically, however, your modem may simply not work or may fail intermittently. In such cases, you may be able to troubleshoot your modem's problem and then change a hardware setting from within the Modems Properties dialog box. To view your modem's current hardware properties, perform these steps:

1. Select the Start menu Settings option. Windows 98, in turn, will display the Settings submenu.

2. Within the Settings submenu, select the Control Panel option. Windows 98 will open the Control Panel window.

3. Within the Control Panel window, click your mouse on the Modems icon. Windows 98, in turn, will display the Modems Properties dialog box.

4. Within the Modems Properties dialog box, click you mouse on the Properties button. Windows 98, in turn, will display the Modem Properties dialog box General sheet, as shown in Figure 280.

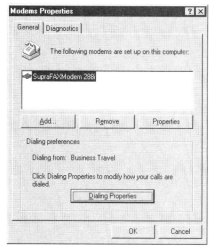

Figure 280 *The Windows 98 Modem Properties dialog box General sheet.*

Several of the Tips that follow discuss ways you can use the Modems Properties dialog box to configure your modem's hardware settings.

281 UNDERSTANDING YOUR MODEM'S COMMUNICATION PORT

Years ago, modems were external devices that you connected to one of the PC's serial ports. Most PCs come with two serial ports, but can support up to four. Your PC calls its serial ports, COM1, COM2, COM3, and COM4. The COM in the serial port name corresponds to the fact that the PC uses the serial ports to communicate with different hardware devices. In the "old days," which were actually only a few years ago, users would connect a serial mouse to one of their serial ports and a serial modem to the second port. The user then had to tell Windows which port he or she was using for the mouse and which port he or she was using for the modem.

Today, most PCs use internal modems which you (or your PC's manufacturer) install within the PC as a hardware card. To communicate with the modem, your PC sends and receives electronic signals over a specific set of wires. Because most PCs do not use all four serial ports, you will usually borrow the wires that correspond to one of the port locations for use by your modem. Therefore, when you install a modem yourself, you must tell your PC (and the modem, usually by using switches or jumpers on the modem card) which port the modem will use. Often, the modem will use the COM2 wires.

If you experience intermittent errors when you use your modem (such as your mouse suddenly stops working when you place a modem call, or each time you move your mouse, your modem disconnects), you probably have two devices trying to use the same port. In such cases, you will need to change your settings on the modem card itself. (Have an experienced user help you assign your modem a new COM port. The documentation that accompanies your modem will tell you how.) Then, you must tell Windows 98 that you have changed the modem's port. To tell Windows 98 that you have changed the modem port, perform these steps:

1. Select the Start menu Settings option. Windows 98, in turn, will display the Settings submenu.

2. Within the Settings submenu, select the Control Panel option. Windows 98 will open the Control Panel window.

3. Within the Control Panel window, click your mouse on the Modems icon. Windows 98, in turn, will display the Modems Properties dialog box.

4. Within the Modems Properties dialog box, click your mouse on the Properties button. Windows 98, in turn, will display the Modems Properties dialog box General sheet.

5. Within the General sheet, click your mouse on the pull-down Port list. Windows 98, in turn, will display a list of available serial ports.

6. Within the pull-down list, click your mouse on the serial port that corresponds to your modem and then click your mouse on the OK button to put your changes into effect.

7. Within the Modem Properties dialog box, click your mouse on the OK button.

282   CONTROLLING YOUR MODEM'S SPEAKER VOLUME

When you use your modem to connect to another computer, you will usually first hear your phone's dialing tone, your modem dial, and then the two computers exchange a series of tones. If you are working with a computer in an office space, your modem's noises may begin to irritate employees who are working nearby.

In such cases, you use the Modems Properties dialog box to turn down your modem's built-in speaker. Likewise, if your modem is having trouble connecting to a remote computer, there may be times when you want to listen to the tones, so that you can ensure your modem is successfully completing the call. In that case, you may want to turn up your modem's speaker volume. To control your modem's speaker volume, perform these steps:

1. Select the Start menu Settings option. Windows 98, in turn, will display the Settings submenu.

2. Within the Settings submenu, select the Control Panel option. Windows 98 will open the Control Panel window.

3. Within the Control Panel window, click your mouse on the Modems icon. Windows 98, in turn, will display the Modems Properties dialog box.

4. Within the Modems Properties dialog box, click your mouse on the Properties button. Windows 98, in turn, will display the Modems Properties dialog box General sheet.

5. Within the General sheet, use your mouse to drag the Speaker Volume slider higher or lower as your needs require and then click your mouse on the OK button.

6. Within the Modems Properties dialog box, click your mouse on OK.

283   UNDERSTANDING THE MODEM PROPERTIES MAXIMUM SPEED SETTING

If you examine the Modems Properties dialog box General sheet, shown in Figure 283, you will find that the sheet provides a Maximum speed field.

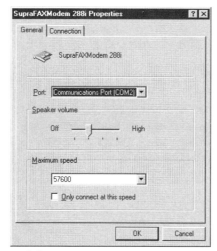

Figure 283 *The Modem Properties dialog box General sheet.*

Most users can ignore Maximum speed setting for their modem. In short, this setting refers to the maximum speed at which the modem can transmit and receive data in an ideal world (such as a direct connection between two modems that did not use standard telephone lines). Usually, the Maximum speed setting contains a value that is faster than your modem speed. Unless you are having problems, ignore this setting's value.

If, however, you have a fast modem, such as a 56Kb modem, and you are having trouble connecting to a slower 14.4Kb modem, for example, you can use this setting to slow down your modem. Usually, the faster modem will determine the speed of the slower modem automatically but, if, for some reason, your modem cannot adjust to the slower speed on its own, you may be able to use the Maximum speed setting to force your modem to slow down.

284 **CUSTOMIZING YOUR MODEM'S DATA CONNECTION SETTINGS**

When you use a modem to communicate with another PC, your modem's hardware and your data-communication software do a lot of work behind the scenes. To begin, both modems must agree on the speed at which they will communicate. If one modem sends information faster than the second modem can receive it, errors will occur and the modems will lose information. Next, the modems must agree on how much data they will send at one time and whether or not they will include extra data (called a parity bit) to help the modems detect transmission errors. These values, upon which the modems must agree, are connection settings. Most users never have to worry about assigning values to the connection settings. Instead, the default settings will work just fine. However, if for some reason, you must change your settings in order to communicate with a specific PC, perform these steps:

1. Select the Start menu Settings option. Windows 98, in turn, will display the Settings submenu.

2. Within the Settings submenu, select the Control Panel option. Windows 98 will open the Control Panel window.

3. Within the Control Panel window, click your mouse on the Modems icon. Windows 98, in turn, will display the Modems Properties dialog box.

4. Within the Modems Properties dialog box, click your mouse on the Properties button. Windows 98, in turn, will display the Modems Properties dialog box General sheet.

5. Within the Modems Properties dialog box, click your mouse on the Connection tab. Windows 98, in turn, will display the Modems Properties dialog box Connection sheet, as shown in Figure 284.

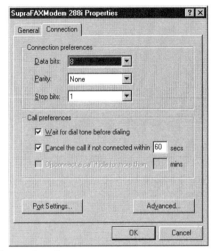

Figure 284 *The Modems Properties dialog box Connection sheet.*

6. Within the Connection sheet, use the Data bits, Parity, and Stop bits pull-down lists to assign the settings you need and then click your mouse on OK.

7. Within the Modems Properties dialog box, click your mouse on OK.

285 **SETTING YOUR MODEM'S CALL PREFERENCE SETTINGS**

When you place a modem call, your modem, much like a phone, will usually wait for a dial tone and then dial its number. If you are traveling in another country, however, a dial tone may be different than the one your modem expects. As a result, if your modem waits to hear a dial tone before dialing, it may never place your call. In addition, when you place a modem call, most modems will wait up to 60 seconds for a modem at the other end of the call to answer. If another modem does not answer the call within the 60-second window, most modems will hang up, terminating the call. Depending from where you are calling and the computer you are calling, there may be times when 60 seconds simply is not long enough for the receiving modem to answer the call. Lastly, there may be times when you simply forget to end your modem call. Rather than let your modem stay connected indefinitely (which might result in your running up a very large long-distance phone bill), you can direct Windows 98 to disconnect your modem when your modem has not sent or received any data over a specific time interval, such as 15 minutes. To control your modem's call preferences, perform these steps:

1. Select the Start menu Settings option. Windows 98, in turn, will display the Settings submenu.

2. Within the Settings submenu, select the Control Panel option. Windows 98 will open the Control Panel window.

3. Within the Control Panel window, click your mouse on the Modems icon. Windows 98, in turn, will display the Modems Properties dialog box.

4. Within the Modems Properties dialog box, click your mouse on the Properties button. Windows 98, in turn, will display the Modems Properties dialog box General sheet.

5. Within the Modems Properties dialog box, click your mouse on the Connection tab. Windows 98, in turn, will display the Modems Properties dialog box Connection sheet, as shown in Figure 285.

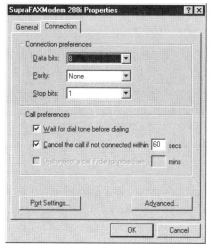

Figure 285 *The Modems Properties dialog box Connection sheet.*

6. Within the Connection sheet, use the Call Preferences fields to customize your modem settings and then click your mouse on the OK button to put your changes into effect.

7. Within the Modems Properties dialog box, click your mouse on OK.

286   CONFIGURING YOUR MODEM'S UART SETTINGS FOR MAXIMUM PERFORMANCE

To communicate over standard telephone lines, the sending modem converts the computer's digital signals into analog signals which it then transmits across the wires. The receiving modem, on the other hand, converts the incoming analog signals back into digital signals its PC can process. At the heart of this analog/digital conversion is a chip on the modem called the UART (the Universal Asynchronous Receiver Transmitter). As you shop for a modem, look for one that comes with a 16550 or 16650 UART chip. These two UART chips are significantly faster than their predecessors and will improve your modem's speed.

Although most users will never know that their modem has a UART, much less want to configure the UART, there are times when you can make a few simple adjustments to the UART settings that will further improve your modem's performance. To view your current UART settings, perform these steps:

1. Select the Start menu Settings option. Windows 98, in turn, will display the Settings submenu.

2. Within the Settings submenu, select the Control Panel option. Windows 98 will open the Control Panel window.

3. Within the Control Panel window, click your mouse on the Modems icon. Windows 98, in turn, will display the Modems Properties dialog box.

4. Within the Modems Properties dialog box, click your mouse on the Properties button. Windows 98, in turn, will display the Modems Properties dialog box General sheet.

5. Within the Modems Properties dialog box, click your mouse on the Connection tab. Windows 98, in turn, will display the Modems Properties dialog box Connection sheet.

6. Within the Connection sheet, click your mouse on the Port Settings button. Windows 98, in turn, will display the Advanced Port Settings dialog box, as shown in Figure 286.

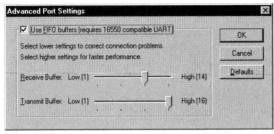

Figure 286 *The Windows 98 Advanced Port Settings dialog box.*

Within the Advanced Port Settings dialog box, you can customize the number of buffers Windows 98 uses to hold the information the UART is to transmit or receive. In general, by increasing the number of the buffers, you will improve your modem performance. Like all system-tuning operations, however, you may need to experiment a little to determine the best setting for your system.

287 TAKING ADVANTAGE OF YOUR MODEM'S ADVANCED SETTINGS

When two PCs use modems to communicate, the modems, as well as your data-communication software, perform many operations behind the scenes. Although most users will never have to control the low-level modem operations, there may be times when you have difficulty connecting to a specific computer (a specific computer that you are trying to dial into, as opposed to a site on the Internet). In such cases, you may need to enable or disable specific data-communication operations by performing these steps:

1. Select the Start menu Settings option. Windows 98, in turn, will display the Settings submenu.

2. Within the Settings submenu, select the Control Panel option. Windows 98 will open the Control Panel window.

3. Within the Control Panel window, click your mouse on the Modems icon. Windows 98, in turn, will display the Modems Properties dialog box.

4. Within the Modems Properties dialog box, click your mouse on the Properties button. Windows 98, in turn, will display the Modems Properties dialog box General sheet.

5. Within the Modems Properties dialog box, click your mouse on the Connection tab. Windows 98, in turn, will display the Modems Properties dialog box Connection sheet.

6. Within the Connection sheet, click your mouse on the Advanced button. Windows 98, in turn, will display the Advanced Connections Settings dialog box as shown in Figure 287.

7. Within the Advanced Connections Settings dialog box, enable or disable the settings that you require and then click your mouse on the OK button to put your changes into effect.

8. Within the Modems Properties dialog box, click your mouse on the OK button.

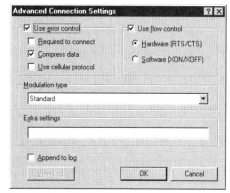

Figure 287 *The Windows 98 Advanced Connections Settings dialog box.*

288 USING THE MODEMLOG.TXT FILE TO TROUBLE SHOOT MODEM OPERATIONS

If Windows 98 has trouble working with your modem, you can request that Windows 98 log all modem operations within a file named *MODEMLOG.TXT* that Windows 98 stores within your Windows folder. Later, using an editor such as the Notepad accessory, you can open the log file and use its contents to troubleshoot your modem connections. To direct Windows 98 to create the *MODEMLOG.TXT* log file, perform these steps:

1.   Click your mouse on the Start menu Settings option and then choose the Control Panel option. Windows 98, in turn, will open the Control Panel window.

2.   Within the Control Panel window, double click your mouse on the Modems icon. Windows 98 will open the Modem Properties dialog box.

3.   Within the Modems Properties dialog box, click your mouse on the entry that corresponds to your modem and then click your mouse on the Properties button. Windows 98, in turn, will display a Properties dialog box specific to your modem. Click your mouse on the Connection tab. Windows 98, in turn, will display the Connection sheet.

4.   Within the Connection sheet, click your mouse on the Advanced button. Windows 98, in turn, will display the Advanced Connection Settings dialog box, as shown in Figure 288.

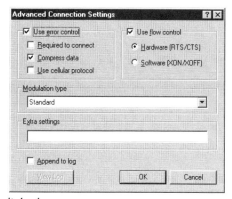

Figure 288 *The Advanced Connection Settings dialog box.*

5. Within the Advanced Connection Settings dialog box, click your mouse on the Record a log checkbox, placing a check mark within the box and then click your mouse on the OK button.

6. Within your Modems Properties dialog box, click your mouse on the OK button to put your changes into effect. If the general Modems Properties dialog box is open, click your mouse on the Close button to close it.

7. Close the Control Panel window.

289 **USING THE WINDOWS 98 ISDN WIZARD TO CONFIGURE AN ISDN MODEM CONNECTION**

To reduce the amount of time they spend waiting for their e-mail or information from sites across the Web to download, many users are turning to ISDN (integrated services digital network) modems and Internet connections. Although ISDN connections are more expensive than traditional phone connections and they require a special modem, users find that the speed and reliability of ISDN makes it well worth the cost. To help you get started with an ISDN modem, Windows 98 provides an ISDN Configuration Wizard. To start the ISDN Configuration Wizard, perform these steps:

1. Click your mouse on the Start menu Programs option and choose Accessories. Windows 98, in turn, will cascade the Accessories submenu.

2. Within the Accessories submenu, click your mouse on the Communications option and then choose ISDN Configuration Wizard. Windows 98 will start the Wizard. Perform each step within the Wizard's dialog box and then click your mouse on the Next button to continue.

290 **USING MULTILINK MODEM CONNECTIONS FOR FAST TELECOMMUNICATIONS**

In addition to using ISDN modems, as discussed in Tip 289, to improve their telecommunications speeds, some users are installing multiple modems within their systems which they then connect simultaneously to their Internet provider over separate phone lines. To use two or more modems in this way, you must first have multiple modems installed in your PC. Next, you must have a separate phone line for each modem. Then, your Internet service provider (your ISP) must support multilink connections. And, finally, you must direct Windows 98 to take advantage of your multilink capabilities by performing these steps:

1. Within your Desktop, click your mouse on the My Computer icon. Windows 98, in turn, will open the My Computer window.

2. Within the My Computer window, double-click your mouse on the Dial-Up Networking icon. Windows 98, in turn, will open the Dial-Up Networking window.

3. Within the Dial-Up Networking window, right-click your mouse on the icon that corresponds to the connection you want to configure. Windows 98 will display a small pop-up menu. Within the pop-up menu, click your mouse on the Properties option. Windows 98 will display

the connection's Properties dialog box.

4. Within the Properties dialog box, click your mouse on the Multilink tab. Windows 98 will display the Multilink sheet, as shown in Figure 290.1.

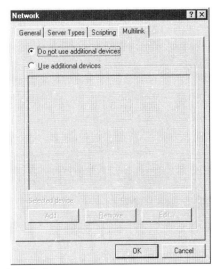

Figure 290.1 *A dial-up network connection's Multilink sheet.*

5. Within the Multilink sheet, click your mouse on the Use additional devices radio button.

6. Within the Multilink sheet, click your mouse on the Add button to specify one of the devices you want the connection to use. Windows 98, in turn, will display the Edit Extra Device dialog box, as shown in Figure 290.2.

Figure 290.2 *The Edit Extra Device dialog box.*

7. Within the Edit Extra Device dialog box, click your mouse on the Device name pull-down list and select the device you want to add. Then, click your mouse on the OK button. (Your ISP may want you to specify a specific phone number for the device as well.)

8. Repeat Steps 6 and 7 to add each modem you want your connection to use. Then, within the Properties dialog box, click your mouse on the OK button to put your changes into effect.

291 CUSTOMIZING YOUR MOUSE WITHIN WINDOWS 98

Within Windows 98, almost every operation you perform will require your use of the mouse. Over time, all Windows users become pretty proficient with the mouse. However, for many new users, simply aiming the mouse pointer can become a frustrating experience. To help users feel comfortable with their mouse, Windows 98 lets users configure several mouse settings. To start, Windows 98 lets left-handed users swap the mouse-select button. In addition, Windows 98 lets you customize several settings that speed up or slow down the mouse. To customize your mouse settings within Windows 98, perform these steps:

1. Select the Start menu Settings option. Windows 98, in turn, will display the Settings submenu.
2. Within the Settings submenu, select the Control Panel option. Windows 98 will open the Control Panel window.
3. Within the Control Panel window, click your mouse on the Mouse icon. Windows 98, in turn, will display the Mouse Properties dialog box.

Several of the Tips that follow discuss how you use the Mouse Properties dialog box to customize your mouse settings.

292 *SWAPPING THE MOUSE-SELECT BUTTONS FOR LEFT-HANDED USERS*

Throughout this book, Tips will tell you to "click your mouse-select button" or "to right-click your mouse." By default, Windows 98 configures the PC mouse for a right-handed user and treats the left-mouse button as its mouse-select button.

If you are left handed, you can swap the mouse buttons to make common operations easier. To swap your mouse buttons, perform these steps:

1. Select the Start menu Settings option. Windows 98, in turn, will display the Settings submenu.
2. Within the Settings submenu, select the Control Panel option. Windows 98 will open the Control Panel window.
3. Within the Control Panel window, click your mouse on the Mouse icon. Windows 98, in turn, will display the Mouse Properties dialog box.
4. Within the Mouse Properties dialog box Button tab, click your mouse on the Right-handed or Left-handed buttons to choose the configuration you desire.
5. Within the Mouse Properties dialog box, click your mouse on the OK button to put your changes into effect.

293 *SPEEDING UP OR SLOWING DOWN THE MOUSE DOUBLE-CLICK SPEED*

Within Windows 98, you use mouse double-click operations to initiate a variety of operations. Depending on your mouse settings, you may find that Windows 98 does not respond to your mouse clicks or that you simply cannot double click your mouse fast enough for Windows 98 to recognize your double-click operation. Luckily, Windows 98 lets you fine-tune its double-click speed. To set your mouse double-click speed, perform these steps:

1. Select the Start menu Settings option. Windows 98, in turn, will display the Settings submenu.

2. Within the Settings submenu, select the Control Panel option. Windows 98 will open the Control Panel window.

3. Within the Control Panel window, click your mouse on the Mouse icon. Windows 98, in turn, will display the Mouse Properties dialog box.

4. Within the Mouse Properties dialog box Button tab, use your mouse to drag the Double-click speed slider to the left or to the right to slow down or speed up the mouse's double-click responsiveness.

5. Within the Buttons sheet, double click your mouse on the jack-in-the-box that appears within the dialog box Test area. If Windows 98 recognizes your double-click operation, Windows 98 will pop the jack-in-the-box, as shown in Figure 293.

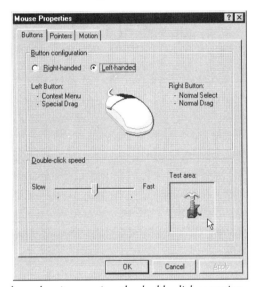

Figure 293 *Windows 98 pops the jack-in-the-box when it recognizes the double-click operation.*

6. After you select the double-click speed you desire, click your mouse on the OK button to put your change into effect.

294 CUSTOMIZING THE WINDOWS 98 MOUSE POINTER

*A*s you perform different operations, Windows 98 will change your mouse pointer to match your context. For example, if you must wait for Windows 98 to complete an operation, Windows 98 will change your mouse pointer into an hourglass. Likewise, if you click your mouse on the "What's this" question mark that starts Windows 98 context-sensitive help, Windows 98 will add a question mark to your mouse pointer, as shown in Figure 294.1.

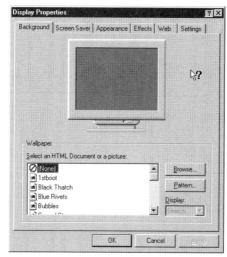

Figure 294.1 *Windows 98 changes your mouse pointer to match the context of your current operation.*

Like many system settings, Windows 98 lets you customize its mouse pointer use. To change the mouse pointer that Windows 98 uses during a specific context, perform these steps:

1. Select the Start menu Settings option. Windows 98, in turn, will display the Settings submenu.
2. Within the Settings submenu, select the Control Panel option. Windows 98 will open the Control Panel window.
3. Within the Control Panel window, click your mouse on the Mouse icon. Windows 98, in turn, will display the Mouse Properties dialog box.
4. Within the Mouse Properties dialog box, click your mouse on the Pointers tab. Windows 98, in turn, will display the Pointers sheet, as shown in Figure 294.2.

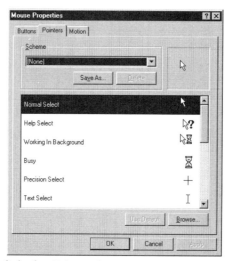

Figure 294 *The Windows 98 Mouse Properties dialog box Pointers sheet.*

5. Within the Pointers sheet, use the scroll bar to locate the Event for which you want to change the mouse pointer, and then click your mouse on the event. Windows 98, in turn, will highlight the event.
6. Within the Properties sheet, click your mouse on the Browse button. Windows 98, in turn, will open a Browse dialog box, which you can use to search your disk for files that contain mouse pointers (files with the ANI extension have animated cursors, whereas files with the CUR

extension contain a traditional mouse cursor). As you highlight files within the Browse dialog box, Windows 98 will preview, within the dialog box, the cursor that the file contains.

7. After you assign mouse pointers to the events you desire, click your mouse on the OK button to put your changes into effect.

295   **USING A MOUSE POINTER SCHEME**

In Tip 294, you learned how to assign a specific mouse pointer to an event within Windows 98. If you assign cursors to a variety of events, you may want to save your settings to a mouse pointer scheme. To save your mouse pointer assignments to a scheme, perform these steps:

1. Within the Mouse Properties dialog box Pointers sheet, assign the mouse pointers to the events you desire.

2. Within the Pointers sheet, click your mouse on the Save As button. Windows 98, in turn, will display the Save Scheme dialog box, as shown in Figure 295.

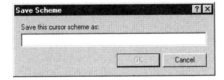

Figure 295 *The Save Scheme dialog box.*

3. Within the Save Scheme dialog box, type in a name that describes your scheme settings and click your mouse on the OK button.

In addition to letting you define your own pointer schemes, Windows 98 predefines several mouse pointer schemes you can apply to your system. To select an existing mouse pointer scheme, perform these steps:

1. Within the Pointers sheet, click your mouse on the Scheme pull-down list. Windows 98, in turn, will display a list of the available schemes.

2. Within the Scheme pull-down list, click your mouse on the Scheme you desire.

3. Within the Properties sheet, click your mouse on the OK button to put your change into effect.

Note: *For more information on animated cursors and icons, refer to Tip 226 which discusses Windows 98 Desktop themes.*

296   **SPEEDING UP OR SLOWING DOWN THE MOUSE POINTER'S MOTION**

When users first learn to use the mouse, they often have trouble aiming the mouse pointers on small objects. In such cases, you can direct Windows 98 to slow down the mouse pointer's motion, which will make it easier for the user to work with the mouse. Likewise, if you are a Windows 98 power user, you may want to speed up the mouse pointer's motion. To change your mouse pointer's speed, perform these steps:

1. Select the Start menu Settings option. Windows 98, in turn, will display the Settings submenu.
2. Within the Settings submenu, select the Control Panel option. Windows 98 will open the Control Panel window.
3. Within the Control Panel window, click your mouse on the Mouse icon. Windows 98, in turn, will display the Mouse Properties dialog box.
4. Within the Mouse Properties dialog box, click your mouse on the Motion tab. Windows 98, in turn, will display the Motion sheet, as shown in Figure 296.

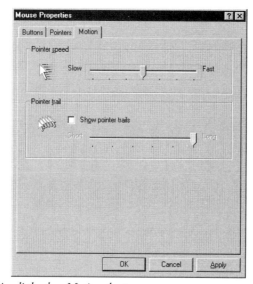

Figure 296 *The Windows 98 Mouse Properties dialog box Motion sheet.*

5. Within the Motion sheet, use your mouse to drag the Pointer speed slider to the right or to the left to speed up or slow down the mouse pointer's responsiveness.
6. After you find the motion speed you desire, click your mouse on the OK button.

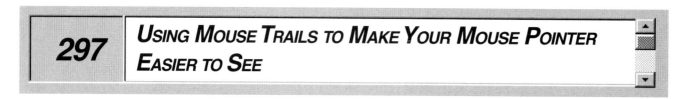

297 USING MOUSE TRAILS TO MAKE YOUR MOUSE POINTER EASIER TO SEE

If you run Windows 98 on a notebook PC, there may be times when you find that your mouse pointer is simply hard to see. In such cases, you may want to direct Windows 98 to display mouse trails, which are a series of mouse pointer icons that chase your mouse pointer, as shown in Figure 297.

To turn the display of mouse trails on or off, perform these steps:

1. Select the Start menu Settings option. Windows 98, in turn, will display the Settings submenu.
2. Within the Settings submenu, select the Control Panel option. Windows 98 will open the Control Panel window.

3. Within the Control Panel window, click your mouse on the Mouse icon. Windows 98, in turn, will display the Mouse Properties dialog box.

4. Within the Mouse Properties dialog box, click your mouse on the Motion tab. Windows 98, in turn, will display the Motion sheet.

5. Within the Motion sheet, click your mouse within the Show pointer trails checkbox, placing a check mark within the box to display mouse trails. To disable the mouse-trail display, click your mouse on the checkbox to remove the check mark.

6. If you enable the mouse-trail display, use your mouse to drag the pointer trail slider to the left or to the right to increase or decrease the length of the pointer trail.

7. Within the Motion sheet, click your mouse on the OK button to put your changes into effect.

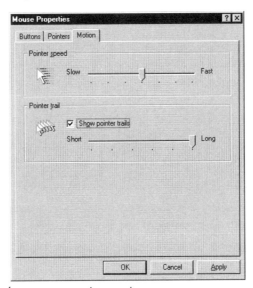

Figure 297 Windows 98 mouse trails may make your mouse pointer easier to see.

298 USING THE WINDOWS 98 CONTROL PANEL TO CUSTOMIZE MULTIMEDIA SETTINGS

Multimedia is the use of text, pictures, sounds, and even video to present information. A multimedia PC is a PC that can record and playback sound, playback video files, and play audio CDs. Windows 98 provides many features that specifically support multimedia. As you have learned, the Windows 98 CD Player accessory program lets you playback audio CDs on your PC. Using Windows 98 autoplay support, you can simply insert an audio CD into your CD-ROM drive and Windows 98 will recognize the audio CD format and start playing the CD's track one. Likewise, using Windows 98 autoplay features, many multimedia programs will automatically run when you insert the CD.

In addition, Windows 98 fully supports digital video discs (DVDs) which store much more information than a traditional CD-ROM. A DVD disc, for example, is capable of storing an entire movie. To play a DVD disc, your PC must have a DVD drive. Also, Windows 98 supports *Polymessaging MIDI*, a technology that lets programs play MIDI sounds without sacrificing CPU performance. Several of the Tips this book presents examine Windows 98 multimedia features in detail.

Almost every PC sold today includes a CD-ROM and sound card—the standard multimedia hardware devices. Just as Windows 98 lets you customize your other hardware devices, Windows 98 also lets you customize your system's audio, video, MIDI, and audio CD settings. Several of the Tips that follow discuss specific multimedia device settings. To configure your multimedia devices, perform these steps:

1. Click your mouse on the Start button. Windows 98, in turn, will display the Start menu.

2. Within the Start menu, click your mouse on the Settings option and then click your mouse on the Control Panel option. Windows 98, in turn, will open the Control Panel window.

3. Within the Control Panel, double click your mouse on the Multimedia icon. Windows 98, in turn, will display the Multimedia Properties dialog box, as shown in Figure 298.

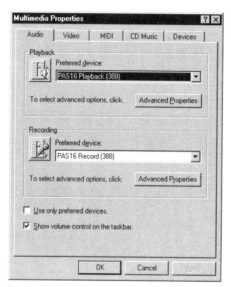

Figure 298 *The Multimedia Properties dialog box.*

4. Within the Multimedia Properties dialog box, click your mouse on the tab that corresponds to the multimedia setting you want to configure.

299 CONTROLLING YOUR PC'S SPEAKER VOLUME

As you work, there will be times when you want to turn up or turn down your PC's speaker volume. For example, if you are listening to an audio CD, you may want to turn up your speaker's volume. Likewise, if you are going to connect to the Internet using your PC's modem, you may want to turn down your speaker volume. Windows 98 provides several ways you can control your speaker volume. In addition, many notebook PCs have small volume controls that you can use to adjust the speaker volume. To start, within your Taskbar, you should see a small speaker icon, as shown in Figure 299.1.

Figure 299.1 *The Taskbar speaker icon.*

Click your mouse on the speaker icon. Windows 98, in turn, will display a volume slider similar to that shown in Figure 299.2.

Figure 299.2 *The Windows 98 speaker volume slider.*

Using your mouse, drag the speaker volume slider up to increase your speaker volume or move the slider down to decrease your speaker volume. If you double-click your mouse on the Taskbar speaker icon, Windows 98 will open the Volume Control dialog box, as shown in Figure 299.3.

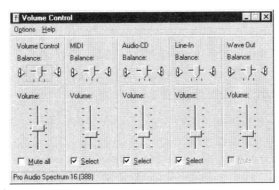

Figure 299.3 *The Volume Control dialog box.*

Within the Volume Control dialog box, you can use your mouse to drag the volume control slider up or down to increase or decrease the speaker volume. Also, within the Multimedia Properties dialog box, you can click your mouse on the small icon that appears within the Playback settings to display the Volume Control dialog box.

300 CONTROLLING YOUR SPEAKER VOLUME USING THE SOUND CARD'S BUILT-IN VOLUME CONTROL

In Tip 299, you learned how to use the Taskbar Speaker icon to control your PC's speaker volume. If, as you adjust your speaker volume, you find that you cannot hear a difference, you may first need to adjust your sound card's built-in volume control. If you are using a desktop PC, you will usually find the sound card's built-in volume control at the back on your PC, near the sound card ports into which you plug your speaker cables. If you are using a notebook PC, you will usually find the PC's volume control on the front or side of your system. Use your PC's built-in volume-control knob to set your computer's volume to the level you desire. Later, you can use the Windows 98 Volume Control to fine-tune the volume.

301 | **CONTROLLING YOUR SOUND CARD'S RECORDING LEVEL**

In Tip 551, you will learn how to use the Windows 98 Sound Recorder program to record, playback, and edit sound files. When you record your own sounds, you may need to adjust the volume at which your system records sounds to ensure that your sounds play back at a reasonable volume on your own and other systems.

To adjust the volume at which your system records sounds, perform these steps:

1. Click your mouse on the Start button. Windows 98, in turn, will display the Start menu.

2. Within the Start menu, click your mouse on the Settings option and then click your mouse on the Control Panel option. Windows 98, in turn, will open the Control Panel window.

3. Within the Control Panel, double click your mouse on the Multimedia icon. Windows 98, in turn, will display the Multimedia Properties dialog box.

4. Within the Multimedia Properties dialog box, click your mouse on the Audio tab. Windows 98, in turn, will display the Audio sheet.

5. Within the Audio sheet, click your mouse on the small icon that appears within the Recording section. Windows 98, in turn, will display the Recording Control dialog box, as shown in Figure 301.

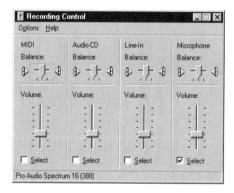

Figure 301 *The Recording Control dialog box.*

6. Within the Recording Control dialog box, use your mouse to slide the volume control to increase or decrease your system's recording volume.

302 | **CUSTOMIZING YOUR PC'S AUDIO SETTINGS**

In Tip 298, you learned how to use the Multimedia Properties dialog box Audio sheet to control the volume at which your system records or plays back an audio file. In addition to letting you control the volume settings, the Audio sheet contains Advanced Properties buttons that let you control the audio quality. If, for example, you click your mouse on the Playback field Advanced Properties button, Windows 98 will display the Advanced Audio Properties dialog box Speakers sheet, as shown in Figure 302.1.

Figure 302.1 *The Advanced Audio Properties dialog box Speakers sheet.*

Within the dialog box, you can use the Speaker Setup pull-down list to select the type of speakers that best matches your PC configuration. Next, if you click your mouse on the Performance tab, Windows 98 will display the Performance sheet, as shown in Figure 302.2.

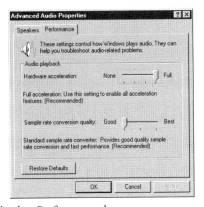

Figure 302.2 *The Advanced Audio Properties dialog box Performance sheet.*

Within the Performance sheet, you can control how Windows 98 plays back audio files. Usually, you will want to select Full hardware acceleration and the Best sampling rate. However, if you experience errors when Windows 98 plays back audio, you can use this sheet to change the settings and to troubleshoot your error. In a similar way, if you click your mouse on the Recording field Advanced Properties button, Windows 98 will display the Performance sheet, as shown in Figure 302.3

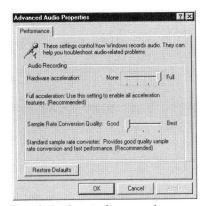

Figure 302.3 *The Recording field's Advanced Properties dialog box Performance sheet.*

Within the Performance sheet, you can control how Windows 98 records audio. Usually, you will want to use Full hardware acceleration. The sample rate quality lets you select between quality levels that users may best associate with CD quality (the best), radio quality, and telephone quality (the worst) sampling rates.

---

303 | **USING THE EXPLORER TO DISPLAY AUDIO FILE DETAILS**

Audio files may differ in quality based on whether they use 8-bit or 16-bit quality, a high or low sampling rate, and whether they are stereo or monotone files. Using the Explorer, you can display specifics about an audio file, as shown in Figure 303.1.

Figure 303.1 *Using the Explorer to display specifics about an audio file.*

To display specifics about an audio file, perform these steps:

1. Within the Explorer, right-click your mouse on the audio file you desire. Windows 98, in turn, will display a pop-up menu.

2. Within the pop-up menu, click your mouse on the Properties option. Windows 98 will display the audio file's Properties dialog box General sheet.

3. Within the Properties dialog box, click your mouse on the Details tab. Windows 98, in turn, will display the Details sheet which contains specifics about the audio file.

4. If you want to preview (hear) the current audio file, click your mouse on the Preview tab. Windows 98 will display the Preview sheet, as shown in Figure 303.2.

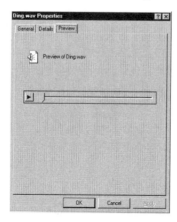

Figure 303.2 *Previewing an audio file.*

5. Within the Preview sheet, click your mouse on the Play button.

304   CUSTOMIZING YOUR SYSTEM'S VIDEO PLAYBACK WINDOW

As you have learned, Windows 98 stores the sound that you record within WAV files. In a similar way, Windows 98 stores video within AVI files. In Tip 546, you will learn how to play back video files using the Windows 98 Media Player. As you search the Internet, you can find a wide variety of video files which you can download and then play on your system. When you playback a video within Windows 98, your PC's speed and video-card type determine how large a window your system can use to display the video. (Also, if you are playing the video from a CD-ROM, your CD-ROM drive's speed will also influence your system's ability to display video.) In general, as you increase the window size, the video's appearance will become choppier. To control the size that the Media Player uses to play back a video, perform these steps:

1. Click your mouse on the Start button. Windows 98, in turn, will display the Start menu.

2. Within the Start menu, click your mouse on the Settings option and then click your mouse on the Control Panel option. Windows 98, in turn, will open the Control Panel window.

3. Within the Control Panel, double-click your mouse on the Multimedia icon. Windows 98, in turn, will display the Multimedia Properties dialog box.

4. Within the Multimedia Properties dialog box, click your mouse on the Video tab. Windows 98, in turn, will display the Video sheet, as shown in Figure 304.

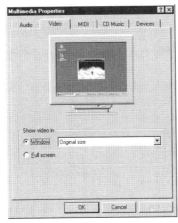

Figure 304 *The Multimedia Properties dialog box Video sheet.*

5. Within the Video sheet, click your mouse on the pull-down list and select the screen size at which you want Windows 98 to display your video.

6. Within the Video sheet, click your mouse on the OK button to save your changes.

305   USING THE WINDOWS EXPLORER TO DISPLAY A VIDEO FILE'S PROPERTIES

As you have learned, using the Windows 98 Media Player accessory, you can play back video files within a window. Depending on the video's quality, the size of one video's window or the number of frames the video displays per second may differ from a second video. Using the Windows 98 Explorer, however, you can display specifics about a video file by performing these steps:

1. Within the Explorer, right-click your mouse on the video file you desire. Windows 98, in turn, will display a pop-up menu.

2. Within the pop-up menu, click your mouse on the Properties option. Windows 98 will display the video file's Properties dialog box General sheet.

3. Within the Properties dialog box, click your mouse on the Details tab. Windows 98 will display the Details sheet which contains specifics about the video file as shown in Figure 305.1.

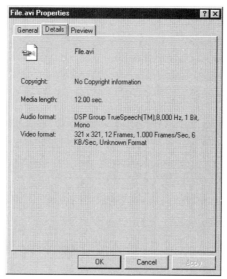

Figure 305.1 Displaying specifics about a video file.

4. If you want to preview the video file, click your mouse on the Preview tab. Windows 98 will display the Preview sheet, as shown in Figure 305.2.

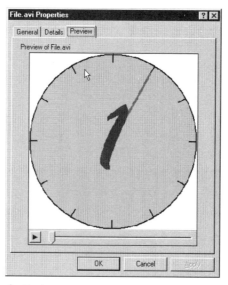

Figure 305.2 Previewing a video file within the Explorer.

5. Within the Preview sheet, click your mouse on the Play button.

306 CUSTOMIZING YOUR SOUND CARD'S *MIDI* SETTINGS

In addition to playing back audio files, most sound cards also provide MIDI (*Musical Instrument Digital Interface*) capabilities which use a music synthesizer built into the sound card to simulate various musical instruments. The best way to understand MIDI is simply to hear your sound card play back a MIDI file. To play the MIDI file *CANYON.MID* which Windows 98 provides, perform these steps:

1. Click your mouse on the Start menu Run option. Windows 98, in turn, will display the Run dialog box.

2. Within the Run dialog box Open field, type **\WINDOWS\MEDIA\CANYON.MID** and press ENTER. Windows 98, in turn, will play the MIDI sound file.

Just as Windows 98 lets you customize your system's audio settings, Windows 98 also lets you control how your sound card plays a MIDI file. Think of a MIDI file as containing a symphony of notes. Just as a conductor controls when each instrument within an orchestra plays, so too, does the MIDI file. Rather than referring to instruments, however, the MIDI file refers to 16 musical channels. Your sound card, in turn, associates each MIDI channel with a specific instrument. Using the Multimedia Properties dialog box MIDI sheet, you can select a single instrument (usually, your sound card) which Windows 98 will use to play back the MIDI sounds, or, if you have attached other MIDI devices to your PC, you can tell Windows 98 which device should play which MIDI channel. To customize the Windows 98 MIDI properties, perform these steps:

1. Click your mouse on the Start button. Windows 98, in turn, will display the Start menu.

2. Within the Start menu, click your mouse on the Settings option and then click your mouse on the Control Panel option. Windows 98, in turn, will open the Control Panel window.

3. Within the Control Panel, double click your mouse on the Multimedia icon. Windows 98, in turn, will display the Multimedia Properties dialog box.

4. Within the Multimedia Properties dialog box, click your mouse on the MIDI tab. Windows 98, in turn, will display the MIDI sheet, as shown in Figure 306.

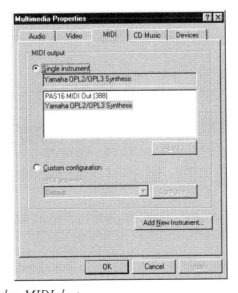

Figure 306 The Multimedia Properties dialog box MIDI sheet.

Within the MIDI sheet, most users will select the Single instrument button. However, if you have MIDI devices connected to your PC, you can use the Custom configuration button to assign a device to a specific channel.

Note: Before you can assign a device to a specific MIDI channel, you may need to add a device (the instrument) to your system by selecting the MIDI sheet Add New Instrument button.

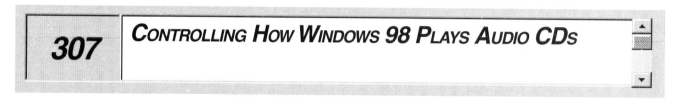

307 CONTROLLING HOW WINDOWS 98 PLAYS AUDIO CDS

As you have learned, if you place an audio CD into your PC's CD-ROM drive, Windows 98 will play the CD's contents, just as if you placed the CD into a stereo CD player. Usually, to play an audio CD, you simply need to insert the CD into your drive. Windows 98, in turn, will recognize that the CD contains audio data (as opposed to programs and data) and will start the CD Player accessory program to play the CD. If Windows 98 does not automatically play your CD, you can start the CD Player yourself, as discussed in Tip 539.

When you use your system to play back an audio CD, your system will usually play the CD through your PC's speakers. In addition, if your CD-ROM drive has a headphone jack, you can attach headphones to the jack and listen to the audio CD privately. When you use the drive's headphone jack, you can adjust the volume by performing these steps:

1. Click your mouse on the Start button. Windows 98, in turn, will display the Start menu.
2. Within the Start menu, click your mouse on the Settings option and then click your mouse on the Control Panel option. Windows 98, in turn, will open the Control Panel window.
3. Within the Control Panel, double click your mouse on the Multimedia icon. Windows 98, in turn, will display the Multimedia Properties dialog box.
4. Within the Multimedia Properties dialog box, click your mouse on the CD Music tab. Windows 98, in turn, will display the CD Music sheet, as shown in Figure 307.

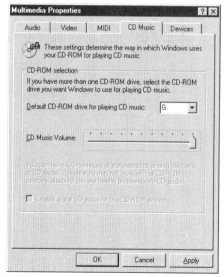

Figure 307 *The Multimedia Properties dialog box CD Music sheet.*

5. Within the CD Music sheet, use your mouse to drag the CD Music Volume slider to the left or to the right to decrease or increase the volume.

6. Within the CD Music sheet, click your mouse on the OK button to save your changes.

308 CUSTOMIZING WINDOWS 98 ADVANCED MULTIMEDIA SETTINGS

When you have trouble running a multimedia application, you may eventually have to chase down which device drivers Windows 98 is using for your multimedia hardware, and possibly update specific device settings. To view your system's multimedia device drivers, perform these steps:

1. Click your mouse on the Start button. Windows 98, in turn, will display the Start menu.

2. Within the Start menu, click your mouse on the Settings option and then click your mouse on the Control Panel option. Windows 98, in turn, will open the Control Panel window.

3. Within the Control Panel, double click your mouse on the Multimedia icon. Windows 98, in turn, will display the Multimedia Properties dialog box.

4. Within the Multimedia Properties dialog box, click your mouse on the Devices tab. Windows 98, in turn, will display the Devices sheet, as shown in Figure 308.

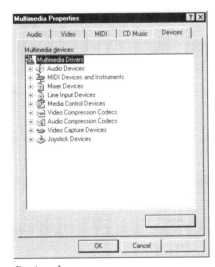

Figure 308 *The Multimedia Properties dialog box Devices sheet.*

5. Within the Devices sheet, click your mouse on the plus sign (+) that appears next to a device type to display the list of available devices.

6. Within the Device sheet, click your mouse on the device you desire and then click your mouse on the Properties button. Windows 98, in turn, will display a Properties dialog box specific to the device. Within the Properties dialog box, you can often view the current device driver information and possibly set various settings.

7. Within the Device sheet, click your mouse on the OK button to put your changes into effect.

Note: *In addition to displaying your system's multimedia hardware devices, the Devices sheet lists the video and audio codecs (compression and decompression software) that are available for use on your system. Tip 309 discusses codecs in detail.*

---

309 WINDOWS 98 USES VIDEO AND AUDIO CODECS TO COMPRESS AND LATER DECOMPRESS MULTIMEDIA DATA

Video and audio files contain huge amounts of data and thus require vast amounts of disk space. A one-minute video file, for example, can consume over 100Mb of disk space. In addition to their very large file size, video files also require that your system transfer large amounts of data from one device to another. For example, if the video file resides on your CD-ROM, your PC must transfer the video data to your video card and the audio data to your sound card before your PC can play back the video. Depending on your CD-ROM drive's speed, for example, there may be times when your drive cannot keep up with the data-transfer requirements. To reduce the amount of disk space that audio and video files consume and to reduce the amount of data the PC must transfer to play back such files, hardware and software manufacturers have developed a series of compression schemes, which they commonly call *audio* and *video codecs*. As shown in Figure 309, the Multimedia Properties dialog box Device sheet contains two general categories of codecs: Video Compression Codecs and Audio Compression Codecs.

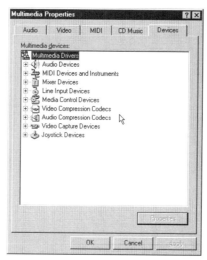

Figure 309 *The Multimedia Properties dialog box Device sheet.*

Within the Device sheet, you can click your mouse on the plus sign (+) that precedes the Codecs entries to display a list of the specific compression algorithms you can use for your video and audio files. Windows 98 assigns each audio and video codec a specific priority number (which you can change). When Windows 98 must select a codec to compress or decompress a file, Windows 98 will chose the codec with the lowest priority. To view or to change a codec's priority, click your mouse on the codec within the list and then click your mouse on the Properties button. Windows 98, in turn, will display a Properties dialog box for the codec, within which you can change the codec's priority.

---

310 UNDERSTANDING WINDOWS 98 NETWORK SUPPORT

Today, computer networks are one of the fastest growing technologies. Within a network, users connect computers to share resources, such as files, printers, and other hardware devices. The Tips that follow examine Windows 98 network operations in detail. If your PC is part of a network, you can display your network's resources using the Network Neighborhood icon. When you double-click the Network Neighborhood icon, Windows 98 will open the Network Neighborhood window, which displays all the networked computers and network workgroups your computer can access, as shown in Figure 310.

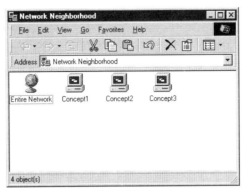

Figure 310 Exploring computers and printers within your network neighborhood.

The Network Neighborhood window is an Explorer window. As a result, within the Network Neighborhood window, you can use drag-and-drop operations to copy files from your computer to a remote network computer or to print a document on a remote printer.

311 MOVING AND COPYING FILES ACROSS A NETWORK

As you learned in Tip 310, using the Network Neighborhood, you can view PCs and printers within your network. Within a PC folder, you will find the folders the PC's user lets you share. To copy files to or from a remote PC, you can use drag-and-drop file operations using the Network Neighborhood and the Windows 98 Explorer. Specifically, to copy a file to or from a remote PC, perform these steps:

1. Open the Network Neighborhood window and then locate the remote PC and the shared folder to or from which you want to copy files.

2. Start the Explorer and open the folder on your system to which you want to, or from which you want to, copy files.

3. Within the Network Neighborhood or the Explorer window, select the files that you want to copy. Next, hold down your mouse-select button and drag the files to the destination window.

312 TO UNDERSTAND NETWORKS, START WITH KEY DEFINITIONS

Although many users make extensive use of networks on a daily basis to send and receive e-mail or to exchange files, most users still have little understanding of how networks operate. Several of the Tips that follow will discuss Windows

98 network operations in detail. Before you examine Windows 98, networking, however, it is important that you understand several key terms. After you understand a few key terms, you will better understand the steps you must perform to configure Windows 98 network settings. To start, a *network* is simply two or more computers connected (via cables) to exchange information. Users connect computers to a network to share resources, such as files and printers.

313   A NETWORK'S ORGANIZATION DEFINES HOW USERS ARRANGE PCs WITHIN THE NETWORK

As you learned in Tip 312, a network consists of two or more computers, connected to share information. The manner in which users connect the computers, in other words, the shape within which the computers are arranged, defines the network's organization (which network administrators refer to as *network topology*). In general, the topology determines how electronic signals travel between computers within the network. The two most common network topologies are the star and ring networks. Within a star network topology, network administrators connect PCs to a central *hub*, as shown in Figure 313.1. If the central hub crashes, the network will not function. However, a breakdown on one network computer will not disable the network.

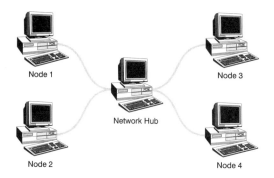

Figure 313.1 *The star topology.*

Computers in a ring network topology, in contrast, do not use a central hub. Instead, to create a ring network, network administrators connect a cable from one computer to the next, often in a circular fashion, as shown in Figure 313.2. Within a ring network topology, data passes through each network computer that resides between the sending and receiving computers. In such configurations, if one computer within the network fails, the entire network fails until the network administrator routes a cable past the broken computer.

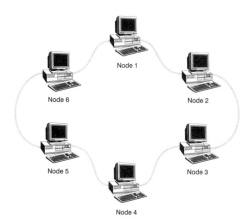

Figure 313.2 *The ring topology.*

314 YOUR NETWORK'S TECHNOLOGY DEFINES THE NETWORK'S CABLE AND CARD TYPES

Just as there are different types of PCs, modems, and even printers, there are different network types. A *network's technology* defines the type of cables and network cards a network uses to connect computers. The three most common network technologies include Ethernet, token ring, and Arcnet. If, for example, your network uses Ethernet cards and cable, you are using the Ethernet network technology. Within an Ethernet network, the most common network technology, network administrators connect PCs (and printers) using coaxial or twisted-pair cables. Ethernet cards, which have become inexpensive, offer fast networking speeds (from 10 to 100 megabits per second).

The token-ring technology, developed by IBM and Texas Instruments, is used primarily by IBM-only computer sites. The token ring architecture is the fastest of the three technologies but one of the most expensive. If you work in a small network environment (2 to 10 networked computers), the Ethernet typically offers more efficient networking speeds. Within a larger network, a token-ring topology is often more efficient than Ethernet. ArcNet is an older but expensive network technology. Unfortunately, the ArcNet technology does not work well in many PC environments, which makes ArcNet the least used network technology.

315 YOUR PC'S NETWORK CARD IS YOUR NETWORK ADAPTER

One of the first steps you must perform to configure Windows 98 network support is to install software to support your network adapter, which, is simply the network card you install within your PC into which you plug the network cable. As you shop for networks, you will encounter a variety of network cards. As you shop, you must keep your network's technology (Ethernet, token-ring, or Arcnet) in mind. You cannot connect a PC with an Ethernet card, for example, to a token-ring network. Likewise, although you may use different brands of network cards, it is a good practice to pick a brand whose card you can get working and then stick with that brand. Otherwise, you will increase the amount of work you must perform to administer the network, because you now have more network cards for which you must track and maintain device drivers as well as card settings. After you install a network adapter within your PC, you must install software specific to the card.

316 THE SOFTWARE YOU USE TO ACCESS THE NETWORK IS YOUR NETWORK INTERFACE

As you have learned, the Windows 98 operating system exists to let you run programs, use your hardware devices, such as your printer, and to help you store information within files on your disk. In a similar way, within a network, programs must run software that lets the PCs send and receive e-mail messages, exchange files, share printers, and so on. The software users run so that they can use a network defines the network's interface. Usually, users will use the name of the network-software developer, such as Novell, Banyan, or Microsoft to specify their network interface.

Windows 98 provides built-in support for a variety of network interfaces. Within your system, you will install client software that lets your PC connect to the network. Figure 316, for example, shows the Select Network Client dialog box that you will use to install client software on your system for a specific network interface.

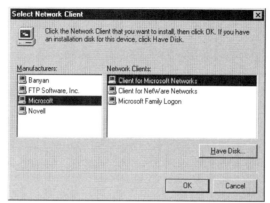

Figure 316 The Select Network Client dialog box.

317 UNDERSTANDING CLIENTS AND SERVERS WITHIN A NETWORK

With today's widespread use of networks, users often talk in terms of *client/server applications*. In general, a *server* is a computer that contains specific information (such as a company database or Web site) that client computers can access. In other words, the server provides a specific service to the client computers—and hence the server's name. When you surf the Web, for example, your browser (the client software) requests documents from a Web server. Likewise, when you receive electronic mail at your PC, you get the messages from a mail server.

Usually, network administrators select the network's fastest computer, or the computer with the most disk space, as the *file server*. Such a server computer serves files (which may be data files or programs) to *client* computers. In a similar way, the network administrator may designate another computer as the network's *print server*, to which users send their printer output. When network administrators configure a network, they often designate one computer as the file server, one (perhaps the same computer) as the print server. The rest of the network PCs become clients. Today, most networks use Windows NT as the operating system they run on their server PCs. Windows NT has higher performance and offers more security than Windows 98.

318 UNDERSTANDING PEER-TO-PEER NETWORKING

In Tip 317, you learned that within a client/server network, network administrators usually select a small number (usually one or two) of the computers as network servers while the remaining PCs function as clients. As Tip 317 discussed, network administrators usually use Windows NT as the server's operating system.

In contrast, within a *peer-to-peer network*, all computers on the network act as both clients and servers. As such, one computer on the network can access another computer's shared resources (its shared files, folders, and printers). Within peer-to-peer networks, network traffic is generally high. As a result, peer-to-peer networking typically works best in small computing environments with less than 10 systems. Tip 330 discusses Windows 98 direct-connection networking which lets two PCs create a network by exchanging information over a null-modem cable connected to each PC's serial port. Within a direct-connection network, both PCs are equals, or peers, thus forming a peer-to-peer network.

319 NETWORK PROTOCOLS ARE SIMPLY RULES PROGRAMS MUST FOLLOW TO COMMUNICATE OVER A NETWORK

As you have learned, networks let users share files and printers and exchange information using electronic mail. To perform such tasks, computers within the network must communicate with each other. For example, for one PC to copy a file from another PC across the network, the client PC must first tell the server the name of the file it wants to copy. Then, the server must send the file to the client, which requires additional communication. In general, the client will say "Ok, I'm ready, send me some data." The server, in turn, will say "Ok, here comes 500 bytes." After the client receives the data, it will tell the server "Ok, got it. Send me some more." By communicating in this fashion, the two PCs can exchange information across the network.

As you may have guessed, depending on the operation the two PCs are performing across the network, the messages they must exchange may become quite complex. As the programs exchange messages with one another, they follow a specific set of rules, or protocols.

In short, a network protocol might specify how fast the PCs exchange information or which PC goes first or second. When programmers create network software, they must follow the protocols to define their program's behavior. For example, when you surf the Web, your browser uses the hypertext transport protocol (HTTP) to request information from a Web server. Likewise, to download information from across the Web, you might use the file transport protocol (FTP). In each case, the protocol defines the rules the programs follow to communicate.

Across the Internet, most programs make extensive use of TCP/IP, the Transmission Control Protocol/Internet Protocol. Before you can use programs, such as your browser or chat program on the Internet, you must first install TCP/IP support within Windows 98. To add software support for a specific network protocol, such as TCP/IP, you will select the Protocol option from within the Select Network Component Type dialog box, shown in Figure 319, and then you will click your mouse on the Add button.

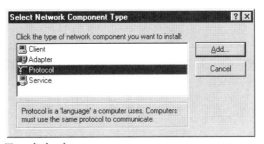

Figure 319 *The Select Network Component Type dialog box.*

---

320 | **THE NETBEUI PROTOCOL LETS WINDOWS 98 COMMUNICATE WITH WINDOWS FOR WORKGROUPS**

Within a PC network, some PCs may be running Windows NT, some Windows 98 or Windows 95, and some older PCs may be running Windows for Workgroups. To let such PCs communicate across a network, network administrators must install a myriad of network software programs. As you configure Windows 98 network settings, you may encounter the term *NetBEUI*, which stands for *Networking BIOS Extended User Interface* protocol. The NetBEUI protocol lets Windows 98 clients and servers communicate with network computers running Microsoft Windows for Workgroups, Windows NT, and Microsoft LAN Manager. For example, Figure 320 shows the Select Network Protocol dialog box. As you can see, the NetBEUI protocol appears within the list of protocols Microsoft provides.

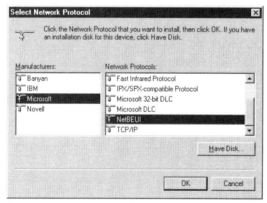

Figure 320 *The NetBEUI protocol lets Windows 98 communicate with servers running Windows for Workgroups, Windows NT, or the Microsoft LAN Manager.*

---

321 | **UNDERSTANDING NDIS AND ODI NETWORK STANDARDS**

Just as there are many different PC, modem, and printer manufacturers, there are an equally large number of companies creating network cards and writing network software. Because such cards and software must work within a network which may use other manufacturer's cards and software, network hardware and software developers must follow a set of industry standards when they create a new device or write new programs. One such standard is the Network Driver Interface Standard, or NDIS, which defines how an operating system, such as Windows 98, will interact with a network device driver (the software that lets the operating system use the network card). Because Windows 98 complies with NDIS, you can use an NDIS-compliant network card within Windows 98.

In a similar way, the Open Datalink Interface, or ODI, is a network standard developed by Novell and Apple. As you shop for network cards and software, make sure the card or software is compliant with the latest network standards. You will not select an ODI or NDIS option as you configure Windows 98 network operations. NDIS and ODI are standards your hardware and software developers follow so that Windows 98 can later interact with your network device.

322

NFS IS THE UNIX NETWORK FILE SYSTEM

As you have learned, Windows 98 uses the FAT32 file system to store files on your disk. In a similar way, the Unix operating system uses the NFS or Network File System. In general, FAT32 and NFS define how the operating systems store files on disk. Windows 98 and Unix store files differently. As a result, using the FAT32 file system, Windows 98 could not read a Unix disk. Likewise, using NFS, Unix could not read a Windows 98 disk. If you connect to a Unix computer that resides on your network or to which you dial in, you may need to install software support within Windows 98 that lets your system access files stored on an NFS disk. In most cases, your network administrator will install and configure the NFS software for you. Figure 322, for example, shows the Select Network Client software dialog box that shows FTP Software, Inc.'s NFS client.

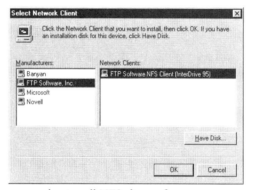

Figure 322 *To access files on a Unix disk, you may need to install NFS client software on your system.*

323

UNDERSTANDING THE UNIVERSAL NAMING CONVENTION (UNC)

As you have learned, within the Windows 98 Network Neighborhood, you can traverse network resources by clicking your mouse on PC and printer icons. Depending on the program you are running, there may be times when you must specify a network resource using its name. In such cases, the name you will use follows the Universal Naming Convention (UNC). In short, UNC defines a naming standard for networks. To start, every computer within the network must have a name, such as Production_1 or Editorial_2. Following the PC name is a volume name, which usually corresponds to a shared folder, as shown here:

> *server**volume*

Note that the UNC format precedes the PC name with two slashes (\\) and the volume name with only one slash. Examples of valid UNC names include:

> \\Production_1\Layout\ThisBook
>
> \\Production_1\Marketing\Flier
>
> \\RemotePC\SharedFiles\DataFile

324   **WINDOWS 98 DIAL-UP NETWORKING**

Today, most users are comfortable with the process of using their modem to dial into an Internet service provider or online service. In a similar way, Windows 98 lets you use your modem to dial into a remote PC. After you connect to the remote PC, Windows 98 lets you share files and folders with the remote user, run remote programs, and even print documents to a remote printer. By using Windows 98 dial-up networking, you can use your laptop, for example, to connect to your office computer from home or from the road. To create a Windows 98 dial-up network connection for a remote PC, perform these steps:

1. Within the Windows 98 Desktop, double click your mouse on the My Computer icon. Windows 98, in turn, will open the My Computer window.

2. Within the My Computer window, double click your mouse on the Dial-Up Networking folder. Windows 98, in turn, will open the Dial-Up Networking folder.

3. Within the Dial-Up Networking folder, double-click your mouse on the Make New Connection icon. Windows 98 will start the Make New Connection Wizard which will walk you through the steps you must perform to name your connection and to assign the connection's phone number.

Later, to use your connection to access the remote computer, perform these steps:

1. Within the My Computer window, double-click your mouse on the icon that corresponds to your connection. Windows 98, in turn, will display the Connect To dialog box, as shown in Figure 324.

Figure 324 *The Connect To dialog box.*

2. Within the Connect To dialog box, type in the username and password the remote computer will use to authenticate your access and then click your mouse on the Connect button to start the connection.

Note: *Before you can dial into a remote computer, the remote computer must be running dial-in server software. Tip 325 discusses the Windows 98 Dial-Up Server.*

325 USING THE WINDOWS *98* DIAL-UP SERVER

In Tip 324, you learned that using the Windows 98 dial-up networking, you can use your modem to connect to a remote computer. Usually, the remote computer to which you connect will be a server running an operating system, such as Windows NT. Depending on your needs, however, there may be times when you need other users to dial into your PC. To let a user connect to your PC, you can use the Windows 98 Dial-Up Server.

To start, you may have to install the Windows 98 Dial-Up Server software using the Control Panel Add/Remove Programs option. Next, to enable the Windows 98 Dial-Up Server, perform these steps:

1. Within the Windows 98 Desktop, double-click your mouse on the My Computer icon. Windows 98, in turn, will open the My Computer window.

2. Within the My Computer window, double-click your mouse on the Dial-Up Networking folder. Windows 98, in turn, will open the Dial-Up Networking folder.

3. Within the Dial-Up Networking folder, click your mouse on the Connections menu and choose the Dial-Up Server option. Windows 98, in turn, will display the Dial-Up Server dialog box, as shown in Figure 325.1.

Figure 325.1 *The Dial-Up Server dialog box.*

4. Within the Dial-Up Server dialog box, click your mouse on the Allow caller access radio button to let users dial into your PC.

5. If you want to force users to specify a password before they can access your system, click your mouse on the Change Password button. Windows 98, in turn, will display the Dial-Up Networking Password dialog box. Within the dialog box, type in the password you desire.

6. Within the Dial-Up Server dialog box, click your mouse on the OK button. Windows 98, in turn, will enable the Dial-Up Server which, in turn, will listen for an incoming call. In addition, Windows 98 will display a Dial-Up Server icon within the Taskbar, as shown in Figure 325.2.

Figure 325.2 *The Dial-Up Server Taskbar icon.*

326   *TURNING OFF THE WINDOWS 98 DIAL-UP SERVER*

In Tip 325, you learned how to turn on the Windows 98 Dial-Up Server. To turn off the Windows 98 Dial-Up Server later, perform these steps:

1. Within the Taskbar, locate the Dial-Up Server icon shown in Figure 326.

Figure 326 *The Dial-Up Server Taskbar icon.*

2. Double-click your mouse on the Dial-Up Server icon. Windows 98, in turn, will display the Dial-Up Server dialog box.
3. Within the Dial-Up Server dialog box, click your mouse on the No caller access radio button and then click your mouse on the OK button. Windows 98 will turn off the Dial-Up Server and will remove the Server's icon from the Taskbar.

327   *DISCONNECTING A REMOTE USER FROM A DIAL-UP SESSION*

In Tip 325, you learned how to enable the Windows 98 Dial-Up Server which lets a remote user dial into your PC and access your system's shared resources. In Tip 326, you learned how to turn off dial-up access to your system. Depending on your needs, there may be times when you want to disconnect the current remote user without turning off the dial-up server. To disconnect the current remote user, perform these steps:

1. Double click your mouse on the Dial-Up Server Taskbar icon. Windows 98, in turn, will display the Dial-Up Server dialog box.
2. Within the Dial-Up Server dialog box, click your mouse on the Disconnect User button. The Dial-Up Server, in turn, will log the current remote user off of your system.

328   *UNDERSTANDING VIRTUAL PRIVATE NETWORKING*

In Tip 324, you learned how to use the Windows 98 Dial-Up networking to dial into a remote computer. In addition to dial-up network operations, Windows 98 provides a virtual private networking, a new technology that lets you access a corporate network across the Internet. Using virtual private network operations, you can, for example, connect your notebook PC to the Internet and, from there, connect to your corporate network. Before you can use Windows 98 virtual private networking, you must use the Dial-Up Network Wizard to create two connections. The first connection is to your Internet service provider. The second is to your corporate network. Later, to connect to your corporate network, you first connect to your Internet service provider and then, while connected to the Internet, you connect to your corporate network. To support virtual private networking, your Internet service provider and your corporate network must support a "tunneling" protocol, such as the point-to-point tunneling protocol (PPTP). Follow the steps Tip 325 discusses to create a dial-up network connection to your Internet service provider. Next, perform these steps to create a connection to your corporate Internet:

1. Within the Windows 98 Desktop, double-click your mouse on the My Computer icon. Windows 98, in turn, will open the My Computer window.

2. Within the My Computer window, double-click your mouse on the Dial-Up Networking folder. Windows 98, in turn, will open the Dial-Up Networking folder.

3. Within the Dial-Up Networking folder, double-click your mouse on the Make New Connection icon. Windows 98 will start the Make New Connection Wizard.

4. Within the Make New Connection Wizard, click your mouse on the Select a device pull-down list and select the Microsoft VPN Adapter option and then click your mouse on the Next button. The Make New Connection Wizard, in turn, will display a dialog box that prompts you for your corporate network's host name (such as microsoft.com) or the network's Internet protocol (IP) address.

5. Type in your company's host-name or IP address and then click your mouse on the Next button to continue the Wizard's processing.

Note: *If the Make New Connection Wizard does not display the Microsoft VPN Adapter, you must install the VPN Adapter using the Control Panel Network option.*

329 ADDING THE MICROSOFT VIRTUAL PRIVATE NETWORK (VPN) ADAPTER

In Tip 328, you learned how to create a virtual private network connection using the Windows 98 Make New Connection Wizard. If, however, the Wizard does not display the Microsoft VPN Adapter option, you must first install network software for the adapter by performing these steps:

1. Click your mouse on the Start button. Windows 98, in turn, will display the Start menu.

2. Within the Start menu, select the Settings menu Control Panel option. Windows 98, in turn, will open the Control Panel window.

3. Within the Control Panel, double-click your mouse on the Network icon. Windows 98 will display the Network dialog box.

4. Within the Network dialog box, click your mouse on the Add button. Windows 98, in turn, will display the Select Network Component Type dialog box.

5. Within the Select Network Component Type dialog box, click your mouse on the Adapter option and then choose Add. Windows 98 will display the Select Network Adapters dialog box.

6. Within the Select Network Adapters dialog box Manufacturers list, click your mouse on the Microsoft option.

7. Within the Select Network Adapters dialog box Network Adapters list, click your mouse on the Microsoft Virtual Private Networking Adapter option and then click your mouse on OK.

8. Restart your system for your software installation to take effect.

330 **USING WINDOWS 98 DIRECT-CONNECTION NETWORKING**

If you must move files from one system to another, you could save all the files on disk, physically carry them to the second system, and load them in. However, this file-transfer process may be time-consuming, especially if the files you want to transfer are very large, do not fit on a floppy, and thus require you to use software (such as the Winzip shareware program to compress and later decompress the files). If the systems between which you want to exchange files are running Windows 98 (or Windows 95), you can use a direct-cable connection between the two systems to create a simple network. Known by some as a "poor man's network," a direct cable connection lets you quickly and easily connect two computers together using a null-modem, parallel cable, or even an infrared connection. Later Tips discuss the steps you must perform to create a direct-connection network. You will find such a network is a convenient way to exchange files between your laptop and desktop PCs.

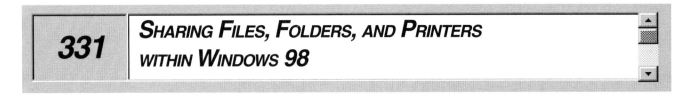

331 **SHARING FILES, FOLDERS, AND PRINTERS WITHIN WINDOWS 98**

As you have learned, computers within a network share resources, such as files, folders, and printers. Before two or more computers can use a resource, the resource owner (usually, the person who created the file or folder or to whose system a printer is attached) must declare that resource as *sharable*. If a resource, such as a file is not sharable, only the user at the computer on which the resource resides can use the resource. When you make a resource sharable, other users within your network can access the resource. Depending on your security concerns, you may let everyone within your network use a resource or only those users who know a specific password (that you specify and can change). When you use the Network Neighborhood to traverse your network, you can only view shared objects. In other words, if a user wants to protect files on his or her system, he or she can do so simply by not sharing the files (or the folders or disk upon which the files reside). If, however, a user shares an entire disk (not a good idea—the user should only share specific folders), users in the network can access all the information on the user's disk. In later Tips, you will learn how to enable file sharing within Windows 98 and how to share and protect specific folders and files.

332 **UNDERSTANDING THE WINDOWS LOGON**

As you have learned, within Windows 98, you will make extensive use of the Network dialog box, shown in Figure 332, to configure your network components. Near the middle of the Network dialog box, you will find the Primary Network Logon pull-down list.

As you can see in Figure 332, the Primary Network Logon pull-down list contains two (or possibly three, depending on your network configuration) entries. The first, Client for Microsoft Networks, will log you into Microsoft Network and Windows 98 will use it to determine your user-profile settings. If you usually use the network each time you log into your PC and you are using a Microsoft Network client, you should select the Client for Microsoft Networks option. If, on the other hand, you do not always use the network and it takes a while for the network to process your logon request, you can select the Windows Logon option. Later, when you log onto your computer, Windows 98 will use your username and password to select your user profile, but it will not log you into the network.

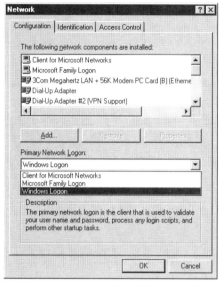

Figure 332 *The Network dialog box Primary Network Logon pull-down list.*

333 CONTROLLING NETWORK SECURITY WITHIN WINDOWS 98

Within Windows 98, you can use two basic types of Windows 98 network security: *share-level access control* and *user-level access control*. With share-level access, you specify a password for each file, folder, disk drive, or printer that you want to share. Before another network user can use your resource, the user must specify the password. For example, assume that you want your assistant to be able to access your schedule, which you keep within the file, *MySchedule.DOC*. First, you would make the file shareable, by performing the steps discussed in Tip 340. Then, you would assign a password to the file and tell that password to your assistant. Later, using his or her Network Neighborhood, your assistant can select the file. Windows 98, in turn, will display a dialog box that prompts your assistant for a password. If your assistant specifies the correct password, Windows 98 will let your assistant access the file. Otherwise, Windows 98 will not allow the user to access the file.

With user-level access, you create a list of users and workgroups who can access shared resources. Then, for each shared resource, you specify the users or workgroups you want to access the resource. If a different user tries to use the resource, Windows 98 will not allow him or her access. A workgroup is simply a list of related users. For example, assume that you have 10 programmers who you want to share a specific folder or files. Rather than continually having to type in each programmer's name, you can instead create a workgroup that contains the names, such as a workgroup named *Programmers*. Then, you would give the workgroup access to the resource. Should you hire or terminate a programmer, you can then simply add or remove the programmer's name within the workgroup. To use user-level access, your network must support it. Usually, the network will keep the access lists on a specific server. When a user tries to access a shared resource, Windows 98 will check with the server to see if the user is authorized to use the resource.

Within Windows 98, you will use the Network dialog box Access Control sheet, shown in Figure 333, to select your network security. Check with your network administrator to determine if your network supports user-level access control and, if so, which domain contains the access list.

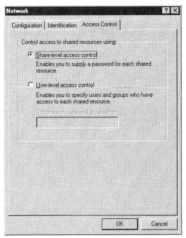

Figure 333 *The Network dialog box Access Control sheet.*

334 VIEWING YOUR SYSTEM'S CURRENT NETWORK COMPONENTS

When you install Windows 98, the Setup program should install the software you need for your network adapter (your network card). Usually, your network administrator will configure the client software you will use to connect to your network. To view your current Network components (your network adapter, the protocols Windows 98 supports, and your client software), perform these steps:

1. Click your mouse on the Start menu Settings option and choose Control Panel. Windows 98 will open the Control Panel window.

2. Within the Control Panel window, double-click your mouse on the Network icon. Windows 98, in turn, will display the Network dialog box, as shown in Figure 334.

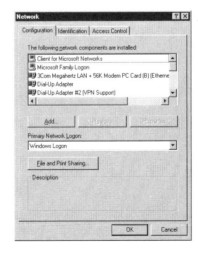

Figure 334 *The Network dialog box.*

3. Within the Network dialog box Configuration sheet, use your mouse to scroll through the network components installed on your system.

4. Within the Identification sheet, you can view your computer's name, your workgroup, and the description Windows 98 displays for your computer within other user's Network Neighborhoods.

5. Within the Access Control sheet, you can determine if your system is using share-level or user-level security.

335 ADDING A NETWORK COMPONENT WITHIN WINDOWS 98

As briefly discussed in several preceding Tips, your network components consist of the items that let you use the network, such as your network adapter (the network card), the client software you use to connect to the network, the protocols such as TCP/IP that Windows 98 supports, and services, such as a network printer that plugs into the network directly.

As you change or add network hardware or software, you must add Windows 98 support for the new component. To add a network component, perform these steps:

1. Click your mouse on the Start menu Settings option and choose Control Panel. Windows 98 will open the Control Panel window.

2. Within the Control Panel, double-click your mouse on the Network icon. Windows 98 will display the Network dialog box.

3. Within the Network dialog box, click your mouse on the Add button. Windows 98 will display the Select Network Component Type dialog box, as shown in Figure 335.

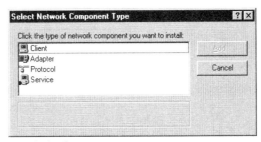

Figure 335 *The Select Network Component Type dialog box.*

4. Within the Select Network Component Type dialog box, click your mouse on the component you want to install and then click your mouse on the Add button. Windows 98, in turn, will display a dialog box within which you can select the component manufacturer and then the specific component. Do so and select OK. Windows 98 may ask you to insert your Windows 98 CD-ROM. Insert the CD and click your mouse on the OK button. Windows 98, in turn, will install the component software.

5. Finally, Windows 98 may display a dialog box telling you that you must restart your system for the change to take effect. Restart your system now.

336   REMOVING A NETWORK COMPONENT

In Tip 335, you learned how to add Windows 98 support for a network component. If, for example, you install a new network adapter (network card), you will then want to remove Windows 98 support for the old adapter to free up disk space and other resources. To remove a network component, perform these steps:

1. Click your mouse on the Start menu Settings option and choose Control Panel. Windows 98 will open the Control Panel window. Within the Control Panel, double-click your mouse on the Network icon. Windows 98 will display the Network dialog box.

2. Within the Network dialog box, click your mouse on the component that you want to remove and then click your mouse on the Remove button. Windows 98 will remove the component.

3. To close the Network dialog box, click your mouse on the OK button.

4. Finally, Windows 98 may display a dialog box telling you that you must restart your system for the change to take effect. Restart your system now.

337   CUSTOMIZING A NETWORK COMPONENT'S PROPERTIES

In Tip 334, you learned how to install Windows 98 support for a new network component. Depending on your network configuration, there may be times when your network administrator will ask you to customize a network component's settings. To change a network component's settings, perform these steps:

1. Click your mouse on the Start menu Settings option and choose Control Panel. Windows 98 will open the Control Panel window.

2. Within the Control Panel, double-click your mouse on the Network icon. Windows 98 will display the Network Properties dialog box.

3. Within the Network Properties dialog box, click your mouse on the component that you want to configure and then click your mouse on the Properties button. Windows 98, in turn, will display a dialog box you can use to specify the component's settings.

4. Within the component's Properties dialog box, change the settings you require and then click your mouse on the OK button. To close the Network dialog box, click your mouse on OK.

338   INSTALLING A NETWORK ADAPTER WITHIN WINDOWS 98

As you have learned, your network adapter is the network card you install within your PC. After you install a network card, you then install Windows 98 software to support the card. To install Windows 98 software for a network adapter, perform these steps:

1. Click your mouse on the Start menu Settings option and choose Control Panel. Windows 98 will open the Control Panel window.

2. Within the Control Panel, double-click your mouse on the Network icon. Windows 98 will display the Network dialog box.

3. Within the Network dialog box, click your mouse on the Add button. Windows 98 will display the Select Network Component Type dialog box.

4. Within the Select Network Component Type dialog box, click your mouse on the Adapter icon and then click your mouse on the Add button. Windows 98 will display the Select Network Adapters dialog box, as shown in Figure 338.

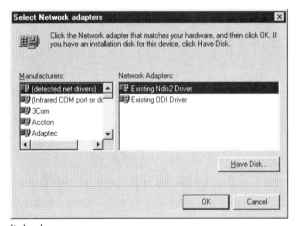

Figure 338 *The Select Network adapters dialog box.*

5. Within the Select Network Adapters dialog box Manufacturers list, select the manufacturer that created your network card.

6. Within the Network Adapters list, click your mouse on the specific adapter type. Then, click your mouse on the OK button. Windows 98, in turn, will install your adapter driver software.

Note: *If you buy a true plug-and-play network adapter card, Windows 98 will probably recognize and install the card without your intervention when you start your system and will then prompt you to insert the disk that accompanied your card so it can install the adapter's software.*

339 **IDENTIFYING YOUR PC TO THE NETWORK**

As you have learned, when you traverse the Windows 98 Network Neighborhood, Windows 98 displays each PC within your network, as shown within Figure 339.1.

Figure 339.1 *Windows 98 displays PC names within the Network Neighborhood.*

As you can see in Figure 339.1, each PC within the network has a name. Using the Network dialog box Identification sheet, shown in Figure 339.2, you can assign your PC's name.

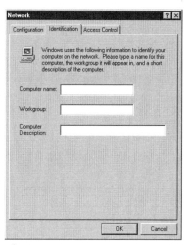

Figure 339.2 *The Network dialog box Identification sheet.*

Within the Identification sheet's Computer name, you can type in the name the Network Neighborhood displays for your computer. You should not change your PC name, however, until you check with your network administrator. Changing your PC name may cause problems with other network software. To display the Network dialog box Identification sheet, perform these steps:

1. Click your mouse on the Start menu Settings option and choose Control Panel. Windows 98 will open the Control Panel window.

2. Within the Control Panel, double-click your mouse on the Network icon. Windows 98 will display the Network dialog box.

3. Within the Network dialog box, click your mouse on the Identification tab. Windows 98 will display the Identification sheet.

340 **CONTROLLING HOW YOUR PC SHARES FILES, FOLDERS, AND PRINTERS**

In Tip 333, you learned that Windows 98 supports share-level and user-level access to shared resources within a network. You also learned that before your system can use user-level access, your network administrator must provide software to support it. To specify the security control your system uses for shared resources, perform these steps:

1. Click your mouse on the Start menu Settings option and choose Control Panel. Windows 98 will open the Control Panel window.

2. Within the Control Panel, double-click your mouse on the Network icon. Windows 98 will display the Network dialog box.

3. Within the Network dialog box, click your mouse on the Access Control tab. Windows 98 will display the Access Control sheet, as shown in Figure 340.

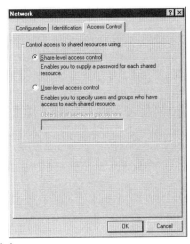

Figure 340 *The Network dialog box Access Control sheet.*

4. Within the Access Control sheet, click your mouse on the radio button that corresponds to your network's access-control type. If you are using user-level access control, type in the name of the server that contains the access-control list.

5. Click your mouse on the OK button to close the Network dialog box and to put your changes into effect.

---

341 ENABLING FILE AND PRINTER SHARING WITHIN WINDOWS 98

As you know, within a network, users share resources such as files, folders, and printers. Before you can share resources on your system, however, you must enable File and Print sharing by performing these steps:

1. Click your mouse on the Start menu Settings option and choose Control Panel. Windows 98 will open the Control Panel window.

2. Within the Control Panel, double-click your mouse on the Network icon. Windows 98 will display the Network dialog box.

3. Within the Network dialog box, click your mouse on the File and Print Sharing button. Windows 98 will display the File and Print Sharing dialog box, as shown in Figure 341.

4. Within the File and Print Sharing dialog box, click your mouse on the checkbox that corresponds to the resources on your system you want to share. Then, click your mouse on OK.

5. To close the Network dialog box and to put your changes into effect, click your mouse on the OK button.

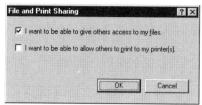

Figure 341 *The File and Print Sharing dialog box.*

342   LOGGING ONTO YOUR PC NETWORK

To use the network, you must log onto it. Usually, your network administrator will assign you a username and password. Then, you can use the Passwords Properties dialog box to change your password to one that only you know. As a rule, you should not tell other users your password. You can and should, however, tell users your username. In fact, the users must know your username to send you electronic mail. To log onto your network, simply type your username and password within the Welcome to Windows dialog box that Windows 98 displays when you first start your system.

343   PRINTING TO A SHARED PRINTER WITHIN YOUR NETWORK

In Tip 341, you learned how to enable printer and file sharing on your system. After you enable sharing, you must then tell Windows 98 which printers and files you want to share. To share a specific printer that's attached to your PC, perform these steps :

1. Click your mouse on the Start menu Settings option and choose Printers. Windows 98, in turn, will open the Printers window.

2. Within the Printers window, right-click your mouse on the icon that corresponds to the printer you want to share. Windows 98 will display a pop-up menu.

3. Within the pop-up menu, click your mouse on the Sharing option. Windows 98 will display the printer's Properties dialog box Sharing sheet, as shown in Figure 343.

4. Within the Sharing sheet, click your mouse on the Shared As option. Windows 98, in turn, will activate other dialog box fields.

5. Within the Sharing sheet Share name field, type in the printer name that other users on the network will select to use the shared printer.

6. Within the Sharing sheet Comment field, type an optional description of the printer, such as Fast Color Printer.

7. Within the Sharing sheet Password field, you can type an optional password that other users must enter before they can use the shared printer. If you do not specify a password, all users can share the printer.

8. To close the Properties dialog box, click your mouse on the OK button.

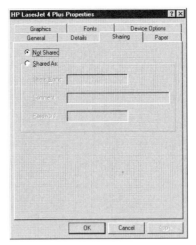

Figure 343 *The Properties dialog box Sharing sheet.*

Note: *Before a remote user can print to your shared printer, the user must have the printer driver installed on his or her system. To install the driver, the user can use the Printers window Add Printer icon to start the Add Printer Wizard. Within the Add Printer Wizard, the user must install the software for a network printer.*

344   *SHARING A FOLDER WITHIN YOUR NETWORK*

In Tip 341, you learned how to enable printer and file sharing on your system. After you enable file sharing, you must tell Windows 98 which folders you want to share. To share a specific folder, perform these steps:

1. Click your mouse on the Start menu Programs option and then choose Windows Explorer. Windows 98 will start the Explorer.

2. Within the Explorer, right-click your mouse on the folder you want to share. Windows 98 will display a pop-up menu.

3. Within the pop-up menu, click your mouse on the Sharing option. Windows 98 will display the file's Properties dialog box Sharing sheet, as shown in Figure 344.

4. Within the Sharing sheet, click your mouse on the Shared As option. Windows 98 will activate the other dialog box fields.

5. Within the Share Name field, type in a name other network users will see for this folder.

6. Within the Comment field, type in an optional comment for the folder, such as Company Budget Information.

7. Within the Access Type field, click your mouse on the radio button that corresponds to the type of access you want to grant to other users.

8. If you want to password-protect your folder, type in your passwords within the sheet's Passwords field. Windows 98 lets you specify one password for users to whom you want to grant read-only access and a different password for users to whom you want to grant full access.

9. To close the Properties dialog box, click your mouse on the OK button.

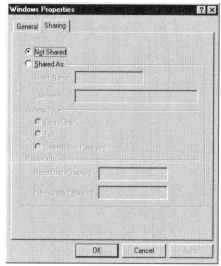

Figure 344 The Properties dialog box Sharing sheet.

345 **PAY ATTENTION TO AN UPPER-LEVEL FOLDER'S SHARING SETTINGS**

In Tip 344, you learned how to share a folder using the Windows 98 Explorer. As you enable sharing on your system, keep in mind that when you share a folder, you also automatically share its subfolders. As a rule, you should only share the lowest-level folder that you require. In that way, you will reduce the possibility of granting access to files or folders the user does not need. Windows 98, for example, will let you share your entire hard drive.

However, in doing so, you grant users access to all the folders on your disk. Rather than granting access to a number of files, you should limit sharing to specific files and then use a password to limit users who can access the folder to only those users with a "need to know."

346 **CHANGING THE PASSWORD FOR A SHARED FOLDER OR PRINTER**

In Tips 343 and 344, you learned how to share a printer and folder within your network. As a rule, you should change the resource's password on a regular basis to protect the resource from use by others who have learned the password or from users who are no longer authorized access. To change a printer's password, perform these steps:

1. Click your mouse on the Start menu Settings option and choose Printers. Windows 98, in turn, will open the Printers window.

2. Within the Printers window, right-click your mouse on the icon that corresponds to the printer you want to share. Windows 98 will display a pop-up menu.

3. Within the pop-up menu, click your mouse on the Sharing option. Windows 98 will display the printer's Properties dialog box Sharing sheet.

4. Within the Sharing sheet, type in the new password that you desire and then click your mouse on the OK button.

To change a folder's password, perform these steps:

1. Click your mouse on the Start menu Programs option and then choose Windows Explorer. Windows 98 will start the Explorer.

2. Within the Explorer, right-click your mouse on the folder you want to share. Windows 98 will display a pop-up menu.

3. Within the pop-up menu, click your mouse on the Sharing option. Windows 98 will display the file's Properties dialog box Sharing sheet.

4. Within the Sharing sheet, type in the password you desire and then click your mouse on the OK button.

---

347   DISABLING USER ACCESS TO A PREVIOUSLY SHARED FOLDER OR PRINTER

In Tips 343 and 344, you learned how to share a printer and folder within a network. Over time, users may no longer need access to the printer or folder. At that time, you can turn off the resource sharing which will make your system more secure. To turn off sharing for a printer, perform these steps:

1. Click your mouse on the Start menu Settings option and choose Printers. Windows 98, in turn, will open the Printers window.

2. Within the Printers window, right-click your mouse on the icon that corresponds to the printer you no longer want to share. Windows 98 will display a pop-up menu.

3. Within the pop-up menu, click your mouse on the Sharing option. Windows 98 will display the printer's Properties dialog box Sharing sheet.

4. Within the Sharing sheet, click your mouse on the Not Shared button and then click your mouse on OK.

To turn off sharing for a folder, perform these steps:

1. Click your mouse on the Start menu Programs option and then choose Windows Explorer. Windows 98 will start the Explorer.

2. Within the Explorer, right-click your mouse on the folder you no longer want to share. Windows 98 will display a pop-up menu.

3. Within the pop-up menu, click your mouse on the Sharing option. Windows 98 will display the file's Properties dialog box Sharing sheet.

4. Within the Sharing sheet, click your mouse on the Not Shared button and then click your mouse on the OK button.

348 | CHANGING YOUR NETWORK PASSWORD

If you work within a network environment, you should change your network password on a regular basis. By changing your password, you prevent another user who may have guessed your old password from getting to your files. To change your network password, perform these steps:

1. Click your mouse on the Start menu Settings option and choose Control Panel. Windows 98, in turn, will display the Control Panel window.

2. Within the Control Panel window, double-click your mouse on the Passwords icon. Windows 98 will open the Passwords Properties dialog box.

3. If you use the Novell NetWare client protocol, click your mouse on the Change Other Password button. Otherwise, click your mouse on the Change Windows Password button.

4. Enter both your old and new passwords. Enter your new password again to verify it.

5. Click your mouse on the OK button. Windows 98 will save your changes.

349 | USING DIAL-UP NETWORKING WITHIN WINDOWS 98

In later Tips, you will learn how to use Windows 98's Dial-Up Networking support and your modem to connect to an Internet service provider's computer for access to the Internet and World Wide Web or to dial into a remote server, such as a computer at your office.

If you use Windows 98 dial-up networking to connect to a remote server, you can then use the Network Neighborhood to access the server's shared resources. In addition, you may be able to access resources at systems that are connected to the server. Figure 349 shows the Dial-Up Networking window within which you can click your mouse on the icon that corresponds to the remote computer to which you want to connect.

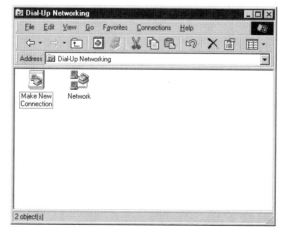

Figure 349 *Using Windows 98 Dial-Up networking to connect to a remote computer.*

350   LOGGING OFF THE NETWORK

If your PC is connected to a local-area network, you may spend considerable time logged into the network so you can send and receive electronic mail. After you are done using your PC, make sure you log off the network before you leave. Otherwise, if another user gains access to your PC, they not only gain access to the files on your system, but also to the files you can share on the network. To log off the network, perform these steps:

1.   Within Windows 98, close all open programs.

2.   Click your mouse on the Start menu Log Off option. Windows 98, in turn, will display the Log Off Windows dialog box, as shown in Figure 350.

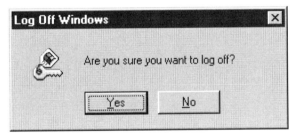

Figure 350 *The Log Off Windows dialog box.*

3.   Within the Log Off Windows dialog box, click your mouse on the Yes option. Windows 98 will log you off the network and will display its Welcome to Windows dialog box that you or another user can then use to log onto the network.

351   CONTROLLING REMOTE ADMINISTRATION OF YOUR PC

If your PC is connected to a network within an office, you may have an assistant whom you want to let manage the files and folders that reside on your disk. In such cases, you can allow your assistant access to your files without having to enable file sharing. To enable remote administration of your files and folders, perform these steps:

1.   Click your mouse on the Start menu Settings option and then choose Control Panel. Windows 98 will display the Control Panel window.

2.   Within the Control Panel, double-click your mouse on the Passwords icons and then click your mouse on the Remote Administration tab. Windows 98, in turn, will display the Password Properties dialog box, as shown in Figure 351.

3.   Within the Password Properties dialog box, click your mouse on the Enable remote administration of this server checkbox, placing a check mark within the box.

4.   Within the Password Properties dialog box Password field, type the password your assistant will use to access your files. Then, type the password a second time within the Confirm Password field and click your mouse on the OK button.

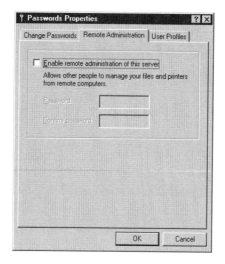

Figure 351 *The Password Properties dialog box.*

352 CHANGING WINDOWS 98 LOGON PASSWORD

In Tip 413, you learned that Windows 98 lets you assign a username and password that specifies a user profile (which lets users who share systems customize settings). In addition, you learned that if your PC is connected to a network, your username and password may also let you log onto the network. Never let another user know your password. If another user learns your password, that user can log onto the network as you, access your files, and even send e-mail messages that appear to come from you.

As a rule, you should change your password on a fairly regular basis. In this way, if another user has learned your password, you disable the user's access by changing your old password. To change your password within Windows 98, perform these steps:

1. Click your mouse on the Start button. Windows 98, in turn, will display the Start menu.

2. Within the Start menu, select the Settings option and then choose Control Panel. Windows 98 will open the Control Panel window.

3. Within the Control Panel, double click your mouse on the Passwords icon. Windows 98, in turn, will display the Password Properties dialog box.

4. Within the Password Properties dialog box, click your mouse on the Change Windows Password button. Windows 98, in turn, will display the Change Windows Password dialog box, as shown in Figure 352.

Figure 352 *The Change Windows Password dialog box.*

5.   Within the Change Windows Password dialog box, click your mouse within the Old password text file and type in your current password. As you type the password, Windows 98 will display an asterisk for each character to prevent another user from reading your password.

6.   Click your mouse within the New password field and type in the new password you desire.

7.   Click your mouse in the Confirm new password text field and type your new password a second time and then click your mouse on the OK button.

8.   Within the Password Properties dialog box, click your mouse on the OK button.

Depending on your network configuration, you may have the ability to log onto a variety of computers, some of which may not be Windows-based systems. Using the Change Password dialog box, you may be able to change your password for those systems from within Windows 98. If you click your mouse on the Change Other Passwords button, Windows 98 will display the Select Password dialog box. Within the dialog box, Windows 98 will list systems for which you can specify a password. For more information on accessing remote systems within your network, refer to your network administrator.

353 CONTROLLING YOUR COMPUTER'S POWER-MANAGEMENT SETTINGS

If you run with a notebook PC using the PC's battery, the less power your PC consumes, the longer your battery will last. Likewise, if you use a Desktop PC at home or in an office, you can direct Windows 98 to reduce the PC's power consumption when the system is not in use—which, in turn, may reduce your power bills and help conserve energy. To help you conserve your PC's power consumption, Windows 98 provides several power-management features.

The Windows 98 power-management features let you specify how soon, after Windows 98 recognizes that your system is not in use, it turns off your monitor and spins down your hard drive. Several of the Tips that follow discuss ways you can conserve your PC's power consumption. To use the power-management features, perform these steps:

1.   Select the Start menu Settings option and choose Control Panel. Windows 98, in turn, will open the Control Panel window.

2.   Within the Control Panel window, double-click your mouse on the Power Management icon. Windows 98, in turn, will display the Power Management Properties dialog box, as shown in Figure 353.

Within the Power Management Properties dialog box, you can use the pull-down lists to control the amount of time Windows 98 waits, when you are not currently using your system, before Windows 98 puts your PC into a low power consumption standby mode, spins down your hard drive, or shuts off your monitor.

When your PC is in standby mode, Windows 98 automatically spins down the hard drive and shuts off the monitor. When you are again ready to use your PC, you simply need to move a mouse or press a key. Windows 98, in turn, will immediately wake up your system, directing it to turn on your monitor and be ready to use your drive.

Note: *To disable Windows 98 Power Management features, simply select the Never option from each pull-down list within the Power Management Properties dialog box.*

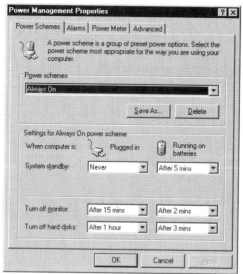

Figure 353 *The Power Management Properties dialog box.*

354 **USING AN EXISTING POWER-MANAGEMENT SCHEME**

In Tip 353, you learned that using the Windows 98 power-management features, you can control how long Windows 98 waits, when you are not using the system, before it will spin down your hard drive, shut off your monitor, or invoke your PC's standby mode. To help you configure your system's power-management settings, Windows 98 predefines power-management schemes which you can select from the Power schemes pull-down list within the Power Management Properties dialog box, as shown in Figure 354.

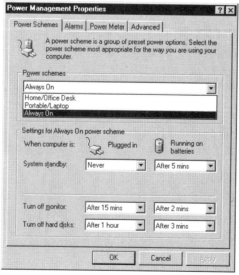

Figure 354 *Selecting a power-management scheme.*

Each scheme automatically configures the times for various power-management features. In Tip 355, you will learn how to create your own power-management scheme that uses the times you specify.

355 SAVING YOUR OWN SETTINGS TO A POWER-MANAGEMENT SCHEME

In Tip 354, you learned how to use the power-management schemes that Windows 98 predefines. However, there may be times when the existing power-management schemes do not meet your needs. For example, if you use your notebook PC for multimedia presentations, you may want to disable your PC's power-management features. To simplify the process of turning power management off and on, you can create your own power-management scheme, perhaps that you name Presentation. Then, by following the steps Tip 354 presents, you can switch between power-management schemes, as your needs require. To create your own power-management scheme, perform these steps:

1. Select the Start menu Settings option and choose Control Panel. Windows 98, in turn, will open the Control Panel window.

2. Within the Control Panel window, double-click your mouse on the Power Management icon. Windows 98, in turn, will display the Power Management Properties dialog box.

3. Within the Power Management Properties dialog box, use the pull-down lists to select the standby, monitor, and hard disk settings that you desire and then click your mouse on the Save As button. Windows 98 will display the Save Scheme dialog box.

4. Within the Save Scheme dialog box, type in the scheme name that you desire and then click your mouse on the OK button.

5. Within the Power Management Properties dialog box, select the power-management scheme you currently want to use and then click your mouse on the OK button to put your changes into effect.

356 SETTING ALARMS TO NOTIFY YOU OF THE CURRENT BATTERY LEVEL

When you run your PC notebook using its battery, it is important that you keep track of your current battery level so you have time to close your programs and save your documents before your system simply shuts off. Rather than having to continually click your mouse on the Taskbar's battery meter to check your current battery level (although it is not a bad idea to do so every once in a while), you can direct Windows 98 to sound an alarm when your battery reaches specific levels (such as 10% power remaining). To configure your system's battery-level alarms, perform these steps:

1. Select the Start menu Settings option and choose Control Panel. Windows 98, in turn, will open the Control Panel window.

2. Within the Control Panel window, double-click your mouse on the Power Management icon. Windows 98, in turn, will display the Power Management Properties dialog box.

3. Within the Power Management Properties dialog box, use the Power schemes pull-down lists to select the scheme to which you want to apply your settings. Next, click your mouse on the Alarms tab. Windows 98, in turn, will display the Alarms sheet, as shown in Figure 356.1.

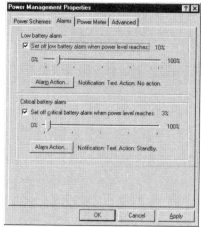

Figure 356.1 The Power Management Properties dialog box Alarms sheet.

4. Within the Alarms sheet, use the Low battery alarm checkbox and Critical battery alarm checkbox to enable or disable the specific power-management alarms. Next, use your mouse to drag the power-level sliders to the percentage of battery power at which you want Windows 98 to generate each alarm. Next, click your mouse on each Alarm Action button to configure how Windows 98 will notify you of the alarm. Windows 98, in turn, will display the Low Battery Alarm Actions dialog box, as shown in Figure 356.2.

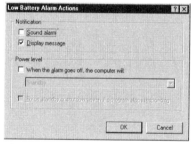

Figure 356.2 The Low Battery Alarm Actions dialog box.

5. Within the Low Battery Alarm Actions dialog box, use the Notification checkboxes to control how Windows 98 will notify you of the alarm. Next, within the Power level field, use the checkboxes and pull-down list to control what actions Windows 98 performs to save power when an alarm occurs. Then, click your mouse on the OK button.

6. Within the Power Management Properties dialog box, click your mouse on the OK button to put your changes into effect.

---

357   U*SING THE* P*OWER* M*ETER TO* D*ISPLAY A* B*ATTERY'S* C*URRENT* P*OWER* L*EVELS*

As discussed in Tip 356, when you run your notebook PC using its battery, you will periodically want to view the battery's current power level. To view the battery level, perform these steps:

1. Select the Start menu Settings option and choose Control Panel. Windows 98, in turn, will open the Control Panel window.

2. Within the Control Panel window, double-click your mouse on the Power Management icon. Windows 98 will display the Power Management Properties dialog box.

3. Within the Power Management Properties dialog box, click your mouse on the Power Meter tab. Windows 98, in turn, will display the Power Meter sheet, as shown in Figure 357.1.

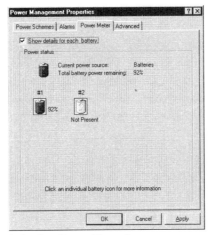

Figure 357.1 *The Power Management Properties dialog box Power Meter sheet.*

4. Within the Power Meter sheet, you can view your battery's current power level. If you want to view specifics about your battery, double-click your mouse on the battery icon that appears within the Power Meter sheet. Windows 98, in turn, will display the Detailed Information for Battery dialog box, as shown in Figure 357.2.

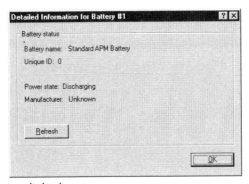

Figure 357 *The Detailed Information for Battery dialog box.*

5. Click your mouse on the OK button to close the Detailed Information for Battery dialog box. Then, click your mouse on the OK button to close the Power Management Properties dialog box.

Note: *If you perform the steps Tip 358 discusses, you can direct Windows 98 to display a battery icon within the Taskbar. To view the Power Management Properties dialog box, you can simply double-click your mouse on the Taskbar's battery icon.*

6. Click your mouse on Next. The Wizard, in turn, will display a dialog box within which you can select the port to which you connected the null-modem or bi-directional parallel cable.

7. Within the dialog box, click your mouse on the port to which you connected the cable and then click your mouse on Next. The Wizard, in turn, will display its final dialog box telling you that you have successfully set up the guest computer.

358 CUSTOMIZING OTHER POWER MANAGEMENT SETTINGS

In Tip 357, you learned how to view a notebook PC's current battery level within the Power Management Properties dialog box. As the Tip discussed, it is not a bad idea for you to periodically check your battery level as you work. To simplify the number of steps you must perform to check your battery level, Windows 98 lets you place a battery icon on the Taskbar. Later, to view the current battery level, you must simply hold your mouse pointer over the icon. Windows 98, in turn, will display a small pop-up window that contains the battery level, as shown in Figure 358.1.

Figure 358.1 *Viewing a battery's power level from the Taskbar.*

If you double-click your mouse on the Taskbar battery icon, Windows 98 will display the Power Meter dialog box previously shown in Tip 357. To place a battery icon on the Windows 98 Taskbar, perform these steps:

1. Select the Start menu Settings option and choose Control Panel. Windows 98, in turn, will open the Control Panel window.

2. Within the Control Panel window, double-click your mouse on the Power Management icon. Windows 98 will display the Power Management Properties dialog box.

3. Within the Power Management Properties dialog box, click your mouse on the Advanced tab. Windows 98, in turn, will display the Advanced sheet, as shown in Figure 358.2.

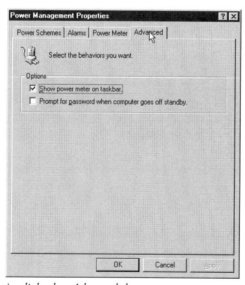

Figure 358.2 *The Power Management Properties dialog box Advanced sheet.*

4. Within the Advanced sheet, click your mouse on the Show power meter on Taskbar checkbox, placing a check mark within the box. Next, click your mouse on the OK button to put your changes into effect.

359 *USING WINDOWS 98 POWER-MANAGEMENT FEATURES TO PASSWORD PROTECT YOUR PC*

As you have learned, Windows 98 power-management features let you specify the amount of time Windows 98 will wait, when you are not using your system, before it will place your PC into a low power consumption standby mode. To better protect your system, you can direct Windows 98 to prompt you for your Windows password each time it returns from the standby mode. To direct Windows 98 power-management software to prompt you for a password in this way, perform these steps:

1. Select the Start menu Settings option and choose Control Panel. Windows 98, in turn, will open the Control Panel window.

2. Within the Control Panel window, double-click your mouse on the Power Management icon. Windows 98, in turn, will display the Power Management Properties dialog box.

3. Within the Power Management Properties dialog box, click your mouse on the Advanced tab. Windows 98, in turn, will display the Advanced sheet, as shown in Figure 359.

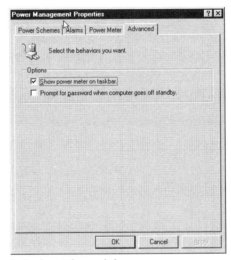

Figure 359 *The Power Management Properties dialog box Advanced sheet.*

4. Within the Advanced sheet, click your mouse on the Prompt for password when computer goes off standby checkbox, placing a check mark within the box. Next, click your mouse on the OK button to put your changes into effect.

360 *INSTALLING A PRINTER UNDER WINDOWS 98*

When you connect a new computer to your system, you may also need to install software specific to that printer before Windows 98 can access the printer. Depending on your printer type, Windows 98 may actually recognize (using its plug-and-play capabilities) your new printer after you connect the printer to your system. However, before Windows

98 can use the printer, you will quite likely have to install a device driver for the printer, which lets Windows 98 communicate with the printer hardware. The Windows 98 CD-ROM contains device drivers for the most common printer types.

Windows 98 may prompt you to insert the CD into your CD-ROM drive. If Windows 98 fails to find a driver for your printer on its CD, you will need to install the driver using the floppy disk or CD-ROM that accompanied your printer. If Windows 98 fails to recognize your printer automatically, you will need to use the Windows 98 Add Printer Wizard to set up your printer. To start the Add Printer Wizard, perform these steps:

1. Click your mouse on the Start button. Windows 98, in turn, will display the Start menu.
2. Within the Start menu, select the Settings option and then choose Control Panel. Windows 98 will open the Control Panel window.
3. Within the Control Panel, double-click your mouse on the Printers icon. Windows 98 will display Printers window, as shown in Figure 360.

Figure 360 *The Windows 98 Printers window.*

Note: *Depending on your Start menu configuration, you may be able to select the Printers option directly from the Settings submenu to open the Windows 98 Printers window.*

4. Within the Printers window, double click your mouse on the Add Printer icon. Windows 98, in turn, will start the Add Printer Wizard which will walk you through the printer installation.

Note: *If your new printer does not appear within the Printer Wizard's printer list, click your mouse on the Have Disk button that appears to the right of the printer list. The Wizard, in turn, will display a dialog box that prompts you for the location of the disk. Insert the floppy disk or CD-ROM that accompanied your printer into the corresponding disk drive and then type in the disk drive letter within the dialog box to tell the Wizard where it can locate the printer's device driver files.*

361   **CHANGING YOUR PRINTER SETTINGS**

Depending on your printer type, your printer may let you customize a variety of settings. For example, your printer might let you control how it prints graphics images (the level sharpness or resolution), which font cartridges it is currently using, whether it prints in landscape or portrait mode, and whether other users in your network can share the printer. To customize your printer's settings, perform these steps:

1. Select the Start menu Settings options. Windows 98, in turn, will display the Settings submenu.

2. Within the Settings submenu, click your mouse on the Printers option. Windows 98 will open the Printers menu. If your Settings menu does not have a Printers option, select the Control Panel option and then double-click your mouse on the Printers icon from within the Control Panel.

3. Within the Printer's window, right-click your mouse on the printer whose options you want to change. Windows 98, in turn, will display a pop-up menu.

4. Within the pop-up menu, select the Properties option. Windows 98 will display the printer's Properties dialog box, which appear similar to that shown in Figure 361.

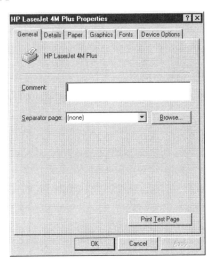

Figure 361 *A printer's Properties dialog box.*

5. Depending on your printer type, the options you can change within its Properties dialog box will differ. After you assign the settings you desire, click your mouse on the OK button to put your changes into effect.

362 PRINTING A TEST PAGE FROM WITHIN A PRINTER'S PROPERTIES DIALOG BOX

In Tip 361, you learned how to use a printer's Properties dialog box within Windows 98 to change printer settings. If, as you use an application program within Windows 98, such as Microsoft Word, you encounter problems with your printer (such as your printer not printing or simply printing unrecognizable characters), you can use the printer's Properties dialog box to print a test page to the printer. If you can successfully print a test page from within the Properties dialog box, the problem is not your current printer configuration but, rather, is somehow related to the application program that is experiencing the errors. To print a test page for a specific printer, perform these steps:

1. Select the Start menu Settings options. Windows 98, in turn, will display the Settings submenu.

2. Within the Settings submenu, click your mouse on the Printers option. Windows 98 will open the Printers menu. If your Settings menu does not have a Printers option, select the Control

Panel option and then double-click your mouse on the Printers icon from within the Control Panel.

3. Within the Printer's window, right-click your mouse on the printer whose options you want to change. Windows 98, in turn, will display a pop-up menu.

4. Within the pop-up menu, select the Properties option. Windows 98 will display the printer's Properties dialog box.

5. Within the printer's Properties dialog box, click your mouse on the General tab. Windows 98, in turn, will display the General sheet.

6. Within the General tab, click your mouse on the Print Test Page button. Windows 98, in turn, will send a test page to your printer. In addition, Windows 98 will display a dialog box asking you if the page printed successfully. If you click your mouse on the Yes button, Windows 98 will remove the dialog box. If you, instead, click your mouse on the No button, Windows 98 will start a Troubleshooting Wizard to help you determine the cause of your printer error.

363 **REMOVING A PRINTER FROM THE WINDOWS 98 PRINTERS LIST**

After you install a printer on your system, Windows 98 and most of your application programs will list the printer as available for use each time a program displays the Print dialog box, as shown in Figure 363.

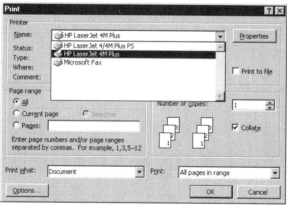

Figure 363 A list of available printers from within a Windows 98 application.

If you disconnect a printer from your system, Windows 98 and your programs will still display the printer within the list of available printers. To remove the printer from the list, you must remove the printer from within the Printers window by performing these steps:

1. Select the Start menu Settings options. Windows 98, in turn, will display the Settings submenu.

2. Within the Settings submenu, click your mouse on the Printers option. Windows 98 will open the Printers menu. If your Settings menu does not have a Printers option, select the Control Panel option and then double-click your mouse on the Printers icon from within the Control Panel.

3. Within the Printer's window, right-click your mouse on the printer whose options you want to change. Windows 98, in turn, will display a pop-up menu.

4. Within the pop-up menu, select the Delete option. Windows 98 will display a dialog box that asks you to confirm that you want to delete the printer.

5. Click your mouse on the Yes button. Windows 98 will remove the printer icon from the Printers window and will remove the printer from its printers list. In addition, Windows 98 may display a dialog box asking you if you want to remove files from your disk that were specific to the printer.

6. Click your mouse on the Yes button to remove the printer-specific files.

7. Close the Printers window.

364   *UNDERSTANDING WINDOWS 98 PRINT SPOOLING*

Compared to your computer's fast electronic components, such as the CPU and random-access memory, your mechanical printer is very slow. Even the fastest laser printers are much slower than the PC itself. As a result, if you print large documents, you may often find yourself waiting on the printer.

In the "old days," which were not that many years ago, after you started printing a document, you had to wait for your print job to complete before you could do any other work. If your printer was slow, you might sit and wait for a long time. Today, however, Windows 98 lets you work as your documents print. To do so, Windows 98 copies the documents you print to a file on disk (which users refer to as "spooling the document"). Then, Windows 98 periodically checks your printer to see if it is ready to receive more data. If so, Windows 98 sends the data to the printer. Otherwise, Windows 98 lets you continue your work. By printing jobs in the background using print spooling, Windows 98 eliminates your need to wait for your print jobs to complete before you can perform useful work.

Because Windows 98 spools files to a disk, you must ensure that your disk has sufficient space to hold the file (by default, Windows 98 spools files into the directory Windows\Spool). If Windows 98 runs out of disk space as it spools your job, Windows 98 will display a dialog box telling you that you have insufficient disk space to print the file. If Windows 98 displays such a dialog box, use the Windows Tune-Up Wizard to delete unnecessary files from your disk and then try to print your document. As you will learn in Tip 365, Windows 98 lets you customize each printer's spool settings.

Note: *If you are trying to print a large document, and you have minimal disk space, you can turn off print spooling and print directly to the printer. Although turning off print spooling will let you bypass the insufficient disk space problem, you will have to wait to perform any work within the application that is printing until it completes.*

365   *CUSTOMIZING A PRINTER'S SPOOL SETTINGS*

In Tip 364, you learned that to improve your system performance, Windows 98 spools the information that you print to a file on your disk and then to Windows 98 itself, rather than to the application that originally printed the data, and sends data to the printer whenever the printer is ready to receive it. Depending on your printer types, there may be times when you want to customize a printer's spool settings. For example, you may not spool jobs to a label printer. To change a printer's spool settings, perform these steps:

1. Select the Start menu Settings options. Windows 98, in turn, will display the Settings submenu.

2. Within the Settings submenu, click your mouse on the Printers option. Windows 98 will open the Printers menu. If your Settings menu does not have a Printers option, select the Control Panel option and then double-click your mouse on the Printers icon from within the Control Panel.

3. Within the Printers window, right-click your mouse on the printer whose options you want to change. Windows 98, in turn, will display a pop-up menu.

4. Within the pop-up menu, select the Properties option. Windows 98 will display the printer's Properties dialog box.

5. Within the printer's Properties dialog box, click your mouse on the Details tab. Windows 98, in turn, will display the Details sheet, as shown in Figure 365.1.

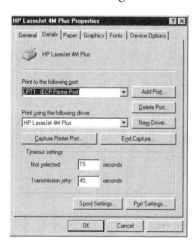

Figure 365.1 A printer's Details sheet.

6. Within the Details sheet, click your mouse on the Spool Settings button. Windows 98, in turn, will display the Spool Settings dialog box, as shown in Figure 365.2.

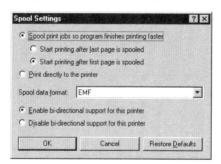

Figure 365.2 The Spool Settings dialog box.

7. Within the Spool Settings dialog box, you can enable or disable the printer's spooling and control when Windows 98 starts printing a job when the printer is spooling. Several of the Tips that follow discuss other options within the Spool Settings dialog box.

8. After you assign your spool settings, click your mouse on the OK button to close the Spool Settings dialog box.

9. Within the printer's Properties dialog box, click your mouse on the OK button to put your changes into effect.

366 UNDERSTANDING *ECP* AND *EPP*

A few years ago, a printer port was a one-directional device. In other words, your PC sent data out of the printer port to your printer. The printer, however, did not send information back to the PC. Today, however, most PCs use bi-directional printer ports. When your printer experiences an error, or runs out of paper, your printer can send a message back to the PC through the port. Users refer to such bi-directional printer ports as *ECP* (*Extended Capability Ports*) and *EPP* (*Enhanced Parallel Ports*). When you attach a new printer to a bi-directional port, the printer can send information about itself to Windows 98, making your printer a plug-and-play device. In Tip 367, you will learn how to view your printer port's properties.

367 PROVIDING SUPPORT FOR *ECP* AND *EPP* PRINTERS

In Tip 366, you learned that if your PC has a bi-directional printer port (either an ECP or EPP port) Windows 98 can use the port to get printer-status information. Usually, if your printer port supports ECP operations, Windows 98 will use them. To determine if your printer is using an ECP port, perform these steps:

1. Click your mouse on the Start menu Settings option and choose Printers. Windows 98, in turn, will open the Printers window.

2. Within the Printers window, right-click your mouse on your printer icon. Windows 98 will display a pop-up menu.

3. Within the pop-up menu, click your mouse on the Properties option. Windows 98, in turn, will display the Properties dialog box.

4. Within the Properties dialog box, click your mouse on the Details tab. Windows 98 will display the Details sheet as shown in Figure 367.

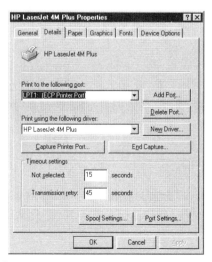

Figure 367 *The Properties dialog box Details sheet.*

5. Within the Details sheet, examine the Print to the following Port pull-down list. Usually, your ECP-based LPT ports will include the text (ECP Printer Port) within the port name.

368 SPOOL *EMF* FILES TO YOUR PRINTER FOR BETTER PERFORMANCE

When you spool a print job within Windows 98, you have two choices for the format which Windows 98 will use to send your data to the printer. First, Windows 98 can spool RAW data, which Windows 98 must first convert from its current format into a printer-specific format. Usually, Windows 98 will only use RAW data for printers that support PostScript files or to fax modems. Second, Windows 98 can spool your data using an enhanced metafile format (EMF) that converts the data into a more generic format which the printer will later interpret. Because Windows 98 does not have to convert the data into the printer's exact format, Windows 98 can spool EMF data faster. To select the RAW or EMF data formats, perform these steps:

1. Click your mouse on the Start menu Settings option and choose Printers. Windows 98, in turn, will open the Printers window.

2. Within the Printers window, right-click your mouse on your printer icon. Windows 98 will display a pop-up menu.

3. Within the pop-up menu, click your mouse on the Properties option. Windows 98, in turn, will display the Properties dialog box.

4. Within the Properties dialog box, click your mouse on the Details tab. Windows 98 will display the Details sheet.

5. Within the Details sheet, click your mouse on the Spool Settings button. Windows 98, in turn, will display the Spool Settings dialog box, as shown in Figure 368.

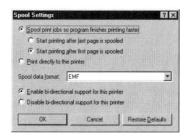

Figure 368 The Spool Settings dialog box.

6. Within the Spool Settings dialog box, click your mouse on the Spool data format pull-down list and then select the format you desire. Click your mouse on the OK button to put your changes into effect.

369 CREATING A PRINTER SHORTCUT ON YOUR WINDOWS *98* DESKTOP

In Tip 101, you learned that Windows 98 lets you print a file by using your mouse to drag and drop the file on a printer's icon. Usually, to drag and drop a file onto a printer icon, you must have the Printers window open, which may not be likely or convenient. As an alternative, you can create a shortcut to the printer on your Desktop, as shown in Figure 369, to which you can drag and drop a document.

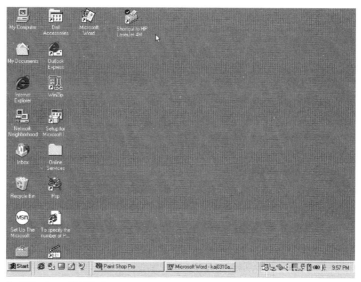

Figure 369 *A printer shortcut on the Windows 98 Desktop.*

To create a printer shortcut on the Windows 98 Desktop, perform these steps:

1. Select the Start menu Settings options. Windows 98, in turn, will display the Settings submenu.

2. Within the Settings submenu, click your mouse on the Printers option. Windows 98, in turn, will open the Printers menu. If your Settings menu does not have a Printers option, select the Control Panel option and then double-click your mouse on the Printers icon from within the Control Panel.

3. Within the Printer's window, hold down your keyboard's CTRL key and use your mouse to drag the printer you desire onto the Desktop. After you release your keyboard's CTRL key and the mouse-select button, Windows 98, in turn, will display the printer shortcut.

4. Close the Printers window.

370 MANAGING PRINTER PORTS WITHIN WINDOWS 98

When you connect a printer to your computer, Windows 98 must associate the printer with a specific port, such as LPT1 or LPT2. When you use the Add Printers Wizard to install software for a new printer, you must tell Windows 98 the printer's port. If you later move the printer to a different port, you must update the printer's setting within Windows 98. To change a printer's port setting within Windows 98, perform these steps:

1. Select the Start menu Settings options. Windows 98, in turn, will display the Settings submenu.

2. Within the Settings submenu, click your mouse on the Printers option. Windows 98, in turn, will open the Printers menu. If your Settings menu does not have a Printers option, select the Control Panel option and then double-click your mouse on the Printers icon from within the Control Panel.

3. Within the Printer's window, right-click your mouse on the printer whose options you want to change. Windows 98, in turn, will display a pop-up menu.

4. Within the pop-up menu, select the Properties option. Windows 98 will display the printer's Properties dialog box.

5. Within the printer's Properties dialog box, click your mouse on the Details tab. Windows 98, in turn, will display the Details sheet, as shown in Figure 370.

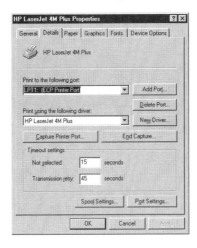

Figure 370 *A printer's Details sheet.*

6. Within the Details sheet, click your mouse on the pull-down Print to the following port list. Windows 98, in turn, will display a list of available ports.

7. Within the port list, select the port to which you have connected your printer.

8. Within the printer's Properties dialog box, click your mouse on the OK button to put your changes into effect.

Note: *Should you later add or remove printer ports from your system, you can use the Details sheet, Add Port and Delete Port buttons to notify Windows 98 of your hardware change.*

371 **CAPTURING AND RELEASING A PRINTER PORT'S OUTPUT**

In Tip 360, you learned how to share your printer with other users within your network. As briefly discussed, before a remote user can use your printer, the user must use the Add Printer Wizard to install software to support the printer.

When you use a remote printer (a printer that is connected to another user's computer), an easy way to use the printer is to direct Windows 98 to capture any output a program sends to your local printer port (such as LPT1) and to send the output to the remote printer. To capture a printer port's output and to direct Windows 98 to send the port's data to a network printer, perform these steps:

1. Select the Start menu Settings options. Windows 98, in turn, will display the Settings submenu.

2. Within the Settings submenu, click your mouse on the Printers option. Windows 98 will open the Printers menu. If your Settings menu does not have a Printers option, select the Control Panel option and then double-click your mouse on the Printers icon from within the Control Panel.

3. Within the Printers window, right-click your mouse on the printer whose options you want to change. Windows 98, in turn, will display a pop-up menu.

4. Within the pop-up menu, select the Properties option. Windows 98, in turn, will display the printer's Properties dialog box.

5. Within the printer's Properties dialog box, click your mouse on the Details tab. Windows 98, in turn, will display the Details sheet.

6. Within the Details sheet, click your mouse on the Capture Printer Port button. Windows 98, in turn, will display the Capture Printer Port dialog box, as shown in Figure 371.

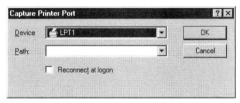

Figure 371 *The Capture Printer Port dialog box.*

7. Within the Capture Printer Port dialog box, click your mouse on the Device pull-down list and then select the port whose output you want Windows 98 to capture. Windows 98, in turn, will highlight the port name.

8. Within the Capture Printer Port dialog box, click your mouse on the Path pull-down list and click your mouse on the network printer to which you want Windows 98 to send the printer port's output.

9. Within the Capture Printer Port dialog box, click your mouse on OK.

10. Within the printer's Properties dialog box, click your mouse on the OK button to put your changes into effect.

Note: *When you no longer want Windows 98 to capture the port's output, use the Details sheet End Capture button to turn off the port capture.*

372 **CONTROLLING PRINTER PORT SETTINGS WITHIN WINDOWS 98**

In Tip 364, you learned that to improve your system performance, Windows 98 spools the information that your applications print to a file on disk and then, Windows 98, itself, oversees the document's printing. If, while you run programs from within an MS-DOS window, you experience problems printing information, you may need to disable Windows 98 spool for MS-DOS-based print jobs. To control Windows 98 spooling for MS-DOS-based programs, perform these steps:

1. Select the Start menu Settings options. Windows 98, in turn, will display the Settings submenu.

2. Within the Settings submenu, click your mouse on the Printers option. Windows 98, in turn, will open the Printers menu. If your Settings menu does not have a Printers option, select the Control Panel option and then double-click your mouse on the Printers icon from within the Control Panel.

3. Within the Printer's window, right-click your mouse on the printer whose options you want to change. Windows 98, in turn, will display a pop-up menu.

4. Within the pop-up menu, select the Properties option. Windows 98 will display the printer's Properties dialog box.

5. Within the printer's Properties dialog box, click your mouse on the Details tab. Windows 98, in turn, will display the Details sheet.

6. Within the Details sheet, click your mouse on the Port Settings button. Windows 98, in turn, will display the Configure LPT Port dialog box, as shown in Figure 372.

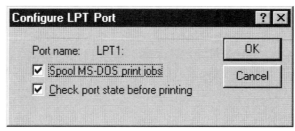

Figure 372 *The Port Settings dialog box.*

7. Within the Port Settings dialog box, click your mouse on the Spool MS-DOS print jobs checkbox to remove the check mark from the box. Click your mouse on the OK button. Windows 98, in turn, will no longer spool MS-DOS-based printer output.

8. Within the printer's Properties dialog box, click your mouse on the OK button to put your changes into effect.

373 SHARING YOUR PRINTER ACROSS YOUR NETWORK

Computer networks exist to help users exchange information (most often via e-mail) and to let users share resources. Depending on your printer type and network configuration, you may want to share your printer with other users. For example, if you have a fast printer, it makes sense to let others take advantage of your printer's capabilities. Likewise, if you have a slow printer, but you have the only printer on your end of the office, other users will probably want you to share the printer. Before you can share your printer with other users within your network, you must first enable file and printer sharing within your computer's network settings, as discussed in Tip 333. Then, to enable sharing for the printer itself, perform these steps:

1. Select the Start menu Settings options. Windows 98, in turn, will display the Settings submenu.

2. Within the Settings submenu, click your mouse on the Printers option. Windows 98 will open the Printers menu. If your Settings menu does not have a Printers option, select the Control Panel option and then double-click your mouse on the Printers icon from within the Control Panel.

3. Within the Printers window, right-click your mouse on the printer whose options you want to change. Windows 98, in turn, will display a pop-up menu.

4. Within the pop-up menu, select the Properties option. Windows 98 will display the printer's Properties dialog box.

5. Within the printer's Properties dialog box, click your mouse on the Sharing sheet. Windows 98, in turn, will display the Sharing sheet, as shown in Figure 373.

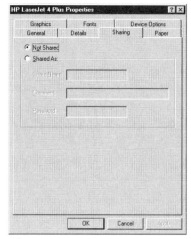

Figure 373 *A printer's Properties dialog box Sharing sheet.*

6. Within the Sharing sheet, click your mouse on the Shared As button. Windows 98, in turn, will enable the sheet's three text fields.

7. Within the Share Name field, type in the name other users use to access your printer. You should include the printer type within the name, such as LaserJet 4000.

8. Within the Comment field, type in a general comment that network users can view about the printer, such as Located next to office 27.

9. Lastly, if you want to restrict which users can share your printer, you can assign a password to the printer that a network user must specify before he or she can print to the printer. Then, only give the password to those users with whom you want to share the printer.

Note: *Before a remote user can print to your printer, the user must install a device driver for your printer on his or her system and then configure the printer as a network printer. To install the device driver for a network printer, the user can use Add Printer Wizard which Tip 360 discusses.*

374   **PRINTING SEPARATOR PAGES TO ORGANIZE PRINT JOBS**

In Tip 373, you learned how to share a printer with other network users. When multiple users send documents (print jobs) to the printer, it is not uncommon for one user to accidentally carry off another user's printout as part of his or her own document. To help users identify each new job, you can direct your printer to print a separator page between print jobs. In short, a separator page simply identifies the start of the next printout, as well as the user who initiated the job.

To direct a printer to print separator pages, perform these steps:

1. Select the Start menu Settings options. Windows 98, in turn, will display the Settings submenu.

2. Within the Settings submenu, click your mouse on the Printers option. Windows 98 will open the Printers menu. If your Settings menu does not have a Printers option, select the Control Panel option and then double-click your mouse on the Printers icon from within the Control Panel.

3. Within the Printers window, right-click your mouse on the printer whose options you want to change. Windows 98, in turn, will display a pop-up menu.

4. Within the pop-up menu, select the Properties option. Windows 98, in turn, will display the printer's Properties dialog box. If the General sheet is not visible, click your mouse on the General tab.

5. Within the General sheet, click your mouse on the Separator page pull-down list. Windows 98, in turn, will display a list of the printer's supported separator pages.

6. Within the pull-down list, click your mouse on the separator page type you desire. In addition to using the pages that appear within the pull-down list, Windows 98 will let you use any Windows metafile as a separator page. If you have a Windows metafile on your disk that you want to use as a separator page, click your mouse on the Browse button and use the Browse dialog box to locate the file.

7. After you specify the separator page type you desire, click your mouse on the OK button to put your changes into effect.

375 DISPLAYING THE JOBS CURRENTLY PRINTING ON A PRINTER

As you have learned, when you print a document, Windows 98 spools the document's contents to disk. If you print several documents, Windows 98 will spool each of the documents and later print each document in the order that you printed them. Windows 98 stores each spooled document in a list that users refer to the print queue. Windows 98 keeps such a list for each printer connected to your system.

To view the list of jobs a printer is currently printing, perform these steps:

1. Select the Start menu Settings options. Windows 98, in turn, will display the Settings submenu.

2. Within the Settings submenu, click your mouse on the Printers option. Windows 98 will open the Printers menu. If your Settings menu does not have a Printers option, select the Control Panel option and then double-click your mouse on the Printers icon from within the Control Panel.

3. Within the Printers window, double-click your mouse on the printer whose jobs you want to view. Windows 98, in turn, will display a printer window within which it will list all the jobs you have sent to the printer, as shown in Figure 375.1.

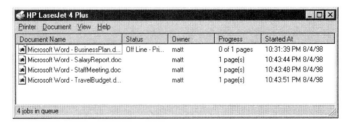

Figure 375.1 A list of printer jobs.

In addition to using Steps 1-3 just discussed to view a printer's jobs, you can also display a printer's queue quickly using the Windows 98 Taskbar. Each time you print a job, Windows 98 will display the printers icon within the Taskbar, as shown in Figure 375.2. If you double-click your mouse on the printer icon, Windows 98, in turn, will display the printer's current list of jobs.

Figure 375.2 *Windows 98 displays a printer's icon within the Taskbar.*

Several of the Tips that follow discuss ways you can use the printer's window to manage your printer's processing.

376 TEMPORARILY PAUSING AND LATER RESUMING A PRINTER'S PRINTING

In Tip 375, you learned that Windows 98 lets you view the jobs you have spooled to a printer. By viewing your job list, you can determine, for example, how much of a current job Windows 98 has printed or how many other jobs must print before your document. Depending on the document you are printing (or about to print), there may be times when you must temporarily suspend a printer. For example, you may need to change the type paper the printer will use to print the document. To suspend a printer's printing, perform these steps:

1. Select the Start menu Settings options. Windows 98, in turn, will display the Settings submenu.

2. Within the Settings submenu, click your mouse on the Printers option. Windows 98, in turn, will open the Printers menu. If your Settings menu does not have a Printers option, select the Control Panel option and then double-click your mouse on the Printers icon from within the Control Panel.

3. Within the Printer's window, double-click your mouse on the printer whose jobs you want to view. Windows 98, in turn, will display the printer's window.

4. Within the printer's window, click your mouse on the Printer menu. Windows 98, in turn, will display the Printer menu, as shown in Figure 376.

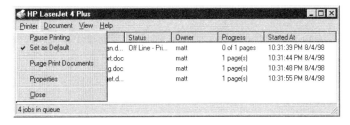

Figure 376 *The Printer menu.*

5. Within the Printer menu, click your mouse on the Pause Printing option, placing a check mark next to the option. Windows 98, in turn, will pause the printer. When you are ready to resume the printer's operations, again click your mouse on the Printer menu Pause Printing option to remove the check mark.

377 DELETING (PURGING) A PRINTER'S CURRENT JOBS

As you have learned, Windows 98 spools each job that you send to a printer. Often, when a job does not immediately print, users try to print the document several more times. As a result, the printer may end up with several copies of the document spooled, as shown in Figure 377.

Figure 377 *Several copies of the same document spooled to the printer.*

Rather than forcing the printer to print each of the documents you have spooled, you may, instead, want the printer to delete its current print jobs so you can start over. To delete the current printer jobs (which users refer to as purging the current print jobs), perform these steps:

1. Select the Start menu Settings options. Windows 98, in turn, will display the Settings submenu.
2. Within the Settings submenu, click your mouse on the Printers option. Windows 98, in turn, will open the Printers menu. If your Settings menu does not have a Printers option, select the Control Panel option and then double-click your mouse on the Printers icon from within the Control Panel.
3. Within the Printer's window, double-click your mouse on the printer whose jobs you want to view. Windows 98, in turn, will display the printer's window.
4. Within the printer's window, click your mouse on the Printer menu. Windows 98, in turn, will display the Printer menu.
5. Within the Printer menu, click your mouse on the Purge Print Documents option. Windows 98, in turn, will stop printing the current job and will remove the remaining jobs from the printer's queue.

378 SUSPENDING OR CANCELING A SPECIFIC PRINT JOB

In Tip 377, you learned how to suspend your printer's printing. Likewise, in Tip 377, you learned how to purge a printer's current print jobs. As you work, there may be times when, rather than suspending the printer or canceling all the printer jobs, you simply want to suspend or delete a specific job. To suspend or delete a specific print job, perform these steps:

1. Select the Start menu Settings options. Windows 98, in turn, will display the Settings submenu.
2. Within the Settings submenu, click your mouse on the Printers option. Windows 98, in turn, will open the Printers menu. If your Settings menu does not have a Printers option, select the Control Panel option and then double-click your mouse on the Printers icon from within the Control Panel.
3. Within the Printer's window, double-click your mouse on the printer whose jobs you want to view. Windows 98, in turn, will display the printer's window.
4. Within the printer's list of jobs, click your mouse on the job you want to suspend or delete.
5. Within the printer's window, click your mouse on the Document menu. Windows 98, in turn, will display the Document menu, as shown in Figure 378.

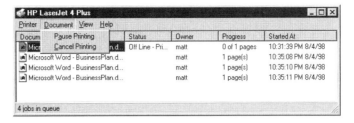

Figure 378 *The Documents menu.*

6. Within the Document menu, click your mouse on the Pause Printing option to suspend the document's printing or click your mouse on the Cancel Printing option to delete the print job.

379 CHANGING THE ORDER OF JOBS IN A PRINTER'S PRINT QUEUE

As you have learned, Windows 98 spools the jobs that you print in the order that you print them. Depending on your needs, there may be times when you need one job to print before another or possibly before several other jobs. Within a printer's list of queued jobs, Windows lets you move jobs up and down within the list, essentially changing the job's print priority. To change a job's priority within a printer's queue, perform these steps:

1. Select the Start menu Settings options. Windows 98, in turn, will display the Settings submenu.

2. Within the Settings submenu, click your mouse on the Printers option. Windows 98 will open the Printers menu. If your Settings menu does not have a Printers option, select the Control Panel option and then double-click your mouse on the Printers icon from within the Control Panel.

3. Within the Printers window, double-click your mouse on the printer whose jobs you want to view. Windows 98, in turn, will display the printer's window.

4. Within the printer's window, click your mouse on the job whose priority you want to change and then use your mouse to drag the document to the location within the list of queued files that you desire. Windows 98 will not let you replace the job that it is currently printing. When you release your mouse-select button, Windows 98 will move the document to its new location within the print queue.

380 SELECTING A WINDOWS 98 DEFAULT PRINTER

Windows 98 lets you connect multiple printers to your PC. Within your applications, you can use the Print dialog box to select the printer to which you want to print. When you use multiple printers, you must pick one printer that Windows 98 treats as the default printer—the printer to which your programs will send their output if you do not select a specific printer within the Print dialog box. To select a default printer, perform these steps:

1. Select the Start menu Settings options. Windows 98, in turn, will display the Settings submenu.

2. Within the Settings submenu, click your mouse on the Printers option. Windows 98, in turn, will open the Printers menu. If your Settings menu does not have a Printers option, select the Control Panel option and then double-click your mouse on the Printers icon from within the Control Panel.

3. Within the Printers window, right-click your mouse on the printer that you want to select as the default printer. Windows 98, in turn, will display the pop-up menu, as shown in Figure 380.

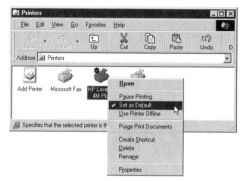

Figure 380 *The pop-up menu Windows 98 displays when you right-click your mouse on a printer icon.*

4. Within the pop-up menu, click your mouse on the Set as Default option.

Note: *In addition to using Steps 1-4 just discussed to select a default printer, Windows 98 also lets you select a printer as the default from within the printer's window by choosing the Printer menu Set As Default option.*

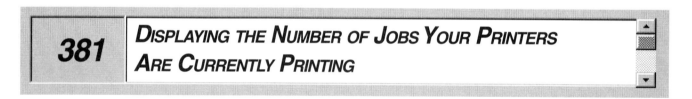

381 DISPLAYING THE NUMBER OF JOBS YOUR PRINTERS ARE CURRENTLY PRINTING

If you have several printers available to which you can print, you may want to select the printer that is the least busy as the printer to which you will send your output. Within Windows 98, you can quickly view the number of jobs each printer is printing by performing these steps:

1. Select the Start menu Settings options. Windows 98, in turn, will display the Settings submenu.

2. Within the Settings submenu, click your mouse on the Printers option. Windows 98, in turn, will open the Printers menu. If your Settings menu does not have a Printers option, select the Control Panel option and then double-click your mouse on the Printers icon from within the Control Panel.

3. Within the Printers window, click your mouse on the View menu and choose the Details option. Windows 98, in turn, will change the Printers window to display a count of the number of jobs each printer is currently printing, as shown in Figure 381.

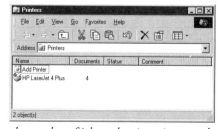

Figure 381 *Using the Printers window to display the number of jobs each printer is currently printing.*

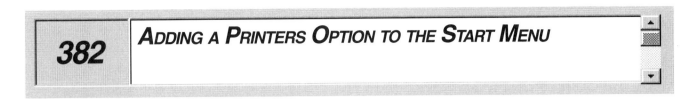

382 ADDING A PRINTERS OPTION TO THE START MENU

As you learned in Tip 361, using the Control Panel Printers folder, you can add a new printer to your system or change an existing printer's properties. If you use the Printers folder on a regular basis, you may find that you can save time and mouse clicks by adding the Printers folder to your Start menu, as shown in Figure 382.

Figure 382 *Adding the Printers folder to the Start menu.*

To add the Printers folder to your Start menu, perform these steps:

1. Right-click your mouse on the Taskbar's Start button. Windows 98, in turn, will display a pop-up menu.
2. Within the pop-up menu, click your mouse on the Explore option. Windows 98, in turn, will start the Explorer.
3. Within the Explorer's right window, right click your mouse within a blank location. The Explorer, in turn, will display a pop-up menu.
4. Within the Explorer pop-up menu, click your mouse on the New Folder option. The Explorer, in turn, will display a new folder icon.
5. Within the new folder icon's name field, type the following folder name, including the period and brackets:
   Printers.{2227A280-3AEA-1069-A2DE-08002B30309D}
6. Select the Explorer File menu Exit Explorer option to close the Explorer window.

Should you later decide that you want to remove the Printers menu from the Startup menu, use Explorer to open the Startup Menu folder and then use your mouse to highlight the folder. Press the DEL key. Windows 98, in turn, will delete the folder, restoring your Start menu to its previous state.

383   *TROUBLESHOOTING A SLOW PRINTER*

Because your printer is a mechanical device, your printer is always going to be one of your slowest pieces of hardware. However, if you feel that your printer is printing especially slowly, perform the following steps to improve your printer's performance:

1. Run the Windows Maintenance Wizard discussed in Tip 636 to fine-tune your system's performance.

2. Using the Windows Explorer, examine your disk to ensure it has sufficient free space within which it can place the temporary spool files. If your system is low on disk space, empty the Recycle Bin, as discussed in Tip 152.

3. Open the Printers folder and display your printer's Properties sheet, as discussed in Tip 361. Within the Properties sheet, click your mouse on the Details tab and the click your mouse on the Spool Settings button. Windows 98, in turn, will display the Spool Settings dialog box, as shown in Figure 383.

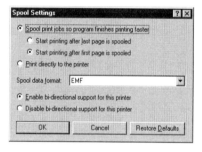

Figure 383 *The Spool Settings dialog box.*

4. Within the Spool Settings dialog box Spool data format pull-down list, select the EMF option which directs Windows 98 to take advantage of the enhanced meta-format discussed in Tip 368. If your printer supports bi-directional communication, make sure you select the Enable bi-directional support for this printer radio button within the Spool Settings dialog box.

5. If your system has multiple disks, assign the TEMP environment entry to point to a folder on your fastest disk. Later Tips discuss the TEMP entry in detail. Windows 98, in turn, will spool the files you print to the TEMP directory.

6. Depending on your printer type, its Properties dialog box may have a variety of settings you can use to trade print quality for faster output or to perform other performance options.

384   *CUSTOMIZING WINDOWS 98 REGIONAL SETTINGS*

Over the past five years, Windows has become the most popular operating system in the world. Each day, tens of millions of users around the world use Windows. As you may know, different countries use different formats to represent numbers, times, and dates. Using the Control Panel's Regional Settings icon, you can select the regional settings you want Windows 98 and its applications to use. To select the settings for a specific region, perform these steps:

1. Select the Start menu Settings options. Windows 98, in turn, will display the Settings submenu.

2. Within the Settings submenu, click your mouse on the Control Panel option. Windows 98, in turn, will open the Control Panel window.

3. Within the Control Panel, double-click your mouse on the Regional Settings icon. Windows 98, in turn, will open the Regional Settings Properties dialog box, as shown in Figure 384.

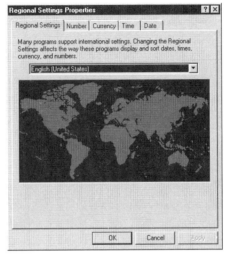

Figure 384 *The Regional Settings Properties dialog box.*

4. Within the Regional Settings Properties dialog box, click your mouse on the pull-down list of regions.

5. Within the pull-down region list, click your mouse on the region that you desire.

6. Within the Regional Settings Properties dialog box, click your mouse on the OK button.

7. Windows 98, in turn, will display a dialog box telling you that you must restart your system for your changes to take place. Within the dialog box, click your mouse on the Yes button to restart your system.

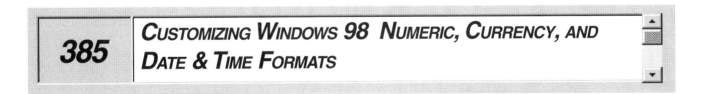

385 CUSTOMIZING WINDOWS 98 NUMERIC, CURRENCY, AND DATE & TIME FORMATS

In Tip 384, you learned how to use the Windows 98 Regional Settings Properties dialog box to select a region's numeric, currency, date, and time formats in one step. Depending on your needs, there may be times when you need to change a specific setting. In such cases, you can use the Regional Settings Properties dialog box Number, Currency, Date, and Time sheets. To change a specific regional setting, perform these steps:

1. Select the Start menu Settings options. Windows 98, in turn, will display the Settings submenu.

2. Within the Settings submenu, click your mouse on the Control Panel option. Windows 98, in turn, will open the Control Panel window.

3. Within the Control Panel, double-click your mouse on the Regional Settings icon. Windows 98, in turn, will open the Regional Settings Properties dialog box.

4. Within the Regional Settings Properties dialog box, click your mouse on the tab that corresponds to the setting you want to change. Windows 98 will display the corresponding sheet.

5. Within the properties sheet, change the settings you desire.

6. Within the Regional Settings dialog box, click your mouse on the OK button.

386 | ASSIGNING SOUNDS TO WINDOWS 98 EVENTS

As you perform various operations, Windows 98 may generate different sounds. In some cases, Windows 98 generates the sound to notify you of an error (to get your attention). At other times, Windows 98 generates the sound, well, just because. Using the Windows 98 Control Panel Sounds icon, you can customize how and when Windows 98 generates such sounds by specifying which sounds (if any) Windows 98 generates when a specific event occurs. To assign a sound to a specific Windows 98 event, perform these steps:

1. Select the Start menu Settings options. Windows 98, in turn, will display the Settings submenu.

2. Within the Settings submenu, click your mouse on the Control Panel option. Windows 98, in turn, will open the Control Panel window.

3. Within the Control Panel, double-click your mouse on the Sounds icon. Windows 98, in turn, will open the Sounds Properties dialog box, as shown in Figure 386.

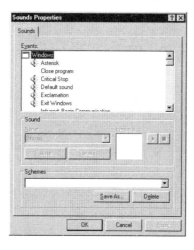

Figure 386 *The Sounds Properties dialog box.*

4. Within the Sounds Properties dialog box Events list, use your mouse to scroll through the events to which you can assign a sound. As you highlight an event, Windows 98 will display the name of the current sound Windows 98 generates when the event occurs. To hear the current sound, click your mouse on the right-facing arrow (the play button) that appears next to the Preview icon.

5. To change the event's sound, click your mouse on the pull-down Name list. Windows 98 will display a list of available sounds. Within the sound list, click your mouse on the sound you desire. (Again, you can Preview the sound by clicking your mouse on the play button.)

6. After you assign the sounds to events as you desire, click your mouse on the OK button to put your changes into effect.

---

387 USING WINDOWS 98 SOUND SCHEMES TO SAVE YOUR SOUND SETTINGS

In Tip 386, you learned how to assign specific sounds to different Windows 98 events. After you customize your sound settings, you should save your settings within a sound scheme. To save your settings within a sound scheme, perform these steps:

1. Select the Start menu Settings options. Windows 98, in turn, will display the Settings submenu.
2. Within the Settings submenu, click your mouse on the Control Panel option. Windows 98, in turn, will open the Control Panel window.
3. Within the Control Panel, double-click your mouse on the Sounds icon. Windows 98, in turn, will open the Sounds Properties dialog box.
4. Within the Sounds Properties dialog box, click your mouse on the Save As button. Windows 98, in turn, will display the Save Scheme As dialog box, as shown in Figure 387.

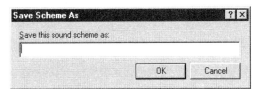

Figure 387 The Save Scheme As dialog box.

5. Within the Save Scheme dialog box, type in a meaningful name that describes your sound settings and click your mouse on the OK button. Later using the Sounds Properties dialog box Schemes pull-down list, you can choose the sound scheme you want Windows 98 to use.
6. Within the Sounds Properties dialog box, click your mouse on the OK button.

---

388 ASSIGNING A *WAV* SOUND FILE TO A WINDOWS 98 EVENT

In Tip 387, you learned how to assign one of the Windows 98 predefined sounds to a system event. In addition to using the predefined sounds, Windows 98 lets you assign any WAV file (a sound file with the WAV file extension) to an event. You can buy WAV files, download WAV files from the Internet, and even record your own WAV files using the Windows 98 Sound Recorder accessory program. To assign a WAV file to a Windows 98 event, perform these steps:

1. Select the Start menu Settings options. Windows 98, in turn, will display the Settings submenu.
2. Within the Settings submenu, click your mouse on the Control Panel option. Windows 98 will

open the Control Panel window.

3. Within the Control Panel, double-click your mouse on the Sounds icon. Windows 98, in turn, will open the Sounds Properties dialog box.

4. Within the Sounds Properties dialog box Events list, use your mouse to scroll through the events to which you can assign a sound. Click your mouse on the event that you desire.

5. Within the Sound Properties dialog box, click your mouse on the Browse button. Windows 98, in turn, will display the Browse dialog box.

6. Within the Browse dialog box, you can search the folders on your directory for the WAV file that you desire. After you locate the WAV file, click your mouse on the file and then click your mouse on the OK button.

7. Within the Sound Properties dialog box, you can click your mouse on the Preview button to hear the WAV file's contents. Then, click your mouse on the OK button to put your changes into effect.

389 USING THE CONTROL PANEL SYSTEM PROPERTIES OPTION TO DISPLAY HARDWARE AND SOFTWARE INFORMATION

As you have learned, the Windows 98 Control Panel exists to provide you with ways to customize your system settings and hardware devices for maximum performance. Eventually, if you must troubleshoot a hardware error or if you are trying to fine-tune your system's performance, you will use the Control Panel System Properties dialog box, as shown in Figure 389.

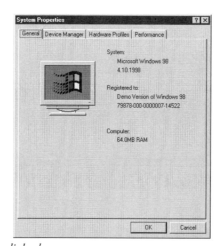

Figure 389 *The Control Panel System Properties dialog box.*

Using the System Properties dialog box, you can view specifics about each of your hardware devices, the low-level PC components, and even fine-tune various system settings. Several of the Tips that follow examine specific operations you can perform within the System Properties dialog box. To open the System Properties dialog box, perform these steps:

1. Select the Start menu Settings option and choose Control Panel. Windows 98, in turn, will open the Control Panel window.

2. Within the Control Panel window, double-click your mouse on the System icon. Windows 98, in turn, will display the System Properties dialog box.

Within the System Properties dialog box General sheet, you will see a general summary that describes your current operating system version as well as the amount of RAM your PC contains. Depending on your hardware manufacturer, you may find other information on the General sheet.

390 *VIEWING DEVICE SETTINGS WITHIN THE WINDOWS 98 DEVICE MANAGER*

Compared to the "old days" when users had to configure jumpers and switches on their hardware cards, new technologies such as "plug and play" let most users forget about hardware settings. However, if you find yourself needing to view low-level hardware settings, the place to start is the Windows 98 Device Manager, as shown in Figure 390.1.

Figure 390.1 *The Windows 98 Device Manager.*

As you can see, the Windows 98 Device Manager lists your system's hardware devices. If you click your mouse on the plus sign (+) that precedes a device category, Windows 98 will expand the device tree to display your system's specific devices, as shown in Figure 390.2. Several of the Tips that follow will tell you how to use the Device Manger to view or change specific settings.

Figure 390.2 *Expanding a Device Manager category to display specific devices.*

391 | **VIEWING DEVICES WITHIN THE DEVICE MANAGER BY CONNECTION**

In Tip 390, you learned that the Windows 98 Device Manager lists each of your system's hardware devices. Usually, the Device Manager displays devices sorted by category, such as your CD-ROM drives followed by your disk drives, followed by your display adapter, and so on. In addition to letting you view devices by category, the Device Manager can also display the device list by connection, as shown in Figure 391.

When you list devices by connection, the Device Manager lists your system devices based upon how the device is connected to your PC. For example, the Device Manager will group together all the devices that connect to a SCSI controller. To switch between the Device Manger's category and connection display, simply click your mouse on the radio button (that appears near the top of the Device Manager sheet) that corresponds to the list type that you desire.

Figure 391 *Viewing devices within the Device Manager by connection.*

392 | **DISPLAYING DEVICE PROPERTIES WITHIN THE WINDOWS 98 DEVICE MANAGER**

In Tip 391, you learned that within the Device Manager, you can click your mouse on the plus sign that precedes a device category to display your system's specific devices. To display the properties for a specific device within the Device Manager, perform these steps:

1. Within the Device Manager sheet, click your mouse on the plus sign that precedes the device category you desire. The Device Manager, in turn, will expand its device list.

2. Within the Device Manager's device list, click your mouse on the device you desire and then click your mouse on the Properties button. The Device Manager will display the device's Properties dialog box. Depending on the device you select, the contents of the Properties dialog box will differ.

393 **PRINTING THE DEVICE MANAGER SUMMARY**

As you have learned, using the Windows 98 Device Manager, you can display specifics about your system's hardware devices. If you are troubleshooting a hardware problem, using the Device Manager is a convenient way to identify hardware conflicts. In fact, you may want the Device Manager to print a copy of your current hardware settings. To print your current device settings, perform these steps:

1. Select the Start menu Settings option and choose Control Panel. Windows 98, in turn, will open the Control Panel window.

2. Within the Control Panel window, double-click your mouse on the System icon. Windows 98 will display the System Properties dialog box.

3. Within the System Properties dialog box, click your mouse on the Device Manager tab. Windows 98 will display the Device Manager sheet.

4. Within the Device Manager sheet, click your mouse on the Print button. Windows 98, in turn, will display the Print dialog box, as shown in Figure 393.

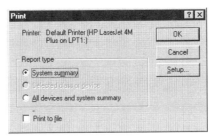

Figure 393 The Device Manager Print dialog box.

5. Within the Print dialog box, click your mouse on the report type that you desire and then click your mouse on the OK button.

394 **USING THE DEVICE MANAGER TO REMOVE A DEVICE FROM YOUR SYSTEM**

In Tip 216, you learned how to use the Control Panel Add New Hardware option to install device-driver software onto your system for a new hardware device. Should you later remove the hardware device from your system, you can free up disk space, (and possibly some RAM) by removing the device's software from your system. To remove a device's software, perform these steps:

1. Select the Start menu Settings option and choose Control Panel. Windows 98, in turn, will open the Control Panel window.

2. Within the Control Panel window, double-click your mouse on the System icon. Windows 98 will display the System Properties dialog box.

3. Within the System Properties dialog box, click your mouse on the Device Manager tab. Windows 98 will display the Device Manager sheet.

4. Within the Device Manager sheet, expand the device category that corresponds to the device you desire. Next, click your mouse on the device you want to remove, and then click your mouse on the Device Manager Remove button. Windows 98, in turn, will display the Confirm Device Removal dialog box asking you to confirm the operation.

5. Within the Confirm Device Removal dialog box, click your mouse on the OK button.

6. Within the System Properties dialog box, click your mouse on the Close button to close the dialog box.

Note: *If you use the Device Manger to remove the plug-and-play device which you have not yet taken out of your system, Windows 98 will not remove the device's software until after you remove the device.*

395 RESERVING RESOURCES WITHIN THE WINDOWS 98 DEVICE MANAGER

As you have learned, the Windows 98 Device Manager lets you display specifics about your hardware devices. When you install new hardware within your system, there may be times when your new device conflicts with an existing device. In some cases, you may be able to resolve the conflict by using jumpers and switches that reside on your hardware card.

In the case of a plug-and-play device, you may be able to use the Device Manager to reserve specific resources for the device's use. To reserve resources for a device, perform these steps:

1. Select the Start menu Settings option and choose Control Panel. Windows 98, in turn, will open the Control Panel window.

2. Within the Control Panel window, double-click your mouse on the System icon. Windows 98 will display the System Properties dialog box.

3. Within the System Properties dialog box, click your mouse on the Device Manager tab. Windows 98 will display the Device Manager sheet.

4. Within the Device Manager sheet, expand the device category that corresponds to the device you desire. Next, click your mouse on the device for which you want to reserve resources and then click your mouse on the Properties button. Windows 98, in turn, will display the device's Properties dialog box, which will differ from one device to another.

5. Within the device's Properties dialog box, click your mouse on the Resources tab. Windows 98, in turn, will display a dialog box that shows the current device settings. Within the Resources tab, reserve the device settings you desire and then click your mouse on the OK button to put your changes into effect (unfortunately, the device settings will vary from one device to the next and may vary given your current hardware configuration, making it impossible to provide you with more information here).

6. Within the Properties dialog box, click your mouse on the OK button.

396 | **VERIFYING YOUR PC DOES NOT HAVE THE PENTIUM MATH BUG**

If you are using an older PC, one from 1994, your PC's central processing unit (CPU) may have the "famous Pentium math bug" which causes math errors in certain high-precision calculations. Actually, Intel estimated that the "typical spreadsheet user" would encounter the error once every 27,000 years. Intel estimates that in 1994, it spent over $500,000,000 dollars to replace Pentium chips that contained the floating-point error. To determine if your processor has the Pentium math bug, perform these steps:

1. Click your mouse on the Start menu Settings option and choose the Control Panel option. Windows 98, in turn, will display the Control Panel window.

2. Within the Control Panel window, double-click your mouse on the System icon. Windows 98 will display the System Properties dialog box.

3. Within the System Properties dialog box, click your mouse on the Device Manager tab. Windows 98, in turn, will display the Device Manager sheet.

4. Within the Device Manager sheet, click your mouse on the plus sign that Windows 98 displays next to the System Devices option. Windows 98 will expand the System Devices branch.

5. Within the System Devices branch, click your mouse on the Numeric data processor option and then click your mouse on the Properties button. Windows 98 will display the Numeric data processor Properties sheet, as shown in Figure 396.

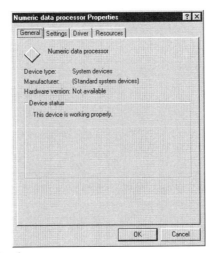

Figure 396 The Numeric data processor Properties sheet.

6. Within the Numeric data processor Properties sheet, look for the message "This device is working properly." If you find the message, your Pentium is working properly and does not have the math bug.

Note: *If your Pentium has the math bug, contract your PC manufacturer; they may let you exchange your CPU. Also, keep in mind that the math bug errors are very rare and only affect a small number of users. If you do not perform high-precision mathematics using your PC, the math bug will not effect you.*

397 UNDERSTANDING HARDWARE PROFILES

If you use a notebook PC, there may be times when your PC is connected to a docking station and, at other times, the PC is disconnected. Depending on the hardware the docking station contains, you may want Windows 98 to use one set of hardware configuration values when your PC is docked and a second set when it is undocked. Using the System Properties dialog box, you can define and later select your own hardware profiles. If you define multiple hardware profiles, Windows 98 will display a dialog box each time your system starts, asking you which profile you want to use. To display your current hardware profiles, perform these steps:

1. Select the Start menu Settings option and choose Control Panel. Windows 98, in turn, will open the Control Panel window.

2. Within the Control Panel window, double-click your mouse on the System icon. Windows 98 will display the System Properties dialog box.

3. Within the System Properties dialog box, click your mouse on the Hardware Profiles tab. Windows 98 will display the Hardware Profiles sheet, as shown in Figure 397.

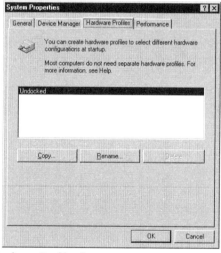

Figure 397 The System Properties dialog box Hardware Profiles sheet.

Within the Hardware Profiles sheet, you can create your own hardware profiles, within which you can configure your device settings. To create a hardware profile, perform these steps:

1. Within the Hardware Profiles sheet, click your mouse on an existing profile and then click your mouse on the Copy option. Windows 98, in turn, will display the Copy Profile dialog box.

2. Within the Copy Profile dialog box To field, type in the name you want to assign to your new profile and then click your mouse on the OK button. Windows 98 will copy the system settings to the profile and display the profile within your current profile list.

Should you later decide to rename or to delete a hardware profile, select the profile within the Hardware Profile sheet's list and then click your mouse on the Rename or Delete option.

398 FINE-TUNING WINDOWS 98 SYSTEM PERFORMANCE SETTINGS

As several of the Tips in this book have discussed, users are always interested in ways they can improve their system performance. Several of the tips that follow discuss ways you can use the System Properties dialog box to improve the Windows 98 file system, video display, and virtual-memory use. To perform these Tips, you will start at the System Properties dialog box Performance sheet, as shown in Figure 398. Within the Performance sheet, you can view how much RAM your PC contains, how much of its resources Windows 98 is currently using, as well as information about your file system, virtual memory, and disk compression, and PC cards.

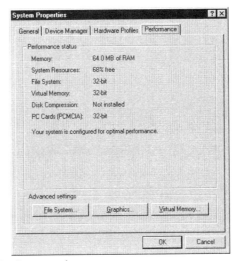

Figure 398 *The System Properties dialog box Performance sheet.*

To display the Performance sheet, perform these steps:

1. Select the Start menu Settings option and choose Control Panel. Windows 98, in turn, will open the Control Panel window.
2. Within the Control Panel window, double-click your mouse on the System icon. Windows 98 will display the System Properties dialog box.
3. Within the System Properties dialog box, click your mouse on the Performance tab. Windows 98 will display the Performance sheet, previously shown in Figure 398.

399 FOR OPTIMAL PERFORMANCE, ENSURE THAT YOUR SYSTEM IS USING 32-BIT DEVICE DRIVERS

To improve performance, Windows 98 makes extensive use of protected-mode 32-bit device drivers. Unfortunately, depending on your hardware (or age of your hardware), Windows 98 may have to use real-mode 16-bit drivers for specific hardware devices. Unfortunately, real-mode device drivers are much slower than their 32-bit protected-mode counterparts and will slow down your system performance.

As a rule, you should use 32-bit drivers whenever possible. By using the Windows 98 Update Wizard discussed in Tip 196, you can locate and install new device drivers much easier than users could in the past. To determine if a device driver is using a real-mode 16-bit or a virtual 32-bit mode device driver, perform these steps:

1. Click your mouse on the Start menu and then select the Settings menu Control Panel option. Windows 98, in turn, will open the Control Panel window.

2. Within the Control Panel window, double-click your mouse on the System icon. Windows 98 will display the System Properties dialog box.

3. Within the System Properties dialog box, click your mouse on the Performance tab. Windows 98, in turn, will display the Performance sheet.

4. Within the Performance sheet, look for the message "Your system is configured for optimal performance." If you find the message, your system is using all available virtual 32-bit device drivers. If you see a different message, click your mouse on the Device Manager tab. Windows 98, in turn, will display the Device Manager sheet. Within the Device Manager, examine the various devices and check if they are using 32-bit drivers. If you find an older driver, use the Windows Update (as discussed in Tip 196, to locate and install a newer device driver).

400 — USING THE DEVICE MANAGER TO DETERMINE IF A DEVICE IS USING A 32-BIT OR 16-BIT DRIVER

In Tip 399, you learned that to improve your system performance, you should use 32-bit device drivers whenever possible. Using the Windows 98 Device Manager shown in Figure 400.1, you can determine whether a device is using a 32-bit or 16-bit driver.

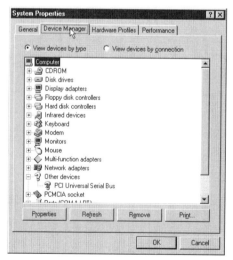

Figure 400.1 *The Windows 98 Device Manager.*

To determine a device's driver type using the Device Manager, perform these steps:

1. Click your mouse on the Start menu Settings option and choose Control Panel. Windows 98, in turn, will open the Control Panel window.

2. Within the Control Panel window, double-click your mouse on the System icon. Windows 98 will display the System Properties dialog box.

3. Within the System Properties dialog box, click your mouse on the Device Manager tab. Windows 98 will display the Device Manager sheet previously shown in Figure 400.1.

4. Within the Device Manager sheet, click your mouse on the plus sign that appears next to the device you want to check. The Device Manager, in turn, will expand its device tree to list the specific device types.

5. Within the Device Manager's device list, double-click your mouse on the device you desire. Windows 98, in turn, will display the device's Properties dialog box.

6. Within the Properties dialog box, click your mouse on the Driver tab. Windows 98 will display the Driver sheet.

7. Within the Driver sheet, click your mouse on the Driver Files Details button. Windows 98, in turn, will display the Driver File Details dialog box, similar to that shown in Figure 400.2, which displays the driver name. If the driver uses the *.VxD* filename extension, Windows is using a 32-bit driver. If, instead, the driver uses the *.DRV* filename extension, Windows is using a 16-bit driver. Some devices, such as many display adapters, use both 16-bit and 32-bit drivers.

Figure 400.2 *The Driver File Details dialog box.*

Depending on the age of your hardware, there may be times when you have no choice but to use a 16-bit driver. If you find that your system is using 16-bit drivers, contact the device manufacturer to see if you can get a 32-bit Windows 98 driver. You may, for example, be able to download the 32-bit driver from the manufacturer's Web site. A *VxD* (*Virtual Device Driver)* is a 32-bit *protected mode driver* which manages a system resource such as a disk drive or a CD-ROM. Protected drivers often have fewer conflicts (with other device drivers) than the older 16-bit real device drivers used in Windows 3.1. The *x* in *VxD* refers to a type of device driver. VDD is a virtual device display (video) driver, VTD is a virtual device timer driver, and VPD is a virtual device printer driver. Using virtual device drivers, Windows 98 is able to make each multitasking application think that it has its own printer, display, and so on, without affecting other running tasks.

401 CUSTOMIZING THE WINDOWS 98 FILE SYSTEM

As you have learned, an operating system such as Windows 98 exists to serve three key functions: letting you run programs, letting your programs interact with your PC's hardware, and letting you store information on disk. The

Windows 98 file system is the software responsible for letting you store information within files and folders on your disk. Windows 98 provides a new file system, FAT32, to which you should upgrade, as discussed in Tip 618. Next, you can fine-tune your hard disk using the File System Properties dialog box shown in Figure 401. Several of the Tips that follow will display the dialog box settings in detail.

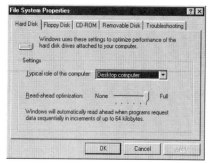

Figure 401 *The File System Properties dialog box.*

To display the File System Properties dialog box, perform these steps:

1. Select the Start menu Settings option and choose Control Panel. Windows 98, in turn, will open the Control Panel window.

2. Within the Control Panel window, double-click your mouse on the System icon. Windows 98 will display the System Properties dialog box.

3. Within the System Properties dialog box, click your mouse on the Performance tab. Windows 98 will display the Performance sheet.

4. Within the Performance sheet, click your mouse on the File System button.

402 UNDERSTANDING DISK CACHING AND READ-AHEAD BUFFERS

As you will learn in Tip 403, Windows 98 lets you specify the size of its disk cache and the number of read-ahead buffers Windows 98 uses to reduce slow disk-input operations. To understand how the cache and read-ahead buffers influence your system performance, you must first understand how Windows 98 uses each. To start, keep in mind that your disk is a mechanical device and, as such, it is much slower than your computer's electronic components, such as your CPU and random-access memory (RAM). One way to improve your system performance is to reduce the number of slow disk operations that Windows 98 must perform.

A disk read-ahead buffer is a location in RAM into which Windows 98 can read a little extra data from your disk each time it performs a disk-input operation. Assume, for example, that you are using a large database. When Windows 98 reads the disk sectors that contain specific database information, Windows 98 will read a few extra sectors hedging on the fact that you will probably end up needing them. Should you later need the information that resides within the sectors, Windows 98 can get the information that it has preloaded into RAM and avoid a slow disk operation. As a result, your performance increases. If you do not use the preloaded sectors, Windows 98 can overwrite them the next time it performs an input operation. By directing Windows 98 to increase the size of its disk read-ahead buffer, you increase the likelihood that Windows 98 will locate the information that it needs within the read-ahead buffer. However, you must keep in mind that the buffers consume RAM which Windows 98 might better use for other purposes.

As such, you may need to experiment with a few different read-ahead buffer sizes until you find one that offers the best performance.

A disk cache is similar to a read-ahead buffer in that it is storage location in RAM within which Windows 98 stores data it will read from or write to a disk. Assume, for example, that you are working on a large word processing document. Usually, as you move throughout your document, Windows 98 may have to continually read information from disk—a slow operation. To reduce disk operations, Windows 98 reads the information from the disk into a cache (a storage location) in RAM. Later, as you scroll back through your document, Windows 98 can get the information from the cache rather than having to reread the information from your disk. As before, the larger your disk cache, the greater the likelihood that Windows 98 will find information that it has previously read from disk within the cache, which lets Windows 98 eliminate slow disk operations.

In addition to using a disk cache when its reads information from disk, Windows 98 also uses the cache when it writes data (a write-behind cache). By placing information into the cache, Windows 98 can later write the information to disk at a more convenient time (which usually occurs within a few seconds after Windows 98 places the data in the cache). Unfortunately, if your system loses power or experiences a serious error before Windows 98 records the data to disk, you may lose the data (which your program will believe was successfully stored). For that reason, many users choose to turn off Windows 98 write-behind caching, trading security for a slight decrease in performance.

403 OPTIMIZING THE WINDOWS 98 FILE SYSTEM FOR YOUR HARD DISK

Depending on how you use your PC, you may be able to improve your system performance by letting Windows 98 optimize its hard-disk settings to match your needs. For example, if you usually work with a large database, Windows 98 may want to allocate more disk buffers into which it can preload database information. In contrast, if you simply use your PC to send and receive e-mail messages, Windows 98 might reduce the number of disk buffers, freeing up memory for other users. To customize your hard-disk settings, perform these steps:

1. Select the Start menu Settings option and choose Control Panel. Windows 98, in turn, will open the Control Panel window.

2. Within the Control Panel window, double-click your mouse on the System icon. Windows 98 will display the System Properties dialog box.

3. Within the System Properties dialog box, click your mouse on the Performance tab. Windows 98 will display the Performance sheet.

4. Within the Performance sheet, click your mouse on the File System button. Windows 98 will display the File System Properties dialog box.

5. Within the File System Properties dialog box Hard Disk sheet, click your mouse on the Typical role of this computer pull-down list and select the option that best describes how you use your computer. Next, use your mouse to drag the Read-ahead optimization slider to the right or to the left to increase or decrease the amount of information Windows 98 preloads from your disk into memory each time it performs a disk read operation. By preloading information in this way, Windows 98 hopes to reduce subsequent (slow) disk read operations. Finally, click your mouse on the OK button.

6. Within the System Properties dialog box, click your mouse on the Close button to close the dialog box.

Determining the read-ahead buffer size that is best for you may take some experimentation. If you are like many users, you will drag the slider completely to the right to select Full optimization. Unfortunately, depending on how you actually use your hard disk, you may be wasting memory on disk buffers you do not use or you may have Windows 98 preloading information from disk that you do not need. So, you may want to take a little time and experiment with the setting that appears to give you the best performance.

---

404 DIRECTING WINDOWS 98 NOT TO SCAN YOUR NOTEBOOK PC'S FLOPPY DRIVE EACH TIME YOUR SYSTEM STARTS

As you probably know, each time your system starts, your PC first checks your floppy disk drive for a bootable disk and then tries your hard disk. Today, however, most newer PCs let you specify the disk order your PC checks for a boot system. For example, you can tell your PC to check your hard drive first, then your CD-ROM, and then, finally, your floppy drive. Depending on how you use your notebook PC, there may be times when you start your PC with the floppy drive connected and other times when your start your system without the floppy drive.

By default, Windows 98 will search for floppy drives each time your system starts. By telling Windows 98 not to search for connected floppy disks when it starts, you can speed up your system startup. Windows 98 will instead use its last floppy disk drive settings. To direct Windows 98 not to scan for floppy disks when it starts, perform these steps:

1. Select the Start menu Settings options. Windows 98, in turn, will display the Settings submenu.

2. Within the Settings submenu, click your mouse on the Control Panel option. Windows 98 will open the Control Panel window.

3. Within the Control Panel, double-click your mouse on the System icon. Windows 98, in turn, will display the System Properties dialog box.

4. Within the System Properties dialog box, click your mouse on the Performance tab. Windows 98, in turn, will display the Performance sheet.

5. Within the Performance sheet, click your mouse on the File System button. Windows 98, in turn, will display the File System Properties dialog box.

6. Within the File System Properties dialog box, click your mouse on the Floppy Disk tab. Windows 98, will display the Floppy Disk sheet, as shown in Figure 404.

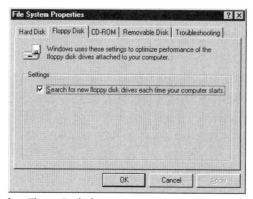

Figure 404 *The File System Properties dialog box Floppy Disk sheet.*

7. Within the Floppy Disk sheet, click your mouse on the Search for new floppy disk drives each time your computer starts checkbox, removing a check mark within the box, and then click your mouse on the OK button.

8. Within the System Properties dialog box, click your mouse on the OK button.

405 | **OPTIMIZING THE WINDOWS 98 FILE SYSTEM FOR YOUR CD-ROM DRIVE**

In previous Tips, you learned how to customize your hard disk's settings within Windows 98 to achieve maximum performance. In a similar way, Windows 98 lets you customize your CD-ROM drive's settings. In general, Windows 98 lets you give up a little memory for Windows 98 to use for buffers into which it reads information from your CD-ROM. The more buffers you provide, the better your performance. To customize your CD-ROM drive settings under Windows 98, perform these steps:

1. Select the Start menu Settings options. Windows 98, in turn, will display the Settings submenu.

2. Within the Settings submenu, click your mouse on the Control Panel option. Windows 98 will open the Control Panel window.

3. Within the Control Panel, double-click your mouse on the System icon. Windows 98, in turn, will display the System Properties dialog box.

4. Within the System Properties dialog box, click your mouse on the Performance tab. Windows 98, in turn, will display the Performance sheet.

5. Within the Performance sheet, click your mouse on the File System button. Windows 98, in turn, will display the File System Properties dialog box.

6. Within the File System Properties dialog box, click your mouse on the CD-ROM tab. Windows 98, will display the CD-ROM sheet, as shown in Figure 405.

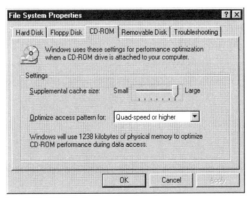

Figure 405 The File System Properties dialog box CD-ROM sheet.

7. Within the CD-ROM sheet, use your mouse to drag the Supplemental cache size slider to the right or to the left to increase or decrease the amount of memory Windows 98 allocates for CD-ROM input buffers.

8. Within the CD-ROM sheet, click your mouse on the Optimize access pattern for pull-down list. Windows 98, in turn, will display a list of CD-ROM drive types. Within the pull-down list, click your mouse on the entry that matches your CD-ROM drive speed.

9. Within the File System Properties sheet, click your mouse on the OK button to put your changes into effect.

10. Within the System Properties dialog box, click your mouse on the OK button to close the dialog box.

406 — OPTIMIZING THE WINDOWS 98 DISK-CACHE SETTINGS

In Tip 402, you learned that to improve your system performance, Windows 98 takes advantage of disk caches which reside in your PC's fast electronic RAM. As Tip 402 discussed, Windows 98 can perform read and write caching. As you learned, when Windows 98 performs write-behind caching, Windows 98 will temporarily place the information that your programs write to disk into its disk cache. Later, when Windows 98 has a free moment, it will write the cache's contents to disk. Because your program does not have to wait for the slow disk-write operation to complete, your program's performance improves. Unfortunately, if in the short interval of time between when Windows 98 places the information into the cache and when Windows 98 records the information on your disk, your system experiences a power outage or disk error, you may lose the information in cache. Worse yet, your program thinks the information was correctly written to disk. Because of this potential data loss, users often turn off write-behind caching.

Depending on your willingness to trade off risk of data loss for improved performance, you may want to let Windows 98 perform write-behind caching. In Tip 407, you will learn how to disable write-behind caching. If, you are using write-behind caching and you are experiencing disk errors on a removable drive, you can perform these steps to disable write-behind caching for that drive:

1. Select the Start menu Settings options. Windows 98, in turn, will display the Settings submenu.

2. Within the Settings submenu, click your mouse on the Control Panel option. Windows 98 will open the Control Panel window.

3. Within the Control Panel, double-click your mouse on the System icon. Windows 98, in turn, will display the System Properties dialog box.

4. Within the System Properties dialog box, click your mouse on the Performance tab. Windows 98, in turn, will display the Performance sheet.

5. Within the Performance sheet, click your mouse on the File System button. Windows 98, in turn, will display the File System Properties dialog box.

6. Within the File System Properties dialog box, click your mouse on the Removable Disk tab. Windows 98, will display the Removable Disk sheet, as shown in Figure 406.

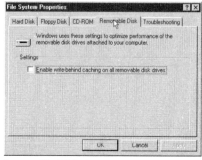

Figure 406 *The File System Properties dialog box Removable Disk sheet.*

7. Within the Removable Disk sheet, remove the check mark from the Enable write-behind caching on all removable drives checkbox and then click your mouse on the OK button.

8. Within the System Properties dialog box, click your mouse on the Close button to close the dialog box.

407 TROUBLESHOOTING THE WINDOWS 98 FILE SYSTEM

If, as you work with Windows 98, you experience intermittent disk errors, you may be able to determine the cause of the error by turning off one or more Windows 98 low-level disk I/O operations. In general, you may simply have to experiment a little to see if the disk errors stop as you change various settings. To troubleshoot disk errors within Windows 98, perform these steps:

1. Select the Start menu Settings options. Windows 98, in turn, will display the Settings submenu.

2. Within the Settings submenu, click your mouse on the Control Panel option. Windows 98 will open the Control Panel window.

3. Within the Control Panel, double-click your mouse on the System icon. Windows 98, in turn, will display the System Properties dialog box.

4. Within the System Properties dialog box, click your mouse on the Performance tab. Windows 98, in turn, will display the Performance sheet.

5. Within the Performance sheet, click your mouse on the File System button. Windows 98, in turn, will display the File System Properties dialog box.

6. Within the File System Properties dialog box, click your mouse on the Troubleshooting tab. Windows 98, will display the Troubleshooting sheet, as shown in Figure 407.

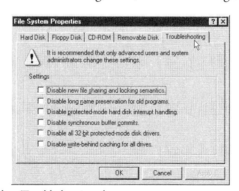

Figure 407 *The File System Properties dialog box Troubleshooting sheet.*

7. If you do not understand the purpose of each entry on the sheet, try to locate another user who does and who can help you. Next, if you are not sure which entry might be causing the error, you may simply want to try to disable the entries one at a time until the disk errors stop.

8. After you have selected the item or items you want to disable, click your mouse on OK.

9. Within the System Properties dialog box, click your mouse on the OK button. Windows 98, in turn, will display a message telling you that it must restart your system for the changes to take effect. Click your mouse on the Yes button to restart your system.

Note: *Within the File System Properties dialog box Troubleshooting sheet, you can disable write-behind caching by placing a check mark within the Disable write-behind caching for all drives checkbox.*

408 | **CHANGING A DISK DRIVE LETTER ASSIGNMENT**

When you install software on your system, Windows 98 will often create shortcuts and menu options that correspond to the software's location on your disks. If you later remove a hard drive from your system, Windows 98 may reassign your disk drive letters, which causes your programs not to run from the menu option or shortcut. In such cases, you may be able to change the disk drive's letter assignment (which may you may find convenient for changing your CD-ROM drive letter) by performing these steps:

1. Select the Start menu Settings options. Windows 98, in turn, will display the Settings submenu.

2. Within the Settings submenu, click your mouse on the Control Panel option. Windows 98 will open the Control Panel window.

3. Within the Control Panel, double-click your mouse on the System icon. Windows 98, in turn, will display the System Properties dialog box.

4. Within the System Properties dialog box, click your mouse on the Device Manager tab. Windows 98, in turn, will display the Device Manager sheet.

5. Within the Device Manager sheet, expand the drive list, and then double-click your mouse on the disk drive. Windows 98 will display the drive's Properties dialog box.

6. Within the Properties dialog box, click your mouse on the Settings tab. Windows 98 will display the Settings sheet, as shown in Figure 408.

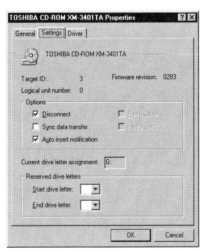

Figure 408 *The Properties dialog box Settings sheet.*

7. Within the Settings sheet, use the Reserved drive letters field to select the drive letter you desire. Then, click your mouse on the OK button.

8. Within the System Properties dialog box, click your mouse on the OK button.

409 TAKING ADVANTAGE OF YOUR VIDEO CARD'S ACCELERATION CAPABILITIES

As you know, Windows 98 makes extensive use of computer graphics. Essentially, each window, icon, and menu is a computer graphic. One way to improve your system performance is to install a high-speed video card which, in turn, will perform all your screen's graphics operations. Depending on your video card type, you may be able to enhance your system performance by directing Windows 98 to take full advantage of your video card's acceleration techniques. Likewise, if you experience intermittent video errors, you may need to turn off your video card's acceleration. To control your video card settings within Windows 98, perform these steps:

1. Select the Start menu Settings options. Windows 98, in turn, will display the Settings submenu.
2. Within the Settings submenu, click your mouse on the Control Panel option. Windows 98 will open the Control Panel window.
3. Within the Control Panel, double-click your mouse on the System icon. Windows 98, in turn, will display the System Properties dialog box.
4. Within the System Properties dialog box, click your mouse on the Performance tab. Windows 98, in turn, will display the Performance sheet.
5. Within the Performance sheet, click your mouse on the Graphics button. Windows 98, in turn, will display the Advanced Graphics Settings dialog box.
6. Within the Advanced Graphics Settings dialog box, use your mouse to drag the Hardware acceleration slider to the right or to the left to increase or decrease your video card's hardware acceleration and then click your mouse on the OK button.
7. Within the System Properties dialog box, click your mouse on the OK button.

410 UNDERSTANDING WINDOWS 98 VIRTUAL MEMORY

As you have learned, Windows 98 is a multitasking operating system that lets your run two or more programs at the same time. As you may know, before your PC can run a program, the program must reside within your computer's random access memory (RAM). As you might guess, to run multiple programs at the same time, Windows 98 may consume a lot of memory. In fact, there may be times when Windows 98 requires more memory than your system contains. To handle its memory demand, Windows 98 uses a technique called *virtual memory* for which Windows 98 sets aside part of your disk to temporarily hold programs when Windows 98 runs out of RAM. In other words, when Windows 98 requires more RAM than your PC contains, Windows 98 uses its virtual memory (the space on the disk) to hold one or more programs. Essentially, Windows 98 moves parts of programs (the parts it is not using) from your PC's memory to disk.

Windows 98 does not just use virtual memory when you are running multiple programs. In some cases, a single program may require more memory than your computer contains. For example, assume that your computer contains 8Mb of random access memory. Likewise, assume your program is manipulating a 16Mb graphics image. In such cases, Windows 98 will load part of the graphic into your computer's RAM and part to the virtual memory on disk. The more RAM your PC contains, the less virtual memory Windows 98 must use.

Because your computer's random access memory is electronic, it is much faster than your computer's mechanical disk. As a rule, the less virtual memory Windows 98 must use, the faster your system will perform.

When you use Windows 98 to run multiple programs at the same time, there may be times when the programs may require more memory than your computer contains. To make space in memory for a new program, Windows 98 may swap one program from memory to a special file on disk called the *swap file*. When Windows 98 must swap a program from RAM to disk, Windows 98 will try to select a program that you are not currently using. When you later want to use the program (you click on the program's Taskbar icon, for example), Windows 98 will reload the program from the swap file back into RAM. Depending on the amount of RAM that your PC has available, Windows 98 may need to swap a second program to disk to make room for the program it is placing back into RAM. By *swapping* programs between RAM and disk, in this way, Windows 98 can run multiple programs at the same time, despite the amount of RAM your system contains.

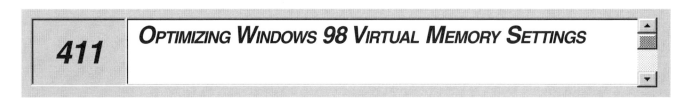

411   OPTIMIZING WINDOWS 98 VIRTUAL MEMORY SETTINGS

In Tip 410, you learned that Windows 98 uses virtual memory to provide programs with the illusion that your PC actually contains more random access memory than the PC contains. Usually, you do not need to be concerned with Windows 98 virtual memory operations unless, of course, your system starts to slow down. If, while you work, you hear your PC's disk drive make extensive noise (from a lot of disk activity), you can improve your PC's performance by adding more RAM. By adding RAM, you reduce the number of programs that Windows 98 must swap into or out of memory to disk. By reducing slow disk operations, you improve your system's performance.

In addition to adding more memory to improve your system performance, Windows 98 also lets you control several virtual memory settings. Most users, however, should adjust Windows 98 virtual memory settings. If, however, you have some overriding reason to change the settings, perform these steps:

1. Select the Start menu Settings options. Windows 98, in turn, will display the Settings submenu.
2. Within the Settings submenu, click your mouse on the Control Panel option. Windows 98 will open the Control Panel window.
3. Within the Control Panel window, double-click your mouse on the System icon. Windows 98, in turn, will display the System Properties dialog box.
4. Within the System Properties dialog box, click your mouse on the Performance tab. Windows 98, in turn, will display the Performance sheet.
5. Within the Performance sheet, click your mouse on the Virtual Memory button. Windows 98, in turn, will display the Virtual Memory dialog box, as shown in Figure 411.
6. Within the Virtual Memory dialog box, click your mouse on the Let me specify my own virtual memory settings radio button. Windows 98, in turn, will then let you change the location and size of the Windows 98 swap file or even turn off Windows 98 virtual memory use.
7. After you change the virtual memory settings that you require, click your mouse on the OK button.
8. Within the System Properties dialog box, click your mouse on the OK button.

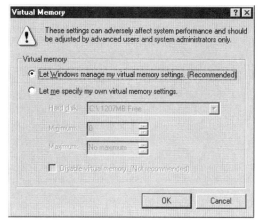

Figure 411 *The Virtual Memory dialog box.*

412   **FORCING WINDOWS *98* TO USE A PERMANENT SWAP FILE**

As you have learned, when you run several programs at the same time, Windows 98 may, depending on the number and the size of your programs, run out of RAM. In such cases, Windows 98 will use a *swap file* into which it will move one program out of memory to disk, in order to make room for a different program in memory. The more programs you run simultaneously, the more Windows 98 may have to swap programs between RAM and your swap file on disk. As a rule, the more RAM your computer has, the less Windows 98 will have to swap to and from the disk.

Usually, Windows 98 will reserve space on your hard disk for the swap file. In previous versions of Windows, you had to configure your Windows swap file settings yourself. In contrast, Windows 98 uses a dynamic swap file that it can grow or shrink as its needs require.

Although Windows 98 configures its own swap file settings, you can take control and configure your own swap file, as your needs require (most users will not have a need to configure the swap-file settings). To force a permanent swap-file size within Windows 98, perform these steps:

1. Click your mouse on the Start menu Settings option and choose Control Panel. Windows 98 will open the Control Panel window.

2. Within the Control Panel window, double-click your mouse on the System icon. Windows 98 will display the System Properties sheet.

3. Within the System Properties sheet, click your mouse on the Performance tab. Windows 98 will display the Performance sheet.

4. Within the Performance sheet, click your mouse on the Virtual Memory button. Windows 98 will display the Virtual Memory dialog box, as shown in Figure 412.

5. Within the Virtual Memory dialog box, click your mouse on the Let me specify my own virtual settings and then enter a minimum and maximum size value for your swap file. Next, click your mouse on the OK button.

6. To put your changes into effect, you must restart your system.

Figure 412 The Virtual Memory dialog box.

413 USING USER PROFILES TO HELP USERS SHARE A PC

In general, Microsoft designed Windows 98 for users who do not share PCs. Windows 98, for example, does not provide security features that protect your files from another user who walks up and simply starts your system. Despite the fact that Windows 98 does provide security features that protect a user's files, Microsoft did recognize that users do share PCs. It is not uncommon, for example, for workers who work different shifts to use the same PC. To allow each user to customize the PC settings, such as the Desktop look and feel, how Windows 98 uses sounds, and so on, Windows 98 provides user profiles. In short, each user can define his or her own settings within his or her user profile without changing the settings for any other user who shares their system. Before the user starts working, the user types in his or her username and password in the Enter Windows Password dialog box.

Based on the username and password the user enters, Windows 98 will select a user profile. As the user works, any changes the user makes to Desktop settings only affect the current user profile. When the user is done working for the day, the user should log out of the current user profile by selecting the Start menu Log off option.

Note: User profiles exist only to let users configure system settings on a shared PC. The user profile does not protect one user's files from another user. To bypass the password dialog box, a user can simply press the ESC key instead of typing a password.

414 CREATING A USER PROFILE WITHIN WINDOWS 98

In Tip 413, you learned that user profiles let users who share a PC customize their own system settings without changing the settings of the other users. To create a user profile within Windows 98, perform these steps:

1. Click your mouse on the Start button. Windows 98, in turn, will display the Start menu.

2. Within the Start menu, select the Settings option and then choose Control Panel. Windows 98 will open the Control Panel window.

3. Within the Control Panel window, double-click your mouse on the User icon. If you are creating the first user profile on your system, Windows 98 will immediately start the Add User Wizard. If user profiles exist on your system, Windows 98 will display the User Settings dialog box, as shown in Figure 414. Click your mouse on the New User button and Windows 98 will start the Add User Wizard.

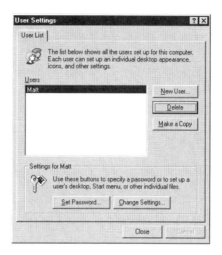

Figure 414 *The User Settings dialog box.*

4. Follow the Add User Wizard's screen instructions to create the user profile. After the Wizard completes, Windows 98 will restart your system.

415 **CUSTOMIZING A USER PROFILE ENTRY WITHIN WINDOWS 98**

In Tip 414, you learned how to use the Windows 98 Add User Wizard to create a user profile. As you learned, each time you add a user profile to your system, Windows 98 will later display the user's name within the Enter Password dialog box. If a user stops sharing your system, you can delete the user's profile and remove the user's name from the user list. In addition, Windows 98 lets you change each user's settings by letting you specify which elements each wants to customize. To change the settings for a specific user, perform these steps:

1. Click your mouse on the Start button. Windows 98, in turn, will display the Start menu.
2. Within the Start menu, select the Settings option and then choose Control Panel. Windows 98 will open the Control Panel window.
3. Within the Control Panel window, double-click your mouse on the User icon. Windows 98 will display the User Settings dialog box.
4. Within the User Settings dialog box, you can change the user's password (so if a user forgets their password, you can change their password for them), delete a user, or you can copy a user's profile for use by another user (copying a user's profile does not copy the user's settings, it copies the profile that defines which items the user can customize). Within the User List dialog box Users list, click your mouse on the name of the user profile you want to change, copy, or delete.
5. Within the User Settings dialog box, click your mouse on the button that corresponds to the operation you want to perform. For example, if you click your mouse on the Change Settings

option, Windows 98 will display the Personalized Items Settings dialog box, as shown in Figure 415, within which you can select the items the user can customize.

Figure 415 *The Personalized Items Settings dialog box.*

6. After you perform the operation you desire, click your mouse on the Close button to close the User Settings dialog box.

416   INSTALLING A SCANNER OR DIGITAL CAMERA

If you purchase a digital camera or scanner, the device should come with software on a floppy disk or CD-ROM that you can install on your system. Usually, Windows 98 will recognize your device when you attach it to your system. If, however, Windows 98 does not recognize your scanner or digital camera, you can use the Scanners and Cameras Properties dialog box, as shown in Figure 416, to add your device to your system.

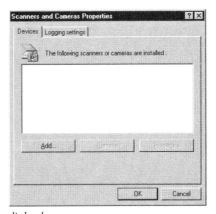

Figure 416 *The Scanners and Cameras Properties dialog box.*

Within the Scanners and Cameras Properties dialog box, click your mouse on the Add button. Windows 98, in turn, will start the Scanner and Camera Installation Wizard that will walk you through the installation process. To display the Scanners and Cameras Properties dialog box, perform these steps:

1. Click your mouse on the Start menu Help option. Windows 98 will start its on-line help facility.

2. Within the Help window, click your mouse on the Index tab. Windows 98 will display the Index sheet.

3. Within the Index sheet, type the keyword **scanners** and then click your mouse on the Display button. The Windows 98 on-line Help system will display a link upon which you can click your mouse to display the Scanners and Cameras Properties dialog box.

417 *GETTING TO AN MS-DOS PROMPT WITHIN WINDOWS 98*

Each time you turn on your PC's power, Windows 98 is the first program your PC runs. Years ago, (before Windows 98), the MS-DOS operating system was the first program that the PC ran. In fact, for many years, MS-DOS was the most widely used operating system in the world. Today, millions of users still use Windows 3.1 which runs on top of the MS-DOS operating system. In other words, when the users first turn on their PCs, the first program that runs is MS-DOS. After the MS-DOS operating system is running, the user can start Windows 3.1.

Windows 98, like its predecessor, Windows 95, replaces the MS-DOS operating system. When you first start your PC, your system runs Windows 98. MS-DOS is no longer in the picture. When Windows 98 was first released, many users still ran MS-DOS-based programs. In fact, many users would run the MS-DOS-based programs from within Windows 95. Today, there are still a few MS-DOS stragglers that run either old-key programs or computer games from an MS-DOS system prompt. To access an MS-DOS system prompt from within Windows 98, perform these steps:

1. Click your mouse on the Start menu Programs option. Windows 98, in turn, will display the Programs menu.
2. Within the Programs menu, select the MS-DOS Prompt option. Windows 98 will open an MS-DOS window, similar to that shown in Figure 417.

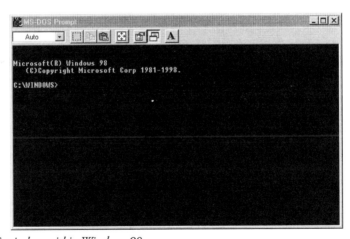

Figure 417 *Opening an MS-DOS window within Windows 98.*

Within the MS-DOS window, you will find a system prompt, at which you can issue commands, such as DIR, CD, COPY, REN and DEL. To close the MS-DOS window, and to return to Windows 98, type EXIT at the MS-DOS prompt and press ENTER, or click your mouse on the window's Close button.

Note: *To run an MS-DOS-based program without opening an MS-DOS window, select the Start menu Run command. Within the Run dialog box, type the path and name of the MS-DOS program and press ENTER.*

418   CREATING A SHORTCUT TO *MS-DOS* ON THE DESKTOP

In Tip 417, you learned how to open an MS-DOS window using the Programs menu MS-DOS Prompt option. If you find that you open an MS-DOS window on a regular basis, you can place a shortcut to the MS-DOS prompt on your Desktop, upon which you can click your mouse to quickly open an MS-DOS window. To place a shortcut for the MS-DOS prompt on your Desktop, perform these steps:

1. Right-click your mouse on an unused location on the Desktop. Windows 98 will display a pop-up menu.

2. Within the pop-up menu, click your mouse on the New option and choose Shortcut. Windows 98 will start the Create Shortcut Wizard.

3. Within the Create Shortcut Wizard's Command line field, type COMMAND and then click your mouse on the Next button. The Create Shortcut Wizard will display the Select a Title for the Program dialog box, within which it asks you to specify your shortcut's name.

4. Within the Select a Title for the Program dialog box, type in the shortcut name that you desire and then click your mouse on the Finish button. Windows 98 will create the shortcut to an MS-DOS prompt on your Desktop.

To open an MS-DOS window, you can also use the Start menu Run option by performing these steps:

1. Click your mouse on the Start button. Windows 98 will display the Start menu.
2. Within the Start menu, click your mouse on the Run option. Windows 98, in turn, will display the Run dialog box.

3. Within the Run dialog box Open field, type COMMAND and press ENTER. Windows 98, in turn, will open an MS-DOS window. Later, to close the window, type EXIT at the system prompt and press ENTER.

419   SIZING AN *MS-DOS* WINDOW WITHIN *WINDOWS 98*

In previous Tips, you learned how to maximize and minimize a window within Windows 98. You also learned how to size a window by dragging the window's frame. To Windows 98, an MS-DOS window is not much different than a standard window. Using your mouse, for example, you can drag the window's frame to size the window. You can also minimize an MS-DOS window into a Taskbar icon and later restore the window from an icon to its previous size.

In addition, if you press the ALT-ENTER keyboard combination within an MS-DOS window, Windows 98 will expand the MS-DOS window to fill the entire screen (with no window frame or title bar). If you press ALT-ENTER within a maximized MS-DOS window, Windows 98 will restore the window back to its previous size.

420 OLD *MS-DOS* PROGRAMS MAY NOT RUN WITHIN *WINDOWS 98*

If you are still using old MS-DOS-based programs, you may encounter programs that will not run within an MS-DOS window under Windows 98. Depending on the program's problem, you may find that by changing the program's memory settings you may get the program to run. At other times, however, you may have to restart Windows 98 using its special MS-DOS mode (which you can access from the Windows 98 Shut Down dialog box). Within MS-DOS mode, Windows 98 will not display a graphical-user interface. Instead, Windows 98 will display a system prompt at which you can run your MS-DOS-based programs. Later, when you are ready to run Windows 98 within its standard mode, you can simply type the WIN command at the system prompt, as shown here:

```
C:\> WIN  <ENTER>
```

To restart Windows 98 in MS-DOS mode, perform these steps:

1. Close any open program windows.
2. Click your mouse on the Start menu and select the Shut Down option. Windows 98, in turn, will display its Shut Down Windows dialog box, as shown in Figure 420.

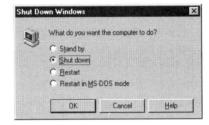

Figure 420 *The Shut Down Windows dialog box.*

3. Within the Shut Down Windows dialog box, select the Restart in MS-DOS mode option and then click your mouse on OK. Windows 98, in turn, will shut down and your computer will restart in MS-DOS mode.
4. Within Windows 98 MS-DOS mode, run your MS-DOS-based programs.
5. To restart Windows 98, type **WIN** at the system prompt and press ENTER.

421 WINDOWS *98* USES *CONFIG.SYS* AND *AUTOEXEC.BAT* DIFFERENTLY THAN *MS-DOS*

If you are familiar with the MS-DOS operating system, you know that each time DOS starts, it searches your boot disk's root directory for two special files named *CONFIG.SYS* and *AUTOEXEC.BAT* files. MS-DOS uses these two files to help you configure your system settings. Within the *CONFIG.SYS* file, you would load device drivers and assign values to specific operating-system attributes. Within *AUTOEXEC.BAT*, you would specify the names of one or more commands that you want MS-DOS to run, automatically, each time your system starts.

When you start Windows 98 for normal operations, Windows 98 will examine each of the two files' contents, executing commands *AUTOEXEC.BAT* contains and applying *CONFIG.SYS* settings. In general, however, because Windows 98 will then display your Desktop and its windows-based environment, you probably do not want to start commands from within *AUTOEXEC.BAT*. Instead, you should probably restrict your *AUTOEXEC.BAT* commands to a PATH entry that defines the MS-DOS command path, and possibly one or more SET entries that define where Windows 98 should place your temporary files. The following commands illustrate the contents of a typical *AUTOEXEC.BAT* file for Windows 98:

```
@ECHO OFF
PATH C:\WINDOWS;C:\WINDOWS\COMMAND
SET TEMP=C:\WINDOWS\TEMP
```

In a similar way, Windows 98 will examine and use the CONFIG.SYS entries each time your system starts, which gives you an opportunity to define specific settings you want Windows 98 to put into effect within your MS-DOS windows. When you later open an MS-DOS window or run an MS-DOS-based program, Windows 98 will use the settings you defined within your *AUTOEXEC.BAT* file. Likewise, if you start your system in MS-DOS mode, Windows 98 will apply your *AUTOEXEC.BAT* and *CONFIG.SYS* settings.

As was the case with MS-DOS, for Windows 98 to use these two files when you open an MS-DOS window, you must store the files within your boot disk's root directory. In later Tips, you will learn how to use a program's Properties dialog box to assign specific *CONFIG.SYS* and *AUTOEXEC.BAT* values to an MS-DOS-based program that Windows 98 will use when you run that program within MS-DOS mode. In this way, you can, as necessary, assign an MS-DOS-based program its own settings.

422 TAKING ADVANTAGE OF THE TOOLBAR WITHIN AN MS-DOS WINDOW

Throughout this book, you have used the toolbar within a variety of programs to perform common tasks. If you examine the MS-DOS window, you will find that it, too, offers a toolbar. If your window does not display a toolbar, right-click your mouse on the MS-DOS window's title bar. Windows 98, in turn, will display a pop-up menu. Within the pop-up menu, click your mouse on the toolbar option, placing a check mark next to the option. Figure 422 briefly describes the MS-DOS window's toolbar buttons.

Selects the font size Windows 98 displays within the MS-DOS window

Marks text for selection

Copies select text to the Windows 98 Clipboard

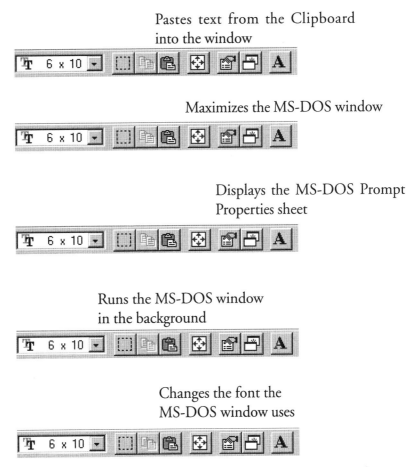

Pastes text from the Clipboard
into the window

Maximizes the MS-DOS window

Displays the MS-DOS Prompt
Properties sheet

Runs the MS-DOS window
in the background

Changes the font the
MS-DOS window uses

Figure 422 The MS-DOS toolbar buttons.

423

SELECTING THE MS-DOS WINDOW FONT SIZE

When you run a program within an MS-DOS window, there may be times when you have trouble reading the screen's content, either because the current font is too small or too large. Fortunately, Windows 98 lets you customize the font size that it uses within an MS-DOS window. To select an MS-DOS window font size, perform these steps:

1. Within the MS-DOS window, click your mouse on the Font size pull-down list, as shown in Figure 423.

2. Within the pull-down list, click your mouse on the font size that you desire.

The entries within the pull-down list specify a font's width and height in pixels. For example, a 5 x 12 font is 5 pixels wide by 12 pixels tall. If you select the Auto option, Windows 98 will select a font so that it is capable of displaying 25 lines of text, each of which are 80 characters wide.

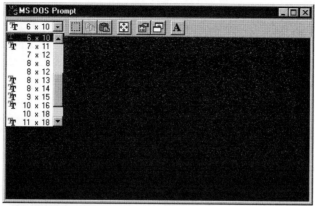

Figure 423 *The MS-DOS window Font size pull-down list.*

---

424 COPYING AND PASTING TEXT TO AND FROM THE WINDOWS 98 CLIPBOARD WITHIN AN MS-DOS WINDOW

Throughout this book, several of the Tips have used cut-and-paste operations to perform a variety of operations, from moving or copy text within a document to moving and copying files within the Windows 98 Explorer. As it turns out, from within an MS-DOS window, you can access the Windows 98 Clipboard. To copy text from the MS-DOS window into the Clipboard, perform these steps:

1. Within the MS-DOS window's toolbar, click your mouse on the Mark button.
2. Within the MS-DOS window, aim the mouse pointer to the first character you want to mark. Next, hold down your mouse-select button and drag your mouse over the characters that you want to select. Windows 98, in turn, will highlight each character you select using reverse video.
3. Within the MS-DOS window's toolbar, click your mouse on the Copy button. Windows 98, in turn, will copy your selected text to the Clipboard.

Just as you can copy text from the MS-DOS window into the Clipboard, Windows 98 also lets you paste text from the Clipboard into the MS-DOS window at the current cursor position.

To paste the Clipboard text into an MS-DOS window, perform these steps:

1. Within the MS-DOS window, position the text cursor at the location at which you want Windows 98 to insert the text from the Clipboard. You might, for example, open the EDIT text editor and position the cursor at a specific location.
2. Within the MS-DOS window's toolbar, click your mouse on the Paste button. Windows 98, in turn, will paste the Clipboard text at the current cursor location.

Note: *If you cannot paste text from the Clipboard into an MS-DOS window, you will have to use the MS-DOS Prompt Properties sheet Misc page to disable the Windows 98 fast pasting feature, as discussed in Tip 422.*

425 *THE WINDOWS 98 PROPERTIES SHEET REPLACES THE WINDOWS 3.1 PIF EDITOR*

If you are upgrading to Windows 98 from Windows 3.1 or Windows for Workgroups, you may know that Windows 3.1 uses a special file, called a PIF (*Program Information File*) file, to learn specifics about an MS-DOS-based program's characteristics. Within the PIF file, Windows 3.1 would learn about the program's memory requirements, hot keys, and so on. If an MS-DOS program did not have its own corresponding PIF, Windows 3.1 would use the MS-DOS PIF, whose settings were suitable for most DOS-based programs. Within Windows 3.1, users would use the PIF editor to create a PIF file for an MS-DOS program that defined the program's settings. To define an MS-DOS program's settings within Windows 98, users no longer use PIFs. Instead, Windows 98 users assign the program's settings using the program file's Properties sheet, as shown in Figure 425.

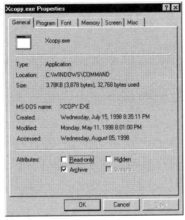

Figure 425 An MS-DOS program's Properties dialog box.

As you know, to run an MS-DOS-based program, users often simply open an MS-DOS window by selecting the MS-DOS Prompt option from the Start menu Programs submenu. The characteristics that Windows 98 uses to run the programs, therefore, correspond to the MS-DOS Prompt's settings. To display the MS-DOS Prompt's settings, perform these steps:

1. Open an MS-DOS window by clicking the Start menu Programs option and then choosing MS-DOS Prompt.

2. Within the MS-DOS window, right-click your mouse on the window's title bar. Windows 98, in turn, will display a pop-up menu.

3. Within the pop-up menu, click your mouse on the Properties option. Windows 98 will display the window's Properties dialog box.

Several of the Tips that follow examine the MS-DOS Properties dialog box in detail. To display the Properties dialog box for a specific program, perform these steps:

1. Click your mouse on the Start menu Programs option and then choose the Explorer. Windows 98 will open the Explorer window.

2. Within the Explorer, open the folder that contains the MS-DOS program of interest and then right-click your mouse on the program file. Windows 98 will display a pop-up menu.

3. Within the pop-up menu, click your mouse on the Properties option. Windows 98 will display the program's Properties dialog box.

426 CONTROLLING AN MS-DOS-BASED PROGRAM'S COMMAND LINE

As you have learned, to run MS-DOS-based programs, users often open an MS-DOS window and then start their programs from the system prompt. When you run an MS-DOS program from the system prompt, you must know that program's command-line requirements and optional command line switches.

Within Windows 98, there may be times when you run a program by double-clicking your mouse on the program file from within the Explorer. When you start a program from within the Explorer, you may need a way to specify the program's command-line arguments. Using the Properties dialog box Program sheet's Cmd line field, you can specify the program's command line arguments. To specify the command line settings, perform these steps:

1. Within the Windows Explorer, right-click your mouse on the MS-DOS program's icon. Windows 98 will display a pop-up menu.

2. Within the pop-up menu, click your mouse on the Properties option. Windows 98 will display the Properties dialog box.

3. Within the Properties dialog box, click your mouse on the Program tab. Windows 98 will display the Program sheet.

4. Within the Program sheet, click your mouse within the Cmd line field and type in the command line you desire.

5. Click your mouse on the OK button to put your changes into effect.

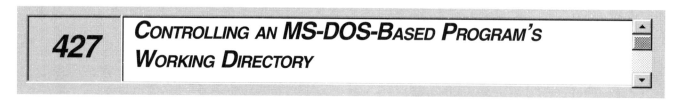

427 CONTROLLING AN MS-DOS-BASED PROGRAM'S WORKING DIRECTORY

As you have learned, within Windows 98, you use folders to organize the files on your disk. When you install a program on your disk, you will usually place the program files within its own folder (MS-DOS users refer to folders as directories). When you run a program, you will usually first select the program's directory and then start the program. Users refer to the directory within which you store the program and its data files as the program's *working directory*. As you run MS-DOS programs, there may be times when the files the program uses do not reside within the program's directory.

For example, assume that you share a PC at work. To separate your files from those other users create, you might create your own directory. If you run an MS-DOS-based program from the system prompt, you can first use the CD command to select the directory that contains your files as the current working directory. If you, instead, run the program by double-clicking your mouse on the program icon from within the Explorer, you will need to specify a working directory within the Properties dialog box. To specify the working directory, perform these steps:

1. Within the Windows Explorer, right-click your mouse on the MS-DOS program's icon. Windows 98 will display a pop-up menu.

2. Within the pop-up menu, click your mouse on the Properties option. Windows 98 will display the Properties dialog box.

3. Within the Properties dialog box, click your mouse on the Program tab. Windows 98 will display the Program sheet.

4. Within the Program sheet, click your mouse within the Working field and type in the working directory that you desire.

5. Click your mouse on the OK button to put your changes into effect.

---

428 RUNNING A BATCH FILE BEFORE AN MS-DOS-BASED PROGRAM

When you run an MS-DOS program within Windows 98, there may be times when you will want Windows 98 to execute a specific set of commands before a program runs. For example, you might want Windows 98 to change the command path or change an environment entry. In such cases, you can create a batch file that contains the commands you want Windows 98 to perform and then you can tell Windows 98 to run the batch file before it runs the program. By associating a batch file with the program in this way, you can later double-click your mouse on the MS-DOS program file and Windows 98 will perform all the operations you need. To associate a batch file within an MS-DOS program, perform these steps:

1. Create the batch file using the MS-DOS Editor program, placing the commands that you want Windows 98 to run within the batch file.

2. Within the Windows Explorer, right-click your mouse on the MS-DOS program's icon. Windows 98, in turn, will display a pop-up menu.

3. Within the pop-up menu, click your mouse on the Properties option. Windows 98 will display the Properties dialog box.

4. Within the Properties dialog box, click your mouse on the Program tab. Windows 98 will display the Program sheet.

5. Within the Program sheet, click your mouse within the Batch file field and type in the name of the batch file you created in Step 1.

6. Click your mouse on the OK button to put your changes into effect.

---

429 USING A SHORTCUT KEY TO ACTIVATE AN MS-DOS-BASED PROGRAM

As you have learned, Windows 98 lets you run MS-DOS programs within a window. If you are running multiple programs at the same time, you can click on Taskbar buttons to select the program you desire. In addition, you can define a shortcut key for the program that you can press to immediately activate the MS-DOS program window.

Your MS-DOS program shortcut keystrokes must begin with either the CTRL or ALT keys followed by another character that you choose as a second key. For example, you use might use a keyboard combination, such as CTRL-P to activate an MS-DOS-based payroll program. The shortcut key lets you quickly activate the MS-DOS program. The shortcut will not run the program if it is not currently running. To assign a shortcut key to an MS-DOS program, perform these steps:

1. Within the Windows Explorer, right-click your mouse on the MS-DOS program's icon. Windows 98 will display a pop-up menu.

2. Within the pop-up menu, click your mouse on the Properties option. Windows 98 will display the Properties dialog box.

3. Within the Properties dialog box, click your mouse on the Program tab. Windows 98 will display the Program sheet.

4. Within the Program sheet, click your mouse within the Shortcut key field and then press the keyboard combination you desire.

5. Click your mouse on the OK button to put your changes into effect.

430 CONTROLLING AN MS-DOS-BASED PROGRAM'S OPENING WINDOW

As you have learned, Windows 98 lets you run MS-DOS programs within a window. Depending on the program's purpose, you may want Windows 98 to start the program with a normal window size, minimized to a Taskbar icon, or maximized to fill the screen. To specify an MS-DOS program's opening window size, perform these steps:

1. Within the Windows Explorer, right-click your mouse on the MS-DOS program's icon. Windows 98 will display a pop-up menu.

2. Within the pop-up menu, click your mouse on the Properties option. Windows 98 will display the Properties dialog box.

3. Within the Properties dialog box, click your mouse on the Program tab. Windows 98 will display the Program sheet.

4. Within the Program sheet, click your mouse within the Run pull-down list and select the opening window size that you desire.

5. Click your mouse on the OK button to put your changes into effect.

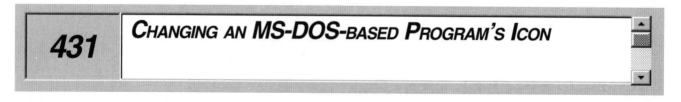

431 CHANGING AN MS-DOS-BASED PROGRAM'S ICON

As you have learned, Windows 98 lets you run an MS-DOS program by double-clicking your mouse on the program's icon or filename within the Explorer or My Computer window. Depending on your MS-DOS program's purpose, there may be times when you will want to assign a specific icon to the program file—which may help you locate the program at a later time. To change an MS-DOS program's current icon, perform these steps:

1. Within the Windows Explorer, right-click your mouse on the MS-DOS program's icon. Windows 98 will display a pop-up menu.

2. Within the pop-up menu, click your mouse on the Properties option. Windows 98 will display the Properties dialog box.

3. Within the Properties dialog box, click your mouse on the Program tab. Windows 98 will display the Program sheet.

4. Within the Program sheet, click your mouse on the Change Icon button. Windows 98, in turn, will display the Change Icon dialog box, as shown in Figure 431.

Figure 431 *The Change Icon dialog box.*

5. Within the Change Icon dialog box, double-click your mouse on the icon you desire.

6. Within the Properties dialog box, click your mouse on OK to put your changes into effect.

432 *PREVENTING AN MS-DOS-BASED PROGRAM FROM KNOWING IT IS RUNNING WITHIN WINDOWS*

As you have learned, Windows 98 lets you run MS-DOS programs within a window. Unfortunately, there may be times when one of your older programs may refuse to run within a window. In such cases, you may be able to hide from the program the fact that it is running within a window. To prevent an MS-DOS program from knowing that it is running within a window, perform these steps:

1. Within the Windows Explorer, right-click your mouse on the MS-DOS program's icon. Windows 98 will display a pop-up menu.

2. Within the pop-up menu, click your mouse on the Properties option. Windows 98 will display the Properties dialog box.

3. Within the Properties dialog box, click your mouse on the Program tab. Windows 98 will display the Program sheet.

4. Within the Program sheet, click your mouse on the Advanced button. Windows 98 will display the Advanced Program Settings dialog box, as shown in Figure 432.

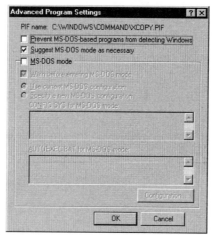

Figure 432 *The Advanced Program Settings dialog box.*

5. Within the Advanced Program Settings dialog box, click your mouse on the Prevent MS-DOS-based programs from detecting Windows checkbox, placing a check mark within the box. Then, click your mouse on the OK button.

6. Within the Properties dialog box, click your mouse on OK to put your changes into effect.

---

433 DIRECTING WINDOWS 98 TO RUN AN MS-DOS-BASED PROGRAM USING MS-DOS MODE

In Tip 432, you learned that there may be times when you can trick an MS-DOS program into not knowing that it is running within a window. Despite such tricks, you may still have programs that refuse to run within Windows 98. In such cases, you must run the program using MS-DOS mode. To run the program in MS-DOS mode, you have two choices. First, you can close all your open program windows and then use the Start menu Shut Down option to restart windows in MS-DOS mode. Second, you can direct Windows 98 to perform these operations for you by performing these steps:

1. Within the Windows Explorer, right-click your mouse on the MS-DOS program's icon. Windows 98 will display a pop-up menu.

2. Within the pop-up menu, click your mouse on the Properties option. Windows 98 will display the Properties dialog box.

3. Within the Properties dialog box, click your mouse on the Program tab. Windows 98 will display the Program sheet.

4. Within the Program sheet, click your mouse on the Advanced button. Windows 98, in turn, will display the Advanced Program Settings dialog box.

5. Within the Advanced Program Settings dialog box, click your mouse on the MS-DOS checkbox, placing a check mark within the box. Then, click your mouse on the OK button.

6. Within the Properties dialog box, click your mouse on OK to put your changes into effect.

---

434 | **CONTROLLING A PROGRAM'S MS-DOS MODE AUTOEXEC.BAT AND CONFIG.SYS SETTINGS**

In Tip 433, you learned how to direct Windows 98 to run an MS-DOS program using MS-DOS mode. When you run a program using MS-DOS mode, Windows 98 will shut down and restart within MS-DOS mode to run the program. As Windows 98 starts within MS-DOS mode, it will usually use the contents of your root directory *CONFIG.SYS* and *AUTOEXEC.BAT* files. Some programs, however, may have special system requirements. In such cases, you can use the Advanced Program Settings dialog box to define the specific *CONFIG.SYS* and *AUTOEXEC.BAT* entries that Windows 98 will use for the program, by performing these steps:

1. Within the Windows Explorer, right-click your mouse on the MS-DOS program's icon. Windows 98 will display a pop-up menu.

2. Within the pop-up menu, click your mouse on the Properties option. Windows 98 will display the Properties dialog box.

3. Within the Properties dialog box, click your mouse on the Program tab. Windows 98 will display the Program sheet.

4. Within the Program sheet, click your mouse on the Advanced button. Windows 98, in turn, will display the Advanced Program Settings dialog box.

5. Within the Advanced Program Setting dialog box, click your mouse on the MS-DOS checkbox, placing a check mark within the box. Then, click your mouse on the Specify a new MS-DOS configuration radio button. Windows 98 will activate the *CONFIG.SYS* and *AUTOEXEC.BAT* fields within the dialog box.

6. Within the *CONFIG.SYS* and *AUTOEXEC.BAT* fields, type in the settings and commands that your program requires. Then, click your mouse on the OK button.

7. Within the Properties dialog box, click your mouse on the OK button.

Note: *To help you customize your CONFIG.SYS and AUTOEXEC.BAT file settings, you can click your mouse on the Advanced Program Settings dialog box Configuration button. Windows 98, in turn, will display the Select MS-DOS Configuration Options dialog box, within which you can select the types of operations you want MS-DOS to perform. Windows 98, in turn, will place the entries it requires within the CONFIG.SYS and AUTOEXEC.BAT fields.*

---

435 | **CONTROLLING AN MS-DOS-BASED PROGRAM'S FONT**

In previous Tips, you learned how to use the MS-DOS window's Font pull-down list to control the font size within an MS-DOS window. When you run an MS-DOS program by double-clicking your mouse on the program's icon within the Explorer, you may want Windows 98 to start the program using a specific font setting. In such cases, you can use the program's Properties dialog box to choose the font you desire. To specify the font for an MS-DOS program, perform these steps:

1. Within the Windows Explorer, right-click your mouse on the MS-DOS program's icon. Windows 98 will display a pop-up menu.

2. Within the pop-up menu, click your mouse on the Properties option. Windows 98 will display the Properties dialog box.

3. Within the Properties dialog box, click your mouse on the Font tab. Windows 98 will display the Font sheet, as shown in Figure 435.

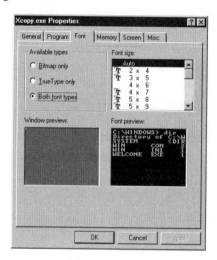

Figure 435 *The Properties dialog box Font sheet.*

4. Within the Font sheet, select the font type and size you desire. As you make your selections, Windows 98 will preview your font within the dialog box's preview field. After you select the font settings you desire, click your mouse on the OK button to put your changes into effect.

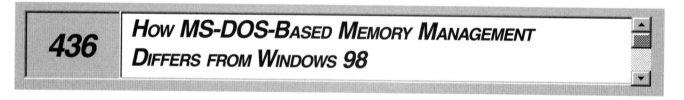

436 HOW MS-DOS-BASED MEMORY MANAGEMENT DIFFERS FROM WINDOWS 98

As you have learned, when you run Windows-based programs, Windows 98 uses virtual memory to give each program the illusion that it has almost unlimited available memory. Unfortunately, MS-DOS-based programs do not use virtual memory. Instead, MS-DOS-based programs use the following memory technologies:

*   Conventional memory

*   High memory

*   Upper memory

*   *DPMI* (DOS Protected Mode Interface) memory

*   Expanded memory

*   Extended memory

When you run an MS-DOS-based program within Windows 98, you can use the program's Properties dialog box to tell Windows 98 the types of memory the program uses. The following Tips discuss the various DOS-based memory technologies in detail.

437 CONTROLLING AN *MS-DOS-BASED* PROGRAM'S CONVENTIONAL MEMORY

Within your PC, conventional memory comprises your computer's first 640Kb of RAM. To run, all MS-DOS programs must reside within your PC's conventional memory. When you run an MS-DOS-based program, Windows 98 will provide the program with as much conventional memory as the program requires, up to 640Kb. If you know your program's specific memory requirements, you can reduce the amount of memory that Windows 98 reserves for the programs use by specifying the program's conventional memory requirements within the program's Properties dialog box Memory sheet. Usually, you will select the Auto value for the Memory sheet's Total and Initial environment fields, which lets Windows 98 allocate conventional memory for the program automatically. However, using either pull-down list, you can specify the memory amount you desire. If you click your mouse on the Protected checkbox, Windows 98 will monitor the program's memory use (which will slow down the program's execution) to ensure that the program does not change conventional memory locations in ways that may disrupt other programs.

438 CONTROLLING AN *MS-DOS-BASED* PROGRAM'S EXPANDED MEMORY

Because of the PC's hardware limitations, MS-DOS programs were originally restricted to the PC's 640Kb of conventional memory. Unfortunately, as programs became more complex and the amount of data the programs required increased, programs quickly outgrew the available 640Kb. As a solution, Lotus, Intel, and Microsoft designed the *expanded memory specification* (also known as *EMS*)—a memory-management technique that tricked the PC into thinking it had more available memory than 640K. The EMS standard was actually designed for very old 8088-based machines (the original IBM PC). In general, using special hardware (called an EMS card) and software, programs divided their data into 64Kb sections, storing all the data within the EMS memory. Next, the software would allocate a 64Kb memory region within conventional memory that it would use to hold pieces of data. When the program needed to access specific data, the EMS software would move the data from the EMS memory card into the 64Kb region (within conventional memory) the PC could access. In this way, a program could access a large spreadsheet by moving parts of the spreadsheet to and from EMS memory. However, this continual swapping of data between expanded and conventional memory, was time consuming. Over time, therefore, expanded memory was replaced by extended memory. To run a program that requires expanded memory, you must direct Windows 98 to use it. To activate expanded memory, perform these steps:

1. Within Explorer, right-click your mouse on the icon of the program you desire. Windows 98 will display a pop-up menu. Within the pop-up menu, select the Properties option. Windows 98 will display the program's Properties dialog box.

2. Within the Properties dialog box, click your mouse on the Memory tab. Windows 98 will display the Memory sheet. Within the Memory sheet, the Expanded (EMS) memory area will let you know if you are using expanded memory or if your system is configured to use expanded memory.

3. To configure your system to use expanded memory, you must edit your *CONFIG.SYS* file to remove the term *noems* (if it exists) from the line in *CONFIG.SYS* that contains the *EMM386.EXE* driver (you may have to add an entry for the driver itself).

4. After you enable expanded memory support within CONFIG.SYS and restart your system, you can use the Memory sheet's Details button to configure your expanded memory settings.

---

439 CONTROLLING AN MS-DOS-BASED PROGRAM'S EXTENDED MEMORY

In Tip 438, you learned that expanded memory let the original IBM PC (the 8088-base system) trick programs into thinking they had memory available beyond 640Kb. As discussed, however, expanded memory was slow. With the advent of the 286-based PC-AT came a new memory-management technique called *extended memory*. The extended memory specification (also known as XMS) defines PC memory that resides above 1Mb. When you add RAM to your PC, that RAM almost always increases your amount of extended memory. When you run an MS-DOS-based program within Windows 98, you can use the program's Properties dialog box Memory sheet to specify the program's extended-memory requirements by performing these steps:

1. Within the Explorer, right-click your mouse on the icon of the program you desire. Windows 98 will display a pop-up menu.

2. Within the pop-up menu, select the Properties option. Windows 98 will display the program's Properties dialog box.

3. Within the Properties dialog box, click your mouse on the Memory tab. Windows 98 will display the Memory sheet.

4. Within the Memory sheet, use the Extended (XMS) memory pull-down list to specify the program's extended-memory requirements. If you select Auto, Windows 98 will allocate extended memory to the program as the program requires. If you select None, you will disable the program's extended memory use. Finally, the list's other values let you allocate 1Mb, 2Mb, 3Mb, of extended memory, and so on.

5. If you want the program to use the high memory area (the first 64Kb of extended memory), click your mouse on the Uses HMA checkbox, placing a check mark within the box.

6. After you specify the program's extended memory requirements, click your mouse on the OK button.

---

440 CONTROLLING AN MS-DOS-BASED PROGRAM'S USE OF DOS PROTECTED MODE INTERFACE (DPMI) MEMORY

Usually, MS-DOS-based programs will use either expanded or extended memory. If, however, your program uses DOS protected mode interface (DPMI) memory (the documentation that accompanied your software will tell you the program's DPMI requirements), you can specify the program's DPMI memory requirements using the Properties dialog box Memory sheet. To tell Windows 98 how much DPMI memory an MS-DOS program requires, perform these steps:

1. Within the Explorer, right-click your mouse on the icon of the program you desire. Windows 98 will display a pop-up menu.

2. Within the pop-up menu, select the Properties option. Windows 98, in turn, will display the program's Properties dialog box.

3. Within the Properties dialog box, click your mouse on the Memory tab. Windows 98 will

display the Memory sheet.

4. Within the Memory sheet, click your mouse on the MS-DOS protected-mode (DPMI) memory pull-down list and change the value, as needed. In most cases, you should simply set the value to Auto.

5. Within the Properties dialog box, click your mouse on the OK button.

441 CONTROLLING AN MS-DOS PROGRAM'S SCREEN AND WINDOW USE

As you have learned, Windows 98 lets you run MS-DOS-based programs within a window. Depending on the information your program displays to the screen, there may be times when you will want Windows 98 to run your MS-DOS program using the entire screen, without a window. To toggle the program's display between full-screen and window mode, press the ALT-ENTER keyboard combination. In addition, Figure 441 shows the Properties dialog box Screen sheet that you can use to control the appearance of an MS-DOS program's window.

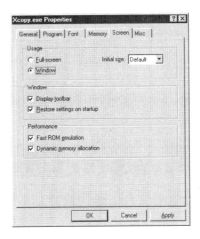

Figure 441 *The Properties dialog box Screen sheet.*

To customize an MS-DOS program's window settings, perform these steps:

1. Within Explorer, right-click your mouse on the icon of the program you desire. Windows 98 will display a pop-up menu.

2. Within pop-up menu, select the Properties option. Windows 98 will display the program's Properties dialog box.

3. Within the Properties dialog box, click your mouse on the Screen tab. Windows 98 will display the Screen sheet.

4. Within the Screen sheet, click your mouse on the Full-screen or Window radio button to control how Windows 98 displays the program.

5. Usually, Windows 98 displays 25 rows of text within an MS-DOS window. However, using the Initial size pull-down list, you can direct Windows 98 to use 25, 43, or even 50 lines.

6. Within the Window field, you can use the Display toolbar checkbox to control whether or not Windows 98 displays a toolbar within the MS-DOS window.

7. After you select the settings you desire, click your mouse on the OK button to put your changes into effect.

| 442 | IMPROVING AN MS-DOS-BASED PROGRAM'S VIDEO OUTPUT |

As you have learned, Windows 98 lets you run MS-DOS programs within a window. If the MS-DOS program that you are running within a window is a game or requires high-performance of its video output, you may be able to improve the program's performance by letting Windows 98 take control of the program's low-level output operations (which the PC's BIOS would usually perform). To direct Windows 98 to perform an MS-DOS program's low-level video operations, perform these steps:

1. Within the Explorer, right-click your mouse on the icon of the program you desire. Windows 98 will display a pop-up menu.

2. Within the pop-up menu, select the Properties option. Windows 98 will display the program's Properties dialog box.

3. Within the Properties dialog box, click your mouse on the Screen tab. Windows 98 will display the Screen sheet.

4. Within the Screen sheet, click your mouse on the Performance field's Fast ROM emulation checkbox, placing a check mark within the box.

5. Within the Properties dialog box, click your mouse on OK to put your changes into effect.

Note: *Should you experience errors when Windows 98 performs a program's low-level video operations, you can use the settings discussed in this Tip to disable Windows 98 performance of the video operations.*

| 443 | CONTROLLING AN MS-DOS-BASED PROGRAM'S VIDEO MEMORY |

As you have learned, Windows 98 lets you run an MS-DOS-based program within a window. Depending on the program's processing, it may display its output in a text-based mode or using graphics. Depending on which mode the program uses to display its output, the amount of video memory that Windows 98 must reserve for the program will differ. Usually, to conserve memory, Windows 98 makes assumptions about how your MS-DOS-based programs will use your computer's video memory and then allocates memory later, as necessary. Using the Properties dialog box Screen sheet, you can control whether Windows 98 allocates memory for text and graphics video output or whether Windows 98 simply allocates the memory dynamically. If you experience video errors when you run an MS-DOS-based program, you may need to disable Windows 98 dynamic video-memory allocation for the program by performing these steps:

1. Within the Explorer, right-click your mouse on the icon of the program you desire. Windows 98, in turn, will display a pop-up menu.

2. Within the pop-up menu, select the Properties option. Windows 98 will display the program's Properties dialog box.

3. Within the Properties dialog box, click your mouse on the Screen tab. Windows 98, in turn, will display the Screen sheet.

4. Within the Screen sheet, click your mouse on the Performance field Dynamic memory allocation checkbox, removing the check mark from the box.

5. Within the Properties dialog box, click your mouse on OK to put your changes into effect.

444 **CONTROLLING SCREEN SAVER OPERATIONS FOR MS-DOS PROGRAMS**

When you run MS-DOS programs within Windows 98, you may encounter conflicts between the program and the Windows 98 screen saver. Should, as you are interacting with the program, the screen saver start, you may want Windows 98 to disable the screen saver whenever you are running the MS-DOS program (as the current foreground task). To disable the screen saver for a specific MS-DOS program, perform these steps:

1. Within the Explorer, right-click your mouse on the icon of the program you desire. Windows 98 will display a pop-up menu.

2. Within the pop-up menu, select the Properties option. Windows 98, in turn, will display the program's Properties dialog box.

3. Within the Properties dialog box, click your mouse on the Misc tab. Windows 98 will display the Misc sheet, as shown in Figure 444.

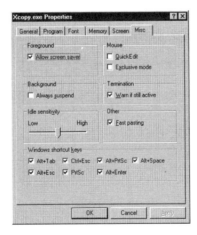

Figure 444 The Properties dialog box Misc sheet.

4. Within the Misc sheet, click your mouse on the Allow screen saver checkbox to remove the check mark. Then, click your mouse on the OK button to put your changes into effect.

445 **SUSPENDING OR ALLOWING MS-DOS PROGRAMS IN THE BACKGROUND**

When you run multiple programs at the same time within Windows 98, the program with which you are currently interacting is the *foreground task*. As you have learned, Windows 98 will pass the keys you type at the keyboard and your mouse operations to the foreground (or active) task. Your other programs, in turn, are *background tasks*. Depending on a program's processing, many programs continue to run as background tasks. For example, assume that you start the Internet Explorer and direct it to download the Microsoft Web site. As the Internet Explorer is downloading data, you switch to Outlook Express and type a quick e-mail message. As you are typing within Outlook Express, it is a foreground task. However, Internet Explorer, which is now a background task, will continue to run, downloading the Microsoft Web site.

Certain MS-DOS programs, unfortunately, will not run as background tasks—usually because they need resources that Windows 98 might have tied up for the foreground task. Rather than having the MS-DOS program fail when you select a different foreground task, you can direct Windows 98 to simply suspend the MS-DOS program's execution. To prevent an MS-DOS-based program from running as a background task, perform these steps:

1. Within the Explorer, right-click your mouse on the icon of the program you desire. Windows 98 will display a pop-up menu.

2. Within the pop-up menu, select the Properties option. Windows 98 will display the program's Properties dialog box.

3. Within the Properties dialog box, click your mouse on the Misc tab. Windows 98, in turn, will display the Misc sheet.

4. Within the Misc sheet, click your mouse on the Background field's Always suspend checkbox, placing a check mark within the box.

5. Within the Properties dialog box, click the OK button to put your changes into effect.

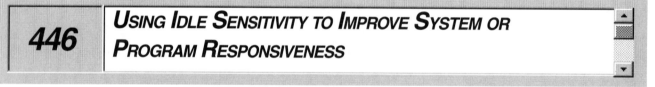

446 USING IDLE SENSITIVITY TO IMPROVE SYSTEM OR PROGRAM RESPONSIVENESS

When you ran a program within the MS-DOS operating system, that program was the only program you could run at one time. MS-DOS is not a multitasking operating system. Unfortunately, when you run an MS-DOS program within Windows 98, there may be times when the program will act as if it is the only program running on your system. In other words, the MS-DOS program ties up virtually all your CPU's processing time, which makes your Windows-based programs that are running within the background appear to stop.

Within the program's Properties dialog box Misc sheet, you can use the Idle sensitivity slider to either monopolize or minimize its use of the CPU. To control an MS-DOS program's CPU use, perform these steps:

1. Within the Explorer, right-click your mouse on the icon of the program you desire. Windows 98 will display a pop-up menu.

2. Within the pop-up menu, select the Properties option. Windows 98 will display the program's Properties dialog box.

3. Within the Properties dialog box, click your mouse on the Misc tab. Windows 98 will display the Misc sheet.

4. Within the Misc sheet, use your mouse to drag the Idle sensitivity slider to the right to reduce the program's CPU use or to the left to increase its use.

5. Within the Properties dialog box, click your mouse on OK to put your changes into effect.

447 CONTROLLING MOUSE OPERATIONS IN AN MS-DOS-BASED WINDOW

As you know, Windows-based programs make extensive use of mouse operations. If you encounter errors or problems when you try to use a mouse within an MS-DOS-based program, you can use the Properties dialog box Misc sheet to customize the program's mouse settings. Figure 447 shows the Misc sheet.

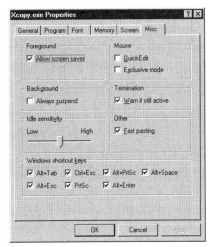

Figure 447 *A program's Properties dialog box Misc sheet.*

Within the Misc sheet's Mouse field, you can use the check boxes to control the way your MS-DOS program will interpret mouse movements. Usually within a DOS-based window, when you want to select text for a cut-and-paste operation, you must click the Mark toolbar button. If, within the Properties dialog box Misc page, you check the QuickEdit check box, you will be able to select MS-DOS text directly with your mouse without having to first click the Mark toolbar button. Many MS-DOS programs run poorly with QuickEdit checked; therefore, Windows 98 usually leaves the QuickEdit option unchecked.

Also, if your MS-DOS program does not respond well to mouse operations, place a check mark within the Mouse field's Exclusive Mode checkbox. When you activate the Exclusive Mode setting, the MS-DOS program exclusively controls the mouse; no other program running will be able to use the mouse until you close the MS-DOS-based program's window. Because Windows 98 programs rely heavily on the mouse, you do not want to activate the Exclusive mode setting unless a specific MS-DOS program requires it. To control an MS-DOS program's mouse operations, perform these steps:

1. Within the Explorer, right-click your mouse on the icon of the program you desire. Windows 98 will display a pop-up menu.
2. Within the pop-up menu, select the Properties option. Windows 98 will display the program's Properties dialog box.
3. Within the Properties dialog box, click your mouse on the Misc tab. Windows 98, in turn, will display the Misc sheet.
4. Within the Misc sheet's Mouse field, click your mouse on the checkboxes you require.
5. Within the Properties dialog box, click your mouse on the OK button to put your changes into effect.

448 CONTROLLING HOW WINDOWS 98 TERMINATES AN MS-DOS-BASED PROGRAM

Usually, when you close an MS-DOS program's window, one of two things will happen. First, Windows 98 may simply end the program and close the window. Or, second, Windows 98 will display a warning box to give you one last chance to save the program's data before the program ends. Because they were not originally designed to run within a window, many MS-DOS programs do not always recognize that you are closing the MS-DOS window. Therefore, if you have not saved the program's data before you close the program's window, you might lose your work. To reduce your chance of losing unsaved data in this way, you can request that Windows 98 always warn you before it closes your MS-DOS program's window. To direct Windows 98 to warn you before it closes an MS-DOS program, perform these steps:

1. Within the Explorer, right-click your mouse on the icon of the program you desire. Windows 98 will display a pop-up menu.

2. Within the pop-up menu, select Properties. Windows will display the Properties dialog box.

3. Within the Properties dialog box, click your mouse on the Misc tab. Windows 98 will display the Misc sheet.

4. Within the Misc sheet, click your mouse on the Termination field's Warn if still active checkbox, placing a check mark in the box.

5. Within the Properties dialog box, click your mouse on OK to put your changes into effect.

449 CONTROLLING SHORTCUT KEYS FOR AN MS-DOS-BASED PROGRAM

As you have learned, Windows 98 defines shortcut keys that help you perform a variety of common operations. For example, if you press the CTRL-ESC keyboard combination, Windows 98 will display the Start menu. Likewise, if you press the ALT-TAB combination, Windows 98 will display a small pop-up box within which you can select the program you want to make active. When you run an MS-DOS-based program, there may be times when one or more of the Windows 98 shortcut keys conflict with the program's shortcut key definitions. In such cases, you can use the program's Properties dialog box Misc sheet to reserve the shortcut key for the program's use. Table 449 defines the shortcut keys which you can reserve for the program's use.

Key	Purpose
ALT-TAB	Displays a pop-up box containing the icons for programs Windows 98 is currently running within which you can select the program you desire
ALT-ESC	Toggles through the active program windows
CTRL-ESC	Displays the Start menu
PRTSC	Copies the current screen contents to the Clipboard
ALT-PRTSC	Copies the current window contents to the Clipboard
ALT-ENTER	Toggles a program's display between a window and full screen
ALT-SPACEBAR	Displays a program's Control menu

Table 449 The shortcut key combinations you can reserve for an MS-DOS program's use.

To reserve a Windows 98 keyboard shortcut for an MS-DOS-based program's use, perform these steps:

1. Within the Explorer, right-click your mouse on the icon of the program you desire. Windows 98 will display a pop-up menu.
2. Within the pop-up menu, select the Properties option. Windows 98 will display the program's Properties dialog box.
3. Within the Properties dialog box, click your mouse on the Misc tab. Windows 98, in turn, will display the Misc sheet.
4. Within the Misc sheet's Windows shortcut keys field, remove the check mark from each shortcut key you want to reserve for the program's exclusive use.
5. Within the Properties dialog box, click your mouse on OK to put your changes into effect.

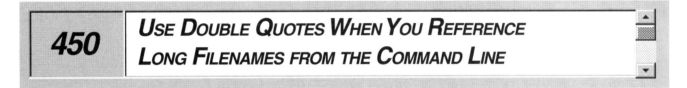

450 USE DOUBLE QUOTES WHEN YOU REFERENCE LONG FILENAMES FROM THE COMMAND LINE

As you learned in Tip 75, Windows 98 supports long filenames, up to 255 characters, that let you assign meaningful names to the documents you store within files on your disk. When you create files within Windows 98, you should take advantage of long filenames to assign meaningful names to your files that accurately describe the file's contents. Provided you only use Windows 98 or Windows 98-based programs, you will not experience problems by using long filenames. However, if you work from the command prompt, you can only refer to files using an eight-character filename and a three-character extension (users refer to this filename format as the 8.3 format). Should you need to work with long filenames from the MS-DOS command-line prompt, simply enclose the long filenames in double-quote marks, as shown in following commands:

```
C:\WINDOWS> DIR "This is a long Filename.DOC"  <ENTER>

C:\WINDOWS> COPY "C:\Long Directory Path\Some Filename.DOC" A:  <ENTER>
```

451 UNDERSTANDING THE TILDE (~) CHARACTER WITHIN MS-DOS FILENAMES

As you know, Windows 98 lets you assign long filenames to your documents. At the same time, Windows 98 must let your computer remain compatible with systems, such as MS-DOS, that do not use long filenames. If you use the DIR command to display a directory listing within an MS-DOS window, you will find that Windows 98 lists two filenames for each file: a short filename that conforms to the MS-DOS 8.3 (8 character filename and 3 character extension) format and the long filename.

Figure 451 Using the DIR command to view filenames within an MS-DOS window.

To convert a long filename to an 8.3-compatible filename, Windows 98 uses the first six characters of the long filename, followed by a tilde (~) and a number that begins at 1. For example, Windows 98 might abbreviate the long filename "Budget Information for the Year 2000.DAT" as *Budget~1.DAT*.

If you copy files with long filenames to a floppy disk and use that diskette in a non-Windows 98 computer, the other computer will have no trouble reading the files because it will see only the short, valid filenames. Although the filenames may look unusual, the other computer can use the files.

452 DRAGGING AND DROPPING A FILE TO THE MS-DOS COMMAND-LINE PROMPT

When you work from within an MS-DOS window, Windows 98 abbreviates long filenames using a tilde (~) character. If you are having trouble typing a filename at the command prompt, you can use your mouse to drag the filename from an Explorer window to the command line. When you release your mouse-select button within the MS-DOS window, Windows 98, in turn, will type the file's complete pathname for you within the command line.

453 WINDOWS 98 STORES MOST MS-DOS COMMANDS WITHIN THE C:\WINDOWS\COMMAND DIRECTORY

If you are upgrading to Windows 98 from an MS-DOS (or Windows 3.1 environment), you know that your DOS commands, such as DelTree or Xcopy, usually reside within a directory on your boot disk named *DOS*. When you install Windows 98, the installation program removes the *DOS* directory and places the MS-DOS commands that you can run from within Windows 98 within the *C:\WINDOWS\COMMAND* directory.

If you define a command path using the AUTOEXEC.BAT file, as discussed in Tip 421, you should place the *C:\WINDOWS\COMMAND* directory within the path.

454 MOVING UP MULTIPLE DIRECTORY LEVELS USING THE CD COMMAND

As you have learned, to help you organize the files on your disk, Windows 98 provides folders. If you have used MS-DOS in the past, you probably referred to folders as directories. Within the MS-DOS operating system, users move from one directory to another using the CD (or CHDIR) command. Using the CD command, users simply specified the directory they desired. To select the Windows directory, for example, the user would use the CD command as follows:

```
C:\> CD \Windows <ENTER>
```

To move from a subdirectory using CD, users took advantage of the double period abbreviation. For example, to move from the Windows directory back up to the root, the user would issue the following CD command:

```
C:\WINDOWS> CD .. <ENTER>
```

If the user was working a directory that was several layers deep, the user could issue multiple CD commands to move up one level at a time, as shown here:

```
C:\WINDOWS\TEMP\DATA> CD  ..  <ENTER>

C:\WINDOWS\TEMP> CD  ..  <ENTER>

C:\WINDOWS> CD  ..  <ENTER>

C:\>
```

Windows 98 further enhances the CD command's ability to move up levels of the directory tree. Using the CD command, if you want to move up more than one directory at a time, you simply add an extra dot for each level. The previous three MS-DOS CD commands would become:

```
C:\WINDOWS\TEMP\DATA> CD .... <ENTER>

C:\>
```

The first two dots tell CD to back up one parent directory; the third dot tells CD to back up one more parent directory, and the final dot requests that CD back up to one more parent directory.

455 **TAKING ADVANTAGE OF WINDOWS 98 SUPPORT FOR NOTEBOOK PCS**

If you use a notebook PC, you will find that Windows 98 provides several utility programs you can run to simplify such tasks as exchanging files between your notebook PC and desktop PC, spooling a print file to disk for printing at a later time, and utilities you can use to configure your PCMCIA-based devices, such as a modem. In addition, Windows 98 provides several power-management features that will help you get the most from your notebook PC's battery life. Several of the Tips that follow examine Windows 98 notebook PC features in detail. Before you continue with these Tips, however, you should take time to record your name, address, and phone number within your notebook PC bag and possibly on to a file you store on your disk, as discussed next. As more travelers hit the road with their notebook PCs, more and more people either fall victim to PC theft or simply forget their notebooks in the airport or a rental car in their rush to catch a flight. If you travel with a notebook PC, make sure you place your name, address, and phone number within your PC's carrying case. Next, use the WordPad accessory program to create a document that offers a reward for your PC's safe return, similar to the one shown in Figure 455. (You might, for example, name your document *PCReward.DOC*.)

Figure 455 *A WordPad document that offers a reward for a PC's safe return.*

Next, using the Windows 98 Explorer, you can place the document within the Startup menu, which will cause Windows 98 to display the document's contents each time your system starts. That way, should someone find and turn on your PC, the first thing they will see is your offer of a reward. To place your document within the Startup menu, perform these steps:

1. Click your mouse on the Start menu Settings option and choose the Taskbar & Start Menu option. Windows 98, in turn, will display the Taskbar Properties dialog box.

2. Within the Taskbar Properties dialog box, click your mouse on the Start Menu Programs tab. Windows 98 will display the Start Menu Programs sheet.

3. Within the Start Menu Programs sheet, click your mouse on the Add button. Windows 98 will display the Create Shortcut dialog box.

4. Within the Create Shortcut dialog box, click your mouse on the Browse button. Windows 98 will display the Browse dialog box.

5. Within the Browse dialog box, locate the document, then double-click your mouse on the document file that contains your reward text. Windows 98, in turn, will return you to the Create Shortcut dialog box.

6. Within the Create Shortcut dialog box, click your mouse on the Next button. Windows 98, in turn, will display the Select Program Folder dialog box.

7. Within the Select Program folder dialog box, scroll through the list of folders until you encounter the Startup folder. Click your mouse on the Startup folder and then click your mouse on the Next button. Windows 98 will display the Select a Title for the Program dialog box.

8. Within the Select a Title for the Program dialog box, type in the text PC Reward and then click your mouse on the Finish button. Windows 98 will add your document to the Startup menu. The next time you start your system, Windows 98 will display the document's contents.

Note: *Should you later decide that you no longer want Windows 98 to display your document each time your system starts, remove the document from the Startup folder.*

456	### KEEP A STARTUP FLOPPY DISK IN YOUR PC BAG

If you travel with a notebook PC, you should keep a startup floppy disk in your PC bag that you can use to boot your notebook PC should you encounter a system error while you are on the road. By booting your notebook using a floppy disk, you may be able to copy key files from your hard disk which you can then use on a different PC (such as a PC within your hotel's business center). To create a startup, bootable floppy disk, perform these steps:

1. Insert an unused floppy disk into your disk drive.

2. Click your mouse on the Start menu Settings option and choose Control Panel. Windows 98, in turn, will open the Control Panel window.

3. Within the Control Panel window, double-click your mouse on the Add/Remove Programs icon. Windows 98, in turn, will display the Add/Remove Programs Properties dialog box.

4. Within the Add/Remove Programs Properties dialog box, click your mouse on the Startup Disk tab. Windows 98, in turn, will display the Startup Disk sheet, as shown in Figure 456.

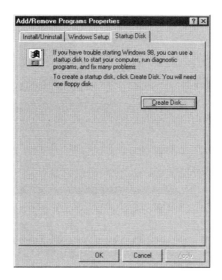

Figure 456 *The Startup Disk Sheet.*

5. Within the Startup Disk sheet, click your mouse on the Create Disk button. Windows 98 may display a dialog box prompting you to insert your Windows 98 CD-ROM into your CD-ROM drive (so Windows 98 can copy the system files from the CD). Insert the CD-ROM and click your mouse on the OK button. Windows 98, in turn, will copy the system files to the floppy disk.

6. Remove the floppy disk drive from the drive and label the disk as Windows 98 Startup Floppy. Store the disk in a safe location within your PC bag.

457   **CONNECTING YOUR NOTEBOOK PC TO A DOCKING STATION**

Because of their small size, most notebook computers do not have the same peripherals as a desktop PC. Luckily, to gain the benefits of full-size and full-capacity peripheral equipment, you do not have to purchase a notebook and a desktop PC. Instead, you can buy a notebook PC that supports a *docking station*. In general, a docking station provides you with a chassis into which you slide your notebook PC. In turn, you connect external devices, such as a large monitor, to the docking station. In this way, when you use your notebook PC at your home or office, the docking station lets you use your notebook as if it were a desktop computer. Later, when you travel, you can remove your notebook from the docking station, leaving the larger peripherals behind.

The challenging part about using a docking station is that, depending on whether or not you are plugged into the docking station, your hardware devices will differ, and Windows 98 may think that you have hardware devices available that really are not there. To help Windows 98 manage your hardware configuration, you should create two hardware profiles, one for when you dock your notebook and one for when your notebook is undocked. Later, when you start your system, Windows 98 will display a prompt asking you which profile you want to use. To create hardware profiles for your notebook PC, perform these steps:

1. Click your mouse on the Start button. Windows 98, in turn, will display the Start menu.

2. Within the Start menu, click your mouse on the Settings option and then click your mouse on the Control Panel option. Windows 98, in turn, will open the Control Panel window.

3. Within the Control Panel window, double-click your mouse on the System icon. Windows 98, in turn, will display the System Properties dialog box.

4. Within the System Properties dialog box, click your mouse on the Hardware Profiles tab. Windows 98, in turn, will display the Hardware Profiles sheet, as shown in Figure 457.

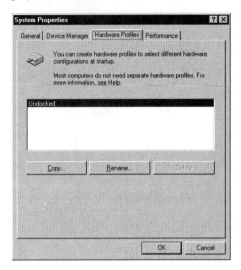

Figure 457 *The Hardware Profiles sheet.*

5. Within the Hardware Profiles sheet, click your mouse on the profile upon which you want to base your new profile and then click your mouse on the Copy button. Windows 98, in turn, will display the Copy Profile dialog box.

6. Within the Copy Profile dialog box, type in the name for your new hardware profile, such as Docked, and then click your mouse on the OK button.

7. Within the System Properties dialog box, click your mouse on the Close button.

Later, when you start your system, Windows 98 will prompt you to select the hardware profile that you desire. After you choose a profile, you can add or delete device drivers based on your profile's configuration. Likewise, should you later dock your notebook PC, Windows 98 will automatically detect the docking station, so you do not need to reboot. Next, Windows 98 will update your notebook's configuration automatically. To later undock your PC, select the Start menu's Eject PC option (non-docking notebooks will not offer this option on the Start menu). Windows 98 will reconfigure itself for notebook use. Again, Windows 98 does not require you to turn off your computer to undock it.

458 **USING PCMCIA CARDS TO EXTEND A NOTEBOOK PC'S HARDWARE CAPABILITIES**

If you are using a desktop PC, you can add new hardware, such as a modem, to your PC by inserting a hardware card into one of the PC's expansion slots, Notebook PCs, on the other hand, don't have expansion slots. Instead, most notebook PCs have two slots for PCMCIA cards. A PCMCIA card (which stands for Personal Computer Memory Card Interface Association) lets you easily add or remove devices on a notebook PC. If you want to install a faster modem, for example, simply purchase a PCMCIA modem card and insert the card into your notebook PC. Today, you can purchase PCMCIA cards for modems, networks, external CD-ROM drives, tape backup drives, and even memory. Several of the Tips that follow detail Windows 98 support for PCMCIA cards.

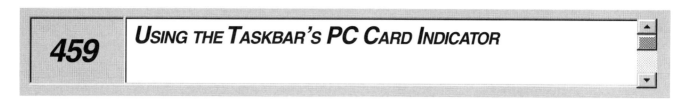

459 USING THE TASKBAR'S *PC CARD INDICATOR*

As you have learned, within Windows 98, the Taskbar is your control center with which you can quickly switch from one application to another or to control system settings, such as the date and time or your scheduled events. In addition, if you are using PCMCIA-based devices, you can display an icon on the Taskbar which gives you access to card's settings, as shown in Figure 459.1.

Figure 459.1 *Displaying a PC card icon on the Windows 98 Taskbar.*

To display the Taskbar's PC card indicator, perform these steps:

1. Click your mouse on the Start button. Windows 98, in turn, will display the Start menu.
2. Within the Start menu, click your mouse on the Settings option and then choose Control Panel. Windows 98, in turn, will open the Control Panel window.
3. Within the Control Panel window, double-click your mouse on the PC Card icon. Windows 98, in turn, will display the PC Card (PCMCIA) Properties dialog box, as shown in Figure 459.2.

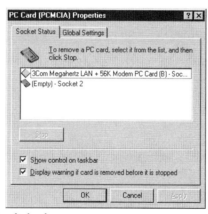

Figure 459.2 *The PC Card (PCMCIA) Properties dialog box.*

4. Within the PC Card (PCMCIA) Properties dialog box, click your mouse on the Show control on taskbar checkbox, placing a check mark within the box, and then click your mouse on OK

460 INSTALLING A *PCMCIA-BASED DEVICE* WITHIN *WINDOWS 98*

When you insert a PCMCIA into a notebook PC for the first time, you may need to install software for the card (a device driver) onto your system before Windows 98 can access the device. Windows 98 lets you insert a PCMCIA card while your notebook is turned on or turned off. Usually, Windows 98 will display a dialog box telling you that it has identified your new hardware and that it will install any new software it requires. If, for some reason, Windows 98 fails to recognize a PCMCIA-based device when you insert the card, you may need to run the Windows 98 Add New Hardware Wizard by performing these steps:

1. Click your mouse on the Start button. Windows 98, in turn, will display the Start menu.
2. Within the Start menu, click your mouse on the Settings and then click your mouse on the Control Panel option. Windows 98, in turn, will open the Control Panel window.
3. Within the Control Panel window, double-click your mouse on the Add New Hardware icon. Windows 98, in turn, will start the Add New Hardware Wizard which, in turn, will search your PC for a new hardware device.

After you install your PCMCIA card's device driver, the device is ready for use. Should you later decide to remove the card from your PC, perhaps so you can insert a different card, the card's device driver software will remain on your system. When you later insert the card again (with your PC powered on or off), Windows 98 will be immediately ready to use your device.

461 INSERTING AND LATER REMOVING A *PCMCIA* CARD FROM A NOTEBOOK *PC*

As you have learned in the previous Tips, to use a PCMCIA-based device, you simply insert the PCMCIA card into your notebook PC. Windows 98, in turn, will recognize your new device. Windows 98 lets you insert a PCMCIA card while it is running (users call this process "hot swapping" the card) or while your PC is powered off.

Likewise, Windows 98 lets you remove a PCMCIA card while your system is on or off. If your PC is off, you can simply remove the card. However, if your PC system is on, you should first turn off the card before you remove it by performing these steps:

1. If your Taskbar contains a PC Card icon, double-click your mouse on the icon. Otherwise, within the Windows 98 Control Panel, double-click your mouse on the PC Card icon. Windows 98, in turn, will display the PC Card (PCMCIA) Properties dialog box, as shown in Figure 461.

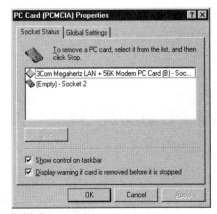

Figure 461 *The PC Card (PCMCIA) Properties dialog box.*

2. Within the PC Card (PCMCIA) Properties dialog box, click your mouse on the entry for the PC card you want to remove and then click your mouse on the Stop button. Windows 98, in turn, will stop the device and will then display a dialog box telling you that it is safe for you to remove the device.

3. Within the PC Card (PCMCIA) Properties dialog box, click your mouse on the OK button.

462   EXCHANGING DOCUMENTS BETWEEN YOUR NOTEBOOK AND DESKTOP PC

If you use a notebook PC when you are away from your office and you use a desktop PC at work, there will be times when you end up with copies of files on both systems. The challenging part of managing files you store on different PCs is keeping track of which computer has the latest version. (In later Tips, you will learn how to transfer files between your notebook and desktop PC.)

In previous Tips, you learned how to use the Windows 98 Explorer to view specifics about a file, such as the file's date and time stamps, that tell you when the file was last modified. By using the Explorer to look at both system's files, you can determine your most current files by examining their date and time stamps. Then, you can copy the newer file to either your desktop or notebook PC, as your needs require. Fortunately, however, Windows 98 provides an easier way for you to manage files, the My Briefcase utility.

The Windows 98 My Briefcase utility is so named because it functions much like a leather briefcase within which you would carry files between your home and the office. Using the Briefcase utility, you can direct Windows 98 itself to determine the most recent version of a file and to perform the file updates for you. To move files between your desktop and notebook PC, you will use the My Briefcase folder to store all the files you move between PCs.

In general, the My Briefcase utility lets you create one or more special Briefcase folders. If your Desktop does not have a My Briefcase folder visible, you can create one by performing these steps:

1. Right-click your mouse on an unused location on the Desktop. Windows 98, in turn, will display a pop-up menu.

2. Within the pop-up menu, click your mouse on the New option and choose Briefcase. Windows 98, in turn, will create a special Briefcase folder on your Desktop.

The easiest way to understand how the My Briefcase utility works is simply to try it. To "test drive" the Briefcase, this Tip will use your floppy disk drive to simulate a remote notebook computer. (To exchange files between your notebook and desktop PC, you can use a local-area network, a direct connect parallel, serial, or infrared connection or, as you will see here, a floppy disk.) To try out the My Briefcase utility, perform these steps:

1. To begin, you will use the WordPad accessory to create a short document named *Demo.DOC*, that you will exchange between your notebook and desktop PC. To create the document, click your mouse on the Start menu Programs options and choose Accessories. Windows 98 will display the Accessories submenu. Within the Accessories submenu, select the Wordpad option. Windows 98 will open the WordPad window.

2. Within the WordPad window, type the text **This is my sample document**. Using the File menu Save As option to store your document within the My Documents folders with the file name *Demo.DOC*. Then, close the WordPad window.

3. Next, you will use the Explorer to copy your file from the My Documents folder into the Briefcase folder that resides on your Desktop. To start the Explorer, click your mouse on the Start menu Programs option and choose Explorer. Windows 98 will open the Explorer window. Using your mouse, drag the Explorer window to the right so you can see the Briefcase folder's icon on your Desktop.

4. Within the Explorer window, open the My Documents folder and locate the *Demo.DOC* file. Hold down the CTRL key and use your mouse to drag the file onto the Briefcase icon. Windows 98, in turn, will copy your document file into the My Briefcase folder.

5. Insert an unused floppy disk into your floppy disk drive.

6. Using your mouse, drag the Briefcase icon that appears on your Desktop onto the floppy disk drive icon that appears within the Explorer window. Windows 98, in turn, will copy the Briefcase folder's contents to the floppy disk.

7. Follow Step 1 to start the WordPad accessory. Within WordPad, open the file *Demo.DOC* that resides on your floppy disk. (You will find the file within the Briefcase folder on the floppy disk.) Within the document, add the text **I am changing my demo file**. Use the File menu Save option to save your change and then close the WordPad window. At this point, the file that resides on the floppy disk is now different than the file that resides within the My Briefcase folder on your PC. Although you used the same PC to modify the file, you could have just as easily taken the floppy to another PC, made your change, and then inserted the disk back into your system.

8. On your Desktop, double-click your mouse on the My Computer icon. Windows 98, in turn, will open the My Computer window. Within the My Computer window, double-click your mouse on the floppy disk drive icon and then, within the floppy disk folder, double-click your mouse on the Briefcase icon. Windows 98, in turn, will display the Briefcase folder, as shown in Figure 462.1.

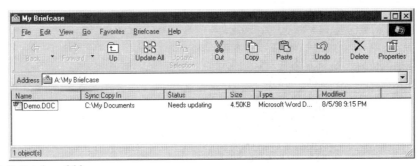

Figure 462.1 *The floppy disk's Briefcase folder.*

9. Within the floppy disk's Briefcase folder, locate the Status column for the *Demo.DOC* file. As you can see, the Status column shows that the file needs updating. In other words, the Briefcase utility realizes that the file's contents have changed.

10. Within the floppy disk's My Briefcase folder, click your mouse on the Briefcase menu Update All option. The Briefcase program, in turn, will display the Update My Briefcase dialog box, as shown in Figure 462.2.

11. Within the Update My Briefcase dialog box, the Briefcase utility will display specifics about how the file on the floppy disk and the file on your PC differ. Within the dialog box, the Briefcase program displays an arrow that indicates which files the Briefcase will use to perform the update.

12. Within the Update My Briefcase dialog box, click your mouse on the Update button to perform the file update operation.

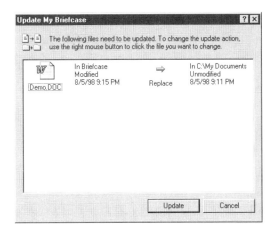

Figure 462.2 *The Update My Briefcase dialog box.*

Note: *If the Update My Briefcase dialog box shows the update arrow in the opposite direction that you desire, simply right-click your mouse on the arrow. Windows 98, in turn, will display a pop-up menu with which you can change the direction of the arrows or direct the software not to update the file.*

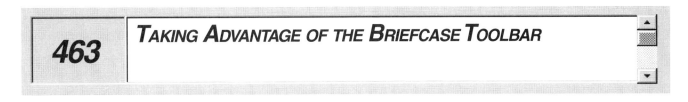

463 TAKING ADVANTAGE OF THE BRIEFCASE TOOLBAR

Like most Windows-based programs, the Briefcase utility provides a toolbar you can use to simplify common operations. If your Briefcase window is not currently showing the toolbar, click your mouse on the View menu Toolbar option, placing a check mark next to the option.

Figure 463 briefly explains each of the Briefcase toolbar buttons.

Lets you move between folders.

Moves you up one level within the directory tree.

Updates all the files in the My Briefcase folder that need updating.

Updates only selected files within the My Briefcase folder.

Cuts one or more selected files or folders from
the My Briefcase folder to the Clipboard.

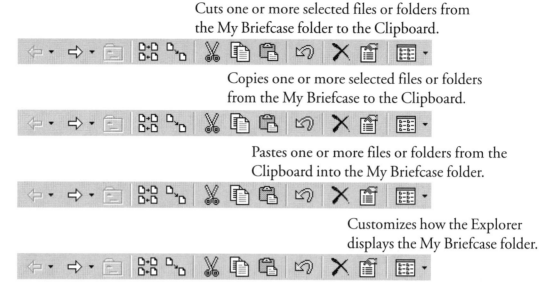

Copies one or more selected files or folders
from the My Briefcase to the Clipboard.

Pastes one or more files or folders from the
Clipboard into the My Briefcase folder.

Customizes how the Explorer
displays the My Briefcase folder.

Figure 463 Using the Briefcase toolbar.

464 **BEFORE YOU USE THE BRIEFCASE, MAKE SURE YOUR
SYSTEM DATE AND TIME ARE CORRECT**

Each time you create or change a file, Windows 98 records the current date and time within the file's date-and-time stamp. In previous Tips, you learned how to display the file's date-and-time stamp within the Windows 98 Explorer. Before you use the Windows 98 Briefcase to manage files, make sure that your system time and date are correct. To determine the latest version of a file, the Briefcase examines the file's date-and-time stamp. If your system date and time are incorrect, the file's date-and-time stamp will be invalid and the Briefcase may overwrite a recent file with a file whose contents are out of date. To view your system's current date and time, aim your mouse pointer at the Taskbar clock. As shown in Figure 464, Windows 98 will display the current date above the clock.

Figure 464 Displaying the current date and time using the Taskbar clock.

If your current system date and time are not correct, double-click your mouse on the Taskbar clock. Windows 98, in turn, will display the Date/Time Properties dialog box, within which you can set the current system time.

465 **USING THE WINDOWS 98 BRIEFCASE TO UPDATE
A SPECIFIC FILE**

As you have learned, using the Windows 98 Briefcase, you can manage files that you keep on two different computers, such as your notebook and desktop PC. Usually, when you use the Briefcase program, the Briefcase will update files on both computers so that each system has the latest version of a file. As you work, there may be times when you only want the Briefcase to update specific files. For example, assume that while you are traveling, another user updates a file on your desktop PC. When you return from your trip, you decide that you want to keep the user's changes and that you do not want the Briefcase to update the file. To use the Briefcase to update only one specific file, perform these steps:

1. Within the Briefcase window, click your mouse on the file you want to update.
2. Click your mouse on the Briefcase menu and then choose the Update Selection option. The Briefcase, in turn, will update only your selected file.

If you want to update several specific files, simply hold down the CTRL key as you click your mouse on the files. Then, as discussed, select the Briefcase menu Update Selection option.

466 SPLITTING A BRIEFCASE FILE FROM THE ORIGINAL FILE

When you use the Briefcase programs, you may find that there are times when you must break (split) the relationship between an original file and a Briefcase file. Assume, for example, that while you are traveling, you make changes to a file on your notebook PC. Next, assume that while you are gone, one of your coworkers makes changes to the same file on your Desktop system. In this case, both files probably have changes that you will want to keep. If you simply let the Briefcase perform its update using the file last modified, you will lose information. Instead, you want to save two separate files. To split a Briefcase file from the desktop PC's file, open the Briefcase window, as discussed in Tip 462. Then, within the Briefcase window, click your mouse on the file you want to split and choose the Briefcase menu Split From Original option, as shown in Figure 466.

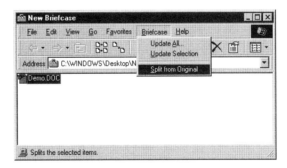

Figure 466 The Briefcase menu.

467 DEFERRING A PRINT JOB UNTIL A LATER TIME

If you work with a notebook computer, there may be many times when you do not have a printer connected to your PC. Usually, you would wait to print your documents until you connected a printer to your notebook. However, if you are really busy, you may want Windows 98 to spool the document so that it can later print the document as soon as you connect your PC to your printer. In other words, you want Windows 98 to defer your print jobs, meaning Windows 98 will spool the jobs, but will wait to actually print them. Likewise, if you work in a network environment, there may be times when you want to print a job to a network printer that, for some reason, is not currently available. By performing the steps discussed here, you can spool the job to the printer for printing at a later time.

Usually, if you print a job when your PC does not have a printer attached, Windows 98 will display an error message telling you that it cannot find a printer. To defer your print jobs, you must tell Windows 98 that you want to "work offline" by performing these steps:

1. Click your mouse on the Start button. Windows 98, in turn, will display the Start menu.
2. Within the Start menu, click your mouse on the Settings option. Windows 98, in turn, will display the Settings submenu.
3. Within the Settings submenu, click your mouse on the Printers option. Windows 98, will open the Printers window.
4. Within the Printers window, click your mouse on the File menu Work offline. Windows 98, in turn, will display a check mark next to the menu option.

After you tell Windows 98 that you want to work offline, you can then spool documents to your printers. Later, after you attach a printer to your PC, you can perform Steps 1 through 4 again to inform Windows 98 that you want to work online and to print the documents.

468 USING A DIRECT CABLE CONNECTION TO EXCHANGE FILES BETWEEN TWO PCS

If you use both a notebook and a desktop PC, there will be many times when you must transfer a file from one system to the other. Depending on the file's size, you may be able to copy the file to a floppy, e-mail the file to an account you can access on the second system, or if both PCs are connected to a network, you can transfer the file across the network. In addition to using these techniques, Windows 98 provides a special program that supports a *direct cable connection* between the two PCs. Using this feature, you can connect a null-modem cable to each computer's serial port, or you can connect a bi-directional parallel cable to each computer's parallel port, or you can use an infrared link. Next, you can use the Windows 98 Direct Cable Connection program to transfer files between the two PCs as if the two computers were networked together. When you use the Windows 98's Direct Cable Connection feature, you must designate one computer as the *host* computer and one as the *guest*. The guest computer copies files to or from the host system. The Tips that follow discuss how to use the Windows 98 Direct Cable Connection software to establish a guest and a host PC.

469 SETTING UP A GUEST COMPUTER FOR A DIRECT CABLE CONNECTION

As you learned in Tip 468, Windows 98 provides the Direct Cable Connection software program that lets you exchange files between two computers that you connect using a null-modem or bi-directional parallel cable. When you use the Direct Cable Connection software, you must set up one computer as the guest computer, before you set up the host. After you physically connect the host and guest computers, perform these steps to create a guest computer:

1. Click your mouse on the guest computer's Start menu. Windows 98, in turn, will display the Start menu.

2. Within the Start menu, elect the Programs menu Accessories option. Windows 98, in turn, will display its Accessories submenu.

3. Within the Accessories submenu, select the Communications menu Direct Cable Connection option. Windows 98, in turn, may display the Direct Cable Connection Wizard, as shown in Figure 469.1. (If you are using the Wizard for the first time, the Wizard will display the dialog box shown in Figure 469.2.)

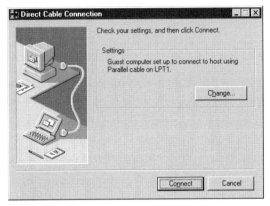

Figure 469.1 *Setting up the guest computer.*

4. Within the Direct Cable Connection Wizard, click your mouse on the Change button. The Wizard, in turn, will display a dialog box similar to that shown in Figure 469.2, within which you can select a host or guest computer.

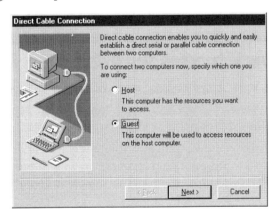

Figure 469.2 *Selecting a guest or host computer.*

5. Within the dialog box, click your mouse on the Guest radio button and then click your mouse on Next. The Wizard, in turn, will display a dialog box within which you can select the port to which you connected the null-modem or bi-directional parallel cable.

6. Within the dialog box, click your mouse on the port to which you connected the cable and then click your mouse on Next. The Wizard, in turn, will display its final dialog box telling you that you have successfully set up the guest computer.

7. Within the dialog box, click your mouse on the Finish button.

470 | SETTING UP A HOST COMPUTER FOR A DIRECT CABLE CONNECTION

As you have learned in Tip 468, using the Windows 98 Direct Cable Connection software, Windows 98 lets you exchange files between two connected computers. In Tip 469, you learned how to create a guest computer. After you define the guest computer, you must designate the host computer by performing these steps:

1. Click your mouse on the host computer's Start menu. Windows 98, in turn, will display the Start menu.
2. Within the Start menu, elect the Programs menu Accessories option. Windows 98 will display its Accessories submenu.
3. Within the Accessories submenu, select the Communications menu Direct Cable Connection option. Windows 98 will display the Direct Cable Connection Wizard.
4. If you connected a null-modem cable to the host's COM1 serial port, simply click your mouse on the Listen button. The Direct Cable Connection software, in turn, will start to listen for a guest connection. If, however, you connected the cable to different a port, click your mouse on the Change button and use the Wizard's dialog boxes to select the correct port.

After the host computer connects with a guest, the host computer will display a dialog box telling you that it has established a connection with the guest. The guest computer, in turn, can then connect to the host computer and access its shared files, folders, and printers.

471 | USING THE WINDOWS 98 ACCESSORY PROGRAMS

In addition to providing you with software to configure your system, Windows 98 also includes several "accessory" programs, such as a calculator, a word processor, and a simple drawing program. To run the Windows 98 accessory programs, select the Programs menu Accessories submenu, as shown in Figure 471.

Several of the Tips that follow discuss the accessory programs listed in Table 471.1. If you do not find these programs within your Accessories submenu, you can install the programs from the Windows 98 CD-ROM as discussed in Tip 218 (In some cases, the programs may appear on a different menu, such as the Internet Explorer submenu, that you will find within the Programs submenu.

Each of this book's Tips will direct you to the correct menu.) Although you will find the programs that Table 471.1 lists within the Accessories menu or one of its submenus, this book presents the programs with the most closely related Tips. In other words, rather than presenting the Tips in the same order as Table 471.1, this book groups together the Internet-related programs, the system utility programs, the multimedia programs, and so on. To locate the Tips that correspond to a specific program, turn to the index that appears at the back of this book.

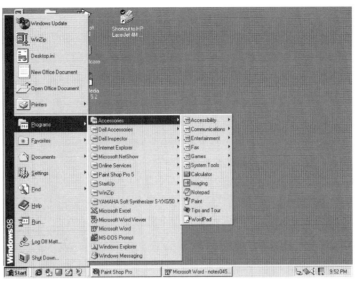

Figure 471 *The Programs menu Accessories submenu.*

Accessory Program	Purpose
Accessibility Wizard	Helps you configure a system to better support a user's hearing, sight, or mobility needs
Backup	Lets you backup your hard disk files to removable disks or tape
Character Map	Lets you copy characters of a specific font to the Clipboard from which you can later paste the character into your application
CD Player	Lets you play an audio CD using your PC's CD-ROM drive, sound card, and speakers
Clipboard Viewer	Lets you view or save the Clipboard's current contents
Compression Agent	Lets you specify the compression Windows 98 should apply to selected files on a disk you have compressed using DriveSpace 3
Dial-Up Networking	Lets you connect to a remote computer using your modem and then perform network operations over the connection, sharing files, folders, and printers
Direct Cable Connection	Lets you connect two computers using a serial, parallel, or infrared connection and then perform network operations over the connection, sharing files, folders, and printers
Disk Cleanup	Helps you increase your disk space by removing temporary files or Windows components that you no longer need
Drive Converter	Converts a disk from a 16-bit file-allocation table (FAT) to a higher-performance 32-bit file-allocation table
Disk Defragmenter	Improves your system performance by repairing fragmented files
DriveSpace	Increases your disk storage capacity by storing your files in a compressed format
Games	Includes the FreeCell, Hearts, Minesweeper, and Solitaire interactive computer games
HyperTerminal	Lets you connect to a remote computer using your modem and then access the computer as if your PC was a terminal

Table 471 *The Windows 98 accessory programs. (continued on the following page)*

Accessory Program	Purpose
Imaging	Provides software to scan images and to edit scans or faxes
Interactive CD Sampler	Provides an interactive catalog that presents Microsoft products
ISDN Configuration Wizard	Helps you configure an ISDN modem for a remote connection
Magnifier	Uses a portion of the screen to magnify the current display, making the screen easier to view
Maintenance Wizard	Lets you perform common operations, such as defragmenting your disks, at regular time intervals
Media Player	Lets you play back a variety of multimedia files and devices, including audio, video, and MIDI files, as well as audio CDs
Microsoft Chat	Lets you participate in on-line chats with remote users
Microsoft FrontPage Express	Lets you create HTML documents
Microsoft NetMeeting	Lets you communicate and share applications with users across a local-area network or the Internet
Microsoft Netshow Player 2.0	Lets you play back streaming multimedia (such as video and audio) across the Web
Microsoft Outlook Express	Lets you exchange electronic mail and view newsgroups
Microsoft VRML 2.0 Viewer	Lets you view virtual reality documents that follow the VRML 2 specification
Microsoft Wallet	Lets you perform secure shopping on the Internet
Net Watcher	Lets you monitor remote user connections to your computer
Personal Web Server	Lets you create your own personal Web site
Phone Dialer	Lets you use your modem to dial your phone calls
Quick View	Lets you preview a document without opening the document
Real Audio Player 4.0	Lets you play back audio, video, and animations across the Web
Resource Meter	Lets you monitor Windows 98 user, system, and GDI resource use
Scheduled Tasks	Lets you direct Windows 98 to run specific programs at a given time
Sound Recorder	Lets you record and play back your own audio files
System Information	Lets you display and print specifics about hardware and software
System Monitor	Lets you monitor Windows 98 operations to identify bottlenecks which may impact your system performance
Trial Programs	Lets you install trial versions for a variety of Microsoft programs
Virtual Private Networking	Lets you perform secure network operations across the Internet
Volume Control	Lets you adjust your PC speaker volume and balance
Web TV	Lets you use a TV receiver card within your PC to display television within a window
Welcome to Windows	A multimedia program that introduces the Internet, Windows 98, and helps you configure your system
Windows Scripting Host	Lets you create scripts to automate tasks
WinPopup	Lets you send pop-up messages to other users whose systems are connected to your network
WordPad	Lets you create simple word-processing documents

Table 471 *The Windows 98 accessory programs. (continued from previous page)*

If you upgraded your system to Windows 98 from Windows 3.1, Windows for Workgroups, or Windows 95 your Accessories menu may contain the programs Table 471.2 lists.

Accessory Program	Purpose
Calendar	A simple scheduling program that lets you keep track of appointments
Card File	A simple database program that records data using electronic index cards
Notepad	A simple text editor you can use to create and edit small (64Kb or less) text files

Table 471.2 *Older Windows accessory programs that may appear within your Accessories submenu.*

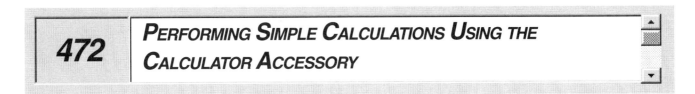

472 PERFORMING SIMPLE CALCULATIONS USING THE CALCULATOR ACCESSORY

As you work, there may be times when you need to quickly calculate numbers. You might, for example, have to multiply numbers that you are including in an e-mail message. In such cases, you no longer have to search your desk drawers for a calculator or an adding machine. Instead, you can use the Windows 98 Calculator accessory program, as shown in Figure 472.

Figure 472 *The Calculator program.*

After you use the Calculator to perform your calculation, you can cut your result from the Calculator and then paste it into your document. To start the Calculator accessory, perform these steps:

1. Click your mouse on the Start button. Windows 98, in turn, will display the Start menu.

2. Within the Start menu, click your mouse on the Programs option and then choose Accessories. Windows 98 will display the Accessories submenu.

3. Within the Accessories submenu, click your mouse on the Calculator option. Windows 98, in turn, will display the Calculator window previously shown in Figure 472.

Note: *If your Calculator window appears more advanced than the one shown in Figure 472, select the Calculator window View menu Standard option to display the Standard Calculator.*

To perform a simple calculation within the Calculator accessory, perform these steps:

1. If your PC's NUM LOCK light is off, press your keyboard NUM LOCK key to illuminate the light.

2. Within the Calculator program, use your keyboard's numeric keypad to type a number, such as **369**, or click your mouse on the numbers within the Calculator window.

3. To add a number to the number you just typed, press your keyboard's + (plus) key. To subtract, press the minus (-) key. To multiply, press the asterisk (*) key. And, to divide, press the forward slash (/) key. In addition to using your keyboard to specify these operations, you can also click your mouse on the corresponding keys within the Calculator window.

4. Within the Calculator window, enter the next number, such as **21**.

5. Press the ENTER key, the equal sign, or click your mouse on the = button. The Calculator, in turn, will display your result. If you want to copy the result into the Clipboard (so you can paste it into a different application), click your mouse on the Edit menu Copy option.

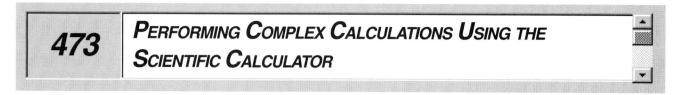

473 **PERFORMING COMPLEX CALCULATIONS USING THE SCIENTIFIC CALCULATOR**

In Tip 472, you learned how to start and use the Windows 98 Calculator accessory program. As it turns out, the Calculator accessory provides a standard calculator, which you used in Tip 472, and a more complex scientific calculator. Using the scientific calculator, you can perform simple statistics and trigonometric calculations. To display the Scientific Calculator, select the Calculator window's View menu Scientific option. The Calculator, in turn, will switch from the standard to scientific mode, as shown in Figure 473.

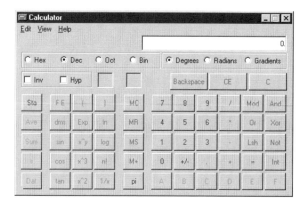

Figure 473 *The Scientific Calculator.*

474 **USING YOUR KEYBOARD TO ACCESS CALCULATOR BUTTONS**

As you usually use the numeric keypad to enter numbers within the Calculator accessory, you may find having to click your mouse on the operator buttons is time consuming. To save you time, the Calculator lets you press various keyboard combinations to access different Calculator buttons. Table 474 contains the Calculator's keyboard combinations.

Button	Keyboard	Button Function
C	Esc	Clears the current calculation.
CE	Del	Clears the current value.
Back	Backspace	Clears the current value's rightmost digit.
MC	Ctrl-L	Clears the Calculator's memory.
MR	Ctrl-R	Recalls the Calculator's memory.
M+	Ctrl-P	Adds the current value to the Calculator's memory and stores the result in memory.
MS	Ctrl-M	Stores the current value in the Calculator's memory.
+/-	F9	Changes the current value's sign.
1/x	R	Calculates the current value's reciprocal.
sqrt	@	Calculates the current value's square root.
%	%	Treats the current value as a percentage.
Mod	%	Calculates the remainder from division.
Or	|	Performs a bitwise OR.
Lsh	<	Performs a bitwise shift to the left. Inv+Lsh performs a bitwise shift to the right
And	&	Performs a bitwise exclusive AND.
Xor	^	Performs a bitwise exclusive OR.
Not	~	Performs a bitwise inverse.
Int	;	Displays the current value's integer portion.
A-F	A-F	Enters a hexadecimal digit.
PI	p	Displays the value of PI. Inv+PI displays 2 times PI.
Sta	Ctrl-S	Activates the Statistics Box.
Ave	Ctrl-A	Displays the average of the Statistics Box values.
Sum	Ctrl-T	Displays the sum of the Statistics Box values.
s	Ctrl-D	Calculates the standard deviation of the Statistics Box values.
Dat	Ins	Places the current value into the Statistics box.
F-E	v	Toggles scientific notation on and off.
dms	m	Converts the current value into the degrees-minutes-seconds format. Inv+dms converts the value back.
sin	s	Displays the current value's sine. Inv+sin displays the arc sine.
cos	o	Displays the current value's cosine. Inv+cos displays the arc cosine.
tan	t	Displays the current value's tangent. Inv+tan displays the arc tangent.
()	()	Groups expressions.
Exp	x	Enables the entry of exponential numbers.
x^y	y	Displays the value of X raised to the power of Y. Inv+x^y displays the result of X to the Y root.
x^3	#	Displays the value of X cubed. Inv+x^3 displays the cube root of X.

Table 474 *The Calculator accessory's keyboard combinations. (continued from previous page)*

Button	Keyboard	Button Function
x^2	@	Displays the value of X squared. Inv+x^2 displays the square root .
ln	n	Displays the current value's natural logarithm.
log	L	Displays the current value's base 10 log.
n!	!	Calculates the current value's factorial.

Table 474 The Calculator accessory's keyboard combinations. (continued from previous page)

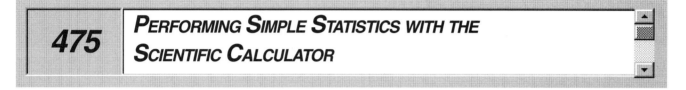

475 PERFORMING SIMPLE STATISTICS WITH THE SCIENTIFIC CALCULATOR

Although spreadsheet programs, such as Microsoft Excel, now provide a powerful set of statistical functions, if you get in a crunch and you do not have your spreadsheet software available, you can perform some simple statistics (such as calculating the sum, average, and standard deviation of a set of numbers) using the Scientific Calculator. To start, you must enter your number set into the Statistics Box by performing these steps:

1. Within the Scientific Calculator, click your mouse on the Sta button. The Scientific Calculator, in turn, will open the Statistics Box, as shown in Figure 475.

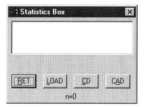

Figure 475 The Statistics Box.

2. Next, within the Calculator, enter a value and then click your mouse on the DAT button. The Calculator will place the number into the Statistics Box. Repeat this step to enter each value in your number set. If you happen to enter an incorrect value, click your mouse on the number and then click your mouse on the CD button to delete the entry from the list.

3. To calculate the sum, average, or standard deviation of your values, click your mouse on the Sum, Ave, or s button. The Calculator, in turn, will display your result within the Result window.

476 MANAGING FONTS ONE CHARACTER AT A TIME USING THE CHARACTER MAP

As you create documents, there may be times when you must insert a specific character, such as a copyright symbol (©) or a trademark (™). Unfortunately, you will not find these characters on your keyboard. Instead, you must insert the character using a specific font. If your word processor does not provide you with the ability to insert characters in this way, you can use the Character Map accessory shown in Figure 476.1 to copy the character to the Clipboard, from which you can later paste the character back into your document.

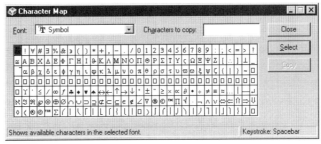

Figure 476.1 *The Character Map accessory program.*

Within the Character Map window, you can click your mouse on the pull-down Font list to select the font you desire. The Character Map, in turn, will display the symbols the font defines. To better view a symbol, hold down your mouse-select button and drag your mouse over the characters. The Character map, in turn, will zoom in on the current symbol, as shown in Figure 476.2.

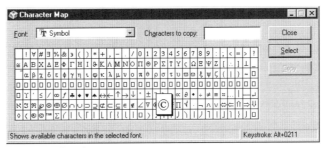

Figure 476.2 *Zooming in on a character within the Character Map.*

To start the Character Map program, perform these steps:

1. Click your mouse on the Start menu Programs option and choose Accessories. Windows 98, in turn, will display the Accessories submenu.

2. Within the Accessories submenu, click your mouse on the Character Map option (depending on your system configuration, you may find the Character Map within the System Tools submenu). Windows 98, in turn, will start the Character Map, as previously shown in Figure 476.1.

Note: *If you cannot locate the Character Map accessory on your system, you can install the program from the Windows 98 CD-ROM by performing the steps Tip 218 presents.*

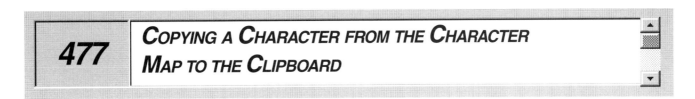

477 COPYING A CHARACTER FROM THE CHARACTER MAP TO THE CLIPBOARD

In Tip 476, you learned how to start the Character Map accessory program. Using the Character Map, you can view the symbols each of your system font's define. After you locate a specific symbol within the Character Map, you can copy the symbol into the Clipboard. Then, from within your application program (such as Microsoft Word), you can paste the symbol from the Clipboard into a document. To copy a Character Map symbol to the Clipboard, perform these steps:

1. Within the Character Map window, use the Font pull-down list to select the font that contains the symbol that you desire.

2. Within the symbol window, click your mouse on the symbol you desire and then click your mouse on the Select button. The Character Map, in turn, will display the symbol within the Characters to copy field, as shown in Figure 477. If you want to copy more than one character from the current font to the Clipboard, repeat this step for each character you desire.

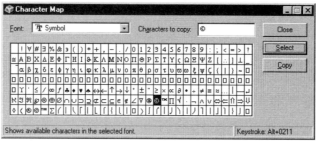

Figure 477 *Placing characters into the Character Map's Characters to copy field.*

3. Within the Character Map window, click your mouse on the Copy button. The Character Map, in turn, will copy the characters to the Clipboard. You can now use your application program to paste the characters from the Clipboard.

4. Within the Character Map window, click your mouse on the Close button to close the Character Map window.

478 DISPLAYING AND SAVING THE CURRENT CLIPBOARD CONTENTS

In Tip 106, you learned how to perform cut-and-paste operations using the Windows Clipboard. If you experience errant results when you perform a cut-and-paste operation (the item your application pastes, for example, does not match the item you expected), you can use the Clipboard Viewer accessory to display the Clipboard's current contents. To open the Clipboard Viewer, perform these steps:

1. Click your mouse on the Start button. Windows 98, in turn, will display the Start menu.

2. Within the Start menu, click your mouse on the Programs option and then choose Accessories. Windows 98 will display the Accessories submenu.

3. Within the Accessories submenu, click your mouse on the Clipboard Viewer option. (Depending on your system configuration, you may find the Clipboard Viewer option within the Accessories menu System Tools submenu.) Windows 98, in turn, will display the Clipboard Viewer window, as shown in Figure 478.

To troubleshoot a cut-and-paste error, you may need to again copy the data you desire to the Clipboard and then use the Clipboard Viewer to display the Clipboard's contents.

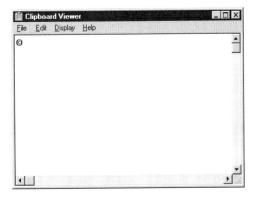

Figure 478 *The Clipboard Viewer window.*

479 **CHANGING THE CLIPBOARD VIEWER'S DISPLAY FORMAT**

In Tip 478, you learned how to use the Clipboard Viewer accessory to display the Clipboard's current contents. Depending on the data you cut or copied to the Clipboard, the format the Clipboard uses to hold the data may vary. In some cases, when you use the Clipboard Viewer to display the Clipboard's current contents, the Clipboard Viewer may not choose the correct display format. In such cases, you can direct the Clipboard Viewer to use a different display format by selecting the Display menu, as shown in Figure 479.

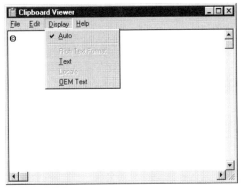

Figure 479 *The Clipboard Viewer Display menu.*

When you change the Clipboard Viewer's display type, the actual Clipboard data does not change. Instead, the Clipboard Viewer program simply changes the format it uses to display the data.

480 **SAVING THE CLIPBOARD CONTENTS USING THE CLIPBOARD VIEWER**

In Tip 479, you learned how to use the Clipboard Viewer to display the Clipboard's current contents. As you perform cut-and-paste operations, there may be times when you want to save the information you copy or cut to the Clipboard to a file on your disk. When you save data from the Clipboard to a file, the Clipboard Viewer will create a file on your disk that uses the CLP (for Clipboard) file extension. Later, when you are ready to use the information, you can use the Clipboard Viewer to open the file's contents which, in turn, loads the information into the Clipboard. To save the current Clipboard contents to a file on disk, perform these steps:

1. Start the Clipboard Viewer, as discussed in Tip 478.
2. Within the Clipboard Viewer window, click your mouse on the File menu Save As option. The Clipboard Viewer, in turn, will display the Save As dialog box.
3. Within the Save As dialog box, specify the folder and file within which you want the Clipboard Viewer to store the current Clipboard contents, and then click your mouse on the OK button.

To later load your file's contents back into the Clipboard, perform these steps:

1. Start the Clipboard Viewer, as discussed in Tip 478.
2. Within the Clipboard Viewer window, click your mouse on the File menu Open option. The Clipboard Viewer, in turn, will display the Open dialog box.
3. Within the Open dialog box, locate and select the file within which you previously stored the Clipboard contents, and then click your mouse on the OK button. The Clipboard Viewer, in turn, will load the file's contents into the Clipboard.

---

481   TAKING A BREAK WITH THE WINDOWS 98 INTERACTIVE GAMES

In addition to providing you with accessory programs you can use to create word processing documents, send and receive faxes, and to customize your system, Windows 98 also provides four interactive games that you can run from the Accessories menu Games submenu, as shown in Figure 481. Several of the Tips that follow discuss each of the games in detail. If you do not have a Games submenu within your Accessories menu, you can install the Games from the Windows 98 CD-ROM, as discussed in Tip 218.

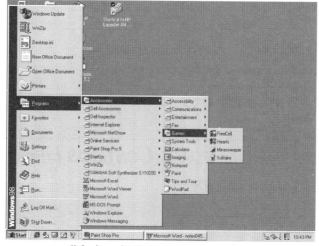

Figure 481 Windows 98 provides four games you will find on the Games submenu.

482 PLAYING THE FREECELL INTERACTIVE CARD GAME

FreeCell is an interactive card game within which your goal is to transfer every card from the bottom of the window into the *home cells* that appear in the window's upper-right corner. Figure 428 shows the FreeCell game board.

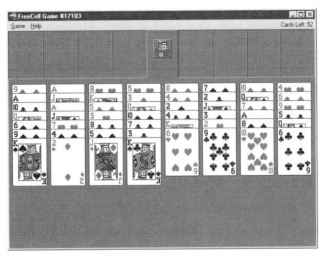

Figure 482 *The FreeCell game board.*

Within FreeCell, the first card you place in a home cell must be an Ace. After that, your second card can be another Ace, which you place next to the first one, or a 2, which you place on top of the Ace (provided the 2 is the same suit as the Ace). As you play your cards, you will build up the home cells from Aces to Kings, and each of the four home cells will hold a suit. You win in FreeCell if you place all 52 cards in the four home cell stacks. Likewise, when you can no longer make a move, you lose and the game is over.

To move a card, click your mouse on the card's initial position and then click your mouse on the location at which you want to place the card. If you move a card to an illegal position, FreeCell will display a dialog box that informs you of the error.

If you need a card that another card is covering, you can move the top card to one of the four *FreeCells* that appear in the window's upper-left corner, using the FreeCell as a temporary storage location. FreeCell only lets you place one card at a time within a FreeCell. Also, after you place a card within a FreeCell, you can only move the card to a home cell, to an empty FreeCell, to an empty column between the card stacks, or to a card stack with a cover card that is the opposite color and one number higher than the card. To start a FreeCell game, perform these steps:

1. Click your mouse on the Start menu Programs options and choose Accessories. Windows 98, in turn, will display the Accessories submenu.

2. Within the Accessories submenu, click your mouse on the Games menu and choose FreeCell. Windows 98 will open the FreeCell window.

3. Within the FreeCell window, you will start your game with four FreeCells and four home cells. If an Ace is showing, move it directly to a home cell. If not, move cards to FreeCells and on top of opposite-color cards whose number is one higher until you encounter your first Ace.

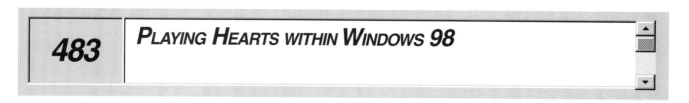

Like the FreeCell game Tip 482 presents, Hearts is also a card game. However, unlike FreeCell, which you play by yourself, you can play hearts against your computer or with other users across a network. When you play Hearts by yourself, the Hearts game will create and play for your three other opponents. Figure 483.1 presents the Hearts game board. Within Hearts, your goal is to end the game with the lowest score. A game consists of several hands, and the first person to achieve a score of 100 or more loses, and the game ends.

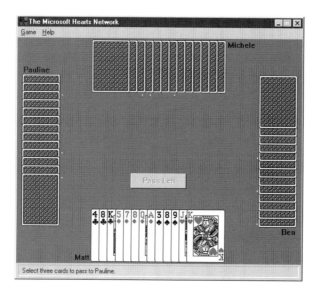

Figure 483.1 *The Hearts game board.*

Within Hearts, your score is based on the number of Hearts cards you have when a hand ends (a hand ends when all cards have been played). Specifically, at the end of a hand, you will get one point for each Heart you hold, and an additional thirteen points if you hold the Queen of Spades. No other card counts against you. As you play, your goal is to avoid taking Hearts and the Queen of Spades.

Within Hearts, you are always the player at the bottom of the window. To begin each hand, you must select three cards and pass those cards to the player on your left. The *Hearts* program will walk you through this process. Usually, you will want to send your highest cards to the person at your left. You will pass cards to the another user in this manner every three hands.

To play a hand, the player who has the two of Clubs throws the card into the middle of the window (which Hearts refers to as starting the *trick*). Other players must then throw out cards of that suit. The person who throws out the highest card in the suit loses and must take all the cards. If a player does not have a card of the matching suit, he or she can throw out any card (ideally, a high Heart or the Queen of Spades) and will not have to take the trick. The person who loses the trick will start the next hand.

If any Hearts, or the Queen of Spades, exist in the trick's set of cards, the person who loses the hand will accumulate points. When you start a trick, do not throw out a high value Hearts card because you might lose the hand and get stuck with all the Hearts. After you have played all the cards, the current hand will end and Hearts will display a scoreboard similar to that shown in Figure 483.2.

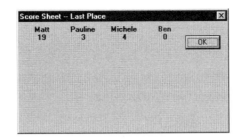

Figure 483.2 *The Hearts scoreboard.*

484   **PLAYING HEARTS AGAINST YOUR COMPUTER**

In Tip 483, you learned how to play the Windows 98 Hearts interactive card game. To play a game of Hearts against your computer, perform these steps:

1. Click your mouse on the Start menu Programs options and choose Accessories. Windows 98, in turn, will display the Accessories submenu.

2. Within the Accessories submenu, click your mouse on the Games menu and choose Hearts. Windows 98 will open the Hearts window, displaying the Microsoft Hearts Network dialog box, as shown in Figure 484.

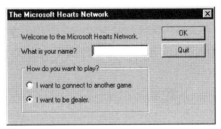

Figure 484 *The Microsoft Hearts Network dialog box.*

3. Within the Microsoft Hearts Network dialog box, type in your name and then click your mouse on the I want to be dealer button. Next, click your mouse on OK to start the game.

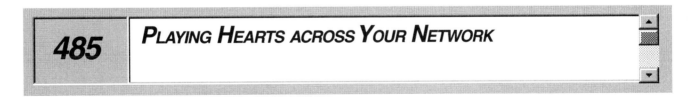

485   **PLAYING HEARTS ACROSS YOUR NETWORK**

In Tip 483, you learned how to play the Windows 98 Hearts interactive card game. As you learned, if you play Hearts by yourself, the Hearts game will create and play for your three opponents. If, however, you are connected to a local-area network, you can play Hearts against other users across the network. When you play Hearts across the network, one of the players will be the *dealer*—whose function is simply to start the game before others can join in. To play Hearts across a network, perform these steps:

1. The player who will serve as the dealer must start the game by selecting the Games submenu Hearts option. Hearts, in turn, will display the Microsoft Hearts Network dialog box.

2. Within the Microsoft Hearts Network dialog box, the dealer must enter his or her name, select the I want to be dealer button, and then click his or her mouse on the OK button.

3. The other players across the network should then start Hearts. Within the Microsoft Hearts Network dialog box, those players should enter their own names, and click their mouse on the I want to connect to another game option. Hearts, in turn, will display the Locate Dealer dialog box, as shown in Figure 485.

Figure 485 *The Locate Dealer dialog box.*

4. Within the Locate Dealer dialog box, each user must type the name of the dealer's computer. The dealer, in turn, will see each player's name as the player joins the game.

5. When all players are at the card table, the dealer should press the F2 function key to start the game. If fewer than four people are playing, Hearts will create and play for the remaining opponents.

486 | **PLAYING MINESWEEPER WITHIN WINDOWS 98**

Minesweeper is an interactive board game within which your goal is to locate all the land mines within a mine field without getting blown up. Figure 486.1 shows the Minesweeper game board before you start to play.

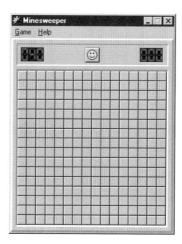

Figure 486.1 *Starting a Minesweeper game.*

Each square on the Minesweeper game board represents an empty location or a mine. To hunt for mines, you click your mouse over a square. Within each square, you will find either a mine (which ends the game), an empty location, or a number that represents how mines reside within the current box's surrounding squares. For example, if a square contains the number 1, only one of the box's surrounding squares contains a mine. Likewise, if the box contains the number 2, two of its surrounding squares have mines. By examining the values within multiple squares, you can determine where the mines reside on your game board. Figure 486.2 illustrates a Minesweeper game in progress.

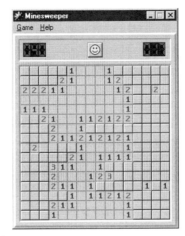

Figure 486.2 *Uncovering squares within Minesweeper.*

If, as you click your mouse on a square, you uncover a mine, the game will end and Minesweeper will uncover all the mines, as shown in Figure 486.3.

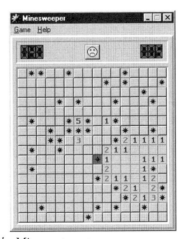

Figure 486.3 *Clicking your mouse on a mine ends the Minesweeper game.*

As you hunt for mines within Minesweeper, you must uncover many squares. As long as the squares contain numbers or spaces, you can keep hunting. After you play one or two games, you will start to understand when you have located a square that contains a mine. At that time, you can right-click your mouse on the mine to mark its location with a red flag. If you think that the square may contain a mine, you can right-click your mouse on the square two times to mark the square with a question mark. Figure 486.4 shows a mine field with marked squares.

As you play, Minesweeper will keep track of the fastest successful wins for each level of play. When you win a game, Minesweeper asks for your name if your time at that level beat the previous best score. To display the high scores, click your mouse on the Game menu Best Times option. To reset the scores, click your mouse on the Game menu Reset Scores button.

Within Minesweeper, you can start a new game by selecting the Game menu New button or by clicking your mouse on the Smiling Face icon.

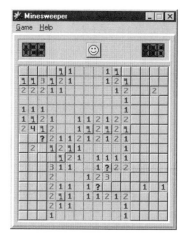

Figure 486.4 *Marking squares within Minesweeper.*

As you play, Minesweeper will keep track of the fastest successful wins for each level of play. When you win a game, Minesweeper asks for your name if your time at that level beat the previous best score. To display the high scores, click your mouse on the Game menu Best Times option. To reset the scores, click your mouse on the Game menu Reset Scores button.

Within Minesweeper, you can start a new game by selecting the Game menu New button or by clicking your mouse on the Smiling Face icon. Depending on your level of success, you may want Minesweeper to increase or decrease its level of difficulty. Minesweeper provides a beginner level with an 8 x 8 playing field and 10 hidden mines, an intermediate level with a 16 x 16 playing field and 40 hidden mines, and an advanced level with a 16 x 30 playing field and 99 hidden mines. To change the Minesweeper level, display the Minesweeper window's Game menu and select the Beginner, Intermediate, or Advanced option.

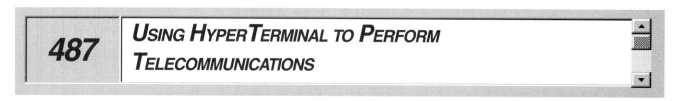

487 USING HYPERTERMINAL TO PERFORM TELECOMMUNICATIONS

Telecommunications is the process of using your PC and standard telephone lines to communicate with a remote computer. When you use your PC modem to connect to the Internet, for example, you are performing telecommunications. Today, most users rely on the Internet for their telecommunication's needs. However, using Windows 98 dial-up networking, you can connect your PC to a remote computer and work as if you were connected to that PC via a local-area network. In addition to providing you with Internet and dial-up networking, Windows 98 also provides the HyperTerminal accessory program that lets you dial into a remote computer and then work from that computer as if your PC was a terminal. By using your PC as a terminal in this way, you can interact with programs running on the remote computer and possibly even upload and download files. Before users connected to the Internet and World Wide Web, users used to connect to remote Bulletin Board Systems (BBS, as the users called them) to exchange files and electronic mail. To start the HyperTerminal accessory program, perform these steps:

1. Click your mouse on the Start menu Programs option and choose Accessories. Windows 98, in turn, will display the Accessories submenu.

2. Within the Accessories submenu, click your mouse on the Communication option and then choose HyperTerminal. Windows 98 will open the HyperTerminal folder, as shown within Figure 487.

Figure 487 *Displaying the HyperTerminal folder.*

Within the HyperTerminal folder, you will find icons that correspond to telecommunications profiles that HyperTerminal has defined for you. By clicking your mouse on a profile option, such as the MCI Mail icon, you can use HyperTerminal to connect to the corresponding service. As you will learn, HyperTerminal also provides a Wizard you can use to define your own profiles.

HyperTerminal, like most Windows-based programs, provides a toolbar of icons you can use to simplify many common operations. Figure 488 describes the HyperTerminal toolbar buttons. If your HyperTerminal window is not displaying the toolbar, click your mouse on the View menu Tool Bar option, placing a check mark next to the option.

Creates a new communications profile.

Opens an existing communications profile.

Connects to the current profile's remote computer.

Disconnects from the remote computer.

Sends a file to the remote computer.

Receives a file from the remote computer.

Displays the HyperTerminal
Properties sheet.

Figure 488 *The HyperTerminal toolbar buttons.*

489 USING AN EXISTING HYPERTERMINAL PROFILE

In Tip 487, you learned that using the HyperTerminal accessory program, you can connect your PC to a remote computer. Within the HyperTerminal folder, you found icons that correspond to profiles that HyperTerminal will use to connect to the remote computer. The profile contains the phone number HyperTerminal will use to dial the remote computer, as well as the remote computer's data-communication settings. In Tip 490, you will learn how to create profiles for other remote computers. After you create a profile, you will double-click your mouse on the profile's icon within the HyperTerminal folder to connect to the profile's remote computer. For example, if you have a CompuServe user ID, you can double-click your mouse on the CompuServe icon that appears within the HyperTerminal folder. HyperTerminal, in turn, will display the Connect dialog box, as shown in Figure 489.

Figure 489 *The HyperTerminal Connect dialog box.*

Within the Connect dialog box, you can use your modem to dial the remote computer or you can change the profile's current settings. Depending on the service you connect to, the steps you must perform will differ. In the case of CompuServe, for example, your HyperTerminal window will display a prompt for your user ID and password. After you successfully logon, you can interact with the remote computer. To end your call, click your mouse on the Call menu Disconnect option. You can then use the File menu Exit option or click your mouse on the Close button to close the HyperTerminal window.

490 CREATING A HYPERTERMINAL PROFILE

In Tip 489, you learned how to use an existing HyperTerminal profile to connect to a remote computer. Before you can connect a computer within HyperTerminal, you must create a profile for that computer which, at a minimum, will contain the computer's phone number. To create a profile for a remote computer, perform these steps:

1. Within the HyperTerminal window, click your mouse on the Hypertrm icon. HyperTerminal, in turn, will display the Connection Description dialog box, as shown in Figure 490.1, that prompts you for your profile name.

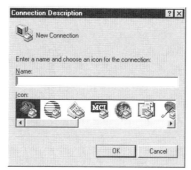

Figure 490.1 *The Connection Description dialog box.*

2. Within the Connection Description dialog box, type in a name that meaningfully describes the remote computer. Next, within the icon field, use the scroll bar to locate the icon you want HyperTerminal to display for your profile. After you click your mouse on the icon you desire, click your mouse on the OK button. HyperTerminal, in turn, will display the Connect To dialog box, as shown in Figure 490.2.

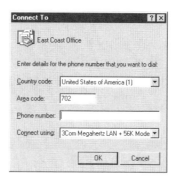

Figure 490.2 *The Connect To dialog box.*

3. Within the Connect To dialog box, type in the phone number you will use to connect to the remote computer and then click OK. HyperTerminal, in turn, will display the Connect dialog box that you can use to dial into the remote computer.

4. Within the Connect dialog box, click your mouse on the Dial button to connect to the remote computer. After you end your telecommunication session, use the File menu Save As option to save your profile. Then, use the File menu Exit option to close the HyperTerminal window. When you later open the HyperTerminal folder, you will find an icon that corresponds to the profile you created.

491 ESTABLISHING DATA COMMUNICATION SETTINGS FOR A HYPERTERMINAL CONNECTION

A few years ago, connecting to a remote computer often required consider technical expertise and an equal amount of luck. Before you could connect to a remote computer, you had to know the remote cmputer's data-communication settings (such as its baud rate, number of start, stop, and data bits, and its use of parity). After you knew the remote computer's settings, you then had to configure your software to use the same settings for your PC.

Today, to connect to a remote computer using HyperTerminal, you usually do not need to configure such settings. Instead, when you connect to a remote computer, HyperTerminal will determine the remote computer's settings and adjust your settings accordingly. Should you experience errors within HyperTerminal, however, you may need to configure the settings yourself. To start, find out the remote computer's settings. Usually, someone will tell you their PC's data-communication settings in the form "28.8 8E1." The first number, 28.8, in this case, specifies the baud rate; the second number, 8, specifies the number of data bits the remote computer sends and receives in each transmission; the letter indicates odd, even (E is for even), or no parity; and the final digit represents the number of stop bits. To change HyperTerminal's settings for a specific profile, perform these steps:

1. Within the HyperTerminal folder, double-click your mouse on the icon of the profile whose data communication settings you want to configure. HyperTerminal will display the Connect dialog box.

2. Within the Connect dialog box, click your mouse on the Modify button. HyperTerminal will display the profile's Properties dialog box.

3. Within the Properties dialog box, click your mouse on the Configure button. HyperTerminal will display the Modem Properties dialog box.

4. Within the Modem Properties dialog box set the maximum speed to at least that of the remote computer's baud rate. Then, click your mouse on the Connection tab. HyperTerminal will display the Connection sheet.

5. Within the Connection sheet, select settings that match the remote computer's data bits, parity, and stop bits. Then, click your mouse on the OK button. HyperTerminal will redisplay the Properties dialog box. Click your mouse on the OK button to put your changes into effect.

492 UNDERSTANDING HYPERTERMINAL'S TERMINAL EMULATION

When you use HyperTerminal to dial into a remote computer, such as a computer at your office or at a university, the remote computer will treat your PC as if it were a *terminal*. In other words, to the remote computer, your PC will appear simply as a screen and keyboard that connects directly to a terminal port. Using a terminal, you can run programs that reside on the remote computer. The programs will process the keystrokes you type at your keyboard and they will display each program's output to your screen. Depending on the computer to which you are connecting, there may be times when you must tell HyperTerminal to behave as if it is a specific terminal type (the most common terminal type is the Digital Equipment Corporation VT100). HyperTerminal, in turn, will send electronic signals to the remote computer that mimic (or emulate) the specific terminal type. To control HyperTerminal's terminal emulation, perform these steps:

1. Within the HyperTerminal folder, double-click your mouse on the icon of the profile whose data communication settings you want to configure. HyperTerminal will display the Connect dialog box.

2. Within the Connect dialog box, click your mouse on the Modify button. HyperTerminal will display the profile's Properties dialog box.

3. Within the Properties dialog box, click your mouse on the Settings tab. HyperTerminal will display Settings sheet, as shown in Figure 492.

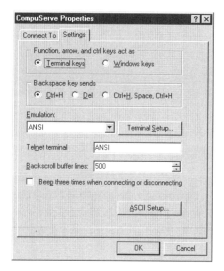

Figure 492 *The HyperTerminal Settings sheet.*

4. Within the Settings sheet, click your mouse on the Emulation pull-down list and select the terminal you want HyperTerminal to emulate. Then, click your mouse on the OK button to put your changes into effect.

493 CONTROLLING HOW HYPERTERMINAL INTERPRETS *ASCII* CONTROLS

Computers represent characters using ASCII files. In general, ASCII, which stands for the *American Standard Code for Information Interchange*, simply assigns a numeric value to each character. The letter A, for example, is an ASCII 48. Likewise, the letter B is ASCII 49, and so on. Usually, you do not need to worry about how your PC represents ASCII characters. However, if you use HyperTerminal to connect to a remote computer, there may be times when your computer and the remote computer interpret ASCII characters differently. For example, some UNIX-based systems may convert a carriage-return character into a linefeed and a carriage return, which may cause your PC to double space every line. Likewise, some systems use 8 bits to represent ASCII characters, while others use only 7. If HyperTerminal appears to display characters incorrectly, you may have to configure the ASCII control settings for your current profile. To specify ASCII settings within HyperTerminal, perform these steps:

1. Within the HyperTerminal folder, double-click your mouse on the icon of the profile whose data communication settings you want to configure. HyperTerminal will display the Connect dialog box.

2. Within the Connect dialog box, click your mouse on the Modify button. HyperTerminal will display the profile's Properties dialog box.

3. Within the Properties dialog box, click your mouse on the Settings tab. HyperTerminal will display the Settings sheet.

4. Within the Settings sheet, click your mouse on the ASCII Setup button. HyperTerminal, in turn, will display the ASCII Setup dialog box, as shown in Figure 493.

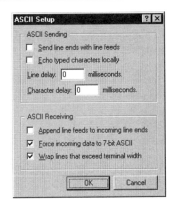

Figure 493 *The ASCII Setup dialog box.*

5. Within the ASCII Setup dialog box, select the settings that correspond to the remote computer and then click your mouse on the OK button. HyperTerminal will return you to the Properties dialog box. Click your mouse on the OK button to put your changes into effect.

494   **SELECTING A FILE-TRANSFER PROTOCOL WITHIN HYPERTERMINAL**

When users discuss telecommunications or the Internet, users often use the term protocol. In general, a *protocol* is simply a set of rules for how the participants in an operation must behave. For example, for two computers to communicate, both computers must agree on how fast each will send and receive data, the amount of data they will send or receive at one time, and so on.

As briefly discussed in Tip 487, using HyperTerminal, you can upload and download files to or from a remote computer. Before you can perform upload and download operations, your computer and an the remote computer must agree on the file-transfer protocol. Usually, when you transfer a file to or from a remote computer, you will tell the remote computer which protocol you want to use (you will usually select the protocol from a menu). Then, you must tell HyperTerminal to use that protocol. In Tips 495 and 496, you will learn how to send and receive files within HyperTerminal. As you will find, the Send File and Receive File dialog boxes each contain pull-down Protocol lists from which you can select a protocol.

495   **USING HYPERTERMINAL TO RECEIVE (DOWNLOAD) A FILE FROM A REMOTE COMPUTER**

As you have learned, using the HyperTerminal program, you can download (receive) a file from a remote computer. To start, you must connect to the remote computer, as discussed in previous Tips. Next, after you connect, you must direct the remote computer to use a specific file-transfer protocol and then to start the file download operation. Usually, you will start the download by selecting one or more menu options on the remote computer, however, the actual steps you must perform will differ from one system to the next. After you start the remote computer's download process, you must tell HyperTerminal to receive the file by performing these steps:

1. Within the HyperTerminal window, click your mouse on the Transfer menu Receive File option. HyperTerminal, in turn, will display the Receive File dialog box, as shown in Figure 495.

Figure 495 *The Receive File dialog box.*

2. Within the Receive File dialog box, type the pathname and filename within which HyperTerminal will store the file (or use the Browse button to select a folder). Next, click your mouse on the pull-down protocol list and select the same protocol you directed the remote computer to use.

3. Within the Receive File dialog box, click your mouse on the Receive button. HyperTerminal will display a Download status dialog box, which shows you the progress of the download and estimated time for completion. When the dialog box disappears, the file will reside on your computer.

496 **USING HYPERTERMINAL TO SEND (UPLOAD) A FILE TO A REMOTE COMPUTER**

As you have learned, using the HyperTerminal program, you can upload (send) a file from a remote computer. To start, you must connect to the remote computer as discussed in previous Tips. Next, after you connect, you must direct the remote computer to use a specific file-transfer protocol and then to start the file upload operation. Usually, you will start the upload by selecting one or more menu options on the remote computer, however, the actual steps you must perform will differ from one system to the next. After you start the remote computer's upload process, you must tell HyperTerminal to send the file by performing these steps:

1. Within the HyperTerminal window, click your mouse on the Transfer menu Send File option. HyperTerminal will display the Send File dialog box, as shown in Figure 496.

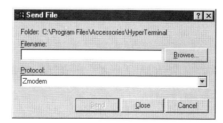

Figure 496 *The Send File dialog box.*

2. Within the Send File dialog box, type the pathname and filename of the file you want to upload (or use the Browse button to select a folder). Next, click your mouse on the pull-down protocol list and select the same protocol you directed the remote computer to use.

3. Within the Send File dialog box, click your mouse on the Send button. HyperTerminal will display a Upload status dialog box, which shows you the progress of the upload and estimated time for completion. When the dialog box disappears, the file will reside on the remote computer.

497 UPLOADING A TEXT FILE TO A REMOTE COMPUTER USING HYPERTERMINAL

When you connect to a remote computer, there may be times when you will want to send a text file's contents to a remote computer. For example, assume that you want to run a word processor on the remote computer and that you have already typed much of your document on your PC. To upload the text to the remote computer, you have two choices. First, you can upload the file to the remote computer, as discussed in Tip 496. Second, you can start the word processor on the remote computer and then you can use HyperTerminal to send your text file to the remote computer, as if you typed the text from the keyboard. To the remote computer's word processor, the operation will appear as if you typed the text from the keyboard, within the word processor itself. To send a text file to a remote computer in this way, perform these steps:

1. Within the HyperTerminal window, click your mouse on the Transfer menu Send Text File option. HyperTerminal will display the Send Text File dialog box, as shown in Figure 497.

Figure 497 *The Send Text File dialog box.*

2. Within the Send Text File dialog box, type the pathname and filename of the file you want to send (or use the Browse button to select a folder) and then click your mouse on the Open button. HyperTerminal, in turn, will open the text file and send it to the remote computer.

498 CAPTURING SESSION TEXT FROM A REMOTE COMPUTER TO A FILE OR PRINTER

In Tip 497, you learned how to send a text file's contents to a remote computer just as if you had typed the text at the keyboard. In a similar way, there may be times when you will want to save the text the remote computer displays on your screen (the session text) to a file on your PC. Later, after you disconnect from your remote session, you can use the WordPad accessory to view or print the file's contents. To save your session text to a file, you must direct HyperTerminal to capture the text by performing these steps:

1. Within the HyperTerminal window, click your mouse on the Transfer menu Capture Text option. HyperTerminal will display the Capture Text dialog box.

2. Within the Capture Text dialog box, type the pathname and filename of the file you want to send (or use the Browse button to select a folder) and then click your mouse on the Start button. HyperTerminal, in turn, will send the session text to the file. Later, when you are ready to stop capturing the session text, click your mouse on the Transfer menu Capture Text option and choose Stop.

When you capture your HyperTerminal session text to a text file, HyperTerminal will place your entire session text with that file. Depending on the information you are trying to view, you may be able to scroll through the HyperTerminal window view text from earlier in your session. If you find that you need to increase the size of HyperTerminal's text buffer, perform these steps:

1. Within the HyperTerminal window, click your mouse on the File menu Properties option. HyperTerminal, in turn, will display the Properties dialog box. Within the Properties dialog box, click your mouse on the Settings tab. HyperTerminal will display the Settings sheet.

2. Within the Settings sheet Backscroll buffer lines field, type a value that corresponds to the number of lines you want HyperTerminal to buffer. Click your mouse on the OK button to put your changes into effect.

499 USING THE KODAK IMAGING SOFTWARE

If you receive fax documents on your PC, you can use the Kodak Imaging software Microsoft includes within the Windows 98 to view and annotate your image files. Also, you can use the Imaging software to view images you scan from your scanner. Figure 499, for example, shows the software with a scanned image.

Figure 499 *Using the Kodak Imaging software to view a scanned image.*

To start the Kodak Imaging software, perform these steps:

1. Click your mouse on the Start menu Programs option and choose Accessories. Windows 98 will display the Accessories submenu.

2. Within the Accessories submenu, click your mouse on the Imaging option. Windows 98, in turn, will start the Kodak Imaging software. Using the File menu Scan New option, you can scan an image. Likewise, you can use the File menu Open option to view an existing scan or fax. As you view an image, the Imaging software lets you add text or graphics annotations to the image, change the image's color and compression settings, or even rotate the image.

---

500 | **USING THE WINDOWS 98 PAINT ACCESSORY TO CREATE SIMPLE GRAPHICS**

With the explosive growth of the World Wide Web and the use of electronic mail, more and more users want the ability to create, edit, and save their own graphics. For example, a user may want to use a graphic he or she received within an e-mail message as the background image that Windows 98 displays on the Desktop. Or, the user might want to edit the image, possibly by adding text, so he or she can send the message to another user via e-mail. To help you create, manipulate, print, and later save graphics images, Windows 98 provides the Paint accessory, as shown in Figure 500.

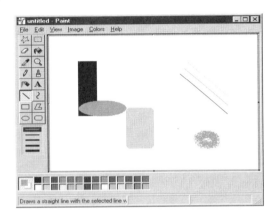

Figure 500 *A Windows Paint image.*

Within Paint, you can use brushes, pencils, pens, and colors to create a graphic image. To start the Paint accessory program, perform these steps:

1. Click your mouse on the Windows Start button. Windows 98 will display the Start menu.
2. Within the Start menu, click your mouse on the Programs menu and then choose the Accessories option. Windows 98 will display the Accessories submenu.
3. Within the Accessories submenu, click your mouse on the Paint option.

Within the Paint accessory program, you will create graphics images that users refer to as bitmap files. Just as you should use the DOC filename extension when you create a word processing document file, you should use the BMP file extension when you create a bitmap file. You might, for example, name the image shown in Figure 500, *MyDog.BMP*. If you use the Windows 98 Explorer to search the *Windows* folder on your disk, you will find that Windows 98 provides several different bitmap files, which you can use as the background image on your Desktop. Using the Paint accessory, you can open, view, and even edit each of these BMP files.

---

501 | **UNDERSTANDING PAINT ACCESSORY'S TOOLS**

In Tip 500, you learned how to start the Paint accessory program. Within Paint, you will find a toolbar that contains the tools you will use to draw or edit your image. To choose the tool, such as an eraser or pencil, with which you want to work, simply click your mouse on the tool within the toolbar. Table 501 briefly explains each tool's purpose.

Icon	Name	Purpose
![Free-Form Selection icon]	Free-Form Selection	Selects any shape within the image.
![Select icon]	Select	Selects a rectangular shape within the image.
![Eraser icon]	Eraser	Erases the area within an image over which you drag your mouse.
![Fill with Color icon]	Fill with Color	Fills in a shape with the current color.
![Pick Color icon]	Pick Color	Selects a color from the color palette.
![Magnifier icon]	Magnifier	Magnifies an object's editing area.
![Pencil icon]	Pencil	Draws free-form lines.
![Brush icon]	Brush	Paints free-form strokes using the current brush size.
![Airbrush icon]	Airbrush	Spray paints the current color.
![Text icon]	Text	Inserts text within the image.
![Line icon]	Line	Draws a straight line within the image.
![Curve icon]	Curve	Draws a curve within the image.
![Rectangle icon]	Rectangle	Draws a rectangle within the image.
![Polygon icon]	Polygon	Draws a polygon (a multi-sided enclosed shape) within the image.
![Ellipse icon]	Ellipse	Draws an ellipse within the image.
![Rounded Rectangle icon]	Rounded Rectangle	Draws a rectangle within rounded corners within the image.

Table 501 *The Paint accessory toolbar buttons.*

502   **ERASING PARTS OF AN IMAGE WITHIN PAINT**

As you create images within Paint, there will be times when you will want to erase all or part of your image. In such cases, you can use Paint's Eraser tool. When you use the Eraser tool to "erase" parts of your image, Paint will replace the image with the current background color. To erase part of an image within Paint, perform these steps:

1. Within the Paint toolbar, click your mouse on the Eraser tool. Paint, in turn, will change your mouse pointer from an arrow into a small square. In addition, beneath the toolbar, Paint will display a box that contains icons that correspond to four different eraser sizes.

2. Within the box of eraser icons, click your mouse on the eraser size you desire.

3. As you erase, Paint uses the current background color to overwrite the current image. To change the background color, follow the steps Tip 509 presents.

4. Move your mouse pointer to the location on your canvas at which you want to erase the image.

5. To erase, hold down your mouse-select button and drag the mouse pointer around your image. To lift your eraser off the image, simply release the mouse button.

503   *ZOOMING IN ON AN IMAGE WITHIN PAINT*

As you create images within Paint, there will be times when you will want to "zoom in" on your image so you can edit your drawing at the pixel level. Paint lets you zoom in on the entire image, as shown in Figure 503.1, or you can use Paint's Magnifier tool to zoom in on a specific area within the image, as shown in Figure 503.2.

Figure 503.1 Zooming in on a Paint image.

Figure 503.2 Zooming in on a specific area within a Paint image.

To zoom in on your entire image, perform these steps:

1. Click your mouse on the View menu and choose the Zoom option. Paint, in turn, will display the Zoom submenu.

2. Within the Zoom menu, you can select the image's normal size, large size (400% zoom), or you can use the Custom option to select the zoom percentage from the Custom Zoom dialog box, as shown in Figure 503.3.

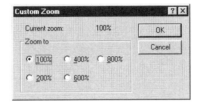

Figure 503.3 *The Custom Zoom dialog box.*

To zoom in on a specific area within your image, you can use Paint's Magnifier tool by performing these steps:

1. Within Paint's toolbox, click your mouse on the Magnifier button. Paint, in turn, will change the mouse pointer from an arrow into a rectangle which it displays within the image.

2. Using your mouse, move the rectangle over the image area you want to zoom and then click your mouse-select button. Paint will zoom in on the region, displaying the image area so large that you can edit individual pixels. To resume the previous image size, simply click your mouse on the Magnify tool a second time and then click your mouse on the enlarged image.

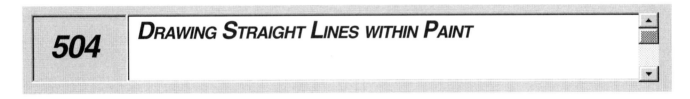

504   DRAWING STRAIGHT LINES WITHIN PAINT

As you create images within Paint, there will be many times when you need to draw a straight line. To draw a straight line within Paint, you will use Paint's Line tool to specify the line's start and end points. Figure 504, for example, illustrates several simple shapes you can create using only straight lines.

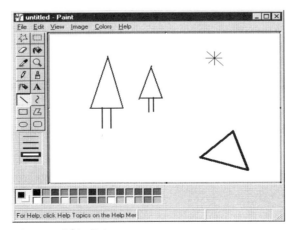

Figure 504 *Using straight lines to create images within Paint.*

Paint will draw a straight line between the two points. To draw a straight line within Paint, perform these steps:

1. Within the Paint toolbox, click your mouse over the Line tool. Paint, in turn, will change your mouse pointer from an arrow into a cross-hair.

2. Beneath the toolbar, Paint will display five line thicknesses from which you can choose a line width. Click your mouse on the line width you desire.

3. Within your image canvas (your drawing area), move the mouse pointer to the location at which you want to begin the line.

4. Hold down your mouse-select button and drag your mouse pointer to the location at which you want to end the line. As you move your mouse, Paint will drag a line.

5. Release your mouse-select button. Paint, in turn, will drop the line at its current location.

In Tip 504, you used Paint's Line tool to draw straight lines within an image. As your drawings increase in complexity, you may need to draw curved as well as straight lines. To create curved lines, you will use Paint's Curve tool. Figure 505, for example, illustrates an image that uses curved lines.

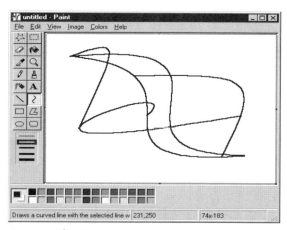

Figure 505 *Using curved lines to create images within Paint.*

To draw a curved line within Paint, perform these steps:

1. Within the Paint toolbar, click your mouse on the Curve tool. Paint, in turn, will change your mouse pointer from an arrow into a cross-hair.

2. Beneath the toolbar, Paint will display five line thicknesses from which you can choose a line width. Click your mouse on the line width you desire.

3. Within your image canvas (your drawing area), move your mouse pointer to the location at which you want to begin the line.

4. Drag the mouse to the end point and release the mouse to draw a straight line.

5. Click your mouse at a location on the straight line and hold down your mouse-select button. As you drag your mouse, Paint will bend the line in response to your mouse movements.

6. After you create the curved line that you desire, release your mouse-select button. Paint, in turn, will place the line into your image.

506 DRAWING RECTANGLES AND SQUARES WITHIN PAINT

In Tips 504 and 505, you have learned how to draw straight and curved lines within Paint. In addition to providing the Line and Curve tools, Paint provides a Rectangle tool that you can use to create rectangles and squares. To create a rectangle within Paint, you will simply specify where, within your image, you want to place the rectangle's upper-left and lower-right corners. Paint, in turn, will draw the lines that connect the corners. Figure 506, for example, shows rectangles within a bitmap image.

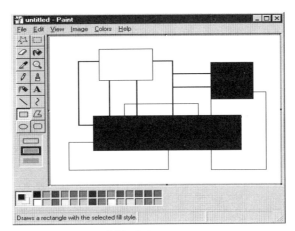

Figure 506 Using rectangles and squares to create images within Paint.

To draw a rectangle or square within Paint, perform these steps:

1. Within the Paint toolbar, click your mouse on the Rectangle tool. Paint, in turn, will change your mouse pointer from an arrow into a cross-hair.

2. Beneath the toolbar, Paint will display three rectangle types. If you select the top icon, Paint will draw an outline of a rectangle. If you select the second icon, Paint will draw the rectangle, filling the rectangle with the current *background* color. If you select the third icon, Paint will draw a rectangle using the current background color to fill and to outline the shape.

3. Within the image canvas, move your mouse pointer to the location at which you want to start the rectangle. If you want to draw a square, hold down the SHIFT key.

4. Hold down your mouse-select button and drag your mouse pointer to the location at which you want to end the line. As you move your mouse, Paint will drag a rectangle.

5. Release your mouse-select button. Paint, in turn, will drop the rectangle at its current location.

Note: *To draw a rounded square or rectangle within Paint, click your mouse on the toolbar Rounded Rectangle icon and then perform Steps 2 through 5.*

507   DRAWING A POLYGON WITHIN PAINT

In previous Tips, you have learned to draw lines and squares within Paint. As your drawings become more complex, you may need to draw polygons. A *polygon* is simply a shape with multiple sides. Figure 507, for example, illustrates polygons. As you might guess, within Paint you can draw filled and unfilled polygons.

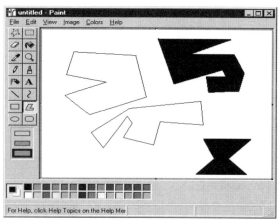

Figure 507 *Using polygons to create images within Paint.*

To draw a polygon within Paint, perform these steps:

1. Within the Paint toolbar, click your mouse on the Polygon tool. Paint, in turn, will change your mouse pointer from an arrow into a cross-hair.

2. Beneath the toolbar, Paint will display three polygon types. If you select the top icon, Paint will draw an outline of a polygon. If you select the second icon, Paint will draw the polygon, filling the shape with the current *background* color. If you select the third icon, Paint will draw a polygon using the current background color to fill and to outline the shape.

3. Within the image canvas, move your mouse pointer to the location at which you want to draw the polygon's first end point and click your mouse.

4. Drag your mouse pointer to the location within your image at which you want to draw the polygon's second end point and release your mouse-select button. Paint, in turn, will connect the two end points.

5. Repeat Steps 3 and 4 until you complete the polygon. After you draw the final point, double click your mouse. Paint, in turn, will connect the first point to the last point.

508   DRAWING CIRCLES AND ELLIPSES WITHIN PAINT

In Tip 506, you learned how to use Paint's Rectangle tool to draw rectangles and squares. In a similar way, you can use Paint's Ellipse tool to create ellipses and circles. Just as Paint lets you create filled or empty rectangles and squares, the same is true for ellipses and circles. Figure 508 illustrates several circles and ellipses within a Paint image. Fortunately, when you use Paint, you do not need to hold a can or glass up to your monitor to draw a perfect circle. Instead, you can use Paint's Ellipse tool to draw filled and unfilled circles and ellipses.

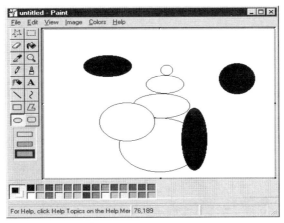

Figure 508 *Using circles and ellipses to create images within Paint.*

To draw circles and ellipses, perform these steps:

1. Within the Paint toolbar, click your mouse on the Ellipse tool. Paint, in turn, will change your mouse pointer from an arrow into a cross-hair.

2. Beneath the toolbar, Paint will display three ellipse types. If you select the top icon, Paint will draw an outline of a ellipse. If you select the second icon, Paint will draw the ellipse, filling the shape with the current *background* color. If you select the third icon, Paint will draw a ellipse using the current background color to fill and to outline the shape.

3. Within the image canvas, move your mouse pointer to the location at which you want to start the ellipse. If you want to draw a square, hold down the SHIFT key.

4. Hold down your mouse-select button and drag your mouse pointer to the location at which you want to end the line. As you move your mouse, Paint will drag an ellipse.

5. Release your mouse-select button. Paint, in turn, will drop the ellipse at its current location.

509 ***SELECTING THE FOREGROUND AND BACKGROUND COLORS WITHIN PAINT***

In previous Tips, you learned how to draw a variety of shapes within the Windows 98 Paint accessory. Within Paint, each shape you draw has a *foreground color* and a *background color*. The foreground color defines the shape's outline color. The background color defines the color inside the shape. For example, to draw a yellow rectangle with a blue outline, you would select yellow as the shape's background color and blue for the foreground color. At the bottom of the Paint window, you should see Paint's color box, as shown in Figure 509.

If the color box is not visible within your Paint window, select the View menu Color Box option. At the left of the color box, you will find two boxes within which Paint displays the current foreground and background colors. The top box displays the foreground color and the lower, partially-hidden box, displays the background color.

To change the foreground color, click your mouse on a color in the color palette. To change the background color, right-click your mouse on a color in the color palette. Paint, in turn, will assign those colors to the next shape you draw and Paint will update the two boxes to reflect your color selection.

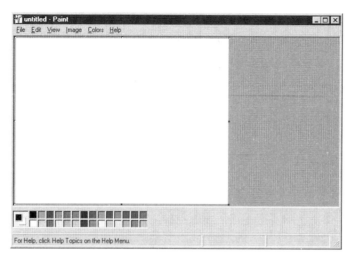

Figure 509 *The Paint color box.*

510 SELECTING AN IMAGE COLOR USING THE PAINT COLOR PICKER

In Tip 509, you learned how to select the current foreground and background colors. As you create images within Paint, there will be times when you want to use a color that matches an object you have already drawn. In such cases, you can use Paint's Pick Color tool to copy the color from one object to the background or foreground color. To use the Pick Color tool, perform these steps:

1. Within Paint's toolbar, click your mouse on the Pick Color button. Paint, in turn, will change your mouse pointer from an arrow into an eye dropper.

2. To change the foreground color, click your mouse-select button on the object whose color you want to copy. To change the current background color, right-click your mouse on the object.

511 FILLING A SHAPE WITH A SPECIFIC COLOR WITHIN PAINT

When you create images using the Paint accessory, there will be times when you will want to "color in" various shapes. Within Paint, you can fill any closed shape with any color. For example, if you draw a rectangle and later want to fill the shape with the color blue, you can easily do so. Figure 511 illustrates several "filled" shapes within Paint. Using Paint's Fill with Color tool, you can fill in any closed shape (a shape such as a box, circle, or triangle whose surrounding outline connects so the color cannot "leak through") using the current foreground color.

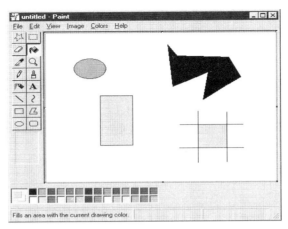

Figure 511 *Filling shapes within a Paint image.*

To fill a shape within Paint, perform these steps:

1. Within Paint's color pallet, click your left mouse button on the color you desire.
2. Within Paint's toolbar, click your mouse on the Fill tool. Paint, in turn, will change your mouse pointer from an arrow into a small paint bucket.
3. Within your image canvas, move your mouse pointer inside the shape you want to fill. (Make sure that the shape you want to fill is completely enclosed or the color will spill out and fill your entire canvas.)
4. Click your left mouse button. Paint will fill the shape with the current foreground color.

512 DRAWING FREE-FORM IMAGES WITHIN PAINT

In several of the previous Tips, you have learned how to draw standard shapes, such as rectangles and circles, within Paint. As your images become more complex, you can use Paint's Pencil tool to draw free-form shapes. Figure 512, for example, illustrates shapes drawn using Paint's free-form pencil.

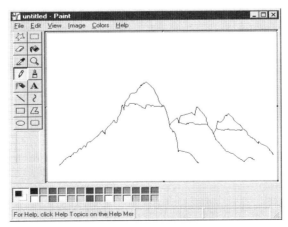

Figure 512 *Drawing free-form shapes using Paint's Pencil tool.*

To use the Pencil tool within Paint, perform these steps:

1. Within the Paint toolbar, click your mouse on the Pencil tool. Paint, in turn, will change your mouse pointer from an arrow into a pencil.

2. Move your mouse pointer to the canvas location at which you want to begin your image.

3. To draw, hold down your mouse-select button and drag the mouse pointer (the pencil) around your image. To lift your pencil off the image, simply release the mouse button.

If you want to use the Pencil tool to draw an image in a specific color, simply select the color you desire, such as the foreground color (discussed in Tip 509), before you start drawing.

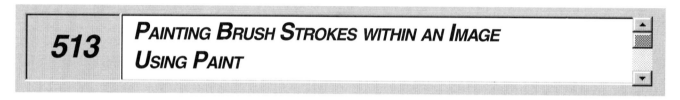

In Tip 512, you learned how to use Paint's Pencil tool to draw free-form images. Depending on your image, there may be times when you will want to use Paint's Brush tool to create stroke-like objects similar to those shown in Figure 513. When you use the Brush tool, Paint will paint your strokes using the current foreground color. In addition, Paint provides several different brush types.

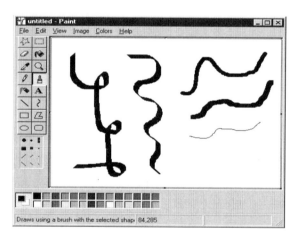

Figure 513 *Using Paint's Brush tool to create stroke-like images.*

To use the Brush tool within Paint, perform these steps:

1. Within the Paint toolbar, click your mouse on the Brush tool. Paint, in turn, will change your mouse pointer from an arrow into a cross-hair. In addition, beneath the toolbar, Paint will display a box that contains various brush types. Each brush type will create a different stroke.

2. Within the box of brushes, click your mouse on the brush type you desire.

3. Move your mouse pointer to the canvas location at which you want to begin your image.

4. To draw, hold down your mouse-select button and drag the mouse pointer around your image. To lift your brush off the image, simply release the mouse button.

To use the Brush tool to draw an image in a specific color, simply select the color you desire, such as the foreground color (discussed in Tip 509), before you start drawing.

514 | **SPRAY PAINTING AN IMAGE WITHIN PAINT**

In Tip 513, you learned how to use Paint's Brush tool to create stroke-like objects within your image. Depending on your image, there may be times when you will want to "spray" the current foreground color onto your image, much like you would use a can of spray paint. In such cases, you can use Paint's Airbrush tool. Figure 514 illustrates an image within which the Airbrush tool has "sprayed" the current foreground color.

Figure 514 *Using the Airbrush tool to create a spray-paint-like image.*

Like a can of spray paint, the longer you hold the Airbrush in one location, the darker and more complete the color becomes. The faster you drag the Airbrush, the lighter the spray. To use the Airbrush tool, perform these steps:

1. Within the Paint toolbar, click your mouse on the Airbrush tool. Paint, in turn, will change your mouse pointer from an arrow into a spray can. In addition, beneath the toolbar, Paint will display a box that contains various spray patterns.

2. Within the box of spray patterns, click your mouse on the pattern you desire.

3. Move your mouse pointer to the canvas locationat which you want to begin your image.

4. To spray the current foreground color, hold down your mouse-select button and drag the mouse pointer around your image. To turn off the spray, simply release the mouse button.

To use the Airbrush tool to draw an image in a specific color, simply select the color you desire, such as the foreground color (discussed in Tip 509), before you start drawing.

515 | **ADDING TEXT TO A GRAPHIC IMAGE WITHIN PAINT**

When you create or edit images within Paint, there will be many times when you will want to add text to the image. For example, Figure 515.1 illustrates an image that contains text.

Figure 515.1 *Adding text to a graphics image within Paint.*

To add text to an image within Paint, you will use Paint's Text tool. When you add text, Paint lets you select a font style and size. To add text to an image, perform these steps:

1. Within Paint's toolbar, click your mouse on the tool box Text button. Paint, in turn, will change your mouse pointer from an arrow to a cross-hair. Paint will also display two icons beneath the toolbar that let you specify the text background type. The top icon directs Paint to display the current background color behind the text. The bottom icon directs Paint to display the text with a transparent background (which lets the image show behind the text).

2. Beneath the toolbar, click your mouse on the icon that corresponds to the text background style that you desire.

3. Move your mouse pointer to a location at which you want to place your text.

4. Hold down your mouse-select button and drag your mouse pointer down and to the right to create a *text frame* within which you will type your text. After you release your mouse button to anchor the text frame, Paint will display the Fonts dialog box, as shown in Figure 515.2.

Figure 515.2 *The Fonts dialog box.*

5. Within the Fonts dialog box, select the font name, size, and style that you desire.

6. When you type text within an image, Paint uses the current foreground color for the text. If you want to use a different color, perform the steps Tip 509 discusses.

7. Click your mouse on the frame and type the text. If your text takes more room than the frame provides, use your mouse to drag one of the frame's sizing handles to increase the frame's size.

Within a text frame, you can change the text's font, size, style, or color attributes. To do so, simply click your mouse over the text frame and then change the attributes you desire. After you select another tool, however, you cannot edit the text again. To change the text at that point, you must completely erase it and start over.

---

516   SAVING YOUR PAINT IMAGE TO DISK

As you create or edit an image within Paint, you will want to save your changes to a file on disk on a regular basis. Like most Windows-based applications, the Paint File menu provides Save and Save As options which you can use to save your work. The first time you save your image, Paint will display the Save As dialog box. Within the Save As dialog box, you will specify the filename and folder within which you want to save your image. In addition, you can specify the image's color settings when you save an image to disk. Within the Save As dialog box, if you click your mouse on the Save as type pull-down list, Paint, as shown in Figure 516, will display a list of four different types of BMP file formats you can use to store your image.

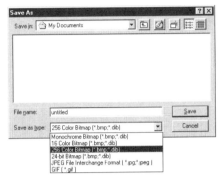

Figure 516 *Specifying the number of colors within a Paint image.*

Each BMP file format corresponds to a specific number of colors the image can contain. If you select the Monochrome Bitmap format, for example, Paint will store your image using only black and white. The fewer the colors an image contains, the smaller the image's file size.

517 PRINTING A GRAPHICS IMAGE WITHIN PAINT

After your create your image within Paint, you will quite likely want to print a copy of your image. If you are using a color printer, your printout should appear in colors that are close to those that appear on your screen (the colors may not be exact due to your monitor's or printer's color-calibration settings). If you are using a black and white printer, your printout will represent different colors using various shades of gray (called a grayscale printout). To print your image, you will use the File menu Print option. However, before you print the image, you should select the File menu Page Setup option. Paint, in turn, will display the Page Setup dialog box, as shown in Figure 517.

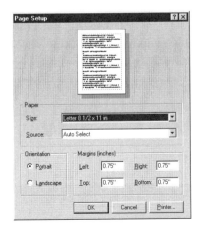

Figure 517 *The Page Setup dialog box.*

Within the Page Setup dialog box, select paper size, output orientation, and the margins you desire and then click your mouse on the OK button.

518 SENDING YOUR PAINT IMAGE TO ANOTHER USER

As you create images within Paint, there may be times when you will need to send your image to another user. Fortunately, Paint's File menu Send option makes it easy for you to send your current image to another user. To send your image to another user, perform these steps:

1. Select the File menu Send option. Paint, in turn, will display the Choose Profile dialog box, within which you can select the communication profile Microsoft Exchange will use to send the file. In most cases, you can simply click your mouse on the OK button to select the Default profile. Paint will then display the New Message window, as shown in Figure 518.

Figure 518 *The New Message window.*

2. Within the New Message window To field, type in the e-mail address of the user to which you want to send your image and then select the File menu Send option.

519 UNDOING AN OPERATION WITHIN PAINT

As you draw, erase, or paint images within Paint, there may be times when you do not want or do not need your last operation. You might have, for example, filled an image that is not completely enclosed and the foreground color leaked onto your canvas. In such cases, Paint lets you undo your three most recent changes. To undo a recent edit, select Paint's Edit menu and choose the Undo option. Paint, in turn, will undo your last operation.

520 USING YOUR PAINT IMAGE AS WALLPAPER ON YOUR DESKTOP

As you learned in Tip 232, Windows 98 lets you use graphics images as the Desktop wallpaper. For example, Figure 520 shows an image within Paint and the same image tiled as Desktop wallpaper.

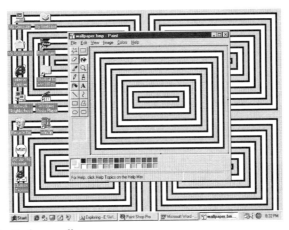

Figure 520 *Using a Paint image as the Desktop wallpaper.*

To use your current Paint image as the Desktop wallpaper, perform these steps:

1. Within Paint, click your mouse on the File menu and save your image to a file.

2. Again, within the File menu, select the Set As Wallpaper (Tiled) option or the Set As Wallpaper (Centered) option, depending on your image size and your desire.

521 SELECTING OBJECTS WITHIN PAINT FOR CUT-AND-PASTE OPERATIONS

As the images you create within Paint become more complex, there may be times when you will need to cut or copy an object that appears within your image so you can paste it somewhere else within the image or even within a different image. Before you can perform such cut-and-paste operations, you must first select the object within your image. Paint provides two tools you can use to select objects: the Select tool and the Free-form Select tool. In addition, to select the entire image, you can use the Edit menu Select All option. Using Paint's Select tool, you can select rectangular portions of your image. For example, Figure 521.1 illustrates an image before and after a rectangular cut-and-paste operation.

Figure 521.1 *Using the Select tool to select a rectangular image for a cut-and-paste operation.*

Using Paint's Free-Form Select tool, drag your mouse to define the shape you want to select. Figure 521.2, for example, illustrates an image before and after a free-form cut-and-paste operation.

Figure 521.2 Using the Free-form Select tool to select an object for a cut-and-paste operation.

After you select an object, you can use the Edit menu Clear Selection option to erase the area and to fill the area with the current background color. To cancel a selection, click your mouse on the Edit menu Cancel Selection option.

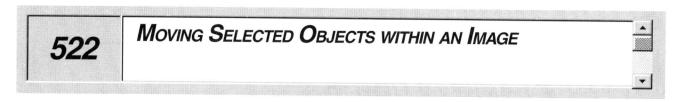

522 MOVING SELECTED OBJECTS WITHIN AN IMAGE

In Tip 521, you learned how to use Paint's Select tool and Free-form Select tool to select an object within an image. In addition to letting you perform cut-and-paste operations with a selected object, Paint also lets you move a selected object within your image by dragging the object with your mouse. After you select an object, Paint will change your mouse cursor into a four-way arrow, indicating to you that you can now use your mouse to drag the selected object.

After you position the object at the location you desire, simply click your mouse at any location outside the object to cancel your selection. Figure 522 illustrates a move operation within Paint.

Figure 522 Dragging a selected object to a new image location.

523 COPYING GRAPHICS IMAGES TO OR FROM A FILE

When you create images within Paint, there may be times when you want to use an image that you have stored within a different file within your current image. In such cases, Paint lets you copy the existing image from its file onto your current canvas. To copy an existing image from a file into your current image, perform these steps:

1. Select the Edit menu Paste From option. Paint, in turn, will display the Paste From dialog box, as shown in Figure 523.

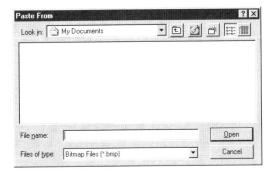

Figure 523 The Paste From dialog box.

2. Within the Paste From dialog box, select the file that contains the image you want to use and click your mouse on the Open button. Paint, in turn, will place the image onto your canvas, selecting the image so you can use your mouse to drag the image to the location you desire.

3. After you position the image at the location you desire, click your mouse at any location outside of the image to deselect it.

Just as Paint lets you paste an existing image from a file, Paint also lets you copy the currently selected portion of an image to a file. To copy the selected portion of an image to a file, perform these steps:

1. Within the image, use a selection tool to choose the portion you desire.

2. Select the Edit menu Copy To option. Paint, in turn, will display the Copy To dialog box.

3. Within the Copy To dialog box, type in the filename into which you want to save the image and then click your mouse on the Save button.

524 FLIPPING OR ROTATING AN IMAGE WITHIN PAINT

As you create or manipulate images within Paint, there may be times when you will want to flip an image, as shown in Figure 524.1, or to rotate an image by 90, 180, or 270 degrees.

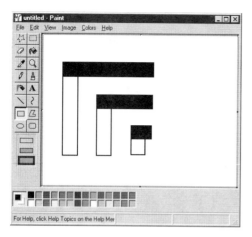 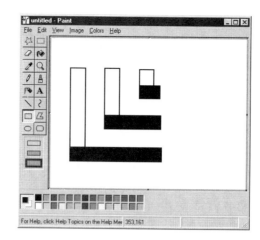

Figure 524.1 *Flipping an image vertically and horizontally.*

To rotate or flip an image within Paint, or to rotate or flip a select part of the image, perform these steps:

1. Click your mouse on the Image menu Flip/Rotate option. Paint, in turn, will display the Flip and Rotate dialog box, as shown in Figure 524.2.

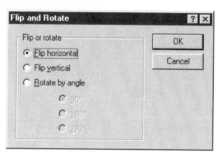

Figure 524.2 *The Flip and Rotate dialog box.*

2. Within the Flip and Rotate dialog box, click your mouse on the option you desire and then choose OK.

525 STRETCHING AND SKEWING AN IMAGE WITHIN PAINT

As you create images, there may be times when your image is not quite the size you need. In such cases, you can use Paint to stretch or shrink your image to the size you desire. To size an image within Paint, you simply specify a percentage value that tells Paint how much it should increase or decrease the image's size along the x and y access.

If you use a different percentage value for each access, Paint will size the image accordingly. Also, Paint will let you skew the object a specific number of degrees along the x or y axis. Figure 525.1, for example, illustrates an image that Paint has stretched and an image that Paint has skewed.

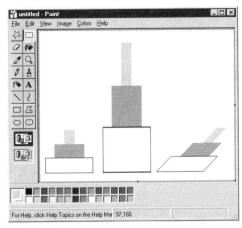

Figure 525.1 *Skewing and stretching images within Paint.*

To stretch, shrink, or skew an image, or a selected image object, within Paint, perform these steps:

1. Click your mouse on the Image menu Stretch/Skew option. Paint, in turn, will display the Stretch and Skew dialog box, as shown in Figure 525.2.

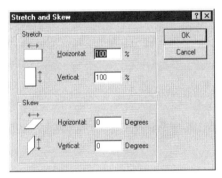

Figure 525.2 *The Stretch and Skew dialog box.*

2. To stretch the image, click your mouse within the Horizontal and Vertical textboxes within the Stretch field and type in the size percentage that you desire. To skew the image, click your mouse within the Horizontal and Vertical textboxes within the Skew field and type in the angle you desire.

3. Click your mouse on the OK button. Paint, in turn, will apply your settings to the image.

526 CONTROLLING IMAGE ATTRIBUTES WITHIN PAINT

When you create an image within Paint, you can specify the image size, colors, and the image's background transparency by selecting the Image menu Attributes option. Paint, in turn, will display the Attributes dialog box, as shown in Figure 526.

Within the Attributes dialog box Width and Height fields, you can specify the image size using inches, centimeters, or pixel measurements. If you decrease the image size, Paint may crop off some of the original picture. Using the Colors field, you can convert a color image into a black-and-white image. Lastly, using the Transparency field, you can control whether or not Paint creates the image with a transparent or opaque background.

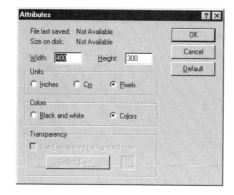

Figure 526 *The Attributes dialog box.*

527   EDITING PAINT'S COLOR PALETTE

By default, Paint displays 28 colors within its color box. As discussed in Tip 509, you can use the color box to select the current foreground and background colors. However, depending on your image needs, there may be times when you need more colors than the color box contains. In such cases, you can select the Colors menu Edit Colors option. Paint, in turn, will display the Edit Colors dialog box, as shown in Figure 527.1.

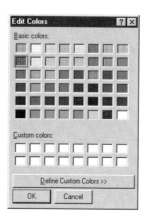

Figure 527.1 *The Edit Colors dialog box.*

Within the Edit Colors dialog box, you can click your mouse on a color within the palette to select a foreground or background color. In addition, you can perform these steps to define up to 16 custom colors:

1. Select the Colors menu Edit Colors option. Paint will display the Edit Colors dialog box.
2. Within the Edit Colors dialog box, click your mouse on the Define Custom Colors button. Paint, in turn, will expand the Edit Colors dialog box, as shown in Figure 527.2.
3. Within the Edit Colors dialog box, drag the arrow pointing to the vertical color bar up and down to change the current color's intensity. To change the current color, drag your mouse pointer within the color spectrum box. As you drag past different color combinations, Paint will change the Color|Solid box to show your new color.
4. After you define the color you desire, click your mouse on the Add to Custom Colors button. Paint, in turn, will add your color to the set of 16 custom colors.

5. Within the Edit Colors dialog box, click your mouse on the OK button to close the dialog box and save your changes. Paint's color palette will now include your custom color.

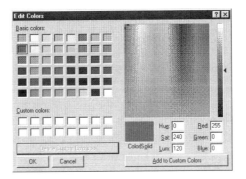

Figure 527.2 *Creating a custom color.*

528 USING GRIDS TO ALIGN OBJECTS WITHIN PAINT

As you place images within Paint, there may be times when you must align two or more, either horizontally or vertically. To help you align objects, Paint lets you turn on a display of grid lines, as shown in Figure 528.

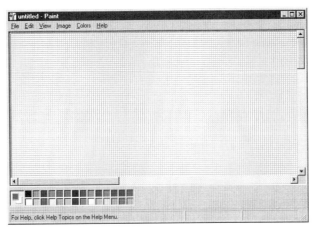

Figure 528 *Using grid lines to align objects within Paint.*

Using the grid lines, you can position objects more accurately. When you later save or print your image, the grid lines will not appear. To turn on editing grid lines within Paint, perform these steps:

1. Click your mouse on the View menu Zoom option. If the Zoom menu displays the Show Grid option in gray (the option is not available), select the Zoom menu Large Size option to magnify your picture. Paint only displays grid lines for zoomed pictures. After you change the magnification, click your mouse on the View menu Zoom option once again and the Show Grid option should be active.

2. Click your mouse on the Zoom menu Show Grid option. Paint will display grid lines in the editing area.

To later turn off the grid-line display, select the View menu Zoom option and select Show Grid.

529   ## DISCARDING YOUR CURRENT IMAGE WITHIN PAINT

As you create images within Paint, there may be times when you want to discard your current drawing without saving your changes to disk. In such cases, you have two choices. First, you can simply select Paint's File menu New option. However, before Paint discards your image, Paint will display a dialog box asking you if you want to save your current changes. Second, you can simply clear your image canvas by selecting the Image menu Clear Image option, as shown in Figure 529.

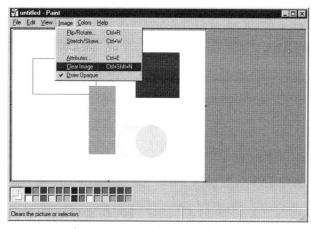

Figure 529 *Discarding your current image using the Image menu Clear Image option.*

530   ## CREATING AN IMAGE WITH A TRANSPARENT BACKGROUND WITHIN PAINT

When you combine one or more images to create a drawing, there will be times when you need to make your image background transparent so you can lay the image on top of a second image. For example, Figure 530 shows two images on top of a background image. The first image has a transparent background and the second image does not.

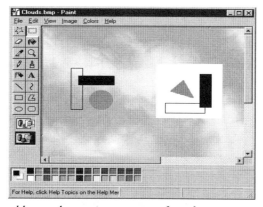

Figure 530 *Using a transparent background lets you lay one image on top of another.*

To create an image with a transparent background, click your mouse on the Image menu Draw Opaque option, placing a check mark next to the option. If you do not want a transparent background, select the option and add the check mark.

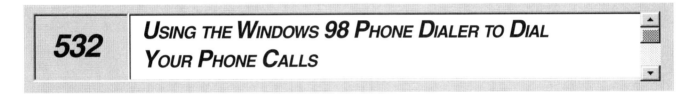

When you shut down your system, Windows 98 displays two messages. The first message informs you that the shutdown is taking place and that you are to wait before turning off your computer. Once Windows 98 successfully shuts down your system, Windows 98 displays a second message that informs you that you can safely turn off your computer. These messages are nothing more than graphic bitmap images that you can edit and change using Paint. Therefore, you can create your own customized message screens that you and other users see when you shut down Windows 98. Windows 98 uses the file names *LOGOW.SYS* and *LOGOS.SYS* for these two files. To create the message images, you must create images that are 320-pixels wide by 400-pixels tall. The easiest way to start is for you simply to open either file within Paint and then change the file's contents as your needs require.

If you examine your PC's modem, you may find that the modem has two phone plugs, the first labeled Line and the second labeled Phone. To use your modem, you connect a phone cable to a wall jack and then to the plug labeled Line. Next, if your modem and phone will share the phone line, you then connect your telephone to the modem plug labeled Phone. When you connect your telephone to your modem in this way, you can use the Windows 98 Phone Dialer accessory program to dial your phone calls for you. To start the Phone Dialer accessory program, perform these steps:

1. Click your mouse on the Start button. Windows 98, in turn, will display the Start menu.

2. Within the Start menu, click your mouse on the Programs option. Windows 98, in turn, will display the Programs submenu.

3. Within the Programs submenu, click your mouse on the Accesssories option and then click your mouse on the Communications option. Windows 98, in turn, will display the Communications submenu. Within the Communications submenu, click your mouse on the Phone Dialer option. Windows 98 will open the Phone Dialer window, as shown in Figure 532.2.

Figure 532.2 *The Windows 98 Phone Dialer accessory program.*

When you hear the speaker sound the ring of the remote phone, you simply pick up your phone's handset and prepare to talk. Several of the Tips that follow discuss the Phone Dialer accessory program in detail.

As you learned in Tip 532, using the Windows 98 Phone Dialer accessory program, you can use your PC's modem to dial your phone calls for you . Using the Phone Dialer, you can manually dial numbers or you can create speed-dial entries to which you assign specific phone numbers. To manually dial a number within the Phone Dialer accessory, perform these steps:

1. Within the Phone Dialer window, click your mouse within the Number to dial field and then type the number you want to dial or click your mouse on the Phone Dialer's number buttons.

2. After you type in or click on the phone number you desire, click your mouse on the Phone Dialer's Dial button or simply press ENTER. The Phone Dialer, in turn, will dial the number and display the Call Status dialog box shown in Figure 533.

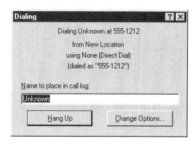

Figure 533 *Talk when the call-recipient answers.*

3. When you hear the remote phone ring, lift your phone receiver and click your mouse on the Phone Dialer's Talk button. If you hear a busy signal or no one answers your call, click your mouse on the Phone Dialer's Hang Up button.

When you use Phone Dialer to place a call, the program will add an entry to your phone log. Within the Call Status dialog box, you can type a name or other information that you want the Phone Dialer to record within the log file.

In Tip 533, you learned how to manually place phone calls within the Phone Dialer accessory program by typing the number or by clicking your mouse on the Phone Dialer's buttons. To make it easier for you to dial the numbers you call on a regular basis, the Phone Dialer lets you define ten speed-dial buttons. You might, for example, assign one speed-dial button that dials your office, a second that dials your house, and a third that dials Microsoft's technical support. To define a speed-dial button within the Phone Dialer, perform these steps:

1. Within the Phone Dialer, click your mouse on the Edit menu and then choose the Speed Dial option. The Phone Dialer will display the Edit Speed Dial dialog box shown in Figure 534.1.

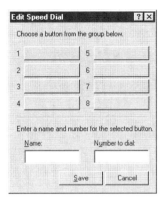

Figure 534.1 *The Edit Speed Dial dialog box.*

2. Within the Edit Speed Dial dialog box, click your mouse on the speed-dial button you want to add (or change).

3. Within the Edit Speed Dial dialog box, click your mouse within the Name field and type the name you want the Phone Dialer to display within the speed-dial button.

4. Within the Edit Speed Dial dialog box, click your mouse within the Number to dial field and type in the number you want the Phone Dialer to associate with the speed-dial button.

5. Within the Edit Speed Dial dialog box, click your mouse on the Save button to save your settings.

Using the Edit Speed Dial dialog box, you can define a new speed-dial button as just discussed or you can edit an existing button. To edit a button, simply click your mouse on the Name or Number to dial field and update the setting as you require. In addition to adding a speed-dial button using the steps just discussed, if you click your mouse on an unused speed-dial button, the Phone Dialer will display the Program Speed Dial dialog box, shown in Figure 534.2, within which you can add a name and phone number.

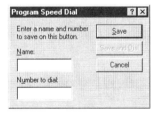

Figure 532.2 *The Program Speed Dial dialog box..*

---

535   SELECTING THE PHONE DIALER MODEM

As you have learned, using the Phone Dialer accessory program, you can direct your modem to dial your phone calls. If your PC has more than one modem, you must tell the Phone Dialer which modem it should use to dial your calls. To tell the Phone Dialer which modem to use, perform these steps:

1. Within the Phone Dialer, click your mouse on the Tools menu. The Phone Dialer, in turn, will display the Tools menu.

2. Within the Tools menu, click your mouse on the Connect Using option. The Phone Dialer will display the Connect Using dialog box, as shown in Figure 535.

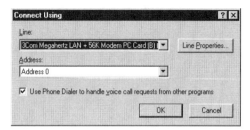

Figure 535 *The Connect Using dialog box.*

3. Within the Connect Using dialog box, click your mouse on the Line pull-down list to display your available modems.

4. Within the Phone Dialer's pull-down modem list, click your mouse on the modem you want the Phone Dialer to use, and then click your mouse on the OK button.

536   CREATING PHONE DIALER PROFILES FOR YOUR HOME AND OFFICE

If you use the Phone Dialer on a laptop computer, there may be times when the locations from which you place your calls may require different dialing properties. For example, to place a call from your office, you may need to dial 9 to get an outside line or a specific access code before you can place a long-distance call. In such cases, you can define dialing schemes that define the dialing properties for each location. To define a dialing scheme, perform these steps:

1. Within the Phone Dialer, click your mouse on the Tools menu and then click your mouse on the Dialing Properties option. Windows 98, in turn, will display the Dialing Properties dialog box, as shown in Figure 536.

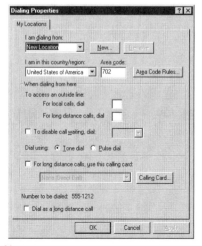

Figure 536 *Specifying a new Phone Dialer profile.*

2. Within the Dialing Properties dialog box, click your mouse within the I am dialing from field and type in your dialing profile name, such as *Work Office*, overwriting the *New Location* name.

3. Within the Dialing Properties dialog box, change the phone settings to match the location for which you are defining your new profile.

4. Within the Dialing Properties dialog box, click your mouse on OK to save your new scheme.

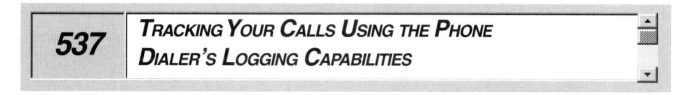

537 TRACKING YOUR CALLS USING THE PHONE DIALER'S LOGGING CAPABILITIES

In addition to dialing your phone calls for you, the Phone Dialer can also log the number, date, and time, as well as the duration of your calls. Each time you use Phone Dialer to place a call, the Phone Dialer will add an entry to your call log. In addition to logging your outgoing calls, the Phone Dialer can also log your incoming calls. To view the Phone Dialer's call log, click your mouse on the Tools menu and then select the Show Log option. The Phone Dialer, in turn, will display its log as shown in Figure 537.

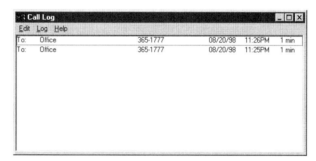

Figure 537 *The Phone Dialer call log.*

After the Phone Dialer displays the log, you can copy or delete information from it. You cannot, however, change specific information within the log, such as the number or person you called. By copying information from the Phone Dialer log to your clipboard, you can later paste the information into a word processor for printing.

Depending on the number of calls you place or receive, your Phone Dialer log may become quite large. Over time, you may want to remove old entries from the log. To remove an entry, click your mouse on it and then select the File menu Cut option. To select multiple entries, hold down the CTRL key as you click your mouse on each entry or hold down the SHIFT key to select a series of files.

538 USING THE WINDOWS 98 ENTERTAINMENT (MULTIMEDIA) ACCESSORIES

Today, almost every PC sold comes with a sound card and speakers. To help you get the most from your PC investment, Windows 98 provides several programs you can use to play back multimedia files, to record your own sounds, and even to let you play audio CDs from your PC. Several of the Tips that follow examine Windows 98 multimedia features in detail. To run the Windows 98 multimedia accessory programs, perform these steps:

1. Click your mouse on the Start menu Programs option and choose Accessories. Windows 98, in turn, will display the Accessories submenu.

2. Within the Accessories submenu, click your mouse on the Entertainment option. Windows 98 will display the Entertainment submenu, as shown in Figure 538.

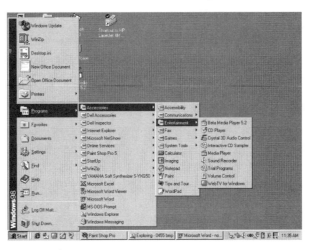

Figure 538 *The Windows 98 Entertainment submenu.*

Note: *Depending on your Windows 98 installation, you may find the multimedia accessory programs within the Entertainment submenu or the Multimedia submenu.*

3. Within the Entertainment submenu, click your mouse on the option that corresponds to the program that you desire.

Note: *If your system does not display one or more of the Windows 98 multimedia accessory programs shown in Figure 538, you can install the programs from the Windows 98 CD-ROM, as discussed in Tip 218.*

539 **USING THE WINDOWS 98 CD PLAYER TO PLAY AUDIO CDs**

In Tip 307, you learned that you can play an audio CD within Windows 98 simply by inserting the audio CD into your CD-ROM drive. Windows 98, in turn, will recognize the audio CD format and will start playing the CD automatically. As it turns out, to play the audio CD, Windows 98 uses the CD Player accessory program, as shown in Figure 539.1.

Figure 539.1 *The CD Player accessory program.*

If the CD Player is not currently running and you have an audio CD in your CD-ROM drive, you can start the CD Player by performing these steps:

1. Click your mouse on the Start menu Programs option and choose Accessories. Windows 98, in turn, will display the Accessories submenu.
2. Within the Accessories submenu, click your mouse on the Entertainment option. Windows 98 will display the Entertainment submenu.
3. Within the Entertainment submenu, click your mouse on the CD Player option.

Within the CD Player, you can play, pause, stop, or select tracks using the buttons shown in Table 539.

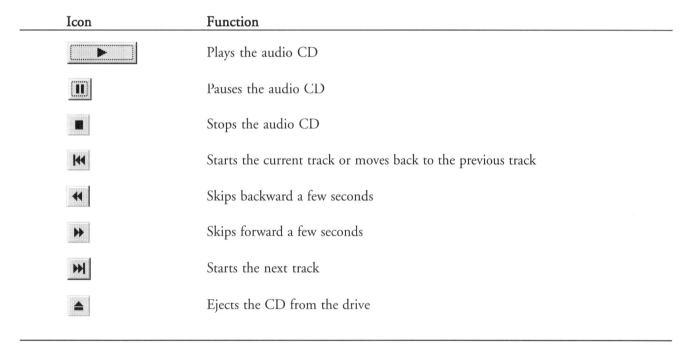

Icon	Function
▶	Plays the audio CD
❚❚	Pauses the audio CD
■	Stops the audio CD
⏮	Starts the current track or moves back to the previous track
⏪	Skips backward a few seconds
⏩	Skips forward a few seconds
⏭	Starts the next track
⏏	Ejects the CD from the drive

Table 539 *Buttons within the CD Player.*

540 **TAKING ADVANTAGE OF THE CD PLAYER TOOLBAR**

Like most Windows-based programs, the CD Player provides a toolbar you can use to simplify common operations. Figure 540 briefly describes each of the CD Player toolbar buttons. If your CD Player window is not currently displaying the toolbar, click your mouse on the View menu Toolbar option, placing a check mark next to the option.

Displays the Play List window

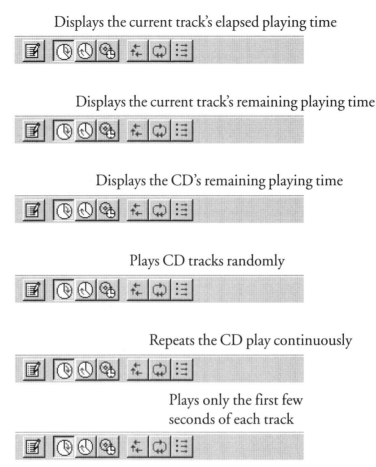

Displays the current track's elapsed playing time

Displays the current track's remaining playing time

Displays the CD's remaining playing time

Plays CD tracks randomly

Repeats the CD play continuously

Plays only the first few
seconds of each track

Figure 540 *The CD Player toolbar buttons.*

In addition to using the View menu to display information about the current CD, you can also use View menu options to direct the CD Player to display the elapsed track time, the track time remaining, or the disc time remaining.

541 USING PLAY LISTS TO CONTROL WHICH CD TRACKS THE CD PLAYER PLAYS

As you know, audio CDs store each song within a track. Usually, when you insert an audio CD into your CD-ROM drive, the CD Player will start with the first track and play through each of the tracks that follow. If you have songs that you really like or dislike on a specific audio CD, you can use a play list to control how the CD Player plays back the CD. For example, your play list might tell the CD-ROM to play your favorite song (which is on track 2) twice and to skip your least favorite song (which is on track 5). Within the CD Player, you can create a play list for each of your audio CDs. After you create a play list for a particular audio CD, the CD Player program will play only those tracks you specify. To create a play list, perform these steps:

1. Insert the audio CD for which you want to define the play list into your audio. Windows 98, in turn, will start the CD Player automatically. (If, for some reason, the CD Player does not start, follow the steps Tip 307 presents to start the program.)

2. Within the CD Player, select the Disc menu Edit Play List. The CD Player displays the Disc Settings dialog box, as shown in Figure 541.

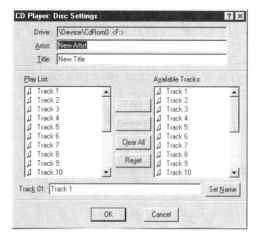

Figure 541 *The Disc Settings dialog box.*

3. Within the Disc Settings dialog box, you will find a Play List field that defines which audio CD tracks the CD Player will play. To remove a track from the play list, click your mouse on the track and then click your mouse on the Remove button.

4. To add a track to the play list, click your mouse on the Track within the Available Tracks list and then click your mouse on the Add button.

5. If you want to place a track at a specific location, use your mouse to drag the track from the Available Tracks list to the location you desire within the Play List.

6. Within the Disc Settings dialog box, click your mouse on the OK button to put your settings into effect.

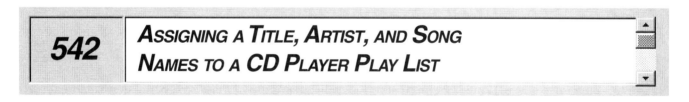

542 ASSIGNING A TITLE, ARTIST, AND SONG NAMES TO A CD PLAYER PLAY LIST

In Tip 541, you learned how to create a play list for an audio CD that defined which tracks of an audio CD the CD Player plays and in what order. Within the Disc Settings dialog box which you used to create your play list, you can also title your audio CD and assign a name to its artist as well as to each track's song. Later, if you insert the same audio CD back into your system, the CD Player software will remember your settings. To title your audio CD, perform these steps:

1. Insert the audio CD for which you want to define the play list into your audio. Windows 98, in turn, will start the CD Player automatically.

2. Within the CD Player, select the Disc menu Edit Play List. The CD Player displays the Disc Settings dialog box, as shown in Figure 542.

3. Within the Disc Settings dialog box, click your mouse on the Artist field and type in the name of the CD's artist. Next, click your mouse on the Title field and type in the CD's title.

4. Next, you must type in the name of the song that corresponds to each track. (You will usually find the songs listed by tracks on the back of your CD case.)

5. Within the Disc Settings dialog box Available Tracks field, click your mouse on a track. Next, within the track name textbox that appears at the bottom of the dialog box, type in the name of the track's corresponding song and then click your mouse on the Set Name button. The Disc Settings dialog box, in turn, will display the name within Available Tracks. Also, if the Play List field contains the track, the dialog box will also display the track name within that list.

6. Repeat Step 5 to assign a title to each of the CD's tracks.

7. Within the Disc Settings dialog box, click your mouse on the OK button to put your changes into effect.

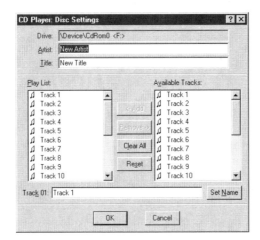

Figure 542 *The Disc Settings dialog box.*

543 **C**ONTROLLING THE **T**RACK **O**RDER THE **CD** **P**LAYER **U**SES TO **P**LAY AN **A**UDIO **CD**

In Tip 542, you learned how to create track lists that control which tracks the CD Player plays and in what order. If you have not yet defined a track list for the current CD, you can use the CD Player Option menu, shown in Figure 543, to control the order in which the CD Player plays audio tracks.

Figure 543 *The CD Player Options menu.*

If you select the Options menu Random Order option, the CD Player will play a CD's tracks in a random sequence. If you, instead, select the Continuous Play option, the CD Player will play the track list over and over until you finally stop the CD Player. Lastly, if you select the Intro Play option, the CD Player will play only the first ten seconds of each song, moving from one song to the next, to help you locate a specific song on the CD.

544 CUSTOMIZING THE CD PLAYER PREFERENCES

By default, when you exit the CD Player, Windows 98 will stop playing the current song. There may be times, however, when you will want Windows 98 to keep playing the CD after you stop the CD Player. Likewise, in Tip 543, you learned that if you select the CD Player Options menu Intro Play option, the CD Player will move through the available tracks by playing a 10-second introduction to the track. If you use the CD Player on a regular basis, you may want to customize these and other CD Player preferences. To customize the CD Player preferences, perform these steps:

1. Within the CD Player window, click your mouse on the Options menu Preferences option. The CD Player, in turn, will display the Preferences dialog box, as shown in Figure 544.

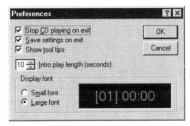

Figure 544 The CD Player Preferences dialog box.

2. Within the Preferences dialog box, customize the settings that you desire and then click your mouse on the OK button to put your changes into effect.

Table 544 briefly explains the Preferences dialog box options.

Setting	Purpose
Stop CD Playing on exit	Directs Windows 98 to stop playing the audio CD when you close the CD Player program. If you remove the check mark, Windows 98 will continue to play the CD after you close the CD Player program.
Save settings on exit	Saves your preferences and view menu selections to disk each time you exit the CD Player, so your settings will take effect the next time you start the program.
Show tool tips	Directs the CD Player to display pop-up tips that describe a toolbar button's purpose when you hold the mouse pointer over a toolbar button.
Intro play length	Controls the length of time the CD Player uses to introduce an audio track when you select the Options menu Intro Play option.
Display font	Controls whether the CD Player uses a large or small font within its digital display.

Table 544 The CD Player Preferences dialog box options.

545

VIEWING MICROSOFT'S INTERACTIVE CATALOG FROM THE WINDOWS 98 CD-ROM

In addition to providing you with the software you need to upgrade your system to Windows 98, the Windows 98 CD-ROM also provides a CD-ROM based catalog of several Microsoft products that you can preview on your screen. To experience the interactive catalog, perform these steps:

1. Click your mouse on the Start menu Programs option and choose Accessories. Windows 98, in turn, will display the Accessories submenu.

2. Within the Accessories submenu, click your mouse on the Entertainment option and choose Interactive CD Sampler. Windows 98 will display the Microsoft Interactive CD Sampler dialog box, as shown in Figure 545.1.

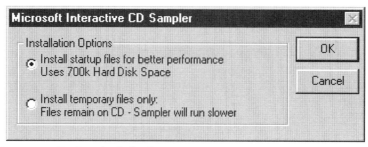

Figure 545.1 *The Microsoft Interactive CD Sampler dialog box.*

3. Within the Microsoft Interactive CD Sampler dialog box, click your mouse on the OK button. Windows 98 will install the catalog software onto your hard disk, eventually displaying the Sampler window, as shown in Figure 545.2.

Figure 545.2 *The Sampler window.*

4. Within the Sampler window, click your mouse on a product category to display the related Microsoft products. Then, click your mouse on a specific product to hear a brief audio presentation on the product's features.

546 **PLAYING BACK MULTIMEDIA FILES USING THE MEDIA PLAYER**

To let you play back just about any type of multimedia file, Windows 98 provides the Media Player accessory program. Using the Media Player, you can play back audio files, MIDI sound files, audio CDs, and even video files. Depending on the type of file you are playing, the Media Player's appearance will differ. Figure 546.1, for example, shows the Media Player window as it plays back a MIDI file and the window as the Media Player plays back an audio CD.

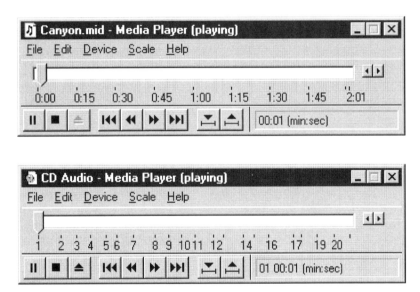

Figure 546.1 *Using the Media Player to play back multimedia files and devices.*

To start the Media Player, perform these steps:

1. Click your mouse on the Start menu Programs option and choose Accessories. Windows 98, in turn, will display the Accessories submenu.

2. Within the Accessories submenu, click your mouse on the Entertainment menu and then click your mouse on the Media Player option. Windows 98 will open the Media Player window.

547 **OPENING A MULTIMEDIA FILE OR A DEVICE WITHIN THE MEDIA PLAYER**

In Tip 546, you learned that the Windows 98 Media Player lets you play back a variety of multimedia files and devices. To open a multimedia file for play back within the Media Player, perform these steps:

1. Within the Media Player, select the File menu Open option. The Media Player, in turn, will display the Open dialog box.

2. Within the Open dialog box, select the file that you want to play back and then click your mouse on the Open button. (By using the Open dialog box Files of type pull-down list, you can direct the Media Player to only display files of a specific type, such as WAV audio files, within the Open dialog box.)

In addition to opening files within the Media Player, you can also open a specific device type, such as an audio CD. To prepare the Media Player to use a specific device type, click your mouse on the Media Player Device menu. Depending on the device-driver software you have installed on your system, the entries that the Media Player displays within the Device window may differ. Also, note that within the Media Player Device menu, you can also control your system's speaker volume by choosing the Volume Control option.

548 **DISPLAYING THE MEDIA PLAYER PROGRESS BAR USING TRACKS, TIME, OR FRAMES**

As you have learned, depending on the type of file or device the Media Player is using, the Media Player's appearance may differ slightly. Within the Media Player window, you can further customize the display by directing the Media Player to display its progress meter in terms of tracks (for audio CDs), time (for WAV or MIDI files), or frames (for video files). To control the Media Player's display, click your mouse on the Media Player Scale menu, as shown in Figure 547, and then choose the display type that you desire.

Figure 548 The Media Player Scale menu.

549 **COPYING MEDIA TO THE CLIPBOARD FROM WITHIN THE MEDIA PLAYER**

In previous Tips, you learned how to perform cut-and-paste operations to move or copy information from one document to another. In a similar way, the Media Player lets you copy part of a media file to the Clipboard. Later, depending on the other software programs that you have available, you can paste the media from the Clipboard into a different application. Unfortunately, the Media Player itself will not let you paste the Clipboard contents back into its current media file.

To copy media to the Clipboard from within the Media Player, perform these steps:

1. Within the Media Player window, click your mouse to drag the current position indicator to the starting location of the media you want to copy.

2. Within the Media Player button bar, click your mouse on the Start selection button. The Media player will display a small marker at the current position.

3. Within the Media Player window, click your mouse to drag the current position indicator to the ending location of the media you want to copy.

4. Within the Media Player button bar, click your mouse on the Stop selection button. The Media player will display a small marker at the current position and will highlight the media that appears between the start and stop markers.

5. Click your mouse on the Media Player Edit menu and choose Copy. The Media Player will copy your selection into the Clipboard.

In addition to using your mouse to mark your media selection, you can also select the Media Player Edit menu Selection option. The Media Player, in turn, will display the Set Selection dialog box, as shown in Figure 549, from which you select the range of media that you desire.

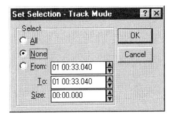

Figure 549 *The Media Player Set Selection dialog box.*

550 **CONTROLLING OTHER MEDIA PLAYER OPTIONS**

Depending on how you are using the Media Player, there may be times when you will want the Media Player to automatically to repeat the media play back or times when you will want the Media Player to run from within a different program's window. To customize such Media Player settings, click your mouse on the Media Player Edit menu and choose Options. The Media Player, in turn, will display the Options dialog box, as shown in Figure 550. Table 550 briefly describes the Options dialog box settings.

Figure 550 *The Media Player Options dialog box.*

Option	Description
Auto Rewind	Directs the Media Player to automatically rewind the media after the clip finishes
Auto Repeat	Directs the Media Player to automatically repeat the current media
OLE Object	Directs the Media Player to display its button bar and caption when you copy a clip to an OLE-compatible program
Border around object	Directs the Media Player to display a border around an object after you copy the object from the Clipboard into another application
Play in client document	Directs the Media Player to start playing the object when a user double-clicks on the embedded object within another program
Dither picture to VGA color	Directs the Media Player to adjust video clips (dither the colors) to compensate for a system's current color settings

Table 550 *The Media Player Options dialog box settings.*

551 RECORDING YOUR OWN SOUNDS USING THE WINDOWS 98 SOUND RECORDER

In previous Tips, you learned how to assign sounds to various Windows 98 events. As you learned, Windows 98 usually stores audio files within files that use the WAV extension. If your PC has a sound card and microphone, you can record your own sounds using the Sound Recorder, as shown in Figure 551.1.

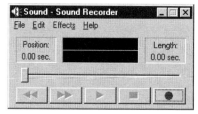

Figure 551.1 *The Windows 98 Sound Recorder.*

To start the Sound Recorder accessory, perform these steps:

1. Click your mouse on the Start menu Programs options and choose Accessories. Windows 98, in turn, will display the Accessories submenu.

2. Within the Accessories submenu, choose the Entertainment menu Sound Recorder option. Windows 98 will open the Sound Recorder window previously shown within Figure 551.1.

If you examine the Sound Recorder window shown in Figure 551.1, you will find that the Sound Recorder provides buttons which are very similar to those you would find on a traditional cassette recorder.

552 RECORDING AND SAVING AN AUDIO FILE WITHIN THE WINDOWS 98 SOUND RECORDER

In Tip 551, you learned how to run the Sound Recorder accessory program which you can use with a sound card and a microphone to record and edit your own sounds. To create a sound file using the Sound Recorder, perform these steps:

1. If your PC microphone has an on/off switch, move the switch to the on position.

2. Within the Sound Recorder, click your mouse on the Record button.

3. Using your microphone, record the sound you desire. As the Sound Recorder records your sound, it will display the sound's wave signal within its display window.

4. After you record your sound, click your mouse on the Stop button to stop recording.

5. Select the Sound Recorder's File menu Save As option. Windows 98, in turn, will display the Save As dialog box.

6. Within the Save As dialog box, type in the filename within which you want to store your sound. The Sound Recorder automatically adds the WAV extension to the filename. Click your mouse on the OK button to save your file.

553 CONTROLLING A SOUND FILE'S FORMAT WITHIN THE SOUND RECORDER

In Tip 298, you learned how to use the Control Panel Multimedia option to configure your sound card's recording and play-back quality. If you are not satisfied with the quality of the sounds you record within the Sound Recorder, or if you feel that your audio files are consuming too much disk space, you can use the Sound Recorder to change your current audio settings by performing these steps:

1. Within the Sound Recorder window, click your mouse on the Edit menu Audio Properties option. The Sound Recorder will display the Audio Properties dialog box, shown in Figure 553.

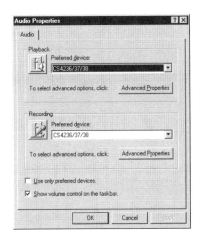

Figure 553 *The Audio Properties dialog box.*

2. Within the Audio Properties dialog box, click your mouse on the Advanced Properties button. Windows 98 will display the Advanced Audio Properties dialog box.

3. Within the Advanced Audio Properties dialog box, you can configure your speaker setup and specify the recording or play back quality that you desire.

---

554 **DELETING THE START OR END OF A RECORDING WITHIN THE SOUND RECORDER**

In Tip 552, you learned how to record sounds within the Sound Recorder. After you record a sound, you may find that you want to delete part of the sound. As you will learn in this Tip, the Sound Recorder makes it easy for you to remove sound from the start or end of your recording. To remove sound from the start of your recording, perform these steps:

1. Within the Sound Recorder window, drag the position slider just past the sound you want to delete (or simply play the recording until just after the sound you want to delete).

2. Select the Sound Recorder Edit menu and choose the Delete Before Current Position option. The Sound Recorder, in turn, will discard the sound that precedes the position slider.

To remove sound from the end of a recording, perform these steps:

3. Within the Sound Recorder window, drag the position slider just past the sound you want to delete (or simply play the recording until just after the sound you want to delete).

4. Select the Sound Recorder Edit menu and choose the Delete After Current Position option. The Sound Recorder, in turn, will discard the sound that follows the position slider.

---

555 **INSERTING AN AUDIO FILE INTO THE CURRENT RECORDING WITHIN THE SOUND RECORDER**

As your collection of audio files grow, there may be times when you will want to combine two or more existing recordings to create a new sound file. For example, assume that you have a recording of your company's president making a short speech and you want to precede the speech with a musical introduction.

Within the Sound Recorder, you can insert an audio file (in this case, a file that contains the musical introduction) into the current recording. To insert an audio file into a recording, perform these steps:

1. Within the Sound Recorder window, drag the position slider to the location within the audio file at which you want to insert the recording (or simply play the recording to the location).

2. Select the Sound Recorder Edit menu and choose the Insert File option. The Sound Recorder, in turn, will display the Insert File dialog box, as shown in Figure 555.

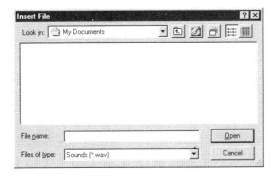

Figure 555 *The Insert File dialog box.*

3. Within the Insert File dialog box, open the audio file you want the Sound Recorder to insert at the current location.

4. Within the Sound Recorder, play back your new recording. If the recording meets your needs, select the File menu Save As option and save your file. If the recording does not meet your needs, use the File menu Open option to reopen the original file, without saving your changes.

556	**MIXING TWO OR MORE RECORDINGS TO CREATE A NEW SOUND**

In Tip 555, you learned how to use the Sound Recorder to insert an existing recording into the current sound. As you edit sounds, there will be times when you will want to mix two sounds together. For example, assume that rather than playing a musical introduction to your company president's speech you want to play a musical background. In this case, you would *mix* the two recordings. To mix two recordings within the Sound Recorder, perform these steps:

1. Within the Sound Recorder window, drag the position slider to the location within the audio file at which you want the mixing to begin (or simply play the recording to the location).

2. Select the Sound Recorder Edit menu and choose the Mix with File option. The Sound Recorder, in turn, will display the Mix With File dialog box, as shown in Figure 556.

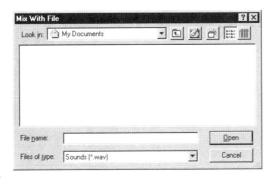

Figure 556 *The Mix With File dialog box.*

3. Within the Mix With File dialog box, open the audio file you want the Sound Recorder to mix at the current location.

4. Within the Sound Recorder, play back your new recording. If the recording meets your needs, select the File menu Save As option and save your file. If the recording does not meet your needs, use the File menu Open option to reopen the original file, without saving your current changes.

Note: *If you have stored a sound clip on the Clipboard, you can mix a sound from the Clipboard using the Edit menu Paste Mix option.*

557 DELETING SOUNDS FROM THE MIDDLE OF A RECORDING WITHIN THE SOUND RECORDER

In Tip 554, you learned how to use the Sound Recorder to delete sounds from the start or end of a recording. In some cases, however, the sound that you want to delete may occur in the middle of a recording. To delete a sound from the middle of a recording, perform these steps:

1. Select the Sound Recorder File menu Save As option. The Sound Recorder will display the Save As dialog box. Within the Save As dialog box, save the current sound to a file named *OldSound.WAV*.

2. Within the Sound Recorder window, drag the position slider just past the sound you want to keep (or simply play the recording until just after the sound you want to keep).

3. Select the Sound Recorder Edit menu and choose the Delete After Current Position option. The Sound Recorder, in turn, will discard the sound that follows the position slider.

4. Select the Sound Recorder File menu Save As option. The Sound Recorder, in turn, will display the Save As dialog box. Within the Save As dialog box, save the current sound to a file named *Start.WAV*.

5. Select the Sound Recorder File menu Open option. The Sound Recorder will display the Open dialog box. Within the Open dialog box, open the sound file *OldSound.WAV*.

6. Within the Sound Recorder window, drag the position slider just past the sound you want to delete (or simply play the recording until just after the sound you want to delete).

7. Select the Sound Recorder Edit menu and choose the Delete Before Current Position option. The Sound Recorder, in turn, will discard the sound that precedes the position slider.

8. Within the Sound Recorder window, drag the position slider to the start of the sound.

9. Select the Sound Recorder Edit menu and choose the Insert File option. The Sound Recorder, in turn, will display the Insert File dialog box. Within the Insert File dialog box, open the file *Start.WAV*. The Sound Recorder, in turn, will insert the file's contents at the start of your current sound file.

10. Select the File menu Save As option. The Sound Recorder will display the Save As dialog box. Within the Save As dialog box, save your new sound to a file on your disk.

558 CUTTING AND PASTING SOUNDS WITHIN THE SOUND RECORDER

In Tip 557, you learned how to use multiple files to edit sound from the middle of a recording. In addition to using files to temporarily hold a sound file, you can also use the Windows Clipboard. Within the Sound Recorder, you can select the Edit menu Copy option to copy the current sound to the Clipboard. Later, using the Edit menu Paste option, you can paste the sound from the Clipboard into your recording at the current position. To edit sound from the middle of a recording using cut-and-paste operations, perform these steps:

1. If you have not already saved the current recording to a file, use the Sound Recorder File menu Save As option to do so now.

2. Within the Sound Recorder window, drag the position slider just past the sound you want to keep (or simply play the recording until just after the sound you want to keep).

3. Select the Sound Recorder Edit menu and choose the Delete After Current Position option. The Sound Recorder, in turn, will discard the sound that follows the position slider.

4. Select the Sound Recorder Edit menu Copy option. The Sound Recorder will copy the current sound to the Clipboard.

5. Select the Sound Recorder File menu Open option. The Sound Recorder will display the Open dialog box. Within the Open dialog box, open your original sound file.

6. Within the Sound Recorder window, drag the position slider just past the sound you want to delete (or simply play the recording until just after the sound you want to delete).

7. Select the Sound Recorder Edit menu and choose the Delete Before Current Position option. The Sound Recorder, in turn, will discard the sound that precedes the position slider.

8. Within the Sound Recorder window, drag the position slider to the start of the sound.

9. Select the Sound Recorder Edit menu and choose the Paste Insert option. The Sound Recorder, in turn, will insert the Clipboard's contents at the start of your current sound file. Select the File menu Save As option. The Sound Recorder will display the Save As dialog box. Within the Save As dialog box, save your new sound to a file on your disk.

559 APPLYING SPECIAL EFFECTS TO A RECORDING WITHIN THE SOUND RECORDER

As you record sounds, there may be times when you must increase or decrease the recording's volume or when you will want to speed up or slow down the sound. To perform these operations, as well as others, you will use the Sound Recorder Effects menu, as shown in Figure 559.

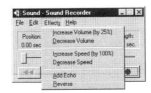

Figure 559 *The Sound Recorder Effects menu.*

Table 559 briefly describes the Effects menu options.

Option	Description
Increase Volume (by 25%)	Increases the sound's volume level by 25%
Decrease Volume	Decreases the sound's volume level by 25%
Increase Speed (by 100%)	Doubles the speed at which the sound plays
Decrease Speed	Reduces the sound's speed in half
Add Echo	Adds an echo to the sound
Reverse	Reverses the sound so it plays backward

Table 559 The Sound Recorder Effects menu options.

560 ASSIGNING YOUR OWN SOUNDS TO WINDOWS SYSTEM EVENTS

As you have learned, using the Control Panel Sounds option you can assign WAV audio files to various Windows events. If you record your own sounds using the Sound Recorder, you can later assign those sounds to various system events. For example, you might want Windows 98 to play a recording that greets you by name each time you start your system. To assign your own sounds to a Windows event, perform these steps:

1. Click your mouse on the Start menu Settings option and choose Control Panel. Windows 98, in turn, will open the Control Panel window.

2. Within the Control Panel window, double-click your mouse on the Sounds icon. Windows 98 will display the Sounds Properties dialog box, as shown in Figure 560.

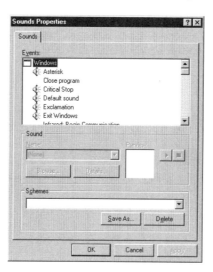

Figure 560 The Sounds Properties dialog box.

3. Within the Sounds Properties dialog box Events field, click your mouse on the event to which you want to assign your own sound. Next, click your mouse on the Browse button. Windows 98, in turn, will display the Browse dialog box.

4. Within the Browse dialog box, locate your sound file and then click your mouse on the OK button.

5. Within the Sounds Properties dialog box, assign sounds to other events as you desire and then click your mouse on the OK button to put your changes into effect.

561 | *TAKING THE WINDOWS 98 TRIAL PROGRAMS FOR A TEST DRIVE*

In addition to containing the software that you must use to upgrade your system to Windows 98, the Windows 98 CD-ROM also contains trial versions of several Microsoft programs that you can install and use on your system. Some of the programs will only run for a 30 to 90 day period, while others are a scaled-back version. Within the trial software, you will find Microsoft Money, Microsoft Golf, Microsoft PictureIt!, and much more. To install the trial software programs, which you can later run from the Programs menu, perform these steps:

1. Click your mouse on the Start menu Programs option and choose Accessories. Windows 98, in turn, will display the Accessories menu.

2. Within the Accessories menu, click your mouse on the Entertainment option and choose Trial Programs. Windows 98 will start the Microsoft Trial Versions Setup window, first displaying a license agreement and eventually a Setup window, as shown in Figure 561.

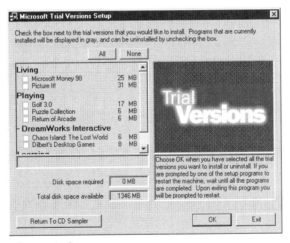

Figure 561 *The Microsoft Trial Versions Setup window.*

3. Within the Microsoft Trial Versions Setup window, click your mouse on the Setup program. The Setup program, in turn, will change the window's contents to display information about the program.

4. To install a program onto your system, click your mouse on the program name, placing a check mark within the checkbox, and then click your mouse on the OK button. The Microsoft Trial Versions Setup program will run a second Setup program that will install the software on your disk.

5. After you install the software that you desire onto your disk, click your mouse on the Exit button to close the Microsoft Trial Versions Setup window.

---

562 | **USING THE WINDOWS 98 VOLUME CONTROL**

As you work with different multimedia devices, there may be times when you must control a specific device's volume. In such cases, you can use the Windows 98 Volume Control accessory program, as shown in Figure 562. Using the Volume Control accessory program, you can change the volume for all your devices in one step, for audio file recording or play back, for MIDI files, and for audio CDs.

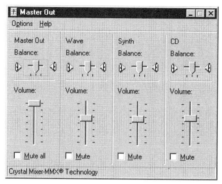

Figure 562 *The Volume Control accessory program.*

To start the Volume Control program, perform these steps:

1. Click your mouse on the Start menu Programs option and choose Accessories. Windows 98 will display the Accessories submenu.
2. Within the Accessories submenu, click your mouse on Entertainment and then choose Volume Control.

Note: *You can also start the Volume Control accessory program by double-clicking your mouse on the Taskbar speaker icon.*

---

563 | **CONTROLLING YOUR SOUND CARD'S SPEAKER BALANCE**

Most multimedia PCs provide two speakers so they can produce stereo-quality sound. To fine-tune your sound quality, most sound cards and speakers let you control the speaker *balance* (the amount of volume each speaker produces). Within the Windows 98 Volume Control accessory, you can control the speaker balance for your different multimedia devices. To adjust a device's speaker balance, use your mouse to drag the device's Balance slider to the left or to the right.

Note: *Within the Volume Control window, you can use the Mute checkbox to enable or disable a device's output. When you mute a device, Windows 98 will keep playing the sound—you simply will not hear it. The Mute All checkbox lets you mute all of your devices in one step.*

564 **SELECTING WHICH DEVICES THE WINDOWS 98 VOLUME CONTROL DISPLAYS**

In Tip 562, you learned how to use the Windows 98 Volume Control accessory to control your multimedia device volume. Usually, the Volume Control accessory will display a Volume Control box for each of your devices. However, if you do not use a specific device, you can hide the device's volume-bar display within the Volume Control. To specify which devices the Volume Control displays, perform these steps:

1. Within the Volume Control window, click your mouse on the Options menu Properties option. Windows 98 will display the Volume Control Properties sheet, as shown in Figure 564.

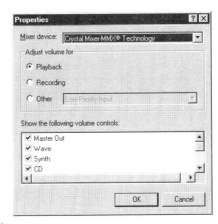

Figure 564 *The Volume Control Properties sheet.*

2. Within the Volume Control Properties sheet, click your mouse on the checkbox that appears next to the device name, placing a check mark in the box. To remove a device from the Volume Control window, remove the check from the device's checkbox.
3. Click your mouse on the OK button to put your changes into effect.

565 **USING THE WORDPAD WORD PROCESSOR TO CREATE, VIEW, AND PRINT DOCUMENTS**

Today, three of the most commonly used PC applications are e-mail, Web browsing, and word processing. Windows 98 provides built-in programs you can use to perform each of these applications. In the Tips that follow, you will examine WordPad, the word processing software that Microsoft bundles with Windows 98. Using WordPad, you can create, edit, view, and print documents. Like most word processors, WordPad lets you format text, use character attributes such as bold and italic highlights, and even create bulleted lists. Unlike a full-scale word processor, such as Microsoft Word, WordPad does not provide a spell checker, thesaurus, or advanced formatting capabilities. However, for most simple word processing documents, WordPad will meet most of your needs. To start the WordPad accessory program, perform these steps:

1. Click your mouse on the Start menu. Windows 98, in turn, will display the Start menu.

2. Within the Start menu, click your mouse on the Programs option and then click your mouse on the Accessories option. Windows 98 will display the Accessories submenu.

3. Within the Accessories submenu, click your mouse on the WordPad option. Windows 98 will open the WordPad window, as shown in Figure 565.

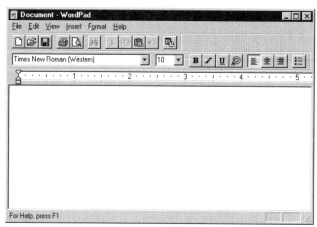

Figure 565 *The Windows 98 WordPad word processor.*

Within WordPad, you can create and edit documents. For now, type several lines of text. As WordPad reaches the end of the line, WordPad will automatically wrap the cursor to the start of the next line. You do not have to press the ENTER key to advance the cursor. In fact, as you will learn in Tip 569, you only press the ENTER key at the end of each paragraph. To print your text, select the File menu Print option. To save your text to a document on disk, select the File menu Save As option. Lastly, to discard your text, without saving it to a file on disk, select the File menu New option to create a new document or the File menu Exit option to close WordPad.

566 SAVING STEPS USING WORDPAD'S TOOLBAR BAR AND FORMAT BAR

Like most Windows-based programs, WordPad provides a toolbar of icons that you can use to perform specific operations quickly. Figure 566.1 illustrates the WordPad toolbar. If WordPad is not currently displaying its toolbar, select the WordPad View menu Toolbar option, placing a check mark next to the option.

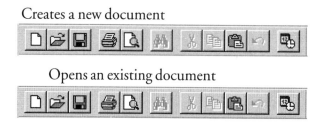

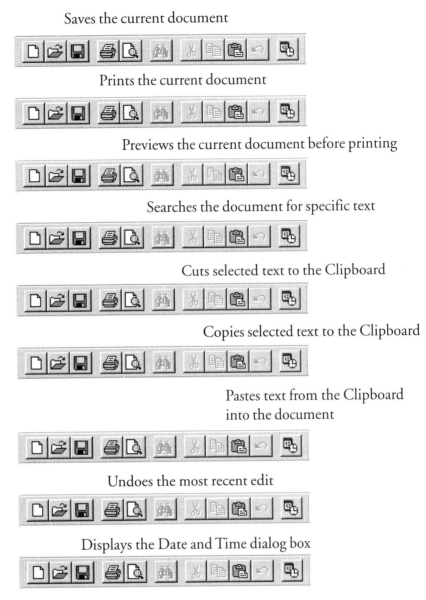

Saves the current document

Prints the current document

Previews the current document before printing

Searches the document for specific text

Cuts selected text to the Clipboard

Copies selected text to the Clipboard

Pastes text from the Clipboard
into the document

Undoes the most recent edit

Displays the Date and Time dialog box

Figure 566.1 *The WordPad toolbar.*

In addition to providing the toolbar, WordPad also provides a format bar (a second toolbar), as shown in Figure 566.2 that contains icons you can use to quickly format text. If WordPad is not currently displaying its format bar, select the WordPad View menu Format option, placing a check mark next to the option.

Figure 566.2 *The WordPad's format bar.*

567 HIGHLIGHTING YOUR TEXT USING BOLD, ITALIC, OR UNDERLINE ATTRIBUTES

Within word processing documents, users often use font attributes, such as italic or bold text to highlight key text. Within WordPad, you have two ways to assign such attributes. First, you can turn on (or turn off) an attribute and then type your text. WordPad, in turn, will add the new text to your document using your selected attributes. For example, within the WordPad format bar, you might click your mouse on the Bold icon (the icon with the letter B). WordPad, in turn, will display the icon as depressed (pressed in) to indicate that you have selected the attribute. As you type, WordPad will bold your text. If you click on the button again, turning off the attribute, and then type, WordPad will display normal text. Second, you can select characters, words, or even paragraphs to which you then apply the attribute. WordPad, in turn, will assign the attribute to your selected text. For example, if you select a word or paragraph (see Tip 570 for a discussion on selecting text within WordPad), and then click your mouse on the format bar Bold icon, WordPad will bold your selected text. In addition to setting font attributes using WordPad's format bar, you can also set font attributes from within the Font dialog, box as discussed in Tip 568.

568 MANAGING FONTS WITHIN A WORDPAD DOCUMENT

In Tip 567, you learned two ways to assign a font attribute, such as italics or underlining, to text within a WordPad document. In addition to letting you use such attributes within your documents, WordPad also lets you control the current font and font size. If you examine WordPad's format bar, you will find a pull-down font list from which you can select the current font, and you will find a pull-down font size list. As is the case when you assign the font attributes, WordPad lets you apply a new font or font size to text you previously selected or you can choose a font or font size and then type new text. In addition to using the format bar to select fonts and font attributes, you can select the Format menu Font option to display the Font dialog box, as shown in Figure 568. Using the Font dialog box, you can select the current font, font color, size, and even assign the strikeout attribute which causes WordPad to display a line through your text: ~~This text is struck out.~~

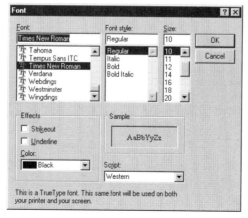

Figure 568 The WordPad Font dialog box.

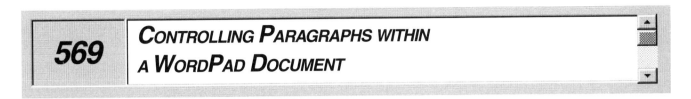

569 | **CONTROLLING PARAGRAPHS WITHIN A WORDPAD DOCUMENT**

Like most word processors, WordPad automatically wraps your text to the start of the next line when your text reaches the right-hand margin. Thus, when you type text within a WordPad document, the only time you press ENTER is when you reach the end of a paragraph. By default, WordPad *left-justifies* your text, meaning it aligns each line of text within your document along the left margin and it does not align text along the right margin. However, depending on your needs, you can direct WordPad to right justify or center your text.

WordPad provides you with two ways to change your document's paragraph alignment. First, if you want to change the alignment for existing paragraphs, you must first select the paragraphs (see Tip 570 for a discussion on selecting text within WordPad). Next, you can use the format bar alignment buttons. To format your subsequent paragraphs, click your mouse on the format bar alignment button that you desire and then type. WordPad, in turn, will apply the alignment that you have selected to your new paragraphs. In addition to letting you select your paragraph alignment, WordPad lets you control paragraph indentation. You might, for example, want to indent your first line of a paragraph one inch, or you might want to indent subsequent lines within the paragraph to create a hanging indent. To control your paragraph indentation, select the WordPad Format menu Paragraph option. WordPad, in turn, will display the Paragraph dialog box, as shown in Figure 569.

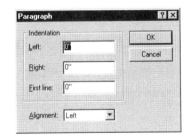

Figure 569 *The WordPad Paragraph dialog box.*

Within the Paragraph dialog box, select the indentation you desire and then click your mouse on the OK button. Note that the Paragraph dialog box also lets you select your paragraph alignment.

570 | **SELECTING TEXT WITHIN A WORDPAD DOCUMENT**

As you create and edit text within a WordPad document, you will perform many operations that require you to first select text. For example, you might want to italicize a specific word or phrase within your document or you may want to move or copy text from one location to another. Before you can perform these operations, you must first select the text. As is the case with most Windows-based programs, within WordPad you can select text using either your mouse or keyboard. To select text using your keyboard, use the ARROW keys to position the cursor in front of the first character you want to select. Next, hold down the SHIFT key and press the ARROW keys to select the characters you desire. After you select the last character that you desire, release the SHIFT key.

To select text using your mouse, move your mouse pointer to the first character you want to select. Next, hold down your mouse-select button and drag your mouse pointer over the characters you desire. As you drag your mouse, WordPad will highlight the text you select. After you select the last character that you desire, release your left mouse button.

Note: *In Tip 579, you will learn how to use the WordPad Options dialog box, within which you can direct WordPad to select a word at a time when you drag your mouse.*

571 USING CUT-AND-PASTE OPERATIONS TO MOVE OR COPY TEXT WITHIN A WORDPAD DOCUMENT

As you create documents within WordPad, there will be times when you will want to move or copy text from one location to another. Like most Windows-based programs, WordPad fully supports cut-and-paste operations. To move text from one location to another within in a WordPad document, perform these steps:

1. Select the text you want to move (Tip 570 discusses the steps you must perform to select text).
2. Click your mouse on the WordPad Edit menu and choose the Cut option. WordPad, in turn, will remove the text from the document, placing the text within the Windows clipboard.
3. Using your keyboard ARROW keys or your mouse, move the cursor to the location within your document at which you want to place the text.
4. Click your mouse on the WordPad Edit menu and then choose the Paste option. WordPad, in turn, will insert the text into the document at the current location.

To copy text from one location to another within a WordPad document, perform these steps:

1. Select the text you want to copy (Tip 570 discusses the steps you must perform to select text).
2. Click your mouse on the WordPad Edit menu and choose the Copy option. WordPad, in turn, will place a copy of the text within the Windows clipboard.
3. Using your keyboard ARROW keys or your mouse, move the cursor to the location within your document at which you want to place the text.
4. Click your mouse on the WordPad Edit menu and then choose the Paste option. WordPad, in turn, will insert the text into the document at the current location.

Note: *Using cut-and-paste operations, you can also copy or move text from one WordPad document to another.*

572 SEARCHING FOR SPECIFIC TEXT WITHIN A WORDPAD DOCUMENT

As the documents that you create within WordPad become large, finding specific words or phrases within your document may become difficult. Fortunately, WordPad provides a Find command you can use to quickly locate text. To find text within a WordPad document, perform these steps:

1. Click your mouse on the WordPad Edit menu and choose the Find option. WordPad, in turn, will display the Find dialog box, as shown in Figure 572.

Figure 572 *The Find dialog box.*

2. Within the Find dialog box Find what field, type the text you want WordPad to locate.

3. Within the Find dialog box, click your mouse on the Match whole words only checkbox if you want WordPad to distinguish between full and partial words. (WordPad would not, therefore, match *Win* with *Windows.*)

4. Within the Find dialog box, click your mouse on the Match case checkbox, if you want WordPad to distinguish between uppercase and lowercase letters. (WordPad would not, therefore, match *WINDOWS* with *Windows.*)

5. Within the Find dialog box, click your mouse on the Find Next button to start your search. If WordPad finds a match, WordPad will highlight the matching word within your document, leaving the Find dialog box open. To search for the next occurrence of the word, click your mouse on the Find Next button. To close the Find dialog box, click your mouse on the Cancel button.

Note: *WordPad lets you quickly search for the next occurrence of the text by clicking your mouse on the Edit menu Find Next option or by simply pressing the F3 function key.*

573 **REPLACING SPECIFIC TEXT THROUGHOUT A WORDPAD DOCUMENT**

In Tip 572, you learned how to use WordPad's find capabilities to locate a specific word or phrase within your document. As you edit documents within WordPad, there may be times when you will want to replace one word or phrase with another. To use WordPad to replace a word or phrase within a WordPad document, perform these steps:

1. Select the WordPad Edit menu and choose the Replace option. WordPad, in turn, will display the Replace dialog box, as shown in Figure 573.

Figure 573 *The Replace dialog box.*

2. Within the Replace dialog box Find what field, type in the text you want WordPad to replace.

3. Press T*AB* to move the text cursor into the Replace with field and type in your replacement text.

4. Within the Replace dialog box, click your mouse on the Match whole words only checkbox, if you want WordPad to distinguish between full and partial words. (WordPad would not, therefore, match *Win* with *Windows.*)

5. Within the Replace dialog box, click your mouse on the Match case checkbox, If you want WordPad to distinguish between uppercase and lowercase letters. (WordPad would not, therefore, match *WINDOWS* with *Windows.*)

6. If you want WordPad to replace every occurrence of the text, click your mouse on the Replace All button.

7. If you want to review the text before you replace it, click your mouse on the Find Next button. WordPad will highlight the next occurrence of the text within your document. If you want to replace the highlighted text, click your mouse on the Replace button. If you want WordPad to search for the next occurrence, leaving the highlighted text unchanged, click your mouse on the Find Next button.

8. To end the replacement operation, click your mouse on the Cancel button.

574 **D*ATE AND* T*IME* S*TAMPING* Y*OUR* E*DITS WITHIN A* W*ORD*P*AD* D*OCUMENT***

Depending on the type of document you are creating, there may be times when you want to insert the current date and time into your text. For example, using WordPad, you might keep track of the phone calls you make or receive:

15-Jun-99

> 12:30:21 Phone call from Microsoft regarding new software
>
> 12:45:11 Phone call to Marketing department regarding new catalog schedule
>
> 13:01:12 Phone to call to data processing regarding sales reports

One way to insert the date and time is simply to type them. However, WordPad makes it easy for you to insert the date or time into your document without having to type anything. To insert the date or time into your document, perform these steps:

1. Within your WordPad document, use your keyboard or mouse to position the cursor at the location at which you want to insert the date and time.

2. Select the WordPad Insert menu and choose the Date and Time option. WordPad, in turn, will display the Date and Time dialog box, as shown in Figure 574.

3. Within the Date and Time dialog box, click your mouse on the date or time format you desire and then click your mouse on the OK button. WordPad, in turn, will insert the date or time at the current cursor location within your document.

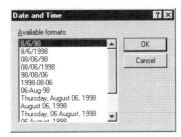

Figure 574 *The WordPad Date and Time dialog box.*

575	**INSERTING GRAPHICS OR OTHER OBJECTS INTO A WORDPAD DOCUMENT**

In Tip 574, you learned how to insert the current date and time into a WordPad document. In addition to letting you insert the date and time, WordPad also lets you insert other objects into your documents, such as graphics, sound effects, and even video clips. When you insert an object other than a graphics image into your document, WordPad will display an icon that corresponds to the object's type. If you double-click your mouse on the icon, Windows 98 will run the program that corresponds to the object. For example, if you insert a WAV sound file into a WordPad document and you later double-click your mouse on the sound's icon, Windows 98 will play back the sound. To insert an object into a WordPad document, perform these steps:

1. Within your document, use your keyboard or mouse to position the cursor to the location at which you want to insert the object.

2. Select the WordPad Insert menu and choose the Object option. WordPad, in turn, will display the Insert Object dialog box, as shown in Figure 575.

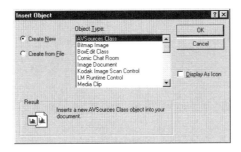

Figure 575 *The Insert Object dialog box.*

3. Within the Insert Object dialog box, select the Display As Icon option if you want WordPad to display an icon for the object within your document, rather than the object itself.

4. Within the Insert Object dialog box, select the Create New object if you want to create the object now (you might, for example, record a sound effect now) or select the Create from File option if the object you want to insert already resides within a file on your disk.

5. Within the Insert Object dialog box, scroll through the Object Type list and highlight the type of object you want to insert. Click your mouse on the OK button. If you are creating the object, WordPad will start a program that you can use. If you are inserting the object from a file on disk, WordPad will change the Insert Object dialog box so you can type in the object's filename or you can use the Browse dialog box to locate the object's file on your disk.

576 USING BULLETS TO HIGHLIGHT TEXT WITHIN A WORDPAD DOCUMENT

Within word-processing documents, users often highlight lists using bullets, similar to those shown here:

- WordPad lets you assign font attributes, such as bolding and italics
- WordPad lets you align and indent paragraphs
- WordPad lets you insert objects, such as a graphic, into your documents

To create a bulleted list within WordPad, perform these steps:

1. Using your keyboard or mouse, move the cursor to the location at which you want the bulleted list to begin.
2. Select the WordPad Format menu and chose the Bullet Style option, placing a check mark next to the option. WordPad, in turn, will insert a bullet at the beginning of the line.
3. Type the first item in the list and press ENTER. WordPad will automatically insert a bullet for the next item.
4. Repeat Steps 3 and 4 to complete your bulleted list.
5. Select the WordPad Format menu and choose the Bullet Style option, removing the check mark next to the option. WordPad, in turn, will turn off bulleting.

577 DEFINING TAB STOPS WITHIN A WORDPAD DOCUMENT

As you create documents within WordPad, there will be times when you will need to align two or more columns. For example, you might need to create a table of information similar to that shown in Figure 577.1.

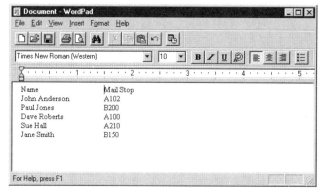

Figure 577.1 *A table within a WordPad document.*

Within WordPad, the easy way to align columns of text is to place one or more tab characters between the text. By default, WordPad places tab stops (the next location to which WordPad will advance the cursor when you press the TAB key) at half-inch intervals. Depending on the information that you are placing in each column, there may be times when you will need to change the location of WordPad's tab stops. To define tab stop locations within WordPad, perform these steps:

1. Select the WordPad Format menu and choose the Tabs option. WordPad, in turn, will display the Tabs dialog box, as shown in Figure 577.2.

Figure 577.2 *The Tabs dialog box.*

2. Within the Tabs dialog box, type in the location at which you want WordPad to create a tab stop. Type your location in inches or centimeters. For example, to place a tab stop one and one quarter inches from the margin, you would type **1.25"** or **1.25 inch**. Likewise, to place a tab stop 2 centimeters from the margin, you would type **2 cm**.

3. Press ENTER or click your mouse on the Set button. WordPad, in turn, will place the tab stop within the Tab stop position list box.

4. Repeat Steps 2 and 3 to add the tab stop locations you desire.

5. Click your mouse on the OK button to save your settings.

To remove a tab stop, display the Tabs dialog box, select a tab stop in the Tab stop position list box, and then click your mouse on the Clear button. To remove all tab stops, select the Clear All button.

578 **CONTROLLING MARGIN AND TAB SETTINGS USING THE WORDPAD RULER**

As you edit and create documents within WordPad, you may find it convenient to use WordPad's built-in ruler, shown in Figure 578, to monitor tab stops, your margins, and your current cursor position. If WordPad is not currently displaying its ruler, select the View menu and choose the Ruler option, placing a check mark next to the option. Using the WordPad ruler, you can set the selected paragraph's margin and indentation settings (you can make the selected paragraph's margin smaller than the page margins, but not wider). To increase or decrease margin settings, use your mouse to drag the left or right margin markers which appear at the ruler's top-left and top-right corners. To change the indentation, use your mouse to drag the indentation marker which appears at the ruler's lower-left and lower-right corners.

Using the ruler, you can also add or remove tab stops. To add a tab stop, click your mouse at the ruler locations at which you want the tab stop to reside. WordPad, in turn, will display a L-shaped bracket within the ruler to indicate the tab stop. To remove a tab stop using the ruler, click your mouse on the tab stop and then hold down your mouse-select button and drag the tab stop off the ruler.

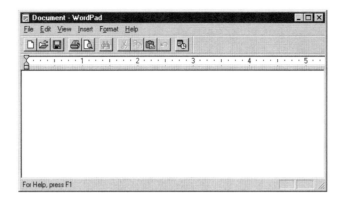

Figure 578 *The WordPad ruler.*

579	### CUSTOMIZING WORDPAD OPTIONS TO MEET YOUR NEEDS

Like many Windows-based programs, WordPad provides many options which you can customize as your needs require. A few of the options control how WordPad always behaves, such as whether WordPad selects a word or character when you drag your mouse over text, as discussed in Tip 570. Other WordPad options control how WordPad behaves when you edit specific document types, such as text, Word, or Write documents. To customize the WordPad settings, select the View menu and choose Options. WordPad, in turn, will display the Options dialog box, as shown in Figure 579. Within the Options dialog box, configure the options you desire and then click your mouse on the OK button to put your changes into effect.

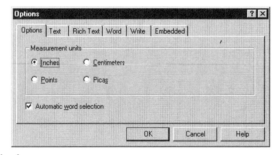

Figure 579 *The WordPad Options dialog box.*

580	### PREVIEWING YOUR WORDPAD DOCUMENT BEFORE YOU PRINT IT

In Tip 565, you learned that to print the current WordPad document, you can click your mouse on the toolbar printer icon, or you can select the File menu Print option. By using the vertical scroll bar, you can scroll through your document's text. Before you print a document, however, you may want to preview how the document looks on a page.

To preview a document within WordPad, select the WordPad File menu and choose the Print Preview option or click your mouse on the toolbar Print Preview icon. WordPad, in turn, will display a full-page representation of your document, as shown in Figure 580.

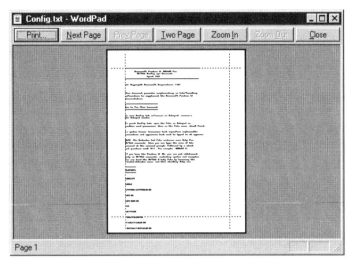

Figure 580 *Getting a print preview.*

Using WordPad's print preview, you can view how WordPad will print your document. If, for example, your margins or tab stops are not what you want, you can use the print preview to view the document without wasting paper.

Within the print preview, you cannot edit your document. You can, however, zoom in and out of the document to better read its contents. To view the print preview close up, click your mouse on the Zoom In button. Likewise, to return to the full-page view, click your mouse on the Zoom Out button.

To view a specific part of the document close up, move your mouse pointer (WordPad will change your mouse pointer to a magnifying glass) to the location you want to view and click your mouse-select button. To leave the print preview mode, click your mouse on the Close button.

581 DEFINING A DOCUMENT'S PAGE SETTINGS WITHIN WORDPAD

In Tip 580, you learned how to use WordPad's print preview mode to view how WordPad will print your document. Depending on your document's contents, there may be times when you will want to change its orientation from portrait to landscape or change the type of paper on which you will be printing the document (you might be printing on legal-sized paper). In such cases, you can change the document's page settings.

To view or change the document's page settings, click your mouse on the WordPad File menu and then choose the Page Setup option. WordPad, in turn, will display the Page Setup dialog box, as shown in Figure 581. Within the Page Setup dialog box, change the page settings you desire and then click your mouse on the OK button to put your changes into effect.

582	USING THE WINDOWS 98 SYSTEM TOOLS TO TAKE CHARGE OF YOUR SYSTEM

In addition to providing you with software you can use to run other programs, to store information within files on your disk, as well as the accessory programs you can use to perform common tasks, Windows 98 also provides you with a powerful collection of utility programs you can use to fine-tune your system performance. Windows 98 places these system utilities within the Accessories menu System Tools submenu, as shown in Figure 582.

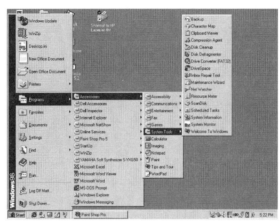

Figure 582 *The Windows 98 System utilities.*

The Tips that follow examine the Windows 98 system utilities in detail. For now, Table 582 briefly describes each program's purpose. If your system does not have one or more of the programs the table lists, you can install the program from your Windows 98 CD-ROM, as discussed in Tip 218. To display your System Tools menu, perform these steps:

1. Click your mouse on the Start menu Programs option and choose Accessories. Windows 98, in turn, will display the Accessories submenu.

2. Within the Accessories submenu, click your mouse on the System Tools option. Windows 98 will display the System Tools submenu.

Utility Program	Purpose
Backup	Creates backup copies of your files
Compression Agent	Lets you use Windows 98 disk compression to compress specific files
Disk Cleanup	Helps you free up space on your disk by deleting unnecessary files
Disk Defragmenter	Improves your disk performance by correcting fragmented files
Drive Converter	Converts your disk's file system to FAT32
DriveSpace	Compresses files on your disk to increase your disk's storage capacity
Maintenance Wizard	Helps you perform (and schedule) common system maintenance operations
Net Watcher	Monitors your system's network activity
Resource Meter	Monitor's Windows 98 resources
ScanDisk	Searches for and corrects disk and file errors
Scheduled Tasks	Lets you direct Windows 98 to run specific programs at specific times
System Monitor	Monitors Windows 98 low-level (behind-the-scenes) system operations

Table 582 *Programs you can run from within the System Tools menu.*

583 **To Protect Your Files, Back Them Up to Another Disk or Tape**

As you have learned, your hard disk is a mechanical device, and like many things with moving parts, your hard disk may eventually break, causing you to lose the information it contains. To protect yourself (and your files) against a hard-disk error, you must backup (copy) your files to another disk or tape on a regular basis. To help you create backup copies of your files, Windows 98 provides the Backup utility program, as shown in Figure 583.1. Using the Backup utility, you can make copies of your key files. Should you ever need to restore files back to your disk from your backup tape or disks, you will use the Backup utility to perform the file restoration.

Figure 583.1 Using the Windows 98 Backup utility to make copies of your files.

By backing up your files to another disk or tape on a regular basis, you reduce your risk of losing information due to a disk error. In addition to getting into the habit of performing regular backups, you should also get into the practice of keeping your backup disks or tapes off-site. That way, should a fire or other disaster destroy your computer, your data will be safe elsewhere. Several of the Tips that follow examine the Windows 98 Backup utility in detail. To start Backup, perform these steps:

1. Click your mouse on the Start menu Programs option and choose Accessories. Windows 98, in turn, will display the Accessories submenu.

2. Within the Accessories submenu, click your mouse on the System Tools option and choose Backup. Windows 98 will open the Backup window, displaying the Microsoft Backup dialog box, as shown in Figure 583.2, within which you can select the option you want to perform.

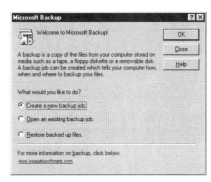

Figure 583.2 The Microsoft Backup dialog box.

3. Within the Microsoft Backup window, if you select the Create a new backup job button, Backup will start its Backup Wizard. Likewise, if you select the Restore backed up files, Backup will start its Restore Wizard. Finally, if you select the Open an existing backup job, Backup will display a dialog box within which you can open a file that contains the backup job.

4. For now, simply click your mouse on the Close button to display the Backup window, previously shown in Figure 583.1.

584 TO SIMPLIFY YOUR BACKUPS, YOU SHOULD PURCHASE A TAPE DRIVE

Today, very large hard drives have become very inexpensive. As a result, it is almost impossible to backup your hard disk to floppy disks—it would simply take too many floppies. As an alternative, you should purchase a tape drive to which you can copy the files on your disk.

If you have only one PC, you can purchase an inexpensive internal tape drive. If you have several PCs to backup, you should consider buying an external tape drive which you can later move from one PC to the next as you perform your backups (most external tape drives will connect to a PC's parallel port).

As a rule, most users really only have to backup a few key files (as opposed to their entire disk). As an alternative to using a tape drive, many users are buying Zip drives whose disks act like a very large floppy disk (one that can store over 100Mb of data). An advantage of using a Zip drive over a tape is that many users now have Zip drives and often exchange documents that reside on Zip disks much like they exchanged floppy disks in the past. In short, Zip disks are easy to use. Whether you use a tape or Zip disk, you need a device to which you can create backup copies of your key files.

585 UNDERSTANDING WHICH FILES ON YOUR DISK YOU REALLY MUST BACKUP

As hard disk storage capacity continues to increase, backing up everything on your hard disk can become quite time consuming (and can consume a very large number of disks or magnetic tape). Before you perform your backups, think about which items on your system you really must backup. Usually, for example, you do not need to backup your programs, such as Windows 98, Microsoft Word, Microsoft Excel, and so on. If you encounter a disk error, you can simply reinstall such programs from the program's original CD-ROMs.

What you must backup are your data files, such as the word-processing documents that you create within Microsoft Word or the spreadsheets you create with Excel. In Tip 74, you learned that Windows 98 provides folders to help you organize the files that you store on disk. By grouping your files within folders, you will simplify your backups.

The Tips that follow will teach you how to backup your entire disk as well as specific files or folders on your disk. If you have a small hard disk and you have a tape backup, backing up your entire disk may be an easy operation. Usually, however, you will simply want to direct the Backup utility to backup specific folders and files.

586 | *TAKING ADVANTAGE OF BACKUP'S TOOLBAR*

Throughout this book, you have learned how to take advantage of toolbars within an application to simplify common operations. Backup, like most Windows-based programs, provides a toolbar with buttons you can use to perform common tasks. Figure 586 briefly describes each button's use. If Backup is not currently displaying its toolbar, select the Backup View menu Toolbar option, placing a check mark next to the option.

Creates a new Backup job

Opens an existing Backup job

Saves the current settings to a Backup job

Selects items for inclusion within a Backup job

Deselects items (so they are not
included) within a Backup job

Starts the Backup Wizard

Starts the Restore Wizard

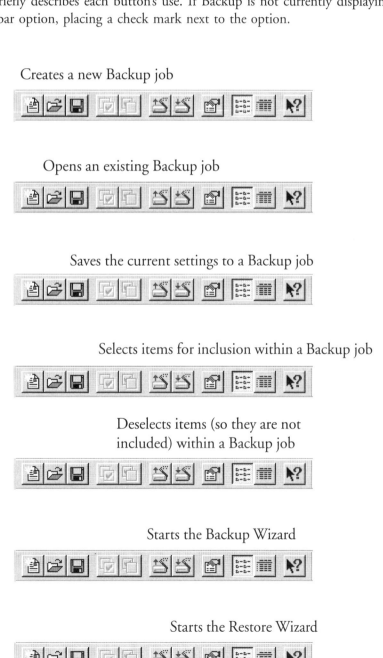

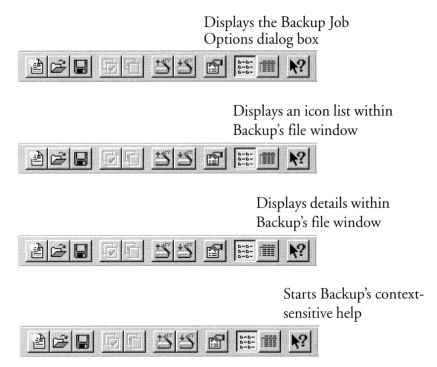

Displays the Backup Job
Options dialog box

Displays an icon list within
Backup's file window

Displays details within
Backup's file window

Starts Backup's context-
sensitive help

Figure 586 *The Backup toolbar buttons.*

587 BACKING UP YOUR ENTIRE HARD DISK

As Tip 585 briefly discussed, because you can reinstall your program files should you encounter an error, you will usually not backup your entire disk. However, should you decide that you want a backup copy of everything on your disk, perform these steps:

1. Within the Backup window's drive-and-folder window, click your mouse on the checkbox that appears to the left of the drive you want to backup, placing a check mark within the box.

2. Within the Where to back up field, select the tape drive or disk drive to which you will backup your files.

3. Click your mouse on the Job menu Save As option. Windows 98, in turn, will display the Save Backup Job As dialog box.

4. Within the Save Backup Job As dialog box, type in the Backup job name **Drive x**, replacing the letter x, within the drive letter of the disk you are backing up.

5. Click your mouse on the Start button. Backup, in turn, may display a dialog box asking you if you want to save your job. Select Yes. Backup will then begin the backup process, displaying the Backup Progress dialog box, as shown in Figure 587.

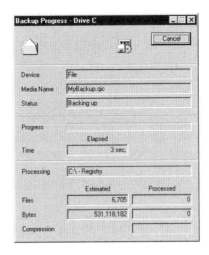

Figure 587 *The Backup Progress dialog box.*

588 **SAVING YOUR FILE SELECTIONS AND SETTINGS WITHIN A BACKUP JOB**

When you use the Backup utility to backup files on your disk, you will usually select specific files and folders that you want to backup. In addition, you may want to assign a password to your backup files which prevents another user from restoring your files on his or her system should they find your backup tape or disk, and you may want to change other Backup settings you will examine in the Tips that follow.

After you make your file and setting selections within Backup, you must then store them within a file that Backup refers to as a *backup job*. In short, a backup job is simply a file that contains your backup selections. If you later want to backup the same files on your system again, you simply tell Backup to use your backup job. By storing your settings within a backup job, the Backup utility makes it easy for you to backup specific files on specific disks.

589 **SELECTING SPECIFIC FILES OR FOLDERS FOR A BACKUP JOB**

As discussed in Tip 585, to save time, you will usually only backup specific files on your disk, such as the folders that contain your working documents. Within Backup, you select a disk or folder that you want to backup by placing a check mark next to the object's name within Backup's drives and folders list, as shown in Figure 589.1.

Within the drives and folders list, you select a folder by placing a check mark within the checkbox that appears next to the object's name. If you do not want to backup the object, remove the check mark. As is the case with the Windows 98 Explorer, you can expand or collapse a folder's tree by clicking your mouse on the plus sign (+) or minus sign (-) that precedes the folder.

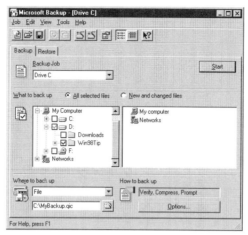

Figure 589.1 *Selecting the folders you want to backup.*

After you select a folder from within Backup's drives and folders list, Backup will then display the corresponding folder within its selected files and folders list (which Backup displays in the right-hand window pane). Depending on your needs, there may be times when you only want to backup specific files that reside within a selected folder. In such cases, double-click your mouse on the selected folder. Backup, in turn, will display the folder's contents. Then, within the folder's list of files and subfolders, click your mouse on a file or subfolder's checkbox to select or deselect the object for backing up. Figure 589.2, for example, shows some selected and not selected files within a folder's contents list. After you select the files and folders you want to backup, save your selections within your backup job.

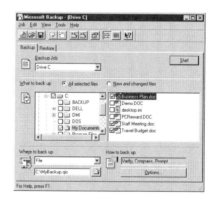

Figure 589.2 *Selected and not selected files within a folder's contents list.*

590 BACKING UP YOUR FILES TO A NETWORK DRIVE

If your PC is connected to other computers within a local-area network, there may be times when you will want to backup your local files to a disk that resides on a remote computer. To backup your files to a network disk, perform these steps:

1. The remote folder to which you want to backup your files must be shareable. Check with your network administrator to determine if you must specify a password to use the remote folder.

2. Within the Backup window, click your mouse on the Where to back up pull-down list and select the File option. Then, click your mouse on the file-open icon that appears beneath the pull-down list. Backup, in turn, will display the Where to back up dialog box, as shown in Figure 590.

Figure 590 *The Where to back up dialog box.*

3. Within the Where to back up dialog box, click your mouse on the Look in pull-down list and locate the shared folder within the Network Neighborhood. Then, type in the filename within which you want Backup to place your files. You might include the date within your filename, such as *98-12-25 System Backup*. Then, click your mouse on the Open option.

4. Within the Backup window, select the files and folders you want to backup and your backup settings. Then, use the Job menu Save As option to save your selections to a backup job.

5. Within the Backup window, click your mouse on the Start button to begin your backup.

591 VIEWING INFORMATION ABOUT YOUR SELECTED FILES

In Tip 583, you learned how to use the Backup utility program to select files and folders you want to backup. After you select the files and folders that you desire, you may want to see just how much information (in bytes or the number of files) that you are backing up. To view specifics about your current selections, click your mouse on the Backup View menu and choose Selection Information. Backup will display the Selection Information dialog box, as shown in Figure 591.

Figure 591 *The Selection Information dialog box.*

592 VIEWING AND PRINTING THE BACKUP STATUS REPORT

If you ever have to restore one or more files from your backup disks or tape, you will want to determine when you last backed up your system. To help you track your backup operations, Backup creates a log file, as shown in Figure 592.

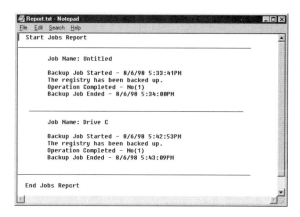

Figure 592 *The Backup log file.*

Within the log file, you will find a listing of your backup operations that tells you which backup job the operation used as well as the operation's success. To view the log file, perform these steps:

1. Click your mouse on the Backup Tools menu and select Report. Backup, in turn, will cascade the Report submenu.
2. Within the Report submenu, click your mouse on the View option to display the log or on the Print option to print a copy of the log file.

593 **CUSTOMIZING THE BACKUP LOG REPORT**

In Tip 592, you learned how to view and print Backup's log report that tells you information about your previous backup operations. Depending on your needs, there may be times when you want Backup to include or exclude specific information from within the report. To customize the information that Backup includes in its report, perform these steps:

1. Within the Backup window, click your mouse on the Options button. Backup, in turn, will display the Backup Job Options dialog box.
2. Within the Backup Job Options dialog box, click your mouse on the Report tab. Backup, in turn, will display the Report sheet, as shown in Figure 593.

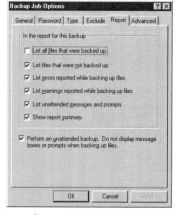

Figure 593 *The Backup Job Options dialog box Report sheet.*

3. Within the Report sheet, use the checkboxes to select the items you want Backup to include in the log and then click your mouse on the OK button.

594 VERIFYING THAT BACKUP SUCCESSFULLY COPIED YOUR FILES

As you have learned, by backing up the files on your disk, you reduce your chance of losing information should you encounter a disk error or inadvertently delete files from your disk. If you backup your files on a regular basis, you will minimize your risk of losing information. Unfortunately, you can never be 100% risk free. By keeping your backup copies at a location away from your computer, you reduce the risk of fire or theft destroying both your PC and your backups at the same time. Second, by verifying that Backup successfully recorded your files when it copied them to your backup media, you reduce the chance that an error on your magnetic tape or floppy disk will prevent you from restoring a file in the future.

Within Backup, you can enable *backup verification* which directs Backup to reread the information that it records on your tape or backup disks to ensure that it correctly recorded the information. In other words, Backup compares each byte of data on the backup tape or disk to the original file, to ensure that they match. If a byte on the backup media differs from the original, Backup can notify you that it has experienced a disk or tape error, so you can start the operation again using new media. Although the verification process ensures that Backup has successfully recorded your data on the backup media, the comparison process is very time consuming. Because recording errors are quite rare, many users disable verification so their backups complete faster. To control whether or not Backup performs verification, perform these steps:

1. Within the Backup window, click your mouse on the Options button. Backup will display the Backup Job Options dialog box.
2. Within the General sheet, click your mouse on the Compare original and backup files to verify data was successfully backed up checkbox. To enable verification, place a check mark within the box. To disable verification, remove the checkbox.

595 SAVING FLOPPY DISK OR MAGNETIC TAPE BY COMPRESSING YOUR BACKUP FILES

Depending on the size and number of files you are backing up, the number of floppy disks or the amount of magnetic tape your backups will consume will vary. To reduce the amount of space your backups consume, you can direct Backup to compress files it stores on your backup media. When you direct Backup to compress files, you will reduce the amount of space your backups consume, but you will increase the amount of time Backup requires to backup your disk because it must now compress your files as it stores them. If your target media has sufficient space, you may want to save time by disabling Backup's file compression. To control how Backup compresses files on the target media, perform these steps:

1. Within the Backup window, click your mouse on the Options button. Backup will display the Backup Job Options dialog box, as shown in Figure 595.

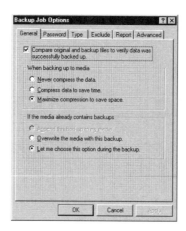

Figure 595 *The Backup Job Options dialog box.*

2. Within the General sheet, you will find three radio buttons you can use to control Backup's compression settings. Click your mouse on the Option you desire. Then, click your mouse on the OK button to put your selection into effect.

596 CONTROLLING WHETHER BACKUP APPENDS TO OR OVERWRITES A PREVIOUS BACKUP FILE

When you perform backup operations, you can backup to a tape, floppy disks, or even to a file. If you have previously performed a backup operation, your disk or tape may contain the previous backup information. In such cases, Backup can either overwrite the previous information or append new information to it. If, for example, you are backing up your files to a file that resides on a network disk, you might want Backup to simply overwrite the file's previous contents each time you perform a backup. To control whether Backup appends to or overwrites a previous backup, perform these steps:

1. Within the Backup window, click your mouse on the Options button. Backup, in turn, will display the Backup Job Options dialog box.

2. Within the General sheet, you will find three radio buttons you can use to control Backup whether backup overwrites or appends to a previous backup. Click your mouse on the selection you desire and then click your mouse on the OK button to put your selection into effect.

597 PERFORMING AN UNATTENDED BACKUP

In Tip 651, you will learn how to use the Windows 98 Task Scheduler that lets you perform operations at specific times. Using the Task Scheduler, for example, you might start a backup operation each night at midnight. Because you will not be present to respond to Backup's various dialog boxes, you will want Backup to perform an *unattended-backup operation*. In other words, you will not want Backup to display dialog or message boxes, that might suspend its processing until a user responds. To direct Backup to perform an unattended-backup operation, perform these steps:

1. Within the Backup window, click your mouse on the Options button. Backup will display the Backup Job Options dialog box.

2. Within the Backup Job Options dialog box, click your mouse on the Report tab. Backup, in turn, will display the Report sheet.

3. Within the Report sheet, click your mouse on the Perform an unattended backup checkbox, placing a check mark within the box. Then, click your mouse on the OK button to put your change into effect.

598   PASSWORD PROTECTING YOUR BACKUP FILES

If you have confidential files on your disk, you may want to password protect your backups. In this way, should another user get hold of your backup media, that user cannot then restore your files to his or her disk and access your confidential files. Instead, before someone can restore the files, he or she must type in your password. To password protect your backups, perform these steps:

1. Within the Backup window, click your mouse on the Options button. Backup, in turn, will display the Backup Job Options dialog box.

2. Within the Backup Job Options dialog box, click your mouse on the Password tab. Backup, in turn, will display the Password sheet.

3. Within the Password sheet, click your mouse on the Protect this backup with a password checkbox, placing a check mark in the box. Then, click your mouse on the Password field and type in the password you desire. Next, click your mouse on the Confirm password file and repeat your password.

4. Within the Password sheet, click your mouse on the OK button.

599   EXCLUDING FILES FROM A BACKUP OPERATION

As you have learned, when you perform backup operations, you can save time by not backing program files that you could reinstall from the program's original CD-ROM. Usually, when you do not want to backup your program files, you simply do not select the program's folder for backing up. In addition to letting you omit files or folders from your backup, the Backup utility also lets you omit specific types of files, such as WAV files, AVI files, EXE program files, and so on. To exclude specific file types from your backup operation, perform these steps:

1. Within the Backup window, click your mouse on the Options button. Backup, in turn, will display the Backup Job Options dialog box.

2. Within the Backup Job Options dialog box, click your mouse on the Exclude tab. Backup, in turn, will display the Exclude sheet, as shown in Figure 599.1.

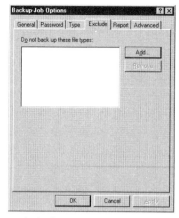

Figure 599.1 *The Backup Job Options dialog box Exclude sheet.*

3. Within the Exclude sheet, click your mouse on the Add button. Backup, in turn, will display the Add Exclude dialog box, as shown in Figure 599.2.

Figure 599.2 *The Add Exclude dialog box.*

4. Within the Add Exclude dialog box, click your mouse on the file type you want to exclude and then click your mouse on the OK button. Backup will add the file type to the list of excluded file types.

5. Within the Exclude sheet, click your mouse on the OK button to put your changes into effect.

600 BACKING UP YOUR SYSTEM REGISTRY SETTINGS

As you have learned, Windows 98 and many Windows-based programs store program settings within the Registry database. The Registry is one of the most important files on your disk. If the Registry becomes damaged, Windows 98, or some of your other programs, may simply not run. When you back up the information on your disk, you will usually want Backup to also make a copy of your current Registry. To direct Backup to include your Registry database within your current backup operation, perform these steps:

1. Within the Backup window, click your mouse on the Options button. Backup, in turn, will display the Backup Job Options dialog box.

2. Within the Backup Job Options dialog box, click your mouse on the Advanced tab. Backup, in turn, will display the Advanced sheet, as shown in Figure 600.

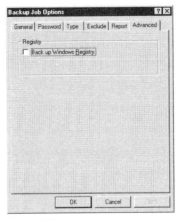

Figure 600 *The Backup Job Options dialog box Advanced sheet.*

3. Within the Advanced sheet, click your mouse on the Back Up Windows Registry checkbox, placing a check mark within the box. Then, click your mouse on the OK button to put your change into effect.

Note: *If you backup your Registry file, you may or may not want Backup to restore the Registry should you later perform a restore operation. Within the Backup utility's Restore sheet, you can use the Restore Options Advanced sheet to control whether or not Backup restores the Registry.*

601 BACKING UP ONLY NEW OR CHANGED FILES

As you learned in Tip 599, when you perform a backup operation, you do not have to backup every file on your disk. For example, you can always reinstall your program files from your original CD-ROMs. Likewise, if you have current backup copies of most of your files, there's probably no need for you to backup the files again. To save time, users often direct the Backup utility to only backup those files that you have created or changed since your last backup operation. Because Backup will not have to backup as many files, it can complete the operation faster. To direct Backup to only backup those files that have changed since your last backup, perform these steps:

1. Make sure you place the file or backup media that contains your previous backup in a safe location because you will now rely on the previous backup's contents.
2. Within the Backup window, click your mouse on the Options button. Backup will display the Backup Job Options dialog box.
3. Within the Backup Job Options dialog box, click your mouse on the Type tab. Backup, in turn, will display the Type sheet, as shown in Figure 601.
4. Within the Type sheet, click your mouse on the New and changed files only radio button. Backup, in turn, will activate the field's radio buttons that let you select a differential or incremental backup. Tip 602 discusses how the two backup operations differ. Click your mouse on the backup type you desire and then click your mouse on the OK button.

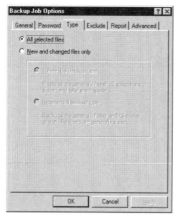

Figure 601 *The Backup Job Options dialog box Type sheet.*

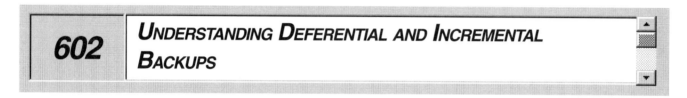

602 UNDERSTANDING DEFERENTIAL AND INCREMENTAL BACKUPS

In Tip 601, you learned that you can direct the Backup utility to only backup new files or files that you have changed since the last backup operation. As it turns out, when you direct Backup to backup only those files that you have created or changed since the last operation, Backup lets you perform either a differential or incremental backup. A *differential backup operation* backs up all of your selected files that have changed since you last performed a backup operation using the Type sheet's All selected files field. In contrast, an incremental backup operation will backup all the files that have changed since you last performed either an All selected files backup operation or a previous incremental backup.

Assume, for example, that on Monday you perform an All selected files backup. Then, on Tuesday and Wednesday, you perform incremental backup operations. On Tuesday, the incremental backup operation will backup only new files or files that you changed between Monday and Tuesday. Likewise, on Wednesday, the incremental backup will backup only new or changed files that occurred since Tuesday's incremental backup. If, on Thursday, you perform a differential backup, the operation will backup all the files that you have created or changed since Monday (since the last All selected files backup).

603 DEFINING BACKUP'S PREFERENCES

As you learned in Tip 583, each time you start the Backup utility, it will display the Microsoft Backup (startup) dialog box, within which you can specify the operation you want to perform. If you find that you usually close the dialog box, you can direct Backup to suppress its display, using the Preferences dialog box, as shown in Figure 603.

As you can see, within the Preferences dialog box, you can control the startup dialog box's display, whether or not Backup backs up the Windows 98 Registry, and whether or not Backup displays a summary of the number files (and their sizes) it will backup or restore. To access the Preferences dialog box, click your mouse on the Backup Tools menu and choose Preferences.

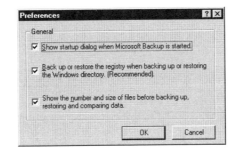

Figure 603 *The Preferences dialog box.*

604 **RESTORING FILES FROM YOUR BACKUP MEDIA**

Hopefully, you will never have to use the backup copies of your files and you can view the time you spend performing backups much like you would view spending money on an insurance policy (hopefully you will never need your insurance but, if you do, it is there). However, should you ever have to restore one or more files, you will use the Backup utilities Restore sheet, as shown in Figure 604, to perform the operation. To display the Restore sheet, simply start the Backup utility, as discussed in Tip 583, and then click your mouse on the Restore tab. Several of the Tips that follow discuss Restore operations in detail.

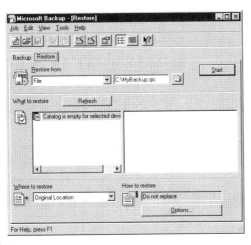

Figure 604 *The Backup utility's Restore sheet.*

605 **SELECTING FILES YOU WANT TO RESTORE**

If you must restore one or more files on your disk from your backup media, you must first determine which backup media (file or tape) contains the files you require. Next, within the Restore sheet's Restore from pull-down list, select the file or device from which you will restore your backup copies. If you are opening a specific file, click your mouse on the file-open icon that appears to the right of the pull-down list. Backup, in turn, will display the Restore from dialog box, as shown in Figure 605, from within which you can select the backup file that you desire.

Figure 605 *The Restore from dialog box.*

After you select your backup file, the Backup utility will display the backup's contents within the Restore sheet. To select a folder or file to be restored, click your mouse on the checkbox that appears next to the file or folder, placing a check mark within the box. Tip 606 discusses how you control which files Backup restores and where Backup places those files. After you select the files that you want to restore and the settings you want Backup to use, click your mouse on the Start button.

606 CONTROLLING WHERE BACKUP PLACES THE FILES YOU RESTORE

When you restore files using the Backup utility, you can direct Backup to place the files back at their original locations or to place the files at a different location. Usually, you will want Backup to place the files back to their original location. However, assume that you deleted some (not all) files from a folder. Using your backup, you can restore your deleted files. If, however, you cannot remember which files you deleted, you may want Backup to restore the entire folder to a new location. Then, later, using the Explorer, you can display both folders side by side. In that way, you can then copy only those files that you need back into the original folder.

To direct Backup to restore files to their original locations, click your mouse on the Where to restore pull-down list and select the Original Location option. If you, instead, want Backup to restore the files to a different location, click your mouse on the pull-down list and select the Alternate Location option. Backup, in turn, will then display a small file-open icon upon which you can click your mouse to select the target location that you desire.

607 CONTROLLING HOW BACKUP RESTORES FILES WHEN A MATCHING FILE ALREADY EXISTS ON YOUR DISK

When you use the Backup utility program to restore files back to your disk, there may be times when a file on your backup tape matches a file that already exists on your disk. In such cases, Backup can perform one of several options. First, Backup can skip the file, leaving the file that exists on your disk unchanged. Second, Backup can overwrite the file on your disk with the file that exists on the backup media. Or, third, Backup can overwrite the file on your disk only if the backup media contains a newer version of the file. To control how Backup resolves an existing file conflict, perform these steps:

1. Within the Restore sheet, click your mouse on the Options button. Backup, in turn, will display the Restore Options dialog box, as shown in Figure 607.

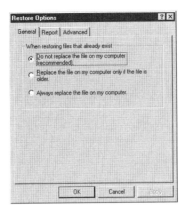

Figure 607 *The Restore Options dialog box.*

2. Within the Restore Options dialog box, click your mouse on the radio button that corresponds to the option that you desire. Then, click your mouse on the OK button to put your changes into effect.

608 USING THE BACKUP AND RESTORE WIZARDS

In several of the preceding Tips, you have learned how to perform backup and restore operations. Usually, to simplify backup and restore operations, you should take advantage of the Backup Wizard and the Restore Wizard, each of which you can start from either the Microsoft Backup startup window shown in Figure 608.1, or from the Backup toolbar.

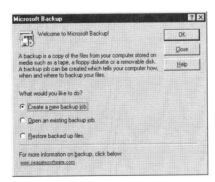

Figure 608.1 *The Microsoft Backup startup window.*

Within the Microsoft Backup startup window, you can direct the Backup Wizard to use an existing Backup job by clicking your mouse on the Open an existing backup job radio button and then clicking your mouse on the OK button. Backup, in turn, will display the Open Backup Job dialog box, within which you can select the backup job that you desire. After Backup opens the Backup job, you can click your mouse on the Start button to begin the backup operation. If you have not yet defined a Backup job, you can use the Backup Wizard to create one by selecting the Microsoft Backup startup window's Create a new backup job radio button and then clicking your mouse on the OK button. The Backup Wizard, in turn, will display a series of dialog boxes within which you can select the files and folders you want to backup.

To perform a restore operation using the Restore Wizard, click your mouse on the Microsoft Backup startup window's Restore backed up files radio button and then click your mouse on the OK button. Backup, in turn, will start the Restore Wizard, as shown in Figure 608.2, within which you can select the files you want to restore.

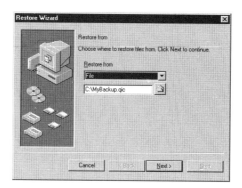

Figure 608.2 *The Restore Wizard.*

609 USING THE WINDOWS 98 COMPRESSION AGENT

In Tip 619, you will learn how to use the Windows 98 DriveSpace utility to increase your disk's storage capacity by compressing the files that reside on your disk. As you will learn, by compressing files you gain storage space on your disk. However, by compressing files you also decrease your system performance because Windows 98 must compress or decompress files as you use them, which requires additional processing.

In Tip 610, you will learn how to change a drive's compression ratio to trade disk space for system performance. When you change a drive's compression ratio, your change effects every file that resides on the disk. Depending on how you use the files on your disk, however, there may be times when it makes more sense for you to change compression settings on a file-by-file basis. In such cases, you can use the Compression Agent, as shown in Figure 609.

Figure 609 *The Windows 98 Compression Agent.*

To start the Compression Agent, perform these steps:

1. Click your mouse on the Start menu Programs option and choose Accessories. Windows 98, will display the Accessories submenu.

2. Within the Accessories submenu, click your mouse on the System Tools option and select Compression Agent.

Several of the Tips that follow examine the Compression Agent in detail.

610 **USING THE COMPRESSION AGENT TO CHOOSE ULTRAPACK OR HIPACK COMPRESSION**

In Tip 619, you will learn how to use the Windows 98 DriveSpace utility to increase your disk's storage capacity by compressing the files on your disk. As you will learn, when you compress files on your disk, you decrease your system performance because Windows 98 must now compress and decompress each file you use—which requires additional processing that slows down your system. When you use DriveSpace to compress the files on your drive, DriveSpace will usually use its UltraPack compression technique that maximizes each file's compression. Unfortunately, the UltraPack compression technique also requires considerable processing. To help you balance your system performance and disk use, the Windows 98 Compression Agent lets you select the HiPack compression technique (which requires less processing, but also achieves lower compression) for the files that you use on a regular basis. To use the Compression Agent to control your compression settings, perform these steps:

1. Click your mouse on the Start menu Programs option and choose Accessories. Windows 98, in turn, will display the Accessories submenu.

2. Within the Accessories submenu, click your mouse on the System Tools option and select Compression Agent. Windows 98 will open the Compression Agent window.

3. Within the Compression Agent window, click your mouse on the Settings button. Windows 98, in turn, will display the Compression Agent Settings dialog box, as shown in Figure 610.

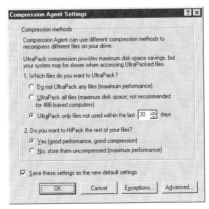

Figure 610 The Compression Agent Settings dialog box.

4. Within the Compression Agent Settings dialog box, you can specify when you want DriveSpace to use UltraPack (for maximum compression and slower performance) or when you want it to use HiPack. After you make your selections, click your mouse on the OK button.

---

611 | **SELECTING COMPRESSION SETTINGS ON A FILE-BY-FILE BASIS**

In Tip 610, you learned how to use the Windows 98 Compression Agent to select the DriveSpace UltraPack or HiPack compression techniques based on specific criteria. In some cases, you may want to control the compression settings on a file-by-file basis. To do so, you can use the Add Exceptions dialog box shown in Figure 611 to specify a file's settings.

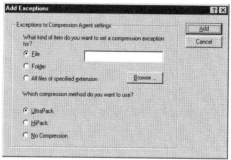

Figure 611.1 *The Compression Agent's Add Exceptions dialog box.*

To control a file's compression settings, perform these steps:

1. Click your mouse on the Start menu Programs option and choose Accessories. Windows 98, will display the Accessories submenu.

2. Within the Accessories submenu, click your mouse on the System Tools option and select Compression Agent. Windows 98, in turn, will open the Compression Agent window.

3. Within the Compression Agent window, click your mouse on the Settings button. Windows 98, in turn, will display the Compression Agent Settings dialog box.

4. Within the Compression Agent Settings dialog box, click your mouse on the Exceptions button. Windows 98, in turn, will display the Exceptions dialog box, as shown in Figure 611.2.

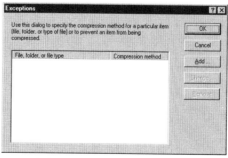

Figure 611.2 *The Compression Agent's Exceptions dialog box.*

5. Within the Exceptions dialog box, click your mouse on the Add button. Windows 98 will display the Add Exceptions dialog box, as shown in Figure 611.3.

Figure 611.3 The Add Exceptions dialog box.

6. Within the Add Exceptions dialog box, use the Browse button to select the file or folder for which you want to specify compression settings. Then, use the radio buttons to select the compression method you desire. Then, click your mouse on the Add button. The Compression Agent, in turn, will add your selected file or folder to the Exceptions dialog box.

7. Within the Exceptions dialog box, click your mouse on the OK button. Then, within the Compression Agents Settings dialog box, click your mouse on the OK button. Finally, within the Compression Agent dialog box, click your mouse on the Start button to put your changes into effect.

612 CONTROLLING THE COMPRESSION AGENT'S ADVANCED SETTINGS

In several of the previous Tips, you have learned to use the Windows 98 Compression Agent to customize your system's disk-compression settings. Using the Compression Agent, you can balance your disk's compression settings with your system performance. In an attempt to improve your system performance, there may be times when the Compression Agent may decompress files automatically. To control such Compression Agent operations, you can use the Advanced Settings dialog box, as shown in Figure 612.

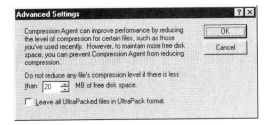

Figure 612 The Compression Agent's Advanced Settings dialog box.

Within the Advanced Settings dialog box, you can direct the Compression Agent not to decompress files if your free disk space reaches a specific level. In addition, you can also prevent the Compression Agent from decompressing files that are currently compressed using the UltraPack compression method. To display the Advanced Settings dialog box, perform these steps:

1. Within the Compression Agent window, click your mouse on the Settings button. Windows 98 will display the Compression Agent Settings dialog box.

2. Within the Compression Agent Settings dialog box, click your mouse on the Advanced button. Within the dialog box, you can select the settings you desire.

613 — USING THE WINDOWS 98 DISK CLEANUP WIZARD TO FREE UP SPACE ON YOUR DISK

As many of the Tips in this book discuss, users just cannot seem to get enough disk space. Before you decide to upgrade your hard disk to a larger drive, or to compress the files on your disk as discussed in Tip 609, you should run the Windows 98 Disk Cleanup Wizard and discard any files you no longer need. To start the Disk Cleanup Wizard, perform these steps:

1. Click your mouse on the Start menu Programs option and choose Accessories. Windows 98, in turn, will display the Accessories submenu.

2. Within the Accessories submenu, click your mouse on the System Tools option and choose the Disk Cleanup option. Windows 98, in turn, will start the Disk Cleanup Wizard which, in turn, will display the Select Drive dialog box, as shown in Figure 613.1.

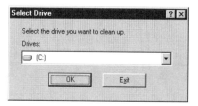

Figure 613.1 *The Select Drive dialog box.*

3. Within the Select Drive dialog box, use the pull-down list to select the disk drive you want to clean up. Then, click your mouse on the OK button. Windows 98, in turn, will display the Disk Cleanup Wizard, as shown in Figure 613.2.

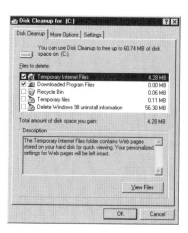

Figure 613.2 *The Disk Cleanup Wizard.*

4. Within the Disk Cleanup Wizard's Disk Cleanup sheet, click your mouse on the checkboxes that correspond to the files you want the Wizard to delete, placing a check mark within the box. (Most users will select each box. To display a list of the files that correspond to each checkbox, click your mouse on the View Files button. Windows 98, in turn, will open an Explorer window that lists the files.)

5. Within the Disk Cleanup sheet, click your mouse on the OK button. The Disk Cleanup Wizard, in turn, will display a dialog box asking you to verify that you want to delete the files. Select Yes.

Note: Within the Disk Cleanup Wizard's Settings tab, you can di]rect Windows 98 to automatically run the Disk Cleanup Wizard each time your disk gets low on disk space.

614 **USING THE DISK CLEANUP WIZARD TO REMOVE PROGRAM FILES FROM YOUR DISK**

In Tip 613, you learned how to free up space on your disk by letting the Windows 98 Disk Cleanup Wizard delete temporary files and to empty your Recycle Bin. In addition to using the Disk Cleanup Wizard to remove temporary files, you can also use the Wizard to remove programs from your system and to start the Drive Conversion Wizard, discussed in Tip 618, which converts your current file system to FAT32. To perform such operations using the Disk Cleanup Wizard, perform these steps:

1. Click your mouse on the Start menu Programs option and choose Accessories. Windows 98, in turn, will display the Accessories submenu.
2. Within the Accessories submenu, click your mouse on the System Tools option and choose the Disk Cleanup option. Windows 98, in turn, will start the Disk Cleanup Wizard which, in turn, will display the Select Drive dialog box.
3. Within the Select Drive dialog box, use the pull-down list to select the disk drive you want to clean up. Then, click your mouse on the OK button. Windows 98, in turn, will display the Disk Cleanup Wizard.
4. Within the Disk Cleanup Wizard, click your mouse on the More Options tab. The Disk Cleanup Wizard, in turn, will display the More Options sheet, as shown in Figure 614.

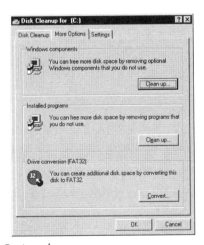

Figure 614 *The Disk Cleanup Wizard's More Options sheet.*

5. Within the More Options sheet, you can direct the Disk Cleanup Wizard to remove Windows components you are not currently using as well as programs you have installed on your system that you no longer use. When you click your mouse on the Cleanup button for either of these options, the Disk Cleanup Wizard will display the Control Panel Add/Remove Program Properties dialog box. Likewise, if you click your mouse on the Convert button to convert your disk to the FAT32 file system, the Disk Cleanup Wizard will start the Disk Conversion Wizard discussed in Tip 618.

615 **IMPROVING SYSTEM PERFORMANCE BY ELIMINATING FRAGMENTED FILES**

When you store information within a file, the Windows 98 file system, behind the scenes, records your data into one or more sectors on your disk. Over time, as you edit a file, the sectors that Windows 98 uses to store your file my become spread out (or fragmented) across your disk. Users refer to such files as *fragmented files* because there is a piece (fragment) here and a piece there. The problem with fragmented files is that they take longer for your disk drive to read than does a file whose contents reside within consecutive disk sectors. If you find your programs or files take longer to load, your files may be fragmented. Fortunately, Windows 98 provides the Disk Defragmenter utility that you can use to "defragment" your disk. When you run the Disk Defragmenter, the program will search your disk for fragmented files and will then move the file's contents to a new location on your disk that lets it store the information in consecutive sectors. To defragment your disk using the Disk Defragmenter, perform these steps:

1. Click your mouse on the Start menu Programs option. Windows 98, in turn, will display the Programs submenu.
2. Within the Programs submenu, click your mouse on the Accessories option and choose the System Tools option. Windows 98, in turn, will display the System Tools submenu.
3. Within the System Tools submenu, click your mouse on the Disk Defragmenter option. Windows 98, in turn, will start the Disk Defragmenter program which, in turn, will display the Select Drive dialog box, as shown in Figure 615.

Figure 615 *The Select Drive dialog box.*

4. Within the Select Drive dialog box, use the pull-down list to select the disk drive you want to defragment. Then, click your mouse on the OK button.

Depending on the number and size of the files on your disk, defragmenting your disk may require up to an hour. However, after the Disk Defragmenter completes its processing your system should seem faster. As a rule, you should defragment your disk at least once a month, and maybe more often, depending on the number of files you create, edit, and change throughout the day. As a rule, you should not run other programs while the Disk Defragmenter is running.

616 **PAUSING, RESUMING, OR ENDING DISK DEFRAGMENTER**

In Tip 615, you learned how to run the Disk Defragmenter to improve your disk performance. As discussed, depending on the number of files on your disk, the defragmentation operation can take a long while. Fortunately, if, after you start the Disk Defragmenter program, you must use your system, you can pause or stop the disk defragmentation process by clicking your mouse on the Pause or Stop button within the Defragmenting dialog box, as shown in Figure 616.

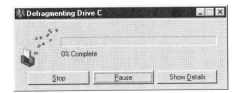

Figure 616 *The Defragmenting dialog box.*

If you pause the Disk Defragmenter, you can run another program to perform a specific task and then you can resume (by clicking your mouse on the Resume button) the Disk Defragmenter after the task is complete. If you end the Disk Defragmenter, you can later run the program by following the steps Tip 615 presents.

617   **VIEWING THE DISK DEFRAGMENTER'S PROCESSING**

As you learned in Tip 615, to defragment the files on your disk, the Disk Defragmenter moves the file's contents from their current disk sectors, which may be spread across your disk, to sectors that reside in consecutive locations. As the Disk Defragmenter performs its processing, you can view the actual processing by clicking your mouse on the Defragmenting dialog box Show Details button. The Disk Defragmenter, in turn, will expand its window to show a series of small squares that represent storage locations on your disk, as shown in Figure 617.1. Within the window, you can watch the Disk Defragmenter move information from one location on your disk to another.

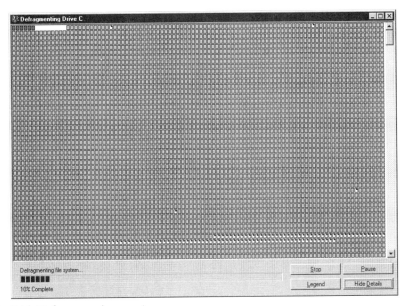

Figure 617.1 *Viewing the Disk Defragmenter's processing.*

To better understand the Disk Defragmenter's processing, click your mouse on the Legend button. The Disk Defragmenter, in turn, will display a legend that explains the color of each square it displays within its disk map, as shown in Figure 617.2.

Figure 617.2 Displaying the Disk Defragmenter's legend.

---

618 USING THE WINDOWS 98 DRIVE CONVERTER TO UPGRADE YOUR DISK TO A FAT32 FILE SYSTEM

As you have learned, Windows 98 exists to let you run programs, to let your programs use your hardware devices (such as your printer, keyboard, and mouse), and to let your programs store information on disk. To manage the files you store on disk, Windows 98 uses special software called the file system. Specifically, within the file system, Windows 98 uses a special table, the file allocation table (FAT), to track the locations on your disk where your files reside. If you are upgrading from an earlier version of Windows (such as 3.1 or 95) to Windows 98, your system is using the FAT16 file system—a file system built around a 16-bit file allocation table. As the size of hard drives continued to increase, the FAT16 file system's 16-bit file allocation table could not manage hard-disk space optimally. As a result, each file a user stored on a disk wasted considerable space. Here's why.

As you may know, to store information on a disk, your programs record the data within disk sectors, which are usually 512 bytes in length. If your program only stores 3 characters of data within a file, such as your initials, 509 bytes of the sector are wasted. If you store 100 small files on your disk, you can quickly waste considerable space. Likewise, if you store 1,000 small files, you will waste even more disk space.

Because of how the file allocation table tracks files, wasted space becomes worse. Here is why. The file allocation table tracks the location of your files on disk. To reduce the number of entries it must track for each file, the file allocation table groups four sectors into *clusters*. When you create a file, the file allocation table allocates a cluster (four sectors) to the file. So, if you create a small file that contains only 3 characters, your disk will now waste 2,045 bytes (one cluster, in this case, contains four 512-byte sectors, or 2,048 bytes). As the size of your hard disk increases, so too does the number of sectors the file allocation table allocates to a cluster. For a very large hard disk, the cluster size might become 64Kb. In that case, a small file will waste considerable space.

Windows 98 provides a new file allocation table, FAT32, which uses a 32-bit file-allocation table. Because the FAT32 has room to track more entries, it can reduce the cluster size for large disks, which results in less wasted space. Likewise, if you want to use a large cluster size with FAT32, you can use a 2Tb disk (a Tb is a terrabyte or trillion bytes). To take advantage of FAT32, you must convert your existing file-allocation table from the FAT16 format into the FAT32 format. Fortunately, Windows 98 provides a Wizard to assist you. To convert your existing file system to FAT32, perform these steps:

1. Click your mouse on the Start menu Programs option and choose Accessories. Windows 98, in turn, will display the Accessories submenu.

2. Within the Accessories submenu, click your mouse on the System Tools option and choose Drive Converter (FAT32). Windows 98, in turn, will start the Drive Converter Wizard, as

shown in Figure 618, which will walk you through the conversion process. Depending on your disk size, the conversion process may take several hours.

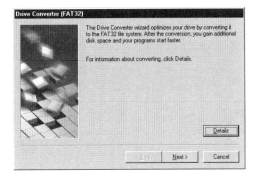

Figure 618 *The Drive Converter Wizard.*

Note: *If your PC has a hibernate mode (you should refer to your system documentation or your manufacturer's technical-support staff), you should not convert your drive to FAT32 until you disable the hibernate mode. Should your PC hibernate while the conversion process is running, you may lose the information on your disk. In addition, before you start the conversion process, you should backup your disk.*

619 ## COMPRESSING FILES TO INCREASE YOUR DISK'S STORAGE CAPACITY

If you are like most users, your system (particularly if you are using a notebook PC with a small drive) simply cannot have enough disk space. Fortunately, like many hardware devices, the prices for larger (and faster) disk drives are steadily dropping. However, before you run out to purchase a new disk drive, you should consider compressing the files on your disk to free up space on your drive. Using the Windows 98 DriveSpace utility program, you can direct Windows 98 to store files in a compressed format, which reduces the amount of disk space each file consumes.

After you enable disk compression on your PC, Windows 98, in turn, will later compress each file's data before it records the data on your disk. When you later use the file's contents, Windows 98 will decompress the data. Best of all, Windows 98 performs its compression and decompression operations behind the scenes.

You simply open and save files as you always have in the past. (However, you may notice that files take just a little longer to open or save because of Windows extra compression and decompression processing.) To compress a disk, you will use the DriveSpace utility which you will find within the Accessories System Tools submenu. Before you compress your hard drive, however, you should practice with a floppy disk, as discussed in Tip 620.

Note: *Usually, the DriveSpace program will successfully compress the files on your disk. Nevertheless, should a power failure or some other hardware error occur during the compression, the operation could damage your files. To be safe, backup the files on your disk before you use DriveSpace to compress it. Also, DriveSpace requires that the drive you want to compress contain some free space. During the compression process, DriveSpace will use the free space as a work area.*

620 COMPRESSING A FLOPPY DISK FOR PRACTICE

In Tip 619, you learned that Windows 98 provides the DriveSpace utility that you can use to compress the files on your disk which, in turn, increases the amount of information your disk can store. Before you use DriveSpace to compress your hard drive, you should take DriveSpace for a test drive using a floppy disk. That way, should something happen to go wrong during your practice session, you will not lose any valuable data. To compress a floppy disk using DriveSpace, perform these steps:

1. Insert an unused floppy disk (or a floppy whose contents you no longer need) within your floppy disk drive.

2. Click your mouse on the Start menu Programs option and choose Accessories. Windows 98, in turn, will display the Accessories submenu.

3. Within the Accessories submenu, click your mouse on the System Tools and choose DriveSpace. Windows 98, in turn, will display the DriveSpace 3 window, as shown in Figure 620.1.

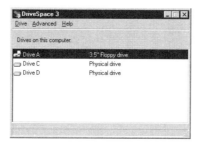

Figure 620.1 *The DriveSpace 3 window.*

4. Within the DriveSpace 3 window, click your mouse on the floppy disk drive icon and then click your mouse on the Drive menu Compress option. DriveSpace, in turn, will display the Compress a Drive dialog box, as shown in Figure 620.2, that shows your disk's before (compression) and after storage capacity.

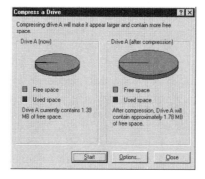

Figure 620.2 *The Compress a Drive dialog box.*

5. Within the Compress a Drive dialog box, click your mouse on the Start button. DriveSpace will first check your disk for errors and if it finds no errors, DriveSpace will start the compression. After DriveSpace compresses the drive, it will display a summary window that shows you the compression results. Click your mouse on the Close button to close the summary window. Within the DriveSpace window, you will now see an extra drive, probably drive H which DriveSpace is labeling the Host drive. Tip 621 discusses the purpose of this new drive.

621   UNDERSTANDING HOW DRIVESPACE COMPRESSES YOUR FILES

When you use the DriveSpace utility to increase a disk's free space, DriveSpace does not actually compress the disk. Instead, DriveSpace creates a compressed file, called the *compressed volume file (CVF)*, for the drive, within which DriveSpace stores the drive's files in a compressed format. (In other words, the compressed volume file is simply a file that contains the disk's original files in a compressed format.) Windows 98, in turn, stores the CVF back on the disk in an uncompressed area which Windows 98 calls the *host drive*. Next, Windows 98 assigns an unused drive letter, such as drive H, to the host drive. For example, when you compressed the floppy disk in Tip 620, you started with only one drive, which was drive A. After you compressed the drive, Windows 98 and your application programs will work as if your system has two drives—the compressed A: drive and an uncompressed H: drive (host drive), which holds the CVF. Because the uncompressed host drive probably will not contain much free space, you should continue using the A: drive for your programs and data and simply ignore the fact that the host drive, drive H:, exists.

Depending on your disk requirements, you can compress an entire drive or you can choose to only compress the drive's free space. For example, drive C: has 50Mb of free space. Using DriveSpace, you can compress 30Mb of the free space, creating a new compressed drive (possibly named drive D:, depending on your system's other drives). For each drive you compress, DriveSpace will create a host drive.

Note: *Unless the host drive has more than 2Mb of free space, the drive will not appear within an Explorer window.*

622   PREVIEWING THE AMOUNT OF ADDITIONAL DISK SPACE DRIVESPACE CAN PROVIDE

Before you decide to compress a disk using the DriveSpace utility, you may want to first determine just how much space you will gain from the operation. Most users will usually double their disk space. However, depending on the files you store on your disk, the amount of space you gain may be much less. That is because some files, such as ZIP files and graphic images (such as GIF images), do not compress well because they are already stored in compressed format. Thus, depending on the types of files the two drives contain, compressing two disks of the same size drives may not yield the same amount of disk space. To determine how much space you will gain by compressing a disk, without actually compressing the disk, perform these steps:

1. Click your mouse on the Start menu Programs option and choose Accessories. Windows 98, in turn, will display the Accessories submenu.

2. Within the Accessories submenu, click your mouse on the System Tools and choose DriveSpace. Windows 98, in turn, will display the DriveSpace window.

3. Within the DriveSpace 3 window, click your mouse on the drive icon for the disk you want to compress and then click your mouse on the Drive menu Compress option. DriveSpace, in turn, will display the Compress a Drive dialog box that shows your disk's before (compression) and after storage capacity.

4. Within the Compress a Drive dialog box, click your mouse on the Close button to cancel the compression operation.

623 | **USING DRIVESPACE TO UNCOMPRESS A DRIVE**

As you have learned, DriveSpace increases the amount of information your disk can store by storing your files in a compressed format. Each time you open a document, Windows 98 decompresses the file's contents behind the scenes. Likewise, each time you create a file, Windows 98 stores the file using the compressed format. Although compressing files in this way increases your disk's storage capacity, it also decreases your system performance because Windows 98 must now perform additional processing for every file you create or open. If system performance is more important to you than disk space, you should not compress your disk. Should you need to decompress, perform these steps:

1. Click your mouse on the Start menu Programs option and choose Accessories. Windows 98, in turn, will display the Accessories submenu.

2. Within the Accessories submenu, click your mouse on the System Tools and choose DriveSpace. Windows 98, in turn, will display the DriveSpace 3 window.

3. Within the DriveSpace 3 window, click your mouse on the drive icon for the disk you want to decompress and then click your mouse on the Drive menu Uncompress option. DriveSpace, in turn, will display the Uncompress a Drive dialog box, as shown in Figure 623, that shows your disk's before (uncompression) and after storage capacity.

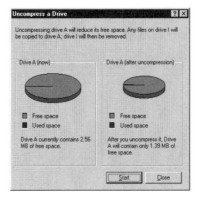

Figure 623 *The Uncompress a Drive dialog box.*

4. Within the Uncompress a Drive dialog box, click your mouse on the Start button to decompress the disk. DriveSpace, in turn, will display a dialog box asking you to verify that you want to uncompress the disk. Click your mouse on the Uncompress Now option.

Note: Depending on the amount of data your compressed disk contains, DriveSpace may not be able to uncompress the disk until you delete files from the disk. For example, if your compressed disk contains 100Mb of data and your uncompressed drive will only have 50Mb of free space, DriveSpace will not be able to uncompress the drive.

624   *MOUNTING AND DISMOUNTING A COMPRESSED DISK*

When you start Windows 98, the operating system checks all drives to determine which are compressed and uncompressed. If you use a compressed hard disk, Windows 98 recognizes that the disk is compressed upon startup. After Windows 98 starts, you can simply access the compressed drive as you would any uncompressed drive. In fact, you'll have no visible indication that the drive is compressed (other than the increased disk space).

However, if you insert a compressed floppy disk into a disk drive, Windows 98 cannot know in advance that the floppy disk is compressed. In such cases, you must tell Windows 98 that you have inserted a compressed floppy disk. The DriveSpace documentation refers to this process as *mounting* the compressed disk for use. To mount the floppy disk, select the Advanced menu Mount option. When you remove the diskette, select the Advanced menu Unmount option so you can insert additional compressed and uncompressed floppy disks.

Note: If you use compressed floppy disks regularly, follow the steps that Tip 625 presents to direct DriveSpace to automatically mount compressed disks when you insert them.

625   *DIRECTING DRIVESPACE TO AUTOMATICALLY MOUNT COMPRESSED DISKS*

As you learned in Tip 624, when you insert a compressed floppy disk into a drive, you usually must tell DriveSpace to mount the compressed disk for use. If you use compressed floppy disks on a regular basis, you can direct DriveSpace to automatically mount and unmount the compressed floppy disks that you insert into your floppy drive. To direct DriveSpace to automatically mount compressed floppy disks, perform these steps:

1. Click your mouse on the Start menu Programs option and choose Accessories. Windows 98 will display the Accessories submenu.
2. Within the Accessories submenu, click your mouse on the System Tools option and choose DriveSpace. Windows 98 will display the DriveSpace 3 window.
3. Within the DriveSpace 3 window, click your mouse on the Advanced menu Settings option. Windows 98 will display the Disk Compression Settings dialog box, as shown in Figure 625.
4. Within the Disk Compression Settings dialog box, click your mouse on the Automatically mount new compressed drives checkbox, placing a check mark within the box. Then, click your mouse on the OK button to put your changes into effect.

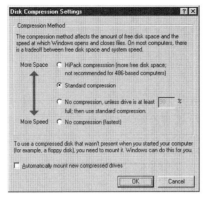

Figure 625 *The DriveSpace Disk Compression Settings dialog box.*

626 USING DRIVESPACE TO COMPRESS YOUR HARD DRIVE

As you have learned, the Windows 98 DriveSpace utility lets you increase your disk's storage capacity—in some cases, you may even double your storage space. However, as you have also learned, the increased disk space is not without its cost. Because Windows 98 must compress and decompress each file as you work, your system performance will decrease. If you are willing to trade some performance for additional disk space, perform these steps to compress your hard drive:

1. Click your mouse on the Start menu Programs option and choose Accessories. Windows 98 will display the Accessories submenu.

2. Within the Accessories submenu, click your mouse on the System Tools option and choose DriveSpace. Windows 98 will display the DriveSpace 3 window.

3. Within the DriveSpace 3 window, click your mouse on the disk that you want to compress.

4. Within the DriveSpace 3 window, click your mouse on the Drive menu Compress option. DriveSpace, in turn, will display the Compress a Drive dialog box that shows you the amount of disk space you have following the compression.

5. Within the Compress a Drive dialog box, click your mouse on the Start button. Windows 98, in turn, will display a dialog box suggesting that you create a bootable floppy disk. If you have not done so in the past, perform the steps the dialog boxes present to create a system disk. Then, DriveSpace will display a dialog box that gives you a chance to backup your files before you compress your drive. If you do not have a current backup copy of your files, click your mouse on the Back Up Files button to make a backup of your hard disk.

6. Click your mouse on the Compress Now button. DriveSpace, in turn, will start compressing the drive. Depending on the size of your hard disk, the compression process may take up to an hour. When DriveSpace completes the compression, DriveSpace will display a status window that shows how much your disk compressed and how much free space it now contains.

7. DriveSpace will then display a dialog box telling you that you must restart your system. Click your mouse on the Yes button to restart the computer. After you restart your system, Windows 98 will recognize the compressed drive and let you resume your work.

627   COMPRESSING PART OF YOUR DRIVE

In Tip 626, you learned how to use DriveSpace to compress your entire hard drive. If you have not yet compressed your drive and your disk has free space available, you can compress part of that free space to gain even more space. For example, assume your drive C: has 200Mb of free space. Using DriveSpace, you might, for example, compress 100Mb of the free space. After DriveSpace completes its compression, drive C: will have 100 Mb free, and D: drive (your new compressed drive) will have about 200Mb of compressed free space. In this case, by compressing only part of your disk, you gain 100Mb of free space. As you have learned, because Windows 98 must compress and decompress every file you store or access with a compressed drive, file compression decreases your system performance. If you only compress part of your disk, you can place the files you use on a regular basis on your uncompressed drive and the files you use less often on the compressed drive. In this way, you will better balance your system performance and disk storage requirements. To compress part of your drive, perform these steps:

1. Within the DriveSpace 3 window, click your mouse on the Advanced menu Create Empty option. Windows 98, in turn, will display the Create New Compressed Drive dialog box, as shown in Figure 627.

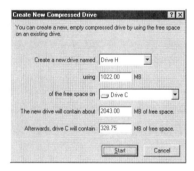

Figure 627 The Create New Compressed Drive dialog box.

2. Within the Create New Compressed Drive dialog box, click your mouse on the using field and type in the amount of disk space you want to use for the compressed drive. Then, click your mouse on the Start button. Windows 98, in turn, will display a dialog box telling you that you should create a startup disk before you compress your drive. If you have already created a startup disk, click your mouse on the No option. If you have not yet created a startup disk, click your mouse on the Yes option and perform the steps Windows 98 requests to create the startup disk. The DriveSpace program will then examine your drive for errors. If DriveSpace does not find any errors, it will then create your compressed drive.

628   DELETING A COMPRESSED DRIVE

In previous tips, you have learned how to compress all or a portion of your disk. If you work with large files, there may be times when you create a compressed drive to temporarily hold one or more files. When you no longer need the files, you can delete the files and leave the compressed drive on your disk for other uses or you can delete the compressed drive as well. When you delete a compressed drive from your disk, DriveSpace will also delete all the data you have stored within the compressed drive as well. To delete a compressed drive from your disk, perform these steps:

1. Click your mouse on the Start menu Programs option and then choose Accessories. Windows 98, in turn, will display the Accessories submenu.

2. Within the Accessories submenu, click your mouse on the System Tools option and then choose DriveSpace. Windows 98 will open the DriveSpace 3 window.

3. Within the DriveSpace window, click your mouse on the compressed drive that you want to delete and then click your mouse on the Advanced menu Delete option. DriveSpace, in turn, will display the Are you sure? dialog box that tells you the data will not be available after DriveSpace deletes the drive.

4. Within the Are you sure? dialog box, click your mouse on the Yes button to delete the drive and its contents. After DriveSpace deletes the drive, DriveSpace will display the DriveSpace Operation Complete dialog box that informs you it has completed the deletion.

5. Within the dialog box, click your mouse on the OK button. If your system does not have any other compressed drives, DriveSpace will display a dialog box asking you if you want to remove its compression software from memory. Within the dialog box, click your mouse on the Yes button (if you later compress another drive, DriveSpace will install the software you need).

Note: *Deleting a drive is different from decompressing a drive. When you delete a drive, DriveSpace discards the compressed drive's contents and returns the space it was using for the compressed drive back to the host. When you decompress a drive, DriveSpace first uncompresses the compressed drive's files, placing the files back onto the host.*

629   VIEWING A DISK'S COMPRESSION PROPERTIES

As you have learned, within the Windows 98 Explorer, you can display a disk's properties by right-clicking your mouse on the drive's icon and then clicking the Properties option from within the pop-up menu. Within the Explorer, when you click your mouse on a compressed drive, the Explorer will display the disk's Properties dialog box, within which you can select the Compression tab to display the compression sheet, as shown in Figure 629.1.

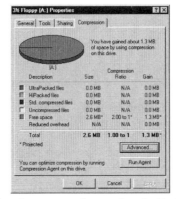

Figure 629.1 Viewing a disk's Properties dialog box Compression sheet within the Explorer.

Within the Compression sheet, you can view information about the disk's current compression ratios. In addition to viewing information about a compressed disk using the Explorer, you can use the DriveSpace utility to display the Properties dialog box shown in Figure 629.2.

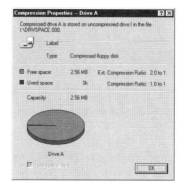

Figure 629.2 *Viewing a disk's Properties dialog box within the DriveSpace utility.*

To display a compressed disk's properties within the DriveSpace utility, perform these steps:

1. Click your mouse on the Start menu Programs option and then choose Accessories. Windows 98, in turn, will display the Accessories submenu.

2. Within the Accessories submenu, click your mouse on the System Tools option and then choose DriveSpace. Windows 98 will open the DriveSpace 3 window.

3. Within the DriveSpace window, click your mouse on the compressed drive you desire. Next, click your mouse on the Drive menu Properties option. DriveSpace, in turn, will display the disk's Properties dialog box.

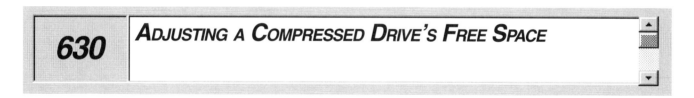

630 | **ADJUSTING A COMPRESSED DRIVE'S FREE SPACE**

In Tip 627, you learned how to compress part of your hard drive. Depending on your disk-storage requirements, there may be times when you want to change the amount of space DriveSpace allocates to a compressed drive. When you increase or decrease a compressed drive's space, you also increase or decrease space within the corresponding host drive. To adjust a compressed drive's free space, perform these steps:

1. Click your mouse on the Start menu Programs option and choose Accessories. Windows 98, in turn, will display the Accessories submenu.

2. Within the Accessories submenu, click your mouse on the System Tools option and choose DriveSpace. Windows 98 will open the DriveSpace 3 window.

3. Within the DriveSpace 3 window, click your mouse on the icon that corresponds to the drive whose free space you want to adjust.

4. Within the DriveSpace 3 window, click your mouse on the Drive menu Adjust Free Space option. DriveSpace, in turn, will display the Adjust Free Space, as shown in Figure 630.

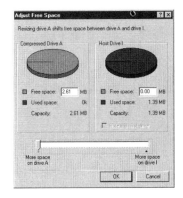

Figure 630 *The Adjust Free Space dialog box.*

5. Within the Adjust Free Space dialog box, use your mouse to drag the slider bar (that appears near the bottom of the window) to the left or the right to transfer free space between the compressed drive and its host drive.

6. Within the Adjust Free Space dialog box, click your mouse on the OK button to put your changes into effect.

631 **UNDERSTANDING AND FINE-TUNING COMPRESSION RATIOS**

To increase your disk's storage capacity, the DriveSpace program compresses the files you store on your disk. As you have learned, by compressing files, you decrease your system performance because Windows 98 must now compress and later decompress your files. Depending on your needs, you can increase or decrease the compression ratio that DriveSpace uses to compress your files to trade performance for disk space. If you increase the compression ratio, for example, DriveSpace may increase your disk's storage capacity, but will also require additional processing. By decreasing the DriveSpace ratio, you may give up a little disk space for slightly better performance. To change a compressed drive's compression ratio, perform these steps:

1. Click your mouse on the Start menu Programs option and choose Accessories. Windows 98, in turn, will display the Accessories submenu.

2. Within the Accessories submenu, click your mouse on the System Tools and choose DriveSpace. Windows 98 will open the DriveSpace 3 window.

3. Within the DriveSpace 3 window, click your mouse on the drive whose compression ratio you want to change.

4. Within the DriveSpace 3 window, click your mouse on the Advanced menu Change Ratio option. DriveSpace, in turn, will display the Compression Ratio dialog box, as shown in Figure 631.

5. Within the Compression Ratio dialog box, use your mouse to drag the slider bar to the left or to the right to increase or decrease the compression ratio.

6. Within the Compression Ratio dialog box, click your mouse on the OK button. DriveSpace, in turn, will change the disk's compression ratio and will then display the DriveSpace Operation Complete dialog box, telling you it has successfully performed the operation. Within the dialog box, click your mouse on the OK button.

Figure 631 *The Compression Ratio dialog box.*

Note: *Depending on the files on your disk, DriveSpace may not be able achieve the compression ratio you select.*

632	**HIDING OR DISPLAYING A COMPRESSED DISK'S HOST DRIVE**

As you have learned, when you compress a drive, the DriveSpace utility creates two drives: the compressed drive and a host (that holds the compressed volume file). Usually, the host drive will also contain free space within which you can store other files. Depending on how you use the host drive, you may want DriveSpace to allow or surpress the host drive's display (within the Explorer or other programs that display drive lists). When you compress a drive, you can use the Hide host drive checkbox within Properties dialog box, shown in Figure 632, to direct DriveSpace to hide or suppress the host drive's display.

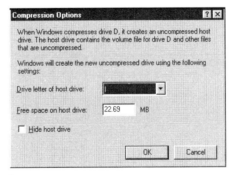

Figure 632 *The Compression Options dialog box.*

To display the Properties dialog box, select the File menu Properties option.

Note: *DriveSpace will hide host drives that contain less than 2Mb of free space. As a result, DriveSpace will hide a floppy disk's host drive.*

633	**USING DRIVESPACE TO FORMAT A COMPRESSED DRIVE**

If you use compressed drives, there may be times when, due to an error within the compressed file, Windows 98 cannot store information within the drive. In such cases, you may need to format the compressed drive to correct the error.

When you format a compressed drive, you will lose the information the compressed drive currently contains. To format a compressed drive, you must use the DriveSpace utility, within which you must perform these steps:

1. Within the DriveSpace window, click your mouse on the compressed drive you want to format.

2. Within the DriveSpace window, click your mouse on the Drive menu Format option. DriveSpace, in turn, will display the Are you sure? dialog box, within which it displays a message telling you that the format operation will delete the files that reside on the compressed drive.

3. Within the Are you sure? dialog box, click your mouse on the Yes button.

634 **CHANGING A HOST DRIVE'S DRIVE LETTER**

As you have learned, when you use DriveSpace to compress a drive, DriveSpace creates the compressed drive and a host drive (within which DriveSpace stores the compressed volume file). When DriveSpace creates the host drive, DriveSpace will assign a drive letter, such as H:, to your host drive. Depending on the drives you have on your system, there may be times when you will want to change the drive letter that DriveSpace assigned to the host drive. To change a host-drive letter, perform these steps:

1. Click your mouse on the Start menu Programs option and choose Accessories. Windows 98 will display the Accessories submenu.

2. Within the Accessories submenu, click your mouse on the System Tools and choose DriveSpace. Windows 98 will open the DriveSpace 3 window.

3. Within the DriveSpace 3 window, click your mouse on the host drive whose drive letter you want to change.

4. Within the DriveSpace 3 window, click your mouse on the Advanced menu Change Letter option. DriveSpace, in turn, will display the Select Drive dialog box, as shown in Figure 634.

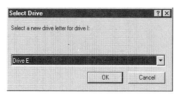

Figure 634 *The Select Drive dialog box.*

5. Within the Select Drive dialog box, click your mouse on the pull-down drive list and select the drive letter that you desire. Then, click your mouse on the OK button.

635 **LOOKING BEHIND-THE-SCENES WITH DRIVESPACE**

As you have learned, when you use DriveSpace to compress a disk, DriveSpace creates a compressed drive and a host drive. To compress the information on your disk, DriveSpace creates a special file on the compressed drive, which

DriveSpace names *DRVSPACE.000*. Within the *DRVSPACE.000* file, DriveSpace stores your disk's files in a compressed format. The DriveSpace documentation refers to the *DRVSPACE.000* file as the compressed volume file, or CVF. In other words, the CVF is a huge file within which DriveSpace stores all your files. When you later use a file that resides on the compressed disk, DriveSpace locates the file's contents within the huge CVF file and then decompresses the file's contents so your application can use the data.

Before you can use a compressed floppy disk, you must first mount the disk for use. After you mount the disk, DriveSpace will use the *DRVSPACE.000* file (that you can find on the floppy disk) to provide you with access to the drive's compressed files.

Using the Explorer, you can list the files on a host disk (if you are viewing a compressed floppy disk, you must first unmount the drive) to view the *DRVSPACE.000* file. Figure 635, for example, shows the *DRVSPACE.000* on a floppy disk within an Explorer file list.

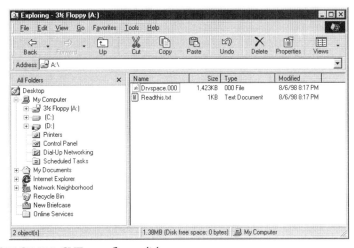

Figure 635 *Viewing the DRVSPACE.000 CVF on a floppy disk.*

636 **USING THE WINDOWS 98 MAINTENANCE WIZARD TO FINE-TUNE YOUR SYSTEM SETTINGS**

Several of the Tips this book presents examine the ScanDisk disk utility that examines your disks and files for errors, the Disk Defragmenter that improves your system performance by defragmenting your files, and the Disk Cleanup Wizard that eliminates unnecessary files from your disk. To help users perform these operations on a regular basis, Windows 98 provides the Maintenance Wizard, which will automatically run each of these utilities. To start the Maintenance Wizard, perform these steps:

1. Click your mouse on the Start menu Programs option and choose Accessories. Windows 98, in turn, will display the Accessories submenu.

2. Within the Accessories submenu, click your mouse on System Tools option and choose Maintenance Wizard. Windows 98, in turn, may start the Maintenance Wizard, as shown in Figure 636 (assuming you have previously configured the Wizard, otherwise, the first time you run

the Wizard, it will display a series of screens that let you change your current maintenance settings and schedules).

3. Using the Maintenance Wizard, you can perform the operations now or you can schedule the operations to run at a later time. If you want the Wizard to perform the operations now, click your mouse on the Perform maintenance now button and then click your mouse on OK. The Wizard, in turn, will automatically run the Windows 98 maintenance programs. If you want to schedule the operations for a later time, click your mouse on the Change my maintenance settings or schedule button and then click OK. (Tip 637 discusses the steps you must perform to change your maintenance settings or schedule.)

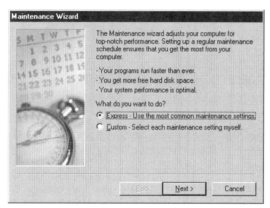

Figure 636 *The Windows 98 Maintenance Wizard.*

637 CUSTOMIZING THE MAINTENANCE WIZARD'S OPERATIONS

In Tip 636, you learned that Windows 98 provides the Maintenance Wizard that you can use to delete unnecessary files from your disk, to defragment files on your disk, and to examine your disk, files, and folders for errors. Using the Maintenance Wizard, you can perform the operations now, or you can schedule the operations to run automatically, at a later time. To control the Maintenance Wizard's schedule or settings, perform these steps:

1. Click your mouse on the Start menu Programs option and choose Accessories. Windows 98, in turn, will display the Accessories submenu.

2. Within the Accessories submenu, click your mouse on the System Tools option and choose Maintenance Wizard. Windows 98, in turn, will start the Maintenance Wizard.

3. Within the Maintenance Wizard, click your mouse on the Change my maintenance settings or schedule button and then click your mouse on the OK button. The Maintenance Wizard, in turn, will display a series of dialog boxes within which you can schedule or disable its specific operations. For example, you might direct the Maintenance Wizard to perform each of its operations every night at midnight.

When you use the Maintenance Wizard to schedule operations, the Maintenance Wizard, in turn, will place an entry for each task within the Scheduled Tasks folder.

638 USING NET WATCHER TO MONITOR HOW NETWORK USERS ACCESS YOUR SYSTEM RESOURCES

As you have learned, users connect PC and printers to a local-area network (LAN) to share resources, such as folders, files, and printers. If you share resources that reside on your system, the operations other users perform on your system may decrease your performance. Fortunately, using the Net Watcher utility program, you can monitor your shared resources and determine which other users access your resources, when, and for how long. In addition, the Net Watcher also lets you disconnect users from specific files that reside on your system. If you have installed the Client for Microsoft Networks client software and have enabled file and printer sharing, you can use Net Watcher to monitor your system's network activities. To start the Net Watcher utility, perform these steps:

1. Click your mouse on the Start menu Programs option and choose Accessories. Windows 98, in turn, will display the Accessories submenu.

2. Within the Accessories submenu, click your mouse on the System Tools option and choose Net Watcher. Windows 98 will start the Net Watcher utility program, as shown in Figure 638.1.

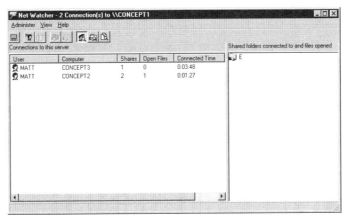

Figure 638.1 *The Net Watcher program.*

Within the Net Watcher, click your mouse on the Administer menu Select Server option. Windows 98, in turn, will display the Select Server dialog box, as shown in Figure 638.2.

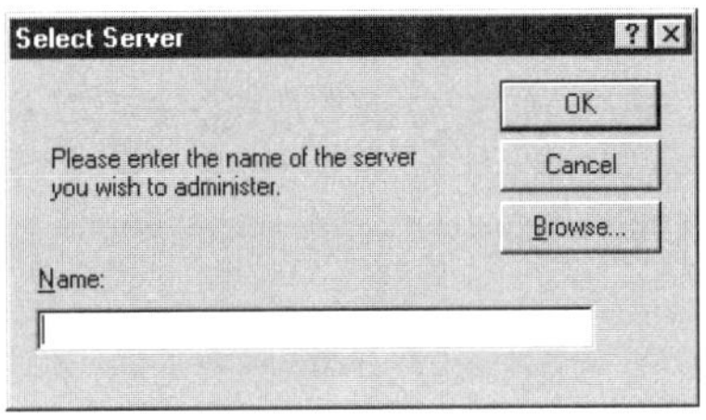

Figure 638.2 *The Select Server dialog box.*

Within the Select Server dialog box, type in the name of the server PC you want to monitor. Usually, you select your own PC.

Note: *If your System Tools menu does not have the Net Watcher option, you can add the program using the Control Panel Add/Remove Programs icon.*

---

639 | **Using Net Watcher to Disconnect Remote Users**

In Tip 638, you learned how to use the Net Watcher to view remote users connected to your system. Within the Net Watcher, you can use the View menu to display users sorted by connections, shared folders, or open files. Figure 639, for example, shows users connected to a system within the Net Watcher.

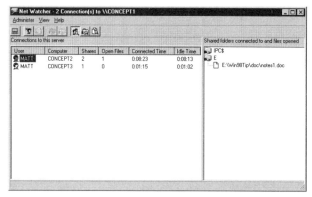

Figure 639 *Viewing open files within the Net Watcher.*

As you have learned, when users connect to your system to share resources, these remote users consume resources on your system which, in turn, reduces your system performance. Depending on the operations you must perform, there may be times when you must disconnect users from your system. To disconnect a user from your system using the Net Watcher, perform these steps:

1. Click your mouse on the Start menu Programs option and choose Accessories. Windows 98 will display the Accessories submenu.

2. Within the Accessories submenu, click your mouse on the System Tools option and choose Net Watcher. Windows 98 will start the Net Watcher utility program.

3. Within the Net Watcher window, click your mouse on the Show users toolbar button. The Net Watcher, in turn, will show you the users connected to the system.

4. Within the Net Watcher's user list, click your mouse on the user you want to disconnect. Then, click your mouse on the Net Watcher's Administer menu and select the Disconnect User option.

Note: *Before you disconnect a user, send an e-mail message to the user that informs the user that you are going to disconnect them from your system and that they should save their current files. The user, in fact, may choose to disconnect themselves from the system after he or she saves his or her work.*

---

640 | **Using Net Watcher to View Which Files Remote Users Have Open on Your System**

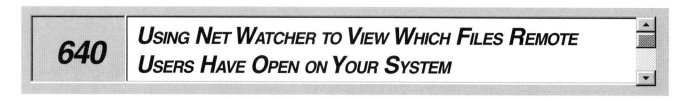

In Tip 638, you learned how to use the Net Watcher to view users who are connected to your system. As you examine the user list, you will next probably want to know which files the users are using. For example, Figure 640 lists files that are opened on your system by remote users.

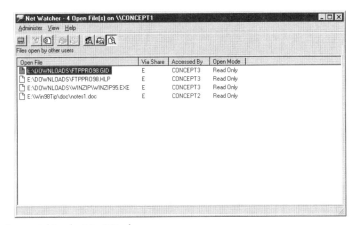

Figure 640 *Viewing open files from within the Net Watcher.*

In addition to viewing open files, you can also use the Net Watcher to close an open file (after you notify the user that you are going to close the file, so he or she can save his or her work). To close a file within the Net Watcher, perform these steps:

1. Click your mouse on the Start menu Programs option and choose Accessories. Windows 98 will display the Accessories submenu.

2. Within the Accessories submenu, click your mouse on the System Tools option and choose Net Watcher. Windows 98 will start the Net Watcher utility program.

3. Within the Net Watcher, click your mouse on the Show files toolbar button and then click your mouse the file that you want to close. Finally, select the Administer menu Close File option.

---

641 USING THE RESOURCE METER TO MONITOR WINDOWS 98 SYSTEM RESOURCES

In Tip 674, you will learn how to use the Windows 98 System Monitor to track various low-level Windows 98 operations. For example, you might use the System Monitor to track Windows 98 memory-management operations or disk read and write operations. In addition to tracking Windows 98 performance using the System Monitor, you can also track the resources Windows 98 has available for use using a second program, the Resource Meter, that this Tip presents. As you have learned, Windows 98, like all operating systems, exists to let you run programs. Like all programs, to run, the operating system must reside within your computer's RAM. As Windows 98 runs, it allocates memory to hold its own program instructions and data. In addition, Windows 98 reserves memory which it may later use to store objects, for its own use, to store objects for a program's use, or to store graphics objects such as dialog boxes or other windows. Windows 98 refers to these three types of objects as system resources, user resources, and GDI (graphic device interface) resources.

Depending on the number of programs you run (and each program's processing), there may be times when Windows 98 appears to slow down. In most cases, you can attribute Windows 98 poor performance to insufficient memory. However, before you run out and buy more memory, you can use the Resource Meter utility to determine how much resource memory Windows 98 currently has available for use, as shown in Figure 641.1.

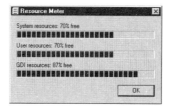

Figure 641.1 *The Windows 98 Resource Meter.*

To run the Windows 98 Resource Meter, perform these steps:

1. Click your mouse on the Start menu Programs option and choose Accessories. Windows 98, in turn, will display the Accessories submenu.

2. Within the Accessories submenu, click your mouse on the System Tools option and choose the Resource Meter option. Windows 98 will start the Resource Meter which, in turn, will display a dialog box telling you that because the Resource Meter is a program, it will consume some resources, which will make the results it displays not exact. Click your mouse on the OK button. Windows 98, in turn, will display a small icon for the Resource Meter on your Taskbar, as shown in Figure 641.2

Figure 641.2 *The Taskbar Resource Meter icon.*

3. To display the Resource Meter, click your mouse on the Taskbar icon. To hide the Resource Meter, click your mouse on the Resource Meter window's Close button.

642   **WATCH FOR PROGRAMS THAT DO NOT GIVE BACK RESOURCES**

If, as you run the Resource Meter discussed in Tip 641, you find that Windows 98 is low on resources despite the fact that you are not running any programs, use the Resource Meter to try to determine which program is consuming resources that it does not give when it ends. Users refer to programs that do not give back their resources as a resource leak (the program consumes and "leaks away" resources rather than giving the resources back to Windows 98 for reuse). To test for such a program, start the Resource Meter as discussed in Tip 641. Next, before you run a program, use the Resource Meter to display the current available resources. Then, after you end the program, use the Resource Meter to determine if the program gave back the resources it consumed.

643   **USING SCANDISK TO REPAIR FILE, FOLDER, AND DISK ERRORS**

As you know, Windows 98 stores your programs and documents within files on your disk. To help you organize your files, Windows 98 lets you group related files into folders. Although the Windows 98 file system is very reliable, there may be times, due to such events as a power outage or a program or hardware error, when Windows 98 cannot successfully read or write your files. In such cases, you can use the ScanDisk utility to detect and, quite possibly, to correct the error. Unfortunately, depending on the problem, ScanDisk may not be able to recover all your data. For example, if a disk error occurs within the middle of a file, ScanDisk will not be able to recover the file's contents. As a rule, you should run the ScanDisk utility once a week to make sure your disks contain no errors that could lead to data loss. To examine your disk using ScanDisk, perform these steps:

1. Click your mouse on the Start menu Programs option and choose Accessories. Windows 98, in turn, will display the Accessories submenu.

2. Within the Accessories submenu, click your mouse on the System Tools option and choose ScanDisk. Windows 98 will open the ScanDisk window, as shown in Figure 643.1.

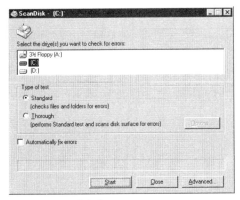

Figure 643.1 *Running the ScanDisk utility to examine a disk for errors.*

3. Within the ScanDisk window, click your mouse on the disk you want to examine.

4. Within the ScanDisk window's Type of test field, click your mouse on the Standard button and then click your mouse on the Start button. ScanDisk, in turn, will start examining your files and folders for errors. If ScanDisk encounters an error, it will display a message describing the error and will ask you how you want to proceed. When ScanDisk completes its examination, it will display the Results dialog box, as shown in Figure 643.2.

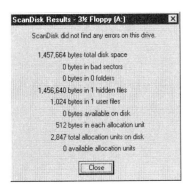

Figure 643.2 *The ScanDisk Results dialog box.*

5. Within the Results dialog box, click your mouse on the OK button to close the box.

6. Within the ScanDisk window, click your mouse on Close to end the ScanDisk program.

Note: *Usually, when ScanDisk encounters a disk error, ScanDisk will display a message describing the error and ask you how you want to correct the problem. If you would prefer that ScanDisk, on its own, determine the best way to correct the error without asking for your intervention, click your mouse on the Automatically fix errors checkbox that appears within the ScanDisk window, placing a check mark into the checkbox.*

644 PERFORMING SCANDISK'S THOROUGH ERROR DETECTION

In Tip 643, you learned how to use ScanDisk's standard-error detection, which checks your disk for folder errors, file errors (such as lost fragments or cross-linked clusters), and for file-allocation-table errors (Windows 98 uses the file-allocation table to track where your files reside on disk). The advantage of running ScanDisk's standard-error checking is that the test is fast and will usually identify the majority of problems you may incur.

ScanDisk also provides a thorough test for which ScanDisk will first perform its standard test and then will examine your disk's surface (each sector) for bad locations, which ScanDisk will mark within the file-allocation table as damaged so Windows 98 will not try to use the locations to store files. Because ScanDisk must examine your disk a sector at a time, the thorough test can be quite time consuming. However, if you start to encounter several disk errors, you should run the thorough test by performing these steps:

1. Click your mouse on the Start menu Programs option and choose Accessories. Windows 98, in turn, will display the Accessories submenu.

2.. Within the Accessories submenu, click your mouse on the System Tools option and choose ScanDisk. Windows 98 will open the ScanDisk window.

3. Within the ScanDisk window, click your mouse on the disk you want to examine.

4. Within the ScanDisk window's Type of test field, click your mouse on the Thorough button and then click your mouse on the Start button. ScanDisk, in turn, will start examining your files and folders for errors and will then scan your disk's surface. If ScanDisk encounters an error, it will display a message describing the error and will ask you how you want to proceed. When ScanDisk completes its examination, it will display the Results dialog box.

5. Within the Results dialog box, click your mouse on the OK button to close the box.

6. Within the ScanDisk window, click your mouse on the Close button to end the ScanDisk program.

645 CONFIGURING SCANDISK'S THOROUGH ERROR CHECK DISK SURFACE SCAN

In Tip 644, you learned how to perform ScanDisk's thorough error checking, which directs ScanDisk to examine the surface of your disk for sector errors. As you learned, depending on your disk size, ScanDisk's thorough test can be quite time consuming. Depending on your needs, there may be times when you want to control how ScanDisk performs the surface test. When you click your mouse on the Thorough test button within the ScanDisk window, ScanDisk will activate the Options button. If you click your mouse on the Options button, ScanDisk will then display the Surface Scan Options dialog box, as shown in Figure 645.

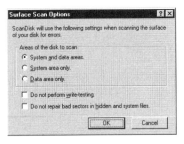

Figure 645 *The Surface Scan Options dialog box.*

Table 645 briefly explains each of the ScanDisk surface scan options.

Surface Scan Option	Description
System and data areas	Directs ScanDisk to test the entire disk for errors.
System area only	Directs ScanDisk to test only those parts of your disk used specifically by the operating system, such as the file-allocation table and root directory.
Data area only	Directs ScanDisk to test only those parts that follow the system area (disk areas that contain your files and folders).
Do not perform write-testing	Directs ScanDisk not to test the disk for recording errors.
Do not repair bad sectors in hidden or system files	Directs ScanDisk not to try to fix errors it encounters within a hidden or system files.

Table 645 *The ScanDisk Thorough test surface scan options.*

646 **CUSTOMIZING SCANDISK OPERATIONS**

If you use the ScanDisk utility on a regular basis (and you should), you may want to use several of ScanDisk's advanced settings to customize specific operations. If, within the ScanDisk window, you click your mouse on the Advanced button, ScanDisk will display the Advanced Options dialog box, as shown in Figure 646.

Figure 646 *The Advanced Options dialog box.*

Using the Advanced Options dialog box, you can customize several operations, as Table 646 explains.

Advanced Option	Description
Display summary	Controls when ScanDisk displays its Summary dialog box that details the number of files and folders on your disk as well as any errors ScanDisk encounters.
Log File	Controls how and if ScanDisk records its processing to the log file *ScanDisk.LOG*.
Cross-linked files	Controls how ScanDisk treats cross-linked files. Tip 649 discusses cross-linked files in detail.
Lost file fragments	Controls how ScanDisk treats lost file fragments. Tip 648 discusses lost file fragments in detail.
Check files for	Directs ScanDisk to check files for specific errors.
Check host drive first	If you use a compressed disk drive, you can direct ScanDisk to first check the host drive for errors before checking the compressed drive, which may be useful if the compressed drive has errors that relate to host drive errors.

Table 646 *The purpose of ScanDisk's Advanced Options.*

647 VIEWING OR PRINTING THE SCANDISK LOG FILE

In Tip 646, you learned how to use ScanDisk's advanced settings to customize various operations. Within the ScanDisk Advanced Options dialog box, you can direct ScanDisk to create a log file within which ScanDisk records the errors it encounters and the steps it performs to correct the error. When you direct ScanDisk to use a log file, ScanDisk will create or append information to the file *ScanDisk.LOG* which resides within your disk's root directory.

Using the Windows 98 WordPad accessory program, you can view or print the log file's contents, as shown in Figure 647.

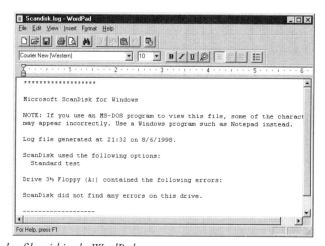

Figure 647 *Viewing the ScanDisk log file within the WordPad accessory program.*

To view the ScanDisk log file within WordPad, simply start the WordPad accessory as discussed in Tip 565 and then use the File menu Open option to open the *ScanDisk.LOG* file from your disk's root directory.

648 — U*SING* S*CAN*D*ISK TO* F*IX* L*OST* F*ILE* F*RAGMENTS*

As your files grow, Windows may store the files in sectors that reside in locations that are spread across your disk. When a file's contents no longer reside in consecutive storage locations, users refer to the file as *fragmented*.

If, as Windows 98 is updating a file on disk, your system loses power or Windows 98 encounters a fatal error, Windows 98 may misplace one or more pieces of the file, which users refer to as *lost fragments*. When you run the ScanDisk utility, the program searches your disk for such lost file fragments and tries to convert the missing pieces into small files, which ScanDisk stores in your disk's root directory with the names *FILE0000.CHK, FILE0001.CHK*, and so on.

Later, after the ScanDisk program ends, you can use an editor, such as the Windows 98 WordPad accessory, to view each file's contents. If the file is part of a word-processing document, for example, you may be able to recognize part of the document and may choose to save the file back to your disk with a more meaningful name (or you might cut and paste the file's contents into another document). If, instead, the file is part of a program, its contents will appear within your word processor as illegible characters and you should simply delete the file to free up the disk space it consumes.

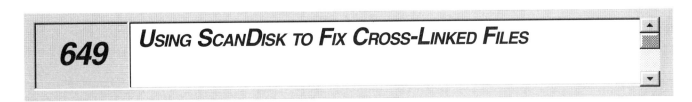

649 — U*SING* S*CAN*D*ISK TO* F*IX* C*ROSS*-L*INKED* F*ILES*

Windows 98 stores your files on disk by recording the file's information into one or more disk sectors. To keep track of where each file resides on disk, Windows 98 uses the file-allocation table, within which it stores information about which sectors contain the file's data. Should your PC experience a loss of power or should Windows 98 experience an error as it records information about your file to disk, Windows may not correctly update the file-allocation table. In such cases, the file-allocation table may point to the same disk location for two or more files, making the files *cross-linked*. Usually, when two files become cross-linked, one of the files is correct, and the second file is damaged. If you can determine which file is correct, you can save that file, and then delete the damaged file.

When the ScanDisk utility examines your disk, the program examines the file-allocation table for such cross-links. Should ScanDisk encounter two cross-linked files, you have two choices. First, you can simply have ScanDisk delete the cross-linked files, which will mean you will then need to restore the files from your backups. Second, you can direct ScanDisk to make copies of both files (you can view the ScanDisk log file to determine the filenames ScanDisk used for the file copies).

Then, using an editor, such as the Windows 98 WordPad accessory, you can view each file's contents. As was the case with lost file fragments, discussed in Tip 649, if you do not recognize cross-linked file contents within your word processor, you should probably delete the file.

650

UNDERSTANDING AND USING THE WINDOWS 98 CABINET FILES

If you use the Windows Explorer to examine the files that reside on the Windows 98 CD-ROM, you will find a large number of cabinet files (which use the CAB extension). In general, a cabinet file is simply a compressed file that stores information more efficiently. Software companies often use cabinet files to compress information into the smallest possible format so that they can fit as much data onto a floppy disk or CD-ROM. When you install the software, the installation program decompresses the cabinet files, extracting the information the file contains.

Usually, you can simply ignore the cabinet files. If you need to install software from the Windows 98 CD, you can use the Control Panel Add/Remove Programs option to install the software for you. If you are an advanced user or system administrator, there may be times when you want to extract one or more files yourself from within a cabinet file. You might, for example, want to extract a specific device driver from within a cabinet. To extract information from a file cabinet file, perform these steps:

1. Using your system documentation (or information you find on a technical support Web site), determine the cabinet file that contains the information you require.
2. Click your mouse on the Start menu Run option. Windows 98, in turn, will display the Run dialog box.
3. Within the Run dialog box, type **COMMAND** and press ENTER. Windows 98 will open an MS-DOS window from within which you can issue commands at the system prompt.
4. At the MS-DOS system prompt, use the CD command to select the directory into which you want to place the files you extract from the cabinet file.
5. At the MS-DOS system prompt, type the command **EXTRACT E:\Path\CabFilename.CAB**, replacing the *E:\Path\CabFilename.CAB* with the name of the cabinet file from which you want to extract data. Windows 98, in turn, will read and decompress the cabinet file placing the files within the current directory.

Note: *In addition to performing the steps this Tip presents to expand a Cab file, you can also double-click your mouse on the Cab file from within the Explorer. The Explorer, in turn, will display a list of the Cab file's contents. Within the file list, click your mouse on the file that you desire and then select the File menu Extract option.*

651

USING THE SCHEDULED TASK WIZARD TO PERFORM OPERATIONS AT A SPECIFIC TIME

To simplify operations that you must perform on a regular basis, Windows 98 provides the Scheduled Tasks folder, within which you can place programs that you want Windows 98 to run at specific times. For example, you must direct Windows 98 to run the Disk Defragmenter utility to defragment your files each Friday night at midnight. Likewise, on Thursday nights, you might want Windows 98 to run ScanDisk to check your disks for errors. To use the Scheduled Task Wizard to schedule a task, perform these steps:

1. Click your mouse on the Start menu Programs options and choose Accessories. Windows 98, in turn, will display the Accessories submenu.

2. Within the Accessories submenu, click your mouse on the System Tools option and then choose Scheduled Tasks. Windows 98, in turn, will open the Scheduled Tasks folder, as shown in Figure 651.1. Depending on the number of tasks you have scheduled, the folder's contents may differ from those shown here.

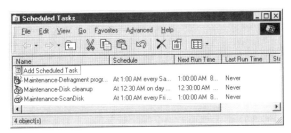

Figure 651.1 *The Scheduled Tasks folder.*

3. Within the Scheduled Tasks folder, double-click your mouse on the Add Scheduled Task icon. Windows 98, in turn, will start the Scheduled Task Wizard. Within the Wizard, click your mouse on the Next button. The Scheduled Task Wizard, in turn, will display a dialog box, as shown in Figure 651.2, within which you can select the program you want to schedule.

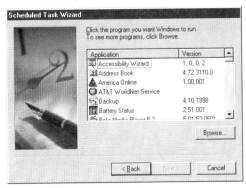

Figure 651.2 *The Scheduled Task Wizard's prompt for the program you want to schedule.*

4. Within the dialog box, click your mouse on the program you want to schedule (or use the Browse button to locate the program you desire). Then, click your mouse on the Next button. The Scheduled Task Wizard, in turn, will display a dialog box within which you can specify how often you want to run the program, as shown in Figure 651.3.

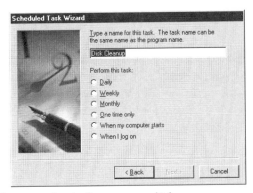

Figure 651.3 *The Scheduled Task Wizard's prompt for the frequency at which you want to run the program.*

5. Within the dialog box, click your mouse on the radio button that corresponds to the frequency at which you want to run the program. Then, click your mouse on the Next button. The Wizard, in turn, will display a dialog box that prompts you for the time at which you want to run the program, as shown in Figure 651.4.

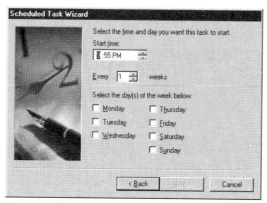

Figure 651.4 *The Scheduled Task Wizard's prompt for the time at which you want to run a program.*

6. Within the dialog box, specify the time that you want to run the program and then click your mouse on the Next button. The Wizard, in turn, will display a dialog box that summarizes your program scheduling. Click your mouse on the Finish button. The Wizard, in turn, will place an icon within the Scheduled Tasks folder that corresponds to your new entry.

652 CHANGING WHEN THE TASK SCHEDULER PERFORMS A TASK

In Tip 651, you learned how to use the Scheduled Task Wizard to schedule a program that you want Windows 98 to automatically run at a specific time. When you use the Scheduled Task Wizard to schedule a task, the Wizard will place an entry within the Scheduled Tasks folder.

Should you later decide to change the time at which a program runs, perform these steps:

1. Click your mouse on the Start menu Programs options and choose Accessories. Windows 98 will display the Accessories submenu.

2. Within the Accessories submenu, click your mouse on the System Tools option and choose Scheduled Tasks. Windows 98 will display the Scheduled Tasks folder.

3. Within the Scheduled Tasks folder, right-click your mouse on the icon that corresponds to the program whose settings you want to change. Windows 98 will display a pop-up menu. Within the pop-up menu, click your mouse on the Properties option. Windows 98 will display the program's Task sheet, as shown in Figure 652.1.

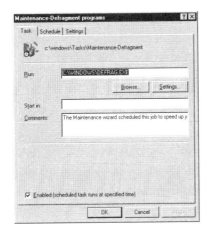

Figure 652.1 *A scheduled task's Task sheet.*

    4. Within the dialog box, click your mouse on the Schedule tab. Windows 98, in turn, will display the Schedule sheet, as shown in Figure 652.2.

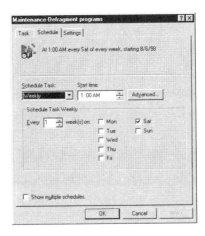

Figure 652.2 *A scheduled task's Schedule sheet.*

    5. Within the Schedule sheet, select the time settings you desire and then click your mouse on the OK button.

Note: *In addition to opening the Scheduled Tasks folder from the System Tools menu, you can also open the folder by clicking your mouse on the Taskbar's Task Scheduler icon, as shown in Figure 652.3.*

Figure 652.3 *Using the Taskbar's Task Scheduler icon to open the Scheduled Tasks folder.*

653   SETTING THE OPTIONS FOR A TASK SCHEDULER'S TASK

In Tip 651, you learned how to use the Windows 98 Scheduled Task Wizard to direct Windows 98 to run a program at a specific time. Then, in Tip 652, you learned how to change the time or frequency at which Windows 98 runs the program. In addition to controlling a scheduled task's time settings, Windows 98 also lets you direct Windows 98 to remove the task from the list of scheduled tasks after Windows 98 runs it, to stop the task after a specific time interval, or to only run the program when the system is not busy. To control a scheduled task's settings, perform these steps:

1. Click your mouse on the Start menu Programs options and choose Accessories. Windows 98 will display the Accessories submenu.

2. Within the Accessories submenu, click your mouse on the System Tools option and choose Scheduled Tasks. Windows 98 will display the Scheduled Tasks folder.

3. Within the Scheduled Tasks folder, right-click your mouse on the icon that corresponds to the program whose settings you want to change. Windows 98 will display a pop-up menu. Within the pop-up menu, click your mouse on the Properties option. Windows 98 will display the program's Task sheet.

4. Within the dialog box, click your mouse on the Settings tab. Windows 98, in turn, will display the Schedule sheet, as shown in Figure 653.

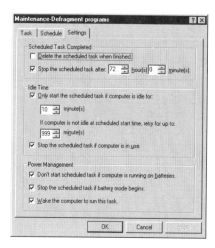

Figure 653 *A scheduled task's Settings sheet.*

5. Within the Settings sheet, select the task settings that you desire and then click your mouse on the OK button.

654 | **USING POWER MANAGEMENT SETTINGS WITH YOUR SCHEDULED TASKS**

Windows 98 provides extensive power-management support that lets it shut down parts of your PC's equipment (such as your monitor) when you are not using your PC. When you schedule tasks for Windows 98 to run at specific times, you can control how Windows 98 runs the task when the system is running on batteries or is currently in a "sleep" mode. Figure 654, for example, shows a scheduled task's Settings sheet. If you examine the sheet's Power Management section, you will find that Windows 98 provides you with checkboxes you can use to prevent the program from running if your PC is running off of a battery and even to prevent the program from starting if the PC is in its battery mode. Likewise, if you select the Wake the computer to run this task checkbox, you direct Windows 98 to bring the PC out of its sleep mode to run your task. By waking the PC in this way, you can schedule tasks to run at specific times and take full advantage of the Windows 98 power-management capabilities.

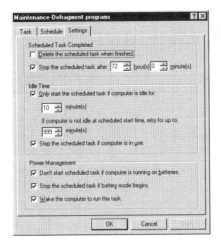

Figure 654 A scheduled task's Settings sheet.

655 **REMOVING A SCHEDULED TASK FROM THE SCHEDULED TASK LIST**

In Tip 651, you learned how to schedule Windows 98 to run a task at a specific time. Over time, you may find that you no longer need or want Windows 98 to run a specific program. To remove the program from the list of Scheduled Tasks, perform these steps:

1. Click your mouse on the Start menu Programs options and choose Accessories. Windows 98 will display the Accessories submenu.

2. Within the Accessories submenu, click your mouse on the System Tools option and choose Scheduled Tasks. Windows 98 will display the Scheduled Tasks folder.

3. Within the Scheduled Tasks folder, right-click your mouse on the icon that corresponds to the program whose settings you want to change. Windows 98 will display a pop-up menu.

4. Within the pop-up menu, click your mouse on the Delete option. Windows 98 will display the Confirm File Delete dialog box, asking you to verify that you want to delete the item.

5. Within the Confirm File Delete dialog box, click your mouse on the Yes button.

656 **USING THE TASK SCHEDULER'S LOG FILE TO MONITOR SCHEDULED TASKS**

In Tip 651, you learned how to use the Scheduled Tasks folder to schedule tasks for Windows 98 to run at a specific time. When you use Windows 98 to automatically run programs for you, you will often want to verify that Windows 98 indeed ran the program at the time you specified. Fortunately, the Task Scheduler provides a log file, whose contents you can view, as shown in Figure 656.

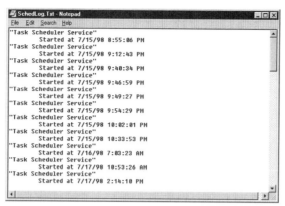

Figure 656 *Viewing the Task Scheduler's log file.*

1. Click your mouse on the Start menu Programs options and choose Accessories. Windows 98 will display the Accessories submenu.

2. Within the Accessories submenu, click your mouse on the System Tools option and choose Scheduled Tasks. Windows 98 will display the Scheduled Tasks folder.

3. Within the Scheduled Tasks folder, click your mouse on the Advanced menu and choose the View Log option. Windows 98, in turn, will open a Notepad window, within which it will display the log file's contents.

657 PERFORMING A TASK SCHEDULER TASK NOW

In Tip 651, you learned how to use the Scheduled Tasks folder to direct Windows 98 to run a program at a specific time. As you view scheduled tasks within the Scheduled Tasks folder, there may be times when you will want Windows 98 to run a specific program now. To run a task from within the Scheduled Task folder, perform these steps:

1. Click your mouse on the Start menu Programs options and choose Accessories. Windows 98 will display the Accessories submenu.

2. Within the Accessories submenu, click your mouse on the System Tools option and choose Scheduled Tasks. Windows 98, in turn, will display the Scheduled Tasks folder.

3. Within the Scheduled Tasks folder, right-click your mouse on the icon that corresponds to the program whose settings you want to change. Windows 98 will display a pop-up menu.

4. Within the pop-up menu, click your mouse on the Run option.

658 CONTROLLING THE WINDOWS 98 TASK SCHEDULER

As you learned in Tip 651, Windows 98 lets you schedule a program to run at a specific time. Each time you schedule a task, Windows 98 will create an entry for the task within the Scheduled Tasks folder. As you learned in Tip 652,

Windows 98 lets you customize each program's time settings. Depending on the operations you are performing, there may be times when you will not want the Task Scheduler to automatically run programs. For example, assume that you are using your PC to perform a large complex task—such as calculating your company's financials. Next, assume that after you start the budget program, it will run for eight hours. In such cases, you usually start the program before you leave for the day. Because the program is so complex, you do not want the Task Scheduler to start other programs which may interfere with the program's processing. Rather than disable tasks individually, you can simply disable the Task Scheduler by performing these steps:

1. Click your mouse on the Start menu Programs options and choose Accessories. Windows 98 will display the Accessories submenu.

2. Within the Accessories submenu, click your mouse on the System Tools option and choose Scheduled Tasks. Windows 98 will display the Scheduled Tasks folder.

3. Within the Scheduled Tasks folder, click your mouse on the Advanced menu Stop Using Task Scheduler option. Later, to resume Task Scheduler operations, click your mouse on the Advanced menu Start Using Task Scheduler option.

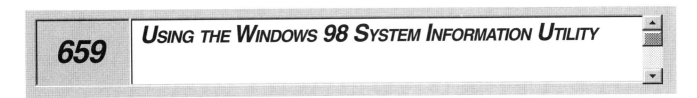

659 USING THE WINDOWS 98 SYSTEM INFORMATION UTILITY

In Tip 390, you learned how to use the Control Panel's System Properties icon to display specifics about your system. In addition to using the System Properties dialog box and its Device Manager sheet to learn about your Windows 98 device-driver and hardware settings, you can use the System Information utility shown in Figure 659.

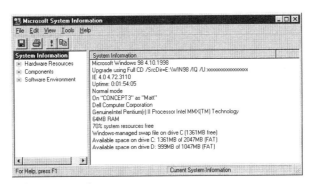

Figure 659 *The Windows 98 System Information utility.*

Within the System Information utility, you can display (and print) information about your system's low-level hardware and software settings. Several of the Tips that follow examine the System Information utility in detail. To run the System Information utility, perform these steps:

1. Click your mouse on the Start menu Programs option and choose Accessories. Windows 98, in turn, will display the Accessories submenu.

2. Within the Accessories submenu, select the System Tools option and then click your mouse on System Information. Windows 98, in turn, will open the System Information window.

660 PRINTING SPECIFICS ABOUT YOUR SYSTEM FROM WITHIN THE SYSTEM INFORMATION UTILITY

In Tip 390, you learned how to use the System Properties dialog box Device Manager sheet to display low-level information about your hardware. As you troubleshoot problems on your system, you can learn more information about your Windows 98, your hardware, device drivers, and even the programs Windows 98 is currently running by using the System Information utility program shown in Figure 660.

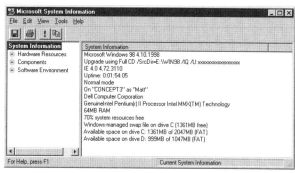

Figure 660 *The System Information utility program.*

Several of the Tips that follow examine the System Information utility program in detail. From within the program's main screen, however, you can view such information as your current version of Windows 98 and Internet Explorer, as well as information about your CPU, RAM, and virtual-memory use.

To start the System Information utility, perform these steps:

1. Click your mouse on the Start menu Programs option and choose Accessories. Windows 98, in turn, will display the Accessories submenu.
2. Within the Accessories submenu, click your mouse on the System Tools option and choose System Information. Windows 98 will display the System Information window.

Within the System Information utility, you can click your mouse on the plus sign (+) and minus sign (-) that precede an entry's name to expand or collapse the entry's list. To print the System Information utility's system information, click your mouse on the Printer icon or select the File menu Print option.

661 VIEWING SHARED RESOURCES AND DEVICE CONFLICTS WITHIN THE SYSTEM INFORMATION UTILITY

In previous Tips, you learned how to display device conflicts within the System Properties dialog box Device Manager sheet. In addition to using the Device Manager to identify device conflicts, you can also use the System Information utility, as shown in Figure 661, to identify conflicts or potential conflicts (due to devices that are sharing the same IRQ or memory settings).

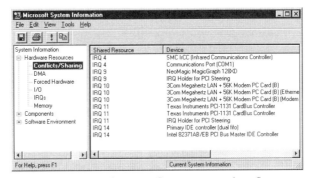

Figure 661 *Using the System Information utility to view device conflicts or potential conflicts.*

To view device conflicts or potential conflicts using the System Information utility, perform these steps:

1. Click your mouse on the Start menu Programs option and choose Accessories. Windows 98, in turn, will display the Accessories submenu.

2. Within the Accessories submenu, click your mouse on the System Tools option and choose System Information. Windows 98 will display the System Information window.

3. Within the System Information window's entry list, click your mouse on the plus sign that precedes the Hardware Resources entry (to expand the entry). The System Information utility will expand its Hardware Resources list.

4. Within the System Hardware Resources utility's component list, click your mouse on the Conflicts/Sharing entry. The System Information utility, in turn, will display your existing or potential device conflicts.

662 VIEWING YOUR SYSTEM'S DIRECT-MEMORY ACCESS (DMA) DEVICES

In computer systems that existed many years ago, the only way a device could transfer information into your computer's random-access memory (RAM) was for the device to send the information to the CPU, which in turn, transferred the information into RAM. Assume, for example, your program read 4,096 bytes of information from a file. Your disk drive would read the information and then transfer the information to the CPU which, would then transfer the information into RAM. Because your CPU was busy transferring information from the drive into RAM, it was not running other programs—which slowed down your system performance.

As a solution, computer designers created direct-memory access (DMA) chips that a device, such as a disk drive, could use to transfer information into RAM without having to bother the CPU. When you install a device that uses DMA into your system, you must specify the channels that the device can use to transfer its data. Using the System Information utility, you can view your system's current DMA settings, as shown in Figure 662.

To display your system's direct-memory access settings, perform these steps:

1. Click your mouse on the Start menu Programs option and choose Accessories. Windows 98, in turn, will display the Accessories submenu.

2. Within the Accessories submenu, click your mouse on the System Tools option and choose System Information. Windows 98 will display the System Information window.

3. Within the System Information window's entry list, click your mouse on the plus sign that precedes the Hardware Resources entry (to expand the entry). The System Information utility will expand its Hardware Resources list.

4. Within the System Information utility's Hardware Resources list, click your mouse on the DMA entry. The System Information utility, in turn, will display your system's direct-memory access settings.

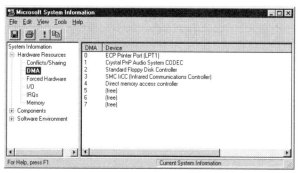

Figure 662 *Using the System Information utility to view your system's DMA settings.*

663 VIEWING YOUR SYSTEM'S UP TIME

As a general rule, to maximize your system performance, you should restart Windows 98 once a day—such as first thing in the morning. By restarting Windows 98, you may correct problems (such as lost memory or resources) caused by one of your application programs that fails to exit correctly or a program that has crashed. When you help troubleshoot someone else's system, you may want to know the last time they restarted their system. Using the System Information utility, you can view the system's up time, as shown in Figure 663.

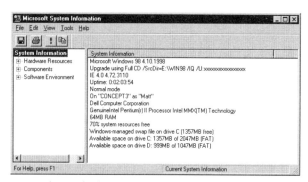

Figure 663 *Using the System Information utility to display a system's up time.*

To display a system's up time using the System Information utility, perform these steps:

1. Click your mouse on the Start menu Programs option and choose Accessories. Windows 98, in turn, will display the Accessories submenu.

2. Within the Accessories submenu, click your mouse on the System Tools option and choose System Information. Windows 98 will display the System Information window.

3. Within the System Information window's entry list, click your mouse on the System Information entry. The System Information utility, in turn, will display its system-overview information that contains your system's up time.

To interact with a hardware device, the CPU will sometime place values within specific memory addresses (or retrieve values from the addresses) that the device reserves for such low-level input/output operations. Depending on the documentation that you read, you may find these memory addresses are called *ports*. In either case, just as your hardware devices require unique interrupt-request settings (Tip 665 discusses interrupt requests), your devices may require unique memory I/O memory addresses.

Usually, when you install a new plug-and-play device, your new device will communicate with your existing devices to determine the I/O memory-address settings it should use. However, should you encounter a conflict, you may need to change settings on your new card (which you can usually do using the software that accompanied your card or the Windows 98 Device Manager). Fortunately, using the System Information utility program, as shown in Figure 664, you can view your system's current I/O memory use.

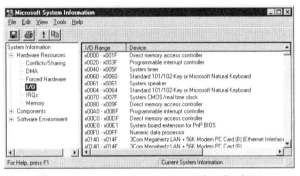

Figure 664 *Using the System Information utility program to view your system's low-level I/O memory use.*

To display your system's I/O memory-address settings within the System Information utility, perform these steps:

1. Click your mouse on the Start menu Programs option and choose Accessories. Windows 98, in turn, will display the Accessories submenu.

2. Within the Accessories submenu, click your mouse on the System Tools option and choose System Information. Windows 98 will display the System Information window.

3. Within the System Information window's entry list, click your mouse on the plus sign that precedes the Hardware Resources entry (to expand the entry). The System Information utility will expand its Hardware Resources list.

4. Within the System Information utility's Hardware Resources list, click your mouse on the I/O entry. The System Information utility, in turn, will display your system's I/O memory-settings.

665	**VIEWING YOUR SYSTEM'S CURRENT INTERRUPT REQUEST (IRQ) SETTINGS**

Within your system, devices such as your mouse or keyboard communicate with the central processing unit (CPU) by interrupting the CPU's current operation and telling the CPU that they need to perform a specific operation. For example, each time you move your mouse, your mouse interrupts the CPU and tells it how much it was moved. The CPU, in turn, runs software specific to the mouse (the mouse's device-driver software), which directs Windows 98 to move the mouse pointer across your screen.

When a device interrupts the CPU in this way, the CPU needs a way to know which software to run. Otherwise, you might move your mouse and the CPU could run your keyboard's software. To tell the CPU which device is interrupting it, your system assigns an interrupt-request line (a wire that connects to the CPU) to each device. If the CPU receives a signal from interrupt-request line number 7, for example, the CPU runs your printer software.

To install a new hardware device in the past (before plug-and-play hardware), users had to determine which IRQ lines their existing devices were using and then use jumpers or switches on their new hardware cards to select an unused IRQ setting. Today, plug-and-play devices resolve such issues themselves, behind the scenes. However, if you encounter a conflict (your modem may hang up each time you move your mouse, for example), you may need to change a device's IRQ setting. Fortunately, using the System Information utility, you can view your system's IRQ settings, as shown in Figure 665.

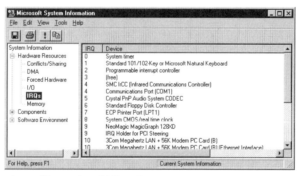

Figure 665 *Using the System Information utility to view IRQ settings.*

To display IRQ settings within the System Information utility, perform these steps:

1. Click your mouse on the Start menu Programs option and choose Accessories. Windows 98, in turn, will display the Accessories submenu.

2. Within the Accessories submenu, click your mouse on the System Tools option and choose System Information. Windows 98 will display the System Information window.

3. Within the System Information window's entry list, click your mouse on the plus sign that precedes the Hardware Resources entry (to expand the entry). The System Information utility will expand its Hardware Resources list.

4. Within the System Information utility's Hardware Resources list, click your mouse on the IRQs entry. The System Information utility, in turn, will display your system's IRQ settings.

666   VIEWING YOUR SYSTEM'S RESERVED MEMORY REGIONS

As you have learned, using the System Information utility, you can display specifics about your hardware devices. Usually, outside of DMA memory discussed in Tip 662, your hardware devices will not reserve specific locations within your computer's random-access memory (the I/O memory locations that Tip 664 discusses do not reside in RAM).

To improve your system's video performance, however, your video card will reserve a section of your computer's random-access memory within which Windows 98 stores the color values for each pixel on your screen display. Using the System Information utility, as shown in Figure 666, you can view the memory region your video card reserves as well as memory reserved by other devices.

If a device's documentation specifies that the device must use a specific region of RAM, you may need to reserve that memory region using the System Properties dialog box Device Manager sheet.

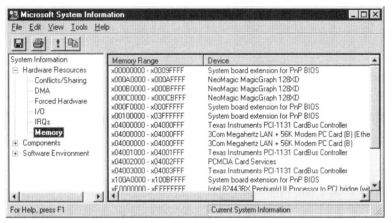

Figure 666 *Using the System Information utility to display your system's reserved memory settings.*

To display your system's reserved memory using the System Information utility, perform these steps:

1. Click your mouse on the Start menu Programs option and choose Accessories. Windows 98, in turn, will display the Accessories submenu.

2. Within the Accessories submenu, click your mouse on the System Tools option and choose System Information. Windows 98 will display the System Information window.

3. Within the System Information window's entry list, click your mouse on the plus sign that precedes the Hardware Resources entry (to expand the entry). The System Information utility will expand its Hardware Resources list.

4. Within the System Information utility's Hardware Resources list, click your mouse on the Memory entry. The System Information utility, in turn, will display your system's reserved-memory settings.

---

667 | **VIEWING INFORMATION ABOUT SPECIFIC HARDWARE DEVICES WITHIN THE SYSTEM INFORMATION UTILITY**

In Tip 390, you learned how to display specifics about your hardware using the System Properties dialog box Device Manager sheet. In addition to using the Device Manger to view specifics about your hardware settings, you can also use the System Information utility.

Within the System Information utility, you can display a device's interrupt-request (IRQ) settings, its direct-memory access (DMA) settings, its Registry key (which you can use within the Registry Editor to view additional settings), its memory buffers, its device-driver software, and much more. For example, Figure 667 shows settings for the current monitor within the System Information utility.

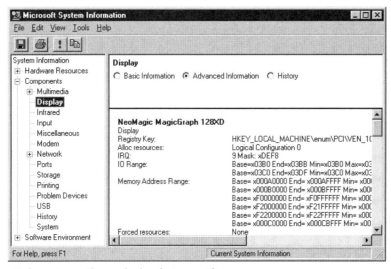

Figure 667 *Using the System Information utility to display device specifics.*

To display specifics about your hardware devices within the System Information utility, perform these steps:

1. Click your mouse on the Start menu Programs option and choose Accessories. Windows 98, in turn, will display the Accessories submenu.

2. Within the Accessories submenu, click your mouse on the System Tools option and choose System Information. Windows 98 will display the System Information window.

3. Within the System Information window's entry list, click your mouse on the plus sign that precedes the Components entry (to expand the entry). The System Information utility, in turn, will expand its Components list.

4. Within the System Information utility's component list, click your mouse on the hardware device you desire. The System Information utility, in turn, will display the device's hardware settings.

668 | VIEWING SPECIFICS ABOUT YOUR SYSTEM'S DEVICE DRIVERS

Before your programs, and even Windows 98 for that matter, can access your hardware devices, you must install device-driver software that the programs will use to interact with the device. Depending on the hardware connected to your system, the device drivers your system uses will differ. Using the System Information utility, you can view your system device drivers, as shown in Figure 668.

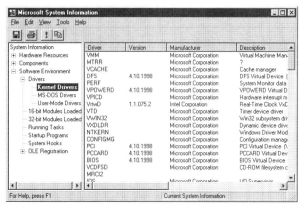

Figure 668 *Viewing your system device drivers within the System Information utility.*

Within the System Information utility, you will find that most of your device drivers are kernel-mode drivers, which means Windows 98 uses these drivers in its special kernel mode (which uses the operating system's lowest-level code that interacts with the hardware directly). When you examined the System Monitor utility in Tip 674, you learned that you can monitor Windows 98 kernel-mode operations. An example of a kernel-mode operation is when Windows 98 interacts with a device driver.

Within the System Information utility, you will also find a list of the additional device drivers that Windows 98 loads into memory when you open an MS-DOS window, as well as a list of user-mode device drivers that usually do not interact directly with the hardware and, thus, do not require Windows 98 kernel mode.

To display your system's device drivers, perform these steps:

1. Click your mouse on the Start menu Programs option and choose Accessories. Windows 98, in turn, will display the Accessories submenu.

2. Within the Accessories submenu, click your mouse on the System Tools option and choose System Information. Windows 98 will display the System Information window.

3. Within the System Information window's entry list, click your mouse on the plus sign that precedes the Software Environment entry (to expand the entry). Then, click your mouse on the plus sign that precedes the Drivers entry. The System Information utility will expand its Drivers list.

4. To view kernel-mode device drivers, click your mouse on the Kernel Drivers entry.

5. To view MS-DOS device drivers, click your mouse on the MS-DOS Drivers entry.

6. To view user-mode device drivers, click your mouse on the User-Mode Drivers entry.

669	IDENTIFYING YOUR SYSTEM'S 16-BIT AND 32-BIT SOFTWARE

In Tip 339, you learned that to improve your system performance, you want Windows 98 to use a 32-bit device driver (as opposed to a 16-bit driver) whenever possible. Just as your older device drivers may use 16-bit software, the same is true for your older programs. When you upgrade your software, such as your word processor, to a new version, the software should take advantage of 32-bit modules. Using the System Information utility, you can display a list of the 16-bit software modules and a list of the 32-bit modules that your system is currently using, as shown in Figure 669. By examining the software list, you may be able to identify programs for which you should determine if a newer 32-bit version is available.

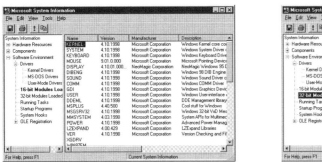 

Figure 669 Using the System Information utility program to display a list of 16-bit and 32-bit software modules.

To view your system's 16-bit and 32-bit software modules, perform these steps:

1. Click your mouse on the Start menu Programs option and choose Accessories. Windows 98, in turn, will display the Accessories submenu.

2. Within the Accessories submenu, click your mouse on the System Tools option and choose System Information. Windows 98, in turn, will display the System Information window.

3. Within the System Information window's entry list, click your mouse on the plus sign that precedes the Software Environment entry (to expand the entry).

4. To display your system's 16-bit drivers, click your mouse on the 16-bit Modules Loaded entry.

5. To display your system's 32-bit drivers, click your mouse on the 32-bit Modules Loaded entry.

670	VIEWING THE PROGRAMS YOUR SYSTEM IS CURRENTLY RUNNING

As you know, Windows 98 usually runs your programs within a window on your screen. Using the Taskbar, you can quickly switch between programs. If you feel that your system is performing slowly, you can use the System Information program's Running Tasks entry to display the foreground and background programs that Windows 98 is currently running, as shown in Figure 670.

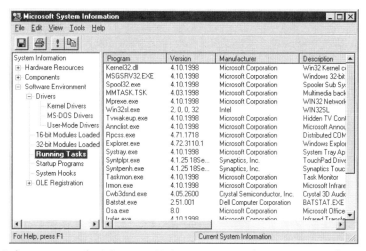

Figure 670 *Using the System Information window's Running Tasks entry to view the programs Windows 98 is currently running.*

If your system is performing slowly, it may be because one of the Windows 98 background tasks is consuming too much processor time or too much memory. By examining the Description field within the System Information program's window, you may be able to determine the function each program performs and decide if you even need to use the program. If you do not need the program, you can use the System Information program, as Tip 671 discusses, to determine the location from which Windows 98 starts the program and then disable the program's use.

To view the programs that Windows 98 is currently running, perform these steps:

1. Click your mouse on the Start menu Programs option and choose Accessories. Windows 98, in turn, will display the Accessories submenu.

2. Within the Accessories submenu, click your mouse on the System Tools option and choose System Information. Windows 98 will display the System Information window.

3. Within the System Information window's entry list, click your mouse on the plus sign that precedes the Software Environment entry (to expand the entry) and then click your mouse on the Running Tasks entry. The System Information program, in turn, will display the names of the foreground and background tasks that Windows 98 is currently running.

---

671 IDENTIFYING FROM WHERE WINDOWS 98 IS LOADING A SPECIFIC PROGRAM

As you have learned, by placing a program shortcut within the Windows 98 Startup folder, you direct Windows 98 to automatically run the corresponding program each time your system starts. Depending on your system configuration, Windows 98 may also start other programs from either the *Registry* database or the *System.INI* file. Using the System Information program's Software Environment folder, you can view the programs your system automatically starts, as shown in Figure 671.

After you determine the location from which Windows 98 is starting a specific program, you can later remove the program's corresponding entry from that location should you want to disable the program's automatic startup.

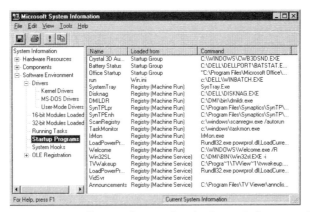

Figure 671 *Viewing programs your system automatically starts from within the System Information Software Environment entry.*

To view the locations from which Windows 98 is automatically starting programs each time your system starts, perform these steps:

1. Click your mouse on the Start menu Programs option and choose Accessories. Windows 98, in turn, will display the Accessories submenu.

2. Within the Accessories submenu, click your mouse on the System Tools option and choose System Information. Windows 98 will display the System Information window.

3. Within the System Information window's entry list, click your mouse on the plus sign that precedes the Software Environment entry (to expand the entry) and then click your mouse on the Startup Programs entry. The System Information program, in turn, will display each of the programs Windows 98 automatically runs each time your system starts.

672 UNDERSTANDING AND VIEWING SYSTEM HOOKS

Assume that you are a programmer who is tasked with writing a program that faxes a user's screen contents to a company's main office each time the user presses the PRTSC key. Your problem is that because Windows 98 is a multitasking operating system, the user may have many different programs running at any time which means your program simply can't enter a loop that waits for the user to press the PrtSc key.

As you have learned, by default, when the user presses the PRTSC key, Windows 98 copies the current screen contents to the Clipboard. To perform its processing, Windows 98 generates an *event* when the user presses the PRTSC key for which Windows 98 has defined software that *handles* the event by copying the current screen contents to the Clipboard. Knowing this, you can write a program that "hooks" the Windows 98 event, lets your program fax the screen contents to the home office, and then passes the event along to Windows 98 which in turn, will copy the screen contents to the Clipboard.

Depending on operations that programs must perform, it is not uncommon for programs to hook Windows 98 events in this way. Unfortunately, if the program does not handle the event correctly or pass the event along to Windows 98, you may experience system errors. Fortunately, using the System Information utility program, you can view your system's current software hooks, as shown in Figure 672. By viewing the software hooks, you may be able to identify the software that is causing the problem.

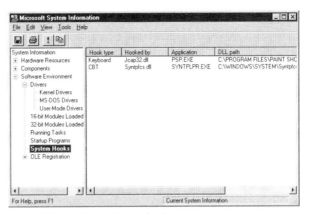

Figure 672 *Using the System Information utility to view software hooks.*

To view software hooks within the System Information utility, perform these steps:

1. Click your mouse on the Start menu Programs option and choose Accessories. Windows 98, in turn, will display the Accessories submenu.

2. Within the Accessories submenu, click your mouse on the System Tools option and choose System Information. Windows 98, in turn, will display the System Information window.

3. Within the System Information window's entry list, click your mouse on the plus sign that precedes the Software Environment entry (to expand the entry) and then click your mouse on the System Hooks entry.

673 IDENTIFYING THE SOURCE OF AN OLE REGISTRATION

Previous Tips introduced object linking and embedding (OLE) which lets you place an object, such as an Excel spreadsheet or Paint graphic, within a document. Later, if you double-click your mouse on the object within the document, Windows 98 will start the corresponding program, in this case, Excel or Paint, loading the object within the program. When you double-click your mouse on an object in this way, Windows 98 knows which program to run by examining the object's file extension. You can associate a program with a document extension using the Explorer's Add Program dialog box. When you associate a program with a file extension in this way, Windows 98 stores the association within its Registry database. Usually, using the Explorer, you can change a document's program association. However, if you find that your change is having no effect, the problem may be that the *System.INI* file (that resides within your *Windows* folder) is overriding your settings.

Fortunately, as shown in Figure 673, using the System Information utility, you can determine the source of a document's OLE registration (which will be either the Registry or the *System.INI* file).

To view the source of an OLE registration within the System Information utility, perform these steps:

1. Click your mouse on the Start menu Programs option and choose Accessories. Windows 98, in turn, will display the Accessories submenu.

2. Within the Accessories submenu, click your mouse on the System Tools option and choose System Information. Windows 98 will display the System Information window.

3. Within the System Information window's entry list, click your mouse on the plus sign that precedes the OLE Registration entry (to expand the entry).

4. To view the OLE registration entries the *System.INI* file assigns, click your mouse on the INI File entry.

5. To view the OLE registration entries the Registry assigns, click your mouse on the Registry entry.

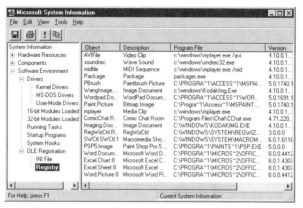

Figure 673 Using the System Information utility to display the source of an OLE registration.

674 USING THE SYSTEM MONITOR TO LOCATE SYSTEM BOTTLENECKS

As quickly as PC makers release faster high-performance PCs, users seem to find new ways to consume the system's computing power. To help you get the most from your system, Windows 98 includes the System Monitor utility which you can run to monitor your system's disk, memory, and network operations. When you use the System Monitor, you can select various graphs that help view your system use. Figure 674, for example, shows System Monitor graphs for a variety of events.

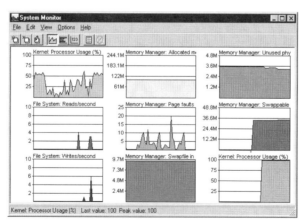

Figure 674 Using the System Monitor to chart system performance.

In general, the System Monitor is not a tool for fine-tuning a system that currently runs well. Instead, you should use System Monitor to locate your system bottlenecks. After you run System Monitor a few times, you will begin to better understand your system's normal performance, which will make it easier for you to identify bottlenecks as they occur.

To run the System Monitor, perform these steps:

1. Click your mouse on the Start menu Programs option and choose Accessories. Windows 98, in turn, will display the Accessories submenu.

2. Within the Accessories submenu, click your mouse on the System Tools option and choose System Monitor. Windows 98 will open the System Monitor window.

Note: *If the System Monitor does not appear within the System Tools menu, perform the steps Tip 218 describes to add the System Monitor from the Windows 98 CD-ROM.*

675	SAVE KEYSTROKES AND MOUSE CLICKS USING THE SYSTEM MONITOR TOOLBAR

Like most Windows-based programs, the System Monitor provides a toolbar whose icons you can use to simplify most operations. If the toolbar is not currently in view, select the View menu Toolbar option. Figure 675 briefly explains each of the System Monitor toolbar buttons.

Adds a system resource for monitoring

Removes a system resource from monitoring

Edits a system resource's monitoring display

Displays line charts

Displays bar charts

Displays numeric charts

Enables logging

Stops logging

Figure 675 System Monitor's toolbar buttons.

676 USING THE SYSTEM MONITOR TO CHART A DIAL-UP ADAPTER OPERATIONS

If you are using a dial-up adapter (a modem) to connect to the Internet or to some other remote computer, you can use the System Monitor to track a variety of items, ranging from the number of bytes you send or receive to the number or type of serial-port errors. To track dial-up adapter operations within the System Monitor, perform these steps:

1. Start the System Monitor as discussed in Tip 675.

2. Within the System Monitor window, click your mouse on the Edit menu Add Item option. The System Monitor, in turn, will display the Add Item dialog box.

3. Within the Add Item dialog box Category list, click your mouse on the Dial-Up Adapter option. The System Monitor, in turn will display a list of dial-up adapter items you can monitor within the Add Item dialog box as shown in Figure 676.

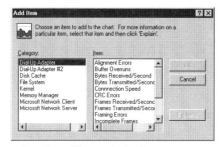

Figure 676 *Displaying dial-up adapter items within the Add Item dialog box.*

4. Within the Category list, hold down the CTRL key and click your mouse on each item you want to monitor and then click your mouse on the OK button. The System Monitor, in turn, will change its charts to show your newly selected items.

Table 676 briefly describes the information the System Monitor will display for each of the dial-up adapter entries. By monitoring various dial-up adapter operations, you may be able to troubleshoot different modem operations or you may find that you need to adjust your data communication settings.

Item	Purpose
Alignment Errors	The number serial port byte alignment errors
Buffer Overruns	The number of times the serial port buffer is overrun by incoming or outgoing data (may be an indication that you must slow down your baud rate for the current connection)
Bytes Received/Second	The number of bytes/second the adapter is receiving
Bytes Transmitted/Second	The number of bytes/second the adapter is sending
Connection Speed	The current adapter connection speed in bits/second
CRC Errors	The number of cyclic redundancy errors (may indicate a poor connection)
Frames Received/Second	The number of data frames/second the adapter is receiving
Frames Transmitted/Second	The number of data frames/second the adapter is sending

Framing Errors	The number of bad frames the adapter is receiving (an indication of a poor connection)
Incomplete Frames	The number of incomplete frames the adapter is receiving (an indication of a poor connection)
Overrun Errors	The number of serial port overrun errors (an indication that you must lower the baud rate for the current connection)
Timeout Errors	The number of timeout errors the adapter is experiencing while waiting for data (an indication of a port connection or a possible remote-modem problem)
Total Bytes Received	A count of the total number of bytes the adapter has received since monitoring was enabled
Total Bytes Transmitted	A count of the total number of bytes the adapter has sent since monitoring was enabled

Table 676 Information the System Monitor displays for the dial-up adapter items.

677 USING THE SYSTEM MONITOR TO CHART WINDOWS 98 DISK-CACHE OPERATIONS

Previous Tips discussed disk-cache operations in detail. Using the System Monitor, you can track various disk-cache settings. You might, for example, monitor your system performance and then use the Control Panel System option to change your current disk-cache settings. Then, using the System Monitor a second time, you can determine the impact of your changes on your system performance. To monitor Windows 98 disk-cache operations within the System Monitor, perform these steps:

1. Start the System Monitor as discussed in Tip 675.

2. Within the System Monitor window, click your mouse on the Edit menu Add Item option. The System Monitor, in turn, will display the Add Item dialog box.

3. Within the Add Item dialog box Category list, click your mouse on the Disk Cache option. The System Monitor, in turn will display a list of disk-cache items you can monitor within the Add Item dialog box as shown in Figure 677.

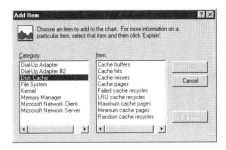

Figure 677 Displaying disk-cache items within the Add Item dialog box.

4. Within the Category list, hold down the CTRL key and click your mouse on each item you want to monitor and then click your mouse on the OK button. The System Monitor, in turn, will change its charts to show your newly selected items.

Table 677 briefly describes the information the System Monitor will display for each of the disk-cache entries.

Item	Purpose
Cache buffers	The number of active buffers within the disk cache
Cache hits	The number of times Windows 98 found data in the disk cache (which eliminated a slow disk operation)
Cache misses	The number of times Windows 98 did not find data in the disk cache (which required Windows 98 to then perform a disk I/O operation)
Cache pages	The number of pages within the disk cache
Failed cache recycles	The number of times Windows 98 could not recycle cache pages, most likely due to insufficient memory
LRU cache recycles	The number of times Windows 98 has recycled the least recently used cache buffer to hold new information
Maximum cache pages	The maximum size, in pages, to which Windows 98 can grow the disk cache
Minimum cache pages	The minimum size, in pages, to which Windows 98 can grow the disk cache
Random cache recycles	The number of times Windows 98 has randomly selected a cache buffer for recycling

Table 677 Information the System Monitor displays for the disk-cache items.

---

678   USING THE SYSTEM MONITOR TO CHART WINDOWS 98 FILE-SYSTEM OPERATIONS

The Windows 98 file system is the software that Windows 98 uses to store and later retrieve information from within files and folders on your disk. Because disks are mechanical devices (with moving parts), disks are much slower than your computer's electronic CPU or RAM. As a result, one way to improve your system performance is simply to reduce the number of disk input and output operations Windows 98 must perform.

Using System Monitor, you can monitor your system's disk activity to identify potential bottlenecks. If, for example, you find that your system continually reads and writes data from or to your disk, you may improve your system performance by upgrading to a faster disk drive. Likewise, if the System Monitor reveals that your system performs minimal disk operations, upgrading to a faster disk drive will have little impact on your system performance. To monitor the Windows 98 File System using the System Monitor, perform these steps:

1. Start the System Monitor as discussed in Tip 675.

2. Within the System Monitor window, click your mouse on the Edit menu Add Item option. The System Monitor, in turn, will display the Add Item dialog box.

3. Within the Add Item dialog box Category list, click your mouse on the File System option. The System Monitor, in turn will display a list of file system items you can monitor within the Add Item dialog box as shown in Figure 678.

4. Within the Category list, hold down the CTRL key and click your mouse on each item you want to monitor and then click your mouse on the OK button. The System Monitor, in turn, will change its charts to show your newly selected items.

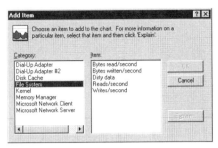

Figure 678 *Displaying file system items within the Add Item dialog box.*

Table 678 briefly describes the information the System Monitor will display for each of the file system entries. Should you find that your system is performing an excessive number of disk input or output operations, run the Windows 98 Tune Up Wizard to fine-tune your disk operations. Also, examine the File System Properties using the Control Panel System icon.

Item	Purpose
Bytes read/second	The number of bytes read per second
Bytes written/second	The number of bytes written per second
Dirty data	The amount of data, in bytes, still in the system cache that the file system must write back to the disk
Reads/second	The number of read requests the file system receives per second
Writes/second	The number of write requests the file system receives per second

Table 678 *Information the System Monitor displays for the file-system items.*

679 **USING THE SYSTEM MONITOR TO CHART *IPX/SPX* NETWORK OPERATIONS**

If you are using a network with Windows NT, Windows 95, and Novell Netware, your system will use the IPX/SPX (Internet Packet Exchange/Sequenced Packet Exchange) protocols to let the systems communicate. Using the System Monitor, you can track various protocol operations. If, for example, you feel that your network operations are slow, or have slowed down since you added a new device, you can use the System Monitor to measure your network's current performance. To monitor IPX/SPX network operations within the System Monitor, perform these steps:

1. Start the System Monitor as discussed in Tip 675.

2. Within the System Monitor window, click your mouse on the Edit menu Add Item option. The System Monitor, in turn, will display the Add Item dialog box.

3. Within the Add Item dialog box Category list, click your mouse on the IPX/SPX compatible protocol option. The System Monitor, in turn, will display a list of file system items you can monitor within the Add Item dialog box.

4. Within the Category list, hold down the CTRL key and click your mouse on each item you want to monitor and then click your mouse on the OK button. The System Monitor, in turn, will change its charts to show your newly selected items.

Table 679 briefly describes the information the System Monitor will display for each of the IPX/SPX protocol entries.

Item	Purpose
IPX packets lost/second	The number of IPX packets/second that the network discarded because no node on the network claimed the packet.
IPX packets received/second	The number of IPX packets/second the system is receiving.
IPX packets sent/second	The number of IPX packets/second the system is sending
Open sockets	The number of sockets (connections to other programs) the system currently has open.
Routing Table entries	The number of IPX routes (paths to other nodes) the system is currently tracking.
SAP Table entries	The number of service advertisements the system is currently tracking. The IPX/SPX network servers use the Service Advertising Protocol to tell other systems (advertise) the services they offer (such as printing or a specific application).
SPX packets received/second	The number of SPX packets/second the system is receiving.
SPX packets sent/second	The number of SPX packets/second the system is sending.

Table 679 *Information the System Monitor displays for the IPX/SPX protocol items.*

680 **USING THE SYSTEM MONITOR TO CHART WINDOWS 98 KERNEL-MODE OPERATIONS**

In general, an operating system, Windows 98 in this case, exists to let you run programs. Within that role, the operating system oversees your mouse and keyboard operations, the display of information your programs send to the monitor or a printer, and even the program's ability to store and later retrieve information from files on disk. As you might guess, an operating system is a very large, complex program (or collection of programs).

At the heart of the Windows 98 operating system is special software called the *kernel* which handles tasks such as memory management, device input and output, and thread management (A thread is an executable entity—the instructions the CPU executes. Windows-based programs can have a single thread—do one thing at a time—or they may use multiple threads. A word processor that can print as it spell checks your document uses multiple threads—one to print and one to spell check). The kernel also loads the programs you run from disk into memory. Because the kernel performs tasks which are essential to every program you run, it is very important that the kernel operate efficiently. Using the System Monitor, you can monitor kernel activities. If your system operations overtask the kernel, your system will slow down. To monitor kernel activities using the System Monitor, perform these steps:

1. Start the System Monitor as discussed in Tip 675.

2. Within the System Monitor window, click your mouse on the Edit menu Add Item option. The System Monitor, in turn, will display the Add Item dialog box.

3. Within the Add Item dialog box Category list, click your mouse on the Kernel option. The System Monitor, in turn, will display a list of kernel-mode items you can monitor within the Add Item dialog box as shown in Figure 680.

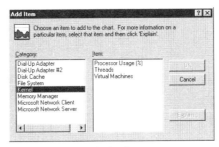

Figure 680 *Displaying kernel-mode items within the Add Item dialog box.*

4. Within the Category list, hold down the CTRL key and click your mouse on each item you want to monitor and then click your mouse on the OK button. The System Monitor, in turn, will change its charts to show your newly selected items.

If you find that your system is spending a lot of time performing kernel-level activities, you may need to add more memory, run fewer programs at one time, or eventually, upgrade to a faster PC.

681 USING THE SYSTEM MONITOR TO CHART WINDOWS 98 MEMORY MANAGEMENT

Within your PC, the two items that influence your system performance the most are your CPU and your random-access memory (RAM). The faster your CPU, the more instructions your PC can execute per second. The more RAM your system contains, the more program instructions your PC can keep in memory, as opposed to keeping the instructions within a swap file on a slower mechanical disk. Using the System Monitor, you can track a wide range of Windows 98 memory-management operations. In general, the only way you can improve the values the System Monitor charts is to add more memory or to run fewer programs at the same time. Fortunately, the cost of memory continues to drop and has now become quite affordable. To monitor Windows 98 memory-management operations within the System Monitor, perform these steps:

1. Start the System Monitor as discussed in Tip 675.

2. Within the System Monitor window, click your mouse on the Edit menu Add Item option. The System Monitor, in turn, will display the Add Item dialog box.

3. Within the Add Item dialog box Category list, click your mouse on the Memory Manager option. The System Monitor, in turn, will display a list of file system items you can monitor within the Add Item dialog box, as shown in Figure 681.

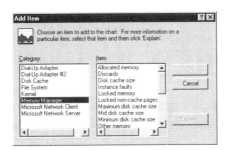

Figure 681 *Displaying memory-management items within the Add Item dialog box.*

4. Within the Category list, hold down the CTRL key and click your mouse on each item you want to monitor and then click your mouse on the OK button. The System Monitor, in turn, will change its charts to show your newly selected items.

Table 681 briefly describes the information the System Monitor will display for each of the file system entries. As you start to add memory to your system, take time to monitor the impact on the Windows 98 memory-management operations. You may find that 32Mb of RAM gives you results which are similar to those you experience when you install 64Mb.

Item	Purpose
Allocated memory	The amount of RAM, in bytes, Windows 98 has currently allocated for its own use as well as for use by other programs.
Discards	The number of virtual-memory pages/second that Windows 98 discards (overwrites or makes available for use).
Disk cache size	The size, in bytes, of the current disk cache.
Instance faults	The number of instance faults per second. An instance fault occurs when a program must access local (or instance) data that resides within a that page contains global (shared) data and local (instance) data.
Locked memory	The amount of memory, in bytes, Windows 98 has locked within physical memory to prevent swapping.
Locked non-cache pages	The amount of memory, in pages, Windows 98 has locked for non-cached memory.
Maximum disk cache size	The maximize size, in bytes, to which Windows 98 can grow the disk cache.
Minimum disk cache size	The minimum size, in bytes, to which Windows 98 can shrink the disk cache.
Other memory	The amount of memory, in bytes, Windows 98 has allocated but is not storing within the swap file, such as the disk cache or memory-mapped file.
Page faults	The number of page faults/second.
Page-ins	The number of times per second Windows 98 must bring a page from disk into memory.
Page-outs	The number of times per second Windows 98 must copy a page's contents from memory to disk.
Pages mapped from cache	The number of pages Windows 98 is mapping directly from the file cache.
Swapfile defective	The number of bytes within the swapfile which are not usable due to a disk error.
Swapfile in use	The number of bytes of swapfile disk space that Windows 98 is currently using.
Swapfile size	The size, in bytes, of the Windows 98 swapfile.
Swappable memory	The number of bytes Windows 98 has allocated from the swapfile.
Unused physical memory	The amount, in bytes, of unused physical RAM.

Table 681 Information the System Monitor displays for the memory-management items.

682	USING THE SYSTEM MONITOR TO CHART MICROSOFT NETWORK OPERATIONS

If your PC is connected to a network that is running Microsoft Network software, you can use the System Monitor to track your system's client or server operations. To monitor Microsoft Network client operations within the System Monitor, perform these steps:

1. Start the System Monitor as discussed in Tip 675.

2. Within the System Monitor window, click your mouse on the Edit menu Add Item option. The System Monitor, in turn, will display the Add Item dialog box.

3. Within the Add Item dialog box Category list, click your mouse on the Microsoft Network Client option. The System Monitor, in turn, will display a list of network system items you can monitor within the Add Item dialog box.

4. Within the Category list, hold down the CTRL key and click your mouse on each item you want to monitor and then click your mouse on the OK button. The System Monitor, in turn, will change its charts to show your newly selected items.

Likewise, to monitor Microsoft Network server operations within the System Monitor, you would simply select the Microsoft Network Server option in Step 3. The System Monitor, in turn, will display a list of server items you can monitor.

Table 682 briefly describes the Microsoft Network items you can monitor using the System Monitor.

Item	Purpose
Buffers	The number of server buffers
Bytes read/second	The number of bytes/second the system is receiving
Bytes/sec	The total, in bytes, of the amount of data the server is reading from or writing to disk
Bytes written/second	The number of bytes/second the system is sending
Memory	The amount of memory, in bytes, the server is using for network operations
NBs	The number of server network buffers
Number of nets	The number of nets the system is currently running
Open files	The number of files the system currently has open on the network
Server Threads	The number of Windows threads the server is using to perform network operations
Sessions	The number of network sessions the system currently has open
Transactions/second	The number of SMB transactions the system is performing per second

Table 682 Information the System Monitor displays for Microsoft Network client and server items.

683 **DIRECTING THE SYSTEM MONITOR TO NO LONGER TRACK AN ITEM**

In several of the previous Tips, you learned how to direct the System Monitor to track specific items. As your requirements change, there will be times when you will no longer want to track a specific item. To direct the System Monitor to stop tracking a specific item, perform these steps:

1. Within the System Monitor, click your mouse on the Edit menu Remove Item option. The System Monitor, in turn, will display the Remove Item dialog box, as shown in Figure 683.

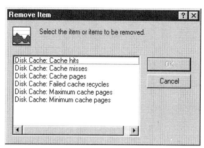

Figure 683 The System Monitor Remove Item dialog box.

2. Within the Remove Item dialog box, click your mouse on the item that you no longer want to track and then click your mouse on the OK button.

684 **DISPLAYING SYSTEM MONITOR GRAPHS USING BAR, LINE, AND NUMERIC CHARTS**

Depending on the information you are displaying within the System Monitor, there may be times when you will want to customize the System Monitor's chart type. For example, Figure 684 shows three System Monitor charts, one using a bar chart, one using a line chart, and one using numeric data. To select a specific chart type, click your mouse on the System Monitor View menu and then choose the chart type you desire.

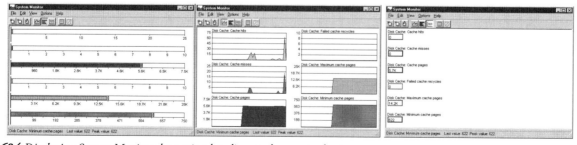

Figure 684 Displaying System Monitor data using bar, line, and numeric charts.

685 CUSTOMIZING A SYSTEM MONITOR CHART

In Tip 684, you learned how to display information within the System Monitor using bar, line, and numeric charts. Depending on your needs and preferences, there may be times when you must customize a specific chart by changing an item's color or scale. To customize the chart for a specific System Monitor item, perform these steps:

1. Within the System Monitor, click your mouse on the Edit menu Edit Item option. The System Monitor, in turn, will display the Edit Item dialog box, as shown in Figure 685.1.

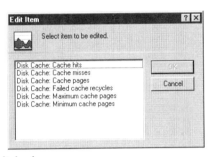

Figure 685.1 *The System Monitor Edit Item dialog box.*

2. Within the Edit Item dialog box, click your mouse on the item for which you want to customize the chart and then click your mouse on the OK button. The System Monitor, in turn, will display the Chart Options dialog box, as shown in Figure 685.2.

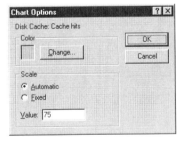

Figure 685.2 *The System Monitor Chart Options dialog box.*

3. Within the System Monitor Chart Options dialog box, select the Color and Scale value that you desire and then click your mouse on the OK button to put your changes into effect.

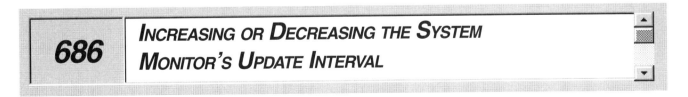

686 INCREASING OR DECREASING THE SYSTEM MONITOR'S UPDATE INTERVAL

Unless you tell the System Monitor to do otherwise, the System Monitor will measure system information every five seconds. Depending on the items you are trying to chart, you may want the System Monitor to record information more or less often. Keep in mind, however, that if you direct the System Monitor to record information at a faster interval, say every one second, the System Monitor's own processing may begin to skew your data (Windows 98, for instance, might spend more time in kernel mode because it is performing System Monitor operations). To increase or decrease the System Monitor update interval, perform these steps:

1. Within the System Monitor, click your mouse on the Options menu Chart option. The System Monitor, in turn, will display the Options dialog box, as shown in Figure 686.

Figure 686 The System Monitor Options dialog box.

2. Within the Options dialog box, use your mouse to drag the Update interval slider to the left or to the right to increase or reduce the update interval.

3. Within the Options dialog box, click your mouse on the OK button.

687 USING THE SYSTEM MONITOR TO OBSERVE A REMOTE COMPUTER

If you are a network administrator, you can use the System Monitor to monitor another computer's operations. (The remote computer must allow remote administration.) To monitor a remote computer, perform these steps:

1. Within the System Monitor, select the File menu Connect option. The System Monitor, in turn, will display the Connect dialog box, as shown in Figure 687.

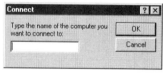

Figure 687 The System Monitor Connect dialog box.

2. Within the Connect dialog box, type in the name of the remote computer to which you want to connect and then click your mouse on the OK button. The System Monitor, in turn, will chart and display the remote computer's operations.

688 LOGGING SYSTEM MONITOR DATA TO A FILE

In addition to charting system information, the System Monitor also lets you record information to a file which you can later preview or manipulate yourself using a spreadsheet, such as Excel. When you direct the System Monitor to log information to a file, the System Monitor will log the items you have currently selected for charting. To record System Monitor information to a file, perform these steps:

1. Within the System Monitor, select the File menu Start Logging option. The System Monitor, in turn, will display the Save As dialog box.

2. Within the Save As dialog box, specify the folder and filename within which you want the System Monitor to log its data, and then click your mouse on the OK button.

3. After you have recorded the information you desire, click your mouse on the System Monitor File menu Stop Logging option. You can now use the WordPad accessory program to view the System Monitor log file.

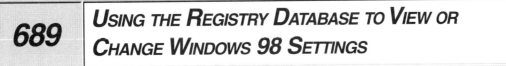

689 USING THE REGISTRY DATABASE TO VIEW OR CHANGE WINDOWS 98 SETTINGS

Throughout this book's Tips, you have performed operations that configure various Windows 98 settings. For example, using the Control Panel, you customized your screen, printer, mouse, keyboard, modem settings, and more. When you configure your programs or hardware properties, Windows 98 stores your settings within a special database file called the Registry. Each time your system starts, Windows 98 uses the Registry's contents to configure your system. If you are familiar with Windows 3.1, you can think of the Registry as similar to the *System.INI* and *Win.INI* initialization files.

Usually, most users will never directly change the Registry's contents. Instead, users will use the Control Panel or program dialog boxes to change hardware or software settings. Behind the scenes, Windows 98 will update the Registry's corresponding entries. If you are a system administrator or "power user," you can learn a considerable amount about Windows 98, your hardware, and your programs by examining entries within the Registry database. Several of the Tips that follow examine a special program, the Registry Editor, that you can use to view or change Registry entries. To start the Registry Editor, perform these steps:

1. Click your mouse on the Start menu Run option. Windows 98, in turn, will display the Run dialog box.

2. Within the Run dialog box, type in the command **RegEdit** and press ENTER. Windows 98, in turn, will open the Registry Editor window, as shown in Figure 689.

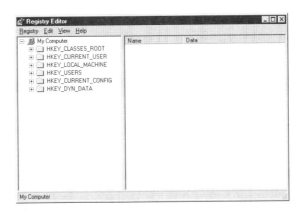

Figure 689 *The Windows 98 Registry Editor.*

---

690 **TO BE COMPATIBLE WITH EARLIER VERSIONS, WINDOWS 98 STILL SUPPORTS .INI FILES**

As you learned in Tip 689, Windows 98 stores your system settings within a special database called the Registry. Each time your system starts, Windows 98 reads the Registry's contents and uses its settings to customize your system. If you are familiar with Windows 3.1 or Windows for Workgroups, you know that those systems stored their system settings within files with the *.INI* extension, such as *System.INI* and *Win.INI*.

Although Windows 98 stores its hardware and software settings within the Registry, Windows 98 still supports *.INI* files, which lets Windows 98 support your older programs. If, when you start your system, Windows 98 displays an error message about a "device not found," the problem may be due to a conflict between your Registry settings and those within the *System.INI* file. Likewise, if you find that a change you make to your Desktop (such as a new color scheme or background image) has no effect, the problem may be a conflict between your Registry and the *Win.INI* file.

So, although Windows 98 supports *.INI* files and thus many of your older software programs, there may be times when you must resolve conflicts between the Registry entries and those Windows 98 finds within the older *.INI* files. In later Tips, you will learn how to edit the *.INI* files using the System Configuration Editor.

---

691 **WINDOWS 98 USES THE REGISTRY'S CONTENTS EACH TIME YOUR SYSTEM STARTS**

Several of the Tips that follow examine values that Windows 98 stores within the Registry database. Each time your system starts, Windows 98 first reads the Registry's contents and assigns the settings the Registry contains. Next, Windows 98 examines the *System.INI* file and uses its contents to further configure older system settings. After that, Windows 98 loads the kernel (*Kernel32.dll*), its graphical user interface (*Gdi.Exe* and *Gdi32.dll*), its user interface software (*User.Exe* and *User32.EXE*), its resources, such as fonts, and, finally, Windows 98 reads and loads the *Win.INI* file's contents.

Next, Windows 98 will load the shell and Desktop components displaying the Welcome to Windows 98 login prompt. After the user logs in, Windows 98 again uses the Registry to determine the user-specific settings.

---

692 **USING THE SYSTEM CONFIGURATION EDITOR TO EDIT KEY .INI FILE SETTINGS**

In Tip 691, you learned that each time Windows 98 starts, it reads the contents of the *System.INI* and *Win.INI* files, using each file's contents to configure your system settings. If you find that a change you make to a system setting appears to have no effect, the problem may be due to a setting within one of these *.INI* files that is overriding your Registry settings. In such cases, you should edit the *.INI* files and look for a conflict. To edit the *.INI* files (which reside within the *Windows* folder), you can use the Notepad accessory. In addition, you can use the System Configuration Editor which, as shown in Figure 692, will open several key *.INI* files and the *CONFIG.SYS* and *AUTOEXEC.BAT* files for editing. Within the System Configuration Editor, you can edit a file's contents and then use the File menu Save option to save the file's contents.

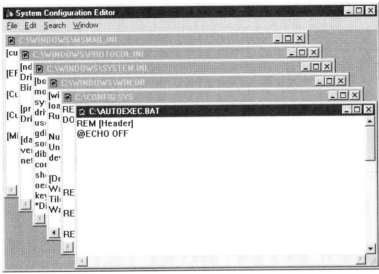

Figure 692 *Using the System Configuration Editor, you can edit key .INI files as well as CONFIG.SYS and AUTOEXEC.BAT files.*

To run the System Configuration Editor, perform these steps:

1. Click your mouse on the Start menu Run option. Windows 98, in turn, will display the Run dialog box.
2. Within the Run dialog box, type the command **Sysedit** and press ENTER. Windows 98, in turn, will open the System Configuration Editor.

---

693   **UNDERSTANDING WHEN AND WHEN NOT TO EDIT ENTRIES WITHIN THE WINDOWS 98 REGISTRY**

As you have learned, Windows 98 stores your hardware and software settings within the Registry database. In previous Tips, you learned how to start the Windows 98 Registry Editor, within which you can view or change Registry entries. However, as a rule, whenever you can change a system setting using a dialog box, such as a Control Panel dialog box, you should use the dialog box to change the setting rather than editing the Registry. As you have learned, Windows 98 uses the Registry's contents each time your system starts. If you introduce an error to the Registry when you edit an entry, you may prevent your system from starting.

Several of the Tips that follow examine Registry entries Windows 98 uses for specific hardware and software settings. In general, the Tips present these entries to help you better understand the Registry's contents and design. And, although you can use the Registry Editor to change each setting's value, whenever possible, you should find the setting's corresponding dialog box entry and then use the dialog box to change the setting.

694 PRINTING YOUR WINDOWS 98 REGISTRY'S CONTENTS

If you spend a few minutes expanding and traversing trees within the Registry database, you will quickly appreciate the Registry's large size. When you use the Registry Editor to view or change values, you may often want to print a range of Registry values. Rather than printing the entire Registry, which would require hundreds of pages of paper, you will usually only want to print a specific Registry tree's value. To print part of the Registry, perform these steps:

1. Within the Registry Editor, click your mouse on the icon of the key you want to print.
2. Within the Registry Editor, click your mouse on the Registry menu Print option. Windows 98, in turn, will display the Print dialog box.
3. Within the Print dialog box's Print Range field, click your mouse on the Selected branch option and then click your mouse on the OK button.

695 EXPORTING THE REGISTRY'S CONTENTS TO A FILE ON DISK

As you learned in Tip 693, whenever possible you should not make changes within the Registry itself, but rather, using Control Panel and program dialog boxes. However, by examining the Registry's contents, you can learn a lot about Windows 98, your hardware, as well as your software settings. One way to safely view the Registry's contents is to create a text file whose contents you can then view with the WordPad accessory program, as shown in Figure 695.1.

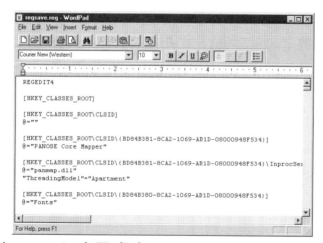

Figure 695.1 *Viewing the Registry's contents using the WordPad accessory program.*

Later, within WordPad, you can make changes to the exported database contents which you can later import back into the Registry to put your changes into effect. To export the Registry's contents to a file on your disk, perform these steps:

1. Click your mouse on the Start menu Run option. Windows 98, in turn, will display the Run dialog box.

2. Within the Run dialog box, type in the command **RegEdit** and press ENTER. Windows 98, in turn, will start the Registry Editor.

3. Within the Registry Editor, click your mouse on the Registry menu Export Registry File option. The Registry Editor, in turn, will display the Export Registry File dialog box, as shown in Figure 695.2.

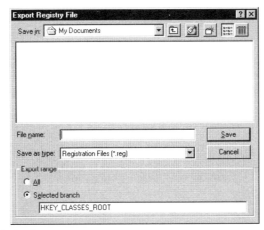

Figure 695.2 *The Export Registry File dialog box.*

4. Within the Export Registry File dialog box, select a path and filename to which you want to export the Registry's contents and then click your mouse on the Save option.

Later, to view your exported file's contents, start the WordPad accessory program and then use the File menu Open option to open your file.

Note: *Some users will export the Registry's contents to a file and then save the file's contents for use as a backup. Should you ever need to restore a Registry entry, you can print the exported file's contents or import the file's contents, as discussed in Tip 694.*

696 IMPORTING THE REGISTRY'S CONTENTS FROM A FILE ON DISK

In Tip 695, you learned how to export the Registry's contents to a file on your disk. As discussed, you can use your exported file as a backup or use it to edit Registry entries. Later, you can import your file back into the Registry. To import a previously exported Registry file's contents back into the Registry, perform these steps:

1. Click your mouse on the Start menu Run option. Windows 98, in turn, will display the Run dialog box.

2. Within the Run dialog box, type in the command **RegEdit** and press ENTER. Windows 98, in turn, will start the Registry Editor.

3. Within the Registry Editor, click your mouse on the Registry menu Import Registry File option. The Registry Editor, in turn, will display the Import Registry File dialog box, as shown in Figure 696.

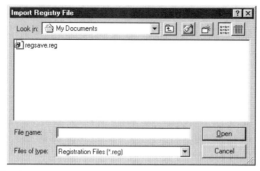

Figure 696 *The Import Registry File dialog box.*

4. Within the Import Registry File dialog box, select the file whose contents you want to import and then click your mouse on the Open button.

697 CHECKING THE REGISTRY'S CONTENTS

As you have learned, Windows 98 stores its system settings within the Registry database. Each time your system starts, Windows 98 reads the Registry's contents and uses its entries to configure your system. If the Registry database contains an error, your system may not start. Fortunately, Windows 98 provides a special program, the Registry Checker, that you can run on a regular basis to check the Registry's contents.

As it turns out, Windows 98 runs the Registry Checker each time your system starts. If the Registry Checker finds an error, the Registry Checker will use a backup copy of Registry settings that Windows 98 used previously to successfully start your system. (Windows 98 keeps five copies of Registry settings that it has used to successfully start your system.) When Windows 98 must "fall back" to previous Registry settings in order to start your system, you will lose the errant settings that prevented your system from starting and possibly valid settings that did not exist within the Registry backup. In such cases, you may have to reinstall software. To run the Registry Checker yourself, perform these steps:

1. Click your mouse on the Start menu Run option. Windows 98, in turn, will display the Run dialog box.

2. Within the Run dialog box, type the command **ScanRegw** and press ENTER. Windows 98 will run the Registry Checker. If the Registry Checker encounters an error, it will load a previous backup of the Registry. If, however, the Registry does not have any errors, the Registry Checker will display the Registry Scan Results dialog box, as shown in Figure 697, within which it asks you if you want to backup the Registry's contents at this time. To backup your Registry, click your mouse on the Yes button.

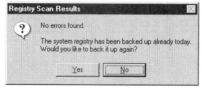

Figure 697 *The Registry Scan Results dialog box.*

698 **UNDERSTANDING THE REGISTRY FILES**

As you have learned, Windows 98 stores your system settings within the Registry database. As it turns out, the Registry database consists of multiple files: *User.dat*, *System.dat*, *Policy.pol*, and *RBxxx.cab* files. Within the *User.dat* file, which is a hidden file that resides within the *Windows* folder, the Registry stores user-profile information. If a system supports multiple users, each user will have their own User.Dat file, which Windows 98 will store within the *Windows\Profiles\User'sName* folder. Within the file *System.dat*, which is also a hidden file within the *Windows* folder, the Registry stores hardware, plug-and-play, and PC-specific settings. If you enable system policies, Windows 98 stores the policy settings which may override the Registry within the file *Policy.pol*. Finally, as you will learn in Tip 699, each time you (or Windows 98, when your system starts) backup your Registry settings, Windows 98 will create a *.Cab* file (Tip 650 discusses cabinet files) within the *Windows\Sysbckup* folder that contains a backup copy of the Registry's contents.

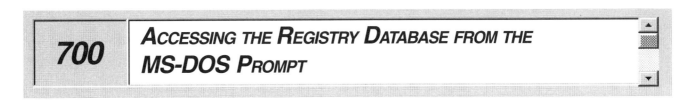

699 **BACKING UP AND RESTORING THE REGISTRY'S CONTENTS**

As you have learned, Windows 98 stores its settings within the Registry database. Each time your system starts, Windows 98 reads the Registry's contents and uses the settings it finds to configure your system. If your Registry contains an errant entry, Windows 98 may not be able to start. If Windows 98 successfully starts, Windows 98 will make a backup copy of the Registry's current contents that it stores within a hidden cabinet file within the *Windows\Sysbckup* folder. By default, Windows 98 will keep copies of the last five Registry copies from which it started successfully. Windows 98 will name these files *RB000.Cab* through *RB004.Cab*. In Tip 697, you learned how to backup the Registry's contents yourself using the Registry Checker. However, because Windows 98 backs up the Registry for you on a regular basis, you usually will not have to backup the Registry yourself. However, you may want to backup the Registry before you install new hardware or software.

If, when Windows 98 starts, the Registry Checker encounters an error, Windows 98 will "fall back" to a previous version of the Registry's contents. When Windows 98 falls back to previous Registry contents, you may lose your most recent changes to Registry settings. Although Windows 98 will keep a current backup copy of your Registry, Windows 98 does not keep backup copies of your *System.INI* and *Win.INI* files, both of which may contain key system settings. As a rule, you should keep a copy of these two files on a floppy disk that you store in a safe location.

700 **ACCESSING THE REGISTRY DATABASE FROM THE MS-DOS PROMPT**

As you have learned, using the Registry Editor, you can view or change entries within the Windows 98 Registry database. If you make a change to the Registry that prevents Windows 98 from starting your system, Windows 98 will usually use one of its backup copies of a "startable" Registry. However, should your system still not start due to a

Registry entry, you can start Windows 98 in MS-DOS mode and then edit the Registry from within the MS-DOS. Using the Registry Editor from the MS-DOS prompt, for example, you might first export the Registry's contents to a file which you can then edit. After you correct the errant Registry settings, you can then run the RegEdit command a second time, this time to import your edited entries.

To run the Registry Editor in MS-DOS mode, perform these steps:

1. Start your system in MS-DOS mode, as discussed in Tip 417.
2. From the DOS system prompt, type the **RegEdit** command using one of the following command formats then and press ENTER:

```
REGEDIT [/L:system] [/R:user] ImportFile.reg

REGEDIT [/L:system] [/R:user] /E ExportFile.reg [regkey]

REGEDIT [/L:system] [/R:user] /C File.reg

REGEDIT [/L:system] [/R:user] /D regkey
```

Table 700 briefly explains the MS-DOS mode RegEdit command-line switches.

Command-Line Argument	Description
/L:*system*	Specifies the location of the *System.DAT* file that contains the Registry, such as *C:\Windows*.
/R:*user*	Specifies the location of the *User.DAT* file that contains the settings for the entries that define user settings, such as *C:\Windows*.
ImportFile.reg	Specifies the *.REG* registry file from which you want to import the new Registry contents (make sure the file contains a complete copy of the Registry).
/E *ExportFile.reg*	Specifies the name of the file to which you want the Registry to export settings.
regkey	Specifies the starting Registry key from which you want to export or which you want the Registry Editor to delete.
/C *File.reg*	Specifies a *.REG* file that you want to use to change Registry settings.
/D *regkey*	Specifies the Registry key you want the Registry Editor to delete.

Table 700 *The MS-DOS mode RegEdit command-line switches.*

---

701 RUNNING THE REGISTRY CHECKER FROM THE MS-DOS PROMPT

In Tip 700, you learned how to run the Registry Editor from the MS-DOS system prompt. If your Registry is corrupt, you can start the Registry Checker from the MS-DOS prompt to restore a previous backup. To run the Registry Checker from the MS-DOS prompt, perform these steps:

1. Start your system in MS-DOS mode as discussed in Tip 417.

2. From the DOS system prompt, type the **ScanReg** command using the command-line switches Table 701 presents and then press ENTER.

Command-Line Argument	Description
/Backup	Directs the Registry Checker to make a backup copy of the Registry.
/Comment=	Lets you add a text comment to a backup that the Registry Checker will later display before it restores the backup.
/Fix	Directs the Registry Checker to try to correct the corruption.
/Restore	Directs the Registry Checker to display a list of available backups (and their comments) from which you can select the backup you want to use to restore the Registry settings.

Table 701 *The MS-DOS mode ScanReg command-line switches.*

---

702 **RUNNING THE REGISTRY CHECKER FROM WITHIN AN MS-DOS BATCH FILE**

In Tip 701, you learned how to run the Registry Checker from an MS-DOS prompt. If you are a network administrator responsible for hundreds of systems, you can simplify the process of restoring registry settings from an MS-DOS prompt by creating a batch file that examines first the Registry's contents and then, based on whether or not the Registry is bad, restores the Registry's contents. To create the batch file, you can use the IF ERRORLEVEL command with the ScanReg command's exit-status values, which Table 702 presents.

Error Status Value	Meaning
-7	Registry file sharing violation
-6	Registry file write operation failed
-5	Registry file read operation failed
-4	Error creating *System.DAT* or *User.DAT*
-3	Error finding *System.DAT* or *User.DAT*
-2	Insufficient memory
0	Successful operation
2	Registry is corrupt

Table 702 *The ScanReg command's exit-status values.*

---

703 **USING COMMAND-LINE SWITCHES TO CONTROL THE REGISTRY CHECKER'S PROCESSING**

In Tip 701, you learned that using the Registry Checker, you can verify that the Registry settings are valid and then you can backup the Registry entries to a cabinet file on your disk. As you learned, to run the Registry Checker, you run the

ScanRegw command (which you can start using the Run dialog box or by creating a shortcut for the command). When you run the ScanRegw command, you can include the command-line switches that Table 703 presents to control the program's processing.

Command-Line Switch	Purpose
/Autoscan	Directs the Registry Checker to examine the Registry each time it runs, but to only backup the Registry one time per day
/Backup	Directs the Registry Checker to create a backup copy of the Registry without prompting the user
/Comment=	Lets you add a text comment to a backup that the Registry Checker will later display before it restores the backup
/Scanonly	Directs the Registry Checker to examine the Registry's contents but not to backup the Registry

Table 703 *The ScanRegw command-line switches.*

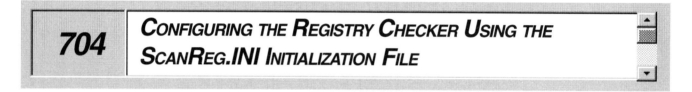

704	CONFIGURING THE REGISTRY CHECKER USING THE SCANREG.INI INITIALIZATION FILE

As you learned in Tip 701, using the Registry Checker utility program, you can verify that your Registry entries are valid and you can then backup the Registry's contents to a cabinet file (a compressed file) on your disk. By default, the Registry Checker will keep five backup copies of your Registry. To customize the Registry Checker's processing, you can use the *ScanReg.INI* initialization file. Like all *.INI* files, the *ScanReg.INI* file contains single-line entries that control its processing. To edit the *ScanReg.INI*, you can use the Notepad accessory, as shown in Figure 704. Table 704 briefly describes the *ScanReg.INI* entries.

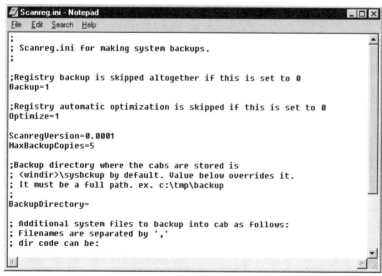

Figure 704 *Using the Notepad accessory to edit the **ScanReg.INI** file.*

Entry	Purpose
Backup=	Enables or disables the Registry Checker's creation of a backup file. Backup=0 turns off backups. Backup=1 turns on backups.
BackupDirectory=	Specifies the folder within which the Registry Checker will place its backup copies. By default, the Registry Checker uses BackupDirectory=C:\Windows\SysBckup.
Files=	Specifies other system files you want the Registry Checker to backup. You must specify a directory code followed by one or more comma-separated filenames. The directory codes are as follows: 10 windir C:\Windows 11 system dir C:\Windows\System 30 boot dir C:\ 31 boot host dir C:\ For example, the following entry would direct the Registry Checker to also backup *Config.SYS* and *AutoExec.Bat*: Files=[30]Config.SYS,AutoExec.BAT
MaxBackupCopies=	Species the number of backup copies the Registry Checker will keep. By default, the Registry Checker uses MaxBackupCopies=5, which directs it to keep five copies.
Optimize	Enables or disables the Registry Checkers optimization of Registry settings. Optimize=0 disables optimization. Optimize=1 enables optimization.

Table 704 *Entries within the **ScanReg.INI** file.*

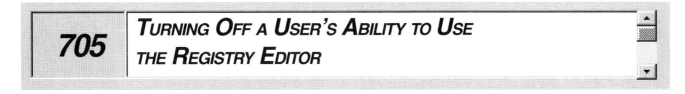

705 TURNING OFF A USER'S ABILITY TO USE THE REGISTRY EDITOR

If you are a system administrator responsible for managing computers within a local-area network or office, you may not want your users running the Registry Editor. To disable a user's ability to run the Registry Editor, you will use the System Policy Editor which Tip 995 presents. Within the System Policy Editor, perform these steps:

1. Click your mouse on the Start menu Programs option and choose Accessories. Windows 98, in turn, will display the Accessories submenu.

2. Within the Accessories submenu, click your mouse on the System Tools option and choose System Policy Editor. Windows 98, in turn, will open the System Policy Editor window.

3. Within the System Policy Editor, select the File menu Open Registry icon. The System Policy Editor will display a list of current users and computers.

4. Within the System Policy Editor's list click your mouse a user or computer. The System Policy Editor will display a list of the users or the computer's available policies.

5. Within the System Policy Editor's policy list, click your mouse on the plus sign that precedes the Windows 98 User and then click your mouse on the plus sign that precedes the Restrictions icon. The System Policy Editor will expand the entry's list.

6. Within the Restrictions list, click your mouse on the Disable Registry Editing Tools option and then click your mouse on the OK button.

7. Select the System Policy Editor's File menu Save option to save your settings.

706   *ADMINISTERING A USER'S REGISTRY FROM ACROSS A NETWORK*

If you are a network administrator responsible for managing computers within a local-area network, you may want to enable the Registry's remote administration capabilities. In this way, you can use the Registry Editor to connect to a remote user's PC and then to edit the user's Registry settings. Before you can perform remote Registry administration, you must first use the Control Panel Network Properties dialog box to install the Remote Registry service on both computers. Then, on the remote PC, you must enable user-level security and remote administration. Within your system, start the Registry Editor and then select the Registry menu Connect Network Registry option. The Registry Editor, in turn, will display the Connect Network Registry dialog box, as shown in Figure 706, within which you can specify the name of the PC to which you want to connect.

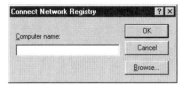

Figure 706 The Connect Network Registry dialog box.

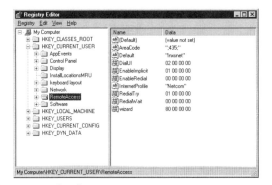

707   *FINDING ENTRIES WITHIN THE WINDOWS 98 REGISTRY DATABASE*

As you have learned, Windows 98 stores your system settings within the Registry database. Using the Registry Editor, you can traverse the Registry's entries much as you would traverse files within the Explorer. In other words, the Registry Editor displays two window frames, as shown in Figure 707.1

Figure 707.1 The Registry Editor displays two window frames.

Within the Registry Editor's left-hand frame, you will encounter a series of file folders that you can expand or collapse by clicking your mouse on the plus or minus sign that precedes the folder icon. If you expand a folder, the Registry Editor will display the folder's subfolders. Within the Registry Editor's right-hand frame, it will display specific setting values. If you spend a few minutes traversing the Registry Editor, you will quickly appreciate that the Registry database is very large. To help you find an entry within the Registry quickly, you can use the Edit menu Find option. The Registry Editor, in turn, will display the Find dialog box, as shown in Figure 707.2.

Figure 707.2 *The Registry Editor Find dialog box.*

Within the Find dialog box, you can search for key names (folders), specific data settings, as well as specific values. After you click your mouse on the Find Next button, the Registry Editor will search its entries for your specified text. If the Registry Editor finds a match, it will highlight the corresponding Registry entry. If the Registry Editor finds a match, but not the match you desire, simply press the F3 function key to direct the Registry Editor to find the next occurrence of the text.

708 RENAMING AN ENTRY WITHIN THE WINDOWS 98 REGISTRY DATABASE

As you have learned, Windows 98 stores its system settings within the Registry database. Using the Registry Editor, you can view or change Registry entries. As a rule, you usually will not rename entries within the Registry. That is because the programs that use the Registry's contents search for specific entries. If you rename an entry, the program will not find the entry and may cause an error. The one exception to renaming entries, however, may be when you want to delete an entry. Rather than simply deleting an entry from the Registry, you should first consider renaming the entry. That way, should your system fail to start after you make your change, you can quickly restore your previous system settings by simply renaming the entry back to its previous name. If your system starts and your programs run successfully, you can then delete the entries you previously renamed. To rename an entry within the Registry Editor, click your mouse on the entry you want to rename. Then, click your mouse on the Edit menu Rename option. The Registry Editor, in turn, will highlight the entry within a small box within which you can type the name that you desire. When you rename an entry in this way, you might simply precede the item's current name with text such as *DELETE_* or *REMOVE_*. After you restart your system, you can use the Registry Editor's Find dialog box to locate the item, which you can then delete.

709 DELETING AN ENTRY WITHIN THE WINDOWS 98 REGISTRY DATABASE

As you have learned, Windows 98 stores its system settings within the Registry database. Usually, you will not have to delete entries from within the Registry. However, should you remove a hardware device from your system, there may be times when you must later delete the device's Registry settings. (Before you delete entries from the Registry, you should use the Control Panel's System Properties dialog box Device Manager to remove the hardware—which should also direct Windows 98 to remove the device's Registry settings.)

Should you have to delete one or more entries from the Registry, you should first rename the entries, as discussed in Tip 708. Then, after you find that your system starts and that your programs run successfully, you can delete an entry by clicking your mouse on the entry and then selecting the Edit menu Delete option.

710   ADDING AN ENTRY TO THE WINDOWS 98 REGISTRY DATABASE

As you have learned, Windows 98 stores its system settings within the Registry database. Usually, Windows 98 or your programs will create the Registry entries they need. In some cases, Windows 98 or your programs will not place entries within the Registry for all their possible settings. Instead, the programs will use default values for settings they do not find within the Registry. When you troubleshoot your hardware or software, there may be times when a technical-support specialist will ask you to create a Registry entry to which you can assign a value that overrides a default setting.

To add an entry to the Registry, perform these steps:

1. Click your mouse on the Start menu Run option. Windows 98, in turn, will display the Run dialog box.

2. Within the Run dialog box, type in the command **RegEdit** and press ENTER. Windows 98 will start the Registry Editor.

3. Within the Registry Editor, locate the key location at which you want to create the new entry and then right-click your mouse on the corresponding key folder. The Registry Editor, in turn, will display a pop-up menu.

4. Within the pop-up menu, select the New option. The Registry Editor, in turn, will cascade the New submenu.

5. Within the New submenu, select the Key, String Value, Binary Value, or DWORD Value option to create the entry you desire. The Registry Editor, in turn, will create the corresponding entry type to which you can assign a name and a value, as appropriate.

711   *EDITING A STRING VALUE WITHIN THE REGISTRY DATABASE*

As you have learned, Windows 98 stores its system settings within the Registry database. As a rule, you should change Windows 98 settings and your program settings using the Control Panel or program-specific dialog boxes. However, as you troubleshoot your system, there may be times when you must change a Registry entry for which there is no corresponding dialog-box entry. Within the Registry, entries have either a character-string, binary, or DWORD value. Tip 712 discusses binary and DWORD values in detail. A character-string value is simply a series of characters, such as a filename. For example, Figure 711.1 shows the current Wallpaper setting within the Registry.

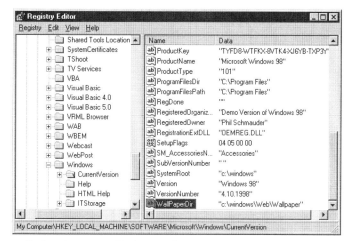

Figure 711.1 *Using the Registry to display the current Desktop wallpaper.*

Within the Registry Editor, you can edit a string value by performing these steps:

1. Within the Registry Editor, locate the entry whose value you want to change. Next, right-click your mouse on the entry's name. The Registry Editor will display a pop-up menu.

2. Within the pop-up menu, click your mouse on the Modify option. The Registry Editor, in turn, will display the Edit String dialog box, as shown in Figure 711.2.

Figure 711.2 *The Edit String dialog box.*

3. Within the Edit String dialog box, type in the entry's new value and then click your mouse on the OK button.

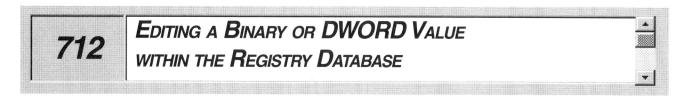

712

EDITING A BINARY OR DWORD VALUE WITHIN THE REGISTRY DATABASE

As you have learned, Windows 98 stores its system settings within the Registry database. As a rule, you should change Windows 98 settings and your program settings using the Control Panel or program-specific dialog boxes. However, as you troubleshoot your system, there may be times when you must change a Registry entry for which there is no corresponding dialog-box entry. Within the Registry, entries have either a character-string, binary, or DWORD value. Tip 711 discusses string values and how you change them within the Registry Editor.

A binary value is a numeric value that, within the Registry Editor, you must specify using the hexadecimal (base 16) format. Unlike a DWORD value that the Registry Editor restricts to four bytes in length, a binary value can be any length.

As discussed, when you specify a binary or DWORD value within the Registry, you must specify the value using the hexadecimal format, which represents numbers using the digits 0 through 9 and the letters A through F. Fortunately, when you change a binary or DWORD value, a technical-support specialist, your system documentation, or information you find on a Web site will provide you with the value you must use.

To change a binary value within the Registry Editor, perform these steps:

1. Within the Registry Editor, locate the entry whose value you want to change. Next, right-click your mouse on the entry's name. The Registry Editor will display a pop-up menu.

2. Within the pop-up menu, click your mouse on the Modify option. The Registry Editor, in turn, will display the Edit Binary Value dialog box, as shown in Figure 712.1.

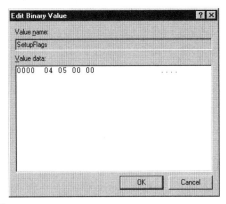

Figure 712.1 *The Edit Binary Value dialog box.*

3. Within the Edit Binary Value dialog box, type in the entry's new value and then click your mouse on the OK button.

To change a DWORD value within the Registry Editor, perform these steps:

1. Within the Registry Editor, locate the entry whose value you want to change. Next, right-click your mouse on the entry's name. The Registry Editor will display a pop-up menu.

2. Within the pop-up menu, click your mouse on the Modify option. The Registry Editor, in turn, will display the Edit DWORD Value dialog box, as shown in Figure 712.2.

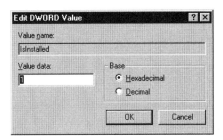

Figure 712.2 *The Edit DWORD Value dialog box.*

3. Within the Edit DWORD Value dialog box, type in the entry's new value and then click your mouse on the OK button.

713 EXAMINING THE REGISTRY'S HKEY_CLASSES_ROOT KEY

As you have learned, Windows 98 makes extensive use of file extensions to determine which program created the file. By associating a file extension with a program, Windows 98 knows which program to run when you double-click your mouse on a document within the Explorer. In addition to the Explorer using the program associations when you double-click your mouse on a document file, Windows 98 also uses the program settings to support object-linking and embedding (Tip 786 discusses OLE) as well as drag-and-drop operations. Using the Explorer's Add New File Type dialog box, shown in Figure 713.1, you can register a file extension with Windows 98.

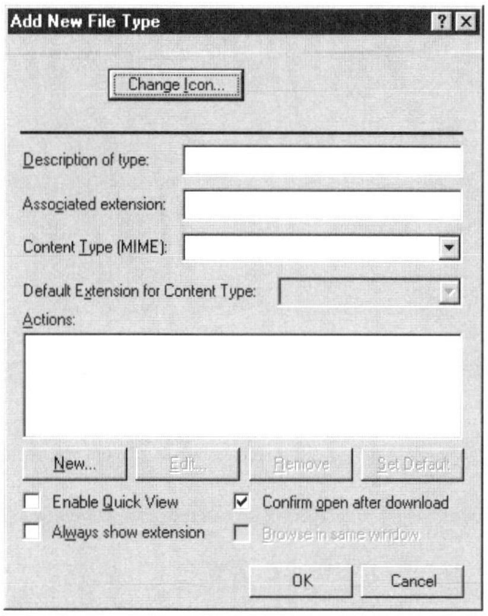

Figure 713.1 Using the Explorer's Add New File Type dialog box to register a file extension.

When you register a file type, Windows 98 stores your setting information within the Registry's *HKEY_CLASSES_ROOT* key, as shown in Figure 713.2. Within the key's entries, you can click your mouse on a file extension to display specifics about the corresponding program.

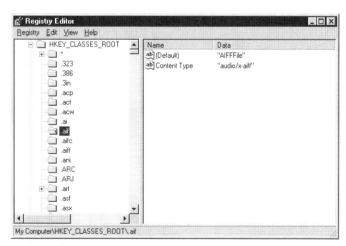

Figure 713.2 Using the Registry to view registered program extensions.

714

EXAMINING THE REGISTRY'S HKEY_CURRENT_USER KEY

As you have learned, to help two or more users share the same PC, Windows 98 supports user profiles. Within a user profile, Windows 98 stores a user's Desktop, document, and possibly even Internet Explorer settings. As Tip 723 discusses, the *HKEY_USERS* key provides information about each user who can log onto a system. In a similar way, the *HKEY_CURRENT_USER* Registry key contains information about the current user. Each time a user logs into a Windows 98 system, Windows 98 copies the user's profile settings to the *HKEY_CURRENT_USER* Registry tree, as shown in Figure 714.

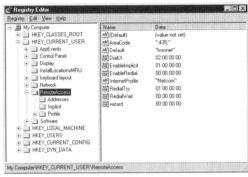

Figure 714 *Using the Registry to view settings about the current user profile.*

715

TAKING A CLOSE LOOK AT HKEY_LOCAL_MACHINE KEY

As you have learned, Windows 98 stores its system settings within the Registry database. Within the Registry, you will find the settings for your system's hardware and software within the *HKEY_LOCAL_MACHINE* key. When you use the Control Panel to make changes to your system settings, Windows 98 will store your changes within the *HKEY_LOCAL_MACHINE* key. As shown in Figure 715, the *HKEY_LOCAL_MACHINE* contains settings for hardware, device driver, as well as your software. In fact, several of the Tips that follow examine subkeys that contain specific settings.

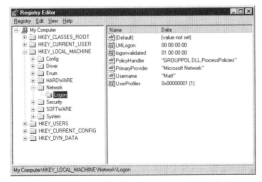

Figure 715 *Using the Registry to view or change your system's hardware, software, and device driver settings.*

716 EXAMINING THE REGISTRY'S HKEY_LOCAL_MACHINE\CONFIG SUBKEY

As you have learned, the Registry's *HKEY_LOCAL_MACHINE* key provides specifics about the local PC, such as the PC's hardware devices and installed software. By traversing the *HKEY_LOCAL_MACHINE\Config* subkey, you can find information about your system's various hardware and software configuration settings. For example, Figure 716 shows information about the current display settings, such as resolution and color settings (bits per pixel).

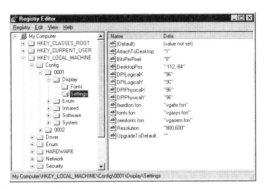

Figure 716 *Viewing information about the current Display settings.*

When you want to view the current display settings, you can use the Display Properties dialog box. When your programs or Windows 98 require such information, they can use the Registry settings.

717 EXAMINING THE REGISTRY'S HKEY_LOCAL_MACHINE\ENUM SUBKEY

As you have learned, the Registry's *HKEY_LOCAL_MACHINE* key provides specifics about the local PC, such as the PC's hardware devices and installed software. By traversing the *HKEY_LOCAL_MACHINE\Enum* subkey, you can view specifics about your system's low-level hardware devices. The subkey, *Enum*, stands for enumerate (which means to list). Within the Enum subkey, you will find specifics about your disks, modems, monitor, tape drives, infrared devices, and so on. Figure 717, for example, uses the Enum subkey to display information about a disk drive, such as the drives type (IDE), manufacturer, and even flags that Windows 98 may use to determine the drive's capabilities.

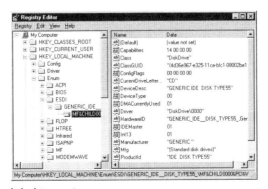

Figure 717 *Using the Registry to display disk-drive settings.*

718

EXAMINING THE REGISTRY'S
KEY_LOCAL_MACHINE\HARDWARE SUBKEY

As you have learned, the Registry's *HKEY_LOCAL_MACHINE* key provides specifics about the local PC, such as the PC's hardware devices and installed software. By traversing the *HKEY_LOCAL_MACHINE\hardware subkey*, you can view specifics about your central processing unit (CPU), such as its manufacturer, information about your floating-point processor, and even settings for your serial ports. Figure 718, for example, shows specifics about the local machine's CPU.

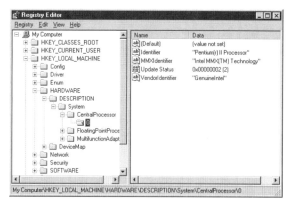

Figure 718 *Viewing specifics about the current CPU.*

719

EXAMINING THE REGISTRY'S
HKEY_LOCAL_MACHINE\NETWORK SUBKEY

As you have learned, the Registry's *HKEY_LOCAL_MACHINE* key provides specifics about the local PC, such as the PC's hardware devices and installed software. By traversing the *HKEY_LOCAL_MACHINE\Network* subkey, you can view specifics about your system's network settings, such as your primary Internet Service Provider and username. In addition, as shown in Figure 719, the Registry provides Windows 98 with information about your user and group profile.

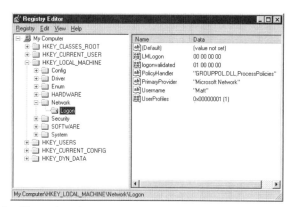

Figure 719 *Using the Registry to display Network settings.*

720 **EXAMINING THE REGISTRY'S
HKEY_LOCAL_MACHINE\SECURITY SUBKEY**

As you have learned, the Registry's *HKEY_LOCAL_MACHINE* key provides specifics about the local PC, such as the PC's hardware devices and installed software. Depending on your system's configuration, you may be able to view your security settings by traversing the *HKEY_LOCAL_MACHINE\Security* subkey, as shown in Figure 720. Depending on your security settings, the entries you will find within the Security subkey may differ.

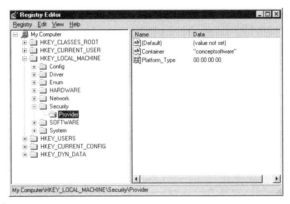

Figure 720 *Using the Registry to display Security settings.*

721 **EXAMINING THE REGISTRY'S
KEY_LOCAL_MACHINE\SOFTWARE SUBKEY**

As you have learned, the Registry's *HKEY_LOCAL_MACHINE* key provides specifics about the local PC, such as the PC's hardware devices and installed software. By traversing the *HKEY_LOCAL_MACHINE\Software* subkey, you can view specifics about the software installed on your system, as shown in Figure 721.1.

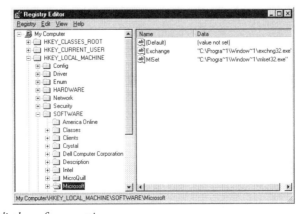

Figure 721.1 *Using the Registry to display software settings.*

As you know, Windows 98 tracks various properties about files which it may later use to automatically start a program when you double-click your mouse on a document file within the Explorer. If you examine the *Software* subkey *Classes* field, you will find a list of the file extensions that Windows 98 associates with those of your system's registered program types. Figure 721.2 displays the *Classes* subkey. Within the program list, you can click your mouse on a file extension to view specifics about that file type.

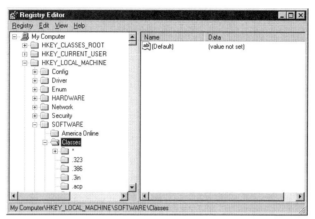

Figure 721.2 *Using the Registry to display information about program types.*

722	EXAMINING THE REGISTRY'S HKEY_LOCAL_MACHINE\SYSTEM SUBKEY

As you have learned, the Registry's *HKEY_LOCAL_MACHINE* key provides specifics about the local PC, such as the PC's hardware devices and installed software. By traversing the *HKEY_LOCAL_MACHINE\System* subkey, you can view specifics about virtually every aspect of your PC, from its file system to Control Panel settings to the values the System Monitor (see Tip 674) tracks and charts. Figure 722 shows a portion of the System subkey. Take time to traverse the System subkey and you will better understand how and where Windows 98 stores your various system settings.

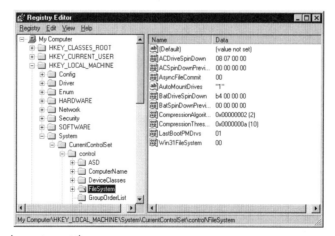

Figure 722 *Using the Registry to view system settings.*

723   EXAMINING THE REGISTRY'S *HKEY_USERS* KEY

As you have learned, to help two or more users share the same PC, Windows 98 provides user profiles. Within a user profile, Windows 98 stores each user's Desktop settings and possibly such information as where the user keeps his or her documents, and so on. For each user, Windows 98 has settings the user can customize as well as default settings that it applies to each user.

Within the Registry, Windows 98 uses the *HKEY_USERS* key to track information about each user who can log into the system (each user profile) as well as the system's default settings, as shown in Figure 723. If you traverse the *HKEY_USERS* key, you will find that many applications also store their default settings within this tree.

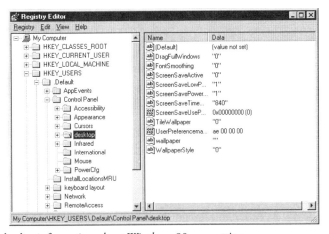

Figure 723 *Using the Registry to display information about Windows 98 user settings.*

724   EXAMINING THE REGISTRY'S
HKEY_CURRENT_CONFIG KEY

In Tip 716, you learned that Windows 98 tracks information about a system's hardware and settings within the *HKEY_LOCAL_MACHINE\Config* key. As you learned in Tip 397, using the Windows 98 Control Panel's System icon, you can define Hardware profiles. For a notebook PC, for example, you might define a profile for when the PC is docked within its docking station and a second profile for when the PC is undocked. Depending on which profile is in use, Windows 98 will employ different hardware and software settings.

Within the Registry, Windows 98 tracks the current hardware and software settings within the *HKEY_CURRENT_CONFIG* key. As shown in Figure 724, within the *HKEY_CURRENT_CONFIG* key, you will find many entries similar to those in the *HKEY_LOCAL_MACHINE\Config* key. Depending on the current user and hardware profile, Windows 98 will assign values to the settings within the *HKEY_CURRENT_CONFIG* tree.

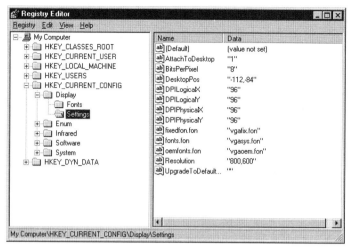

Figure 724 *Using the Registry to display the current system settings.*

725 EXPLORING THE REGISTRY'S HKEY_DYN_DATA KEY

As you have learned, the Registry is a database file that Windows 98 stores on your computer's hard disk. To improve your system performance, Windows 98 loads key registry entries into your PC's fast random-access memory (RAM), so your system does not have to access the entries from your slow disk drive.

Within the Registry, Windows 98 stores these RAM-based entries within its *HKEY_DYN_DATA* key, as shown in Figure 725. Within the *HKEY_DYN_DATA* key, you will find entries Windows 98 tracks for performance statistics as well as a series of uniquely named folders (such as C29CD0F0) within which Windows 98 stores device- or program-specific settings.

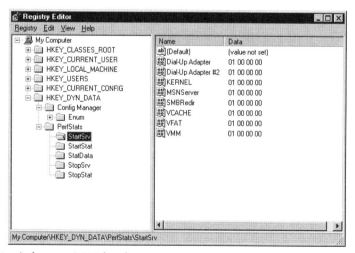

Figure 725 *Displaying the Registry's dynamic RAM-based settings.*

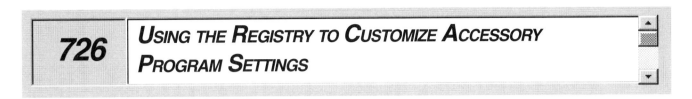

726 USING THE REGISTRY TO CUSTOMIZE ACCESSORY PROGRAM SETTINGS

As you have learned, most Windows-based programs use the Registry to store a variety of settings, such as the current color palette, the list of most recently used files, or even your current printer configuration. Many of the Windows Accessory programs, for example, store their settings within the Registry tree *HKEY_CURRENT_USER\Software\Micro soft\Windows\CurrentVersion\Applets*, as shown in Figure 726.1.

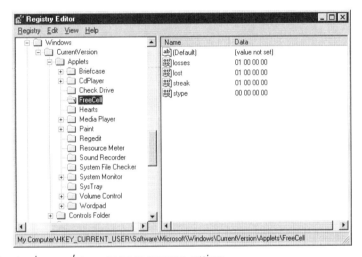

Figure 726.1 *Using the Registry to view or change accessory-program settings.*

If you examine the entries within the *Applets* tree, you may be able to learn more about how the Accessory programs function behind the scenes. For example, the Paint accessory stores its list of recently used files within the *Applets\Paint\Recent File List* subkey, as shown in Figure 726.2. If, for example, you want to eliminate the Paint accessory's list of recently used files, you can edit the Registry entry and delete or change the files the entry lists.

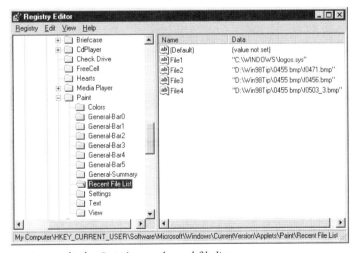

Figure 726.2 *Using the Registry to view or display Paint's recently used file list.*

727   USING THE REGISTRY TO CHANGE YOUR COMPUTER NAME

Within a network, each computer must have a unique name. If your PC is connected to a local-area network, you can use the Control Panel's Network Properties dialog box Identification sheet to change your PC's name. In addition, using the Registry's *HKEY_LOCAL_MACHINE\System\CurrentControlSet\Control\ComputerName\ComputerName* shown in Figure 727, you can view or change your PC's network name.

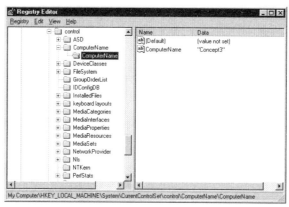

Figure 727 *Using the Registry to view or change your PC's network name.*

728   USING THE REGISTRY TO CONTROL THE CURSOR BLINK RATE

In Tip 265, you learned how to use the Control Panel Keyboard Properties dialog box to set your screen's cursor blink rate. When you assign a cursor blink rate using the Control Panel, Windows 98 will store your settings within the Registry. For example, Figure 728 shows the cursor-blink rate within the Registry. To slow down the blink rate, set the following registry subkey value to 200. To increase the blink rate's speed, change the value to 1200.

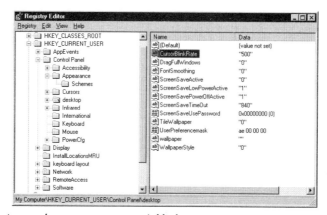

Figure 728 *Using the Registry to view or change your text cursor's blink rate.*

In Tip 226, you learned how to use the Desktop Themes dialog box Pointers sheet to assign different cursors to various Windows events. When you assign cursor settings using the Pointers sheet, Windows 98 stores your settings within the Registry. Figure 729, for example, shows the filenames for icons Windows 98 will use for different cursor settings. To change a cursor setting, simply assign a different cursor file to the cursor type you desire.

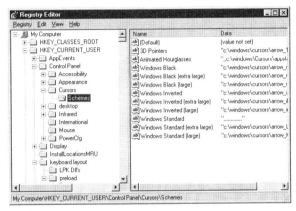

Figure 729 *Using the Registry to view or change your cursor settings.*

In previous Tips, you have learned how to use the Display Properties dialog box to customize various Desktop settings. In addition to using the Display Properties dialog box sheets to configure your display settings, you can also use the Registry. For example, Figure 730 shows various display settings within the *HKEY_CURRENT_USER* key's Control Panel Desktop settings.

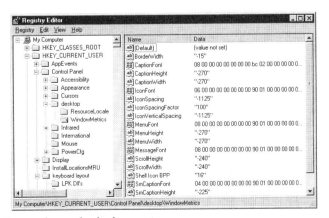

Figure 730 *Using the Registry to view or change the display metrics.*

731 USING THE REGISTRY TO DISPLAY INSTALLED DEVICE DRIVERS

In Tip 309, you learned how to use the Windows 98 Control Panel System Properties dialog box to display your system's device drivers. As it turns out, Windows 98 keeps track of your device drivers using the Registry. For example, Figure 731 displays a list of the device-driver files Windows 98 has installed on your PC.

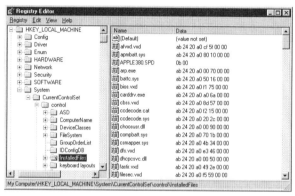

Figure 731 *Using the Registry to view installed device-driver files.*

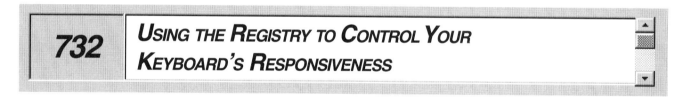

732 USING THE REGISTRY TO CONTROL YOUR KEYBOARD'S RESPONSIVENESS

In Tip 263, you learned how to use the Control Panel Keyboard Properties Speed sheet to customize your keyboard's responsiveness. Within the Keyboard Properties Speed sheet, you can change your keyboard's repeat delay and repeat rate. When you change your keyboard settings, Windows 98 will store the values within the Registry. To view or change your keyboard settings within the Registry, locate the *HKEY_CURRENT_USER* key and then locate the *Control Panel\Keyboard* subkeys, as shown in Figure 732.

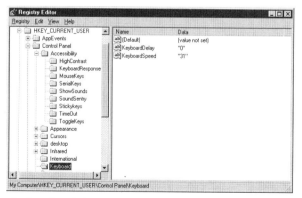

Figure 732 *Using the Registry to view keyboard settings.*

To maximize your keyboard responsiveness, set the *KeyboardDelay* value to 0 and the *KeyboardSpeed* value to 31. To slow down the keyboard's responsiveness and repeat rate, change the *KeyboardDelay* to 3 and the *KeyboardSpeed* to 0.

733 USING THE REGISTRY TO CONFIGURE YOUR MODEM SETTINGS

In Tip 270, you learned how to use the Control Panel Modem Properties dialog box to customize your modem settings. When you use the Modem Properties dialog box to configure your modem settings, Windows 98 stores your settings within the Registry. Using the Registry, you can further customize the modem initialization and response strings that Windows 98 uses to communicate with your modem. To view or change your modem settings, locate the *HKEY_LOCAL_MACHINE\System\CurrentControlSet\Class\Services\Modem* subkey, as shown in Figure 733.

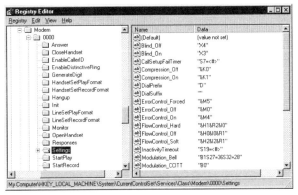

Figure 733 *Using the Registry to view or change low-level modem settings.*

734 USING THE REGISTRY TO CONTROL THE SCREEN-SAVER ACTIVATION INTERVAL

In Tip 235, you learned how to install and configure a screen saver on your system. As you learned, when you assign a screen saver, Windows 98 lets you specify the amount of inactive time Windows 98 must wait before it starts the screen saver. When you use the Display Properties dialog box Screen Saver sheet to configure a screen saver, Windows 98 stores your settings within the Registry. Figure 734, for example, shows the Registry's screen-saver settings. To change the screen-saver interval, assign a value to the *ScreenSaveTimeOut* entry. To assign a one-minute interval, use the value 60. To assign a two-minute interval, use the value 120, and so on.

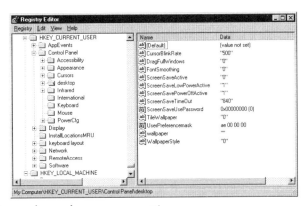

Figure 734 *Using the Registry to view or change the screen-saver settings.*

735 USING THE REGISTRY TO CONTROL SCREEN SAVER PASSWORD PROTECTION

In Tip 237, you learned how to use the Control Panel Display Properties dialog box Screen Saver sheet to password protect your screen saver. When you use the Screen Saver sheet to assign a password to your screen saver, Windows 98 stores your settings within the Registry. To view or change screen-saver settings, you can use the Registry entries shown in Figure 735.

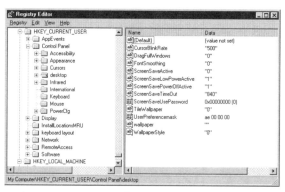

Figure 735 Using the Registry to view or change screen-saver settings.

736 USING THE REGISTRY TO DETERMINE YOUR SYSTEM'S PLUG-AND-PLAY DEVICES

As you learned in Tip 214, when you install a plug-and-play device into your system, Windows 98 will recognize and configure the device automatically. Each time Windows 98 configures a plug-and-play device for use on your system, Windows 98 stores information about the device within the Registry. If you examine the *HKEY_LOCAL_MACHINE\Enum\BIOS* subkey, shown in Figure 736, you will find a series of entries that start with the letters *PNP*. Each PNP entry corresponds to a plug-and-play device type.

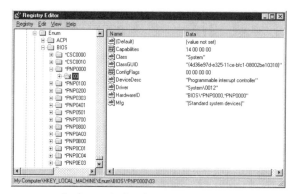

Figure 736 Using the Registry to view your system's plug-and-play device settings.

Each plug-and-play device subkey name corresponds to a specific device type. Table 736 briefly describes how the Registry relates device names to plug-and-play devices.

Registry Name	Device Type
PNP00xx	Interrupt controllers
PNP01xx	System timers
PNP02xx	DMA controllers
PNP03xx	Keyboard controllers
PNP04xx	Printer ports
PNP05xx	Communication ports
PNP06xx	Hard disk controllers
PNP07xx	Floppy disk controllers
PNP08xx	System speaker
PNP09xx	Display adapters
PNP0Axx	Expansion buses
PNP0Bxx	CMOS clock
PNP0Cxx	System board devices
PNP0Exx	PCMCIA controllers
PNP0Fxx	Mouse controllers
PNP8xxx	Network adapters
PNPAxxx	Multimedia CD-ROM controller
PNPBxxx	Unknown adapters

Table 736 Registry device name formats for plug-and-play devices.

737   USING THE REGISTRY TO CONTROL SCREEN COLORS

In Tip 241, you learned how to use the Display Properties dialog box Appearance sheet to assign colors to various Desktop elements. When you assign color values to Desktop items, Windows 98 stores your color assignments within the Registry. For example, Figure 737 shows various color settings for Desktop items within the Registry.

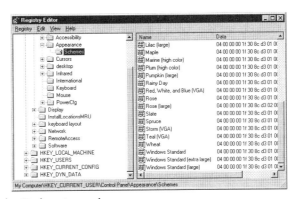

Figure 737 Using the Registry to display Desktop item colors.

As you have learned, Windows 98 assigns colors to items using combinations of the colors red, green, and blue. If you examine the Registry values shown in Figure 737, you will find three color values, ranging from 0 to 255, which specify the red, green, and blue color intensities. If you select the values 255, 255, 255, Windows 98 will display the color white. Likewise, if you use the color values 0, 0, 0, Windows 98 will display the color black.

738 USING THE REGISTRY TO REMOVE THE ARROW FROM SHORTCUT ICONS

As you have learned, within the Explorer, Windows 98 represents shortcuts using an icon that contains a small arrow, similar to those shown in Figure 738.

Figure 738 *Shortcut icons usually contain arrows.*

As Tip 141 discusses, a shortcut is simply a link to an object, as opposed to the object itself. Within your system, for example, you might place shortcuts to a program you use on a regular basis, such as Microsoft Word, within several different folders. Although such shortcuts will give you multiple links to Word, you would still only have one copy of Word on your system. Depending on your preferences, you may want Windows 98 to represent shortcuts using the same icon it would use to represent the object itself. In other words, you want Windows 98 to eliminate the arrow from the shortcut icon. To remove the arrow from shortcut icons, open the Registry's *HKEY_CLASSES_ROOT* and delete the *IsShortCut* settings for the *lnkfile* and *piffile* Registry entries. (To locate the *lnkfile* and *piffile* entries, you may have to scroll through many entries within the *HKEY_CLASSES_ROOT* branch.) After you restart Windows 98, your shortcut icons will no longer appear with arrows.

739 USING THE REGISTRY TO VIEW A SYSTEM'S LOW-LEVEL MICROSOFT *TCP/IP* SETTINGS

To access the Internet from your system, you must enable TCP/IP support. Within the Control Panel Network Properties dialog box, you can configure your system's TCP/IP settings. Windows 98, in turn, will store your TCP/IP settings within the Registry. By examining the entries within the *HKEY_LOCAL_MACHINE\System\CurrentControlSet\Services\VxD\MSTCP* subkey, you can view your current TCP/IP settings and other low-level settings. Figure 739 shows the Microsoft TCP (MSTCP) subtree within the Registry. For more information on the TCP settings you can use within the Registry, visit the Microsoft Web site or use the Microsoft Windows 98 Resource Kit.

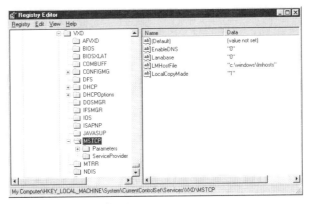

Figure 739 *Using the Registry to view or change Microsoft TCP settings.*

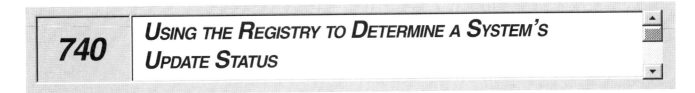

740	**USING THE REGISTRY TO DETERMINE A SYSTEM'S UPDATE STATUS**

If you are a system administer who maintains a number of Windows 98 PCs within a local-area network or large office, there may be times when you need to determine if a PC was upgraded to Windows 98 from a previous version of Windows or if Windows 98 was the PC's original operating system. (A PC that was upgraded from Windows 95, for example, may have device drivers or other files that are not present on an original Windows 98 system.) Using the Registry's *UpdateMode* entry, shown in Figure 740, you can determine the system's upgrade status. If the *UpdateMode* has the value 0, the system was not upgraded from a previous version of Windows. However, if the entry has the value 1, the system was upgraded from a previous version of Windows.

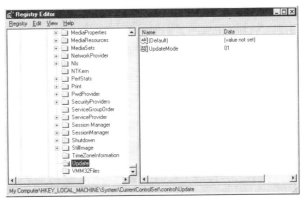

Figure 740 *Using the Registry to determine if a system was upgraded to Windows 98 from a previous version of Windows.*

741	**USING THE REGISTRY TO VIEW A SYSTEM'S USER PROFILES**

In Tip 413, you learned that to help multiple users share the same PC, Windows 98 provides user profiles, within which it stores each user's settings. To create a new user profile, you can use the Control Panel Users Settings option or the user can simply type in his or her username and password at the Welcome to Windows login dialog box. When you create a new user profile, Windows 98 stores information about each user within subfolders within the *Windows\Profiles* folder shown in Figure 741.1.

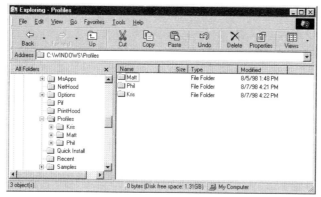

Figure 741.1 *Windows 98 stores specifics about each user profile within subfolders within the **Windows\Profiles** folder.*

In addition to storing user-profile information within files on your disk, Windows 98 also stores information about profiles within the Registry, as shown in Figure 741.2. Using the Registry's profile entries, you can determine which folder Windows 98 uses for each user profile.

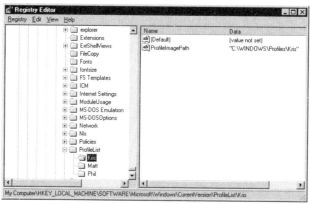

Figure 741.2 *Using the Registry to view information about user profiles.*

742 USING THE REGISTRY TO TILE, CENTER, OR STRETCH WALLPAPER

In Tip 231, you learned how to assign a wallpaper to your Desktop background. Depending on the image you assigned to the background, you may have tiled, centered, or stretched the image to fill the background. When you use the Display Properties dialog box Background sheet to assign a background wallpaper, Windows 98 stores your settings within the Registry. For example, Figure 742 shows the Desktop settings within the Registry. To use the Registry to tile, center, or stretch your wallpaper, assign the value 0, 1, or 2 to the *TileWallPaper* entry.

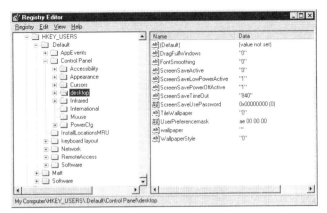

Figure 742 *Using the Registry to view or change the Desktop wallpaper settings.*

---

743 USING THE REGISTRY TO SPECIFY THE DESKTOP WALLPAPER

In Tip 234, you learned how to use the Display Properties dialog box Background sheet to assign a specific image to your Desktop background. When you use the Display Properties dialog box to assign an image to your Desktop, Windows 98 stores your settings within the Registry. For example, Figure 743 shows the Registry's Desktop settings. To change your background wallpaper, assign the filename of the image you desire to the *Wallpaper* entry.

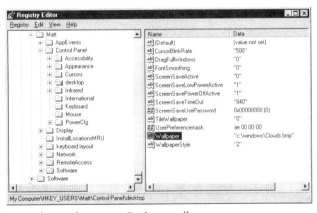

Figure 743 *Using the Registry to view or change the current Desktop wallpaper.*

---

744 USING THE REGISTRY TO CONTROL VIDEO RESOLUTION

In Tip 248, you learned how to use the Control Panels Display Properties dialog box Settings sheet to specify your video-resolution settings. When you use the Settings sheet to assign video settings, Windows 98 stores your values within the Registry. To view or change your video settings, you can use the Registry, as shown in Figure 744.

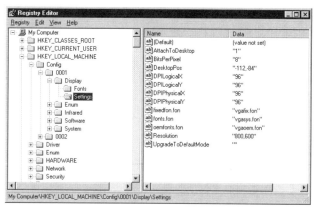

Figure 744 *Using the Registry to view or change video display settings.*

---

745 USING THE REGISTRY TO LIST THE WINDOWS 98 32-BIT VIRTUAL DRIVERS

As you have learned, Windows 98 precedes its 32-bit device-driver names with the letters VxD where the letter x corresponds to the device. To view your system's 32-bit device drivers, you can use the Control Panel System Properties dialog box. In addition, you can use the Registry to display the installed 32-bit drivers, as shown in Figure 745.

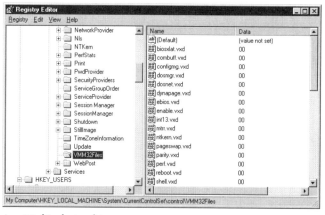

Figure 745 *Using the Registry to view 32-bit device drivers.*

---

746 USING THE WINDOWS 98 REPORT WRITER TO REPORT ERRORS TO MICROSOFT

If you encounter an error running a Windows 98 program, you can (and should) submit a description of the error to Microsoft using the Windows Report Tool, shown in Figure 746. Within the Windows Report Tool, you can describe the error and the steps you can perform to reproduce the error. When you submit the error, you can direct the Windows

Report Tool to also submit your key system files, whose contents may help Microsoft Technical Support Specialists troubleshoot the error. Within the Windows Report Tool, you can click your mouse on the Next buttons to complete and send your report.

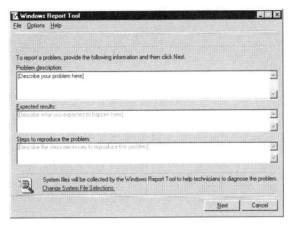

Figure 746 *The Windows Report Tool.*

To start the Windows Report Tool, perform these steps:

1. Click your mouse on the Start menu Programs option and choose Accessories. Windows 98 will display the Accessories submenu.

2. Within the Accessories submenu, click your mouse on the System Tools option and choose System Information. Windows 98 will display the System Information window.

3. Within the System Information Window, click your mouse on the Tools menu Windows Report Tool option. Windows 98, in turn, will open the Windows Report Tool.

747 COMPLETING INFORMATION WITHIN THE WINDOWS REPORT TOOL

In Tip 746, you learned how to start the Windows Report Tool that lets you submit an error report to Microsoft. To complete a report within the Windows Report Tool, perform these steps:

1. Within the Windows Report Tool window, click your mouse within the Problem Description field and type a detailed description of the problem you are encountering. Then, click your mouse on the Expected Results field and type the result you were expecting. Finally, provide a numbered list of the steps you can perform to repeat the error.

2. Within the Windows Report Tool window, click your mouse on the Options menu Collected Information option. Windows 98, in turn, will display the Collected Information dialog box, as shown in Figure 747.1.

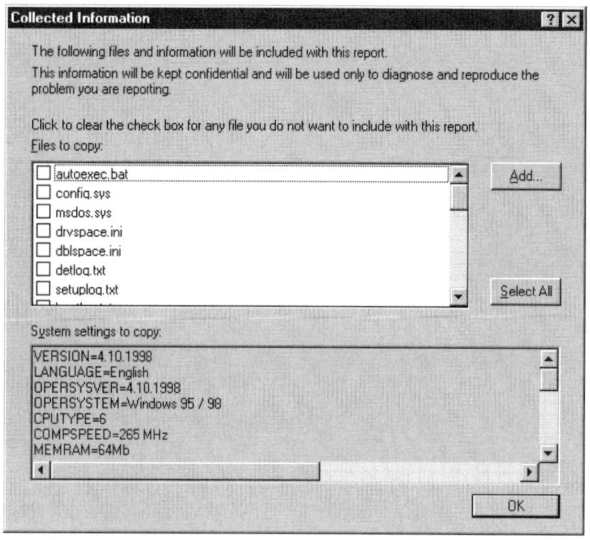

Figure 747.1 *The Collected Information dialog box.*

3. Within the Collected Information dialog box, click your mouse on the checkboxes that correspond to the files you want to submit with your report to Microsoft. Then, click your mouse on the OK button.

4. Within the Windows Report Tool window, click your mouse on the Options menu User Information option. Windows 98 will display the User Information dialog box, as shown in Figure 747.2.

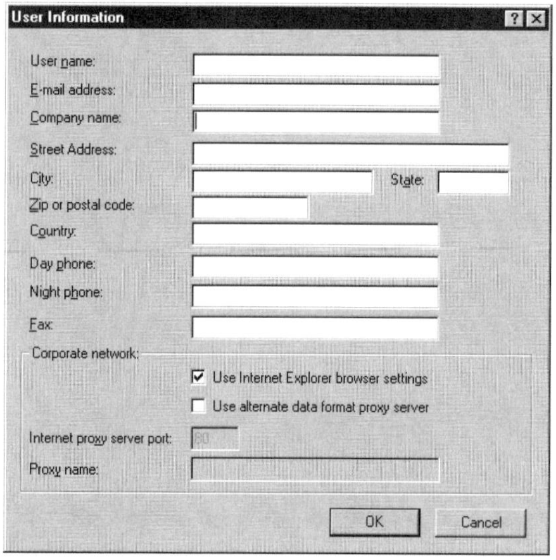

Figure 747.2 *The User Information dialog box.*

5. Within the User Information dialog box, type in the information that the Microsoft Technical Support Specialists can use should they need to contact you in the future. Then, click your mouse on the OK button.

6. Within the Windows Report Tool window, click your mouse on the Next button and perform each of the steps the Wizard presents to send your report.

748   USING THE SYSTEM FILE CHECKER TO EXAMINE KEY FILES

In Tip 643, you learned how to use the ScanDisk utility program to examine your disk, files, and folders. In general, the ScanDisk utility examines your disk's structure and can detect general types of errors. If you experience intermittent or serious errors within Windows 98, there may be times when one or more of your key system files have become corrupt (an error that the ScanDisk utility may not detect). To examine your key system files, you can use the Windows 98 System File Checker. If the System File Checker detects a damage file, it will copy the original file from your Windows 98 CD-ROM. To run the System File Checker, perform these steps:

1. Click your mouse on the Start menu Programs option and choose Accessories. Windows 98 will display the Accessories submenu.

2. Within the Accessories submenu, click your mouse on the System Tools option and choose System Information. Windows 98, in turn, will display the System Information window.

3. Within the System Information Window, click your mouse on the Tools menu System File Checker option. Windows 98, in turn, will open the System File Checker, as shown in Figure 748.

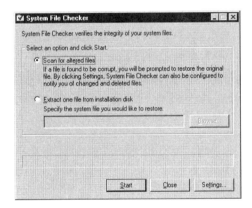

Figure 748 The System File Checker.

4. Within the System File Checker window, click your mouse on the Scan for altered files radio button and then click your mouse on the Start button. The System File Checker will examine your key files. If the System File Checker encounters an error, it will prompt you to insert the Windows 98 CD-ROM from which it can restore the original file.

749   USING THE SYSTEM FILE CHECKER TO RESTORE A SPECIFIC FILE

In Tip 748, you learned how to use the Windows 98 System File Checker to examine your disk for damaged (or altered) system files. As you troubleshoot system problems, there may be times when you will want to restore a specific file from your original Windows 98 CD-ROM. In such cases, you can perform the update using the System File Checker by performing these steps:

1. Click your mouse on the Start menu Programs option and choose Accessories. Windows 98 will display the Accessories submenu.

2. Within the Accessories submenu, click your mouse on the System Tools option and choose System Information. Windows 98, in turn, will display the System Information window.

3. Within the System Information Window, click your mouse on the Tools menu System File Checker option. Windows 98, in turn, will open the System File Checker.

4. Within the System File Checker window, click your mouse on the Extract one file from installation disk radio button and then use the Browse button to locate the file you want to replace. After you select the file you want to replace, click your mouse on the Start button.

USING THE SIGNATURE VERIFICATION TOOL TO FIND SIGNED FILES

750

Across the Web, many sites now let you download programs and utilities that perform specific tasks. You might, for example, download a program which acts as a stock-ticker-tape machine, displaying stock prices on your Desktop. To prevent your computer from being infected by a virus, you usually should not download programs from the Web. However, you can usually feel relatively safe when you download files from reputable sites, such as Microsoft or Netscape.

To further protect your system, sites that offer file downloads often attach a digital signature to the file. When you download a file whose digital signature is in place, you can feel confident that another user has not modified the file's contents. Within your system, you can use the Microsoft Signature Verification Tool to locate signed (or unsigned) files on your system. To search your disk for signed files, perform these steps:

1. Click your mouse on the Start menu Programs option and choose Accessories. Windows 98 will display the Accessories submenu.

2. Within the Accessories submenu, click your mouse on the System Tools option and choose System Information. Windows 98 will display the System Information window.

3. Within the System Information Window, click your mouse on the Tools menu Signature Verification Tool option. Windows 98, in turn, will open the Microsoft Signature Verification Tool, as shown in Figure 750.

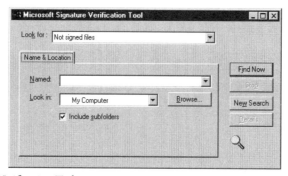

Figure 750 The Microsoft Signature Verification Tool.

4. Within the Microsoft Signature Verification Tool window, select the drive or folder you want to

search and optionally type in a specific filename. (Using the Look for pull-down list, you can search for signed or unsigned files.) To begin your search, click your mouse on the Find Now button. If the utility finds signed files, it will display the file's name within its file list. To display specifics about a file (such as its certificate), click your mouse on the file within the file list and then click your mouse on the Details button.

751 USING DR. WATSON TO TROUBLESHOOT SYSTEM FAULTS

If your system is experiencing intermittent errors, you may be able to identify the cause of the error using the Dr. Watson utility. In general, the Dr. Watson utility captures system faults (errors that occur within your system). Then, you can use Dr. Watson to display specifics about the cause of the error. Usually, Windows 98 does not run the Dr. Watson utility. If your system is experiencing errors, you should restart your system, and start Dr. Watson before you perform other operations. (You might, for example, place the Dr. Watson program within the Startup menu.) To start the Dr. Watson utility, perform these steps:

1. Click your mouse on the Start menu Programs option and choose Accessories. Windows 98 will display the Accessories submenu.

2. Within the Accessories submenu, click your mouse on the System Tools option and choose System Information. Windows 98 will display the System Information window.

3. Within the System Information Window, click your mouse on the Tools menu Dr. Watson option. Windows 98, in turn, will start Dr. Watson, placing a small icon on the Taskbar icon.

4. After Dr. Watson is running, perform the operations that previously caused the error. Then, when the error occurs, click your mouse on the Dr. Watson Taskbar icon. Windows 98, in turn, will display the Dr. Watson dialog box, within which it displays its diagnosis, as shown in Figure 751.

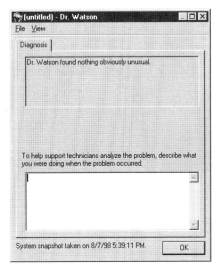

Figure 751 *Displaying the cause of a system error within the Dr. Watson dialog box.*

5. Within the Dr. Watson dialog box, click your mouse on the File menu Print option to print the diagnosis.

752 | USING THE SYSTEM CONFIGURATION UTILITY TO TROUBLESHOOT YOUR SYSTEM

If you are experiencing intermittent system errors, you may be able to troubleshoot the error using the System Configuration Utility program, shown in Figure 752. Within the System Configuration Utility, you can use checkboxes to enable or disable specific *Config.SYS*, *Autoexec.BAT*, *System.INI*, and *Win.INI* settings. In addition, you can disable programs that Windows 98 would usually run each time your system starts.

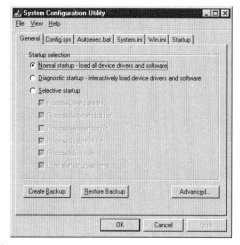

Figure 752 *The System Configuration Utility.*

To run the System Configuration Utility, perform these steps:

1. Click your mouse on the Start menu Programs option and choose Accessories. Windows 98 will display the Accessories submenu.

2. Within the Accessories submenu, click your mouse on the System Tools option and choose System Information. Windows 98 will display the System Information window.

3. Within the System Information Window, click your mouse on the Tools menu System Configuration Utility option. Windows 98, in turn, will start the System Configuration Utility.

4. Within the System Configuration Utility, you should first backup your current system settings by clicking your mouse on the Create Backup button. Later, after you identify the cause of the error, you can restore your previous settings and then disable the entry that is causing the error.

5. Within the System Configuration Utility General sheet, you can click your mouse on the Selective Startup button and then use checkboxes to enable or disable Windows 98's processing of specific files.

6. Next, within the System Configuration Utility, you can click your mouse on a tab that corresponds to a specific system file. The System Configuration Utility, in turn, will display a sheet within which you can enable or disable different settings.

7. After you make the changes to your system settings, click your mouse on the OK button to put your changes into effect. Windows 98, in turn, will display a dialog box that states you must restart your system for your changes to take effect. Click your mouse on the Yes button to restart your system.

---

753 | **USING THE SYSTEM CONFIGURATION UTILITY'S ADVANCED TROUBLESHOOTING OPTIONS**

In Tip 752, you learned that you can use the System Configuration Utility to enable or disable different system settings to help you troubleshoot system errors. In addition to turning on or off Windows 98's processing of specific files and file settings, you can also use the System Configuration Utility's Advanced Troubleshooting Settings dialog box, as shown in Figure 753, to identify possible causes for the system error.

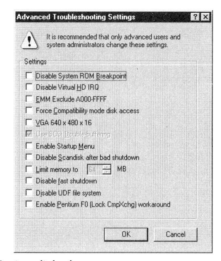

Figure 753 *The Advanced Troubleshooting Settings dialog box.*

To use the Advanced Troubleshooting Settings dialog box to troubleshoot your system, perform these steps:

1. Click your mouse on the Start menu Programs option and choose Accessories. Windows 98 will display the Accessories submenu.

2. Within the Accessories submenu, click your mouse on the System Tools option and choose System Information. Windows 98 will display the System Information window.

3. Within the System Information Window, click your mouse on the Tools menu System Configuration Utility option. Windows 98, in turn, will start the System Configuration Utility.

4. Within the System Configuration Utility, you should first backup your current system settings by clicking your mouse on the Create Backup button. Later, after you identify the cause of the error, you can restore your previous settings and then disable the entry that is causing the error.

5. Within the System Configuration Utility General sheet, click your mouse on the Advanced button. Windows 98, in turn, will display the Advanced Troubleshooting Settings dialog box.

6. Within the Advanced Troubleshooting Settings dialog box, use the checkboxes to enable and disable different settings and to monitor the setting's impact on your system error.

7. After you make the changes to your system settings, click your mouse on the OK button to put your changes into effect. Windows 98, in turn, will display a dialog box that states you must restart your system for your changes to take effect. Click your mouse on the Yes button to restart your system.

754 — USING THE SYSTEM CONFIGURATION UTILITY TO DISABLE STARTUP PROGRAMS

If you are experiencing intermittent system errors, you may want to disable one or more of the programs that Windows 98 runs each time your system starts. To control which programs Windows 98 runs when its starts, you can use the System Configuration Utility's Startup sheet, as shown in Figure 754.

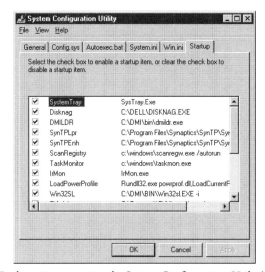

Figure 754 Controlling the programs Windows 98 runs using the System Configuration Utility's Startup sheet.

To use the Startup sheet to control which programs Windows 98 runs each time it starts, perform these steps:

1. Click your mouse on the Start menu Programs option and choose Accessories. Windows 98 will display the Accessories submenu.

2. Within the Accessories submenu, click your mouse on the System Tools option and choose System Information. Windows 98 will display the System Information window.

3. Within the System Information Window, click your mouse on the Tools menu System Configuration Utility option. Windows 98, in turn, will start the System Configuration Utility.

4. Within the System Configuration Utility, you should first backup your current system settings by clicking your mouse on the Create Backup button. Later, after you identify the cause of the error, you can restore your previous settings and then disable the entry that is causing the error.

5. Within the System Configuration Utility General sheet, click your mouse on the Startup tab. Windows 98, in turn, will display the Startup sheet.

6. Within the Startup sheet, use the checkboxes to control which programs Windows 98 runs when your system starts, and then click your mouse on the OK button.

7. After you make your changes to your system settings, click your mouse on the OK button to put your changes into effect. Windows 98, in turn, will display a dialog box that states you must restart your system for your changes to take effect. Click your mouse on the Yes button to restart your system.

755 USING THE VERSION CONFLICT MANAGER

When you install Windows 98, the installation program upgrades many different program files within new versions. During the installation, there may be times when the Setup program replaced a newer version of a specific file that resided on your disk with an older version from the Windows 98 CD-ROM. The Windows 98 installation program places the older file on your disk because it knows the older file is compatible with the rest of Windows 98. However, before the installation program replaces the file, it makes a backup copy of the newer file which it saves on your disk.

If your system is experiencing intermittent errors, the problem may be due to a software version conflict due to your software upgrade. To troubleshoot the error, you can use the Windows 98 Version Conflict Manager, as shown in Figure 755.

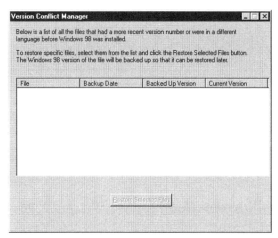

Figure 755 *The Windows 98 Version Conflict Manager.*

Within the Version Conflict Manager, you can view the newer files that the Windows 98 installation replaced with older versions. To direct the Version Conflict Manager to use the newer version of a specific file, click your mouse on the file within the file list and then click your mouse on the Restore Selected Files button.

756 MONITORING THE WINDOWS 98 BOOT
PROCESSING USING BOOTLOG.TXT

Each time you start your system, Windows 98 loads its key operating system files which, in turn, load the device-driver software Windows 98 will use to communicate with your screen display, disk, keyboard, mouse, and so on. If you install new hardware on your system, there may be times when your system will display an error message as it starts, or your system may simply not start at all. To troubleshoot such problems, you can direct Windows 98 to create the root directory file *BootLog.TXT*, whose contents list the device drivers Windows 98 successfully (and possibly unsuccessfully) loaded. After your system starts, you can use an editor, such as the Notepad accessory, to view the log file's contents, as shown in Figure 756.

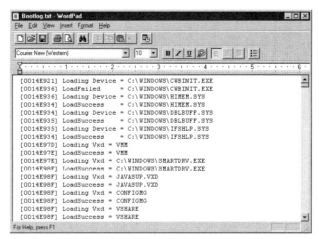

Figure 756 *Viewing the Windows 98 startup log within the file **BootLog.TXT**.*

Within the *BootLog.TXT* file, you will find single-line entries for each startup operation Windows 98 performs. For example, before Windows 98 starts to load a device driver, Windows 98 will write a message logging the action with the file:

```
[000C2763] Loading Device = C:\WINDOWS\HIMEM.SYS
```

If Windows 98 successfully installs (or fails to install the driver), Windows 98 will also log that fact:

```
[000C2764] LoadSuccess = C:\WINDOWS\HIMEM.SYS
```

To direct Windows 98 to create the *BootLog.TXT* file, perform these steps:

1. Start your system in MS-DOS mode.
2. From the MS-DOS system prompt, start Windows 98 using the WIN /B command:

```
C:\Windows> WIN /B   <ENTER>
```

Note: *The Windows 98 Setup program will create a **BootLog.TXT** file within your root directory that you can view to determine the drivers it successfully loaded following your Windows 98 installation.*

757 **DISPLAYING THE WINDOWS 98 SYSTEM MENU**

If you are troubleshooting a system that keeps Windows 98 from starting, you may need to start your system in Real mode so you can correct the error by issuing commands from the system prompt. The easiest way to control your system startup is to use the Windows 98 system menu, as shown here:

```
Microsoft Windows 98 Startup Menu
===================================

 1. Normal
```

```
2. Logged (\BOOTLOG.TXT)
3. Safe mode
4. Step-by-step confirmation
5. Command prompt only
6. Safe mode command prompt only
```

Enter a choice:

To display the Windows 98 Startup menu, use the Shutdown menu Restart option to restart your system (if it is currently running) or simply turn on your PC's power (if your computer is off). As your PC performs its power-on self test, hold down your keyboard's CTRL key. The following Tips examine the Startup menu options in detail.

Note: *Under Windows 95, users would access the system menu by pressing the F8 function key after their screen displayed the message, Starting Windows 95. The Windows 98 operating system does not display a similar message. To display the Startup menu, hold down the CTRL key as your system starts.*

758 STARTING WINDOWS 98 IN NORMAL OR LOGGED MODE

In Tip 757, you learned how to display the Windows 98 Startup menu by pressing the CTRL key as your system starts. Within the Windows 98 Startup menu, the first two options, Normal and Logged direct Windows 98 to start and load the software it would use for normal operations. The difference between the two options is that the Logged option directs Windows 98 to create the startup log file, *BootLog.TXT* that Tip 756 discusses. When you start your system using the Normal or Logged options, Windows 98 will load its startup files, your system's device drivers, and will then process your *CONFIG.SYS* and *AUTOEXEC.BAT* files followed by your *System.INI* and *Win.INI* files.

759 STARTING WINDOWS 98 IN SAFE MODE

In Tip 757, you learned how to display the Windows 98 Startup menu by pressing the CTRL key as your system starts. If, after you install new hardware or new software (or change software settings), your system fails to start, you may be able to start Windows 98 in *safe mode*, from which you can troubleshot and correct the error.

When you select the Windows 98 Startup menu Safe mode option, Windows 98 will start your system using only the minimal settings it must provide in order to start. Specifically, when you select safe mode, Windows 98 will not process the Registry entries, your *CONFIG.SYS* or *AUTOEXEC.BAT* files, or the startup entries within the *System.INI* file. In addition, within safe mode, Windows 98 will not load most device drivers and will not provide network support.

If you can start your system in safe mode, you may then be able to troubleshoot and correct the cause of your system's startup error. After you correct the error, you can restart your system in normal mode by selecting the Start menu Shutdown option and then choosing Restart.

760 USING A STEP-BY-STEP CONFIRMATION TO LOAD WINDOWS 98 SYSTEM FILES

In Tip 759, you learned that when Windows 98 fails to start, you may be able to start your system in safe mode from the Windows 98 Startup menu and then troubleshoot the cause of your system error. If you find that Windows 98 is failing as it processes your *CONFIG.SYS, AUTOEXEC.BAT, System.INI,* or *Win.INI* files, you can select the Startup menu Step-by-step confirmation option to direct Windows 98 to display the following prompt before it processes each entry within the files:

```
[Enter=Y, Esc=N]
```

If you type Y in response to the Yes or No prompt, Windows 98 will process the corresponding entry and will continue its startup operations with the next entry within the startup file. If you instead type N, Windows 98 will skip the entry. By forcing Windows 98 to process the startup file entries one at a time in this way, you can better identify the entry which is causing your system error.

761 STARTING WINDOWS 98 TO A COMMAND PROMPT

In Tip 758, you learned how to display the Windows 98 Startup menu by pressing the CTRL key as your system starts. If you cannot start Windows 98 in safe mode and you cannot start Windows 98 by performing a step-by-step confirmation, as discussed in Tip 760, you may be able to start Windows 98 to a real-mode command prompt, from which you can issue commands to troubleshoot your system error.

In addition to using the real-mode prompt to troubleshoot your system, there may be times when you have an older MS-DOS-based program that will only run within real mode. By selecting the Startup menu Command prompt only option, you can start Windows 98 in real mode. After you correct the error that you were troubleshooting within real mode or after you finish running a real-mode program, you can start Windows 98 for normal operations by typing the WIN command at the system prompt, as shown here:

```
C:\Windows> WIN   <ENTER>
```

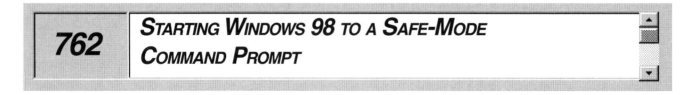

762 STARTING WINDOWS 98 TO A SAFE-MODE COMMAND PROMPT

In Tip 758, you learned how to start Windows 98 from the Startup menu to a command prompt. When you select the Startup menu's Command prompt only option, Windows 98 will start your system in real mode and will process the entries that reside within your system's *CONFIG.SYS* and *AUTOEXEC.BAT* files. If you find that Windows 98 cannot start in real mode due to an errant entry within one of these two files, you can select the Startup menu Safe mode command prompt only option to direct Windows 98 to start in real mode but not to process the *CONFIG.SYS* and *AUTOEXEC.BAT* entries.

From within real mode, you can use an editor such as the Edit command (which resides within the *Windows\Commands* folder) to edit the errant file entry. Then, you can start Windows for normal operations by typing WIN at the command prompt:

```
C:\Windows> WIN   <ENTER>
```

763 UNDERSTANDING HOW WINDOWS 98 USES THE IO.SYS FILE

Within your boot disk's root directory, you will find a hidden file named *IO.SYS*. As it turns out, this file contains a real-mode operating system that your system loads into memory each time it starts. The *IO.SYS* file will load the device drivers that Windows 98 will later require before it can start. If you are familiar with the MS-DOS operating system, you can think of the *IO.SYS* file as combining the MS-DOS *IO.SYS* (which contained software that MS-DOS used to perform hardware input/output operations), *MSDOS.SYS* (which provided the MS-DOS system services), as well as the *CONFIG.SYS* files.

The *IO.SYS* file contains program instructions and data. You cannot edit the file's contents. Table 763.1 lists the device-driver software that the *IO.SYS* file loads. Likewise, Table 763.2 lists default configuration settings the *IO.SYS* defines, that you can override by placing entries within the *CONFIG.SYS* file.

Device Driver	Purpose
HIMEM.SYS	Provides extended-memory support
IFSHLP.SYS	Provides support for the installable file system that traps real-mode network and file system services
SETVER.EXE	Lets MS-DOS report a specific version number back to an inquiring program
DBLSPACE.BIN	Provides support for disk compression

Table 763.1 The device drivers the IO.SYS file loads when your system starts.

Setting	Default Value
BUFFERS	30
FCBS=	4
FILES=	60
LASTDRIVE=	Z
SHELL=	Command.COM
STACKS=	9,256

Table 763.2 Default real-mode settings the IO.SYS file defines when your system starts.

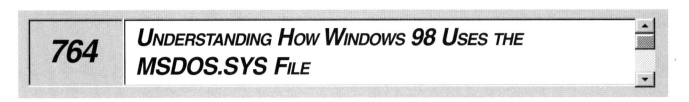

764   *UNDERSTANDING HOW WINDOWS 98 USES THE MSDOS.SYS FILE*

Within your boot disk's root directory, you will find a hidden file named MSDOS.SYS that contains single-line entries that you can edit to control the Windows 98 startup process. Figure 764, for example, shows the contents of the MSDOS.SYS file within the Notepad accessory program.

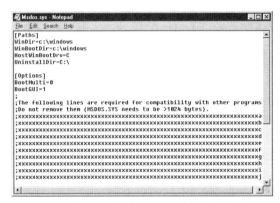

Figure 764 Using the Notepad accessory program to view or edit the contents of the MSDOS.SYS file.

Several of the Tips that follow examine the MSDOS.SYS entries in detail. By default, the MSDOS.SYS file is a read-only, hidden file. Before you can change the file's contents, you must remove its read-only attribute. To change the MSDOS.SYS file's read-only attribute, perform these steps:

1. Click your mouse on the Start menu Programs option and choose Windows Explorer. Windows 98, in turn, will start the Explorer.

2. Within the Explorer window, select the boot disk's root directory and then right-click your mouse on the MSDOS.SYS file. Windows 98 will display a pop-up menu. Within the pop-up menu, select the Properties option. Windows 98 will display the file's Properties dialog box.

3. Within the Properties dialog box, click your mouse on the Read-only checkbox to remove the check mark and then click your mouse on the OK button. You can now use a program such as the Notepad accessory to edit the file's contents.

Note: *Before you edit the MSDOS.SYS file's contents, you should use the Explorer to make a copy of the file's current contents. You might name the copy MSDOS.BAK (for backup). Should you make a change to the file that causes an error, you can simply delete your copy of the file and rename your backup copy back to MSDOS.SYS.*

765   *UNDERSTANDING THE MSDOS.SYS FILE'S CONTENTS*

In Tip 764, you learned that you can use the *MSDOS.SYS* file to control the Windows 98 startup process. Using entries within the *MSDOS.SYS* file, for example, you can control options on the Windows 98 Startup menu. If you use the Notepad accessory to view the contents of the *MSDOS.SYS* file, you will find a series of single-line entries and a series of lines that contain a series of x's. Do not delete the lines containing x's. Windows 98 requires that the file contain at least 1,024 characters. The lines of x's ensure that the file maintains this minimum length.

Within the MSDOS.SYS file, you will find entries within a [Paths] section that defines the location of several key files and an [Options] section that you will use to customize startup settings. Each entry within the file takes the form *Name=Value*. For example, the following *BootMenu* entry directs Windows 98 to display its Startup menu every time your system starts:

```
BootMenu=1
```

By assigning specific values to the file's entries, you control the startup process. Several of the Tips that follow examine the *MSDOS.SYS* entries in detail.

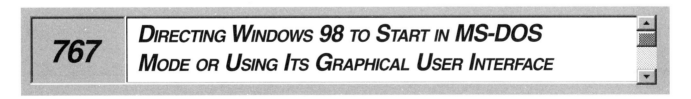

766 CONTROLLING WHEN WINDOWS 98 RUNS THE SCANDISK UTILITY WHEN YOUR SYSTEM STARTS

By default, if your system does not shut down successfully, Windows 98 will run the ScanDisk utility program the next time that your system starts so that ScanDisk can examine your disk and files for possible errors. Usually, Windows 98 will display a dialog box telling you that your system was not shut down correctly and that it will run ScanDisk. Within the dialog box, you can then start or cancel the ScanDisk operation.

Within the *MSDOS.SYS* file, you can use the *AutoScan=* entry to control whether or not Windows 98 automatically starts the ScanDisk utility in this way. If you want to disable Windows 98's automatic starting of the ScanDisk command, assign the value 0 to the *AutoScan=* entry, as shown here:

```
AutoScan=0
```

If you want Windows 98 to prompt you before it starts the ScanDisk command, assign the value 1 to the entry. Likewise, if you want Windows 98 to start ScanDisk without prompting the user, assign the value 2 to the entry, as shown here:

```
AutoScan=2
```

767 DIRECTING WINDOWS 98 TO START IN MS-DOS MODE OR USING ITS GRAPHICAL USER INTERFACE

As you have learned, if you start Windows 98 in real mode (MS-DOS mode), you can later start Windows 98 graphical-user interface by typing the WIN command at the system prompt. If you often use Windows 98 in real mode, or perhaps you run older computer games, you can use the *MSDOS.SYS* file *BootGUI=* entry to direct Windows 98 to start in real mode by assigning the value 0 to the entry, as shown here:

```
BootGUI=0
```

If you later decide that you want Windows 98 to display its graphical-user interface when it starts, assign the value 1 to the entry:

```
BootGUI=1
```

768 CONTROLLING THE WINDOWS *98* STARTUP
SUPPORT FOR THE CTRL KEY

As you have learned, if you hold down your CTRL key as your system starts, Windows 98 will display its Startup menu. If you are a system administrator who is responsible for a local-area network or PCs within a large office, there may be times (possibly for security reasons) that you want to prevent a user from accessing the Startup menu by holding down the CTRL key as the system starts. In such cases, you direct Windows 98 to ignore the CTRL key by assigning the value 0 to the *MSDOS.SYS* file's *BootKeys=* entry, as shown here:

```
BootKeys=0
```

If you want to enable Windows 98 startup support for the CTRL key, assign the value 1 to the entry:

```
BootKeys=1
```

769 DIRECTING WINDOWS *98* TO ALWAYS DISPLAY
ITS STARTUP MENU

As you have learned, if you learned that if you hold down your CTRL key as your system starts, Windows 98 will display its Startup menu. If you are troubleshooting a system, there may be times when you want Windows 98 to display its Startup menu every time that it starts, regardless of whether or not you press the CTRL key. To direct Windows 98 to display its Startup menu each time it starts, assign the value 1 to the *MSDOS.SYS* file *BootMenu=* entry, as shown here:

```
BootMenu=1
```

To turn off the menu's display (which then requires that you press the CTRL key to activate the menu), assign the value 0 to the *BootMenu=* entry.

770 CONTROLLING THE BOOT MENU DEFAULT OPTION

As you have learned, if you learned that when you hold down your CTRL key as your system starts, Windows 98 will display its Startup menu. Within the Startup menu, you can use the MSDOS file *BootMenuDefault=* entry to specify the menu's default entry that Windows 98 will select if the user does not select an option within a specific time interval. In this way, should your system restart when no one is present (perhaps Windows 98 restarts due to a loss of power), Windows 98 will select the default menu option which lets your system start. For example, the following entry selects the normal startup (option 1) as the default Startup menu option:

```
BootMenuDefault=0
```

Note: To specify the menu timeout period, see the BootMenuDelay= entry which Tip 771 presents.

771 **SPECIFYING THE WINDOWS 98 STARTUP MENU DELAY**

As you have learned, if you learned that when you hold down your CTRL key as your system starts, Windows 98 will display its Startup menu. Within the Startup menu, you can specify a default menu that Windows 98 will select if the user does not select an option within a specific time interval. In this way, should your system restart when no one is present (perhaps Windows 98 restarts due to a loss of power), Windows 98 will select the default menu option which lets your system start. To specify the amount of time Windows 98 waits for a menu selection, assign the number of seconds you desire to the *MSDOS.SYS* file *BootMenuDelay=* entry. For example, the following entry specifies a 15-second delay:

```
BootMenuDelay=15
```

As your system displays the Startup menu, it will count down the number of seconds remaining until Windows 98 will select the default menu option.

Note: To specify the default menu option, see the BootMenuDefault= entry which Tip 770 presents.

772 **SUPPORTING MS-DOS AND WINDOWS 98 DUAL-BOOT OPERATIONS**

If your system has the MS-DOS operating system (version 5 or later) and Windows 98 installed on your disk, you can use the *MSDOS.SYS* file *BootMulti=* entry to support dual-boot operations. Before you enable dual-boot support for MS-DOS and Windows 98, make sure your drive C is using a 16-bit file-allocation table. Next, assign the value 1 to the *MSDOS.SYS* file *BootMulti=* entry, as shown here:

```
BootMulti=1
```

To disable dual-boot support, assign the value 0 to the *BootMulti=* entry.

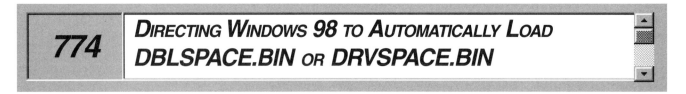

773 SELECTING WINDOWS 98 OR MS-DOS AS THE DEFAULT OPERATING SYSTEM

If your system has the MS-DOS operating system (version 5 or later) and Windows 98 installed on your disk, you can use the *MSDOS.SYS* file *BootWin=* entry to specify the operating system you want your system to start. To specify Windows 98 as the default operating system, set BootWin to 1, as shown here:

```
BootWin=1
```

To select MS-DOS as the default operating system, assign the value 0 to the *BootWin=* entry. To enable dual-boot support for MS-DOS and Windows 98, your drive C must use a 16-bit file-allocation table and you must assign the value 1 to the *MSDOS.SYS* file *BootMulti=* entry.

774 DIRECTING WINDOWS 98 TO AUTOMATICALLY LOAD DBLSPACE.BIN OR DRVSPACE.BIN

In Tip 609, you learned how to increase your disk's storage capacity by compressing the files that reside on your disk. Under Windows 98, if you compress a disk, Windows 98 will load the *DRVSPACE.BIN* device-driver software. If you have upgraded to Windows 98 from Windows 95, your system may load the *DBLSPACE.BIN* device driver. If you are not using disk compression, Windows 98 will not install these device drivers when your system starts. Instead, if you later use a compressed disk (such as a compressed floppy), Windows 98 will automatically load the software it requires. Using the MSDOS.SYS file *DBLSPACE=* and *DRVSPACE=* entries, you can enable or disable Windows 98's automatic loading of these device drivers. To enable the automatic device-driver loading (the default setting), assign the value 1 to the entry that corresponds to your system software:

```
DRVSPACE=1
```

or

```
DBLSPACE=1
```

To disable the driver's automatic loading, assign the value 0 to the entry.

775 DIRECTING WINDOWS 98 TO DOUBLE BUFFER SCSI DEVICES

If you encounter errors with an older SCSI disk drive (or other bus-mastering disk controller), your device may require that Windows 98 *double buffer* device operations. As it turns out, some older SCSI device drivers run in real mode (which uses conventional memory rather than Windows 98 virtual-memory locations). When you direct Windows 98 to perform double buffering, Windows 98 will copy data to be written to disk from its virtual memory into your PC's conventional memory. From there, the real-mode device driver can write the data to the disk. To perform the actual disk operation, Windows 98 changes from protected mode to real mode.

In a similar way, to perform a disk-read operation, Windows 98 will again change to real mode, read the data from disk into conventional memory, and then will change back to protected mode, copying the data to a protected mode buffer. By changing to and from protected mode in this way, Windows 98 insures that data is correctly read from and written to disk. Because Windows 98 must change between real and protected mode and copy data from a real-mode buffer to one in protected mode, double buffering slows down your disk operations. Unfortunately, there may be times when the only way you can get your drive to work is to perform double buffering. To enable double buffering, assign the value 1 to the MSDOS.SYS file *DoubleBuffer* buffer entry, as shown here:

```
DoubleBuffer=1
```

To turn off double buffering, assign the value 0 to the entry:

```
DoubleBuffer=0
```

If you experience errors running Novell Netware within an MS-DOS window, you may need to move COMMAND.COM and DRVSPACE.BIN above 640Kb to free up conventional memory. To direct Windows 98 to move these two files, assign the value 1 to the *MSDOS.SYS* file's *LoadTop=* entry, as shown here:

```
LoadTop=1
```

Note: *To examine how the LoadTop= entry works, you might use the MEM command to display your system's MS-DOS memory use before and after you use the setting.*

Usually, each time Windows 98 starts, its displays an animated logo that highlights the Taskbar and Start menu locations. To perform this animation, Windows 98 captures a series of low-level hooks that some system's may find incompatible. If you find that your system hangs as Windows 98 displays its startup logo, you can use the *MSDOS.SYS* file's *Logo=* entry to disable the animated logos display. To disable the animated logo's display, assign the value 0 to the *Logo=* entry, as shown here:

```
Logo=0
```

778 **REMOVE THE NETWORK= ENTRY FROM YOUR MSDOS.SYS FILE**

If you have upgraded your system from Windows 95, you may have an older *MSDOS.SYS* file that contains a *Network=* entry. Under Windows 95, you could use the *Network=* to start your system in safe mode with network support. Windows 98 does not support safe mode networking. If your *MSDOS.SYS* file contains a *Network=* entry, set the entry's value to 0 or simply remove the entry altogether:

```
Network=0
```

Note: If you must disable network operations, you can do so within the Control Panel Network Properties dialog box.

779 **UNDERSTANDING ENTRIES WITHIN THE MSDOS.SYS [PATHS] SECTION**

As you have learned, each time Windows 98 starts, it examines the boot disk's root directory for the *MSDOS.SYS* file. Within the *MSDOS.SYS* file, you will find a [Paths] section and an [Options] section. Several of the previous Tips examined settings you can place within the *MSDOS.SYS* [Options] section to control your system processing. If you examine the file's [Paths] system, you will find four entries that tell Windows 98 which directories it should use for key operations. Table 779 briefly explains each of the [Paths] section's entries.

Entry	Description
HostWinBootDrv	Defines the Windows 98 boot drive.
UninstallDir	Specifies the directory from which Windows 98 will uninstall its program files. The default is the root directory on your boot disk.
WinBootDir	Defines the directory that contains the Windows 98 startup files. The default is the directory within which you stored Windows 98.
WinDir	Defines the Windows 98 directory. The default is the directory within which you stored Windows 98.

Table 779 The MSDOS.SYS [Paths] section entries.

780 **DISABLING 32-BIT DISK ACCESS WHEN YOU START WINDOWS 98 FROM THE COMMAND PROMPT**

As you learned in Tip 399, to improve performance for systems with newer disk drives, Windows 98 performs 32-bit disk operations (most PCs purchased since 1995 support 32-bit disk operations). Unfortunately, if you are using older hardware, your system may not support 32-bit disk operations. If you try to select 32-bit disk operations, your system may simply not start, or your monitor may display error messages that tell you Windows 98 cannot access your drive. If Windows 98 is currently running, you can disable 32-bit disk operations using the Control Panel System icon. If instead, Windows 98 will not start in normal mode, you can start your system to a system prompt and then disable 32-bit disk access by starting Windows 98 using the WIN command's /D:F switch, as shown here:

```
C:\> WIN /D:F <ENTER>
```

Should your system start successfully with 32-bit disk operations disabled, you can turn off 32-bit disk operations from within Windows 98 by performing these steps:

1. Click your mouse on the Start menu and choose the Settings menu Control Panel option. Windows 98, in turn, will open the Control Panel window.
2. Within the Control Panel window, double-click your mouse on the System icon. Windows 98, in turn, will display the System Properties dialog box.
3. Within the System Properties dialog box, click your mouse on the Performance tab. Windows 98, in turn, will display the Performance sheet.
4. Within the Performance sheet, click your mouse on the File System button. Windows 98, in turn, will display the File System Properties sheet.
5. Within the File System Properties sheet, click your mouse on the Troubleshooting tab. Windows 98, in turn, will display the Troubleshooting sheet.
6. Within the Troubleshooting sheet, click your mouse on the Disable all 32 bit protect-mode disk drivers option, placing a check mark within the checkbox.
7. Within the Troubleshooting sheet, click your mouse on the OK button and restart Windows 98.

781   *STARTING WINDOWS 98 IN SAFE MODE*

As you troubleshoot problems within Windows 98, you can simplify your problem-solving tasks by eliminating factors such as network hardware and software. If, for example, your system fails to start, try starting your system without network support. As your system starts, press the CTRL key to display the Windows 98 Startup menu. Within the Startup menu, select the Command prompt only option. If Windows 98 starts successfully in real mode, try starting Windows 98 in safe mode by using the WIN command's /D:M switch, as shown here:

```
C:\> WIN /D:M <ENTER>
```

If Windows 98 starts successfully, restart your system again to the real-mode command-line prompt.

782   *DISABLING WINDOWS 98 FROM USING THE ROM BREAKPOINT*

When Windows 95 first hit the market a few years ago, it was not uncommon for users still to run older software that ran in the Windows 3.1 "real mode." Unlike the 32-bit protected mode which Windows 95 and Windows 98 support, within real mode, programs had direct access to hardware devices, memory, and even to other programs. When users would run real-mode programs, Windows 95 (and Windows 98) had to continually switch between protected mode and real mode (a slow process). To switch to real mode, Windows 95 (and now Windows 98) used a special location within the PC BIOS called a *ROM breakpoint*.

In general, a ROM breakpoint contains instructions Windows 98 performs to change from protected to real mode. Usually, Windows 98 looks for the breakpoint instructions at a specific address. If, however, you are using a third-party memory manager that moves your BIOS to RAM (to improve your system performance), Windows 98 should not assume that it knows the breakpoint location. If you experience intermittent errors within Windows 98, try disabling Windows 98's use of ROM breakpoints by starting Windows 98 using the following command line:

```
C:\> WIN /D:S  <ENTER>
```

The /D:S command-line switch tells Windows 98 not to use ROM addresses in the range F000:0000 through 1Mb as a breakpoint. If you find that disabling Windows 98's use of ROM breakpoints solves your problem, place the following entry within your *System.INI* file to permanently disable Windows 98's use of ROM breakpoints:

```
SystemROMBreakPoint=False
```

783 DIRECTING WINDOWS 98 TO PERFORM BIOS-BASED DISK OPERATIONS

If your system hangs during disk operations and you have disabled 32-bit disk access as discussed in Tip 780, try telling Windows 98 to access your disk drives using BIOS-based instructions rather than the software-based instructions Windows 98 provides. The BIOS, which is your PC's *Basic Input/Output System*, provides hardware-based instructions that Windows 98 can use to access your disk (as well as other devices, such as your keyboard, monitor, and so on). To try using BIOS-based disk operations, restart Windows 98 to an MS-DOS command-line prompt. Next, from the system prompt, start your system using the WIN command's /D:V switch which directs Windows 98 to perform BIOS-based disk operations:

```
C:\> WIN /D:V  <ENTER>
```

If you find that Windows 98 works successfully by performing BIOS-based disk operations, place the following entry in your *System.INI* file to direct Windows 98 to permanently perform BIOS-based disk operations:

```
VirtualHDIRQ=False
```

784 DISABLING WINDOWS 98'S USE OF ADAPTER MEMORY

Although the price of RAM, your system's random-access memory, has become very affordable, it seems that under Windows a system simply cannot have enough memory. To make the most of the memory your PC contains, Windows

98 will look for available memory within a special region called your system's adapter memory (the range of memory from A000 through FFFF). If Windows 98 finds unused space within the adapter memory, Windows will use it. If you find that your system hangs (possibly intermittently), try directing Windows 98 not to use the adapter memory. To begin, restart Windows 98 at an MS-DOS command-line prompt. Next, start your system using the WIN command's /D:X switch which directs Windows 98 not to use the adapter memory:

```
C:\> WIN /D:X   <ENTER>
```

If you find that Windows 98 runs successfully after you disable its use of the adapter memory, place the following entry within your *System.INI* file to direct Windows 98 to permanently disable the adapter memory use:

```
EMMExclude=A000-FFFF
```

785 | **USING SETUPLOG.TXT TO TROUBLESHOOT WINDOWS 98 INSTALLATION PROBLEMS**

Several of the preceding Tips have looked at utilities you can run to troubleshoot system settings. If, when you try to upgrade your system to Windows 98, the setup operation fails, you may be able to troubleshoot the cause of the error by examining the root directory file *Setuplog.TXT*, whose contents you can view within the WordPad accessory program, as shown in Figure 785.

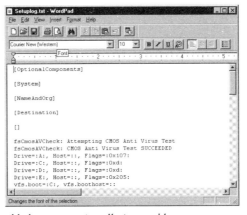

Figure 785 *Using the* **Setuplog.TXT** *to troubleshoot system installation problems.*

To display the contents of the *Setuplog.TXT* file, perform these steps:

1. Click your mouse on the Start menu Programs option and choose Windows Explorer. Windows 98 will open the Explorer window.

2. Within the Explorer window, use the folder list to select the root directory. Then, click your mouse on the *Setuplog.TXT* file. Windows 98 may display an error message stating that the file is too large to open within Notepad and asking you if you want to open the file within WordPad. Within the dialog box, click your mouse on the Yes option. Windows 98 will open the WordPad accessory.

3. Within the Notepad or the WordPad accessory, you can scroll through the file's contents and troubleshoot the installation.

786 USING OBJECT LINKING AND EMBEDDING (OLE) TO PLACE OBJECTS WITHIN YOUR DOCUMENTS

Throughout this book, you have learned how to perform cut-and-paste operations to move text or images from one document into another. In addition to letting you move or copy text or graphics images in this way, Windows 98 also lets you insert other types of objects into your documents, such as a spreadsheet, a word-processing document, or even an audio or video clip. To place such objects into your documents, you use *object linking and embedding* (OLE) to either link or embed the object within a document. When you embed an object within a document, Windows 98 places a copy of that object in your document, similar to when you paste text or an image into a document. However, if you later click your mouse on the object, Windows 98 will start the program that created the object, loading the object for editing (assuming that you have the program that created the object on your system). For example, Figure 786 shows a word-processing document that contains an embedded Excel pie chart. If the user double-clicks his or her mouse on the chart within the document, Windows 98 will start the Excel, within which the user can edit the chart's contents.

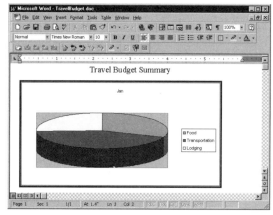

Figure 786 *An embedded Excel pie chart within a word-processing document.*

Linking an object to a document is similar to embedding the object in that the object will appear within the document. The difference between linking and embedding is that when you embed an object, the program places a copy of the object within the document. When you link a document, the application places a link to the object's file that resides on your disk. Assume, for example, that you embed an Excel spreadsheet that contains your company budget within a document. By double-clicking your mouse on the spreadsheet, you can start Excel and make changes to the budget. However, when you make such changes, you are only changing the document's copy of the spreadsheet. Next, assume that you link the spreadsheet to your document. Should you later double-click your mouse on the spreadsheet within the document, Windows 98 will again start Excel, letting you make changes to the spreadsheet's contents. This time, however, your changes will occur within the spreadsheet file that resides on your disk, rather than the document's copy of the file. If, for example, you later make changes to the spreadsheet using Excel, your word processing document (that contains the link to the file) will show your changes the next time you open the document.

If you have linked the spreadsheet to multiple documents (such as a memo, a budget report, and a document you are preparing for the bank), each document will immediately reflect the changes you make to the linked spreadsheet. Had you instead embedded the spreadsheet copy within each document, you would have to edit the spreadsheet individually, within each document, to reflect the same changes.

Several of the Tips that follow examine object linking and embedding in detail.

787 | USING OBJECT EMBEDDING WITHIN MICROSOFT WORD

As you have learned, using object linking and embedding you can embed an object, such as an audio clip, a graphic, or even a spreadsheet, within a document. When you embed an object within a document, you can later double-click your mouse on the object within the document to load the object within the program you used to create it.

For example, if you double-click your mouse on a spreadsheet object, Windows 98 would start Excel (provided you have Excel installed on your system). Likewise, if you double-click your mouse on an embedded audio clip, Windows 98 will start the Sound Recorder accessory, with which you can play back or edit the audio file.

Depending on the program you are running, the steps you must perform to embed an object may differ slightly. To help you understand the process, the following steps tell you how to embed an object into a Word document.

1. Within your Microsoft Word document, position the cursor to the location at which you want to insert the object. Next, click your mouse on the Insert menu Object option. Word, in turn, will display the Object dialog box.

2. Within the Object dialog box, click your mouse on the Create from File tab. Word, in turn, will display the Create from File sheet, as shown in Figure 787.

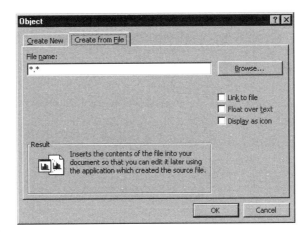

Figure 787 *The Create from File sheet.*

3. Within the Create from File sheet, click your mouse on the Browse button. Word will display the Browse dialog box.

4. Within the Browse dialog box, locate the file you want to embed and then click your mouse on the OK button.

5. Within the Create from File sheet, click your mouse on the OK button. Word, in turn, will insert the object within your document.

Within your document, double-click your mouse on the object. Word, in turn, will start the program that you originally used to create the object, loading the object within the program.

788	USING OBJECT LINKING WITHIN MICROSOFT WORD	

In Tip 787, you learned how to embed an object within a Word document. As you learned, when you embed an object, the application places a copy of the object within the document. If you later make changes to the object, the changes only appear to the object copy that you placed within the document.

In contrast, when you link an object to a document, Windows 98 does not make a copy of the object. Instead, your document will always display the linked object's current contents. For example, if you place a link within a Word document to a graphics image that you create using the Paint accessory and, later, you Paint to update your image, your Word document will reflect your change the next time you open the document.

Depending on the program you are running, the steps you must perform to link an object may differ slightly. To help you understand the process, the following steps tell you how to link an object into a Word document.

1. Within your Microsoft Word document, position the cursor to the location at which you want to insert the object. Next, click your mouse on the Insert menu Object option. Word, in turn, will display the Object dialog box.

2. Within the Object dialog box, click your mouse on the Create from File tab. Word, in turn, will display the Create from File sheet, as shown in Figure 788.

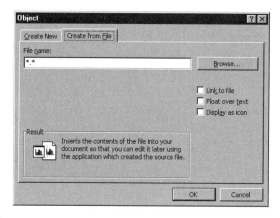

Figure 788 *The Create from File sheet.*

3. Within the Create from File sheet, click your mouse on the Browse button. Word will display the Browse dialog box.

4. Within the Browse dialog box, locate the file you want to link and then click your mouse on the OK button.

5. Within the Create from File sheet, click your mouse on the Link to File checkbox, placing a check mark within the box. Then, click your mouse on the OK button. Word, in turn, will display the linked object within your document.

Next, close your Word document and then change and save the contents of the object you previously linked. Then, open your Word document again. The linked object should reflect the changes you just made to the object.

789   *DECIDING WHEN TO LINK OR EMBED AN OBJECT WITHIN A DOCUMENT*

Several of the previous Tips have examined object linking and embedding. As you have learned, when you embed an image within a document, your application will place a copy of the object's contents within the document. Later, should you make any changes to that object, your changes will only appear within the document's copy. Likewise, if you change the original object's contents, your document will not reflect those changes. If you instead link the object to your document, any changes you make to the object will appear within your document and within the original object file.

To determine whether you should link or embed an object into your document, you must decide how you want Windows 98 to reflect changes to the object. If you want all documents that use an object to see changes to the object, you should link the object to your document. If, instead, you want each document to have its own copy of the object, you should embed the object.

790   *PLACING AN ICON WITHIN YOUR DOCUMENT FOR A LINKED OR EMBEDDED OBJECT*

In Tips 787 and 788, you learned how to embed and to link objects within a Word document. When you place an object within a document, you can place the object itself within the document or you can place an icon that represents the object within the document. Rather than showing an entire spreadsheet within you document, you may prefer to simply put an icon for the spreadsheet within your document, upon which the user can click his or her mouse to open the embedded or linked object. To place an icon for an object within your document, when you embed or link an object, click your mouse on the Create from File sheet Display as Icon checkbox, placing a check mark within the box.

791   *EMBEDDING AN OBJECT THAT YOU CREATE WITHIN A WORD DOCUMENT*

In Tip 787, you learned how to embed an object that exists in a file on your disk into a Word document. As you work, there may be times when you want to create an object that you will simply store within your document. For example, you might want to record an audio clip that explains your reasoning that you insert into your budget document.

Depending on the program you are running, the steps you must perform to create and embed an object may differ slightly. To help you understand the process, the following steps tell you how to create an object that you then embed into a Word document.

1. Within your Microsoft Word document, position the cursor to the location at which you want to insert the object. Next, click your mouse on the Insert menu Object option. Word, in turn, will display the Object dialog box, as shown in Figure 791.

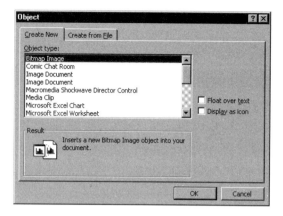

Figure 791 *The Object dialog box.*

2. Within the Object dialog box, use your mouse to scroll through the Object Type list to select the type of object that you want to create. Then, click your mouse on the OK button. Windows 98, in turn, will launch the corresponding program, within which you can create the object that you desire.

3. Within the object's application program, create your object. Then, depending on the program you are using, the steps you must perform to save the object may differ. Usually, however, the program's File menu will have an option that lets you save the object.

4. Within the Object dialog box, click your mouse on the OK button.

792 **UNDERSTANDING DISK PARTITIONS**

When you first purchase and install a hard disk, you may have to "partition" the hard drive before you can use it. In general, partitioning a hard drive defines structures on the disk within which your disk drive stores information about the disk's size and layout. Often, users will use partitions to divide a large disk into several smaller drives. For example, the users might divide a 1Gb disk into four logical drives each containing 250Mb (the drives are logical drives rather than physical drives because you really only have one drive that you can physically touch). Later, rather than having one large drive, the user would have four individual drives. An advantage of using multiple logical drives is that an error on one drive's file system usually does not effect the other drives (which may reduce the amount of information you lose should an error occur).

Previous versions of Windows could not support drives larger than 512Mb. If you purchased a 1Gb, drive, for example, you had to partition the disk into two 512Mb drives. Using the FAT32 file system, Windows 98 now supports disks up to 2,048Gb (over 2 terabytes!).

To partition a disk, you use the FDISK command, which you run from the command prompt. Do not partition a disk that contains data (the partitioning process will overwrite the disk's contents). If you have a new drive you want to partition (or if you are repartitioning a drive whose contents you have recently backed up), start the FDISK command, as shown here:

```
C:\> FDISK  <ENTER>
```

If your disk is larger than 512Mb, FDISK will display a message telling you that Windows 98 now supports larger drives and asking you if you want to enable its large drive support. If you say Yes, Windows 98 will convert your existing drives to the FAT32 file system. If you want to convert your disk using the FDISK command, first make sure that you have a complete backup of your disk's files. You may also want a very experienced user to help you perform the operation.

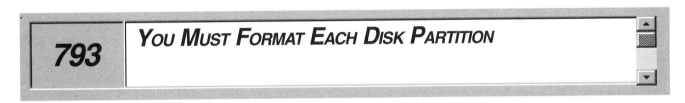

793 YOU MUST FORMAT EACH DISK PARTITION

In Tip 792, you learned that before you can use a new hard drive, you must partition the drive using the FDISK command. After you use FDISK to specify your drive's partition information and logical drives, you must then format each logical drive for use. The disk formatting process creates the file-system structures that Windows 98 will later use to store files and folders on your disk.

To format a drive, you use the FORMAT command which, like FDISK, you issue from the command line. If you are formatting a disk that you will use to boot Windows 98, you must format the disk using the /S switch, as shown here (replacing the words drive_letter with the letter of the drive you are formatting):

```
A:\> FORMAT drive_letter: /S  <ENTER>
```

Note: Do not format a disk that contains files that you need. The disk formatting process will overwrite the disk's current contents.

794 CREATING A SYSTEM DISK THAT CONTAINS THE FDISK AND FORMAT COMMANDS

In Tips 792 and 793, you learned how to use the FDISK command to partition a hard drive and then the FORMAT command to place the file-system structures on your drive. As you learned, you run the FDISK and FORMAT commands from the system prompt. Often, you will run the commands from a floppy disk that you use to boot your system (called a system disk). To create a bootable floppy disk that contains the FDISK and FORMAT commands, perform these steps:

1. Click your mouse on the Start menu Settings option and choose Control Panel. Windows 98, in turn, will open the Control Panel window.
2. Within the Control Panel window, click your mouse on the Add/Remove Programs icons. Windows 98, in turn, will display the Add/Remove Programs Properties dialog box.
3. Within the Add/Remove Programs Properties dialog box, click your mouse on the Startup Disk tab. Windows 98 will display the Startup Disk sheet, as shown in Figure 794.
4. Within the Startup Disk sheet, click your mouse on the Create Disk button. Windows 98, in turn, will display the Insert Disk dialog box asking you to insert a disk onto which it can write the system files. Insert a floppy disk into your drive and click your mouse on the OK button.

5. After Windows 98 transfers the system files to the floppy disk, place a label on the floppy that identifies the disk as a system disk and then store the floppy in a safe location.

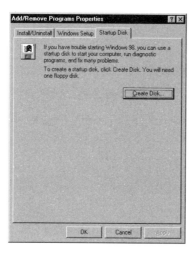

Figure 794 *The Startup Disk sheet.*

795 — UNDERSTANDING THE *FAT32* FILE SYSTEM AND DUAL-BOOT OPERATIONS

To reduce the number of PCs they must own, many programmers, trainers, and consultants install two operating systems on their hard drive. For example, a Windows-based programmer might install Windows NT and Windows 98 onto their hard drive. Each time the user starts his or her system, the user selects the operating system he or she wants to use.

Depending on the operating systems you want to dual boot, the steps you must perform will differ (and will require documentation for both systems). If you are using a dual-boot system, check your operating-system documentation closely before you upgrade Windows 98 to the FAT32 file system. Most operating systems (MS-DOS, Windows NT 4 (and earlier), and Windows 3.1) do not support FAT32. If you install the FAT32 software, you will no longer be able to use dual-boot operations.

796 — GETTING CONNECTED TO THE INTERNET

Today, it is almost impossible to read a magazine article, watch a TV program, or even preview a movie that does not mention a company or product address on the World Wide Web. As you have learned, users connect computers to networks to share resources such as files or printers. The Internet is simply a network of networks. In other words, the Internet is a huge worldwide network to which companies, universities, and even individuals connect their computers or networks. After they connect a system or network to the Internet, users can then run programs that let them exchange files and electronic messages, shop, or simply chat with other users online. No one person owns the Internet. Instead, to become part of the Internet, a company or university will pay for a connection (possibly via phone lines,

ISDN line, fiber-optic cable, or even a satellite link) to the nearest system that is already connected to the "Net." Users usually pay a monthly fee to connect their PCs to the Net by dialing into an Internet Service Provider (ISP) which, in turn, has high-speed connections to the Net that users can share.

Depending on their needs, users will join online services such as America Online (AOL) or the Microsoft Network (MSN). Using such an online service, users can view sites on the World Wide Web, chat with other users, and send and receive electronic mail. The advantage of using an online service is simplicity and cost. The disadvantage of an online service is that their speed may be slightly slower than what an advanced user may desire. Several of the Tips that follow discuss the Microsoft Network, for which Windows 98 includes software that you can use to get up and running on the Net. Depending on where you live, you may find a variety of Internet Service Providers who offer different monthly rates. You may also want to check with your cable TV company to see if it offers high-speed cable-modem connections (you will have to purchase a cable modem, which is different from the standard phone modem that is likely installed in your PC—but the cable modem will provide you with much faster transmission speeds).

To connect your PC to the Internet, you will pay a monthly fee to either an Internet Service Provider or to an online service. After you connect to the Internet, however, you should not have any other fees. If, for example, you download a document from across the globe, you will not pay long distance fVees. Instead, after you are connected to the Internet, you can chat with users around the world, send and receive electronic mail across the globe, or download documents from countries worldwide for free! As you choose your Internet Service Provider or online service, however, make sure that you find a service with a local-access phone number. Otherwise, to dial into your service, you would have to pay long distance charges, which could quickly add up as you surf the Web. Fortunately, almost every major city, worldwide, offers several providers from which you can get Internet service.

---

797 — UNDERSTANDING THE WORLD WIDE WEB

In Tip 796, you learned that the Internet is a worldwide network of networks. Users connect to the Internet to exchange files, to send and receive electronic mail, to chat with other users across the globe, and to find information on a virtually unlimited number of topics. Across the Internet, there are now hundreds of millions of documents. A few years ago, the biggest challenge users faced on the Net was finding the document that contained the information they desired. To help users organize information on the Net, software developers created the World Wide Web (or Web, for short). In general, across the Web, users will find documents that contain images and text. These Web documents reside on computers that users refer to as *Web sites*. Today, most companies, schools, and organizations have sites on the Web. In fact, there are Web sites worldwide that contain information in over 100 languages! Figure 797, for example, shows the Microsoft, Jamsa Press, and Wall Street Journal Web sites.

As you can see, the information Web sites present can include text and graphics as well as multimedia content (such as audio and video clips). To view information on the Web, you must have special software called a Web browser. Several of the Tips in this book present the Internet Explorer, a Web browser that Microsoft bundles with Windows 98. The Web is so named because Web documents consist of links upon which the user can click his or her mouse to move from one document to another. By following such links, a user may move from a document that resides on a Web site at Stanford University to a document that resides on a document at a University in Germany and then to a document that resides on a company Web site in Japan. In other words, by linking related documents, the links create a Web of information that spans the globe.

Best of all, the user does not care where the documents reside. Usually, sites on the Web do not charge the user to view their content. After you are connected to the Web there are no phone costs; it does not matter if the document you want to view resides in San Francisco or London. And, in most cases, you will not see a difference in the amount of time your browser requires to download a document from a site that is near or far from you.

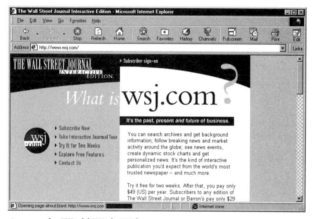

Figure 797 *Viewing information at sites on the World Wide Web.*

---

798 UNDERSTANDING WEB ADDRESSES AND DOCUMENT LINKS

In Tip 797, you learned that the World Wide Web consists of millions of documents that reside at Web sites worldwide. To view the information a Web site contains, you must run special Web browsing software. Today, the two most popular browsers are the Netscape Navigator and the Microsoft Internet Explorer (which comes within Windows 98). After you start your browser, you view a site by typing in the site's Web address (users will sometimes refer to a Web address as a URL—which stands for uniform resource locator).

Most Web addresses take the form *www.name.suffix*, such as *www.microsoft.com*, *www.jamsa.com*, or *www.stanford.edu*. The *www* within a Web address is an abbreviation for World Wide Web. The suffix consists of three characters that tell you the type of site. For example, the letters *com* (the most common suffix) stand for a commercial site. Likewise, the letters *edu* indicate an educational site. Table 798 lists most of the suffixes you will encounter.

To view a site within your browser, you simply type in the site's Web address within your browser's Address field. Your browser, in turn, will download the site's contents, displaying them within the browser window. As you scroll through a site's text and graphics, you will encounter underlined text or graphics images upon which you can click your mouse to display a related document. Such underlined text or graphics are Web *links*. As discussed in Tip 797, by linking related documents, the World Wide Web puts a Web of information a few mouse clicks away.

Suffix	Description
com	Commercial organizations
edu	Educational institutions
gov	Governmental organizations
int	International governmental organizations
mil	Military organizations
net	A network facility, such as an Internet Service Provider
org	An organization that does not fit into another organizational domain category

Table 798 *Common Web address suffixes.*

799 **SURFING THE WEB USING THE INTERNET EXPLORER**

In Tip 820, you will learn how to start the Microsoft Internet Explorer. Within the Internet Explorer, you select Web sites by typing a Web address within the Address field, as shown in Figure 799.

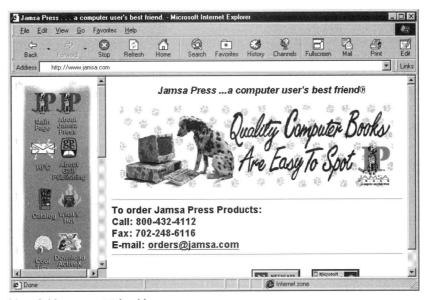

Figure 799 *Using the Address field to type a Web address.*

Within the Internet Explorer, you get can get started surfing the Web by typing in the addresses Table 799 lists.

Site	Address
Microsoft	www.microsoft.com
Jamsa Press	www.jamsa.com
Happy and Max	www.HappyAndMax.com
Business Week	www.businessweek.com
Netscape	www.netscape.com
Yahoo	www.yahoo.com
Wall Street Journal	www.wsj.com
MSNBC	www.msnbc.com

Table 799 Sites to visit on the World Wide Web.

As you surf sites within the World Wide Web, you will encounter underlined text and icons within a sites text that are links upon which you can click your mouse to move to another site. For example, Figure 800 shows the Microsoft Web site. Within the site's text, you will find several underlined text objects (links). When you click your mouse on a Web link, your Web browser will display the link's corresponding page, which may or may not reside at the current site.

For example, a link at the Jamsa Press Web site may link you to the Microsoft Web site. By clicking your mouse on links, you can quickly move from one Web page to another, without having to specify each page's Web address as you did in Tip 799.

Figure 800 Links within the text at the Microsoft Web site.

801	**USING DESKTOP SHORTCUTS FOR QUICK ACCESS TO A SPECIFIC WEB SITE**

If you are like most users, you may have a few specific Web sites, such as Yahoo, that you visit on a regular basis. To simplify the steps you must perform to access these sites, Windows 98 lets you place a shortcut to the site on your Desktop. Then, later, when you are ready to access the site, you simply click your mouse on the shortcut icon. Windows 98, in turn, will load the shortcut's Web address into your browser and, if necessary, start the software you use to connect to the Net. To create a Desktop shortcut to a specific Web site, perform these steps:

1. Right-click your mouse within an unused area on the Desktop. Windows 98, in turn, will display a pop-up menu.

2. Within the pop-up menu, click your mouse on the New option. Windows 98 will display a submenu.

3. Within the submenu, click your mouse on the Shortcut option. Windows 98, in turn, will display the Create Shortcut dialog box, as shown in Figure 801.

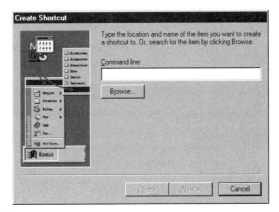

Figure 801 *The Create Shortcut dialog box.*

4. Within the Create Shortcut dialog box Command line field, type in the site's Web address, such as *www.jamsa.com*, and then click your mouse on the Next button. Windows 98, in turn, will display the Select a Title for the Program dialog box.

5. Within the Select a Title for the Program dialog box, type in the text that you want Windows 98 to display below the shortcut icon on your Desktop and then click your mouse on the Finish button. Windows 98, in turn, will create and display the shortcut icon on your Desktop.

802	**LOCATING INFORMATION ON THE WORLD WIDE WEB**

As you have learned, the World Wide Web consists of millions of documents that provide information on a virtually unlimited number of topics. To use the Web effectively, you need a way to locate the sites that contain the information you desire. To help you find such sites, you can take advantage of special sites that offer search engines. In general, using your browser, you will visit the search engine site, such as *www.yahoo.com* or *www.excite.com* (Table 802 lists several sites that offer search engines). The Web site, in turn, will display a text field within which you can type a few words that correspond to the information you desire. For example, if you are interested in learning about Windows 98, you would simply type **Windows 98** within the box and then click your mouse on the Search button. The Web site, in turn, will examine its database of site information and will display a list of sites that discuss your topic (depending on the number of sites that discuss your topic, the Web site may provide many pages of sites which it will try to order based on the likelihood that the site will contain the information you want). Figure 802, for example, shows a list of sites the Yahoo Web site returned for a search on Windows 98.

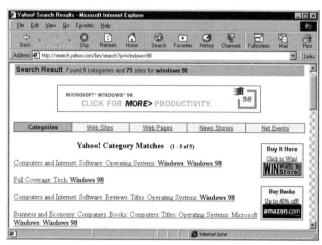

Figure 802 *Using a search engine to find sites that discuss specific topics.*

Within the Web site's list of sites, you can simply click your mouse on a site's link to display that site's content within your browser. If you find that site does not provide all the information you need, you can click your mouse on your browser's Back button to redisplay the search engine's site list. As you surf the Web, you will make extensive use of the search engines to locate sites that discuss topics you desire. Table 802 lists several popular search engines.

Site	Address
Alta Vista	www.altavista.digital.com
Excite	www.excite.com
Info Seek	www.infoseek.com
Lycos	www.lycos.com
Yahoo	www.yahoo.com

Table 802 *Commonly used Web search engines.*

803 UNDERSTANDING HOW YOUR MODEM'S SPEED IMPACTS YOUR SYSTEM PERFORMANCE

Although you can find an almost unlimited amount of information on the World Wide Web, the Web continues to frustrate many users simply because they "have to wait" for the information to download. As it turns out, even if you have the newest and fastest PC available, you may still have to wait for information to download across the Web because of your modem's capabilities.

Today, there are a number of ways that users can connect to the net. If you connect to the net from home, you probably still use a standard phone connection. If you connect to the net from a large office, you may be fortunate enough to have an ISDN or T1 connection available, which provides you with a very fast connection. In the near future, most users will use cable-modem connections for high-speed connections from home.

Regardless of how you connect to the net, you will describe your connection's speed in terms of its baud rate. If you are using a standard modem to connect to the net over phone lines, you are probably connecting at 28.8 baud. In the simplest sense, you can interpret a modem's baud rate to mean the number of bits (a binary 1 or 0) the modem can transfer per second.

When users discuss modem speeds, they often use the term Kb, which stands for kilobits per second. One kilobit is equal to 1,024 bits per second. A 28.8Kb modem, therefore, can transmit 28.8 * 1,024 bits per second or about 30,000 bits per second. Knowing that a byte contains 8 bits, a 28.8Kb modem, in theory, could transmit over 3,000 bytes a second. In reality, however, because electronic noise (static) causes transmission errors and because modems use a few bits of information behind the scenes for error checking and to coordinate communication, most 28.8 modems transmit at about 2500 bytes per second on a clean (static free) connection.

Today, 56Kb modems are readily affordable. In general, because a 56Kb modem is twice as fast as a 28.8Kb modem, upgrading to a 56Kb modem should cut your Web downloading time in half, which will save you considerable time as you surf.

In addition to 28.8Kb and 56Kb modems, you can also purchase an ISDN modem, which requires a special phone line, or a cable modem, which requires your TV cable company to install a special line. Although the ISDN and cable modem lines are more expensive, they are much, much faster than traditional telephone-based modems.

804 ┃ *WINDOWS 98 BUNDLES SEVERAL ONLINE SERVICES*

Several of the Tips that follow examine the Microsoft Network (or MSN), which is Microsoft's online network. Like all online services, you join MSN and then pay a monthly fee. Within MSN, you can send and receive electronic mail, surf the Web, chat with other users, and essentially do everything that anyone else connected to the Internet can do. Although this book's Tips focus on MSN, the Windows 98 CD-ROM provides software for several other online services, including America Online (AOL, the largest online service). Tip 805 discusses the steps you must perform to install MSN. To install the setup software for other online services that Microsoft includes with Windows 98, perform these steps:

1. Click your mouse on the Start button and choose the Settings option. Windows 98, in turn, will display the Settings submenu and choose the Control Panel. Windows 98 will open the Control Panel window.

2. Within the Control Panel window, double-click your mouse on the Add/Remove Programs icon. Windows 98, in turn, will display the Add/Remove Program Properties dialog box.

3. Within the Add/Remove Program Properties dialog box, click your mouse on the Windows Setup tab. Windows 98 will display the Windows Setup sheet.

4. Within the Windows Setup sheet, use your mouse to scroll the Components list box and highlight the Online Services option.

5. Within the Windows Setup sheet, click your mouse on the Details button. Windows 98, in turn, will display the Online Services dialog box within which it lists online services for which you can install software from the Windows 98 CD-ROM.

6. Within the Online Services dialog box, click your mouse on the checkbox that appears to the left of the online service that you desire, placing a check mark within the box.

7. After you select the services you desire, click your mouse on the OK button.

8. Within the Windows Setup dialog box, click your mouse on the OK button to install the setup software. You will need your Windows 98 CD-ROM.

9. After Windows 98 adds the setup software to your system, you can run the programs from within the Online Services submenu that you will find within the Start menu Programs submenu.

805 INSTALLING THE MICROSOFT NETWORK SOFTWARE WITHIN WINDOWS 98

Depending on how Windows 98 was installed on your system, you may need to load the Microsoft Network software before you can connect to MSN. To determine if you must install the MSN software, click your mouse on the Start button. Windows 98, in turn, will display the Start menu. Within the Start menu, look for the Microsoft Network option. If your Start menu does not have a Microsoft Network option, click your mouse on the Start menu Programs option and then examine the Programs submenu for a Microsoft Network option. If you cannot find an option for the Microsoft Network, you must install the MSN software on your system by performing these steps:

1. Click your mouse on the Start button and choose the Settings option. Windows 98, in turn, will display the Settings submenu and choose the Control Panel. Windows 98 will open the Control Panel window.

2. Within the Control Panel, double-click your mouse on the Add/Remove Programs icon. Windows 98, in turn, will display the Add/Remove Program Properties dialog box.

3. Within the Add/Remove Program Properties dialog box, click your mouse on the Windows Setup tab. Windows 98, in turn, will display the Windows Setup sheet.

4. Within the Windows Setup sheet, use your mouse to scroll the Components list box and highlight the Online Services option.

5. Within the Windows Setup sheet, click your mouse on the Details button. Windows 98, in turn, will display the Online Services dialog box within which it lists online services for which you can install software from the Windows 98 CD-ROM.

6. Within the Online Services dialog box, click your mouse on the check box at the left of The Microsoft Network, placing a check mark within the box.

7. Within the Online Services dialog box, click your mouse on the OK button.

8. Within the Windows Setup dialog box, click your mouse on the OK button to install the MSN software. You will need your Windows 98 CD-ROM.

9. After Windows 98 adds the MSN software to your system, you will find an MSN icon on your Desktop.

10. Double-click your mouse on the MSN Desktop icon to continue the software installation. During the installation, you must specify your username and a password you will use to access your account. You will also need a credit card that Microsoft can use to bill you for your service charges.

Note: *To use the Microsoft Network, you must specify a username and a password, both of which you will define. Pick a username which will be easy for other users to remember, such as your first initial and last name, for example, kjamsa. Other users will use your username each time they want to send you an e-mail message. Also, pick a password that other users will not guess. If another user gains access to your account (by guessing your password), he or she can read your e-mail and even send e-mail on your behalf.*

806 — **LOGGING INTO THE MICROSOFT NETWORK**

After you install the MSN software as discussed in Tip 805, you can log into the Microsoft Network. To log into the Microsoft Network, perform these steps:

1. Click your mouse on the Start button. Windows 98, in turn, will display the Start menu.

2. Within the Start menu, click your mouse on the Microsoft Network option. If your Start menu does not contain a Microsoft Network option, click your mouse on the Programs option and select the Microsoft Network option from the Programs submenu. Windows 98, in turn, will open the MSN Sign-In dialog box, as shown in Figure 806.1.

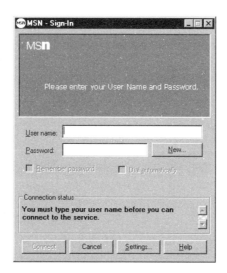

Figure 806.1 *The MSN Sign-In dialog box.*

3. Within the User name, type in the username you selected when you signed up for the Microsoft Network.

4. Within the Password field, type in the password you selected when you signed up for the Microsoft Network.

5. The first time you access the Microsoft Network, you must specify the phone number your PC will dial to connect to MSN. Within the MSN Sign-In dialog box, click your mouse on the Settings button. Windows 98, in turn, will display the Connection Settings dialog box, as shown in Figure 806.2.

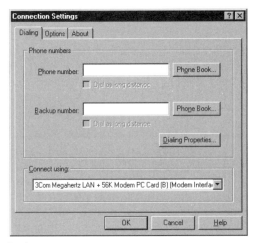

Figure 806.2 *The Connection Settings dialog box.*

6. Within the Connection Settings dialog box, click your mouse the Phone Number field Phone Book button. Windows 98, in turn, will display the Phone Book dialog box, as shown in Figure 806.3.

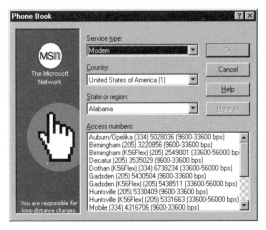

Figure 806.3 *The Phone Book dialog box.*

7. Within the Phone Book dialog box, click your mouse on the Country field and select the country from within which you are going to place your call to connect to MSN.

8. Within the Phone Book dialog box, click your mouse on the State or region field and select the state or region from within which you are going to place your call to connect to MSN.

9. Within the Phone Book dialog box, use your mouse to scroll through the Access numbers list and highlight the city nearest the location from within which you are going to place your call to connect to MSN.

10. Within the Phone Book dialog box, click your mouse on the OK button.

11. Within the Connection Settings dialog box, examine the phone number you have selected to ensure it looks correct. If you are calling from a motel, for example, you may need to dial 9

before the phone number to access an outside line. After you ensure the phone number is correct, click your mouse on the OK button.

12. Within the MSN Sign-In dialog box, click your mouse on the Connect button. Your modem, in turn, will try to dial the number that you have selected.

After you successfully log into MSN, you can use the Internet Explorer (or Netscape Navigator) to traverse the Web or Microsoft Outlook Express to send and receive electronic mail.

807 CHANGING YOUR MSN ACCESS PHONE NUMBER

In Tip 806, you learned that the first time you log into MSN, you must specify the phone number that your modem is to dial in order to connect to the Microsoft Network. If you travel with a notebook computer, you will want to change the MSN access phone number as you move from one city to another. By changing your access number, you can usually dial a local number to access MSN and avoid a long-distance phone bill. The Microsoft Network has local access numbers for most major cities, not just in the United States, but worldwide. To change your number before connecting to MSN, perform these steps:

1. Within the MSN Sign-In dialog box, click your mouse on the Settings button. Windows 98, in turn, will display the Connection Settings dialog box.

2. Within the Connection Settings dialog box, click your mouse on the Phone Number field Phone Book button. Windows 98, in turn, will display the Phone Book dialog.

3. Within the Phone Book dialog box, click your mouse on the Country field and select the country from within which you are going to place your call to connect to MSN.

4. Within the Phone Book dialog box, click your mouse on the State or region field and select the state or region from within which you are going to place your call to connect to MSN.

5. Within the Phone Book dialog box, use your mouse to scroll through the Access numbers list and highlight the city nearest the location from within which you are going to place your call to connect to MSN.

6. Within the Phone Book dialog box, click your mouse on the OK button.

7. Within the Connection Settings dialog box, examine the phone number you have selected to ensure it looks correct. If you are calling from a motel, for example, you may need to dial 9 before the phone number to access an outside line. After you ensure the phone number is correct, click your mouse on the OK button. Within the MSN Sign-In dialog box, click your mouse on the Connect button. Your modem, in turn, will try to dial the number that you have selected.

808 GETTING MAIL FROM YOUR OFFICE OR OTHER E-MAIL ACCOUNTS

Today, many employees like to receive e-mail from their office on their home PC. Depending on the e-mail software your company is using, one of the simplest ways to receive your office e-mail is simply to forward copies of all the e-mail you receive at your office e-mail account to your MSN e-mail account. In this way, you can keep a copy of your messages on your office PC, while having the ability to receive and respond to messages at home. Many offices, for example, use Microsoft Outlook Express as their employee's e-mail software. To forward mail within Outlook Express, you can use the Inbox Assistant to forward mail to your remote e-mail account. For more information on forwarding e-mail in this way, see your system administrator.

809 USING *MSN* TO SEND AND RECEIVE ELECTRONIC MAIL

Today, most users connect to an online service to gain access to the World Wide Web or to send and receive electronic mail (e-mail). If you use MSN to connect to the net, you can then use most common e-mail programs to send and receive electronic mail. In addition, Windows 98 provides Microsoft Outlook Express, a special program you can use to send and receive e-mail. Figure 809 shows the Microsoft Outlook Express window. Tips 858 discuss Microsoft Outlook Express in detail.

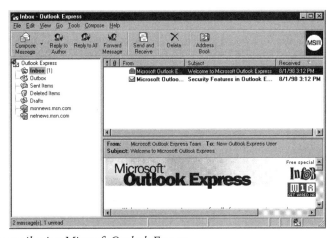

Figure 809 *Sending and receiving mail using Microsoft Outlook Express.*

Before another user can send you electronic mail, that user must know your e-mail address, which combines your username and the characters @msn.com. You pronounce the @ sign as "at". For example, you would say the username bgates@msn.com as "bgates at msn dot com."

Note: *Microsoft Outlook Express is a very powerful e-mail program. In addition to letting you use Outlook Express as your e-mail software when you connect to the Net using MSN, you can also use Outlook Express as your e-mail software should you decide to use a different online service or Internet service provider to access the Net.*

810 USING *MSN* TO BROWSE THE WORLD WIDE WEB

After you connect to the Microsoft Network, you must use Web browsing software to access information on the World Wide Web (or Web, for short). Today, most users use either the Netscape Navigator or Microsoft Internet Explorer to surf the Web. Windows 98 includes the Internet Explorer and, in fact, the Windows 98 Explorer integrates the Internet Explorer into many common operations. To use the Internet Explorer within MSN to surf the Web, perform these steps:

1. If you are using MSN as your Internet service provider, follow the steps discussed in Tip 806 to connect to the Net.
2. Click your mouse on the Start menu and then select the Programs option. Windows 98, in turn, will display the Programs submenu.
3. Within the Programs submenu, click your mouse on the Internet Explorer option. Windows 98, in turn, will display the Internet Explorer submenu.
4. Within the Internet Explorer submenu, click your mouse on the Internet Explorer option. Windows 98 will start the Internet Explorer, as shown in Figure 810.

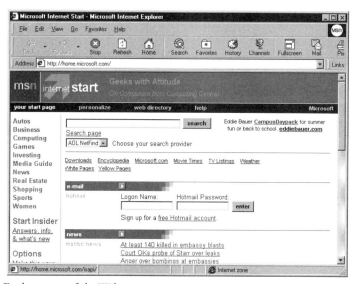

Figure 810 *Using the Internet Explorer to surf the Web.*

811   *USING THE MSN TASKBAR MENU*

To simplify your access to the Microsoft Network, Windows 98 places an MSN icon within the Taskbar, as shown in Figure 811.1.

Figure 811.1 *The MSN Taskbar icon.*

If you click your mouse on the MSN Taskbar icon, Windows 98, in turn, will display the MSN menu, as shown in Figure 811.2. Using the MSN menu, you can log into or log off the Microsoft Network, customize your MSN settings, or quickly jump to various user forums. Several of the Tips that follow discuss operations you can perform using the MSN menu.

Figure 811.2 The MSN menu.

812 **UNDERSTANDING AND USING MSN USER FORUMS**

In addition to wide a number of sites you will encounter on the Web, the Microsoft Network provides a variety of user forums that you can visit to get information on a wide range of topics. The MSN user forums differ from traditional Web sites in that several of the forums let users leave their own information at the site. For example, within a Computer forum, users might ask or answer various questions. Like traditional Web sites, within an MSN forum, you can often upload and download software. To access the MSN user forums, click your mouse on the MSN Taskbar icon. Windows 98, in turn, will display the MSN menu, as shown in Figure 812.

Figure 812 The MSN menu.

Within the MSN menu, the On Stage option will lead you to a variety of forums which include business, computers, education, sports, travel, and more. Likewise, the Essentials option will lead to forums which examine cars, arts, personal finance, and even the arts. Likewise, by selecting the Communicate submenu's MSN Forums option, you will encounter forums on food, books, movies, outdoor activities, and more.

813 **ACCESSING MSN'S MEMBER SERVICES**

In Tip 805, you learned how to sign up for the Microsoft Network. Over time, you may need technical support, want information about your current bill, or you may decide that you no longer want to be an MSN member. In such cases, you can use MSN itself to access its member services. To access MSN's member services, click your mouse on the MSN

Taskbar icon. Windows 98, in turn, will display the MSN menu. Within the MSN menu, click your mouse on the Member Services option. Windows 98, in turn, will display the Member Services submenu, as shown in Figure 813.

Figure 813 *The MSN menu's Member Services submenu.*

Depending on the Member Services submenu option you select, MSN will display a different Web site within which you can get the information you require.

814   USING MSN TO CHAT WITH OTHER ONLINE USERS

Most users communicate across the Net using electronic mail. In addition to e-mail, users often communicate across the Net using chat software which lets two or more users communicate (chat) by typing at their keyboard. In general, to chat with other users, you must use your chat software to join other users who are holding a chat session. Across the Internet, you can find a myriad of chat sessions filled with users who are chatting about any and all topics you might imagine. Within the Microsoft Network, you will chat only with other users who are connected to MSN.

To chat online, you must have chat software. Windows 98 provides Microsoft Chat, which Tip 972 discusses in detail. Figure 814 shows a chat session within Microsoft Chat.

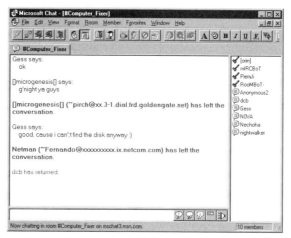

Figure 814 *Using Microsoft Chat to chat with other users online.*

To chat with other users connected to MSN, perform these steps:

1. Log into the Microsoft Network. Click your mouse on the MSN Taskbar icon. Windows 98 will display the MSN menu.

2. Within the MSN menu, click your mouse on the Communicate option. Windows 98, in turn, will display the Communicate submenu.

3. Within the Communicate submenu, click your mouse on the Chat Central option. MSN, in turn, will display the Chat Central Web site which contains the remaining steps you must perform to connect to MSN chat sessions.

815 VIEWING *MSN* CONNECTION INFORMATION

As you work within MSN, there may be times, either due to the network problems or software problems when one of your programs, such as your browser or e-mail software, appears not to be doing anything. In such cases, you can use the Connection dialog box to determine if your system is currently sending or receiving any data across the network. To view information about your current connection, perform these steps:

1. Within your Taskbar, locate the Connection icon shown in Figure 815.1.

Figure 815.1 *The Taskbar Connection icon.*

2. Double-click your mouse on the Connection icon. Windows 98, in turn, will display the Connected to MSN dialog box, as shown in Figure 815.2.

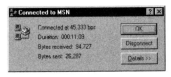

Figure 815.2 *The Connected to MSN dialog box.*

3. Within the Connected to MSN dialog box, watch to see if the number of bytes received or sent changes. If the number does not change, your system is not currently sending or receiving data. If you repeat the current operation and these numbers still do not change, your network connection may be hung. Log off your current connection and then log back into the Microsoft Network.

816 CHANGING YOUR *MSN* PASSWORD

As you have learned, before you can log into the Microsoft Network, you must specify a username and a password. To prevent other users from accessing your account, you should keep your password private. If you think that another user may have learned (or guessed) your password, you can change your password by performing these steps:

1. Log into the Microsoft Network and start the Internet Explorer.
2. Click your mouse on the MSN Taskbar button. Windows 98, in turn, will display the MSN menu.
3. Within the MSN menu, click your mouse on the Member Services button. Windows 98, in turn, will display the Member Services submenu.
4. Within the Member Services submenu, click your mouse on the Check or Change Your Account option. The Internet Explorer, in turn, will display the MSN Web page within which you can specify your new password.

817 CREATING A NEW MSN PASSWORD

If you happen to forget your MSN password and you can no longer log into the Microsoft Network, MSN lets you create a new password. To create a new password, however, you must have the credit-card number MSN is currently billing for your service. Next, to create a new password, perform these steps:

1. Click your mouse on the MSN Taskbar icon or use the Start menu to select the Microsoft Network option. Windows 98, in turn, will display the MSN Sign-In dialog box.
2. Within the MSN Sign-In dialog box, click your mouse on the New button. Windows 98, in turn, will display a dialog box informing you that you will need your credit-card information. Click your mouse on the check box that states you have your credit card information and then click your mouse on the Connect button. Your modem will then connect you to the Microsoft Network.
3. After your modem connects you to the Microsoft Network, a Connection Wizard will walk you through the steps you must perform to change your password.

818 LOGGING OFF MSN

After you are done using the Microsoft Network, you must log off the network to end your current connection. To log off the Microsoft Network, perform these steps:

1. Click your mouse on the MSN Taskbar icon. Windows 98 will display the MSN menu.
2. Within the MSN menu, click your mouse on the Disconnect from MSN option.

If your system does not display a MSN Taskbar button, double-click your mouse instead of the Taskbar connection icon. Windows 98, in turn, will display the Connected to MSN dialog box, as shown in Figure 818.

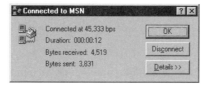

Figure 818 *The Connected to MSN dialog box.*

Within the Connected to MSN dialog box, click your mouse on the Disconnect button to log off the Microsoft Network.

819 **CUSTOMIZING YOUR MSN SETTINGS**

Like other Windows-based software programs, the Microsoft Network lets you customize a variety of settings, such as the fonts, sound effects, and even how and when MSN notifies you of various events, such as new e-mail messages. To customize your MSN settings, perform these steps:

1. Log into MSN.
2. Click your mouse on the MSN Taskbar icon. Windows 98 will display the MSN menu.
3. Within the MSN menu, click your mouse on the MSN Option. Windows 98, in turn, will display the MSN Options submenu.
4. Within the MSN Options submenu, click your mouse on the Customize MSN option. Your browser, in turn, will display a Web site within which you can customize your MSN settings.

820 **STARTING THE INTERNET EXPLORER**

As you have learned, to surf sites on the World Wide Web, you must use special browser software. To help you take full advantage of the Web, Microsoft includes the Internet Explorer, shown in Figure 820.1, that you can use to view sites on the Web. To start the Internet Explorer, perform these steps:

1. Click your mouse on the Start menu Programs option and choose the Internet Explorer. Windows 98, in turn, will cascade the Internet Explorer submenu.
2. Within the Internet Explorer submenu, click your mouse on the Internet Explorer option. Windows 98 will open the Internet Explorer window, shown in Figure 820.1.

Within the Internet Explorer, you can view a Web site's contents by clicking your mouse on the Address field and then typing in the site's Web address. If your PC is not currently connected to the Net and you type in the address of a site on the Web, Windows 98 will start the software that you use to dial into your online service or Internet Service provider. After you connect to the Net, the Internet Explorer will display the Web site's contents.

Figure 820.1 *Windows 98 includes the Internet Explorer with which you can surf the Web.*

Note: *To simplify your access to the Internet Explorer, Windows 98 displays an icon within the Taskbar upon which you can click your mouse to start the program, as shown in Figure 820.2. If your system does not display the Internet Explorer's Taskbar icon, right-click your mouse on the Taskbar and select the pop-up menu Toolbars submenu Quick Launch option.*

Figure 820.2 *Starting the Internet Explorer from the Windows 98 Taskbar.*

821 — USING THE INTERNET EXPLORER TOOLBARS

Like all Windows-based programs, the Internet Explorer provides toolbars whose buttons you can use to help simplify common tasks. However, unlike other programs that provide one tool bar, the Internet Explorer provides four toolbars. To display the Internet Explorer toolbars, click your mouse on the View menu Toolbars option and then click your mouse on the toolbar you desire, placing a check mark next to the option. Figure 821 displays the Internet Explorer's Standard Buttons toolbar, which you can use to move forward or backward between sites you have previously displayed, to refresh the current site, to stop a Web site download, to search for information on the Web, to print the current Web site's content, and more.

Figure 821 *The Internet Explorer's Standard Buttons toolbar.*

Using the Internet Explorer's Address toolbar, you will type in the address of the Web site that you desire. Likewise, using the Internet Explorer's Links toolbar, you can quickly access key sites across the Web.

822 **USING THE EXPLORER BAR**

In Tip 821, you learned how to use the Internet Explorer's toolbars to perform common operations. At it turns out, in addition to providing the toolbars Tip 821 presents, the Internet Explorer provides a special Explorer bar that the Explorer displays along the left-hand-side of its window. Within the Explorer bar, you can view your list of favorite sites, your list of channels (Tip 844 discusses Web channels in detail), your Web history that lists sites you have recently visited, as well as links you can use to search for information on the Web. Figure 822, for example, shows the contents of the Favorites folder within the Explorer bar.

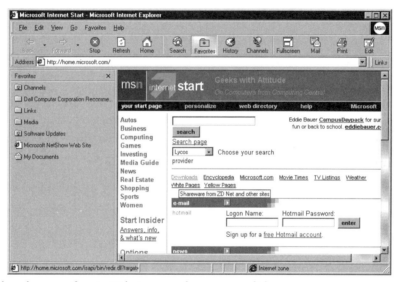

Figure 822 *Using the Explorer bar, your favorite Web sites are only one mouse click away.*

To display the Internet Explorer's Explorer bar, click your mouse on the View menu Explorer bar. The Internet Explorer, in turn, will cascade the Explorer Bar menu. Within the Explorer Bar menu, select the option that corresponds to the contents you want to display or click your mouse on the None option to turn off the Explorer bar display.

Note: *Within the Explorer's Standard Buttons toolbar, you can click your mouse on the Search, Favorites, History, or Channels button to display the corresponding item within the Explorer bar. To close the Explorer bar, you can click your mouse on the Close button that appears at the top right-hand corner of the Explorer bar.*

823 **UNDERSTANDING WEB SITE FRAMES**

As you have learned, when you view a Web site, the Internet Explorer will display the Web site's contents within its window. Depending on the Web site's contents, there may be times when the site will further divide its contents into two or more frames—which you can think of as subwindows. Figure 823.1, for example, shows two Web sites that take advantage of frames.

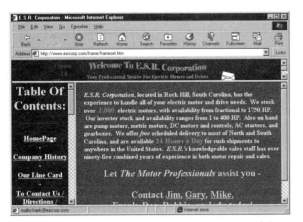 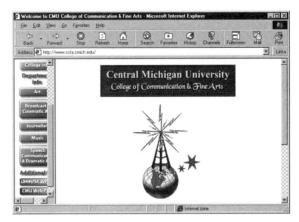

Figure 823.1 *Web sites use frames to present multiple views of their contents.*

Within the Internet Explorer, you can think of each frame as a small window. Depending on the frame's contents, you may be able use vertical or horizontal scroll bars to move through the frame's contents. In addition, as shown in Figure 823.2, you may be able to size the window's frame by using your mouse to drag the frame in or out.

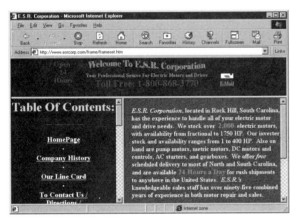 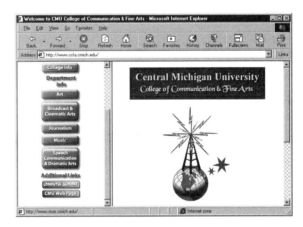

Figure 823.2 *Sizing frames within a Web site.*

824 STOPPING A WEB SITE DOWNLOAD

As you surf the Web, there may be times when, after you initiate a Web site's download, you decide that you no longer want to view the site's contents (possibly because you selected the site by mistake or because the site is taking too long to download). To direct Internet Explorer to stop downloading a site, click your mouse on the toolbar Stop button or press your keyboard's ESC key.

After the Internet Explorer stops the download operation, you can type a different address within the Internet Explorer's Address field to continue on your way about the Web. Should you inadvertently stop a download, you can resume the download by clicking your mouse on the View menu Refresh button or by pressing the F5 function key.

Often, after you locate the information you desire at a Web site, you will want to print the site's contents so you can have a hard copy of the information. To print the current site's content within the Internet Explorer, select the File menu Print option. The Internet Explorer, in turn, will display the Print dialog box, as shown in Figure 825.

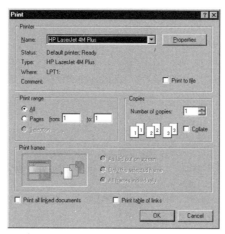

Figure 825 *The Internet Explorer Print dialog box.*

For many sites, you can simply click your mouse on the Print dialog box OK button to print the site's contents. However, if the current site uses frames, you can use radio buttons that appear within the Print dialog box to control how the Internet Explorer prints each frame's contents. First, the Internet Explorer can simply print the site just as it appears on your screen—showing the separate frames. Or, you can direct the Internet Explorer to only print the current frame's contents or to print each frame's contents individually. After you select the radio button that corresponds to the frame format you desire, click your mouse on the Print dialog box OK button.

As you view information on a Web site, there may be times when you will want to copy text from the site to the Clipboard, perhaps so you can send the text to another user within an e-mail message or because you want to cite the text within a document. To copy text from a Web site, you must first select text, either by dragging your mouse pointer over the text you desire or by holding down your keyboard SHIFT key as you press your keyboard arrow keys to highlight the text. After you select the text you desire, you can then use the Internet Explorer's Edit menu Copy option to copy the text to the Clipboard. Then, you can select the program into which you want to paste the text and use the program's Edit menu Paste option to place the text.

Note: *Text you copy from a site on the Web is covered by copyright law. Do not use such text without citing the author and the Web site from which you copied the text.*

827 **SENDING THE CURRENT WEB SITE TO ANOTHER USER**

As you surf the Web, there may be times when you encounter a site whose contents you want another user to see. In such cases, you can direct the Internet Explorer to e-mail the current page or a link to the current page to another user by performing these steps:

1. Within the Internet Explorer, click your mouse on the File menu Send option. The Internet Explorer, in turn, will cascade the Send submenu, as shown in Figure 827.

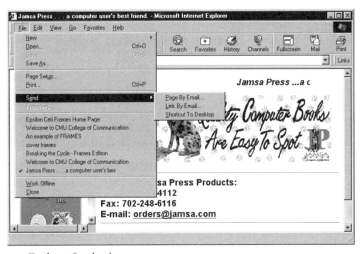

Figure 827 *Cascading the Internet Explorer Send submenu.*

2. Within the Send submenu, select the Page by Email option to send the contents of the current page to another user, and click your mouse on the Page By Email option. To send a link (the site's Web address), click your mouse on the Link By Email option. The Internet Explorer, in turn, will compose an e-mail message using Outlook Express (or the e-mail program you have configured your system to use) that you can then address and send to the recipients that you desire.

828 **OPENING A NEW INTERNET EXPLORER WINDOW**

As you traverse sites on the Web, there may be times that you find a site that contains some of the information that you need, but you still want to continue your search. In such cases, you can use the Internet Explorer's File menu New option to open a second window, within which you can continue your search while you leave your first site's contents in view. For example, Figure 828 shows two Internet Explorer windows. When you are done with either window, you can select the window's File menu Close option to close the window or simply click your mouse on the window's Close button.

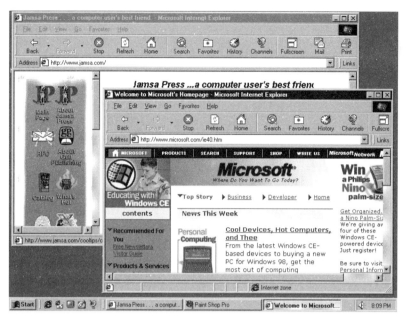

Figure 828 *Using multiple Internet Explorer windows to surf the Web.*

829 SEARCHING THE CURRENT PAGE FOR SPECIFIC TEXT

In Tip 802, you learned how to use a search engine to locate sites on Web that discuss specific topics. When you view a site's contents within the Internet Explorer, there may be times when you will want to search the current document for specific information (some Web pages can actually become quite long). To search the current Web page for information, perform these steps:

1. Within Internet Explorer, click your mouse on the Edit menu Find (on this page) option. The Internet Explorer, in turn, will display the Find dialog box, as shown in Figure 829.

Figure 829 *The Internet Explorer Find dialog box.*

2. Within the Find dialog box, type in the word for which you want the Internet Explorer to search the current page and then click your mouse on the Find Next button. (The Internet Explorer will only search the current page. It will not search pages that correspond to links on the current page.) If the Internet Explorer finds your text, it will highlight the text within the page. Otherwise, the Internet Explorer will display a dialog box telling you that it finished searching the document.

If the page contains multiple occurrences of the word or phrase, you can click your mouse on the Find dialog box Find Next button to move through each occurrence.

830 REFRESHING THE CURRENT PAGE

When you view sites on the Web, there may be times when, due to an error, or because you previously stopped the site's download, Internet Explorer does not download the entire site's text or graphics. In such cases, you can restart the download operation by selecting the Internet Explorer's View menu Refresh option. When you refresh a Web site in this way, the Internet Explorer will only download the files it previously failed to download or content that has changed since you performed the download operation. When you download a site's contents, the Internet Explorer stores the content in temporary files on your disk. If you later revisit the site, the Internet Explorer will use the previously downloaded contents, which lets it quickly display the Web site's contents. Depending on your system's Internet settings, the Internet Explorer may not check if the site's contents have changed since your previous download operation. By selecting the Edit menu Refresh option, you can direct the Internet Explorer to test whether or not the site's contents have changed and, if so, to download the new contents.

831 DISPLAYING THE CURRENT PAGE'S HTML SOURCE CODE

To create a Web site, designers use HTML, a special formatting language. By placing HTML codes within a Web document, designers can direct your browser to display text using italics, a bold typeface, or even large fonts. For example, to display the word *Windows* using italics, the designer would use the *<I>* tag, which turns on italic text, and the *</I>* tag that turns off italics, as shown here:

```
<I>Windows</I>
```

Likewise, to display the word **Windows** as bold, the designer would use the *<B>* tag to turn on bold text and the *</B>* tag to turn off bolding, as shown here:

```
<B>Windows</B>
```

When you view sites on the Web, you can direct the Internet Explorer to display the current page's HTML codes by selecting the View menu Source option. Figure 831, for example, shows the HTML source code from the Microsoft Web site at *www.microsoft.com*. By examining another site's HTML codes, designers can often learn new HTML techniques.

Figure 831 Viewing HTML source code within the Internet Explorer.

As you use the Internet Explorer to view sites on the Web, you will come across sites that you will want to visit again in the future. You might, for example, want to visit the Microsoft site on a regular basis to stay current on Windows 98 or you may want to use the Yahoo search engine on a regular basis to search the Web for specific content (Tip 802 discusses search engines in detail). To make it easy for you to revisit a site in the future, Windows 98 provides a Favorites folder within which you can add a link to a specific site. Later, when you want to revisit the site, you can click your mouse on the Explorer Favorites menu and then click your mouse on the site's link. Figure 832.1, for example, shows the Favorites menu within the Internet Explorer.

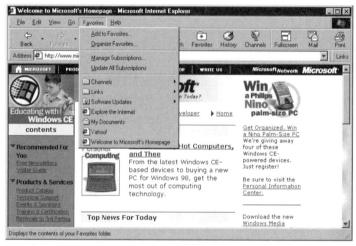

Figure 832.1 *Using the Internet Explorer Favorites menu, you can quickly select a site you want to visit.*

To add your current site to the Favorites menu, perform these steps:

1. Click your mouse on the Internet Explorer Favorites menu and choose Add to Favorites. The Internet Explorer, in turn, will display the Add Favorite dialog box, as shown in Figure 832.2.

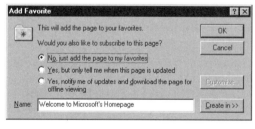

Figure 832.2 *The Add Favorite dialog box.*

2. Within the Add Favorite dialog box, click your mouse on the Name field and then type in the name you want the Favorites menu to display for the current site. Then, click your mouse on the OK button. The Internet Explorer will add the site to the Favorites menu.

Note: If you view the Internet Explorer Favorites menu, you will find that the menu provides several folders within which you can organize your sites. If you want the Internet Explorer to place the current site within a specific folder, perform these steps:

1. Click your mouse on the Internet Explorer Favorites menu and choose Add to Favorites. The Internet Explorer, in turn, will display the Add Favorite dialog box, as shown in Figure 832.2.

2. Within the Add Favorite dialog box, click your mouse on the Name field and then type in the Name you want the Favorites menu to display for the current site. Then, click your mouse on the Create in button. The Internet Explorer, in turn, will expand the dialog box to display the Favorites menu folder list.

3. Within the folder list, click your mouse on the folder within which you want the Internet Explorer to place your site link and then click your mouse on the OK button.

833 | **SELECTING SITES USING THE INTERNET EXPLORER FAVORITES BAR**

In Tip 832, you learned how to add a site to the Internet Explorer Favorites menu. After you add a site to the Favorites menu, you can select the site's menu option to browse the site. In addition to selecting the site from the Favorites menu, you can also direct the Internet Explorer to display the Favorites menu within its Explorer bar, which the Internet Explorer will display along the left-hand-side of its window, as shown in Figure 833.

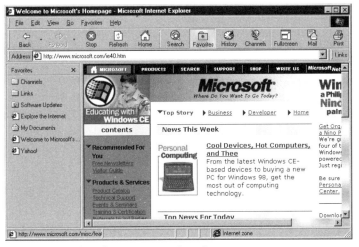

Figure 833 *Displaying the Favorites menu within the Internet Explorer bar.*

To display the Favorites menu within the Internet Explorer bar, click your mouse on the View menu Explorer Bar option and choose Favorites or click your mouse on the toolbar Favorites button.

834 | **ORGANIZING YOUR FAVORITES FOLDER**

In Tip 832, you learned how to add a Web site to the Internet Explorer Favorites menu from which you can then quickly select a specific site. As you learned, when you add a site to the Favorites menu, you can add the site as an upper-level entry within the menu or you can place the site within a folder that appears within the menu. As the number of sites you add to the Favorites menu increases, you may eventually want to remove a site or move a site into a specific folder. To organize the sites that appear within the Favorites menu, perform these steps:

1. Within the Internet Explorer, click your mouse on the Favorites menu and choose the Organize Favorites option. The Internet Explorer, in turn, will display the Organize Favorites dialog box, as shown in Figure 834.1.

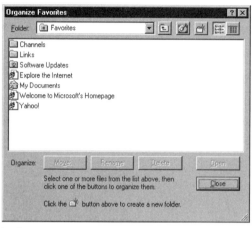

Figure 834.1 *The Organize Favorites dialog box.*

2. To remove a site from the Favorites menu using the Organize Favorites dialog box, click your mouse on the site's entry and then click your mouse on the Delete button. The Internet Explorer, in turn, may display the Confirm File Delete dialog box asking you confirm the operation. Within the dialog box, click your mouse on the Yes button.

3. To move a site into a specific Favorites menu folder, click your mouse on the site and then click your mouse on the Move button. The Internet Explorer, in turn, will display the Browse for Folder dialog box, as shown in Figure 834.2.

Figure 834.2 *The Browse for Folder dialog box.*

4. Within the Browse for Folder dialog box, click your mouse on the folder into which you want the Internet Explorer to move the site and then click your mouse on the OK button.

5. Within the Organize Favorites dialog box, click your mouse on the OK button.

835 **UNDERSTANDING WEB-SITE SUBSCRIPTIONS**

As you use the Internet Explorer to surf sites across the World Wide Web, you will eventually find a set of sites whose contents you want to view on a regular basis. Rather than forcing you to continually visit the site (and wait for the site's content to download), Windows 98 lets you subscribe to a site, which directs Windows 98 to download the site's contents for you (at specific intervals that you define). Later, after Windows 98 downloads the site's contents, you can browse the site offline (without having to wait for downloads).

Several of the Tips that follow discuss Web-site subscriptions in detail. In general, subscribing to a Web site will not cost you any money. Instead, by subscribing to a site, you have the site's contents available when you want it—without a download delay. In other words, just as a magazine to which you subscribe automatically shows up in your mailbox every month, the Web content to which you subscribe will automatically show up on your PC (within the folder that stores temporary Internet files). When you subscribe to a site within Windows 98, you can direct the Internet Explorer to download the site's content each time it changes, or to simply notify you of the change (either by sending you an e-mail message or by highlighting the site's icon within the Favorites menu).

836 **SUBSCRIBING TO A WEB SITE**

In Tip 835, you learned that Windows 98 lets you subscribe to a Web site whose contents you want Windows 98 to download to your system at regular intervals. To subscribe to a channel, perform these steps:

1. As you view the site within the Internet Explorer, click your mouse on the Favorites menu Add to Favorites option. Windows 98, in turn, will display the Add Favorite dialog box, as shown in Figure 836.1, which asks you if you want to subscribe to the site.

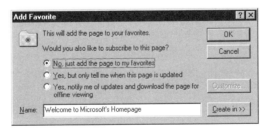

Figure 836.1 The Add Favorite dialog box.

2. When you subscribe to a site, you can direct the Internet Explorer to notify (usually by e-mail) that the site's contents has changed and then, optionally, you can direct the Internet Explorer to download the site's new contents. Within the Add Favorite dialog box, click your mouse on the radio button that corresponds to whether or not you want Internet Explorer to download the current site's contents as it changes.

3. Within the Add Favorite dialog box, click your mouse on the Name field and type in the name you want the Internet Explorer to display for this site on the Favorites menu. Then, click your mouse on the OK button.

Later, should a site's contents change, the Internet Explorer will notify of you of the change either via an e-mail message or by highlighting the icon that appears next to the site's name within the Favorites menu.

837   DIRECTING THE INTERNET EXPLORER TO SEND YOU E-MAIL NOTIFICATION OF A SITE'S CONTENT CHANGE

In Tip 836, you learned how to subscribe to a Web site within the Internet Explorer. As you learned, when you subscribe to a site, you can direct the Internet Explorer to notify you that the site's content has changed. Usually, when a site's content changes, the Internet Explorer will highlight the icon that appears next to the site's name within the Favorites list. If you instead want the Internet Explorer to send you an e-mail message when a site's content changes, perform these steps when you subscribe to the site:

1. As you view the site within the Internet Explorer, click your mouse on the Favorites menu Add to Favorites option. Windows 98, in turn, will display the Add Favorite dialog box which asks you if you want to subscribe to the site.

2. When you subscribe to a site, you can direct the Internet Explorer to notify you (usually by e-mail) that the site's contents have changed and then, optionally, you can direct the Internet Explorer to download the site's new contents. Within the Add Favorite dialog box, click your mouse on the radio button that corresponds to whether or not you want Internet Explorer to download the current site's contents as it changes.

3. Within the Add Favorite dialog box, click your mouse on the Customize button. The Internet Explorer, in turn, will display the Subscription Wizard dialog box, as shown in Figure 837.

Figure 837 *The Subscription Wizard dialog box.*

4. Depending on whether you directed the Internet Explorer to download site changes or to simply notify of you of changes, the boxes that the Subscription Wizard displays will differ. Eventually, however, the Subscription Wizard will display a dialog box that lets you direct the Internet Explorer to send you an e-mail message each time the site's content changes (and that lets you specify the e-mail address to which you want the message sent). Using the Subscription Wizard, customize the settings you desire.

838	CONTROLLING HOW MUCH SUBSCRIPTION INFORMATION THE INTERNET EXPLORER DOWNLOADS

In Tip 836, you learned that within Windows 98, you can subscribe to a Web site, you can direct the Internet Explorer to download each time the site's content changes. By default, when you subscribe to a site, the Internet Explorer will only notify you of the site's content change (by highlighting the icon that appears next to the site's option within the Favorites menu). If you want the Internet Explorer to download the site's contents, perform these steps:

1. As you view the site within the Internet Explorer, click your mouse on the Favorites menu Add to Favorites option. Windows 98, in turn, will display the Add Favorite dialog box which asks you if you want to subscribe to the site.

2. When you subscribe to a site, you can direct the Internet Explorer to notify (usually by e-mail) that the site's contents has changed and then, optionally, you can direct the Internet Explorer to download the site's new contents.

3. Within the Add Favorite dialog box, click your mouse on the Yes, notify me of updates and download the page for offline viewing radio button and then click your mouse on the Customize button. The Internet Explorer, in turn, will display the Subscription Wizard dialog box, as shown in Figure 838.

Figure 838 *The Subscription Wizard dialog box.*

4. Within the Subscription Wizard, you can direct the Internet Explorer to download only the Web page you have specified or also the pages that are linked to the page. Within the Wizard, select the option that you desire and then click your mouse on the Next button to continue the Wizard's processing.

5. Within the Add Favorite dialog box, click your mouse on the Name field and type in the name you want the Internet Explorer to display for this site on the Favorites menu. Then, click your mouse on the OK button.

839	USING THE INTERNET EXPLORER TO BROWSE OFFLINE

In Tip 838, you learned how to direct the Internet Explorer to download a Web site's contents each time the site's contents change. Later, at your convenience, you can view the downloaded contents offline (without the downloading delay). To view a site's contents offline, perform these steps:

1. Click your mouse on the Start menu Favorites option. Windows 98, in turn, will cascade the Favorites submenu, as shown in Figure 839.

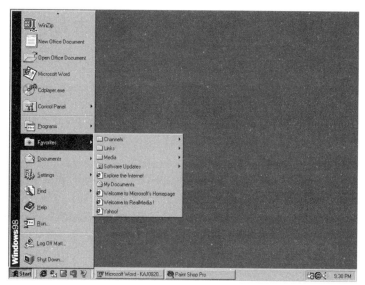

Figure 839 *Cascading the Start menu Favorites submenu.*

2. Within the Favorites menu, click your mouse on the Web site whose contents you want to view offline. Windows 98, in turn, will launch the Internet Explorer, displaying the site's contents.

840 ***MANAGING YOUR SUBSCRIPTIONS***

In Tip 836, you learned how to use the Internet Explorer to subscribe to a Web site. Over time, you may find that you want to cancel a subscription or immediately update the subscription's contents. To manage your subscriptions, you can use the Subscriptions folder, shown in Figure 840. Within the Subscriptions folder, you can click your mouse on the subscription that you want to delete, rename, or update. Then, you can use File menu options to perform the operations you desire. In addition, you can use the Subscriptions folder to determine a subscription's Web site, the site's status (current or out of date), as well as the site's next scheduled update. To display the Subscriptions folder, select the Internet Explorer Favorites menu and choose Manage Subscriptions.

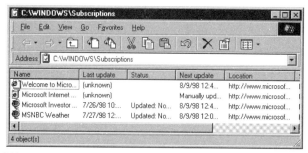

Figure 840 *Using the Subscription folder to manage your subscriptions.*

841 UPDATING A SUBSCRIPTION

In Tip 836, you learned how to use the Internet Explorer to subscribe to a Web site. Using the Subscription folder Tip 840 presents, you can determine whether your subscriptions' contents are current or out of date. In addition, you can determine when the Internet Explorer plans to next update the site's contents. You can use the Subscriptions folder to update the site's contents, by performing these steps:

1. Within the Internet Explorer, click your mouse on the Favorites menu Manage Subscriptions option. The Internet Explorer will display the Subscriptions folder.
2. Within the Subscriptions folder, click your mouse on the subscription whose contents you want to update.
3. Click your mouse on the File menu Update Now option.

Note: *To update all of your subscriptions in one step, select the Favorites menu Update All Subscriptions option.*

842 PERFORMING LATE NIGHT UPDATES

In Tip 836, you learned how to subscribe to a Web site, whose contents you want the Internet Explorer to automatically download each time the site's contents change. In Tip 840, you learned how to use the Subscriptions folder to view the Internet Explorer's download schedule. Depending on the sites to which you subscribe, you may want to schedule your download operations so that the Internet Explorer downloads the site's contents late at night, after you have completed your work.

Then, the following morning, the site's new contents will be present on your system. To schedule a subscription download, perform these steps:

1. Within the Internet Explorer, click your mouse on the Favorites menu Manage Subscriptions option. The Internet Explorer will display the Subscriptions folder.
2. Within the Subscription folder, right-click your mouse on the subscription whose download you want to schedule. Windows 98, in turn, will display a pop-up menu.
3. Within the pop-up menu, click your mouse on the Properties option. Windows 98, in turn, will display the subscription's Properties dialog box.
4. Within the Properties dialog box, click your mouse on the Schedule tab. Windows 98, in turn, will display the Schedule tab, as shown in Figure 842.1.

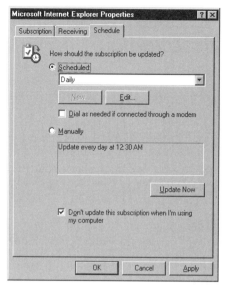

Figure 842.1 *A subscription's Properties dialog box Schedule tab.*

5. Within the Schedule tab, click your mouse on the Edit button. Windows 98, in turn, will display the Custom Schedule dialog box, as shown in Figure 842.2.

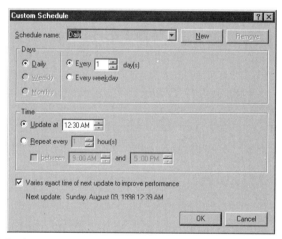

Figure 842.2 *The Custom Schedule dialog box.*

6. Within the Custom Schedule dialog box, select the download schedule and frequency that you desire. Then, click your mouse on the OK button.

7. Within the Properties dialog box, click your mouse on the OK button.

843 CANCELING A SUBSCRIPTION

In Tip 836, you learned how to subscribe to a Web site whose contents you want the Internet Explorer to download (or for which you want the Internet Explorer to notify you of the change). Over time, you may want to cancel one or more of your subscriptions. To cancel a subscription, perform these steps:

1. Within the Internet Explorer, click your mouse on the Favorites menu Manage Subscriptions option. The Internet Explorer, in turn, will display the Subscriptions folder.

2. Within the Subscriptions folder, right-click your mouse on the subscription you want to cancel. Windows 98 will display a pop-up menu.

3. Within the pop-up menu, click your mouse on the Delete option. Windows 98 will display a dialog box asking you to confirm the cancellation. Within the dialog box, click your mouse on the Yes option.

844 *UNDERSTANDING HOW WEB CHANNELS DIFFER FROM SUBSCRIPTIONS*

In Tip 836, you learned how to subscribe to sites on the Web whose contents you want the Internet Explorer to download when the contents change. As you learned, when you subscribe to a Web site, the Internet Explorer will check the corresponding Web site on a regular basis to determine if the site's contents have changed. In addition to supporting subscriptions, Windows 98 also supports channels—which are quite similar.

To start, a channel, like a subscription, corresponds to a Web site. Like a subscription, you subscribe to a channel, which directs Windows 98 to either download the site's new contents or to notify you of the change. Unlike a subscription, however, a channel requires a special channel definition file (CDF) that the Web site will provide to Windows 98 that defines the site's attributes—such as how often or when the site will offer new contents.

Second, you can display a channel's contents on your Desktop or use the channel as a Desktop screen saver. Several of the Tips that follow discuss Windows 98 channel operations in detail.

845 *VIEWING A CHANNEL'S CONTENTS*

In Tip 844, you learned that you can subscribe to a channel on the Web, for which your system will notify you of or download content changes. To help you get started with channels, Windows 98 provides a channel bar, from which you can select and view several channel sites. To view one of the Windows 98 predefined channels, perform these steps:

1. Click your mouse on the Start menu Favorites option. Windows 98, in turn, will cascade the Favorites submenu.

2. Within the Favorites submenu, click your mouse on the Channels option and then choose the channel that you desire. Windows 98, in turn, will launch the Internet Explorer and will display the channel's Web site. In addition, along the edge of its window, the Internet Explorer will display the channel bar. For example, Figure 845 shows the Disney Web site within the Internet Explorer.

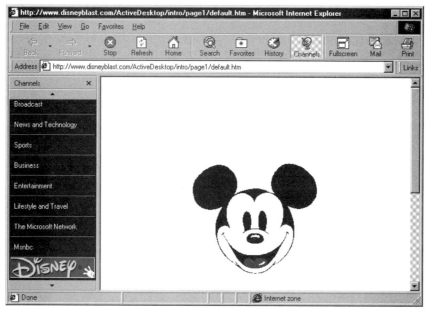

Figure 845 *Viewing the Disney Web site using a Windows 98 channel.*

846   **VIEWING A CHANNEL FROM THE CHANNEL BAR**

In Tip 845, you learned how to use the Start menu Favorites option to view a channel. If you are using the Internet Explorer, you can view a channel's contents by selecting the channel from the Favorites menu Channels submenu. In addition, if you select the View menu Explorer Bar option and choose Channels, the Internet Explorer will display its channel bar along the edge of its window, as shown in Figure 846. Within the channel bar, you can click your mouse on the channel you want to display.

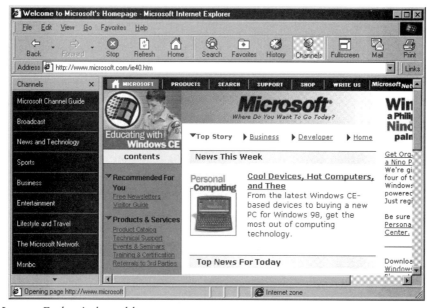

Figure 846 *Using the Internet Explorer's channel bar.*

847 **USING THE CHANNEL VIEWER TO VIEW A SITE'S CONTENTS**

In Tip 846, you learned how to view a channel's contents within the Internet Explorer. When you view channels within the Internet Explorer, you can use the channel bar to choose the channel you want to display. In addition to letting you view a channel within the Internet Explorer, Windows 98 also provides a special program called the Channel Viewer that, as shown in Figure 847.1, you can use to display a channel's contents. The advantage to viewing a channel within the Channel Viewer is that when you move the mouse away from the channel bar, the Channel Viewer will hide the Explorer bar's display. To later display the Explorer bar again, simply move your mouse over the Explorer bar's previous location.

Figure 847.1 *Using the Channel Viewer to view a channel's contents.*

To use the Channel Viewer to display a channel's contents, click your mouse on the Taskbar's Quick Launch toolbar's Channel icon, as shown in Figure 847.2.

Figure 847.2 *The Taskbar's Quick Launch toolbar's Channel icon.*

Note: *If your Taskbar is not currently displaying the Quick Launch toolbar, right-click your mouse on the Taskbar and select the Toolbars Quick Launch option.*

848 **USING A CHANNEL SCREEN SAVER**

As you have learned, a channel is a Web site whose contents you can view within the Internet Explorer or Channel Viewer. Within Windows 98, you can use your current channels as a screen saver. Each time the screen saver becomes active, it will cycle through your current channels, displaying each site's contents on your screen. If you are connected to the Internet, your screen saver will display the site's current contents. If you are not connected to the Internet, your system will cycle through the contents it has previously downloaded for each channel. To use your channels for a screen saver, perform these steps:

1. Right-click your mouse on an unused location on the Desktop. Windows 98 will display a pop-up menu. Within the pop-up menu, click your mouse on the Properties dialog box. Windows 98 will display the Display Properties dialog box.

2. Within the Display Properties dialog box, click your mouse on the Screen Saver tab. Windows 98 will display the Screen Saver sheet.

3. Within the Screen Saver sheet, click your mouse on the pull-down screen-saver list and select Channel Screen Saver option. Then, click your mouse on the Settings option. Windows 98, in turn, will display the Properties dialog box, as shown in Figure 848, within which you can select the channels you want the screen saver to display and for how long.

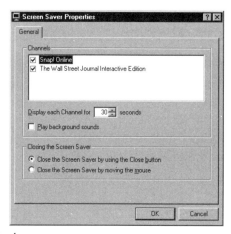

Figure 848 *The screen saver Properties dialog box.*

4. Within the dialog box, select the properties you desire and then click your mouse on the OK button.

5. Within the Display Properties dialog box, click your mouse on the OK button to put your changes into effect.

849 MANAGING THE CHANNELS FOLDER

As the number of channels to which you subscribe increases, you may eventually want to delete, rename, or move one or more channels. To manage your system's channels, perform these steps:

1. Within the Internet Explorer, click your mouse on the Favorites menu Organize Favorites option. The Internet Explorer will display the Organize Favorites dialog box.

2. Within the Organize Favorites dialog box, click your mouse on the Channels folder. The Internet Explorer, in turn, will display your current channels within the Organize Favorites dialog box, as shown in Figure 849.

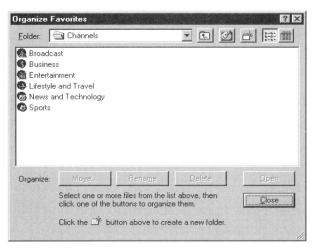

Figure 849 *Using the Organize Favorites dialog box to manage your system's channels.*

3. Within the Organize Favorites dialog box, click on the channel you desire and then use the Move, Rename, or Delete option to perform the operation that you desire.

850 **UNDERSTANDING ACTIVE DESKTOP COMPONENTS**

In addition to letting you subscribe to Web sites and use channels for your Desktop screen saver, Windows 98 also lets you place *active objects* on your Desktop. In general, an active object is a program that interacts with a site on the Web to get and display information as you work. For example, Figure 850 shows two active objects on the Windows 98 Desktop. The first object, a stock ticker tape, displays stock prices (actually prices on a 20-minute delay). The second object displays a weather map for the United States.

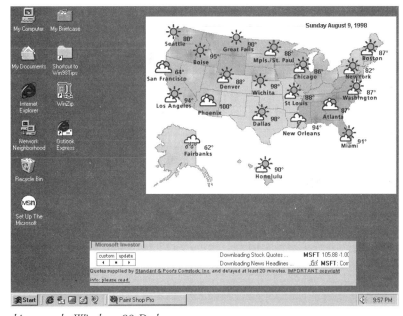

Figure 850 *Placing active objects on the Windows 98 Desktop.*

Across the Web, you will find a variety of active objects that you can install on your system. However, to avoid computer viruses, you should only download active objects from reputable sites, and then, make sure the objects have a digital signature that you can use to verify that the object's file has not been altered.

851 INSTALLING OBJECTS FROM THE ACTIVE DESKTOP GALLERY

In Tip 850, you learned that Windows 98 lets you display active objects on your Desktop. To help you get started with active objects, Microsoft provides an online gallery of objects from which you can download and install the objects that you desire.

To visit the Microsoft Active Desktop Gallery, perform these steps:

1. Right-click your mouse on an unused location on the Desktop. Windows 98 will display a pop-up menu. Within the pop-up menu, select the Properties option. Windows 98, in turn, will display the Display Properties dialog box.

2. Within the Display Properties dialog box, click your mouse on the Web tab. Windows 98 will display the Web sheet, as shown in Figure 851.1.

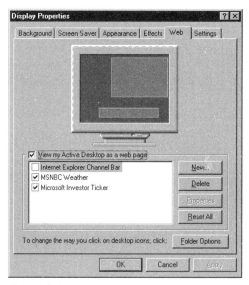

Figure 851.1 *The Display Properties dialog box Web sheet.*

3. Within the Web sheet, click your mouse on the New button. Windows 98, in turn, will display a dialog box asking you if you want to visit the Active Desktop Gallery at this time. Click your mouse on the Yes option. Windows 98, in turn, will start the Internet Explorer which, in turn, will display the Active Desktop Gallery at the Microsoft Web site.

4. Within the Active Desktop Gallery, click your mouse on the active object that you want to download and install.

852 LISTENING TO AND VIEWING REAL-AUDIO SITES FROM ACROSS THE WEB

Across the World Wide Web, designers are creating new ways to present content. Often, a Web site's content will consist only of text and images. At other sites, however, designers are making full use of multimedia video, audio, and animations.

To help the Internet Explorer make better use of sites that integrate audio and video content, Windows 98 includes Real Audio software that your browser can use to play back audio and video from sites across the Web. To install the Windows 98 Real Audio software, perform these steps:

1. Click your mouse on the Start menu Settings menu and choose Control Panel. Windows 98, in turn, will open the Control Panel window.
2. Within the Control Panel window, double-click your mouse on the Add/Remove Programs icon. Windows 98 will display the Add/Remove Programs Properties dialog box.
3. Within the Add/Remove Programs Properties dialog box, click your mouse on the Windows Setup tab. Windows 98 will display checkboxes for the Windows 98 components.
4. Within the Windows 98 component list, click your mouse on the Internet Tools checkbox and then click your mouse on the Details button. Windows 98 will display the Internet Tools dialog box.
5. Within the Internet Tools dialog box, click your mouse on the Real Audio Player 4.0 checkbox, placing a check mark within the box. Then, click your mouse on the OK button.
6. Within the Add/Remove Programs Properties dialog box, click your mouse on the OK button.

After you install the Real Audio software, follow the steps Tip 853 presents to use the Real Audio software.

853 TAKING THE REALPLAYER SOFTWARE FOR A TEST DRIVE

In Tip 852, you learned how to install software that you can use to play back audio and video from across the Web. To start the Real Audio software, perform these steps:

1. If you are not currently connected to the Net, connect to the net now. Click your mouse on the Start menu Programs option and then choose Internet Explorer. Windows 98, in turn, will cascade the Internet Explorer submenu.
2. Within the Internet Explorer submenu, click your mouse on the RealPlayer option. Windows 98, in turn, will display the RealPlayer window, as shown in Figure 853.1.

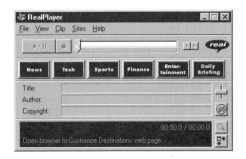

Figure 853.1 *The RealPlayer window.*

3. Within the RealPlayer window, click your mouse on one of the player buttons, such a News, Sports, or Entertainment. Internet Explorer, in turn, will display a list of sites from which you can play back audio or video content, as shown in Figure 853.2.

Figure 853.2 *Displaying RealPlayer sites within the Internet Explorer.*

4. Within the Internet Explorer's list of sites, click your mouse on the site whose contents you want to hear (or view). The RealPlayer, in turn, will start to play back the site's audio content.

If the site you select supports streaming video, the RealPlayer software will display the video content, as shown in Figure 853.3.

Figure 853.3 *Displaying video content within the RealPlayer window.*

Note: *To find more sites across the Web that support Real Audio, visit a search engine, such as Yahoo, and type in Real Audio as your search criteria.*

854 **UPGRADING YOUR REALPLAYER SOFTWARE**

In Tip 852, you learned how to install the RealPlayer software that Microsoft bundles on the Windows 98 CD-ROM. If you follow the steps Tip 852 presents, you will install the RealPlayer version 4 software on your system. As it turns out, the RealPlayer Web site offers regular software upgrades that you download from across the Web. To upgrade your RealPlayer software, perform these steps:

1. Click your mouse on the Start menu Programs option and then choose Internet Explorer. Windows 98, in turn, will cascade the Internet Explorer submenu.

2. Within the Internet Explorer submenu, click your mouse on the RealPlayer option. Windows 98, in turn, will display the RealPlayer window.

3. Within the RealPlayer window, click your mouse on the Help menu About option. The RealPlayer software, in turn, will display its About dialog box, as shown in Figure 854.

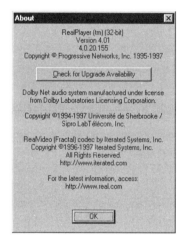

Figure 854 The RealPlayer About dialog box.

4. Within the About dialog box, click your mouse on the Check for Upgrade Availability button. The RealPlayer, in turn, will display a dialog box from which you can download the most recent version of the software.

855 **TAKING ADVANTAGE OF THE WINDOWS 98 SUPPORT FOR VRML 2.0**

Today, many users are familiar with the term *virtual reality*, but few users have ever experienced a virtual reality site. However, using the Internet Explorer, you can view virtual reality sites. For example, Figure 855 shows two sites that support virtual reality.

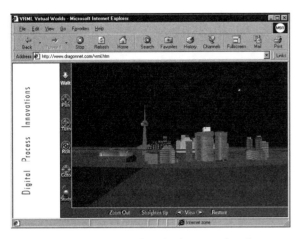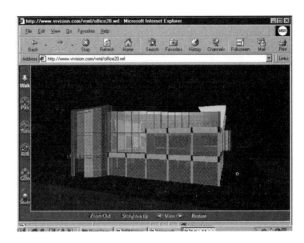

Figure 855 *Viewing sites that display virtual-reality images.*

To create a virtual-reality image, programmers often use the Virtual Reality Modeling Language (VRML). To let the Internet Explorer display the contents of sites that use VRML 2 (the most recent VRML specification), Windows 98 provides software you can install from the Windows 98 CD-ROM. To install support for VRML 2, perform these steps:

1. Click your mouse on the Start menu Settings menu and choose Control Panel. Windows 98, in turn, will open the Control Panel window.
2. Within the Control Panel window, double-click your mouse on the Add/Remove Programs icon. Windows 98 will display the Add/Remove Programs Properties dialog box.
3. Within the Add/Remove Programs Properties dialog box, click your mouse on the Windows Setup tab. Windows 98 will display checkboxes for the Windows 98 components.
4. Within the Windows 98 component list, click your mouse on the Internet Tools checkbox and then click your mouse on the Details button. Windows 98 will display the Internet Tools dialog box.
5. Within the Internet Tools dialog box, click your mouse on the Microsoft VRML 2.0 Viewer checkbox, placing a check mark within the box. Then, click your mouse on the OK button.
6. Within the Add/Remove Programs Properties dialog box, click your mouse on the OK button.

After you install the Windows 98 VRML 2.0 software, perform the steps Tip 856 presents to take a VRML test drive.

856 TAKING THE VRML SOFTWARE FOR A TEST DRIVE

In Tip 855, you learned how to install Windows 98 support for VRML 2.0. After you install the VRML 2.0 software, you may want to test drive some VRML sites using the Internet Explorer. To view a VRML site, you simply type in the site's address within the Internet Explorer's Address field. The site, in turn, will usually provide instructions that tell you how you view its virtual world. To get a better feel for virtual worlds, check out the sites shown in Figures 856.1 through 856.3.

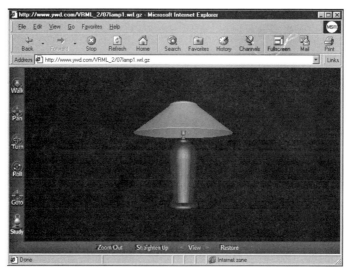

Figure 856.1 Viewing virtual worlds at **www.ywd.com**.

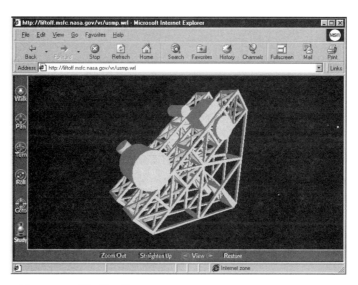

Figure 856.2 Viewing virtual worlds at **www.liftoff.msfc.nasa.gov**.

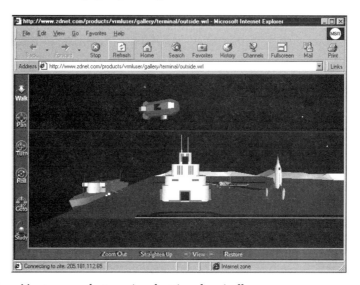

Figure 856.3 Viewing virtual worlds at **www.zdnet.com/products/vrmluser/gallery**.

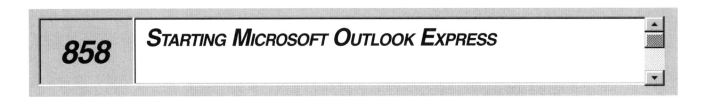

857   **UNDERSTANDING ELECTRONIC MAIL**

Today, business people, students, families, and just about everyone else is making extensive use of the Internet to send and receive electronic mail. In fact, each day hundreds of millions of e-mail messages make their way across the Internet. Using e-mail software, you can type a message that you can send across the Internet to another user. Because the Internet is a worldwide network of networks, you can use the Internet to send an e-mail message to the office down the hall, across town, across the country, or even on the other side of the world. Depending on Internet's current level of electronic traffic, your message will usually reside at its destination in a matter of minutes (or much less). Best of all—electronic mail messages are free! Depending on your needs, your e-mail message can be brief, long, can include pictures of your kids, or you can even attach a document, such as an Excel spreadsheet.

To send another user an e-mail message, you must know the user's e-mail address. E-mail addresses usually follow the format, *Name@someprovider.com*, such as *kris@jamsa.com*. When you send an e-mail message, your recipient does not have to be online. Instead, the next time the user connects to their online service or Internet account, your message will be there waiting for them.

Just as you have to have Web browsing software before you can surf the World Wide Web, you must also have e-mail software and an online service account before you can send and receive electronic mail. In Tip 858, you will learn that Windows 98 includes the Outlook Express program that you can use to send and receive electronic mail messages.

858   **STARTING MICROSOFT OUTLOOK EXPRESS**

As you learned in Tip 857, one of the PC's most common uses today is to send and receive electronic mail messages. Just as Windows 98 includes the Internet Explorer program that you can use to surf the Web, Windows 98 provides Outlook Express, as shown in Figure 858.1, that you can use to send and receive electronic mail.

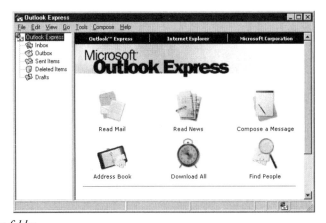

Figure 858.1 The Outlook Express folder.

To start Outlook Express, perform these steps:

1. Click your mouse on the Start menu Programs option and choose Internet Explorer. Windows 98, in turn, will cascade the Internet Explorer submenu.

2. Within the Internet Explorer submenu, click your mouse on the Outlook Express option. Windows 98, in turn, will display the Outlook Express folder previously shown in Figure 858.1.

Note: *To simplify your access to Outlook Express, Windows 98 displays an icon within the Taskbar upon which you can click your mouse to start the program, as shown in Figure 858.2. If your system does not display the Outlook Express Taskbar icon, right-click your mouse on the Taskbar and select the pop-up menu Toolbars submenu Quick Launch option.*

Figure 858.2 *Starting Outlook Express from the Windows 98 Taskbar.*

859 UNDERSTANDING YOUR INBOX AND OTHER FOLDERS

To help you manage the e-mail messages that you send and receive, Outlook Express provides you with several folders within which you can store related messages. To start, each time you receive an e-mail message, Outlook Express places your message within the Inbox folder, much like someone might place an envelope within the in-box on your desk. When you send a message, Outlook Express places the message into your Outbox until it has a chance to send the message. After Outlook Express sends your message, it will move the message from the Outbox into the Sent Items folder. Finally, when you delete an e-mail message, Outlook Express will move your message into the Deleted Items folder. Figure 859 shows folders within the Outlook Express folder list.

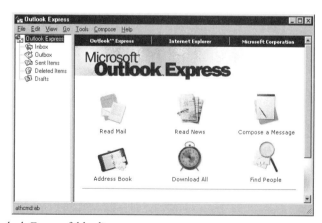

Figure 859 *Folders within the Outlook Express folder list.*

Within Outlook Express, you can display a folder's contents by clicking your mouse on the folder's icon within the folder list. In Tip 882, you will learn how to create your own folders to further organize your e-mail messages. As you create your own folders, there may be times when you create subfolders (folders within a folder). To display a folder's subfolders, simply click your mouse on the plus sign that precedes the folder's name within the folder list. Outlook Express, in turn, will expand the folder's list of subfolders. Later, to collapse the expanded folder list, click your mouse on the minus sign that precedes the folder name.

| 860 | **USING THE OUTLOOK EXPRESS TOOLBAR** |

Like most Windows-based programs, Outlook Express provides a toolbar that contains icons you can use to simplify common operations. Figure 860 briefly describes the toolbar's icons. If Outlook Express is not displaying its toolbar, click your mouse on the Outlook Express View menu and choose the Toolbar option, placing a check mark next to the option name.

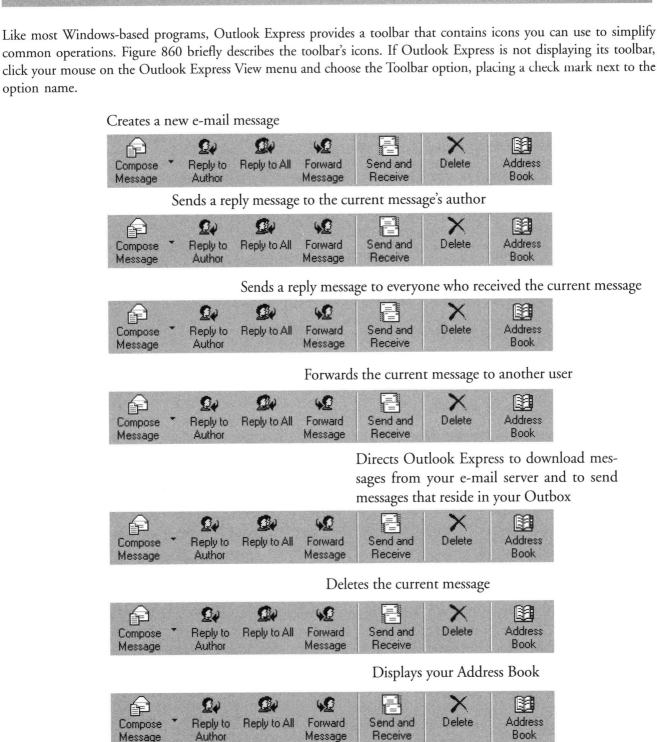

Creates a new e-mail message

Sends a reply message to the current message's author

Sends a reply message to everyone who received the current message

Forwards the current message to another user

Directs Outlook Express to download messages from your e-mail server and to send messages that reside in your Outbox

Deletes the current message

Displays your Address Book

Figure 860 The Outlook Express toolbar buttons.

861 | CUSTOMIZING YOUR OUTLOOK EXPRESS WINDOW LAYOUT

If you use Outlook Express on a regular basis (and most users do), you may want to customize the appearance of the Outlook Express window so that the window better suits your needs. Figure 861.1, shows two Outlook Express windows, each of which uses a different layout.

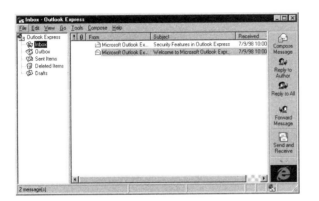 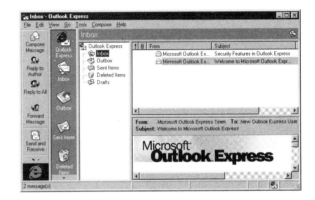

Figure 861.1 Outlook Express lets you customize its window appearance.

To customize the appearance of your Outlook Express window, perform these steps:

1.   Within Outlook Express, click your mouse on the View menu Layout option. Outlook Express, in turn, will display the Window Layout Properties dialog box, as shown in Figure 861.2.

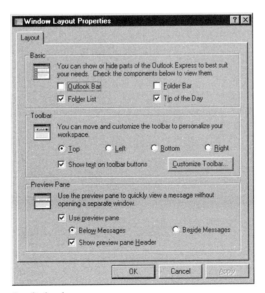

Figure 861.2 The Window Layout Properties dialog box.

2. Within the Window Layout Properties dialog box, use the checkboxes to enable or display specific window components and the radio buttons to position the components.

3. Click your mouse on the OK button to put your changes into effect.

862 CUSTOMIZING THE FIELDS WITHIN YOUR OUTLOOK EXPRESS WINDOW

In Tip 861, you learned how to customize the appearance of the Outlook Express window. In addition to changing the window's appearance, you may want to customize the items Outlook Express displays for each message in its message list. By default, Outlook Express will display the message priority, a paper-clip icon if the message is an attachment, who the message is from (or to), the message subject, and the date and time you received the message, as shown in Figure 862.1.

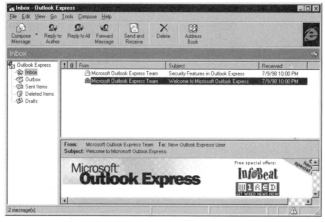

Figure 862.1 Fields within the Outlook Express message list.

Depending on your preferences, you can increase or decrease the amount of space Outlook Express uses for each field by using your mouse to drag the small bars that separate the field names in the bar that appears above the message list. By dragging the bars to the left or the right, you can increase or decrease a field's width. In addition, to add or remove fields, perform these steps:

1. Click your mouse on the Outlook Express View menu can choose Columns. Outlook Express, in turn, will display the Columns dialog box, as shown in Figure 862.2.

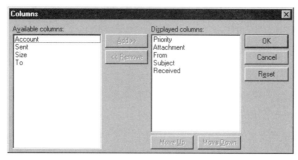

Figure 862.2 The Outlook Express Columns dialog box.

2. To add a field to the current display, click your mouse on the field within the Available columns field and then click your mouse on the Add button. Outlook Express will move the field into the Displayed Columns list.

3. To remove a field from the current display, click your mouse on the field within the Displayed columns list and then click your mouse on the Remove button. Outlook Express will move the field into the Available columns list.

4. Click your mouse on the OK button to put your changes into effect.

863 COMPOSING AN *E-MAIL MESSAGE* WITHIN *OUTLOOK EXPRESS*

Using Outlook Express, you can send and receive e-mail messages. To create and send an e-mail message, you will use the New Message dialog box, as shown in Figure 863.

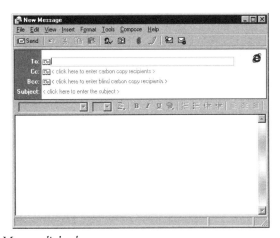

Figure 863 *The Outlook Express New Message dialog box.*

Within the New Message dialog box, you can specify the e-mail address of each user to whom you want to send the message, you can type a single-line entry that summarizes the message subject, and then you can type the message text. Specifically, to send an e-mail message within Outlook Express, perform these steps:

1. Within Outlook Express, click your mouse on the toolbar Compose button or select the Compose menu New Message option. Outlook Express, in turn, will display the New Message dialog box, as previously shown in Figure 863.

2. Within the New Message dialog box, click your mouse on the To field and type in your recipient's e-mail address. Tip 864 discusses the Cc and Bcc which you can use to send courtesy copies of your message to other users.

3. Within the Subject field, type in a one-line message that briefly describes the message contents.

4. Within the message text field, type in your message and then click your mouse on the toolbar Send button or click your mouse on the File menu Send Message option. Outlook Express, in turn, will move your message into the Outbox folder. To direct Outlook Express to immediately send your message, click your mouse on the toolbar Send/Receive button or select the Tools menu Send and Receive option.

For practice, you might send yourself an e-mail message by performing these steps:

1. Within Outlook Express, click your mouse on the toolbar Compose button or select the Compose menu New Message option. Outlook Express, in turn, will display the New Message dialog box, as previously shown in Figure 863.
2. Within the New Message dialog box, click your mouse on the To field and type your own e-mail address, such as *kris@jamsa.com*.
3. Within the Subject field, type the text **Sample Test Message**.
4. Within the message text field, type in the message **This is a sample test message!** and then click your mouse on the toolbar Send button or click your mouse on the File menu Send Message option. Outlook Express will move your message into the Outbox folder. To direct Outlook Express to immediately send your message, click your mouse on the toolbar Send/Receive button or select the Tools menu Send and Receive option.

864 **UNDERSTANDING THE CC AND BCC FIELDS**

As you learned in Tip 863, when you send an e-mail message, you specify the e-mail address of your message recipients within the To, Cc, and Bcc fields. The letters Cc are an abbreviation for courtesy copy. When you send e-mail messages, there will be many times when you are sending a message to a specific person, but you also want other people to be aware of the message. For example, assume that you are sending a note to your project leader that tells him or her that you need to schedule a meeting with the team to discuss the budget. In this case, you would put the project leader's e-mail address within the To field and you would put the e-mail addresses for the team members within the Cc field, with each name separated by semicolons.

In a similar way, there may be times when you want to send a courtesy copy of your message to a user and you do not want others to know that you have done so. In such cases, you can use the blind courtesy copy field (Bcc) to send the message to the user. When your message recipients view the message header to see who received the message, users to whom you Bcc'd the letters will not appear in the list. Given the previous team meeting scenario, you might use the Bcc field to notify your company's accounting director that you will be holding the budget meeting. When your team receives your message, they will be unaware that you have also sent a copy to the accounting director.

865 **SPELL CHECKING YOUR E-MAIL MESSAGE**

Before you send an e-mail message using Outlook Express, you should take time to spell check your message text. To start spell checking your current message within Outlook Express, click your mouse on the Tools menu Spelling option. If the spell checker encounters an error within your message, Outlook Express will display the Spelling dialog box, as shown in Figure 865, within which it highlights the error and displays possible corrections.

Figure 865 *The Outlook Express Spelling dialog box.*

Within the Spelling dialog box, select the Ignore button if your word's spelling is correct (or the Ignore All button if the word appears throughout the document). Likewise, if the Spelling dialog box provides a correction, click your mouse on the Change button (or the Change All button to change the word throughout the document). Lastly, if you want the spell checker to add your word to its dictionary, click your mouse on the Add button.

866 SELECTING E-MAIL MESSAGE RECIPIENTS FROM YOUR ADDRESS BOOK

If you are like many people, you may have a Rolodex on your desk that contains names, addresses, and phone numbers for your key contacts. Within Outlook Express, you can store your contact information within an electronic Address Book. Later, when you want to send an e-mail message to a user, you can look up the user's e-mail address within the Address Book. To help you track e-mail addresses, you can also direct Outlook Express to create an entry within the Address Book each time you reply to an e-mail message. Tip 896 discusses Address Book operations in detail. For now, understand that when you send or forward a message, you can select your recipients from within your Address Book which will eliminate your need to look up or memorize each user's e-mail address. If you examine the New Message dialog box, you will find a small Rolodex card-like icon that appears next to the To:, Cc:, and Bcc: fields. If, as you are addressing your e-mail message, you click your mouse on the index card, Outlook Express, in turn, will display the Select Recipients dialog box, as shown in Figure 866, from within which you can select the users to whom you want to send, courtesy copy, or blind courtesy copy your message.

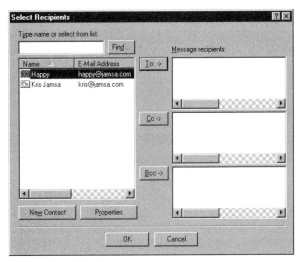

Figure 866 *The Outlook Express Select Recipients dialog box.*

To select a recipient for your message, click your mouse on the user's name within the recipient list and then click your mouse on the To, Cc, or Bcc buttons to assign the user to the corresponding field. After you select the entries you desire, click your mouse on the OK button. Outlook Express, in turn, will return you to the New Message dialog box, within which you can complete and then send your message.

867 **READING A NEW MESSAGE**

Within Windows 98, you can use Outlook Express to send and receive e-mail messages. When you receive an e-mail message, Outlook Express will place the message within your Inbox folder. To display the Inbox folder's contents, click your mouse on the Inbox folder icon within the Outlook Express folder list, or, if Outlook Express is displaying its opening screen, click your mouse on the Read mail icon. Within the Inbox folder, Outlook Express will highlight your unread messages using a bold typeface. In addition, Outlook Express will display a closed envelope to the left of the message, as shown in Figure 867.1.

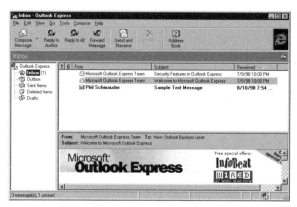

Figure 867.1 Outlook Express highlights your unread messages using a bold typeface.

To read an e-mail message within Outlook Express, click your mouse on the message within the message list. Outlook Express, in turn, will display the message text in the preview frame that usually appears near the bottom of your window, as shown in Figure 867.2. After you read a message, Outlook Express will change the envelope icon that appears next to the message within the message list from a closed to an open envelope.

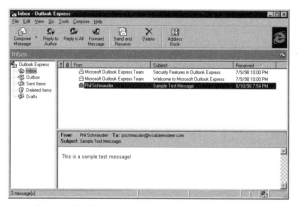

Figure 867.2 To read an e-mail message within Outlook Express, click your mouse on the message within the message list.

Note: *If your Outlook Express window does not contain a preview frame within which you can view a message's contents, you can use the Window Layout Properties dialog box to enable the frame's display or you can double-click your mouse on your messages which will direct Outlook Express to open a window within which it will display the message contents. Most users will find the preview frame more convenient than having to open and close a window for each message.*

Note: *In Tip 882, you will learn how to create your own folders within Outlook Express that you can use to organize your e-mail messages. To view a message within any Outlook Express folder, simply click your mouse on the folder icon within the Outlook Express folder list and then click your mouse on the message you desire within the folder's message list.*

868   PRINTING YOUR CURRENT E-MAIL MESSAGE

As you view an e-mail message within Outlook Express, there will be many times when you will want to print a copy of the message's contents. To print the current message (whose contents you can currently read on your screen display), perform these steps:

1. Click your mouse on the Outlook Express File menu Print option. Outlook Express, in turn, will display the Print dialog box.
2. Within the Print dialog box, click your mouse on the OK button.

To print a message that is not the current message within Outlook Express, perform these steps:

1. Within the Outlook Express message list, right-click your mouse on the message you desire. Windows 98 will display a pop-up menu.

2. Within the pop-up menu, click your mouse on the Print option.

869   FORWARDING AN E-MAIL MESSAGE

As you read through an electronic mail message, there may be times when you will want to forward a copy of the message to another user. To forward the current e-mail message within Outlook Express, perform these steps:

1. If the message you want to send is not the current message (whose contents you can view within the Outlook Express window), click your mouse on the message within the message list to highlight the message.
2. Within the Outlook Express toolbar, click your mouse on the Forward button (or select the Compose menu Forward option). Outlook Express, in turn, will display the Fw: dialog box (Fw is an abbreviation for forward).
3. Within the Fw: dialog box To field, type in the e-mail address (or the addresses separated by semicolons) of the recipient to whom you want to forward the message.

4. Within the message box, you may want to type a short message to the recipient.

5. To send the message, click your mouse on the toolbar Send button or select the File menu Send Message option.

REPLYING TO AN E-MAIL MESSAGE

870

One of the reasons users often become buried with e-mail messages is that it seems that each message he or she receives, requires a response which, in turn, generates a response from another user. To respond to a message within Outlook Express, you have two choices. First, if the message was sent only to you (which you can determine by viewing the To field within the message header that appears at the start of your message), you can reply back to the author. If, however, the message was sent to you and several other people, you can reply to everyone who received the message. Figure 870 shows two message headers. In the first case, the message was sent only to John Doe. In the second case, the message was sent to John Doe and several other users.

Figure 870 *To determine who received the message, examine the To field within the message header.*

To reply to an e-mail message, perform these steps:

1. Within Outlook Express, click your mouse on the toolbar Reply to Author or Reply to All button depending on whether or not you want to reply only to the author or to everyone who received the message. Outlook Express, in turn, will display Re: dialog box (Re: is an abbreviation for Reply). Outlook Express will fill in the To: and Cc: fields for you depending on whether you are replying to the author or to all recipients.

2. Within the Re: dialog box, use the To: Cc: and Bcc: fields to include the e-mail addresses of everyone to whom you want to send the message.

3. Click your mouse within the Re: dialog box's message field and type your reply. Then, click your mouse on the Send button to send your message.

DISPLAYING ONLY UNREAD MESSAGES

871

If you receive a large number of e-mail messages, it may not take long before your Inbox folders fills up with so many messages that you find it difficult to locate specific messages. In fact, there may be times when you have difficulty locating the e-mail messages you have not yet read. To help you locate your unread messages, you can direct Outlook Express to only display your unread messages by selecting the View menu Current View option and then choosing Unread Messages. Outlook Express, in turn, will only display your unread messages.

Later, if you want to view all your messages, again, click your mouse on the View menu Current View option and choose All Messages.

872   SORTING YOUR E-MAIL MESSAGES

Depending on the number of messages you receive, there may be times when your Inbox folder fills up with so many messages that you find locating a specific message difficult. When your Inbox folder becomes cluttered with an excessive number of messages, you should create folders within Outlook Express to group related messages. Next, if you are looking for a specific message, you can direct Outlook Express to sort your messages by the sender, date and time your message was received, or the subject, the message attachment, or even the message priority.

When you are looking for messages from a specific user, for example, you may find it convenient to sort your messages by sender. To sort your messages within Outlook Express, select the View menu Sort by option. Outlook Express, in turn, will cascade the Sort By menu, as shown in Figure 872. Within the Sort By menu, click your mouse on the field by which you want Outlook Express to sort your messages.

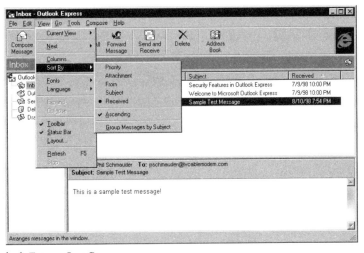

Figure 872 *Cascading the Outlook Express Sort By menu.*

873   FINDING A SPECIFIC E-MAIL MESSAGE

As the number of e-mail messages you receive increases, there may be times when you cannot find a specific message. In such cases, you can use the Find Message dialog box, as shown in Figure 873.

Figure 873 *The Outlook Express Find Message dialog box.*

Within the Find Message dialog box, you can specify the person from which you received the message or the person to whom you sent the message. If you do not specify the sender or receiver, Outlook Express will search all your messages. Within the dialog box's Subject or Message body fields, you can type in the specific text. For example, if you are looking for an e-mail message that discussed your company budget, you might type the word budget within the Message body field. To further refine your message search, you can use the Received field After and Before fields to specify a range of dates within which Outlook Express should limit its search. For example, if you know you received the message in January, you would type in the After date, 1-1-98, and the before date, 2-1-98. Lastly, using the dialog box's Look in field, you can specify the folder within which you want Outlook Express to search your messages and whether or not you want Outlook Express to search subfolders that reside beneath your folder. To search all your messages, you would select the Inbox folder and then direct Outlook Express to search your subfolders. After you specify the settings you desire, click your mouse on the Find Now option. Outlook Express, in turn, will display a list of matching messages at the bottom of the dialog box. To view a message's contents, double-click your mouse on the message within the dialog box list.

874 INSERTING A FILE ATTACHMENT INTO AN E-MAIL MESSAGE

As you work, there will be times when you will want to send copies of your document files, such as a word processing document or a spreadsheet, to another user. In such cases, you can use Outlook Express to *attach* your document to an e-mail message. Later, when your recipient receives your e-mail message, he or she can view or save your attached file. To attach a file to an e-mail message, perform these steps:

1. Within Outlook Express, click your mouse on the Compose button. Outlook Express, in turn, will display the New Message dialog box.

2. Within the New Message dialog box, specify your recipient and message subject and type a message telling your recipient that you have attached a document.

3. Click your mouse on the New Message dialog box Insert menu File Attachment option. Outlook Express will display the Insert Attachment dialog box, as shown in Figure 874.1.

Figure 874.1 *The Insert Attachment dialog box.*

4. Within the Insert Attachment dialog box, locate the folder that contains the file that you want to attach, click your mouse on the file, and then click your mouse on the Attach button. Outlook Express, in turn, will display your attached document at the bottom of your message, as shown in Figure 874.2.

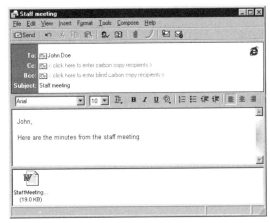

Figure 874.2 Attaching a document file to an e-mail message.

Note: *For your message recipient to view your document, the recipient must have the software that you used to create the document. For example, if you send the recipient a Word document, to view the document, the recipient must have Microsoft Word on his or her system.*

875 INSERTING A FILE'S TEXT CONTENTS INTO AN E-MAIL MESSAGE

In Tip 874, you learned how to attach a document file to an e-mail message. As discussed, for your recipient to view the document's contents, the user must have the software that you used to create the document on his or her system. If you send an attached message to a user that the user cannot view (either because the user does not have the software you used to create the document, or the user's e-mail program does not support attached documents, or the user does not know how to view attached documents), you can direct Outlook Express to insert a file's text within your message. (The file that you specify must be an ASCII text file. Outlook Express will not insert the text from a word-processing document.) To insert the text from a document into an e-mail message, perform these steps:

1. Within Outlook Express, click your mouse on the Compose button. Outlook Express, in turn, will display the New Message dialog box.

2. Within the New Message dialog box, specify your recipient and message subject and type a message telling your recipient that you have attached a document.

3. Click your mouse on the New Message dialog box Insert menu Text from File option. Outlook Express will display the Insert Text File dialog box.

4. Within the Insert Text File dialog box, select the text file whose contents you want to insert within your document. Outlook Express, in turn, will load the file's contents into your message.

876 | **VIEWING OR SAVING A FILE ATTACHMENT**

In Tip 874, you learned how to attach a document, such as a word-processing document or spreadsheet, to an e-mail message. Just as there may be times when you attach documents to the messages that you send to other users, there will be times when users send attached documents to you. When you receive an e-mail message with an attached document, Outlook Express will display a paper-clip icon within your message bar, as shown in Figure 876.1.

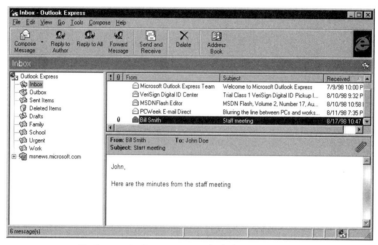

Figure 876.1 Outlook Express uses a paper-clip icon to indicate an attached document.

If you click your mouse on the paper-clip, Outlook Express will display the document name or will list multiple document names, depending on the number of documents the sender attached, as shown in Figure 876.2.

Figure 876.2 Viewing the names of documents attached to an e-mail message.

If you click your mouse on the document, Outlook Express will start the program that the sender used to create the document (provided you have the program on your system) and will load the document for you to view or edit. If you, instead, simply want to save the document to a file on disk, click your mouse on the File menu Save Attachments option. Outlook Express, in turn, will display a submenu that contains the name of each attached document.

Within the submenu, click your mouse on the document that you want to save. Outlook Express, in turn, will display the Save Attachment As dialog box, within which you can select the folder and filename within which you want to save the document file.

877   *INSERTING A SIGNATURE WITHIN AN E-MAIL MESSAGE*

When you send e-mail messages, you may find it convenient to include a signature block at the bottom of your message that includes your name, phone and fax number, e-mail address, and possibly your street address. For example, Figure 877.1 shows a signature block at the bottom of an e-mail message. Within Outlook Express, you can send your signature block with every e-mail message you send, or you can insert the signature into your message, as you desire.

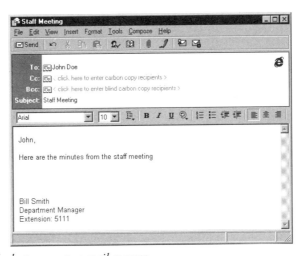

Figure 877.1 A signature block at the bottom on an e-mail message.

To create your signature block, perform these steps:

1. Within Outlook Express, click your mouse on the Tools menu Stationary option. Outlook Express, in turn, will display the Stationary dialog box, as shown in Figure 877.2.

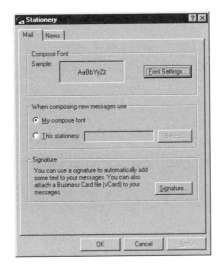

Figure 877.2 The Stationary dialog box.

2. Within the Stationary dialog box, click your mouse on the Signature button. Outlook Express will display the Signature dialog box, as shown in Figure 877.3.

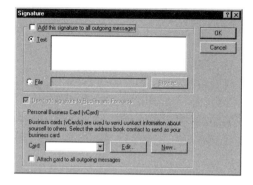

Figure 877.3 *The Signature dialog box.*

3. Within the Signature dialog box, click your mouse on the Text radio button and then type in the signature information you desire. If you want Outlook Express to include your signature on each message you send, click your mouse on the Add this signature to all outgoing messages checkbox, placing a check mark within the box. Then, click your mouse on the OK button.

4. Within the Stationary dialog box, click your mouse on the OK button.

If you do not automatically send your signature with each e-mail message, you can use the Insert menu Signature option to insert your signature text into messages, as you desire.

Note: *Within the Signature dialog box, you can specify that Outlook Express use a specific file's contents for your signature field.*

878 INSERTING YOUR ELECTRONIC BUSINESS CARD WITHIN AN E-MAIL MESSAGE

In Tip 877, you learned how to insert signature text at the end of your e-mail messages. In a similar way, Outlook Express lets you send a virtual business card with your e-mail messages. If your recipient is using Outlook Express, your message window will contain a small card-like icon, as shown in Figure 878.1.

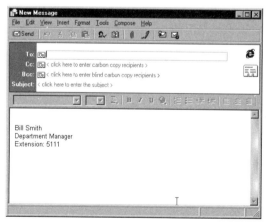

Figure 878.1 *An e-mail message with an attached business card.*

Before you can send a business card with your e-mail messages, you must first create your card by performing these steps:

1. Within Outlook Express, click your mouse on the Tools menu Stationary option. Outlook Express, in turn, will display the Stationary dialog box.

2. Within the Stationary dialog box, click your mouse on the Signature button. Outlook Express will display the Signature dialog box.

3. Within the Signature dialog box, click your mouse on the New button. Outlook Express, in turn, will display the Properties dialog box, as shown in Figure 877.2.

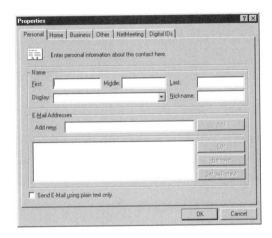

Figure 878.2 *The Properties dialog box.*

4. Within the Properties dialog box, click your mouse on each tab and complete the corresponding sheet's fields. Then, click your mouse on the OK button.

5. Within the Signature dialog box, click your mouse on the Attach card to all outgoing messages checkbox, placing a check mark within the box, if you want to send your card with each e-mail message you send. (If you want to send the card on a message-by-message basis, you can use the Insert menu Business Card option to insert your business card into your current message.)

6. Within the Stationary dialog box, click your mouse on the OK button.

879 INSERTING A GRAPHIC WITHIN AN E-MAIL MESSAGE

In 99 out of 100 cases, your e-mail messages will consist of text and possibly an attached document. Outlook Express, however, will let you insert a graphic within an e-mail message. Figure 879.1, for example, shows an e-mail message that contains picture and text.

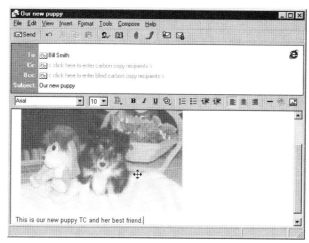

Figure 879.1 An e-mail message that contains a graphics image.

To insert a graphic into your current e-mail message, perform these steps:

1. Within your e-mail message, position the cursor to the location at which you want to insert the graphic.

2. Click your mouse on the Insert menu Picture option (if the Picture option is dim, select the Format menu Rich Text (HTML) option, placing a check mark next to the option). Outlook Express, in turn, will display the Picture dialog box, as shown in Figure 879.2.

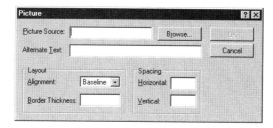

Figure 879.2 The Picture dialog box.

3. Within the Picture dialog box, use the Browse button to locate the image that you want to insert.

4. Within the Picture dialog box, click your mouse on the Alternate Text field and type in a brief description of your image that your recipient's e-mail program will display if it cannot display the image, such as the text A picture of my new Beagle puppy. Then, use the Layout field to align and optionally frame the image and the spacing field to specify the amount of space you want to place around the image. Finally, click your mouse on the OK button.

880 INSERTING A WEB ADDRESS WITHIN AN E-MAIL MESSAGE

As you compose e-mail messages, there may be times when you want to tell the user about a specific Web site. For example, if the user has asked you how to get a digital signature, you send the user an e-mail message that tells the user to visit the Verisign Web site at *www.verisign.com*. To insert a Web address within an e-mail message, simply type in the address within your message text. Later, when the user receives your message, the user's e-mail program will display the link within the his or her message text, as shown in Figure 880. By clicking their mouse on the link within the message text, the user can direct Windows 98 to launch his or her browser to view the corresponding Web site.

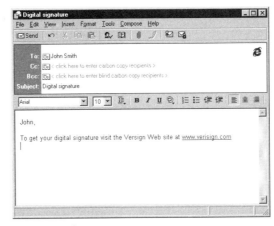

Figure 880 *Including a Web address within an e-mail message.*

881 **VIEWING MESSAGE PROPERTIES**

Within Outlook Express, you can use the View menu Columns option, as discussed in a previous Tip, to specify the information that Outlook Express displays about each message. If Outlook Express is not displaying a field that you desire, such as the message size, you can often view the field's value by examining the message's Properties dialog box, as shown in Figure 881.

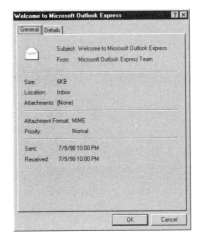

Figure 881 *Viewing a message's Properties dialog box.*

Within the Properties dialog box, you can view a message's size, subject, send and receive times, priority, attachment information, and more. To display a message's Properties dialog box, perform these steps:

1. Within the Outlook Express message list, right-click your mouse on the message you desire. Windows 98, in turn, will display a pop-up menu.

2. Within the pop-up menu, click your mouse on the Properties option. Windows 98, in turn, will display the message's Properties dialog box.

882 CREATING YOUR OWN E-MAIL FOLDERS

As you have learned, when you receive a new e-mail message, Outlook Express places your message within the Inbox folder. If you receive a large number of e-mail messages, you may find that your Inbox folder becomes difficult to manage. In such cases, you should create mail folders within Outlook Express within which you can group related messages. You might, for example, create a folder for *Work*, another for *School*, one for *Family* messages, and even a folder that you name *Urgent*, within which you store messages to which you must respond soon. Figure 882.1, for example, shows an Outlook Express folder list that contains a variety of folders.

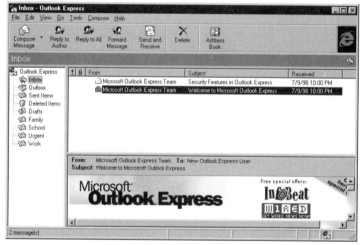

Figure 882.1 *Using folders to organize e-mail messages within Outlook Express.*

To create a folder within Outlook Express, perform these steps:

1. Click your mouse on the Outlook Express File menu and choose Folder. Outlook Express will cascade the Folder submenu.

2. Within the Folder submenu, click your mouse on the New Folder option. Outlook Express will display the Create Folder dialog box, as shown in Figure 882.2.

3. Within the Create Folder dialog box, click your mouse on the folder within which you want to create your subfolder. Next, click your mouse within the Folder name field and type in the folder name that you desire. Finally, click your mouse on the OK button.

Figure 882.2 *The Create Folder dialog box.*

883   *MOVING E-MAIL MESSAGES INTO A DIFFERENT FOLDER*

In Tip 882, you learned how to create your own folders within Outlook Express, within which you later group related messages. To move a message to a specific folder within Outlook Express, simply click your mouse on the message and then hold down your mouse-select button and drag the message on top of the folder you desire. When you release the mouse-select button, Outlook Express will move your message to that folder. To move multiple messages in one step, simply select messages just as you would select files within the Explorer (hold down the CTRL key as click your mouse on each message or hold down the SHIFT key to select consecutive messages). To copy a message to a different folder, simply hold down your keyboard's CTRL key as you perform the drag-and-drop operation.

Note: Outlook Express also provides Edit menu options that you can use to move or copy a selected message to a folder. In most cases, however, you should find simply dragging and dropping messages into the folders that you desire is a fast way to move or copy messages.

884   *PURGING YOUR DELETED E-MAIL MESSAGES*

After you read and no longer need an e-mail message, you should delete the message to reduce clutter within your inbox. To delete a message, simply click your mouse on the message (Outlook Express, in turn, will highlight the message), and then click your mouse on the Delete button or press your keyboard's DEL key.

When you delete an e-mail message, Outlook Express does not delete the message from your system. Outlook Express moves the message from its current folder into the Deleted Items folder—much like Windows 98 moves the files that you delete into the Recycle Bin. Should you later decide that you need the message's contents, you can move the message back from the Deleted Items folder into the folder that you desire. To permanently delete messages from your folders, perform these steps:

1. Within Outlook Express, click your mouse on the Deleted Items folder. Outlook Express, in turn, will display the list of messages you have previously deleted.

2. Within the list of deleted messages, select the messages you want to permanently delete (you can hold down your keyboard CTRL key as you click on messages, you can select the Edit menu Select All option, or you can hold down your keyboard SHIFT key and use your arrow keys to highlight the messages you desire). After you select the messages you want to delete, click your mouse on the toolbar Delete button. Outlook Express, in turn, will display a dialog box asking you to confirm that you want to permanently delete the messages. Within the dialog box, click your mouse on the Yes button.

Note: *As a rule, you should delete messages from your Deleted Items folder on a regular basis. By deleting the messages, you free up disk space the messages consume. In addition, if you work in an office where other users may have access to your system, you prevent other users from viewing messages you have previously deleted.*

885 **DIRECTING OUTLOOK EXPRESS TO EMPTY YOUR DELETED ITEMS FOLDER EACH TIME YOU EXIT**

As you learned in Tip 884, when you delete an e-mail message, Outlook Express does not remove the message from your system. Instead, Outlook Express moves the message into your Deleted Items folder. In Tip 884, you learned how to manually delete messages from within your Deleted Items folder. Depending on your needs, you may want Outlook Express to automatically empty the Deleted Items folder each time you exit the Outlook Express program. To direct Outlook Express to automatically empty your Deleted Items folder in this way, perform these steps:

1. Within Outlook Express, click your mouse on the Tools menu and choose Options. Outlook Express, in turn, will display the Options dialog box, as shown in Figure 885.

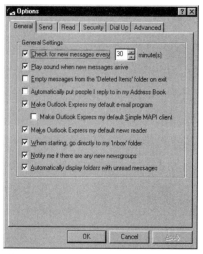

Figure 885 *The Outlook Express Options dialog box.*

2. Within the Options dialog box, click your mouse on the Empty messages from the 'Deleted Items' folder on exit checkbox, placing a check mark within the box. Next, click your mouse on the OK button to put your changes into effect.

886   CREATING E-MAIL MESSAGES OFFLINE

If your PC is not always connected to the Internet (which means you use a dial-up connection that uses your modem to access the Net), there will be times when you will want to reply to your e-mail messages or compose new messages while you are offline. You might, for example, want to catch up on your e-mail messages on an airline flight during which it is difficult to connect your PC to the Net. In such cases, simply start Outlook Express as you usually would. Next, within Outlook Express, click your mouse on the File menu Work Offline option, placing a check mark next to the option. After that, each time you compose, reply to, or forward a message, Outlook Express will place the message within your Outbox folder. When you are done with your messages, you can exit Outlook Express. Later, after you connect your PC to the Net, you can start Outlook Express and click your mouse on the Send and Receive button to send the messages that reside within your Outbox folder.

887   CUTTING AND PASTING MESSAGE TEXT

As you read or compose an e-mail message, there may be times when you will want to copy text from one message that you can then paste into a second message. To start, you must first select the text you want to copy, by either holding down your keyboard SHIFT key as you use your keyboard arrow keys to highlight the text, or by holding down your mouse-select button as you drag your mouse pointer over the text. As you select text within a message, Outlook Express will highlight your selected text using reverse video. After you select the text that you desire, click your mouse on the Edit menu Copy option. Then, click your mouse within the message into which you want to paste the text and position the cursor to the text's starting position. Finally, select the Edit menu Paste option to place the text into the message.

Note: *If you want to select the entire message text for a cut-and-paste operation, click your mouse within the message that contains the text and then select the Edit menu Select All option.*

888   INITIATING A SEND AND RECEIVE OPERATION

By default, Outlook Express checks for new messages every 10 minutes. Likewise, as you have learned, when you first send an e-mail message, Outlook Express places your message within its Outbox until it has time to send the message. By clicking your mouse on the Send/Receive button, or by selecting the Tools menu Send and Receive operation, you can direct Outlook Express to immediately check for new messages and to immediately send messages that reside within your Outbox. When you initiate a Send and Receive operation, Outlook Express will display the Outlook Express dialog box, as shown in Figure 888, within which you can monitor the status of your system's send and receive operation.

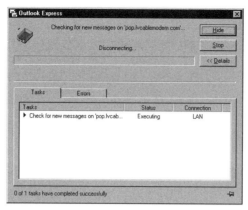

Figure 888 *Monitor e-mail send and receive operations within the Outlook Express dialog box.*

889 STOPPING A RECEIVE OPERATION

If Outlook Express is downloading your e-mail messages or if you want to initiate a download operation, you can click your mouse on the Send/Receive button to display the Outlook Express dialog box within which you can monitor the message download operation. Depending on the number of messages you receive, there may be times when you have more messages to download than you have time to wait. In such cases, you can stop the download operation by clicking your mouse on the Stop button to stop the download after the current message. Later, when you have time to perform the download operation, you can start Outlook Express and use the Send/Receive operation to initiate the e-mail message download.

890 UNDERSTANDING YOUR OUTBOX FOLDER

As you have learned, when you receive e-mail messages, Outlook Express places your messages within its Inbox folder. In a similar way, when you send an e-mail message, Outlook Express first places your message into the Outbox folder. After Outlook Express successfully sends your message, it will move your message into the Sent Items folder. So, for example, if you are working offline (perhaps you are composing your e-mail message on an airline flight), Outlook Express will place all your messages within your Outbox folder. Later, when you connect to the Net, you can click your mouse on the toolbar Send and Receive button (or select the Tools menu Send option) to direct Outlook Express to send the messages.

If you examine your Outbox folder within the Outlook Express folder list, you will find that Outlook Express places a count of the number of messages that it has yet to send next to the folder names. If, for example, your window displays the text Outbox (2), you know that two messages reside in your Outbox that Outlook Express will send the next time you initiate a send operation. If you are not sure if Outlook Express has sent your message, first click your mouse on the Outbox. If the Outbox folder contains messages, click your mouse on the Tools menu Send button to direct Outlook Express to send them. Otherwise, if the Outbox folder is empty, click your mouse on the Sent Items folder within which Outlook Express will display a list of all the messages it has successfully sent.

891 | ***TELLING IF THE RECIPIENT HAS READ YOUR MESSAGE***

Within Outlook Express, you can view the contents of the Sent Items folder to determine which messages you have successfully sent. However, just because you sent the messages does not mean that the messages reached their destination or that the recipient has read them. You might, for example, misspell the user's e-mail address, or the user may have changed their e-mail address since you last sent them mail. Unfortunately, Outlook Express cannot immediately report such errors to you. Instead, Outlook Express will send your message out onto the Internet in an attempt to deliver the message. Eventually, the message will return to your system as undeliverable. Outlook Express, in turn, will place a message within your Inbox folder that tells you that it could not deliver the message. In most cases, the problem that prevented the message delivery is an error in the recipient's address. In addition, Outlook Express has no way of knowing when (or if, for that matter) your message recipient has read your message, just as you have no way of knowing when the recipient of a letter you send by US mail or Federal Express actually opens and reads your message.

892 | ***ASSIGNING A PRIORITY TO YOUR E-MAIL MESSAGE***

Today, it is not uncommon for users to receive dozens, if not hundreds, of e-mail messages each day! When you send an e-mail message to another user, Outlook Express lets you assign a priority (Low, Normal, or High) to the message. When the user receives the message, his or her e-mail software may display an icon next to the message that corresponds to the message priority. As shown in Figure 892, for example, Outlook Express will display an exclamation point for high-priority messages and a down-arrow icon for low-priority messages.

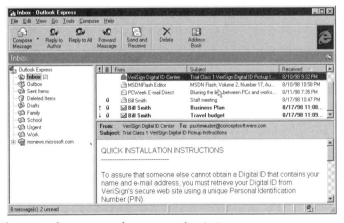

Figure 892 *Outlook Express displays icons that correspond to a message's priority.*

To help manage their e-mail, some users will sort their messages by priority. (These users will also be very unhappy with you if you send them messages marked as high-priority, the contents of which really do not merit the user's urgent response.) To assign a priority to an e-mail message you are about to send, click your mouse on the Outlook Express Tools menu and choose Set Priority. Outlook Express, in turn, will cascade the Set Priority menu, displaying the High, Normal, and Low priority options. Within the Priority submenu, click your mouse on the option that corresponds to the message priority you desire.

893   ENCRYPTING YOUR E-MAIL MESSAGE

When you send an e-mail message to a user across the Internet, your message may travel through or past many computers, each of which is capable of capturing and viewing your message contents. To protect your message contents from being read by anyone except your desired recipient, you must encrypt your message. To encrypt a message within Outlook Express, you must have your recipient's digital signature (an encryption key which your recipient can send to you by sending you a signed message as discussed in Tip 895, or which you can look up on the Web at a site, such as Verisign, which provides the public-portion (the part other users such as you can see) of a user's encryption key. After you record the user's digital signature within the user's Address Book entry, you can send the user an encrypted e-mail message simply by clicking your mouse on the Outlook Express Tools menu Encrypt option.

When the user receives your encrypted message, his or her software will automatically decrypt the message using his or her digital signature. In other words, you will encrypt the message that you send to the recipient using the public portion of the recipient's digital signature (you do not use your digital signature to encrypt the message, you use the recipient's). Then, when the message arrives, the recipient uses the private portion of their digital signature to decrypt the message. Because only the recipient has the private portion of the digital signature, only the recipient can decrypt the message.

Note: *When you receive a signed message from a user, click your mouse on the File menu Properties option to display the message's Properties dialog box. Within the dialog box, click your mouse on the Security tab and then click your mouse on the Add Digital ID to Address Book button to ensure that your Address Book contains the user's digital signature.*

894   OBTAINING A DIGITAL SIGNATURE

In Tip 893, you learned how to encrypt an e-mail message within Outlook Express. As you learned, before you can encrypt a message, you must purchase a digital signature—which you can do online from Verisign. To purchase your digital signature, start the Internet Explorer and then connect to the Verisign Web site at *www.verisign.com.* From within the Verisign Web site, you can perform the steps listed to purchase and download your digital signature. To direct Outlook Express to use the digital signature that Verisign installs on your system, perform these steps:

1. Within Outlook Express, click your mouse on the Tools menu and choose Accounts. Outlook Express, in turn, will display the Internet Accounts dialog box.

2. Within the Internet Accounts dialog box, click your mouse on the Mail tab. Outlook Express will display the Mail sheet.

3. Within the Mail sheet, select the Account for which you created the digital signature. Then, click your mouse on the Properties button. Outlook Express will display the account's Properties dialog box.

4. Within the Properties dialog box, click your mouse on the Security tab. Outlook Express will display the Security sheet.

5. Within the Security sheet, click your mouse on the Use a digital id when sending secure message from checkbox, placing a check mark in the box. Then, click your mouse on the Digital Id button and select your digital id. Finally, click your mouse on the OK button.

6. Within the Internet Accounts dialog box, click your mouse on the Close button.

895   **ASSIGNING A DIGITAL SIGNATURE TO YOUR E-MAIL MESSAGE**

In Tip 894, you learned how to install a digital signature that you download from Verisign. When you send an e-mail message, you can digitally sign your message using your digital signature. When your recipient receives a message with a digital signature, your recipient can feel confident that the message really came from you (meaning another user did not forge a message claiming to be you) and that your message's contents have not changed since you signed the message. To digitally sign your message, simply click your mouse on the Outlook Express Tools menu and choose the Digitally Sign option, placing a check mark next to the option. After you send a user your digital signature, the user can use your signature to the encrypt message that they send back to you.

896   **USING THE OUTLOOK EXPRESS ADDRESS BOOK**

When you address a letter that you send via mail (not e-mail, but traditional mail), you normally look up your recipient's address within your address book. In a similar way, when you send electronic-mail messages, you should not have to memorize each of your recipients' e-mail addresses. As it turns out, Outlook Express provides an Address Book within which you can record information about the people to whom you send e-mail. Each time you reply to an e-mail message, Outlook Express creates an Address Book entry (if necessary) within which it places your recipient's name and e-mail address. Later, when you send, forward, or reply to a message, you can use the Address Book entries. To use the Address Book entries, click your mouse on the small Rolodex card-like icon that Outlook Express displays next to the To:, Cc:, and Bcc: fields. Outlook Express, in turn, will display the Select Recipients dialog box, as shown in Figure 896.

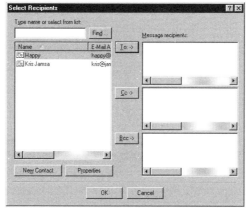

Figure 896 *The Select Recipients dialog box.*

Within the Select Recipients dialog box, click your mouse on a user to whom you want to send the message and then click your mouse on the To:, Cc:, or Bcc:: button. The Select Recipient dialog box, in turn, will move the user into the corresponding list. After you select the recipients that you desire, click your mouse on the OK button. Outlook Express, in turn, will display each of your selected recipients in the appropriate fields within your e-mail message.

| 897 | CUSTOMIZING USER PROPERTIES WITHIN YOUR ADDRESS BOOK |

In Tip 896, you learned how to use the Outlook Express Address Book to select users to whom you wanted to send an e-mail message. As it turns out, you can actually use the Address Book as a contact manager. Within the Address Book, you can store considerable information about an individual, their company, and more.

For example, Figure 897 shows a user's Properties dialog box. Within the Properties dialog box, you can use the various sheets to record the user's address, e-mail address, phone and fax number, home information, company information, and more.

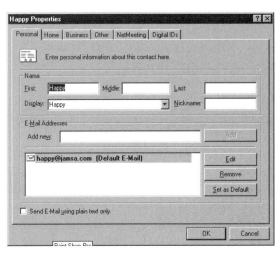

Figure 897 *A user's address book Properties dialog box.*

To display a user's Properties dialog box, perform these steps:

1. Within Outlook Express, click your mouse on the Tools menu and choose Address Book. Outlook Express, in turn, will display the Address Book window.

2. Within the Address Book window, double-click your mouse on the user for whom you want to display the Properties dialog box. Windows 98, in turn, will display the user's Properties dialog box.

3. Within the Properties dialog box, use the sheets to fill in or edit the information that you desire and then click your mouse on the OK button.

Note: *To change the information Outlook Express keeps about you, click your mouse on the Tools menu Stationary option. Within the Stationary dialog box, click your mouse on the Signature button. Within the Signature button, click your mouse on the Personal Business Card field Edit button.*

898   PRINTING YOUR ADDRESS BOOK

In Tip 896, you learned how to use the Outlook Express Address Book. If you keep your address book current, you will find that the information it contains makes a very useful directory of your clients and other contacts. In fact, you may want to print a copy of your address book's contents which you store in your briefcase. To print your address book's contents, perform these steps:

1. Within Outlook Express, click your mouse on the Tools menu Address Book entry. Outlook Express will display the Address Book window. Within the Address Book window, click your mouse on the File menu Print option. Outlook Express will display the Print dialog box.

2. Within the Print dialog box, select the format you want the Address Book to use to print its entries (memo, business card, or phone list) and then click your mouse on the OK button.

899   CREATING AND USING AN E-MAIL GROUP

If you work within an office, there will be many times when you will find yourself sending e-mail messages to the same group of people. If you are on a project team, for example, you will often have messages that you must send to everyone on the team. Rather than forcing you to continually type in each recipient's e-mail address, Outlook Express lets you define an e-mail group, within which you can place the addresses of everyone you want to receive messages that you send to the group. Given the previous project team scenario, you might name your e-mail group Project Team and then assign each team member's e-mail address to the group. To create an e-mail group within Outlook Express, perform these steps:

1. Within Outlook Express, click your mouse on the Tools menu and choose Address Book. Outlook Express, in turn, will display the Address Book window. Within the Address Book window, click your mouse on the File menu New Group option or click your mouse on the toolbar New Group button. Outlook Express, in turn, will display the Group dialog box, as shown in Figure 899.1.

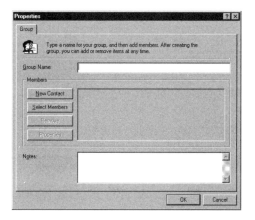

Figure 899.1 The Group dialog box.

3. Within the Group dialog box, click your mouse on the Group Name field and then type in the name that you desire. Next, click your mouse on the Select Members button. Outlook Express, in turn, will display the Select Group Members dialog box, as shown in Figure 899.2.

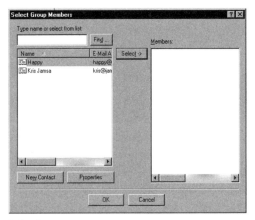

Figure 899.2 The Select Group Members dialog box.

4. Within the Select Group Members dialog box, click your mouse on each user you want to assign to the group, clicking the Select button for each user, or type the user's e-mail address and then click your mouse on the Select button. After you select each of the group members, click your mouse on the OK button.

5. Within the Properties dialog box, click your mouse on the OK button.

6. Within the Address Book window, click your mouse on the File menu Close option.

900 UNDERSTANDING THE OUTLOOK EXPRESS INBOX ASSISTANT

As you have learned, it is not uncommon for users to receive dozens, if not hundreds, of e-mail messages every day. To help users manage the e-mail messages they receive, Outlook Express provides special software called the Inbox Assistant. Using the Inbox Assistant, you can forward the messages that you receive to a different e-mail address (which is convenient when you are traveling), you can also automatically copy the messages that you receive from a specific user into a specific folder, and more. Within the Inbox Assistant, you specify a *rule* that tells the Inbox Assistant how to process specific message types. You might, for example, automatically file copies of all messages you receive from Bill Gates into a specific folder. To display the Inbox Assistant, click your mouse on the Outlook Express Tools menu and then choose Inbox Assistant. Windows 98, in turn, will display the Inbox Assistant dialog box, as shown in Figure 900. Several of the Tips that follow examine operations that you can perform within the Inbox Assistant.

Figure 900 The Inbox Assistant dialog box.

901   FORWARDING YOUR E-MAIL TO ANOTHER ACCOUNT

In Tip 900, you learned that you can use Outlook Express Inbox Assistant to help you manage your electronic mail. For example, if you have multiple Internet accounts (maybe you have one for the office, one for school, as well as a personal account), you may want the Inbox Assistant to forward copies of your new mail to a different account so you can respond to all your messages from one account.

To direct the Inbox Assistant to forward copies of your e-mail, perform these steps:

1. Within Outlook Express, click your mouse on the Tools menu Inbox Assistant option. Outlook Express, in turn, will display the Inbox Assistant dialog box.

2. Within the Inbox Assistant dialog box, click your mouse on the Add button. Outlook Express will display the Properties dialog box, as shown in Figure 901.

Figure 901 The Inbox Assistant's Properties dialog box.

3. Within the Properties dialog box, click your mouse on the All messages checkbox, placing a check mark within the box, to direct the Inbox Assistant to forward all your messages.

4. Within the Properties dialog box, click your mouse on the Forward to checkbox, placing a check mark within the box. Then, in the text field that appears to the right of the box, type in the address to which you want the Inbox Assistant to forward a copy of your message.

5. Click your mouse on the OK button. The Inbox Assistant will display your new rule within its rule list. Within the Inbox Assistant dialog box, click your mouse on the OK button to put your changes into effect.

Note: *Before the Inbox Assistant can forward your e-mail messages, the messages must arrive to your Inbox folder. If your PC is connected to a local-area network, your network software will likely deliver the messages to your Inbox, which lets the Inbox Assistant forward the messages even if you are out of the office. Otherwise, if you use an online service or Internet Service Provider to download your messages, you must connect to the Net and download your messages into your Inbox before the Inbox Assistant can forward your messages as you desire. Tip 902 discusses steps you can perform to let Outlook Express automatically connect to your online service or provider so it can download your new messages.*

902	### SCHEDULING OUTLOOK EXPRESS OPERATIONS WHEN YOU ARE NOT PRESENT

In Tip 901, you learned how to use the Inbox Assistant to automatically forward your e-mail to another account—which may be quite convenient when you traveling. As you learned, however, before the Inbox Assistant can forward your mail, the mail must arrive in your Inbox, which means Outlook Express must first download your messages before your Inbox Assistant can forward them. If you normally access your e-mail messages by dialing into an online service or Internet Service Provider, and then use Outlook Express to download your messages, you may be able to let Outlook Express automatically connect to your online service or provider at regular intervals to download (and then to forward) your messages. To direct Outlook Express to automatically check for new messages in this way, perform these steps:

1. Within your Dial-Up networking folder, you must configure your dial-up settings to remember your password and to allow programs to automatically dial a connection. Depending on your service or provider, the steps you must perform to allow an automatic login will differ.

2. Next, within Outlook Express, click your mouse on the Tools menu and choose Options. Outlook Express, in turn, will display the Options dialog box General sheet, as shown in Figure 902.1.

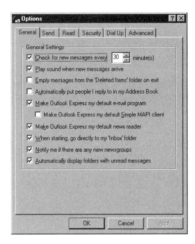

Figure 902.1 *The Options dialog box General sheet.*

3. Within the General sheet, click your mouse on the Check for new messages every *nn* minutes checkbox, placing a check mark in the box. Then, within the text field, specify the interval at which you want Outlook Express to check for messages.

4. Within the Options dialog box, click your mouse on the Dial-Up tab. Outlook Express, in turn, will display the Dial-Up sheet, as shown in Figure 902.2.

5. Within the Dial-Up sheet, click your mouse on the Dial this connection radio button and then select the service that you desire. Next, click your mouse on the Hang up when finished sending, receiving or downloading checkbox, placing a check mark within the box. Then, select the Automatically dial when checking for new messages checkbox, placing a check mark within the box. Finally, click your mouse on the OK button to put your changes into effect.

After you configure Outlook Express to automatically dial and download your messages, you can simply leave Outlook Express running, or you can use the Task Scheduler to start Outlook Express at specific intervals.

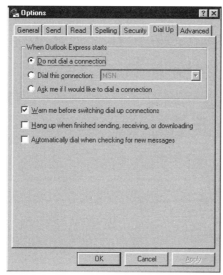

Figure 902.2 *The Options dialog box Dial-Up sheet.*

---

903 CONTROLLING WHICH MESSAGES OUTLOOK EXPRESS DOWNLOADS FROM YOUR E-MAIL SERVER

If you use Outlook Express to send and receive e-mail messages from an online service or dial-up account, depending on your connection speed there may be times when a large message takes a very long time to download (up to an hour, depending on the message size). Rather than sitting through large message downloads, you can direct Outlook Express not to download the messages from the server or to delete such messages.

You might, for example, direct Outlook Express not to download any message larger than 1Mb. To direct the Inbox Assistant to delete large messages from the server, perform these steps:

1. Within Outlook Express, click your mouse on the Tools menu Inbox Assistant option. Outlook Express, in turn, will display the Inbox Assistant dialog box.

2. Within the Inbox Assistant dialog box, click your mouse on the Add button. Outlook Express will display the Properties dialog box.

3. Within the Properties dialog box, click your mouse on the Larger than checkbox, placing a check mark within the box. Then, in the text field that appears to the right of the box, type in the file size above which you want the Inbox Assistant to delete from the server.

4. Within the Properties dialog box, click your mouse on the Delete off server checkbox, placing a check mark within the box and then click your mouse on the OK button. The Inbox Assistant will display your new rule within its rule list.

5. Within the Inbox Assistant dialog box, click your mouse on the OK button to put your changes into effect.

904 SENDING A STANDARD REPLY WHEN YOU ARE AWAY FROM YOUR E-MAIL

In Tip 900, you learned that you can use the Outlook Express Inbox Assistant to help you manage your e-mail messages. If you are going to be traveling and you want to notify people who send you e-mail, you can direct the Inbox Assistant to send a standard reply to everyone who sends you a mail message. You might, for example, send a text reply such as:

John Smith has received your e-mail message but will be out of the Office until Monday,

September 21. If your message is urgent, please call his assistant at 800-555-1212. John

will be checking e-mail nightly and will respond to your message as soon as possible.

To direct the Inbox Assistant to send a standard reply to your messages, perform these steps:

1. Using the Notepad accessory, create a file named *Response.TXT* that contains the message text that you want Outlook Express to send to each user that sends you an e-mail message. Store the file within the My Documents folder.

2. Within Outlook Express, click your mouse on the Tools menu Inbox Assistant option. Outlook Express, in turn, will display the Inbox Assistant dialog box.

3. Within the Inbox Assistant dialog box, click your mouse on the Add button. Outlook Express will display the Properties dialog box.

4. Within the Properties dialog box, click your mouse on the All messages checkbox, placing a check mark within the box, to direct the Inbox Assistant to reply to all your messages.

5. Within the Properties dialog box, click your mouse on the Reply with checkbox, placing a check mark within the box. Then, click your mouse on the Browse button and select the text file that you created in Step 1.

6. Click your mouse on the OK button. The Inbox Assistant will display your new rule within its rule list. Within the Inbox Assistant dialog box, click your mouse on the OK button to put your changes into effect.

Note: *Before the Inbox Assistant can reply to your e-mail messages, the messages must arrive to your Inbox folder. If your PC is connected to a local-area network, your network software will likely deliver the messages to your Inbox which lets the Inbox Assistant forward the messages, even if you are out of the office. Otherwise, if you use an online service or Internet Service Provider to download your messages, you must connect to the Net and download your messages into your Inbox before the Inbox Assistant can reply to your messages as you desire. Tip 902 discusses steps you can perform to let Outlook Express automatically connect to your online service or provider so it can download your new messages.*

905 USING E-MAIL STATIONARY

If you have been sending and receiving e-mail messages for some time, you have probably realized that one e-mail message looks pretty much like the next. To help you dress up your e-mail message appearance, Outlook Express lets you take advantage of e-mail stationary. In general, e-mail stationary lets you place a graphics image within your e-mail message. For example, Figure 905 shows two messages that use stationary.

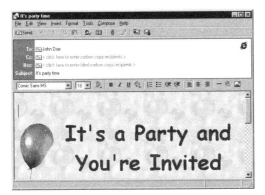 

Figure 905 *Using stationary to dress up your e-mail messages.*

To place stationary within an e-mail message, perform these steps:

1. Within Outlook Express, click your mouse on the Compose button. Outlook Express, in turn, will display the New Message dialog box.

2. Within the New Message dialog box, click your mouse on the Format menu Apply Stationary option. Outlook Express will cascade a menu of available stationary selections.

3. Within the Stationary submenu, click your mouse on the stationary option that you desire.

Should you decide to change the stationary, simply select a replacement stationary from the Format menu Apply Stationary submenu. As it turns out, Outlook Express lets you use any HTML file as an e-mail stationary, which means that if you understand HTML, you can create your own stationary. To select an HTML file as your stationary, perform these steps:

1. Within Outlook Express, click your mouse on the Compose button. Outlook Express, in turn, will display the New Message dialog box.

2. Within the New Message dialog box, click your mouse on the Format menu Apply Stationary option. Outlook Express will cascade a menu of available stationary selections.

3. Within the Stationary submenu, click your mouse on the More Stationary option. Windows 98, in turn, will display the Open dialog box, within which you can select the HTML file that you desire.

Note: *To compose a message using a specific stationary, click your mouse on the down arrow that appears next to the Compose button within the Outlook Express toolbar. Outlook Express, in turn, will display a menu of stationary options. After you click your mouse on an option, Outlook Express will display a New Message dialog box, with the stationary art present, within which you can type and send the message you desire.*

906 CONFIGURING YOUR INTERNET SETTINGS

Today, most users make extensive use of a Web browser and an e-mail program. As you will learn, Windows 98 also provides software you can use to chat with other users across the Net and to hold meetings. To help you configure the

Internet settings that a variety of these programs will use, Windows 98 provides the Internet Properties dialog box, as shown in Figure 906.

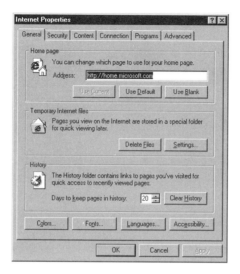

Figure 906 *The Internet Properties dialog box.*

Several of the Tips that follow examine the Internet Properties dialog box in detail. To display the Internet Properties dialog box, perform these steps:

1. Click your mouse on the Start menu Settings button and choose Control Panel. Windows 98, in turn, will open the Control Panel window.

2. Within the Control Panel window, double-click your mouse on the Internet icon. Windows 98, in turn, will display the Internet Properties dialog box.

Note: *In addition to performing the steps this Tip presents to display the Internet Properties dialog box, you can also select the View menu Internet Options choice within the Internet Explorer to display the dialog box.*

907 SPECIFYING YOUR DEFAULT HOME PAGE

In Tip 820, you learned how to start and use the Internet Explorer to browse sites on the World Wide Web. Each time you start the Internet Explorer, it will connect you to your default (or "home") Web site. By default, the Internet Explorer will connect you to the Microsoft Web site. Using the Internet Properties dialog box, you can specify the Web site to which you want the Internet Explorer to connect you each time it starts. For example, you might want the Internet Explorer to automatically display the Yahoo Web site that you can use to search for information on the Web. Likewise, you may want the Internet Explorer to always display your company's Web site. To specify your default Web site, perform these steps:

1. Click your mouse on the Start menu Settings button and choose Control Panel. Windows 98, in turn, will open the Control Panel window.

2. Within the Control Panel window, double-click your mouse on the Internet icon. Windows 98, in turn, will display the Internet Properties dialog box.

3. Within the Internet Properties dialog box, click your mouse on the Address field and type in the Web address of the site you desire, such as *http://www.yahoo.com*, and then click your mouse on the OK button.

908 *PURGING TEMPORARY INTERNET FILES*

If you have spent time surfing the Web, you know that you can spend a considerable amount of time waiting for your system to download files. To improve their performance, most Web browsers will store the files you download within temporary files on your disk. Should you later visit the Web site a second time, your browser can use the files it previously downloaded to immediately display the site's contents. (Actually, your browser will contact the Web site to determine if the files it previously downloaded are current. If the files are current, your browser will use them. Otherwise, your browser will download any files that have changed.)

Although storing downloaded Internet files in this way improves your browser's performance, the temporary files consume disk space that you may want to use for other operations. In addition, if another user gains access to your system, those users can view the temporary file's contents and determine which sites you have been visiting. Your company, for example, could use the temporary files to prove that you were using the Web for non-business purposes during working hours. Fortunately, Windows 98 lets you purge (delete) the temporary files when you no longer need them and it lets you specify how much disk space the temporary files can consume. To purge your temporary Internet files, perform these steps:

1. Click your mouse on the Start menu Settings button and choose Control Panel. Windows 98, in turn, will open the Control Panel window.

2. Within the Control Panel window, double-click your mouse on the Internet icon. Windows 98 will display the Internet Properties dialog box.

3. Within the Internet Properties dialog box Temporary Internet files field, click your mouse on the Delete Files button. Windows 98, in turn, will display the Delete Files dialog box that prompts you to confirm the file deletion.

4. Within the Delete Files dialog box, click your mouse on the OK button.

Note: *In addition to performing the steps this Tip presents to delete your temporary Internet files, you can also use the Windows 98 Disk Cleanup Wizard, which Tip 614 presents, to delete the files.*

909 *CONTROLLING HOW WINDOWS 98 MANAGES TEMPORARY INTERNET FILES*

In Tip 908, you learned how to use the Internet Properties dialog box to purge your temporary Internet files from your disk. Before you delete the temporary files, there may be times when you want to display a listing of files. Or, if you are an employer, you may want to view the Web sites your employees are visiting during working hours. Within the Internet Properties dialog box Settings sheet shown in Figure 909, you can use the View Files button to display a list of the temporary Internet files (within the list, you can double-click your mouse on an entry to view the file's contents). In addition, within the Settings dialog box, you can control how much disk space Windows 98 can allocate for your temporary Internet files and how often, after downloading files, your browser will check for updates to a site's file.

Figure 909 *The Internet Properties dialog box Settings sheet.*

As you have learned, after your browser downloads files from a Web site, your browser can later display those files' contents again should you visit the Web site a second time. Within the Settings dialog box, you can control how often your browser will check for file updates. For example, if you visit Web sites that change their contents very often (such as every few minutes), you will want your browser to check for new files every time you visit a Web site. If you normally start your browser, view a few sites, and then end your browser, you may want your browser to check for file updates for sites that you have visited since you last started your browser. Likewise, if you don't care if you view a site's most current contents, you can direct your browser never to check for new files and to always use its cached file contents if a temporary file is available for the current site.

Within the Settings dialog box Temporary Internet files folder field, you can use the Amount of disk space to use slider to control how much of your disk Windows 98 will allocate for storing temporary Internet files. To increase or decrease the amount of disk space Windows 98 will allocate for temporary files, use your mouse to drag the slider bar to the right or to the left. After Windows 98 consumes the amount of disk space you allow, Windows 98 will delete your oldest files.

---

910 MOVING THE FOLDER WITHIN WHICH WINDOWS 98 STORES YOUR TEMPORARY INTERNET FILES

As you have learned, to improve its performance, your browser stores the information it downloads from the Web sites you visit as temporary files within a folder on your disk. By default, your browser will store the files within the *Windows\Temporary Internet Files* folder. However, depending on your needs, there may be times when you will want your browser to store the temporary files at a different location. For example, if you work within an office, many companies store a user's files within folders that reside on a network server. If your browser is storing your temporary files on a network server, you may encounter two problems. First, because your network must transfer each file you download to the server, your temporary Internet files can consume considerable network bandwidth (which will slow down other network operations) and may consume considerable space on the server's hard disk. Second, because the files now reside on a network server, your network administrator can view the file's contents to determine which Web sites you visit. To change the location at which your browser will store your temporary Internet files, perform these steps:

1. Click your mouse on the Start menu Settings button and choose Control Panel. Windows 98 will open your Control Panel window.
2. Within the Control Panel window, double-click your mouse on the Internet icon. Windows 98 will display the Internet Properties dialog box.
3. Within the Internet Properties dialog box Temporary Internet files field, click your mouse on the Settings button. Windows 98 will display the Settings dialog box.
4. Within the Settings dialog box, click your mouse on the Move Folder button. Windows 98 will display a Warning! dialog box that tells you to move your temporary files, it must delete your subscription data (which means you must resubscribe later). Click your mouse on the OK button. Windows 98, in turn, will display the Browse for Folder dialog box.
5. Within the Browse for Folder dialog box, click your mouse on the folder you desire and then click your mouse on the OK button.

911 **CLEARING YOUR WEB-SITE HISTORY FOLDER**

To make it easier for you to revisit sites across the Web, your browser keeps a history (a list) of the sites you visit. If you want to revisit a site, you can simply click your mouse on the site within your browser's history list. For example, Figure 911 shows the Internet Explorer's pull-down history list from within which you can click your mouse on the site you want to revisit.

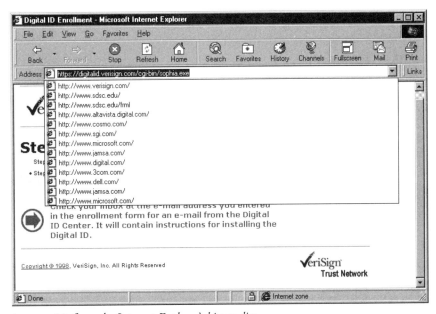

Figure 911 Selecting a site to revisit from the Internet Explorer's history list.

Within the Internet Properties dialog box, you can clear (erase) the current history list and specify the number of days for which Windows 98 will maintain a site's contents (as temporary files) within the history list. If you use a browser within an office, you may want to clear your history list at the end of each day, so your employer cannot use the list to track the Web sites you visit during your working hours. To clear your history list, perform these steps:

1. Click your mouse on the Start menu Settings button and choose Control Panel. Windows 98 will open your Control Panel window.

2. Within the Control Panel window, double-click your mouse on the Internet icon. Windows 98 will display the Internet Properties dialog box.

3. Within the Internet Properties dialog box History field, click your mouse on the Clear History button. Windows 98, in turn, will display a dialog box asking you to confirm the history-list deletion. Click your mouse on the Yes button.

To specify the number of days for which Windows 98 will maintain a site within the history list, perform these steps:

1. Click your mouse on the Start menu Settings button and choose Control Panel. Windows 98 will open your Control Panel window.

2. Within the Control Panel window, double-click your mouse on the Internet icon. Windows 98 will display the Internet Properties dialog box.

3. Within the Internet Properties dialog box History field, click your mouse on the Days to keep pages in history field and type in the number of days you desire. Click your mouse on the OK button to put your changes into effect.

912   CONTROLLING YOUR WEB BROWSER'S COLOR USE

In Tip 241, you learned how to use the Desktop Properties dialog box to specify the colors for items on your Desktop. If you spend a considerable amount of time surfing the Web, you may want to customize your browser's color settings. To specify your browser colors, perform these steps:

1. Click your mouse on the Start menu Settings button and choose Control Panel. Windows 98 will open your Control Panel window.

2. Within the Control Panel window, double-click your mouse on the Internet icon. Windows 98, in turn, will display the Internet Properties dialog box.

3. Within the Internet Properties dialog box, click your mouse on the Colors buttons. Windows 98, in turn, will display the Colors dialog box, as shown in Figure 912.

4. Within the Colors dialog box, you can specify the colors your browser uses for its background color and for text display. By default, the browser will use the current Windows 98 colors. To select your own color settings, click your mouse on the Use Windows colors checkbox to remove the check mark. Then, click your mouse on the Text or Background buttons to specify the colors you desire.

5. Within the Colors dialog box, you can also specify the colors you want your browser to use to display links you can visit as well as links you have visited. In addition, you can choose a color you want your browser to use when you hold your mouse over a link (hover over the link).

6. After you select the colors you desire, click your mouse on the OK button to put your changes into effect.

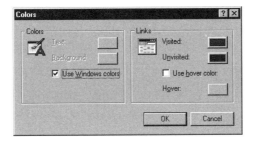

Figure 912 *The Colors dialog box.*

913 CONTROLLING YOUR BROWSER'S FONT USE

In Tip 242, you learned how to use the Display Properties dialog box to select the fonts Windows 98 uses to display items on your Desktop. If you use your browser on a regular basis, there may be times when you will want to customize the browser's font use (you might, for example, select a larger, bolder font that you find easier to see). To customize your browser's font settings, perform these steps:

1. Click your mouse on the Start menu Settings button and choose Control Panel. Windows 98 will open your Control Panel window.

2. Within the Control Panel window, double-click your mouse on the Internet icon. Windows 98 will display the Internet Properties dialog box.

3. Within the Internet Properties dialog box, click your mouse on the Fonts buttons. Windows 98, in turn, will display the Fonts dialog box, as shown in Figure 913.

Figure 913 *The Fonts dialog box.*

4. Within the Fonts dialog box, you can specify the font character set that you desire as well as the specific fonts your browser will use for proportional and fixed-width font operations. In addition, you can choose the font size that you desire.

5. After you select your font settings, click your mouse on the OK button to continue.

914 CONTROLLING YOUR BROWSER'S LANGUAGE SUPPORT

In Tip 384, you learned how to use the Control Panel Regional Settings entry to select your system's language attributes. Depending on the Web sites that you visit, you may encounter sites whose content is based on a different language. Fortunately, using the Language Preferences dialog box shown in Figure 914, you can add software that will let your browser support multiple language attributes.

Figure 914 *The Language Preferences dialog box.*

Within the Language Preferences dialog box, you can add other languages you want your browser to support. By default, when you visit a Web site, your browser will prioritize the languages in the order they appear within the Language list. To change a language's priority, click your mouse on the language within the list and then click your mouse on the Move Up or Move Down button. To add a language to the list, click your mouse on the Add button. Windows 98, in turn, will display the Add Language dialog box, from within which you can select the language that you desire.

915 CONTROLLING YOUR BROWSER'S ACCESSIBILITY SETTINGS

In Tip 197, you learned how to customize various Windows 98 settings to make your system easier to use. For example, you might select a high-contrast screen display to make it easier for a user to view the screen contents. As you surf sites on the Web, there may be times when a site's HTML file specifies specific colors, font styles, or font sizes. Depending on your needs, you may want your browser to ignore the site's settings—so that you find the site's content easier to view. To control your browser's accessibility settings, perform these steps:

1. Click your mouse on the Start menu Settings button and choose Control Panel. Windows 98 will open your Control Panel window.

2. Within the Control Panel window, double-click your mouse on the Internet icon. Windows 98 will display the Internet Properties dialog box.

3. Within the Internet Properties dialog box, click your mouse on the Accessibility buttons. Windows 98, in turn, will display the Accessibility dialog box, as shown in Figure 915.

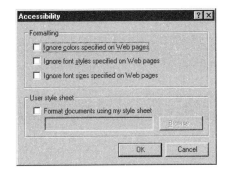

Figure 915 *The Accessibility dialog box.*

4. Within the Accessibility dialog box, use the checkboxes to select attributes you desire and then click your mouse on the OK button to put your changes into effect.

916 **UNDERSTANDING YOUR BROWSER'S ZONE SECURITY SETTINGS**

As you surf sites across the World Wide Web, there will be times when a site may want to download software onto your system that the site uses to play music, play back video or animations, or to perform other specific tasks. To avoid computer viruses, you normally do not want to download programs from across the Web, particularly from sites whose contents you do not know or trust (generally, you can feel safe downloading software from a reputable company's Web site, such as Microsoft, Netscape, Verisign, or even your computer manufacturer).

To help you prevent a site from downloading software that may damage your system, Windows 98 lets you take advantage of security zones. Each security zone lets your browser perform different operations based on the zone's security level. Within your Trusted sites zone, for example, your browser can download and install software. From other zones, however, you might disable software-download operations or require that your browser prompt you before it downloads software. To manage your security-zone settings and the sites that you place in each zone, you will use the Internet Properties dialog box Security sheet, as shown in Figure 916.

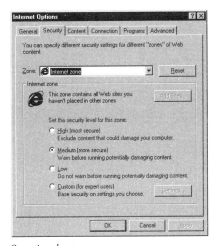

Figure 916 *The Internet Properties dialog box Security sheet.*

If you click your mouse on the Zone pull-down list within the Security sheet, you will find that Windows 98 defines four zones, which Table 916 briefly describes.

Zone	Description
Local intranet zone	Contains a list of sites that reside within your company's intranet
Trusted sites zone	Contains a list of sites that you trust not to damage your system
Internet zone	Contains the majority of sites across the Web—sites you have not assigned to other zones
Restricted sites zone	Contains a list of sites that may potentially download damaging software

Table 916 Windows 98 Internet security zones.

The Internet zone is a catchall zone that your browser will use for all sites that you have not specifically assigned to a different zone. Within each zone, you can define the level of operations that your browser can perform for the zone's sites. Several of the Tips that follow examine security-zone operations in detail.

917   **CONTROLLING AN INTERNET ZONE'S SECURITY SETTINGS**

In Tip 916, you learned that Windows 98 lets you assign Web sites to different security zones. Later, when you surf the Web, your browser will use the zone's settings to determine which operations it can perform for a specific site. To assign security settings to an Internet zone, perform these steps:

1. Click your mouse on the Start menu Settings button and choose Control Panel. Windows 98 will display the Control Panel window.

2. Within the Control Panel window, double-click your mouse on the Internet icon. Windows 98 will display the Internet Properties dialog box.

3. Within the Internet Properties dialog box, click your mouse on the Security tab. Windows 98 will display the Security sheet.

4. Within the Security sheet, click your mouse on the Zone pull-down list and select the zone for which you want to assign security settings. Next, using the security level radio buttons, choose the level of security you want your browser to enforce for the corresponding zone and then click your mouse on the OK button to put your changes into effect.

If you are an advanced user, you can define your own security settings by selecting the Custom radio button and then clicking your mouse on the Settings button. Windows 98, in turn, will display the Security Settings dialog box, as shown in Figure 917.

Within the Security Settings dialog box, you can enable or disable the browser's ability to download plug-ins, ActiveX controls, Java applets, and so on.

Figure 917 *The Security Settings dialog box.*

918 **ADDING A WEB SITE TO A SECURITY ZONE**

In Tip 916, you learned that Windows 98 provides security zones that you can use to control how your browser performs software-download operations as you surf sites on the World Wide Web. In a previous Tip, you learned how define each zone's security settings. If you have Web sites that you visit on a regular basis, you may want to add the site to a specific security zone. For example, you might add the Microsoft Web site to a trusted zone. To add a Web site to a specific Internet security zone, perform these steps:

1. Click your mouse on the Start menu Settings button and choose Control Panel. Windows 98 will display the Control Panel window.

2. Within the Control Panel window, double-click your mouse on the Internet icon. Windows 98 will display the Internet Properties dialog box.

3. Within the Internet Properties dialog box, click your mouse on the Security tab. Windows 98 will display the Security sheet.

4. Within the Security sheet, click your mouse on the Zone pull-down list and select the zone for which you want to assign the Web site. (You cannot add sites to the Internet Zone, it is the catchall zone to which all sites belong until you assign the site to a different zone.)

5. After you select the zone you desire, click your mouse on the Add Sites button. Windows 98, in turn, will display the dialog box specific to the zone within which you can add a site's Web address. After you add the site, click your mouse on the OK button. Within the Internet Properties dialog box, click your mouse on the OK button to put your changes into effect.

919 **UNDERSTANDING THE INTERNET CONTENT ADVISOR**

If your PC is accessible by kids, from whom you want to prevent viewing of various "adult-oriented" Web sites, you can take advantage of the Windows 98 Content Advisor to restrict the sites users can browse. To enable the Content

Advisor, perform these steps:

1. Click your mouse on the Start menu Settings button and choose Control Panel. Windows 98 will display the Control Panel window.

2. Within the Control Panel window, double-click your mouse on the Internet icon. Windows 98 will display the Internet Properties dialog box.

3. Within the Internet Properties dialog box, click your mouse on the Content tab. Windows 98 will display the Content sheet, as shown in Figure 919.

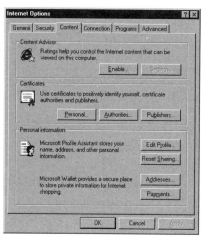

Figure 919 *The Internet Properties dialog box Content sheet.*

4. Within the Content sheet, click your mouse on the Enable button. Windows 98 will display the Supervisor Password Required dialog box, within which you must type (or assign) your supervisor password (the supervisor is the person who will be responsible for enabling and configuring the Content Advisor). Type in the password and click OK. The Content Advisor may display a dialog box that tells you sites you recently viewed may still be accessible. Within the dialog box, click your mouse on the OK button. After you enable the Content Advisor, you can use the Settings button to configure the Content Advisor settings, as discussed in Tip 920.

920 SPECIFYING YOUR SYSTEM'S LANGUAGE, NUDITY, SEX, AND VIOLENCE SETTINGS

In Tip 919, you learned how to use the Windows 98 Content Advisor to restrict the Web sites that users can view from your system. Within the Content Advisor, you can select the level of language, nudity, sex, or violence you will let the browser display. Later, your browser will not display site content that exceeds the settings you have selected. To control the content levels for your system, perform these steps:

1. Click your mouse on the Start menu Settings button and choose Control Panel. Windows 98 will open your Control Panel window.

2. Within the Control Panel window, double-click your mouse on the Internet icon. Windows 98 will display the Internet Properties dialog box.

3. Within the Internet Properties dialog box, click your mouse on the Content tab. Windows 98, in turn, will display the Internet Properties dialog box Content sheet.

4. Within the Content sheet, click your mouse on the Settings button. Windows 98 will display the Supervisor Password Required dialog box, within which you must type in the Supervisor password.

5. Within the Supervisor Password Required dialog box, type in the Supervisor password and then click your mouse on the OK button. Windows 98, in turn, will display the Content Advisor dialog box.

6. Within the Ratings sheet's Category field, click your mouse on the category for which you want to specify the viewing level (such as the Language, Sex, Nudity, or Violence category). The dialog box will display a Rating sliding bar that you can use to select the level you desire. Using your mouse, drag the slider to the left or to the right to decrease or increase the current level. As you select a level, the dialog box will display a description of the level's meaning (Level 0 within the Language field allows inoffensive slang but no profanity).

7. After you select the settings you desire, click your mouse on the Content Advisor dialog box OK button to put your changes into effect.

8. Within the Internet Properties dialog box, click your mouse on the OK button.

The ratings levels are defined by the Recreational Software Advisory Council (RSAC). To assist parents, educators, and others in controlling access to content on the Web, sites can optionally specify their own ratings for language, nudity, sex, and violence. If a site's ratings exceed the Content Advisor levels you have selected, your browser will not display the site. Unfortunately, few sites support such ratings today. In such cases, you can perform the steps Tip 921 discusses to control how your browser handles non-rated sites.

---

921 CONTROLLING USER ACCESS TO NON-RATED SITES AND SUPERVISOR ACCESS TO RATED SITES

As you learned in Tip 920, using the Windows 98 Content Advisor, you can control which Web sites users can view within your browser. However, as you learned, many sites across the Web do not comply with the Content Advisor's ratings system. Using the Content Advisor dialog box General sheet, shown in Figure 921, you can prevent the browser from displaying a non-rated site. In addition, within the sheet you can specify that the supervisor can type in a password that lets the user view restricted content. To adjust settings using the Content Advisor's General sheet, perform these steps:

1. Click your mouse on the Start menu Settings button and choose Control Panel. Windows 98 will open your Control Panel window.

2. Within the Control Panel window, double-click your mouse on the Internet icon. Windows 98 will display the Internet Properties dialog box.

3. Within the Internet Properties dialog box, click your mouse on the Content tab. Windows 98, in turn, will display the Internet Properties dialog box Content sheet.

4. Within the Content sheet, click your mouse on the Settings button. Windows 98 will display the Supervisor Password Required dialog box, within which you must type in the Supervisor password.

5. Within the Supervisor Password Required dialog box, type in the Supervisor password and then click your mouse on the OK button. Windows 98, in turn, will display the Content Advisor dialog box.

6. Within the Content Advisor dialog box, click your mouse on the General tab. Windows 98 will display the General sheet.

7. Within the General sheet, use the checkboxes to specify the settings you desire and then click your mouse on the OK button.

8. Within the Internet Properties dialog box, click your mouse on the OK button to put your changes into effect.

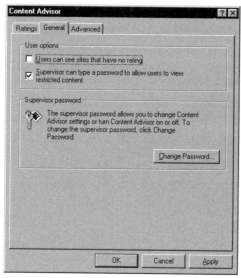

Figure 921 *The Content Advisor dialog box General sheet.*

922 **CONTROLLING YOUR CONTENT ADVISOR PASSWORD**

As you learned in Tip 919, to help you control which Web sites users on your system can view, Windows 98 lets you define a Content Advisor Supervisor who can select various viewing settings. To control the Content Advisor settings, you must type in the correct Supervisor password. If you ever must change your Supervisor password, perform these steps:

1. Click your mouse on the Start menu Settings button and choose Control Panel. Windows 98 will open your Control Panel window.

2. Within the Control Panel window, double-click your mouse on the Internet icon. Windows 98 will display the Internet Properties dialog box.

3. Within the Internet Properties dialog box, click your mouse on the Content tab. Windows 98, in turn, will display the Internet Properties dialog box Content sheet.

4. Within the Content sheet, click your mouse on the Settings button. Windows 98 will display the Supervisor Password Required dialog box, within which you must type in the Supervisor password.

5. Within the Supervisor Password Required dialog box, type in the Supervisor password and then click your mouse on the OK button. Windows 98, in turn, will display the Content Advisor dialog box.

6. Within the Content Advisor dialog box, click your mouse on the General tab. Windows 98 will display the General sheet.

7. Within the General sheet, click your mouse on the Change Password button. Windows 98, in turn, will display the Change Supervisor Password dialog box, as shown in Figure 922.

Figure 922 *The Change Supervisor Password dialog box.* .

8. Within the Change Supervisor Password dialog box, click your mouse on the Old password field and then type your current Supervisor password. Next, click your mouse on the New password dialog box and type in your new password. Then, click your mouse on the Confirm new password dialog box and type your new password a second time. Finally, click your mouse on the OK button to put your changes into effect.

9. Within the Content Advisor dialog box, click your mouse on the OK button. Within the Internet Properties dialog box, click your mouse on the OK button.

923 USING A RATING BUREAU TO GET SITE RATINGS

As you have learned, many (most) sites across the Web do not yet support the Content Advisor's rating system. Rather than simply disallow a site because the site does not provide ratings information, you may be able to get information about the site from a rating bureau (a site on the Web that your browser will contact to determine a site's rating). When you enable the use of a rating bureau, your browser will contact the bureau each time you try to view a site that does not specify a rating. If the rating bureau has rated the site, it will return the rating to your browser which, in turn, can determine whether or not (based on your rating selections) it should display the site's contents.

Although using a rating bureau in this way may let you get ratings for a wider number of sites, it will also slow down the speed at which you browse sites because your browser will have to request and then wait for ratings for each site you visit. Your Internet Service Provider may be able to provide you with the Web address for one or more rating bureaus. To use a rating bureau to rate sites, perform these steps:

1. Click your mouse on the Start menu Settings button and choose Control Panel. Windows 98 will open your Control Panel window.

2. Within the Control Panel window, double-click your mouse on the Internet icon. Windows 98 will display the Internet Properties dialog box.

3. Within the Internet Properties dialog box, click your mouse on the Content tab. Windows 98, in turn, will display the Internet Properties dialog box Content sheet.

4. Within the Content sheet, click your mouse on the Settings button. Windows 98 will display the Supervisor Password Required dialog box, within which you must type in the Supervisor password.

5. Within the Supervisor Password Required dialog box, type in the Supervisor password and then click your mouse on the OK button. Windows 98, in turn, will display the Content Advisor dialog box.

6. Within the Content Advisor dialog box, click your mouse on the Advanced tab. Windows 98 will display the Advanced sheet.

7. Within the Advanced sheet, click your mouse on the Rating bureau field and type in the bureau's corresponding Web address. Then, click your mouse on the OK button.

8. Within the Internet Properties dialog box, click your mouse on the OK button to put your changes into effect.

924 USING THE INTERNET CONNECTION WIZARD TO GET YOU CONNECTED

To help you get connected to the Internet, Windows 98 provides the Internet Connection Wizard. Using the Wizard, you can configure an Internet Service Provider that you access using your modem and phone lines or you can configure a local-area network connection. If you are connected to a local-area network that will provide you with Internet access, you should have your network administrator assist you in configuring your network settings (your system may already be ready to access the Internet). If you want to configure your system to use a new or existing Internet account, perform these steps:

1. Click your mouse on the Start menu Settings button and choose Control Panel. Windows 98 will open your Control Panel window.

2. Within the Control Panel window, double-click your mouse on the Internet icon. Windows 98 will display the Internet Properties dialog box.

3. Within the Internet Properties dialog box, click your mouse on the Connection tab. Windows 98, in turn, will display the Internet Properties dialog box Connection sheet.

4. Within the Connection Sheet, click your mouse on the Connect button. Windows 98, in turn, will start the Internet Connection Wizard, as shown in Figure 924.

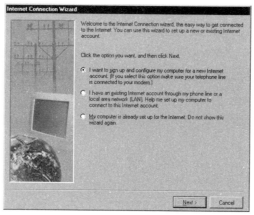

Figure 924 *The Windows 98 Internet Connection Wizard.*

5. Within the Internet Connection Wizard, click your mouse on the radio button that corresponds to the account type you want to connect (a new or an existing account). Then, click your mouse on the Next button. The Wizard, in turn, will display a series of dialog boxes whose content will take you step-by-step through creating your new account or configuring your existing account.

If you are creating a new account, the Internet Connection Wizard can download a list of Internet Service Providers in your area code. From within this list, you can sign up for Internet access from within the Internet Connection Wizard.

925 SELECTING A MODEM OR LOCAL-AREA NETWORK INTERNET CONNECTION

To access the Internet, users will connect their PC to the Net using a modem and phone lines or through a connection on their local-area network. Before you can access the Internet, you must tell Windows 98 how you will connect your PC to the Net. In Tip 924, you learned how to use the Internet Connection Wizard to simplify your connection process. In addition, using the Internet Properties dialog box Connection sheet, shown in Figure 925.1, you can select a modem or local-area network connection.

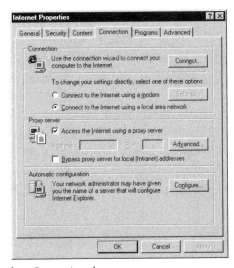

Figure 925.1 *The Internet Properties dialog box Connection sheet.*

If you are using a modem to connect to the Internet, you can click your mouse on the Connection sheet's Settings button to configure your dial-up settings, as shown in Figure 925.2.

Within the Dial-Up Settings dialog box, you can specify the username and password you use to connect to your provider and you can specify the amount of inactive time Windows 98 will wait for this connection before its disconnects (hangs up on) your call.

Note: If you must change the number Windows 98 dials for your provider, you can select the provider within the Dial-Up Settings pull-down list and then click your mouse on the Properties button. Windows 98, in turn, will display the Properties dialog box for your connection within which you can change the phone number and other settings.

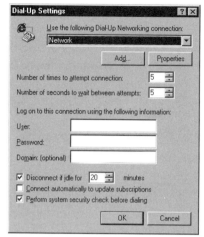

Figure 925.2 *The Dial-Up Settings dialog box.*

926 USING A PROXY SERVER TO ACCESS THE INTERNET

If you are using a PC that is connected to a local-area network, your network may use a special server (a proxy server) to increase your network security. In general, a proxy server sits between the Internet and the computers within your local-area network. When your computer wants to perform an Internet-based operation (such as viewing a Web site), your browser will send its request to the proxy server which, in turn, will send the request on to the Internet.

When the system across the Internet sends back your response, it will send the response to the proxy server which, in turn, will send the information back to your system. You can think of a proxy server as a firewall between your network and the Internet.

If your network uses a proxy server, you must configure your Internet-based software to use the server by performing these steps:

1. Click your mouse on the Start menu Settings button and choose Control Panel. Windows 98 will open your Control Panel window.

2. Within the Control Panel window, double-click your mouse on the Internet icon. Windows 98 will display the Internet Properties dialog box.

3. Within the Internet Properties dialog box, click your mouse on the Connection tab. Windows 98, in turn, will display the Internet Properties dialog box Connection sheet.

4. Within the Connection sheet, click your mouse on the Access the Internet using a proxy server checkbox, placing a check mark within the box. Next, type the proxy server's domain name within the Address field and the proxy server's port number within the Port field. (Your network administrator can provide you with the address and port values.)

5. Within the Connection sheet, click your mouse on the OK button to put your changes into effect.

927 CUSTOMIZING PROXY SERVER SETTINGS

In Tip 926, you learned that to enhance network security, many local-area networks use a proxy server that serves as a firewall between the local-area network and the Internet. If your LAN requires that you use a proxy server, follow the steps Tip 928 presents to configure your Internet software.

Depending on how your network administrator configured your proxy server, there may be times when you must specify different proxy servers for different operations. For example, your browser may request Web pages through one proxy server while an FTP program may perform file-transfer operations through a different server. If your network uses multiple proxy servers, you can use the Proxy Setting dialog box, shown in Figure 927, to define the proxy settings.

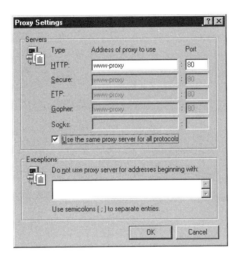

Figure 927 *The Proxy Settings dialog box.*

To display the Proxy Settings dialog box, perform these steps:

1. Click your mouse on the Start menu Settings button and choose Control Panel. Windows 98 will open your Control Panel window.

2. Within the Control Panel window, double-click your mouse on the Internet icon. Windows 98 will display the Internet Properties dialog box.

3. Within the Internet Properties dialog box, click your mouse on the Connection tab. Windows 98, in turn, will display the Internet Properties dialog box Connection sheet.

4. Within the Connection sheet, click your mouse on the Access the Internet using a proxy server checkbox, placing a check mark within the box. Next, click your mouse on the Proxy server section's Advanced button.

Within the Advanced sheet, you can specify the address and port number for your specific proxy servers. In addition, you can direct your software not to use a proxy server for addresses that start with a specific set of characters. (You might, for example, not want to use the proxy server for local addresses within your intranet.)

---

928 **ALLOWING A SERVER TO CONFIGURE YOUR INTERNET EXPLORER SETTINGS**

If you are using a PC that is connected to a local-area network, your network administrator may have specified software on the network that you can use to configure the Internet Explorer. If your network administrator tells you to use a server to configure your Internet Explorer settings, perform these steps:

1. Click your mouse on the Start menu Settings button and choose Control Panel. Windows 98 will open your Control Panel window.

2. Within the Control Panel window, double-click your mouse on the Internet icon. Windows 98 will display the Internet Properties dialog box.

3. Within the Internet Properties dialog box, click your mouse on the Connection tab. Windows 98, in turn, will display the Internet Properties dialog box Connection sheet.

4. Within the Connection sheet, click your mouse on the Configure button. Windows 98 will display the Automatic Configuration dialog box, as shown in Figure 928.

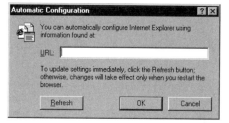

Figure 928 *The Automatic Configuration dialog box.*

5. Within the Automatic Configuration dialog box, type in the Web address of the server file (your network administrator will tell you the address) and then click your mouse on the OK button. (If you are running your browser, you can put the changes into immediate effect by clicking your mouse on the Refresh button.)

6. Within the Internet Properties dialog box, click your mouse on the OK button.

---

929 **SPECIFYING THE PROGRAM YOUR BROWSER WILL USE FOR E-MAIL, NEWSGROUPS, AND AN INTERNET CALL**

As you learned in Tip 799, within the Internet Explorer, you can view Web sites or newsgroups, send and receive electronic mail, and even perform an Internet call. When you perform these operations, the Internet Explorer, in turn, will run a second program, such as Microsoft Outlook Express or NetMeeting, to perform the operation. Using the Internet Properties dialog box Programs sheet, shown in Figure 929, you can specify which program your browser will run to perform these operations.

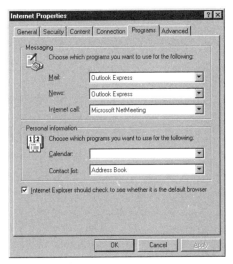

Figure 929 *The Internet Properties dialog box Programs sheet.*

Within the Programs sheet, click your mouse on the pull-down list that corresponds to the operation for which you want to assign a new program and select the program you desire.

In addition to using the Programs sheet to specify the programs your browser will launch for Internet operations, you can also use the sheet to specify the programs you want the browser to launch for your calendar management as well as your contact list. If you use your PC within a local-area network, you may want to take advantage of a "network-aware" program, such as Schedule+ (that comes within Microsoft Office) that helps users coordinate their meetings, appointments, and even conference rooms.

930 **CONTROLLING ADVANCED BROWSER SETTINGS**

Several of the Tips this book presents examine specific operations you can perform to configure your Internet-based program settings. To fine-tune your Internet operations, you can take advantage of the Internet Properties dialog box Advanced sheet, as shown in Figure 930. Within the Advanced sheet, you can control specific browser settings, which HTTP protocol your browser users, how your browser handles Java programs you encounter on the Web, and much more.

To further customize your Internet program settings using the Advanced sheet, perform these steps:

1. Click your mouse on the Start menu Settings button and choose Control Panel. Windows 98 will open your Control Panel window.

2. Within the Control Panel window, double-click your mouse on the Internet icon. Windows 98 will display the Internet Properties dialog box.

3. Within the Internet Properties dialog box, click your mouse on the Advanced tab. Windows 98, in turn, will display the Internet Properties dialog box Advanced sheet.

4. Within the Advanced sheet, use the checkboxes to enable or disable specific settings. After you assign the settings you desire, click your mouse on the OK button to put your changes into effect.

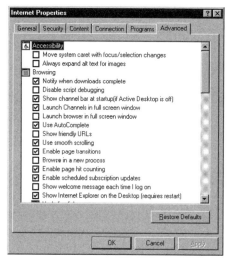

Figure 930 *The Internet Properties dialog box Advanced sheet.*

931 DELETING SAVED PAGES WHEN YOU CLOSE YOUR BROWSER

As you have learned, to improve its performance, your browser stores the information it downloads for the sites that you visit on the Web within temporary files. Should you later revisit a site, your browser can quickly display the site by using the temporary files. In Tip 908, you learned how to purge the temporary Internet files from your disk. If you are using a browser at work, and you do not want another user to determine the sites you visit by examining your temporary Internet files, you can direct your browser to delete its temporary files each time you close the browser window. To direct your browser to delete its temporary files each time you close the browser window, perform these steps:

1. Click your mouse on the Start menu Settings button and choose Control Panel. Windows 98 will open your Control Panel window.

2. Within the Control Panel window, double-click your mouse on the Internet icon. Windows 98 will display the Internet Properties dialog box.

3. Within the Internet Properties dialog box, click your mouse on the Advanced tab. Windows 98, in turn, will display the Internet Properties dialog box Advanced sheet.

4. Within the Advanced sheet, click your mouse on the Delete saved pages when browser is closed checkbox, placing a check mark within the box. Then, click your mouse on the OK button to put your changes into effect.

932 UNDERSTANDING INTERNET COOKIES

When you surf sites on the Web, there are times when the sites you visit want to store information on your computer. For example, the site might record the date and time you visited or it might record information about products you examined. By recording such information about you on your PC, the next time you visit the site, it can pull up the information and hopefully use it to provide you with better service. Users refer to the information that a Web site stores on your disk as an *Internet cookie*. Although many sites use cookies to provide you with better service, the problem with cookies is that most users do not know that the site is creating the cookie on your disk. Within the Internet Properties dialog box Advanced sheet, you can control how your browser handles cookies. To start, you may want your browser simply to accept the cookies with no questions asked. Second, you can direct your browser to prompt you before it accepts or denies a cookie. Third you can simply disable all cookies. To control how your browser handles cookies, perform these steps:

1. Click your mouse on the Start menu Settings button and choose Control Panel. Windows 98 will open your Control Panel window.

2. Within the Control Panel window, double-click your mouse on the Internet icon. Windows 98 will display the Internet Properties dialog box.

3. Within the Internet Properties dialog box, click your mouse on the Advanced tab. Windows 98, in turn, will display the Internet Properties dialog box Advanced sheet. Within the Advanced sheet, scroll through the list of options until you locate the Cookies buttons. Using the buttons, select the settings you desire and then, click your mouse on the OK button to put your changes into effect.

933 **DIRECTING YOUR BROWSER TO PRINT BACKGROUND GRAPHICS AND COLORS**

Within your browser, you can print a site's contents by selecting the File menu Print option or by clicking your mouse on the Printer icon. Normally, to make your printouts easier to read, your browser will not print background graphics or colors that appear on the Web site. Instead, your browser will print the Web site text and graphics images that appear within the text (if the site displays its text on a yellow background, for example, your browser would normally not print the background). To direct your browser to print a site's background color or background image, perform these steps:

1. Click your mouse on the Start menu Settings button and choose Control Panel. Windows 98 will open your Control Panel window.

2. Within the Control Panel window, double-click your mouse on the Internet icon. Windows 98 will display the Internet Properties dialog box.

3. Within the Internet Properties dialog box, click your mouse on the Advanced tab. Windows 98, in turn, will display the Internet Properties dialog box Advanced sheet as shown in Figure 933.

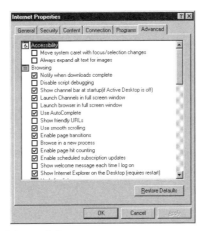

Figure 933 *The Internet Properties dialog box Advanced sheet.*

4. Within the Advanced sheet, click your mouse on the Print background colors and images checkbox, placing a check mark within the box. Then, click your mouse on the OK button to put your changes into effect.

934 | **UNDERSTANDING INTERNET NEWSGROUPS**

In previous Tips, you have learned to send and receive electronic mail, to surf the Web, and, in Tip 972, you will learn how to chat with other users on-line. As you have learned, you can find sites across the Web that present information on a virtually unlimited number of topics. Although the Web provides vast amounts of information, the Web is not well suited for letting you ask questions or debate topics. Fortunately, to interact with other users about a wide range of topics, you can visit newsgroups across the Net.

In general, you can think of a newsgroup as an electronic bulletin board, where users leave their thoughts, facts, questions, and answers to a specific topic. Across the Net, you can find newsgroups that discuss every possible topic, from sports, finance, and computers, to science fiction, vacation resorts, to, well, much more.

Just as each Web site has a unique address, each newsgroup has a unique name. Newsgroup names consist of several parts, which you separate using periods.

Newsgroup names are ordered, by topic, from left to right. To start, each name begins with a major topic name, such as *comp* for computers, *sci* for science, or *soc* for social topics. Following the major topic part of the name are the subtopics which, again, work from left to right.

Within a newsgroup, you can view discussions or post your own thoughts, much like you might post a note on a bulletin board. To view and participate in newsgroups within Windows 98, you can use Outlook Express (which you are probably using to send and receive your e-mail). Figure 934.1, for example, shows a list of the Internet Explorer newsgroups.

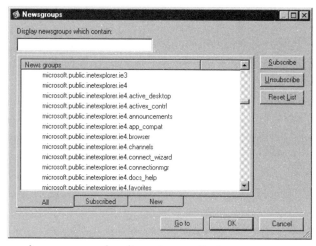

Figure 934.1 *Using Outlook Express to list newsgroups that discuss Internet Explorer.*

After you select a specific newsgroup, Outlook Express will display a list of the newsgroup's current discussions, as shown in Figure 934.2. Several of the Tips that follow discuss ways you can use Outlook Express as you view and contribute to newsgroup discussions.

Figure 934.2 *Viewing a newsgroup's discussions.*

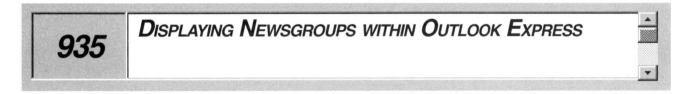

935   D*ISPLAYING* N*EWSGROUPS* *WITHIN* O*UTLOOK* E*XPRESS*

In Tip 934, you learned that a newsgroup is essentially an electronic bulletin board where you can view and contribute to discussions on a wide range of topics. To participate in a newsgroup, you can use Outlook Express. To direct Outlook Express to perform newsgroup operations, rather than e-mail operations, click your mouse on the Outlook Express Go menu and choose News. Outlook Express, in turn, will display its Newsgroups dialog box, as shown in Figure 935.

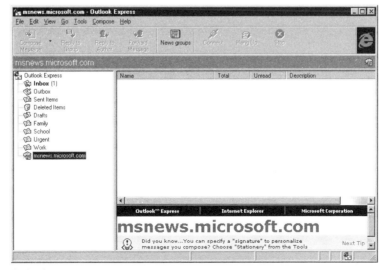

Figure 935 *The Newsgroups dialog box.*

If you have not subscribed to any newsgroups in the past, Outlook Express will display a dialog box telling you that it will now download a list of newsgroups to your system. Click your mouse on the Yes button. Outlook Express, in turn, will start downloading the newsgroup list (that contains thousands of newsgroups).

Depending on the speed of your Internet connection, the newsgroup download may take a few minutes. After Outlook Express downloads the newsgroup list, you can select a newsgroup, as discussed in Tip 936.

936 READING A NEWSGROUP ENTRY

In Tip 935, you learned how to display a list of newsgroups within Outlook Express. Using your mouse, you can scroll through the newsgroups until you find one that interests you. To view the newsgroup's current postings (remember, a newsgroup is somewhat like a bulletin board), click your mouse on the newsgroup and then click your mouse on the Go to button. Outlook Express, in turn, will display the newsgroup's current postings, as shown in Figure 936.1.

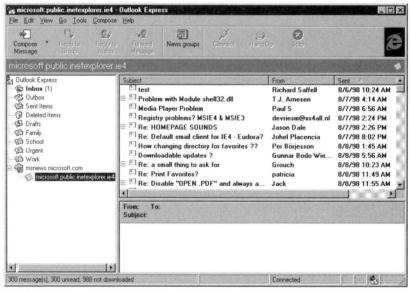

Figure 936.1 Viewing a list of the newsgroups current postings.

Again, using your mouse, you can scroll through the list of postings until you find one that you want to read. To view a specific posting, simply click your mouse on the posting. Outlook Express, in turn, will download the posting, displaying it as a message on your screen, as shown in Figure 936.2.

If you want to print the current posting, simply select the Outlook Express File menu and choose Print. To view a different posting, simply click your mouse on the new posting within the newsgroup's posting list. If you want to select a different newsgroup, click your mouse on the toolbar News groups button. Outlook Express, in turn, will redisplay its newsgroups list.

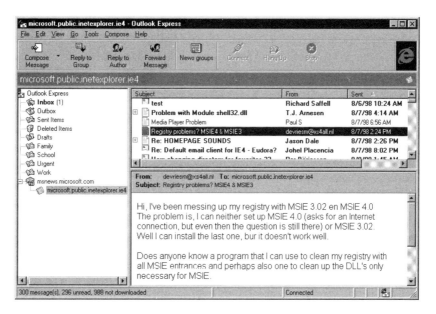

Figure 936.2 *Viewing a specific newsgroup posting.*

937 REPLYING TO A NEWSGROUP POSTING

Within a newsgroup, you can respond to a posting in one of two ways. First, you can simply send an e-mail response to the posting's author. Second, you can place your reply within the newsgroup itself. To reply to a posting's author, perform these steps:

1. Within the newsgroup, click your mouse on the posting you desire. Outlook Express will display the posting's contents.

2. Click your mouse on the toolbar Reply to Author button or select the Compose menu Reply to Author option. Outlook Express will display a reply dialog box within which you can type your response. Within the dialog box, type your message and then click your mouse on the Send button.

To reply to the newsgroup, perform these steps:

1. Within the newsgroup, click your mouse on the posting you desire. Outlook Express will display the posting's contents.

2. Click your mouse on the toolbar Reply to Group button or select the Compose menu Reply to Newsgroup option. Outlook Express will display a reply dialog box within which you can type your response. Within the dialog box, type your message and then click your mouse on the Send button. Within a few minutes, your reply should appear within the newsgroup.

938 **CREATING YOUR OWN NEWSGROUP POSTING**

In Tip 937, you learned how to reply to an existing newsgroup posting. As you traverse newsgroups, there will be times when you will want to place your own posting. For example, if you are visiting a travel newsgroup, you might post a message that asks other users which airline takes the best care of pets that are traveling with you. To post your message to a newsgroup, perform these steps:

1. Within Outlook Express, display the newsgroup to which you want to post a message.

2. Click your mouse on the toolbar Compose Message button or select the Compose menu New Message option. Outlook Express, in turn, will display the New Message dialog box.

3. Within the dialog box, type your message and then click your mouse on the Send button. Within a few minutes, your posting should appear within the newsgroup.

939 **UNDERSTANDING NEWSGROUP TOPICS AND THREADS**

As you have learned, you can think of a newsgroup as an electronic bulletin board to which users post messages. Within a newsgroup, users will often create a series of postings about a specific topic. To help users keep a topic's related discussions in one location, newsgroups support message threads. In general, a thread is simply a message that a user attaches to a specific posting. Within a newsgroup, Outlook Express will place a plus sign in front of postings that have threads. By clicking your mouse on the plus sign, you can expand the posting to display the thread list, as shown in Figure 939.

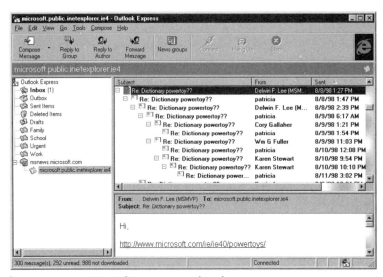

Figure 939 *A plus in front of a newsgroup posting indicates message threads.*

To view a message thread, simply click your mouse on the thread entry. By moving from one thread to the next, you can view the conversations that users have had regarding a specific posting.

940   FINDING A SPECIFIC NEWSGROUP

As you have learned, across the Net there are thousands of newsgroups. To help you find the newsgroup you desire, you can direct Outlook Express to search for a newsgroup whose name contains specific text, such as *travel* or *sports*. To direct Outlook Express to display only newsgroups whose names contain specific text, perform these steps:

1. Within Outlook Express, click your mouse on the toolbar News groups button. Outlook Express, in turn, will display its Newsgroups dialog box.

2. Within the Newsgroups dialog box, click your mouse within the Display newsgroups which contain text field and type the topic you desire. Outlook Express will restrict its newsgroup list to only newsgroups whose name contains the text you type.

941   DOWNLOADING NEWSGROUP MESSAGES

Depending on the number of messages a newsgroup contains, viewing the messages may take you some time. Rather than viewing the newsgroup messages on-line (which may tie up your phone lines), Outlook Express lets you download messages and read them offline. To download a newsgroup's messages for offline viewing, perform these steps:

1. Within Outlook Express, display the newsgroup whose message contents you want to download.

2. Click your mouse on the Tools menu and choose Download this newsgroup. Outlook Express, in turn, will display the Download Newsgroup dialog box, as shown in Figure 941.

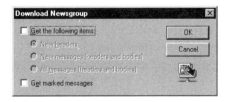

Figure 941 *The Download Newsgroup dialog box.*

3. Within the Download Newsgroup dialog box, click your mouse on the Get the following items checkbox, placing a check mark within the box. Next, click your mouse on the All messages radio button. Then, click your mouse on the OK button. Outlook Express, in turn, will download the newsgroups messages.

Note: *After you download a newsgroup one time, you can save time later by using the Download Newsgroup dialog box to only download new messages.*

942   SUBSCRIBING TO A NEWSGROUP

In Tip 936, you learned how to view a newsgroup's posting by selecting the newsgroup from the Outlook Express newsgroup list and then clicking your mouse on the Go to button. When you select a newsgroup using the Go to button, Outlook Express will later discard the newsgroup's contents when you exit. If you later want to view the newsgroup again, you must locate and select the newsgroup from within the Outlook Express newsgroup list. If you find that you visit the same newsgroup on a regular basis, you can subscribe to that newsgroup. Outlook Express, in turn, will add the newsgroup to your newsgroup folder. Figure 942, for example, shows several newsgroup subscriptions within the newsgroup folder. Later, to display one of the newsgroup's postings, you simply need to click your mouse on the newsgroup's folder. When you exit Outlook Express, the newsgroups to which you have subscribed will remain within your newsgroup tree.

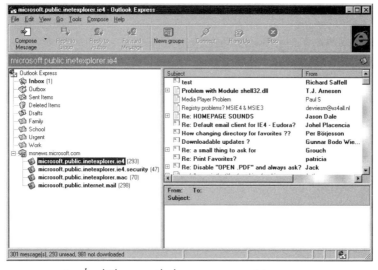

Figure 942 *The folders for your newsgroup subscriptions remain in your newsgroup tree.*

To subscribe to the current newsgroup, simply click your mouse on the Outlook Express Tools menu Subscribe to this newsgroup option. If you later choose to end your newsgroup subscription, simply click your mouse on the newsgroup and then choose the Tools menu Unsubscribe from this newsgroup option.

943   FILTERING NEWSGROUP MESSAGES

A newsgroup is a public forum within which people are pretty much free to post anything they want (and people do). If your PC is accessible by other family members whose "enlightenment" you do not want coming from a newsgroup, you can filter the newsgroups that Outlook Express will display. Unfortunately, the filtering you can perform may not satisfy your requirements—you can only filter messages from a specific user or messages whose Subject field contains specific text. To filter the newsgroup list, perform these steps:

1. Within Outlook Express, click your mouse on the Tools menu Newsgroup Filters option. Outlook Express, in turn, will display the Newsgroup Filters dialog box, as shown in Figure 943.1.

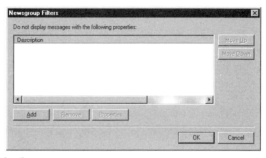

Figure 943.1 *The Newsgroup Filters dialog box.*

2. Within the Newsgroup Filters dialog box, click your mouse on the Add button. Outlook Express will display the Properties dialog box, as shown in Figure 943.2.

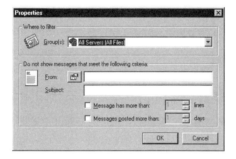

Figure 943.2 *The Properties dialog box.*

3. Within the Properties dialog box, click your mouse on the Group(s) pull-down list and select the newsgroup whose contents you want to filter.

4. If you want to filter messages from a specific user, click your mouse on the From field and type in the user's e-mail name.

5. If you want to filter messages whose subject field contains a specific text, click your mouse on the Subject field and type in the word you want to use as your filter.

6. Click your mouse on the OK button to put your filter into effect.

944 **USING INTERNET-BASED MAILING LISTS FOR YET ANOTHER SOURCE OF INFORMATION**

Throughout this book's Tips, you have learned to search the Web for a vast amount of information, to chat with other users on-line, to view information that resides in newsgroups, and even how to access information in older databases using Telnet. The Internet offers yet another way to exchange information on a variety of topics: mailing lists. In general, a mailing list is a group of individuals that exchange information (using e-mail) on a variety of topics. And, like just about everything else on the Internet, mailing lists are free. Using your e-mail message, you simply send a message to the mailing list that includes the word Subscribe, followed by your e-mail address:

SUBSCRIBE   johndoe@some_server.com

Later, the mailing list will start sending you information on the list's specific topic. Later, to cancel your subscription, you can send an unsubscribe or cancel message to the mailing list (your mailing list will provide you with the steps you must perform to cancel).

Across the Web, you will find sites that provide you with the e-mail addresses for mailing lists you may want to join. Using the Internet Explorer, visit the site *www.list.com* to get a list of mailing list addresses.

945 INSTALLING THE MICROSOFT WALLET

If you use the Internet to shop, you have undoubtedly typed in credit-card and shipping information that you then send across the Net to a Web site. Normally, when you send such information, you do so using a secure connection and your credit-card information is relatively safe. To simplify (and to further secure) your credit-card use across the Net, Internet Explorer now provides the Microsoft Wallet, within which you can store your credit-card and shipping information.

Later, when you shop, you can use the information your wallet contains (no user or application can see the information without your permission). If another user gains access to your system, the user must specify your wallet password before the user can view or use your data. The Microsoft Wallet software will eventually work with a variety of programs that support the Personal Information Exchange (PFX) standard.

Before you can use the Microsoft Wallet, you must install the software on your system by performing these steps:

1. Click your mouse on the Start menu Settings menu and choose Control Panel. Windows 98, in turn, will open the Control Panel window.
2. Within the Control Panel window, double-click your mouse on the Add/Remove Programs icon. Windows 98 will display the Add/Remove Programs Properties dialog box.
3. Within the Add/Remove Programs Properties dialog box, click your mouse on the Windows Setup tab. Windows 98 will display checkboxes for the Windows 98 components.
4. Within the Windows 98 component list, click your mouse on the Internet Tools checkbox and then click your mouse on the Details button. Windows 98 will display the Internet Tools dialog box.
5. Within the Internet Tools dialog box, click your mouse on the Microsoft Wallet checkbox, placing a check mark within the box. Then, click your mouse on the OK button.
6. Within the Add/Remove Programs Properties dialog box, click your mouse on the OK button.

In Tip 947, you will learn how to use the Microsoft Wallet to store your shipping information.

946 **A WORD ON CREDIT CARD TRANSACTIONS ACROSS THE NET**

Each day, across the Web, many more sites support secure credit-card transactions. As a rule, you can feel as confident placing a credit-card order across the Internet as you would giving your credit-card number to a vendor during a telephone call. Admittedly, if you send your credit-card information to a site on the Web using an "unsecure" data transfer, a hacker could potentially capture your credit-card number. However, most sites today offer secure credit-card transactions which are very safe. Should, however, a hacker get your credit-card number and go on a wild shopping spree, in most cases, you will only be responsible for $50 of the amounts charged. Soon, to promote Web-based commerce, you will find many credit-card companies that will reduce or eliminate this $50 liability. The Microsoft Wallet does not increase or decrease the security of your credit-card information. Instead, its purpose is to simplify your transactions by eliminating your need to repeating type in your credit-card information.

947 **STORING YOUR SHIPPING INFORMATION WITHIN THE MICROSOFT WALLET**

In Tip 945, you learned how to install the Microsoft Wallet software, that you can use to store your credit-card and shipping information within the Internet Explorer. To record your shipping information within the Wallet, perform these steps:

1. Click your mouse on the Start menu Settings option and choose Control Panel. Windows 98 will open the Control Panel window.

2. Within the Control Panel window, double-click your mouse on the Internet icon. Windows 98 will display the Internet Properties dialog box.

3. Within the Internet Properties dialog box, click your mouse on the Content tab. Windows 98 will display the Content sheet.

4. Within the Content sheet, click your mouse on the Addresses button. Windows 98 will display the Address Options dialog box.

5. Within the Address Options dialog box, click your mouse on the Add button. Windows 98 will display the Add a New Address dialog box, as shown in Figure 947.

6. Within the Add a New Address dialog box, complete the corresponding fields. Then, within the Display name field that appears near the bottom of the dialog box, type in a name that describes the shipping location, such as Home address. Your software will later display this name when you must select a shipping address. Finally, click your mouse on the OK button.

7. Within the Address Options dialog box, click your mouse on the Close button.

8. Within the Internet Properties dialog box, click your mouse on the OK button to put your changes into effect.

Figure 947 *The Add a New Address dialog box.*

948   **STORING YOUR CREDIT-CARD INFORMATION WITHIN THE MICROSOFT WALLET**

In Tip 945, you learned how to install the Microsoft Wallet software that you can use to store your credit-card and shipping information within the Internet Explorer. To record your credit-card information within the Wallet, perform these steps:

1. Click your mouse on the Start menu Settings option and choose Control Panel. Windows 98 will open the Control Panel window.

2. Within the Control Panel window, double-click your mouse on the Internet icon. Windows 98 will display the Internet Properties dialog box.

3. Within the Internet Properties dialog box, click your mouse on the Content tab. Windows 98 will display the Content sheet.

4. Within the Content sheet, click your mouse on the Payments button. Windows 98 will display the Payment Options dialog box.

5. Within the Payment Options dialog box, click your mouse on the Add button. Windows 98 will display a menu of credit-card options, as shown in Figure 948.

Figure 948 *The Payment Options credit-card list.*

6. Within the pull-down credit-card list, click your mouse on the credit card you desire. Windows 98, in turn, will start the Add a New Credit Card Wizard, which will walk you through the steps you must perform to enter your credit-card information. Perform the Wizard's steps now.

7. Within the Payment Options dialog box, click your mouse on the Close button.

8. Within the Internet Properties dialog box, click your mouse on the OK button to put your changes into effect.

949 CHOOSING AN INTERNET SERVICE PROVIDER

If your PC is connected to a local-area network within an office, you may already have Internet access at your PC—talk to your network administrator to determine the steps you must perform to access the Net. You may simply be able to start the Internet Explorer and Outlook Express and be ready to go.

If you are using a home PC, you can connect to the Internet using an on-line service or an Internet Service Provider (ISP)—each of which will charge you a monthly service charge. Today, in most cities, your Sunday newspaper will advertise several Internet Service Providers—each of which will advertise different specials. Most users will simply want unlimited monthly access at a fixed rate—which will typically run $15 to $30 a month. If you are just getting started, you may find it simpler to subscribe to an on-line service such as the Microsoft Network or America On-line, for which Windows 98 includes the software you need to get started on your Windows 98 CD-ROM.

950 UNDERSTANDING PPP AND SLIP CONNECTIONS

To connect to the Internet using an Internet Service Provider, users normally use either the point-to-point protocol (PPP) or the serial line Internet protocol (SLIP). A few years ago, users made extensive use of SLIP accounts. Today, most Internet Service Providers use PPP accounts, which are faster. Windows 98 provides built-in support for PPP-based Internet access. In fact, when you configure your system to use an Internet Service Provider, Windows 98 will install and configure PPP software on your system. In Tip 382, you learned that to use a virtual private network, your provider had to support a PPP-tunneling protocol. Most users, however, when they shop for an Internet Service Provider, simply need a provider who supports standard PPP operations.

951 PREPARING YOUR SYSTEM TO USE YOUR INTERNET SERVICE PROVIDER

After you choose an Internet Service Provider, you provider will give you a phone number which your system will call (using your PC modem) to gain access to the Internet. To configure your system to dial your provider, you will use the Dial-Up Networking Wizard. Specifically, to prepare your system to access the Internet using your Internet Service

Provider, perform these steps:

1. Within your Desktop, double-click your mouse on the My Computer icon. Windows 98, in turn, will open the My Computer window.

2. Within the My Computer window, double-click your mouse on the Dial-Up Networking icon. Windows 98, in turn, will open the Dial-Up Networking window.

3. Within the Dial-Up Networking window, double-click your mouse on the Make a New Connection icon. Windows 98 will start the Make a Connection Wizard, as shown in Figure 951.1.

Figure 951.1 The Make a Connection Wizard.

4. Within the Make a Connection Wizard, click your mouse on the Type a name for the computer you are dialing field and type in the name of your Internet Service Provider. Next, use your mouse to select your modem from the Select a device pull-down list. Finally, click your mouse on the OK button. The Wizard, in turn, will display a dialog box prompting you to type your provider's phone number.

5. Within the dialog box, type in your provider's area code and phone number and then click your mouse on the Next button. The Wizard, in turn, will display a dialog box that tells you that you have successfully set up your connection. Click your mouse on the Finish button. The Wizard will create an icon for your connection within the Dial-Up Networking dialog box.

6. Using your mouse, drag your newly created icon onto your Desktop to create a shortcut that you can use to access your provider's settings.

952 SETTING YOUR PROVIDER'S TCP/IP SETTINGS

In Tip 951, you learned how to create a connection link that you can use to dial your Internet Service Provider. Most users can create a such connection link and then be ready to connect to the Internet. In some cases, however, depending on your Internet Service Provider's system settings, there may be times when you must customize one or more TCP/IP settings on your system (TCP/IP is the protocol that programs use to communicate across the Net). To configure your system's TCP/IP settings (for your ISP connection), perform these steps:

1. Right-click your mouse on the icon that corresponds to your Internet Service Provider connection. Windows 98 will display a pop-up menu.

2. Within the pop-up menu, click your mouse on the Properties option. Windows 98, in turn, will display the connection's Properties dialog box General sheet.

3. Within the dialog box, click your mouse on the Server Types tab. Windows 98 will display the Server Types sheet, as shown in Figure 952.1.

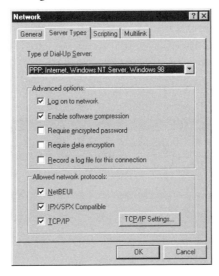

Figure 952.1 *The Server Types sheet.*

4. Within the Server Types sheet, use the checkboxes to select any settings your provider specifies.

5. Within the Server Types sheet, click your mouse on the TCP/IP settings dialog box. Windows 98 will display the TCP/IP Settings dialog box, as shown in Figure 952.2.

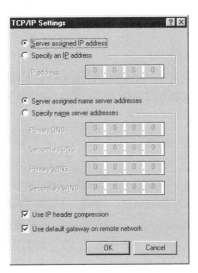

Figure 952.2 *The TCP/IP Settings dialog box.*

6. Within the TCP/IP Settings dialog box, select the settings your provider specifies and then click your mouse on the OK button.

7. Within the Server Types dialog box, click your mouse on the OK button to put your changes into effect.

953 **CONNECTING TO YOUR INTERNET SERVICE PROVIDER**

After you create your dial-up link for your Internet Service Provider, you are ready to use the link to connect and to get on-line. After you connect, you can run programs such as the Internet Explorer to browse the Web or Outlook Express to send and receive electronic mail. To connect to your Internet Service Provider, double-click your mouse on your provider's icon (which you may have copied to the Desktop to simplify your access). Windows 98, in turn, will display the Connect To window, as shown in Figure 953.

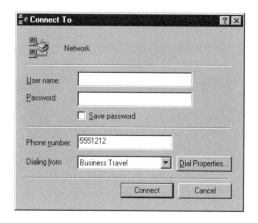

Figure 953 *The Connect To window.*

Within the Connect To window, type in the username and password your Internet Service Provider gave you and then click your mouse on the Connect button. Windows 98, in turn, will dial your Provider. After you establish a connection, you can run your Internet-based programs.

954 **UNDERSTANDING INTERNET PROTOCOL (IP) ADDRESSES**

Across the Internet, each site must have a unique address, which users refer to as the site's Internet Protocol address (or more commonly, IP address). Every IP address consists of four numbers separated by periods, such as 111.222.112.213. When you connect your PC to the Net using an on-line service or Internet Service Provider, your service assigns your PC a temporary IP address. In Tip 958, you will learn how to display your system's IP address.

Fortunately, you normally do not have to use IP addresses. Instead, you can specify a site's domain name, such as *jamsa.com*, that your software will then convert into an IP address. Tip 955 discusses IP addresses in detail.

955 UNDERSTANDING DOMAIN NAMES

As you learned in Tip 954, each PC on the Net must have a unique Internet Protocol address, such as 111.222.101.123. Before two computers can communicate across the Internet, whether to exchange e-mail messages, to chat, or download Web-site information, each computer's software must know the other computer's Internet address.

Fortunately, when you use Internet-based programs, you don't have to use IP addresses. Instead, you can refer to systems using their domain names, such as *www.microsoft.com* or *www.borders.com*. When you use a domain name within a program, the program, in turn, converts the domain name into an IP address. Because your program has no way of knowing every computer's Internet address, it uses a special site on the Net, called a domain-name server, to convert the name into an address (the domain-name server does know every computer's IP address).

In other words, when you use a domain name, such as *jamsa.com*, your program will send a message to a domain-name server (a PC that can reside anywhere on the Net) that contains the domain name. The domain-name server, in turn, will determine the system's corresponding IP address, which it will then send back to your program.

When you type in an invalid Web site address within Internet Explorer, for example, Internet Explorer will not know the address is invalid. Instead, Internet Explorer will send the domain name a domain-name server (which is sometimes called a DNS system) which, in turn, tells the Internet Explorer it cannot find a matching address for the site.

956 CONFIGURING YOUR *TCP/IP* CONNECTION'S DOMAIN-NAME SERVER

As you learned in Tip 955, when you type in a domain name, such as *jamsa.com*, for a site on the Web, your Internet-based programs, in turn, send a message to a special computer, a domain-name server, which, in turn, converts the domain name into the remote system's Internet Protocol address (such as 111.212.222.111).

The domain-name server is a computer that can reside anywhere on the Net. As Tip 955 discussed, the domain-name server knows the domain name and IP address for each system on the Net. Normally, you don't have to worry about the domain-name server. You simply type in a domain name, and your program and the domain-name server do the rest. Your Internet Service Provider will normally specify the domain-name server that your programs will use.

If you find that your software cannot recognize a variety of sites, the problem may reside at the domain-name server. In such cases, your Internet Service Provider may give you the IP address for a different domain-name server that you can use. To configure your system's domain name server, perform these steps:

1. Within your Desktop, double-click your mouse on the My Computer icon. Windows 98 will open the My Computer window.

2. Within the My Computer window, double-click your mouse on the Dial-Up Networking icon. Windows 98 will open the Dial-Up Networking window.

3. Within the Dial-Up Networking window, right-click your mouse on the icon that corresponds to your Internet Service Provider. Windows 98 will display a pop-up menu. Within the pop-up

menu, click your mouse on the Properties option. Windows 98 will display the Properties dialog box.

4. Within the Properties dialog box, click your mouse on the Server Types tab. Windows 98 will display the Server Types sheet.

5. Within the Server Types sheet, click your mouse on the TCP/IP Settings button. Windows 98 will display the TCP/IP Settings dialog box, as shown in Figure 956.

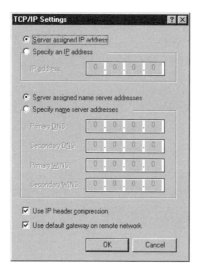

Figure 956 *The TCP/IP Settings dialog box.*

6. Within the TCP/IP Settings dialog box, click your mouse on the Specify name server address radio button and then type in the IP address your Provider gave you for the domain-name server. Then, click your mouse on the OK button.

7. Within the Properties dialog box, click your mouse on the OK button.

957 SPECIFYING YOUR COMPUTER'S IP ADDRESS

As you have learned, every system on the Internet must have a unique Internet Protocol (IP) address. Normally, when you connect to the Internet, your Internet Service Provider will automatically assign your PC the IP address. In some cases, however, an Internet Service Provider may ask you to specify the IP address yourself. To assign an IP address to your system, perform these steps:

1. Within your Desktop, double-click your mouse on the My Computer icon. Windows 98 will open the My Computer window.

2. Within the My Computer window, double-click your mouse on the Dial-Up Networking icon. Windows 98 will open the Dial-Up Networking window.

3. Within the Dial-Up Networking window, right-click your mouse on the icon that corresponds to your Internet Service Provider. Windows 98 will display a pop-up menu. Within the pop-up menu, click your mouse on the Properties option. Windows 98 will display the Properties dialog box.

4. Within the Properties dialog box, click your mouse on the Server Types tab. Windows 98 will display the Server Types sheet.

5. Within the Server Types sheet, click your mouse on the TCP/IP Settings button. Windows 98 will display the TCP/IP Settings dialog box, as shown in Figure 957.

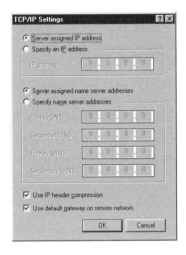

Figure 957 *The TCP/IP Settings dialog box.*

6. Within the TCP/IP Settings dialog box, click your mouse on the Specify IP address radio button and then type in the IP address your Provider gave you for your system. Then, click your mouse on the OK button.

7. Within the Properties dialog box, click your mouse on the OK button.

958 VIEWING YOUR SYSTEM'S INTERNET PROTOCOL (IP) ADDRESS

As you learned in Tip 957, when you connect to the Internet through an Internet Service Provider, your provider will normally assign your system's IP address for you. Depending on the programs that you run, there may be times when you must know your IP address. Within Windows 98, you can use the IPCONFIG to display your system's current IP address, as shown in Figure 958.

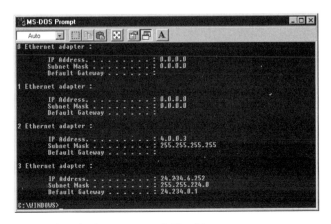

Figure 958 *Using the IPCONFIG command to display your system's IP address.*

To use the IPCONFIG command to display your system's IP address, perform these steps:

1. Click your mouse on the Start menu Run option. Windows 98 will display the Run dialog box.
2. Within the Run dialog box, type in **COMMAND** and press ENTER. Windows 98 will open an MS-DOS window.
3. Within the MS-DOS window, type **IPCONFIG** and press ENTER. Windows 98 will run the IPCONFIG command, which displays your IP address.
4. To later close the MS-DOS window, type **EXIT** at the system prompt and press ENTER.

959 **DISPLAYING *TCP/IP* CONNECTIONS USING *WINIP*CFG**

As you have learned, every system on the Internet must have a unique Internet Protocol (IP) address. In Tip 958, you learned how to use the IPCONFIG command from your system prompt to display your system's current IP address. Within Windows 98, you can run the WinIPcfg (Windows IP-address Configuration command) program to display information about your Internet connection, as shown in Figure 959.1.

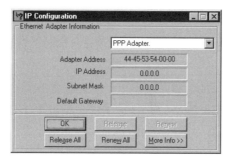

Figure 959.1 *Displaying your system's Internet settings using the WinIPcfg program.*

Within the WinIPCfg window, you can click your mouse on the More Info button to display the advanced IP Configuration information window, as shown in Figure 959.2.

Figure 959.2 *Displaying advanced WinIPcfg information.*

To run the WinIPcfg program, perform these steps:

1. Click your mouse on the Start menu Run option. Windows 98, in turn, will display the Run dialog box.

2. Within the Run dialog box, type **WinIPcfg** and press ENTER.

960 USING THE PING COMMAND TO TEST IF A SITE IS ACCESSIBLE

As you run different programs to connect to computers across the Net, such as your browser or an FTP program, there may be times when the program fails and displays an error message stating that it cannot locate or connect to the remote system. Normally, if you try to make your connection a while later, you will have success. However, if you find that you cannot connect to a remote system, you can use the PING command to determine if the site is running.

The PING command is so named because like a submarine sonar, the PING command essentially bounces a message off a remote site. If the remote site is running, it will send a response. If the remote site fails to respond to the PING, you know the system is not running. Figure 960, for example, shows the results of a PING command of the Jamsa Press Web site, *jamsa.com*.

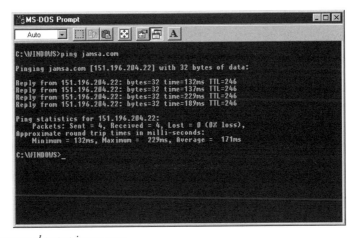

Figure 960 *Using the PING command to test jamsa.com.*

To run the PING command, perform these steps:

1. Click your mouse on the Start menu Run option. Windows 98, in turn, will display the Run dialog box.

2. Within the Run dialog box, type in **COMMAND** and press ENTER. Windows 98 will open an MS-DOS window.

3. Within the MS-DOS window, type PING followed by the name of the site you desire and press ENTER (such as **PING microsoft.com** <ENTER>). Windows 98 will run the PING command.

4. To later close the MS-DOS window, type EXIT at the system prompt and press ENTER.

961	## USING THE TRACERT COMMAND TO TRACE YOUR CONNECTION'S ROUTE

When you send files or documents across the Internet to a remote computer, your software normally does not have a direct link to the remote system. Instead, for example, if you are sending a file from New York to Los Angeles, your file may move from New York, to Boston, and then to Texas, to Idaho, and finally to L.A. To get your file to its final destination, software on the Internet will route your file through various systems, based on network traffic on the links that connect systems.

If you think that your current connection is slow, you can use the Windows 98 TraceRt command to trace the path your files will travel to reach a destination. Figure 961, for example, shows the result of a TraceRt command that traced a route from a PC in Las Vegas to one of the *amazon.com* PCs in Seattle.

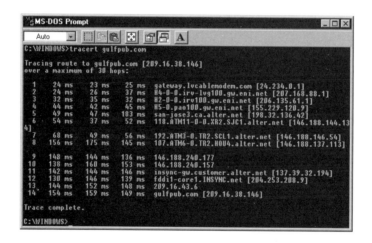

Figure 961 *Using the TraceRT command to trace an Internet connection's route.*

By periodically running the TraceRt command on a regular basis, you can start to "get a feel" for your common connections. If a connection route seems slow or has an excessive number of hops (from one site to another), you may want to stop your current operation and try it again at a later time. To run the TraceRt command, perform these steps:

1. Click your mouse on the Start menu Run option. Windows 98, in turn, will display the Run dialog box.

2. Within the Run dialog box, type in **COMMAND** and press ENTER. Windows 98 will open an MS-DOS window.

3. Within the MS-DOS window, type **TraceRt** followed by the name of the site you desire and press ENTER (such as **TraceRt microsoft.com** <ENTER>). Windows 98 will run the TraceRt command.

4. To later close the MS-DOS window, type **EXIT** at the system prompt and press ENTER.

---

962 USING THE ARP COMMAND TO CONFIGURE YOUR IP TO ETHERNET ADDRESS TRANSLATION

If you are the network administrator for an Ethernet-based local-area network that is running TCP/IP, there may be times when you need to customize your network's address-resolution protocol (ARP) settings that control how the network translates an IP address into an Ethernet address or vice versa. To display or change the settings, you can use the ARP command. To run the ARP command, you must first open an MS-DOS window. The ARP command has three formats:

```
ARP -a [IP_address] [-N [interface_address]]

ARP -d IP_address [interface_address]

ARP -s IP_address ethernet_address [interface_address]
```

To run the ARP command, perform these steps:

1. Click your mouse on the Start menu Run option. Windows 98 will display the Run dialog box.

2. Within the Run dialog box, type in **COMMAND** and press Enter. Windows 98 will open an MS-DOS window.

3. Within the MS-DOS window, type **ARP** and your optional command-line arguments and then press ENTER. Windows 98 will run the ARP command, which displays your network statistics.

4. To later close the MS-DOS window, type **EXIT** at the system prompt and press ENTER.

Table 962 explains each of the ARP command-line arguments.

Argument	Purpose
-a	Displays current ARP entries
-d	Deletes the host specified by the Ethernet address
-s	Associates the *Internet_addresss* with the *ethernet_addr*ess
-N	Displays the ARP tables for the *interface_address* network card
ethernet_address	Specifies a physical ethernet address to use
interface_address	Specifies the interface whose address translation tables need modifying (the default is the first applicable interface)
internet_address	Specifies a dotted IP address

Table 962 ARP's command-line arguments.

963 UNDERSTANDING AND CONFIGURING THE WINDOWS INTERNET NAMING SERVICE (WINS)

As you have learned, within a TCP/IP network, each system has a unique Internet Protocol (IP) address. Within a TCP/IP network, when a user specifies a domain name, programs will use a domain-name server to convert the address into an IP address. In a similar way, if your network runs the NetBIOS protocol on top of TCP/IP, your network may use a similar naming service to convert NetBIOS computer names into a TCP/IP address. In general, WINS software is a service that runs on a Windows NT server that converts a NetBIOS computer name into an IP address. Most users will not have to worry about the WINS software. Instead, the network administrator will configure the WINS settings, using the TCP/IP Properties WINS Configuration sheet as shown in Figure 963.

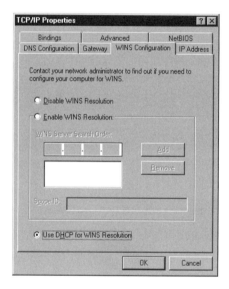

Figure 963 *The WINS Configuration sheet.*

964 USING THE NETSTAT COMMAND TO DISPLAY TCP/IP STATISTICS

If you are trying to troubleshoot your network operations or analyze your network performance, you can use the Netstat command, as shown in Figure 964, which displays statistics on TCP/IP connections. The format of the Netstat command is as follows:

```
Netstat [-a] [-e] [-n] [-s] [-p protocol] [-r] [interval]
```

To run the Netstat command, perform these steps:

1. Click your mouse on the Start menu Run option. Windows 98 will display the Run dialog box.
2. Within the Run dialog box, type in **COMMAND** and press ENTER. Windows 98 will open an MS-DOS window.

3. Within the MS-DOS window, type **Netstat** and your optional command-line arguments and then press ENTER. Windows 98 will run the Netstat command, which displays your network statistics.

4. To later close the MS-DOS window, type **EXIT** at the system prompt and press ENTER.

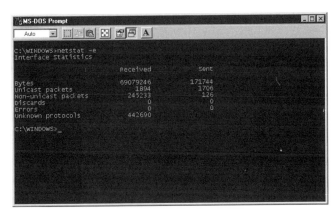

Figure 964 *Using the Netstat command to display network statistics.*

Table 964 explains each of Netstat's command-line arguments.

Argument	Purpose
-a	Produces statistical information on all connections, including server connections that Netstat typically does not show
-e	Produces Ethernet statistics
Interval	Specifies the display interval in seconds
-n	Displays both addresses and port numbers in numerical form instead of by name lookup, as is the default
-s	Often used along with the -e command-line option to produce a per-protocol statistical table
-p protocol	Shows protocol connections where the protocol must be TCP, UDP, or IP
-r	Displays the routing table

Table 964 *Netstat's command-line arguments.*

965 USING THE ROUTE COMMAND TO CONTROL NETWORK ROUTING TABLES

As you have learned, when you send a message across the Internet, your message may travel through many computers. Depending on the network traffic, the route that your message takes may differ from one day to the next. To determine the path your message travels, there are special computers on the net called routers. In general, you can think of a router as a network traffic cop that directs a message between systems.

To perform their traffic routing, network routers keep tables of routing information which help them monitor network traffic. If you are a network administrator, there may be times when you will need to customize router tables. In such cases, you can use the ROUTE command. Figure 965, for example, shows the output of the Route command.

Figure 965 *Using the Route command to display a network route.*

Windows 98's Route program diagnoses and manipulates network router tables. Obviously, only technically-advanced Internet users will have a need for Route. To start Route, open an MS-DOS window and type **ROUTE** followed by one or more arguments. The format of the ROUTE command is as follows:

```
ROUTE [-f] [command [destination] [MASK netmask] [gateway] [METRIC metric]]
```

Table 965 explains each of ROUTE's command-line arguments.

Argument	Purpose
-f	Clears all gateway entry routing tables
command	Specifies either PRINT, ADD, DELETE, or CHANGE, to display, add, delete, or change a route
destination	Specifies the host-to-send command
MASK	Indicates that the next argument is a *netmask* argument
METRIC	Specifies that the metric value is the cost for this connection
netmask	Specifies this route's subnet mask value (the default is 255.255.255.255)
gateway	Specifies the gateway

Table 965 *Route's command-line arguments.*

To run the Route command, perform these steps:

1. Click your mouse on the Start menu Run option. Windows 98 will display the Run dialog box.
2. Within the Run dialog box, type in **COMMAND** and press ENTER. Windows 98 will open an MS-DOS window.
3. Within the MS-DOS window, type **Route** and your optional command-line arguments and then press ENTER. Windows 98 will run the Route command, to display or change network router tables.
4. To later close the MS-DOS window, type **EXIT** at the system prompt and press ENTER.

966

USING TELNET TO MOVE FROM ONE COMPUTER TO ANOTHER

Prior to the World Wide Web, users on the Internet would move from one site to another (either to view information or run specific programs) by running a special program called *Telnet*. In general, Telnet let users connect to a remote computer just as if the user were sitting at a terminal that was connected to the system. From their Telnet connection, users could log into the remote computer and then run specific programs. (Users refer to this type of remote connection as emulating or behaving like a terminal.)

Depending on the remote computer's purpose, the user might be able to log into the system and issue commands from a system prompt, or the system might only let the user perform commands using a series of menu options. Because some users still run Telnet to connect to specific sites (there are almost 2,000 Telnet sites across the Internet), Windows 98 provides a Telnet command that you can run from the system prompt. To use Telnet to visit a site, perform these steps:

1. If you are not currently connected to the Internet, connect now. Click your mouse on the Start menu Run option. Windows 98 will display the Run dialog box.

2. Within the Run dialog box, type **Telnet** and press ENTER. Windows 98 will open the Telnet window, as shown in Figure 966.1.

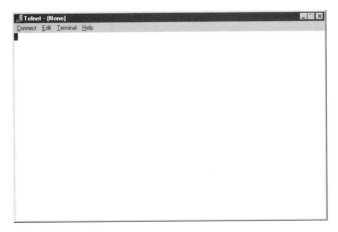

Figure 966.1 *The Telnet window.*

3. Within the Telnet window, click your mouse on the Connect menu Remote System option. Telnet will display the Connect dialog box, as shown in Figure 966.2.

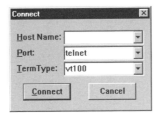

Figure 966.2 The Connect dialog box.

4. Within the Connect dialog box, Host Name field, type in the name of the site to which you

want to connect. Then, within the Port field, type in the site's port number or the word Telnet. Finally, click your mouse on the Connect button. Telnet, in turn, will try to connect you to the remote system. The remote system, in turn, may display a message that tells you which username and password you should use to log into the system.

Note: Tip 967 lists several Telnet sites you may want to visit.

In Tip 966, you learned that Windows 98 provides the Telnet command that you can use to connect to various sites across the Internet. Although many sites are converting their Telnet content to the Web, you can still find a few interesting databases, library card catalogs, and even some crazy sites (a few universities have connected soda machines and other devices to Telnet so students can use Telnet determine if a soda machine has sodas, so the students can eliminate an unnecessary walk down the hall). Table 967 lists a few sites that you can use to test drive Telnet.

Name	Port	Description
martini.eecs.umich.edu	3000	Information about cities (longitude/latitude, elevation)
india.colorado.edu	13	The exact time of day
culine.colorado.edu	859	NBA team schedules
culine.colorado.edu	863	NFL team schedules
duat.gtefsd.com	Telnet	Duat flight planning
spacelink.msfc.nasa.gov	Telnet	NASA information

Table 967 Interesting public Telnet Sites.

Throughout this book, you have learned ways to access information on the Internet using the World Wide Web. Normally, when you download information from a remote site, you can do so from the Web. Likewise, if someone needs you to provide them with information, you can do so by sending an e-mail message. However, when another user requires you to provide a large file, you should consider using the FTP command (e-mail is a very inefficient way to send large files).

The letters FTP are an abbreviation for File Transfer Protocol, a protocol that programs use to exchange files across the Internet. Just as there are Web sites on the Internet, there are also FTP Sites. In general, an FTP site is a computer that runs FTP server software. To connect to an FTP site, you use the FTP command. After you connect to the site (you will have to specify a username and password), you can use FTP commands to upload and download files between your system and the FTP site.

Tip 969 lists several FTP sites that you can visit and download files. To help you get started, Windows 98 provides an FTP command that you run from a system prompt. The following steps will provide you with the information that you need to connect to the Microsoft FTP site, to view a listing of available files, and then to download a specific file. Although the steps listed here connect you to the Microsoft Web site, you can perform these same steps to connect to most FTP sites:

1. If you are not currently connected to the Internet, connect now.

2. Click your mouse on the Start menu Run option. Windows 98 will display the Run dialog box.

3. Within the Run dialog box, type **FTP** and press ENTER. Windows 98 will open an MS-DOS window within which it will display an FTP> prompt.

4. At the FTP> prompt, use the **OPEN** command to connect the Microsoft FTP site:

    OPEN   ftp.microsoft.com <ENTER>

5. The Microsoft FTP site will then ask you for a username. Normally, for most FTP sites, you will type the username **anonymous** and press ENTER.

6. The Microsoft FTP site will then ask you for a password. Normally, for most FTP sites, you will type your e-mail address for a password (such as *JohnDoe@somesite.com*) and then press ENTER.

7. To display a listing of files on the remote site, type the **ls** command and then press ENTER:

    ls <ENTER>

8. To change to a specific directory at the remote site, you can use the **cd** command followed by the directory name and press ENTER:

    cd directory_name <ENTER>

9. After you locate the file you want to download, type the **get** command followed by the filename and then press ENTER (Windows 98 will place the file in the current directory, which is probably the Windows folder):

    get filename.ext <ENTER>

10. If you want to place a file on the remote system, type the **put** command followed by the filename and then press ENTER (Many systems will not let you upload a file. Also, you may need to specify a complete pathname to the file you want to upload to the remote site):

    put filename.ext <ENTER>

11. After you perform your **get** or **put** operation, you can log off the remote system by typing the **quit** command. You can then use the **open** command to connect to a different site or the **exit** command to end your FTP session.

---

969 — *TAKING THE FTP COMMAND FOR A TEST DRIVE*

In Tip 968, you learned that Windows 98 provides an FTP command that you can use to download and upload files from across the Internet. To help you better understand the FTP command, you may want to visit one or more of the sites Table 969 lists. In each case, you can connect to the site by issuing the FTP command from the system prompt, including the site name:

```
C:\Windows> FTP  site_name   <ENTER>
```

When the system prompts you for a username, type **anonymous** and press ENTER. When the system prompts you for a password, type in your e-mail address. After you log into the system, use the **cd /pub** command to change to the public directories where you will find files that you can download using the **get** command. To list the files the remote system contains, use the **ls** command. When you are done, issue the **quit** command.

Name	Description
ftp.books.com	The text for thousands of books (in the public domain)
ftp.microsoft.com	Microsoft support files
ftp.ncsa.uiuc.edu	Tools you can use across the Internet and Web
archive.nevada.edu	Archive of the Constitution

Table 969 *Interesting FTP sites.*

970 DOWNLOADING A WINDOWS-BASED FTP PROGRAM

In Tip 968, you learned that Windows 98 provides an FTP command that you can use from the command line to download and upload files from across the Internet. If you find that you use the FTP command on a regular basis to transfer files, you may want to download a Windows-based FTP program that you can use to perform drag-and-drop file operations.

To download a Windows-based FTP command, visit the *www.ftppro.com* Web site, from which you can download the program. Figure 970 shows the Windows-based FTP program, which you may find much easier to use than the command-line-based FTP commands.

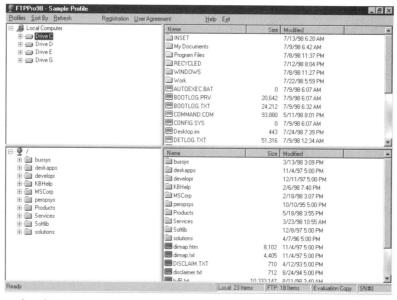

Figure 970 *Using a Windows-based FTP program.*

971   *UNDERSTANDING ON-LINE CHATTING*

Across the Internet, users chat on-line about any and all topics imaginable. To chat, users get together in "virtual rooms" within which the users type messages that appear instantly to all members of the chat. To participate within a chat, you must first run chat software. Then, you must select a chat server which, in turn, will display a list of thousands of chat rooms you can join and start chatting with others. In the past, chat programs were pretty simple. As discussed, to chat, a user simply types a line of text and then presses ENTER. The chat software, in turn, makes the user's line of text immediately visible to all the users within the chat room.

To help you start chatting, Windows 98 provides the Microsoft Chat software, shown in Figure 971. Unlike older chat programs that simply displayed each user's name (or chat nickname), Microsoft Chat lets you select a cartoon character to represent you within the chat. Other users within the chat room that are running Microsoft Chat will see your characters and the expressions you select. Several of the Tips that follow will examine Microsoft Chat on-line.

Figure 971 Chatting on-line within the Microsoft Chat program.

972   *USING MICROSOFT CHAT TO CHAT ON-LINE*

In Tip 971, you learned that Windows 98 provides the Microsoft Chat software that you can use to chat with other users on-line. To start the Microsoft Chat software, perform these steps:

1.   Click your mouse on the Start menu Programs option and choose Internet Explorer. Windows 98 will cascade the Internet Explorer submenu.

2.   Within the Internet Explorer submenu, click your mouse on the Microsoft Chat option. Windows 98, in turn, will start the Microsoft Chat program, displaying the Chat Connection dialog box, as shown in Figure 972.

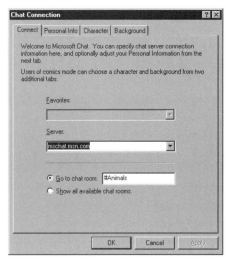

Figure 972 *The Microsoft Chat program Chat Connection dialog box.*

If your Internet Explorer submenu does not include the Microsoft Chat option, you can install the software from the Windows 98 CD-ROM by performing these steps:

1. Click your mouse on the Start menu Settings menu and choose Control Panel. Windows 98, in turn, will open the Control Panel window.

2. Within the Control Panel window, double-click your mouse on the Add/Remove Programs icon. Windows 98 will display the Add/Remove Programs Properties dialog box.

3. Within the Add/Remove Programs Properties dialog box, click your mouse on the Windows Setup tab. Windows 98 will display checkboxes for the Windows 98 components.

4. Within the Windows 98 component list, click your mouse on the Communications checkbox and then click your mouse on the Details button. Windows 98 will display the Communications dialog box.

5. Within the Communications dialog box, click your mouse on the Microsoft Chat 2.1 checkbox, placing a check mark within the box. Then, click your mouse on the OK button.

6. Within the Add/Remove Programs Properties dialog box, click your mouse on the OK button.

973	SELECTING A CHAT SERVER

In several of the previous Tips, you have learned that when your browser connects to a remote site, your browser actually connects to a Web server at the remote site which, in turn, downloads information to your browser. Likewise, when you use the FTP command to connect to a remote site, you actually connect to an FTP server, which, in turn, lets you upload and download files. In a similar way, before you can chat with other users, you must connect to a Chat server. After you select a Chat server, your server will display a list of the Chat rooms you can join. To select a Chat server, click your mouse on the Chat Connection dialog box pull-down Server list and select the server you desire.

If the Chat Connection dialog box is not currently visible, click your mouse on the Room menu Connect option to display the dialog box.

974

CUSTOMIZING YOUR PERSONAL INFORMATION WITH CHAT

As briefly discussed in Tip 971, users will enter chat rooms to discuss a myriad of topics. Before you join into such chats, you may want to change the personal information other users in the chat room can view about you. That way, other users in the chat room cannot determine your true identity. To change your personal information within Microsoft Chat, perform these steps:

1. Within the Chat Connection dialog box, click your mouse on the Personal Info tab or click your mouse on the View menu and choose Options. Microsoft Chat, in turn, will display the Personal Information dialog box, as shown in Figure 974.

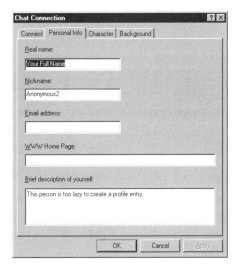

Figure 974 *The Microsoft Chat program Personal Information dialog box.*

2. Within the Personal Information dialog box, you may want to change your name and e-mail address. Within the Nickname field, type in the name by which users will reference you within Chat and then click your mouse on the OK button.

975

SELECTING YOUR COMIC PERSONALITY

Within Microsoft Chat, you can select a comic personality that will represent you within the Chat. For example, Figure 975.1 shows a Microsoft Chat session with multiple comic characters. To select the comic personality that will represent you within Chat, perform these steps:

1. Within the Chat Connection dialog box, click your mouse on the Personal Info tab or click your mouse on the View menu and choose Options. Microsoft Chat, in turn, will display the Microsoft Chat Options dialog box.

Figure 975.1 *Microsoft Chat supports comic characters for chat participants.*

2. Within the Microsoft Chat Options dialog box, click your mouse on the Character tab. Microsoft Chat will display the Character sheet, as shown in Figure 975.2.

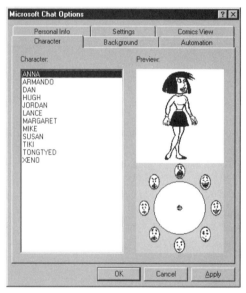

Figure 975.2 *The Microsoft Chat program Character sheet.*

3. Within the Character sheet, Character list, click your mouse on the name of the character that you desire. As you click, your mouse on a character's name, the dialog box will display the characters appearance. After you select the character that you desire, click your mouse on the OK button.

After you select the character you desire, you can also check the background you want Chat to display for the room. To select a background image, perform these steps:

1. Within the Chat Connection dialog box, click your mouse on the Personal Info tab or click your mouse on the View menu and choose Options. Microsoft Chat, in turn, will display the Microsoft Chat Options dialog box.

2. Within the Microsoft Chat Options dialog box, click your mouse on the Background tab. Microsoft Chat will display the Background sheet, as shown in Figure 975.3.

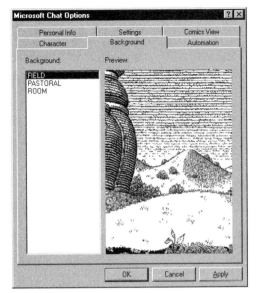

Figure 975.3 *The Microsoft Chat program Background sheet.*

3. Within the Background sheet Background list, click your mouse on the name of the background that you desire. As you click, your mouse on a background's name, the dialog box will display the background's appearance. After you select the background that you desire, click your mouse on the OK button.

Note: *If your Microsoft Chat Options dialog box does not have a Character or Background sheet, select the View menu Comic Strip option.*

976 IGNORING A SPECIFIC USER WITHIN A CHAT ROOM

Within the dictionary, you should find "chat room" somewhere within the definition of free speech. If you participate in on-line chats you will eventually find many users who speak their mind on a variety of topics. If you find that a user's comments offensive or simply a waste of "ones and zeros" you can direct Microsoft Chat to ignore the user, by performing these steps:

1. Within the chat room's member list, right-click your mouse on the user you want to ignore. Windows 98, in turn, will display a pop-up menu.
2. Within the pop-up menu, click your mouse on the Ignore option.

In a similar way, there may be times within a chat that a user simply bombards the discussion with a flurry of messages. To direct chat to discard such message flurries, perform these steps:

1. Within Microsoft Chat, click your mouse on the View menu and choose Options. Microsoft Chat, in turn, will display the Microsoft Chat Options dialog box.
2. Within the Microsoft Chat Options dialog box, click your mouse on the Automation tab. Microsoft Chat will display the Automation sheet as shown in Figure 976.

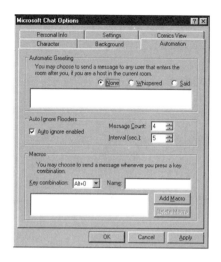

Figure 976 *The Automation sheet.*

3. Within the Automation sheet, click your mouse on the Auto ignore enabled checkbox, placing a check mark within the box. Then, click your mouse on the Message count field and click in the count of the number of messages you consider to be excessive. Then, click your mouse on the Interval field and specify the time interval within which Chat should apply your message count. Finally, click your mouse on the OK button to put your changes into effect.

977 **WHISPERING TO OTHER USERS WITHIN A CHAT**

As you chat with a group of users on-line, there may be times when you want to whisper to a specific user. In other words, you want to monitor the chat room's current discussion while you talk to another user (so that only that user can read your messages). To whisper to another user, perform these steps:

1. Within the chat room's member list, right-click your mouse on the user you to which you want to whisper. Windows 98, in turn, will display a pop-up menu.

2. Within the pop-up menu, click your mouse on the Whisper Box option. Microsoft Chat, in turn, will display a Whisper Box that you can use to talk with that user as shown in Figure 977.

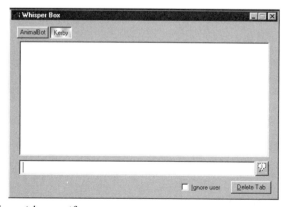

Figure 977 *Using a Whisper Box to chat with a specific user.*

As you chat on-line, you will find that there are many phrases you repeatedly type, such as "That was pretty funny." or "I'm from Houston." Rather than forcing you to continually retype such text, Microsoft Chat lets you define a message macro that contains the text. Later, you can press the keyboard combination you associate with the macro and Chat will send the corresponding text. To create a message macro, perform these steps:

1. Within Microsoft Chat, click your mouse on the View menu and choose Options. Microsoft Chat, in turn, will display the Microsoft Chat Options dialog box.

2. Within the Microsoft Chat Options dialog box, click your mouse on the Automation tab. Microsoft Chat will display the Automation sheet as shown in Figure 978.

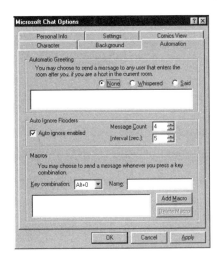

Figure 978 *The Automation sheet.*

3. Within the Automation sheet's Macro field, click your mouse on the text box that appears near the bottom of the dialog box and type in the message text that you want to automate. Then, click your mouse in the Name field and type in a name that describes your text, such as Greeting. Next, click your mouse on the Key-combination pull-down list and select the keyboard combination you want to associate with the macro. Finally, click your mouse on the OK button to put your changes into effect.

Later, to use your macro within Chat, simply press the corresponding keyboard combination.

As you have learned, to join a chat within Microsoft Chat, you simply enter a chat room. As it turns out, Microsoft Chat does let you be "two places at once." In other words, within Microsoft Chat, you can participate within multiple chat rooms, at the same time. Actually, you can only chat in one room at any given time, but you can move from room to room quickly. When you chat within multiple rooms at the same time, Microsoft Chat will display a tab upon which you can click your mouse to view the chat's discussion, as shown in Figure 979.

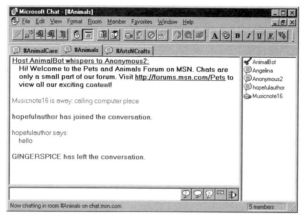

Figure 979 *Chatting within multiple rooms at the same time.*

To open multiple rooms, you simply enter each room, one room at a time, by performing these steps:

1. Click your mouse on the Room menu Room List option. Microsoft Chat, in turn, will display the Chat Room List dialog box that lists the available chat rooms.
2. Within the Chat Room List dialog box, click your mouse on the room you want to enter and then click your mouse on the Go To button.

980   CHANGING YOUR CHAT EXPRESSION

As you send messages within Microsoft Chat, you may want to change your expression to match your conversation. To change your comic character's expression within Chat, click your mouse on the facial expression that you desire within the table of facial expressions that Chat displays at the lower-right-hand side of your window. As you click your mouse on a specific expression, Chat will immediately change your character's expression to match. Figure 980, for example, shows two samples of the facial expressions and their matching character expressions.

Figure 980 *Changing facial expressions within Microsoft Chat.*

981 ENTERING AND LEAVING CHAT ROOMS

A Chat server will normally list thousands of chat rooms that you can enter. To display the chat-room list, click your mouse on the Room menu Room List option. Chat, in turn, will display the room list, as shown in Figure 981.1.

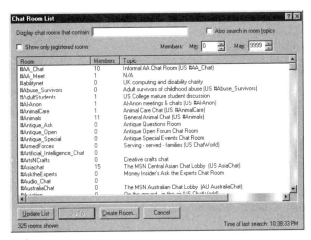

Figure 981.1 *Displaying the chat room list.*

To join a chat room, simply click your mouse on the room within the chat-room list and then click your mouse on the Go To button. Later, to leave a room, you can use these steps to select a different room or you can click your mouse on the Room menu Leave room option. Within Chat, you can create your own chat room, which you can then invite others to join (you can also lock the room to control who enters). To create a room within Chat, perform these steps:

1. Click your mouse on the Room menu Create Room option. Chat, in turn, will display the Create Chat Room dialog box, as shown in Figure 981.2, within which you can specify your room's settings.

Figure 981.2 *The Create Chat Room dialog box.*

2. Within the Create Chat Room dialog box, assign the settings that you desire and then click your mouse on the OK button.

Note: *Within Chat, you can actually join several chat rooms at the same time. When you join multiple chat rooms, Chat will display tabs within the Chat window that you can use to move from one to the next.*

982 SELECTING CHAT'S TEXT VIEW

Although the Comic Chat is pretty entertaining, its performance is still slow. In a busy chat room, users can exchange 100 messages a minute—meaning the text flies. Often, because of graphics operations involved, the Comic Chat simply cannot keep up. In such cases, you may want to revert to Chat's text mode, which simply shows each user's message as a line of text, as shown in Figure 982.

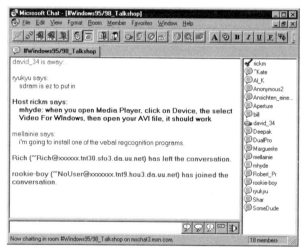

Figure 982 *Using Chat's Text view to display messages within a chat.*

To select Chat's text mode, click your mouse on the View menu Plain text option. Later, if you want to resume the comic view, select the View menu Comic strip option.

983 VIEWING A USER'S IDENTITY WITHIN CHAT

Within Chat, each user has a nickname that appears within the Chat window. Using nicknames, users within the chat can maintain their anonymity. As you chat, however, there may be times when you will want to know more about a user, such as their e-mail name or maybe even their real name.

To display a chat member's profile (Chat will display the profile as text within the Chat window), right-click your mouse on the user's name within Chat's list of users and then select Display Profile from the pop-up menu. To display a user's e-mail name (their identity), right-click your mouse on the user's name and then select the pop-up menu Get Identity option.

Note: *Just as you can use these techniques to display information about other users, other users can use the same techniques to display information about you. Before you chat, you may want to perform the steps that Tip 974 presents to change the information users can view about you.*

984   USING NETSHOW TO WATCH STREAMING VIDEO

In Tip 546, you learned how to use the Windows 98 Media Player to play back video clips that reside on your disk. To help you view video clips that reside on the Web, Windows 98 provides the NetShow Player. Using the NetShow Player, you can view streaming video or listen to streaming audio from sites across the Web. To start the NetShow Player, perform these steps:

1. Click your mouse on the Start menu Programs option and choose Internet Explorer. Windows 98 will cascade the Internet Explorer submenu.

2. Within the Internet Explorer submenu, click your mouse on the NetShow Player option. Windows 98 will open the NetShow Player window.

3. Within the NetShow Player window, click your mouse on the File menu Open File option or Open Location to open the video that you desire.

985   UNDERSTANDING NETMEETING

Throughout this book's Tips, you have learned many ways to use the Internet and the World Wide Web. One of the most exciting programs Windows 98 includes is NetMeeting, a program that users can use to chat, exchange e-mail, exchange files, talk, or even video conference. Using NetMeeting, employees at offices all over the country can get together on-line within a virtual meeting room, as shown in Figure 985.

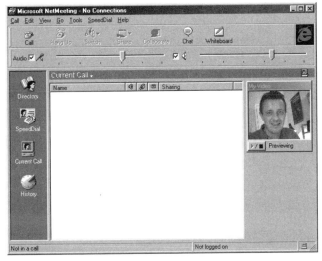

Figure 985 *The NetMeeting virtual meeting room.*

If your PC has a microphone and speakers, you can use NetMeeting to talk with users worldwide, across the Internet for free. Likewise, if your PC has a video camera, you can use NetMeeting for simple video conferencing. In the future, the NetMeeting software may become as valuable as your browser. To run the NetMeeting software, perform these steps:

1. Click your mouse on the Start menu Programs option and choose Internet Explorer. Windows 98 will cascade the Internet Explorer submenu.

2. Within the Internet Explorer submenu, click your mouse on Microsoft NetMeeting. The first time you run NetMeeting, Windows 98 will start a Wizard that will help you configure your NetMeeting settings.

986   CALLING ANOTHER USER WITHIN NETMEETING

To hold a meeting within NetMeeting, each user must agree upon at which NetMeeting server they will meet. You can find a list of NetMeeting servers in the upper-right-hand corner of the NetMeeting window. After you select a server, NetMeeting will display a list of users who are currently using that server. Within the user list, you should begin to see your associates' names. To refresh the list's contents, click your mouse on the toolbar Refresh button or click your mouse on the View menu Refresh option. To call another, user, click your mouse on the user within the user list and then click your mouse on the toolbar Call button. NetMeeting, in turn, will display the Current Call window that lists users who are participating within the call, as shown in Figure 986. If the users are broadcasting video, NetMeeting will display each user's video window.

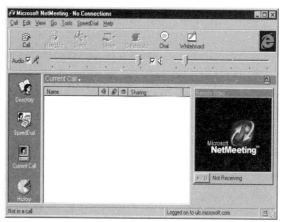

Figure 986 *Viewing users within the current call.*

987   CHATTING WITH USERS WITHIN NETMEETING

Although NetMeeting lets you talk to another user using your PC microphone and speakers and although NetMeeting lets you perform simple video conferencing, many users still find on-line chatting is fast and effective. To chat with another user within NetMeeting, click your mouse on the toolbar Chat button or click your mouse on the Tools menu Chat option. NetMeeting, in turn, will display a Chat window, as shown in Figure 987. Each user in the current call can then participate in the chat. By using the Chat window's File menu, you can later print or save the chat discussion.

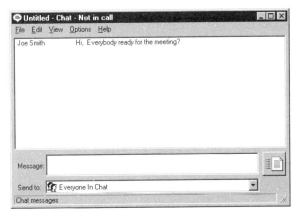

Figure 987 *Using the Chat window within NetMeeting.*

988 EXCHANGING IDEAS USING THE WHITEBOARD

In Tip 500, you learned how to use the Windows 98 Paint accessory program to create simple images. Within NetMeeting, you can use the Whiteboard to draw simple shapes or to preview images, as shown in Figure 988. When you open the Whiteboard, every user in your meeting can view or edit the Whiteboard contents.

In fact, several users can each draw on the Whiteboard at the same time! To display the Whiteboard, click your mouse on the Tools menu and choose Whiteboard.

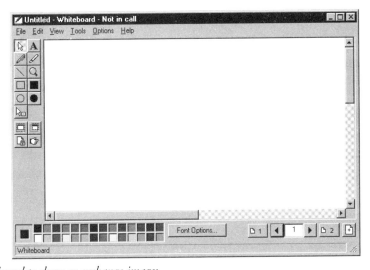

Figure 988 *Using the Whiteboard to draw or exchange images.*

989 CONFIGURING THE NETMEETING CALL, AUDIO, OR VIDEO SETTINGS

As you have learned, within NetMeeting, users can talk using their PC's microphone and speakers and download video to create a simple video conference. If you experience problems with the audio or video that you send or receive, you may need to tune your current settings. To adjust your NetMeeting settings, click your mouse on the Tools menu and choose Options. NetMeeting, in turn, will display the Options dialog box, shown in Figure 989. Using the Options dialog box sheets, you can configure your call, audio, video, and personal information.

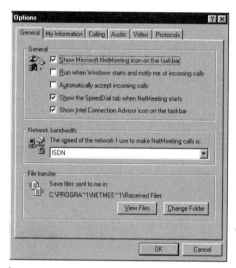

Figure 989 *The NetMeeting Options dialog box.*

Note: *To adjust your audio settings, you may want to use the NetMeeting Audio Tuning Wizard which you can start from the Tools menu.*

990 SHARING AN APPLICATION WITHIN NETMEETING

Within a NetMeeting call, there may be times when you want other users to view or edit a document, such as a Word document or an Excel document that resides on your system. In such cases, you can actually share the application across your call (even if the users in your call do not have the software!). To share an application within NetMeeting, you do not need special application software! You can use your existing programs. To share an application within a NetMeeting call, perform these steps:

1. Start the application program that you want to share.
2. Within the NetMeeting call window, click your mouse on the Tools menu Share Application option and then type the name of the program you want to share.

As you type within the application, the other users in your call can view your work. If a user wants to type within your document, the user must click the Tools menu Collaborate option and then click his or her mouse within the application window. When a user types within the window, NetMeeting will change the mouse pointer to match the initials of the user who is currently typing.

991 UNDERSTANDING THE PERSONAL WEB SERVER

As you have learned, each site across the Web has a corresponding server that is the computer responsible for sending your Web browser the site's text and image files. If you want to have your own Web site, you must place your HTML files on a system that is running Web-server software. Normally, when a user wants to have a Web site, he or she will place his or her files at a location on their Internet Service Provider's Web server. Likewise, if a user within a local-area network wants to have a Web page, he or she will normally place their files on a network server that is running Web-server software. Windows 98, however, provides a simple Web server that you can run on your own system. In this way, if you are part of a local-area network, you can run the Personal Web Server software on your PC and users from across the LAN can use their browser to view HTML files that reside on your PC. Likewise, as you will learn in Tip 993, you can even use the Personal Web Server software to create an Internet-based Web site that users from around the world can access (provided your PC is connected to the Net through your on-line service or Internet Service Provider). To install the Personal Web Server, perform these steps:

1. Click your mouse on the Start menu Run option. Windows 98, in turn, will display the Run dialog box.
2. Within the Run dialog box, use the Browse button select the \add-ons\pws folder from within the Windows 98 CD-ROM and then select the Setup program. Then, click your mouse on the OK button. Windows 98, in turn, will start the Setup program that will install the Personal Web Server on your system.

992 CREATING A WEB SITE USING FRONTPAGE EXPRESS

As you have learned, to create Web sites, designers make extensive use of HTML, a special text-formatting language. To make it easier for designers, and non-designers, for that matter, to create Web sites, Microsoft developed the FrontPage Express software, which it bundles within Windows 98. Using FrontPage Express, you can create your own Web documents that you can later post at a personal Web-site location on your Internet Service Provider's system or that you can display within your company's intranet. To start FrontPage Express, perform these steps:

1. Click your mouse on the Start menu Programs option and choose Internet Explorer. Windows 98, in turn, will cascade the Internet Explorer submenu.
2. Within the Internet Explorer submenu, click your mouse on the FrontPage Express option. Windows 98 will start FrontPage Express, as shown in Figure 992.1.

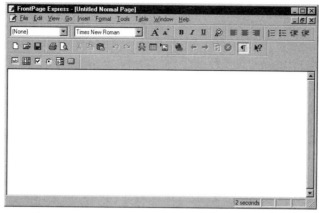

Figure 992.1 *The FrontPage Express window.*

The FrontPage Express program is a very powerful program and includes a wide-variety of features. However, because most users will create a fairly simple Web site to get started, FrontPage provides the Personal Home Page Wizard that you can use to create your Web page. To run the Personal Home Page Wizard, perform these steps:

1. Within FrontPage Express, click your mouse on the File menu New option. FrontPage Express, in turn, will display the New Page dialog box, as shown in Figure 992.2.

Figure 992.2 *The New Page dialog box.*

2. Within the New Page dialog box, click your mouse on the Personal Home Page Wizard option and choose OK. FrontPage Express, in turn, will start the Wizard, which will walk you through the steps you must perform to create a Web page.

After you create your Web site, you can test it by following the steps Tip 993 presents.

In Tip 992, you learned how to create a personal Web site within FrontPage Express. If you store your personal Web site within an HTML file on your disk, you can later use the Internet Explorer to view your site by typing in an address, such as *file:///c:/folder/pathname.html*. By testing your Web site using a file on your disk in this way, you can detect and correct missing graphics, missing links, and other common errors before you post the file to the Internet.

After you feel that your Web site is correct, you can use the Personal Web Server (discussed in Tip 991) to display your Web site from your PC across the Web. If your site works, you can then move the site to a location on the Web that is available 24 hours per day (most Internet Service Providers and on-line services provide a location where you can store your personal Web page).

When you use the Personal Web Server to display a Web page using an Internet connection through an on-line service or Internet Service Provider, your Web page will only be available to other users while you are connected. Next, you must tell the other users your PC's IP address (such as 111.221.121.112). They will need the address to connect to your system.

To display your Web site using the Personal Web Server from across the Internet, perform these steps:

1. Connect to the Internet using your on-line service or Internet Service Provider.

2. Using the Explorer, move the HTML file or files that contain your Web site to the *\InetPub\wwwroot* folder.

3. Click your mouse on the Start menu Run option. Windows will display the Run dialog box. Within the Run dialog box, type WinIPcfg and press ENTER. Windows 98 will run the WinIPcfg program that will display your current IP address.

4. Click your mouse on the Start menu Programs option and choose Internet Explorer. Windows 98 will cascade the Internet Explorer submenu. Within the Internet Explorer submenu, click your mouse on the Personal Web Server option. Windows 98 will cascade the Personal Web Server submenu. Within the Personal Web Server submenu, click your mouse on the Personal Web Manager. Windows 98, in turn, will start the Personal Web Manager, as shown in Figure 993.

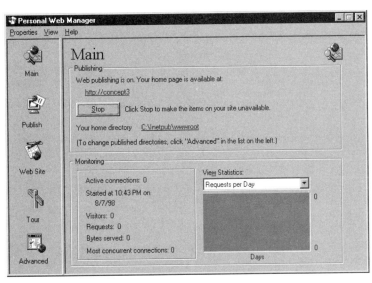

Figure 993 *The Personal Web Manager.*

5. Start the Internet Explorer. Within the Address field, type the letters http://, followed by your IP address, a forward slash, and your HTML file name, such as *http://122.111.221.111/ mypage.html*.

After you have your site up and running, other users can view your site's contents the same way. However, each time you break your Internet connection and then create a new connection, your provider will give you a different IP address, which you must look up using the WinIPcfg program.

994 | UNDERSTANDING THE WINDOWS 98 RESOURCE KIT SAMPLER

If you are a system or network administrator, you should pull out your Windows 98 CD-ROM right now and become familiar with the Windows 98 Resource Kit. In general, the Resource Kit provides a collection of utilities you can use to configure system settings, control network operations, diagnose and troubleshoot errors, and better manage Windows 98 systems within a local-area network environment. To provide you with insight into the Resource Kit, Windows 98 provides a Resource Kit Sampler on the Windows 98 CD-ROM. To load the Windows 98 Resource Kit Sampler onto your system, perform these steps:

1. Insert the Windows 98 CD-ROM into your CD-ROM drive. Windows 98, in turn, should "autorun" the CD's autorun.inf file, which causes it to display the Windows 98 CD-ROM window, as shown in Figure 994.1.

Figure 994.1 *The Windows 98 CD-ROM window.*

2. Within the Windows 98 CD-ROM window, click your mouse on the Browse This CD option. Windows 98, in turn, will open an Explorer window within which you can browse the CD's folders.
3. Within the Explorer window, open the Tools folder and then open the ResKit folder (that contains the Resource Kit Sampler files).
4. Within the ResKit folder, double-click your mouse on the Setup icon. Windows 98 will start a Setup Wizard that will walk you through the installation.
5. Within the ResKit folder, double-click your mouse on the Readme icon. Windows 98 will start Word (or WordPad) and will load the file's contents that describe the utilities the Resource Kit Sampler contains. Within your word processor, print the file's contents.

After the Sampler installation completes, you can access the utilities by performing these steps:

1. Click your mouse on the Start menu Programs option and choose Windows 98 Resource Kit. Windows 98, in turn, will cascade the Windows 98 Resource Kit submenu.

2. Within the Windows 98 Resource Kit submenu, click your mouse on the Tools Management Console. Windows 98 may display a Tip dialog box that describes the Microsoft Management Console—click your mouse on the Close button. Windows 98 will then open the Microsoft Management Console window, as shown in Figure 994.2.

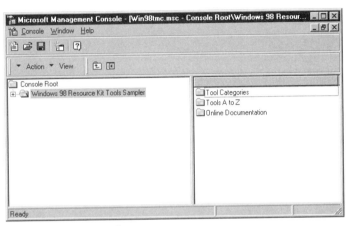

Figure 994.2 *The Microsoft Management Console window.*

3. Within the Microsoft Management Console window, double-click your mouse on the Tool Categories folder. Windows 98, in turn, will display folders that correspond to different operations. Take time now to click on each folder to briefly view the tools the folder contains. The documentation that printed earlier in this Tip will describe each utility's processing.

995 UNDERSTANDING THE SYSTEM POLICY EDITOR

In Tip 994, you learned how to install the Windows 98 Resource Kit Sampler onto your system. In addition to the Resource Kit Sampler's utility programs, Microsoft also bundles a program on the Windows 98 CD-ROM called the System Policy Editor. In general, the System Policy Editor lets you control how people use your computer and its Windows 98 resources. Using the System Policy Editor, you can restrict the operations users can perform from within the Control Panel. If you manage PCs within a local-area network, you may find the System Policy Editor helps you increase your system security and stability by limiting the operations your users can perform, either on their own system or within the network. Using the System Policy Editor, you can define policies that control operations for a user, group of users, or even your entire network. To install the System Policy Editor, perform these steps:

1. Click your mouse on the Start menu Settings option and choose Control Panel. Windows 98 will open the Control Panel window.

2. Within the Control Panel window, double-click your mouse on the Add/Remove Programs icon. Windows 98 will display the Add/Remove Programs Properties dialog box.

3. Within the Add/Remove Program Properties dialog box, click your mouse on the Windows Setup tab. Windows 98 will display the Windows Setup sheet.

4. Within the Windows Setup sheet, click your mouse on the Have Disk button. Windows 98, in turn, will display the Install From Disk dialog box, as shown in Figure 995.1.

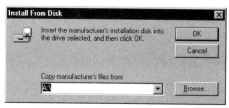

Figure 995.1 *The Install From Disk dialog box.*

5. Within the Install From Disk dialog box, click your mouse on the Browse button and locate the *\tools\reskit\netadmin\poledit* folder on the Windows 98 CD-ROM. Next, click your mouse on the *poledit.inf* option and select OK. Windows 98, in turn, will display the Have Disk dialog box, as shown in Figure 995.2.

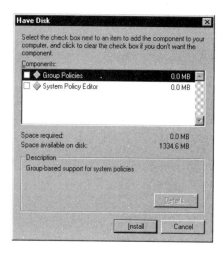

Figure 995.2 *The Have Disk dialog box.*

6. Within the Have Disk dialog box, click your mouse on the Group Policies checkbox and the System Policy Editor checkbox, placing a check mark within each box so that you install both. Then, click your mouse on the OK button.

7. Within the Add/Remove Program Properties dialog box, click your mouse on the OK button.

996 RUNNING THE SYSTEM POLICY EDITOR

In Tip 995, you learned how to install the System Policy Editor on your system, that you can later use to define policies that control how users, groups of users, or network users can access your system. To run the System Policy Editor, perform these steps:

1. Click your mouse on the Start menu Programs option and choose Accessories. Windows 98, in turn, will display the Accessories submenu.

2. Within the Accessories submenu, click your mouse on the System Tools option and choose System Policy Editor. Windows 98, in turn, will open the System Policy Editor window, as shown in Figure 996.

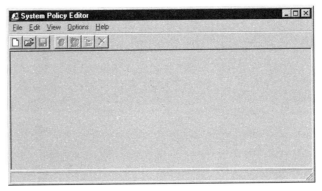

Figure 996 *The System Policy Editor.*

To get you started, the following three Tips will present operations you can perform using the System Policy Editor.

997   TURNING OFF A USER'S ACCESS TO THE NETWORK NEIGHBORHOOD

If you manage PCs in a local-area network, there may be times when specific PCs simply don't "have a need to know" about the network. In such cases, you can use the System Policy Editor to disable the Network Neighborhood icon on those user's systems. To prevent a user from accessing the network. perform these steps to turn off the Network Neighborhood:

1. Click your mouse on the Start menu Programs option and choose Accessories. Windows 98, in turn, will display the Accessories submenu.

2. Within the Accessories submenu, click your mouse on the System Tools option and choose System Policy Editor. Windows 98, in turn, will open the System Policy Editor window.

3. Within the System Policy Editor, select the File menu Open Registry option. The System Policy Editor will display a list of current users and computers.

4. Within the System Policy Editor's list, click your mouse on a user or computer. The System Policy Editor will display a list of the user's or the computer's available policies.

5. Within the System Policy Editor's policy list, click your mouse on the plus sign that precedes the Windows 98 System and then click your mouse on the plus sign that precedes the Shell entry. The System Policy Editor, in turn, will expand the entry.

6. Within the Shell entry's expanded list, click your mouse on the plus sign that proceeds the Restrictions icon. The System Policy Editor will expand the entry's list, as shown in Figure 997.

7. Within the Restrictions list, click your mouse on the Hide Network Neighborhood option and then click your mouse on the OK button.

8. Select the System Policy Editor's File menu Save option to save your settings.

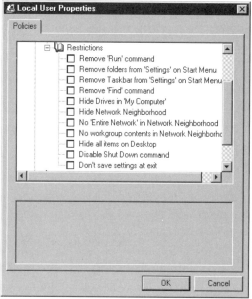

Figure 997 *Expanding a user's or computer's list of restricted objects.*

998 REMOVING THE TASKBAR FROM THE START MENU SETTINGS SUBMENU

As you have learned, Windows 98 makes extensive use of the Taskbar to let users switch quickly from one program to another. To customize the Taskbar, users can use the Start menu Settings options. If you manage PCs within a local-area network, there may be times when you don't want users to customize the Taskbar settings. (You may have shifts of workers who share PCs and you don't want one user changing the PC's behavior.) In such cases, you can use the System Policy Editor to remove the Taskbar from the Settings menu by performing these steps:

1. Click your mouse on the Start menu Programs option and choose Accessories. Windows 98, in turn, will display the Accessories submenu.

2. Within the Accessories submenu, click your mouse on the System Tools option and choose System Policy Editor. Windows 98, in turn, will open the System Policy Editor window.

3. Within the System Policy Editor, select the File menu Open Registry option. The System Policy Editor will display a list of current users and computers.

4. Within the System Policy Editor's list, click your mouse on a user or computer. The System Policy Editor will display a list of the user's or the computer's available policies.

5. Within the System Policy Editor's policy list, click your mouse on the plus sign that precedes the Windows 98 System and then click your mouse on the plus sign that precedes the Shell entry. The System Policy Editor, in turn, will expand the entry.

6. Within the Shell entry's expanded list, click your mouse on the plus sign that proceeds the Restrictions icon. The System Policy Editor will expand the entry's list.

7. Within the expanded list, click your mouse on the Remove Taskbar from Settings on Start Menu checkbox, placing a check mark within the box and then click your mouse on the OK button.

8. Select the System Policy Editor's File menu Save option to save your settings.

PREVENTING A USER FROM SAVING SETTINGS WHEN HE OR SHE EXITS WINDOWS 98

Normally, each time you exit Windows 98, either by shutting down your system or by logging off, Windows 98 saves the current profile settings (such as the Desktop configuration). If you manage PCs that shifts of workers share, you may want to use the System Policy Editor to prevent Windows 98 from automatically saving your system settings by performing these steps:

1. Click your mouse on the Start menu Programs option and choose Accessories. Windows 98, in turn, will display the Accessories submenu.

2. Within the Accessories submenu, click your mouse on the System Tools option and choose System Policy Editor. Windows 98, in turn, will open the System Policy Editor window.

3. Within the System Policy Editor window, select the File menu Open Registry entry. The System Policy Editor will display a list of current users and computers.

4. Within the System Policy Editor's list, click your mouse on a user or computer. The System Policy Editor will display a list of the user's or the computer's available policies.

5. Within the System Policy Editor's policy list, click your mouse on the plus sign that precedes the Windows 98 System and then click your mouse on the plus sign that precedes the Shell entry. The System Policy Editor, in turn, will expand the entry.

6. Within the Shell entry's expanded list, click your mouse on the plus sign that precedes the Restrictions icon. The System Policy Editor will expand the entry's list.

7. Within the Restrictions list, click your mouse on the Don't save settings at exit option and then click your mouse on the OK button.

8. Select the System Policy Editor's File menu Save option to save your settings.

INSTALLING THE TWEAK UI UTILITY

If you are one of those users who just can't seem to get enough performance from Windows 98, you may want to take advantage of the Tweak UI utility program that lets you fine-tune the Windows 98 user interface (the UI in Tweak UI). Using the Tweak UI utility, you can improve the speed at which your system displays menus, your system's use of shortcuts and default names, the icons that appear on your Desktop, and even your mouse sensitivity. To install the Tweak UI utility, perform these steps:

1. Click your mouse on the Start menu Settings option and choose Control Panel. Windows 98 will open the Control Panel window.

2. Within the Control Panel window, double-click your mouse on the Add/Remove Programs icon. Windows 98 will display the Add/Remove Programs Properties dialog box.

3. Within the Add/Remove Program Properties dialog box, click your mouse on the Windows

Setup tab. Windows 98 will display the Windows Setup sheet.

4. Within the Windows Setup sheet, click your mouse on the Have Disk button. Windows 98, in turn, will display the Install From Disk dialog box, as shown in Figure 1000.1.

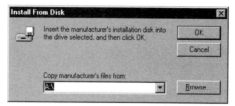

Figure 1000.1 *The Install From Disk dialog box.*

5. Within the Install From Disk dialog box, click your mouse on the Browse button and locate the *\tools\reskit\powertoy* folder on the Windows 98 CD-ROM. Next, click your mouse on the *tweakui.inf* option and select OK. Windows 98, in turn, will display the Have Disk dialog box, as shown in Figure 1000.2.

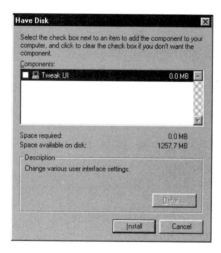

Figure 1000.2 *The Have Disk dialog box.*

6. Within the Have Disk dialog box, click your mouse on the Tweak UI checkbox (and the System Policy Editor checkbox if it is present), placing a check mark. Then, click your mouse on the Install button.

7. Within the Add/Remove Program Properties dialog box, click your mouse on the OK button.

1001   USING THE TWEAK UI UTILITY TO FINE-TUNE (TWEAK) YOUR SYSTEM'S USER INTERFACE

In Tip 1000, you learned how to install the Tweak UI utility from the Windows 98 CD-ROM. As you learned, the Tweak UI utility lets you fine-tune your system's user interface to maximize your system performance and your productivity. To run the Tweak UI utility, perform these steps:

1. Click your mouse on the Start menu Settings option and choose Control Panel. Windows 98, in turn, will open the Control Panel window.

2. Within the Control Panel window, double-click your mouse on the Tweak UI icon. Windows 98, in turn, will open the Tweak UI window, as shown in Figure 1001.1.

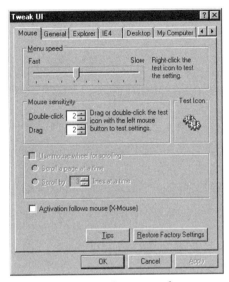

Figure 1001.1 *Using the Tweak UI utility to fine-tune your system's user interface.*

3. Within the Tweak UI utility's Mouse sheet, you can control your system's mouse settings. Likewise, within the Desktop sheet, as shown in Figure 1001.2, you can control which icons Windows 98 displays on your Desktop. Then, in the My Computer sheet, you can control which disk drives Windows 98 displays within the My Computer window.

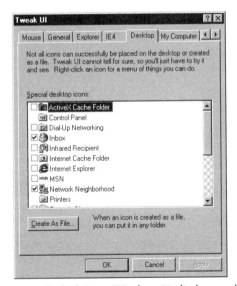

Figure 1001.2 *Using the Tweak UI utility to control which items Windows 98 displays on the Desktop.*

Within the Tweak UI dialog box, select the settings you desire and then click your mouse on the OK button. The Microsoft developers created the Tweak UI utility for tweaking, which means you may have to experiment with a few different settings until you get your system's user interface just right.

Index